Big Data and Armed Conflict

THE LIEBER STUDIES

Professor & Head, Department of Law, Co-Director of the Lieber Institute for Law and Warfare
Colonel Winston Williams

Professor & Co-Director of the Lieber Institute for Law and Warfare
Professor Sean Watts

G. Norman Lieber Distinguished Scholar
Professor Michael N. Schmitt

Board of Advisors
Honorable John Bellinger
Lieutenant General (ret.) Dana Chipman
Professor Mary DeRosa
Sir Christopher Greenwood
Dr. Wolff Heintschel von Heinegg
Sir Adam Roberts
Professor Gary Solis

Senior Fellows
Professor Laurie Blank
Major General (ret.) Blaise Cathcart KC
Professor Robert Chesney
Professor Geoff Corn
Professor Gary Corn
Professor Ashley Deeks
Professor Laura A. Dickinson
Dr. Helen Durham
Brigadier General (ret.) Richard Gross
Colonel (ret.) Richard Jackson
Professor Chris Jenks
Professor Eric Talbot Jensen
Colonel (ret.) Michael Lacey
Professor Rain Liivoja
Professor Naz Modirzadeh
Ms. Jelena Pejic
Professor Daphné Richemond-Barak
Professor Sandesh Sivakumaran
Professor Matthew Waxman

This is not an official publication of the United States Military Academy, Department of the Army, or Department of Defense. The views expressed in this volume represent the authors' personal views and do not necessarily reflect those of the Department of Defense, the United States Army, the United States Military Academy, or any other department or agency of the United States government. The analysis presented stems from their academic research of publicly available sources, not from protected operational information.

The Lieber Studies is the flagship publication of the Lieber Institute for Law and Warfare. It is designed to provide scholars, practitioners, and students with in-depth and critical analysis of the most challenging legal issues related to warfare in the 21st century. Established by the Department of Law of the United States Military Academy at West Point, the mission of the Lieber Institute is to foster a deeper understanding of the complex and evolving relationship between law and warfare in order to educate and empower current and future combat leaders. It does so through global academic engagement and advanced interdisciplinary research. As such, it lies at the crossroads of scholarship and practice by bringing together scholars, military officers, government legal advisers, and members of civil society from around the world to collaboratively examine the role and application of the law of armed conflict in current and future armed conflicts, as well as that of other regimes of international law in situations threatening international peace and security.

Lieber Institute for Law and Warfare
The Lieber Studies

Volume 9

Big Data and Armed Conflict
Legal Issues Above and Below the Armed Conflict Threshold

General Editors

PROFESSOR MICHAEL N. SCHMITT

PROFESSOR SEAN WATTS

Managing Editor

PROFESSOR ROBERT LAWLESS

Volume Editors

PROFESSOR LAURA A. DICKINSON

LIEUTENANT COLONEL (RET.) EDWARD W. BERG

Oxford University Press is a department of the University of Oxford. It furthers the University's objective of excellence in research, scholarship, and education by publishing worldwide. Oxford is a registered trade mark of Oxford University Press in the UK and certain other countries.

Published in the United States of America by Oxford University Press
198 Madison Avenue, New York, NY 10016, United States of America.

© The several contributors 2024

All rights reserved. No part of this publication may be reproduced, stored in a retrieval system, or transmitted, in any form or by any means, without the prior permission in writing of Oxford University Press, or as expressly permitted by law, by license, or under terms agreed with the appropriate reproduction rights organization. Inquiries concerning reproduction outside the scope of the above should be sent to the Rights Department, Oxford University Press, at the address above.

You must not circulate this work in any other form
and you must impose this same condition on any acquirer.

Library of Congress Cataloging-in-Publication Data
Names: Dickinson, Laura A. (Laura Anne) editors. | Berg, Edward W., editors. |
Lieber Institute for Law and Land Warfare (United States Military Academy), sponsoring body.
Title: Big data and armed conflict : legal issues above and below the armed conflict threshold /
[edited by Laura A. Dickinson & Edward Berg]
Description: New York : Oxford University Press, [2024] | Series: Lieber studies ; volume 9 |
Includes bibliographical references and index. |
Identifiers: LCCN 2023004743 (print) | LCCN 2023004744 (ebook) |
ISBN 9780197668610 (hardback) | ISBN 9780197668634 (epub) |
ISBN 9780197668641 (online) | ISBN 9780197668627 (updf)
Subjects: LCSH: Information warfare (International law) | Big data—Law and legislation.
Classification: LCC KZ6718.B54 2024 (print) | LCC KZ6718 (ebook) |
DDC 341.6/3—dc23/eng/20230728
LC record available at https://lccn.loc.gov/2023004743
LC ebook record available at https://lccn.loc.gov/2023004744

DOI: 10.1093/oso/9780197668610.001.0001

Printed by Integrated Books International, United States of America

Note to Readers
This publication is designed to provide accurate and authoritative information in regard to the subject matter covered. It is based upon sources believed to be accurate and reliable and is intended to be current as of the time it was written. It is sold with the understanding that the publisher is not engaged in rendering legal, accounting, or other professional services. If legal advice or other expert assistance is required, the services of a competent professional person should be sought. Also, to confirm that the information has not been affected or changed by recent developments, traditional legal research techniques should be used, including checking primary sources where appropriate.

(Based on the Declaration of Principles jointly adopted by a Committee of the American Bar Association and a Committee of Publishers and Associations.)

You may order this or any other Oxford University Press publication
by visiting the Oxford University Press website at www.oup.com.

CONTENTS

Foreword ix
  Shane R. Reeves
Table of Cases xi
Table of Legislation xiii
Table of Treaties and International Instruments xv
Contributors xix

Introduction 1
  Laura A. Dickinson

Scenario 21
  Mark A. Visger

PART ONE: The *Jus ad Bellum* and Operations Below the Armed Conflict Threshold

1. Big Data: International Law Issues Below the Armed Conflict Threshold 29
   Michael N. Schmitt

2. Threatening Force in Cyberspace 55
   Duncan B. Hollis and Tsvetelina van Benthem

3. "Attacking" Big Data: Strategic Competition, the Race for AI, and the International Law of Cyber Sabotage 91
   Gary P. Corn and Eric Talbot Jensen

4. Attacking Big Data as a Use of Force 135
   Ido Kilovaty

PART TWO: International Humanitarian Law and Military Operations

5. Big Data: International Law Issues During Armed Conflict 151
   Michael N. Schmitt

6. Garbage In, Garbage Out: Data Poisoning Attacks and Their Legal Implications 179
   Mark A. Visger

7. Data Centers and International Humanitarian Law 207
   François Delerue

8. The Duty of Constant Care and Data Protection in War 229
   Asaf Lubin

9. Cyborg Soldiers: Military Use of Brain-Computer Interfaces and the Law of
   Armed Conflict 249
   Noam Lubell and Katya Al-Khateeb

**PART THREE: International Humanitarian Law and the Conduct of
Humanitarian Operations and Atrocity Investigation**

10. Corporate Data Responsibility 275
    Galit A. Sarfaty

11. Leveraging Big Data for LOAC Enforcement: Finding the Needle in a Stack
    of Needles 291
    Beth Van Schaack

PART FOUR: International Human Rights Law

12. The Datafication of Counterterrorism 319
    Fionnuala Ní Aoláin

Index 349

FOREWORD

One of many interesting threads woven into all volumes in the *Lieber Studies* is the impact of massive amounts of data in and around the modern battlefield. Previous volumes on emerging technology, complex battlespaces, the principles of proportionality and necessity, and even evidence collection in Syria have touched on the historically unprecedented effect of digital technology on the legal aspects of armed conflict; subsequent volumes on future conflict will undoubtedly do the same. For this and many more reasons, it is the right time for the Lieber Institute to dedicate a full volume to the study of "Big Data" and its attendant Law of Armed Conflict (LOAC) implications.

This volume is among the first comprehensive efforts to focus, from a legal perspective, on the importance of data to battlefield operations. Current and future combat leaders, scholars, legal advisers, and civil society members will benefit immensely from this scholarly treatment of "Big Data" and the concomitant concept of data literacy—that is, the ability of actors within military operations to draw useful conclusions from immense datasets. Each chapter in this volume not only identifies important questions surrounding the use of data in military operations but, importantly, begins the arduous process of answering such questions.

The "5 V's" of volume, variety, value, velocity, and veracity often characterize the concept of "Big Data." These important traits of datasets are readily apparent in armed conflict, as the sheer volume, variety of sources, and inherent value of data, as well as the velocity at which data travels and reaches combatants and civilians alike, have resulted in changes to doctrine, planning, training, and the actual conduct of hostilities. Yet the veracity, or the trustworthiness and accuracy, of data may be the most important lens through which to view this topic from a legal perspective.

Part I of this work underscores the importance of States' ability to ascertain accurate data in strategic competition with other States and in defense of themselves as part of the *jus ad bellum*. Part II illustrates the critical need for trustworthy information in the operational fight, with *jus in bello* regulation of conduct between parties framing an environment in which commanders receive heretofore unimagined amounts of information prior to making targeting decisions. Parts III and IV reinforce the need for accuracy in evidence collection, investigations, international human rights law, and post-conflict accountability. Regardless of conflict phase, reliable data, notwithstanding its voluminous nature, is of paramount importance to the lawful conduct of operations.

Many States have recognized the need for data literacy throughout all ranks of their militaries. The U.S. Army's XVIIIth Airborne Corps is transitioning to a data-centric operational unit as several other units commit significant resources to similar goals. At West Point, the intellectual engine of the Army's ecosystem, we are educating future officers capable of innovatively solving complex problems in compliance with the LOAC, all while harnessing the potential of ubiquitous data on the modern battlefield. Fortunately, this volume now exists to help with this and many other noble endeavors.

I congratulate the authors and editors on this exceptional work, which truly epitomizes the Lieber Institute's unrivaled efforts to tackle the most challenging legal issues related to current and future warfare.

Brigadier General Shane R. Reeves
Dean of the Academic Board
United States Military Academy
West Point, New York

TABLE OF CASES

EUROPEAN COURT OF HUMAN RIGHTS

Al-Skeini and Others v. U.K., Eur. Ct. H.R., app. no. 55721/07 (July 7, 2011) 40–41
Banković and Others v. Belgium and Others (decision as to admissibility),
    Eur. Ct. H.R., app. no. 52207/99 (Dec. 12, 2001) 40–41
Big Brother Watch and Others v. U.K., Eur. Ct. H.R., App. No. 58170/13
    (May 25, 2021) 34–35, 36–38, 41
Centrum För Rättvisa v. Sweden, Eur. Ct. H.R., app. 35252/08 (May 25, 2021) 35, 36–37
Evans v. U.K., Eur. Ct. H.R., App. No. 6339 (Apr. 10, 2007) 33
Kennedy v. U.K., Eur. Ct. H.R., app. no. 26839/05 (May 18, 2010) 36–37
Leander v. Sweden, Eur. Ct. H.R., app. no. 9248/81 (Mar. 26, 1987) 35
Malone v. U.K., Eur. Ct. H.R., App. No. 8691/79 (Aug. 2, 1984) 33–34
Peck v. U.K., Eur. Ct. H.R., App. No. 00044647/98 (Jan. 28, 2003) .33
Roman Zakharov v. Russia, Eur. Ct. H.R., app. 47143/06 (Apr. 12, 2015) 35, 36–37
Weber and Saravia v. Germany, Eur. Ct. H.R., app.54934/00 (June 29, 2006) 37

EUROPEAN COURT OF JUSTICE

Cases C-293/12 and C-594/12, Digital Rights Ireland and Seitlinger and
    Others, 2014 ECR 238 (Apr. 8) 33–34

INTERNATIONAL COURT OF JUSTICE

Corfu Channel (U.K. v. Alb.), Merits, 1949 ICJ REP. 4, 43 (Apr. 9) 128, 193–94
Military and Paramilitary Activities in and against Nicaragua (Nicar. v. U.S),
    Judgment, 1986 I.C.J. Rep. 14 (June 27) 44, 45, 46, 47, 48–49, 60–61, 63–64, 110–11,
                                        117, 122, 123, 144

INTERNATIONAL CRIMINAL COURT

Prosecutor v. Al-Werfalli, Case No. ICC-01/11/01/17, Warrant of Arrest
    (Aug. 15, 2017) 294–95

INTERNATIONAL CRIMINAL TRIBUNAL FOR THE FORMER YUGOSLAVIA

Prosecutor v. Gotovina et al., Case No, IT-06-90-T, Judgement (Apr. 15, 2011) 313
Prosecutor v. Gotovina, Case No. IT-06-90-A, Judgement, (Nov. 16, 2012) 313
Prosecutor v. Kupreskic´, Case Number IT-95-16-T, Judgment,
    (Int'l Crim. Trib. for the former Yugoslavia Jan. 14, 2000) 167

Prosecutor v. Kupreškić et al., Case No. IT-95-16-T T.Ch.II, Judgment,
  para. 524 (2000) 234–35
Prosecutor v. Tadić, Case No. IT-94-1-T, Judgment, (July 17, 1995) 345
Prosecutor v. Tadić, Case No. IT-94-1-I, Decision on the Defence Motion for
  Interlocutory Appeal on Jurisdiction ¶ 70 (Int'l Crim. Trib. for the Former
  Yugoslavia 2 October 1995 155
Prosecutor v. Tadić, Case No. IT-94-1-A, Appeals Chamber Judgment,
  (Intl'l Crim. Trib. for the Former Yugoslavia July 15, 1999) 155

PERMANENT COURT OF ARBITRATION, PALMAS

Arbitral Tribunal Constituted Pursuant to Article 287, and in Accordance with
  Annex VII, of the United Nations Convention on the Law of the Sea
  (Guyana v. Suriname), 30 RIAA 1, (Perm. Ct. Arb. 2007) 66
Island of Palmas (Neth. v. U.S.) 2 R.I.A.A. 829, 838 (Perm. Ct. Arb. 1928) 44
The Chagos Marine Protected Area Arbitration, In re, (Mar. 18, 2015)............... 230–42

PERMANENT COURT OF INTERNATIONAL JUSTICE

S.S. Lotus (Fr. v. Turk.), 1927 P.C.I.J. (ser. A) No. 10, at 18 (Sept. 7) 128

SPECIAL COURT FOR SIERRA LEONE

Prosecutor v. Norman et al., Case No. SCSL-040140t, Decision on Prosecution's
  Request to Admit into Evidence Certain Documents Pursuant to Rules
  92bis and 89(C) (July 14, 2005)... 313–14

SPECIAL TRIBUNAL FOR LEBANON

Prosecutor v. Ayyash et al., Case No. STL-11-01/T/TC, Decision on the Admission
  of Call Sequence Tables related to the Movements of Mr. Rafiq Hariri and Related
  Events, and Four Witness Statements (Oct. 31, 2016) 298–99
Prosecutor v. Ayyash et al., Case No. STL-11-01/T/TC, Judgment (Aug. 18,2020) 298–99
Prosecutor v. Ayyash, Case No. STL-11-01/A-2/AC, Appeal Judgement
  (Mar. 10, 2022) 298–99

NATIONAL CASES

Austria
De Capitani and others v. Federal Republic of Germany, Criminal Police
  Office of Austria and others 339–40

UNITED STATES
ACLU v. Clapper, 785 F.3d 787 (2nd Cir. 2015)................................ 33–34
Application of the FBI, In re, 2019 WL 5637562................................ 33–34
Carpenter v. United States, 128 S. Ct. 2206 (June 22, 2018)..........33–34, 293–94, 298–99
Ex Parte Quirin, 317 U.S. 1 1942... 104
Green v. Chicago Police Dep't, 2021 IL App. (1st) 200574 (Mar. 31, 2021) 297–98
Hamdan v. Rumsfeld, 548 U.S. (2006) 104
Hamdi v. Rumsfeld, 542 U.S. (2004).. 104
hiQ Labs, Inc. v. LinkedIn Corp., Case: 17-16783 (Nov. 27, 2017) 296–97
hiQ Labs, Inc. v. LinkedIn Corp., 938 F.3d 985 (9th Cir. 2019) 296–97
Smith v. Maryland, 442 U.S. 735 (1979)...............................33–34, 293–94
United States v. Kotey, Indictment, Case 1:20-cr-00239-TSE (Oct. 6, 2020).......... 294–95
U.S. v. Lizarraga-Tirado, 789 F.3d 1107, 1110 (2015) 298–99

TABLE OF LEGISLATION

EUROPEAN UNION

Directives

Council Directive 2016/681 of April 27, 2016, The Use of Passenger Name Record (PNR) Data for the Prevention, Detection, Investigation and Prosecution of Terrorist Offences and Serious Crime (L119) 339–40

Regulations

Regulation (EU) 2016/679, of the European Parliament and the Council of 27 April 2016 on the Protection of Natural Persons with Regard to the Processing of Personal Data and on the Free Movement of Such Data, and Repealing Directive 95/46/EC (General Data Protection Regulation), Art. 83(5), 2016 O.J. (L 119) 1 .... 287–88, 293, 328
Art. 5(1)(b) 287–88

UNITED STATES

Computer Fraud and Abuse Act 1986 (CFAA) 296–97
Military Commissions Act of 2006, HR-6166, Oct. 17, 2006 324–25
Sabotage Act, 18 U.S.C. §§ 2151– 2156 (2018).......... 104–5

TABLE OF TREATIES AND INTERNATIONAL INSTRUMENTS

American Convention on Human Rights, Nov. 22, 1969, Series no. 36, at 1, Organization of American States, Official Record, OEA/Ser.L/V/II.23

Art 11 32–33

Armistice Agreement, 11 November 1918 57–58

ASEAN Declaration, Nov. 19, 2012

Principle 21 32–33

Berkeley Protocol on Digital Open Source Investigations, Dec. 1, 2020 ("Berkeley Protocol") Human Rights Center, University of California, Berkeley/UN Office of the High Commissioner for Human Rights 309

Charter of the United Nations, G.A. Res. 2625 (XXV), U.N. Doc. A/8082 (Sept. 28, 1970) 60–61, 64, 66, 71, 109, 110–11, 123

Ch VII 45, 78–79, 328–29, 331–32

Art 1(1) 60

Art 2 .... 107–8, 138–39

Art 2(1) 88–89

Art 2(4) 9, 38, 44–45, 57–58, 60, 64, 68–69, 77–78, 107–8, 116, 122, 138–39, 141, 142, 143–44

Art 51 .... 45, 48–49, 107–8, 110, 111–12, 138–39, 145

Principle (c). 44

Convention Against Torture and Other Cruel, Inhuman or Degrading Treatment or Punishment, Dec. 10, 1984, 1465 U.N.T.S. 85

Art 3 284–85

Convention on Prohibitions or Restrictions on the Use of Certain Conventional Weapons Which May Be Deemed to Be Excessively Injurious or to Have Indiscriminate Effects, Group of Governmental Experts on Emerging Technologies in the Area of Lethal Autonomous Weapons System 96 (Apr. 19, 2021) 268–69

Convention for the Protection of Individuals with regard to Automatic Processing of Personal Data, Oct. 1 1985, ETS No. 108

Art 1 32–33

Art 11 247

Consolidated Version of the Treaty on European Union (TEU), Oct. 26, 2012, 2012 O.J. (C 326) 15)

Art 4(2) 328

Declaration on the Inadmissibility of Intervention and Interference in the Internal Affairs of States, G.A. Res. 36/103, U.N. Doc. A/RES/36/103 (Dec. 9, 1981)

Annex 44

Declaration on Principles of International Law concerning Friendly Relations and Cooperation among States in accordance with the Charter of the United Nations, G.A. Res. 2625 (XXV), U.N. Doc. A/8082 (Sept. 28, 1970) 60–61, 69–70

Principle (c). 44

European Charter on Fundamental Rights (2000). 339–40

European Convention for the
Protection of Human Rights
and Fundamental Freedoms
(ECHR), Nov. 4, 1950, 213
U.N.T.S. 221...... 33–34, 35, 36–37, 41
s I 40
Art 1 40
Art 8 .... 32–33, 37–38
Art 8(2) 37–38
Geneva Conventions 1949 .... 155, 162–63,
188–89, 211–12, 238,
246, 331–32, 345
Convention (I) for the Amelioration of
the Condition of the Wounded and
Sick in the Armed Forces in the
Field, Aug. 12, 1949, 6 U.S.T.
3114, 75 U.N.T.S. 31 ...... 155, 188–89
Art 2 .... 154, 188–89
Art 3 ....175, 345
Art 12 265–66
Art 24 160–61
Convention (II) for the Amelioration
of the Condition of the Wounded,
Sick, and Shipwrecked Members
of Armed Forces at Sea, Aug. 12,
1949, 6 U.S.T. 3217, 75 U.N.T.S. 85
Art 2 ....154, 188–89,
Art 3 ....175, 345
Convention (III) Relative to the
Treatment of Prisoners of War,
Aug. 12, 1949, 6 U.S.T. 3316, 75
U.N.T.S. 135. .... 155, 331–32
Art 2 .... 154, 188–89
Art 3 ....175, 345
Art 4 331–32
Art 109(1) 265–66
Convention (IV) Relative to the
Protection of Civilian Persons
in Time of War, Aug. 12, 1949,
6 U.S.T. 3516, 75 U.N.T.S. 287 174
Art 2 .... 154, 188–89
Art 3 ....175, 345
Art 32 265–66
Protocol Additional to the Geneva
Conventions of 12 August 1949,
and Relating to the Protection of
Victims of International Armed
Conflicts, June 8, 1977, 1125
U.N.T.S. 3 (Additional
Protocol I) 14–15, 156–57, 176–77,
178, 197–98, 213–14,
234–35, 236, 237,
238, 262
Art 1(2) 240–41

Art 11(5) 265–66
Art 13.3 160–61
Art 36 ....176, 262
Art 37 204
Art 37(1) 173, 267
Art 37(2) 174
Art 38(1) 174
Art 42(1) 162–63
Art 43 .... 160–61, 210–11
Art 43(2) 160–61
Art 48 .... 160–61, 166, 210–11, 221
Art 49 156–57
Art 49(1) 119
Art 50 210–11
Art 50(1) 210–11
Art 51 .... 39–40, 196–97, 221
Art 51(2) 156–57, 161, 169–70,
173, 230–31
Art 51(3) .·.................... 160–61
Art 51(4) 196–97
Art 51(4)(a) 167, 196–97
Art 51(4)(a)(b) 167
Art 51(4)(b). 196–97
Art 51(4)(c) 197
Art 51(5) 221
Art 51(5)(b). 156–57, 169–70, 197–98
Art 52 .... 210–11, 216
Art 52(1) 156–57, 163–64
Art 52(2) 162–63, 211, 212–13,
226–27, 264–65
Art 53 218–19
Art 54 218–19
Art 55 218–19
Art 56 218–19
Art 57 234–35
Art 57(1) 171, 201–2, 221, 234–35
Art 57(2) 156–57, 170
Art 57(2)(a)(ii) 166–67
Art 57(2)(a)(iii) 156–57, 169–70
Art 57(2)(b). 156–57, 169–70
Art 58. .... 171–72, 235
Art 58(c) 235
Additional Protocol II ... 12–13, 238, 345
Art 12 174
Hague Convention (II) Respecting the
Laws and Customs of War on Land
with Annex of Regulations, July
29, 1899, 32 Stat. 1803, 1 Bevans 247
preamble 192, 240–41
Hague Convention (IV) Respecting
the Laws and Customs of War on
Land, 36 Stat. 2277, 207 Consol.
T.S. 277, 18 October 1907 193–94
preamble 240–41

TABLE OF TREATIES AND INTERNATIONAL INSTRUMENTS

International Convention for the Protection of All Persons from Enforced Disappearance, Jan. 12, 2007, U.N. Doc. A/RES/61/177
Art 16 284–85

International Covenant on Civil and Political Rights (ICCPR), Dec. 16, 1966, 999 U.N.T.S. 171 .... 36, 40–41, 175–76
Art 2 41
Art 2(1) 31–32, 40, 41
Art 4 176
Art 4(1) 36
Art 4(3) 36
Art 17(1) 32–33, 36

International Covenant on Economic, Social and Cultural Rights (ICESCR), Dec. 16, 1966, 993 U.N.T.S. 3 40

Kellogg-Briand Pact, 98 L.N.T.S. no. 1-4 (1928) 34

League of Nations Covenant (1920–1946)
Art 12 60

United Nations Convention on the Law of the Sea (UNCLOS) 1982 241–42

United Nations Conventions Relating to the Status of Refugees, Art. 33, Apr. 22, 1954, 189 U.N.T.S. 150
Art 33 284–85

Universal Declaration of Human Rights 1948
Art 12 32–33

CONTRIBUTORS

Katya Al-Khateeb is Senior Research Officer, School of Law & Human Rights Centre, University of Essex.

Edward W. Berg, Lieutenant Colonel (ret.), U.S. Army, is a former Assistant Professor in the Department of Law, United States Military Academy at West Point.

Gary P. Corn is Director of the Technology, Law & Security Program and an Adjunct Professor of Cyber and National Security Law and the Law of Armed Conflict at American University Washington College of Law.

François Delerue is an Assistant Professor of Law at IE University. He is also an Associate Fellow of the Hague Program on International Cyber Security at Leiden University and the GEODE Center at Paris 8 University.

Laura A. Dickinson is the Oswald Symister Colclough Research Professor and Professor of Law at George Washington University School of Law.

Duncan B. Hollis is the Laura H. Carnell Professor of Law, Temple University School of Law and Non-Resident Fellow, Carnegie Endowment for International Peace.

Eric Talbot Jensen is the Robert W. Barker Professor of Law at Brigham Young University Law School.

Ido Kilovaty is an Associate Professor of Law at the University of Arkansas School of Law; an Affiliate at the Center for Law, Innovation and Creativity at Northeastern University Law School; a Visiting Faculty Fellow at the Center for Global Legal Challenges at Yale Law School; and an Affiliated Fellow at the Information Society Project at Yale Law School.

Robert Lawless is an Assistant Professor in the Department of Law and the Research Director of the Lieber Institute for Law and Warfare at the United States Military Academy at West Point.

Noam Lubell is Professor of International Law of Armed Conflict, University of Essex; Senior Research Fellow, Johns Hopkins University Applied Physics

Laboratory; Research Associate, Federmann Cyber Security Research Center, Hebrew University.

Dr. Asaf Lubin is an Associate Professor of Law at Indiana University Maurer School of Law, a Fellow at IU's Center for Applied Cybersecurity Research, a Faculty Associate at the Berkman Klein Center for Internet and Society at Harvard University, an Affiliated Fellow at the Information Society Project at Yale Law School, and a Visiting Scholar at the Federmann Cyber Security Center at Hebrew University of Jerusalem.

Fionnuala Ní Aoláin is Regents Professor and Robina Chair in Law, Public Policy and Society, University of Minnesota Law School and Professor of Law, The Queens University of Belfast, Northern Ireland.

Shane R. Reeves, Brigadier General, U.S. Army, is the Dean of the Academic Board for the United States Military Academy at West Point. Brigadier General Reeves is also the Co-Founder of the Lieber Series.

Galit A. Sarfaty is Canada Research Chair in Global Economic Governance and Associate Professor, Allard School of Law, University of British Columbia.

Michael N. Schmitt is the G. Norman Lieber Distinguished Scholar at the United States Military Academy at West Point; Professor of International Law, University of Reading; and Professor Emeritus, United States Naval War College.

Tsvetelina van Benthem is a Lecturer in international law for the Oxford Diplomatic Studies Programme and researcher at the Oxford Institute for Ethics, Law and Armed Conflict and Merton College, Oxford.

Beth Van Schaack is Leah Kaplan Visiting Professor in Human Rights, Stanford Law School.

Mark A. Visger is an Academy Professor, Army at the Army Cyber Institute, United States Military Academy at West Point.

Sean Watts is a Professor of Law and Co-Director of the Lieber Institute for Law and Warfare at the United States Military Academy at West Point. He is also a Visiting Professor at the University of Reading.

Introduction

Translation or Disruption? International Law, Military Operations, and the Challenges of Big Data

LAURA A. DICKINSON* ■

Data is emerging as a key component of military operations, both on and off the battlefield. Large troves of data generated by new information technologies such as mobile Internet, cloud storage, social networking, and the "Internet of things," as well as the advanced analytics used to process that data—often termed "Big Data"—are growing ever more important to a wide range of military functions.[1] Military forces and other actors will increasingly need to acquire, evaluate, and utilize such data in many combat contexts, such as making probability-based forecasts of enemy behavior, aggregating weather and environmental conditions, anticipating and flagging supply line vulnerabilities, or identifying and tracking targets. At the same time, those forces can gain advantages by targeting adversaries' data and data systems, and acquiring, distorting, or deleting data. And a multitude of actors within armed conflict, including humanitarian and human rights organizations, can also use Big Data from a variety of sources to engage in functions such as delivering aid or identifying atrocities.

The moniker "Big Data" encompasses both "the exponentially increasing amount of digital information being created by new information technologies"[2]

---

* Oswald Symister Colclough Research Professor and Professor of Law, George Washington University School of Law.

1. Paul B. Symon & Arzan Tarapore, *Defense Intelligence Analysis in the Age of Big Data*, 79 JOINT FORCE Q. 5 (2015) (defining "Big Data" as "the exponentially increasing amount of digital information being created by new information technologies–such as mobile Internet, cloud storage, social networking, and the 'Internet of things'–and the advanced analytics used to process that data").

2. *Id.*

Laura A. Dickinson, *Introduction* In: *Big Data and Armed Conflict.* Edited by: Laura A. Dickinson and Edward W. Berg, Oxford University Press. © Laura A. Dickinson 2024. DOI: 10.1093/oso/9780197668610.003.0001

and the analytics used to process that data, as well as its networked quality.[3] The term thus commonly also includes the variety of new technologies and software tools used to create, aggregate, and analyze large datasets.[4] The White House defines "Big Data" as encompassing three V's: the "growing technological ability to capture, aggregate, and process an ever-greater volume, velocity, and variety of data."[5] The utility of Big Data therefore derives not solely from volume, but also "in its nature, which reveals patterns, shows connections about an individual and between individuals, and more."[6] Artificial intelligence (AI) systems, especially those that operate through machine learning, both rely on and evaluate such data. These systems in turn generate an enormous appetite for ever-more data. As contributor Ido Kilovaty has observed, "the technological ecosystem that we have created in the last decade is now also the biggest data mining operation in human history." Data is so important that some have termed it "the new oil."[7] It is arguably the fuel of modern society.

On the battlefield, Big Data is being deployed, and has the potential to be deployed, for an astonishing array of purposes. Increasingly, weapons systems depend on unfathomably large quantities of data in order to operate. And technologies that process and analyze large quantities of data can exponentially increase military capabilities. As contributor Asaf Lubin documents, wartime actors are now employing "machine learning and artificial intelligence to enhance their military capabilities and decision-making."[8] They "use 'Big Data' and algorithmic tools to both predict enemy actions[9] and to enhance their own command-and-control capacities." Militaries are using Big Data and associated technologies "to improve their procurement, transportation, and redeployment of material and personnel" as well as to engage in a variety of battlefield functions, for example, to "launch targeted killing operations and automate the collection and analysis of

---

3. Danah Boyd & Kate Crawford, *Critical Questions for Big Data: Provocations for a Cultural, Technological, and Scholarly Phenomenon*, 15 INFORMATION, COMMUNICATION & SOCIETY 662, 663 (2012).

4. James Manyika et al., *Big Data: The Next Frontier for Innovation, Competition, and Productivity* 1, MCKINSEY GLOBAL INST. (2011), http://www.mckinsey.com/business-functions/business-tec hnology/our-insights/big-data-the-next-frontier-for-innovation.

5. EXEC. OFFICE OF THE PRESIDENT, BIG DATA: SEIZING OPPORTUNITIES, PRESERVING VALUES, THE WHITE HOUSE, 2 (May 2014), https://obamawhitehouse.archives.gov/sites/default/files/docs/big_data_privacy_report_may_1_2014.pdf.

6. Ido Kilovaty, "Chapter 4: Attacking Big Data as a Use of Force," this book, at 137 (citing Boyd & Crawford, *supra* note 3).

7. This quotation is widely attributed to Clive Humby. Charles Arthur, *Tech Giants May Be Huge, but Nothing Matches Big Data*, THE GUARDIAN (Aug. 23, 2013, 3:21 PM), https://www.theguard ian.com/technology/2013/aug/23/tech-giants-data; *see also* Chapter 6, "Garbage In, Garbage Out" (referring to this quotation).

8. *See also* Ashley S. Deeks, *Predicting Enemies*, 104 VIRGINIA L. REV. 1529, 1531 (2018).

9. *Deeks, supra* note 8, at 1531.

Introduction

military intelligence." China and Russia are also incorporating AI into their military weapons systems, a development that requires Big Data.[10] In addition, Big Data is increasingly essential to military detention operations. As discussed by contributor Fionuala Ni Aolain, government and intergovernmental authorities are using biometric data gathered on detainees and others to track and monitor those individuals in counterterrorism initiatives around the globe. And, as contributor François Delerue has observed, all of this data must be stored. Militaries have therefore been housing huge data sets in massive data centers around the globe.

Furthermore, experts suggest that some wartime uses of Big Data that may sound like the stuff of science fiction are in fact just over the horizon. For example, targeting systems could deploy AI-enabled facial recognition technology on a vast scale, which in turn would rely on enormous data sets of facial images.[11] And, as contributors Noam Lubell and Katya Al-Khateeb have noted, brain-computer interface (BCI) Big Data-fueled technology holds the promise for some remarkable battlefield applications in the relatively near future. With BCI technology, computer systems will download and upload large quantities of data from armed forces in the field, thereby enhancing the performance of those forces by enabling "a wide range of superhuman abilities such as extra-sensorial perception, superstrength, or super-precision."[12] Big Data therefore has the potential not only to revolutionize the tools armed forces use to fight, but to transform members of the armed forces themselves.

Big Data is also gaining an increasing role in humanitarian operations on, and adjacent to, the battlefield. Humanitarian organizations are deploying technologies dependent on Big Data to detect atrocities, monitor humanitarian crises, and deliver aid. As contributor Galit Sarfaty notes, such data includes "data exhaust (e.g., cell phone records), online activity (e.g., social media), sensing technologies (e.g., satellite data), and crowdsourced information."[13] Fueled by such data, Big Data analytics can facilitate early warning systems and provide real-time awareness of atrocities. For example, as detailed by Sarfaty, the Syria Tracker project "crowdsourced text, photo and video reports, and data-mining techniques to form a live map of the Syrian conflict."[14] And analytical

10. *See, e.g.*, Patrick Tucker, *New Drones, Weapons Get Spotlight in China's Military Parade*, DEF. ONE (Oct. 1, 2019), https://www.defenseone.com/technology/2019/10/new-drones-weapons-get-spotlight-chinas-military-parade/160291/; Franz-Stefan Gady, *Russia's New Nuclear Torpedo-Carrying Sub to Begin Sea Trials in June 2020*, DIPLOMAT (Sept. 10, 2019), https://thediplomat.com/2019/09/russias-new-nuclear-torpedo-carrying-sub-to-begin-sea-trials-in-june-2020/.

11. Stop Autonomous Weapons, *Slaughterbots*, YOUTUBE (Nov. 12, 2017), https://www.youtube.com/watch?v=9CO6M2HsoIA.

12. Noam Lubell & Katya Al-Khateeb, "Chapter 9: Cyborg Soldiers: Military Use of Brain-Computer Interfaces and the Law of Armed Conflict," this book, at 252.

13. Galit A. Sarfaty, "Chapter 10: Corporate Data Responsibility," this book, at 275.

14. *Id.* at 276. *See also Syria Tracker*, HUMANITARIAN TRACKER, http://www.humanitariantracker.org/#!syria-tracker/cj00.

tools powered by Big Data have also helped address refugee crises related to armed conflict. International organizations are using such tools to "identify potential refugee/migration exoduses; track[] refugee/migrant movements; and resettl[e] . . . refugees/migrants."[15]

Big Data is also serving as a key tool to investigate and prosecute those responsible for wartime atrocities. Whether gleaned from social media or from sensing and "smart technologies," a variety of global actors are gathering and using vast data sets in war crimes accountability efforts. As noted by contributor Beth Van Schaack, "national prosecutors have convicted fighters who have fled the war in Syria for war crimes, including murder and mistreating a corpse, based almost exclusively on trophy photos shared on Facebook, found on their phones, or discovered online."[16] If they can be obtained, datasets "produced in the ordinary course of modern life—such as cell phone and financial records, Internet search histories, bureaucratic reports, and administrative archives"—can be exploited by prosecutors for purposes such as "geolocation of people and events, fugitive tracking, and social network analysis."[17] Governmental, intergovernmental, and nongovernmental war crimes investigators are also purposefully compiling large quantities of information by digitizing found or exfiltrated documents and scraping social media platforms.[18] It is therefore not an exaggeration to say that Big Data has the potential to disrupt and radically change how atrocities are investigated and prosecuted.

Beyond the battlefield, Big Data lies at the epicenter of adversarial activities below the armed conflict threshold. Big Data is the fuel of an emerging AI "arms race" among the United States, China, Russia, and others. Notably, China has announced that it intends to become the leading AI power by 2030, seeking to dominate in advanced computing, Big Data analytics, autonomy, and robotics.[19] And indeed, China has a distinct advantage in achieving this aim because it does not comply with international human rights law (IHRL) principles, such as the right to privacy, when it collects that data. It therefore "is leveraging" the "lower

---

15. Sarfaty, *supra* note 13, at 276.

16. Beth Van Schaack, "Chapter 11: Leveraging Big Data for LOAC Enforcement: Finding the Needle in a Stack of Needles," this book, at 294–95. Such evidence also undergirds the January 6th prosecutions, given the propensity of participants to post incriminating videos of their actions breaching the U.S. Capitol and the prevalence of security cameras in the area. *See* Roger Parloff, *What Do—and Will—the Criminal Prosecutions of the Jan. 6 Capitol Rioters Tell Us?*, LAWFARE (Nov. 4, 2021).

17. Van Schaack, *supra* note 16, at 298.

18. *See id.* at 296.

19. *See* Gary P. Corn & Eric Talbot Jensen, "Chapter 3: 'Attacking' Big Data: Strategic Competition, the Race for AI, and the International Law of Cyber Sabotage," this book (citing Paul Mozur, *Beijing Wants A.I.to Be Made in China by 2030*, N.Y. TIMES (July 20, 2017), https://www.nytimes.com/2017/07/20/business/china-artificial-intelligence.html_).

Introduction

barriers to data collection and lower costs to data labeling to create the large databases on which AI systems train . . . with the potential to have over 30% [of the world's share of data] by 2030."[20] Needless to say, such large quantities of data are essential for AI systems to function.[21]

Because machine learning systems train using enormous data sets, an endless cycle is created: data powers AI systems, which in turn target data, which in turn power AI systems. This relentless quest for more data creates enormous incentives for cyberattacks. As contributors Gary Corn and Eric Jensen emphasize, Big Data has powered AI systems that are engaging in malicious cyber and information operations aimed at data itself. From the recent SolarWinds Orion software hack, which affected as many as 18,000 entities including multiple U.S. government agencies and private sector companies, to the cyberattack on India's Addhaar biometric ID database, which exposed the personal information of more than one billion people, operations to obtain sensitive data can, as contributor Ido Kilovaty observes, "enable the adversary to misuse these credentials in future cyber operations as well as make powerful inferences based on the quality and quantity of the data."[22] And, in this endless cyber-arms race, Big Data can also provide mechanisms to *thwart* these sorts of attacks. As Duncan Hollis and Tsvetelina van Benthem emphasize, Big Data analytics can offer mechanisms to detect and block cyber and other threats that "may be, for their scope and speed, undecipherable to the human mind."[23]

LEGAL CHALLENGES

The growing use of Big Data raises a wide variety of international legal issues and challenges, both with regard to armed conflicts and extraterritorial military and other adversarial actions that might fall below the armed conflict threshold. A significant scholarly and policy literature has touched on some of these issues, primarily in the context of evaluating AI and its application to weapons systems.[24] In addition, debates about cyber operations above and below the armed conflict threshold have grappled with some international legal issues related to

20. *See, e.g.*, Congressional Research Service, *Artificial Intelligence and National Security*, Nov. 21, 2019, at 22-23, at https://fas.org/sgp/crs/natsec/R45178.pdf [hereinafter "*AI and National Security*"].

21. *See* National Security Commission on Artificial Intelligence 32 (Mar. 1, 2021), https://www.nscai.gov/wp-content/uploads/2021/03/Full-Report-Digital-1.pdf.

22. Kilovaty, *supra* note 6, at 136.

23. Duncan B. Hollis & Tsvetelina Van Benthem, "Chapter 2: Threatening Force in Cyberspace," this book, at 82.

24. *See, e.g.*, Ken Anderson & Matthew Waxman, *Debating Autonomous Weapon Systems, Their Ethics, and Their Regulation Under International Law*, in THE OXFORD HANDBOOK OF LAW, REGULATION, AND TECHNOLOGY (2017); *See also* Deeks, *supra* note 8.

the targeting of data.[25] This book, however, is perhaps the first effort to focus specifically on Big Data within military operations and to analyze the variety of legal challenges and issues arising under the international humanitarian law (IHL) and related bodies of international law, including the *jus ad bellum* and IHRL.

To begin with, the increasing role of Big Data across such a broad variety of operations presents enormous challenges for the interpretation and application of IHL. To what extent, and how, does IHL apply to the variety of military operations that involve data, such as targeting? The collection and use of large data sets in weapons systems and for other purposes raise significant questions about data acquisition, retention, and privacy. In addition, biases in data create potential operational risks and the possible misidentification of targets.[26] Do IHL rules and principles that govern targeting and other operations encompass such concerns? To what extent does IHL's principle of distinction impose an obligation to weed out such biases? Does the IHL principle of feasible precautions require testing of algorithms used to distill Big Data in some circumstances to ensure there are no systemic problems that could lead to mistaken targeting of civilians? Is the use of Big Data to operate a particular weapons system itself a weapon that must undergo weapons review procedures? Are there any transparency or "explainability" rules that derive from IHL in this domain, or which should be adopted as a matter of policy?

Furthermore, because of the enormous importance of data to military operations, such data is now itself a target, and adversaries will seek to acquire it, delete it, damage it, or "poison it." As contributor Mark Visger postulates, one likely "vector of attack" in the future will likely be against data. To what extent do IHL principles and rules govern such operations? For example, are operations against data "attacks," as defined in IHL and therefore subject to the IHL rules governing "attacks"? Is data an "object" under IHL targeting rules? When is data civilian, and when is it military in character? May data centers be lawfully targeted if such centers house civilian and military data or are located outside the battlefield? Should harm to civilian data, without any corresponding "kinetic effects," be included as civilian harm in an analysis of the principles of distinction and proportionality? When do operations against data constitute perfidy? And how does IHL encompass the ever-growing role of Big Data in humanitarian relief operations and the efforts of governments and other actors to investigate and prosecute war

---

25. *See, e.g.*, République Francaise, Min. des Armeés, Droit International Appliqué aux Opérations dans le Cyberspace (2019) ["International Law Applicable to Operations in Cyberspace"]; Heather A. Harrison Dinniss, *The Nature of Objects: Targeting Networks and the Challenge of Defining Cyber Military Objectives*, 48 Israel L. Rev. 1 (2015); Michael N. Schmitt, *Wired Warfare 3.0: Protecting the Civilian Population during Cyber Operations*, 101 Int'l Rev. Red Cross 333 (2019).

26. *See, e.g.*, *AI and National Security*, *supra* note 20, at 30, at https://fas.org/sgp/crs/natsec/R45 178.pdf

Introduction 7

crimes? Does IHL include norms prohibiting data bias and privacy intrusions in this context?

The role of "Big Data" on the battlefield also raises important questions under IHRL. International human rights law encompasses more explicit norms that protect privacy rights and prohibit discrimination and bias than other bodies of international law. To what extent do IHRL norms apply to operations that use or target data on the battlefield? This question implicates complex issues related to the extraterritorial application of IHRL rules, as well as the intersection of IHRL and IHL within armed conflict zones. If states interpret IHL narrowly to exclude operations that target data or that use data in ways that infringe on privacy or entail bias, does IHRL fill those gaps? Or might IHRL principles and values influence the understanding of IHL concepts such as civilian harm?

Below the armed conflict threshold, adversarial actions reliant on, or aimed at, Big Data generate challenging questions under the *jus ad bellum* as well. As in the case of IHL, are norms regarding privacy or bias incorporated within the *jus ad bellum*? When do operations against data constitute a prohibited threat or use of force, or amount to an armed attack? When do such operations fall within the generally acceptable domain of cyber espionage? And in what circumstances do operations aimed at acquiring, altering, or deleting data interfere with sovereignty?

Finally, it is significant that states (and non-state actors) may interpret these various questions differently. And of course, because non-state actors play such important roles in producing, collecting, and storing data, the doctrine of state responsibility may come under pressure as well. In the end, the very uncertainty about the scope and content of international legal norms governing Big Data poses its own challenges, not only for the application of these bodies of law independently, but also for questions related to how these bodies of law intersect. Indeed, it may be that the rules incorporated within any of these three bodies of law are inadequate to address a context in which private companies, non-state actors, and individuals are generating, collecting, owning, or seeking access to "Big Data." And what about the increasing number of countries that reject the rules of the international law-based order altogether?

Collectively, the chapters in this book provide a pathbreaking attempt both to define the important legal questions related to the use of Big Data in extraterritorial military operations, and to begin to provide some answers. The volume begins with a detailed scenario developed by the U.S. Army Cyber Institute, West Point Professor Mark Visger, and the co-editors of this volume. The scenario imagines a hypothetical armed conflict between two superpowers, in which Big Data plays a crucial role at every stage. The scenario also includes activities that incorporate Big Data prior to the armed conflict, as well as outside the territory of the battlefield. Rather than imagining the use of data in a far-distant future, the scenario is based on capabilities that either exist now or could be developed in the relatively near future. The goal of the scenario is to set the scene for the legal analyses that follow in the subsequent chapters, which are grouped loosely around questions related to the *jus ad bellum*; IHL and military operations; IHL and the conduct of humanitarian operations and atrocity investigation; and IHRL.

PART ONE: THE *JUS AD BELLUM* AND OPERATIONS BELOW THE ARMED CONFLICT THRESHOLD

One of the most vexing contemporary questions in the interpretation of the *jus ad bellum*, as in the interpretation of other bodies of international law, is whether—and if so how—various legal categories apply to data. We might call this issue a translation problem. To some degree, international lawyers, scholars, and policy makers have been tackling this question in the context of a broader translation exercise: the application of this body of law to cyber operations more generally. Here, the question is whether cyber operations might cross various key thresholds in the law, such as the prohibitions on the use of force and armed attacks. Probably the dominant approach to this issue calls for lawyers to examine whether the effects of any particular cyber activity are kinetic or akin to having kinetic effect.

Yet, operations involving data confound this approach. Such operations can, of course, have kinetic effects. But often, the effects are profound and far-reaching without having any kinetic effect. So, the increasing importance of data pokes a hole into this dominant mode of analysis. Indeed, the emergence of "Big Data" turns that hole into a gaping chasm. The sheer size of data, and its corresponding importance, raises significant questions about the viability of the kinetic effects approach. Several chapters in the book explore key aspects of these important issues.

Michael Schmitt frames the discussion by analyzing the scenario published at the beginning of the book. Using the scenario as a springboard, he highlights the key debates within legal and scholarly circles about how to apply *jus ad bellum* categories to cyber operations involving data.[27] He describes the debates among states and scholars first over whether sovereignty is a flexible principle or a relatively bright-line rule, and then the further debate among states and scholars who view sovereignty as a rule with regard to how to best *apply* that rule to operations involving the collection or targeting of data. Although there is wide agreement that espionage and mis- or dis-information would fall below the line, he observes that it remains to be settled "whether a cyber operation that temporarily interferes with cyberinfrastructure functionality"—such as deletion or alteration of data—violates sovereignty.[28] He then turns to the issue of how the *ad bellum* use of force and armed attack thresholds would apply to operations involving data. With respect to the use of force, he explains that operations involving data can pose a special challenge because states and experts are divided on the question of

27. He also highlights the issues under IHRL, discussed below.

28. Michael N. Schmitt, "Chapter 1: Big Data: International Law Issues Below the Armed Conflict Threshold," this book, at 43.

Introduction

whether an operation "that is neither physically destructive nor injurious . . . ever may qualify as a use of force subject to the prohibition."[29] Although most states and experts would follow a multi-factor "scale and effects" test, wide disagreement abounds over how to apply that test to operations to delete or destroy data that, for example, might result in significant economic harm. He maps out the similar disagreement that reigns over the interpretation of the armed attack threshold.

Duncan Hollis and Tsvetelina van Benthem tackle one particularly challenging aspect of these debates, specifically, the under-explored question of how the prohibition on the "threat" to use force applies in cyberspace, and especially to operations involving data. Article 2(4) of the UN Charter, a foundational provision of the *jus ad bellum*, prohibits not just the use of force but also the "threat" of force. Hollis and van Benthem chart key approaches to analyzing such prohibited threats and then focus on how those approaches might govern cyber operations, particularly those involving "Big Data." Their central claim is that the dominant "effects-based" approach to applying the threat standard is not adequate to address contemporary cyber operations. They point out that, while "[s]ome cyberthreats are overt and readily apparent to victims (e.g., ransomware)," others "function like virtual tunnels *(e.g.,* web shells that afford access to targeted systems via hidden 'back doors')."[30] Furthermore, they observe that the emergence of "Big Data" and Big Data analytics increase capabilities for detecting threats and provide an expanded medium for wielding them. In this data-rich environment, they argue that lawyers and other stakeholders should interpret threats to include credible threats that go beyond those with kinetic effects. They maintain that expanding the conception of "threat" in cyberspace serves an important purpose because of "the polysemous nature of many cyberthreats (they can have multiple meanings for victims and observers) combined with the scale and reach of persistent cyber operations,"[31] which suggests that the need for a theory of prohibited cyberthreats may be greater in cyberspace than in kinetic contexts. Finally, they argue that "*technical* developments—chiefly the rise of Big Data—will increasingly provide States and other actors with a capacity to apply the threat prohibition in more meaningful ways (albeit not without attendant risks/costs)."[32]

Gary Corn and Eric Jensen confront the question of whether cyber-sabotage operations involving data, in the context of tensions between "near-peer" states, can be lawful. They focus primarily on strategic competition between the United States and China, and to a lesser degree the United States and Russia, although their analysis would apply to any such "near-peer" tensions. Corn and Jensen point out that "the race to develop AI is fast becoming a central front in th[is]

---

29. *Id.* at 45.

30. Hollis & Van Benthem, *supra* note 23, at 56.

31. *Id.* at 59.

32. *Id.*

strategic competition" and that a critical component for developing AI systems "is the availability of sufficiently large, relevant, and accurate datasets for AI systems and their underlying algorithms to train on."[33] In other words, competition over the acquisition and use of data lies at the heart of rising tensions between the United States and China. Further, they make the sobering claim that China's authoritarian governance system and lack of respect for the rule of law seem to give the country an edge:

> China's mass data collection and aggregation practices—through unconstrained domestic surveillance programs, nearly unfettered access to Chinese companies' data sets, and relentless theft and exploitation of foreign data— offer China at least one distinct point of comparative advantage in the AI race. Simply put, China is awash in big data.[34]

Yet, at the same time, they note that, "this apparent strength also creates a vulnerability, and hence an opportunity."[35] Specifically, they argue that cyber-sabotage is an important means of tying China's hands and potentially constraining other near-peer competitors. The heart of their chapter, therefore, contains a legal analysis of potential cyber-sabotage operations under the *jus ad bellum* framework. They conclude that many such operations can lawfully sabotage China's AI development without running afoul of the prohibition on the use of force or the doctrine of prohibited intervention, depending on how the cyber means are employed. They maintain that "[c]arefully crafted precision tools might be used to poison China's progress in AI without crossing any thresholds barred by international law."[36]

Like Hollis and van Benthem, Ido Kilovaty examines the application of Article 2(4) to cyber operations. And also like Hollis and van Benthem, Kilovaty argues that states and other stakeholders should move beyond an interpretation that is limited to assessing kinetic effects. Rather than focusing on how to interpret the "threat" to use force, however, Kilovaty addresses the use-of-force threshold itself. Although some states, such as the United States and Israel, interpret the use of force to encompass only those cyber operations that have kinetic effects, Kilovaty agrees with countries such as France and the Netherlands that even non-kinetic operations causing harm to data can constitute the use of force. However, once one dispenses with the kinetic effects test, it can be difficult to draw a principled line for determining what sorts of operation constitute a use of force and what do not. Kilovaty seeks to solve this

---

33. Gary P. Corn & Eric Talbot Jensen, "Chapter 3: 'Attacking' Big Data: Strategic Competition, the Race for AI, and the International Law of Cyber Sabotage," this book, at 92–93.

34. *Id.* at 93.

35. *Id.*

36. *Id.* at 95.

Introduction

conundrum by focusing on the concept of "Big Data" itself. He argues that the sheer scale and scope of data affected by a cyber operation can help states draw this line, because "cyber operations targeting Big Data are much more devastating than cyber operations against Small Data."[37] Thus, he suggests that only cyber operations that impact "Big Data" would constitute the use of force for purposes of Article 2(4).

PART TWO: INTERNATIONAL HUMANITARIAN LAW AND MILITARY OPERATIONS

As in the case of the *jus ad bellum*, military operations that use or target Big Data present an enormous translation exercise under IHL. Operations that target Big Data confound the ordinary application of IHL categories in part because, as discussed in Part One, such operations can have enormous consequences even without kinetic effects. And operations that rely on data present their own set of legal conundrums, including whether principles regarding the treatment of data—such as limits on bias or privacy protections—can be found within armed conflict. Other significant issues derive from the way that operations fueled by Big Data, especially through AI systems using machine learning, generate uncertainty. The acquisition, retention, and use of Big Data prior to armed conflict, or outside hot battlefields, generate further complexity. And added interpretive challenges arise from the fact that so many private actors play a role in collecting and storing Big Data, and this data in turn often commingles military and civilian data sets.

Michael Schmitt contributes a second chapter that uses the opening scenario to highlight key debates, in this case over how IHL might apply to operations involving data. He notes that military activities that rely on or target data do not fit neatly into the existing legal tests for determining whether a conflict even exists. As in the debates about the *jus ad bellum*, the difficulty centers on whether such thresholds are crossed only when "operations result in significant physical damage or injury, as in using cyber means to down an aircraft."[38] States and experts would likely agree that such operations constitute an international armed conflict, whether by the military, other state organs, or proxies under governmental control. But they diverge on "the question of whether non-destructive and non-injurious operations" would qualify.[39] Schmitt suggests that cyber operations targeting data without kinetic effects could in some cases trigger IHL rules for international or non-international armed conflicts because "cyber operations can

37. Kilovaty, *supra* note 6, at 136.

38. Michael N. Schmitt, "Chapter 5: Big Data: International Law Issues During Armed Conflict," this book, at 155.

39. *Id.*

generate highly disruptive nonphysical consequences far more harmful to a State than minor physical damage."[40]

Schmitt then moves on to a series of vexing questions about the applicability of IHL categories to operations involving data, even assuming an armed conflict is underway. He first considers whether operations against data constitute "attacks," thereby activating the relevant IHL rules governing attacks. He notes the consensus that "attacks" should encompass cyber operations (including those against data) that "cause a relatively permanent loss of functionality" to objects. But he then details the disagreement among states and experts over whether "an operation that only temporarily interferes with functionality or causes targeted cyberinfrastructure to misfunction amounts to an attack."[41] He suggests that a policy approach could help bridge differences in legal interpretation here, to ensure that key IHL rules that restrict the targeting of civilian objects could apply as a matter of policy even if not as a matter of law. Next, Schmitt suggests that, if an operation involving data *does* constitutes an attack, we must ask whether data itself is an "object" subject to the IHL rules that limit attacks on civilian objects. Schmitt observes that, on the one hand, if data is an object, then an operation that does not qualify as a military objective—such as a deep fake psychological cyber operation that damages civilian data—would violate the IHL prohibition on attacking civilian objects. But in contrast, "if data is not an object as a matter of IHL . . . cyber operations intended to alter or delete civilian data [are] lawful so long as there are no damaging second order effects to civilian cyberinfrastructure or other systems, or harm to civilians."[42] Under the latter view, "it would be lawful to mount operations that alter or delete civilian databases such as national archives, tax records, educational databases, and social service databases,"[43] and harm to such data alone would not be a civilian harm that must be factored into a proportionality analysis. Schmitt also highlights the challenges of assessing the legality of data poisoning and suggests that, under rules governing attacks, the greater the value of a target, the more uncertainty may be countenanced in an attack, and vice versa. Nevertheless, he argues that the IHL duty of constant care, as established under the general customary principle of precautions in attack, should apply to operations against data—such as data poisoning leading to significant civilian casualties known to the attacker—regardless of whether or not those operations constitute attacks.

Mark Visger directs our attention to a specific, relatively unexplored question under IHL: the legality of attacks on the data upon which military AI systems rely—either during the training phase or when operationally deployed. Visger observes that "[i]f AI artificial agents employed on the battlefield have the decisive

40. *Id.*

41. *Id.* at 157.

42. *Id.* at 164.

43. *Id.*

Introduction

effect that experts are predicting, then enemy forces will accordingly train their fires—both kinetic and cyber—to attempt to neutralize the AI agent."[44] Those efforts, he predicts, will likely focus on the large quantity of data that is necessary to run such systems. He observes that cyber "virtual fires" on an AI system's data are both likely to have significant physical impacts, such as weapons-systems malfunctions that result in civilian casualties, as well as profound non-kinetic effects. Yet, Visger points out that most current scholarship on the question is limited in scope, focusing on operations against data that impact the physical environment. Visger, however, goes beyond this issue and considers non-kinetic consequences of such operations. Drawing on the emerging field of adversarial machine learning, he identifies four types of potential "data poisoning" attacks on the "Big Data" that powers AI weapons systems: data injection, data manipulation, label manipulation, and indirect poisoning. He distinguishes between attacks on data during the training phase, when the system is "learning" from the data, and evasion attacks that take place after the system is operational. He then turns to three core legal questions: First, how should data poisoning activities that take place prior to armed conflict be regulated? He contends that, although such attacks would likely not trigger an armed conflict under conventional tests, the Martens Clause in Additional Protocol II to the Geneva Conventions, which asserts that humanitarian principles apply even when there are gaps in IHL, provides a vehicle for extending IHL rules to pre-conflict data poisoning in limited contexts. Second, he considers how uncertainty about the ultimate impact of such attacks should affect the application of IHL distinction, proportionality, and precautions principles. Third, he assesses how IHL perfidy rules might apply to data attacks on AI weapons systems, arguing that "gaps" in perfidy rules "will only continue to grow with the introduction of machines into the decision cycle."[45] Fundamentally, he maintains that "concepts such as proportionality or perfidy do not neatly map onto data poisoning attacks"[46] and that new approaches are therefore needed.

François Delerue delves into complex questions related to the targeting of data centers during armed conflict. Around the world, such centers store vast quantities of civilian and military data, along with applications that process the data. Delerue considers the circumstances under which such data centers could constitute legitimate military objectives as defined in IHL, a predicate finding necessary to justify any targeting operations. Complicating the analysis, he observes, is the diversity of locations, nature, purposes, and use of data centers, which often commingle military and civilian data and applications, can be owned by public or private actors, and so on. He concludes that, in some cases, data centers may

---

44. Mark A. Visger, "Chapter 6: Garbage In, Garbage Out: Data Poisoning Attacks and Their Legal Implications," this book, at 181.

45. *Id.* at 205.

46. *Id.* at 206.

nevertheless be considered military objectives and thus qualify as lawful objects of attack. The most important elements, he contends, are the purpose and use of the data center. Delerue also considers the challenges of applying the principles of distinction, proportionality, and precautions to the targeting of data centers that do qualify as military objectives, given that such targeting could be achieved through either kinetic or cyber means. (Indeed, he notes that, due to the fragility of environmental conditions for such systems, fires are one of the biggest risks to their functioning.) He also notes that attacks could take the form of temporary or permanent destruction of parts or all of the data center, including the infrastructure necessary to operate the center. He suggests that the commingling of civilian and military data will present significant challenges in determining whether attacks can satisfy distinction and proportionality. With respect to proportionality, a particularly difficult challenge will be to determine "reverberating" effects, especially given the many different uses of data, both public and private.

Asaf Lubin suggests that IHL's duty of constant care provides a mechanism for regulating the use of data by belligerent parties. Drawing on other bodies of law, such as human rights law and domestic law, he argues that military operations involving data threaten to erode a number of digital rights, including "the rights to privacy, anonymity, access to information, online freedom of expression, digital autonomy and dignity, and intellectual property."[47] He then argues that the IHL duty of constant care should be interpreted to protect these rights. Relying on a historical analysis of the First Additional Protocol to the Geneva Conventions (AP I), he contends that the "'precautions in attack principle' . . . reflects, at least in part, a primeval and elementary data protection rule."[48] He observes, to begin with, that the rule applies to all "military operations" and is not limited to "attacks." He further suggests that the duty has always been a "catch-all" open to flexible interpretation and is not limited to the specific practices set forth in Article 57(1) of AP I. He therefore concludes that the duty should be interpreted quite broadly, and specifically that it should apply to "intelligence collection in any of its forms and conducted by any actor (private contractors, civilian intelligence agencies), as well as other broader data collection and management activities."[49] This is quite an expansive view, both as to actors, time frame, and types of harms: in Lubin's formulation, the duty would cover information gathered by private as well as public actors, in preparation for and not just during armed conflict, and would encompass dignitary as well as kinetic harms. Finally, he maps out the duty's possible data protection applications, focusing specifically on two primary categories of obligations: (1) legality and transparency and (2) storage specification and data integrity. Ultimately, he proposes that the duty of constant care might "serve as a temporary gap filler to the lacuna that exists around data

---

47. Asaf Lubin, "Chapter 8: The Duty of Constant Care and Data Protection in War," this book, at 232.

48. *Id.* at 234.

49. *Id.* at 237.

Introduction

protection in IHL,[50] at least until such time as treaties and custom evolve to address data protection more specifically.

Noam Lubell and Katya Al-Khateeb explore the challenges of applying the IHL framework to brain-computer interface (BCI) technology. Although it may sound like the stuff of science fiction, the prospect of such technologies being used on the battlefield is real. And as with many technologies, data—especially "Big Data"—lies at the heart of their deployment. A soldier with a brain implant, which might include, for example, a prosthetic attachment with an offensive capacity, could "stream live data from the battlefield to the Command Base and receive information back from commanders directly to the brain."[51] In addition, the integration of AI in the BCI would enable extensive monitoring and control of soldiers' activities, as well as enhancement of their cognitive capabilities. The technology "would enable the analysis of large volumes of data to improve the soldier's efficiency when assessing a situation on the battlefield," including "a system capable of receiving sensory input data from the soldier's vision," using AI for analysing this "input to identify threats, and relay findings and recommendations back to the soldier's brain as well as to the commanders."[52]

Lubell and Al-Khateeb map out the myriad legal conundrums the use of such systems would pose for IHL. To begin, the integration of BCIs complicates the IHL weapons review process, raising questions about which aspects of the technology even constitute a "weapon" and which are deemed part of the individual person. In addition, the technology would impact the application of IHL targeting rules. For example, BCI-enhanced perception could speed "individual perception and decision-making in a targeting situation."[53] But such enhanced perception, especially if based on AI fueled by "Big Data," might well reflect data biases that could lead to erroneous targeting decisions and violations of distinction and proportionality rules. On the flip side, attackers might seek to use technologies such as electromagnetic pulses to disrupt BCIs, which might violate the principle of unnecessary suffering. BCI technology could also affect assessments of whether service members are hors de combat, for example if they are captured and their brain-implanted devices could continue to gather data. Lubell and Al-Khateeb point out the risks of new forms of torture and cruel treatment, if detaining parties try to extract data from brain implants of captured service members. The ability of the BCIs to continue operating after soldiers are captured also raises challenges for the application of perfidy rules. Finally, the use of BCIs could impact accountability frameworks. By downloading data directly into the brains of service members in the field, BCIs complicate the agency and decision-making of those service members for accountability purposes. At the same time, increased

50. *Id.* at 234.

51. Lubell & Al-Khateeb, *supra* note 12, at 252.

52. *Id.* at 254–55.

53. *Id.* at 260.

monitoring by commanders of soldier-generated data in the field could increase the possibility that commanders could be held responsible for acts of soldiers under the "knew or had reason to know" standard. In sum, BCIs complicate application of IHL because they effectively blur the distinction between human and weapon, brain and machine, and soldier and commander.

PART THREE: INTERNATIONAL HUMANITARIAN LAW AND THE CONDUCT OF HUMANITARIAN OPERATIONS AND ATROCITY INVESTIGATION

Apart from military operations themselves, the rise of Big Data also presents challenges for the interpretation of IHL and IHRL as they apply to humanitarian relief efforts and accountability for atrocities that take place within or in proximity to conflict zones. For example, the same data bias and privacy concerns that arise from military operations also come up in humanitarian relief efforts, which similarly depend on Big Data. The Big Data revolution in the investigation and prosecution of battlefield atrocities likewise raises problems, along with additional concerns about access to and reliability of data gathered and stored by a myriad of actors, public and private.

Galit Sarfaty spotlights the risks of what she refers to as "digital humanitarianism," the "mobilization of data in pursuit of humanitarian goals."[54] While acknowledging the power of data, and especially Big Data, to play a significant role in humanitarian relief and atrocity prevention in or near armed conflict, she shines a light on one big downside: the private sector typically controls much of this data. Whether it involves refugee flow tracking or aid delivery, private companies often own, hold, or store the data that is now essential for such activities. Some companies are willing to engage in "digital philanthropy" to share the data they collect and store, but others refuse to do so, even when such data could facilitate relief efforts or thwart atrocities connected to an armed conflict. Still others are "complicit" in abuses "when they engage in digital surveillance and other forms of data manipulation." Drawing on her background as an anthropologist, Sarfaty uses infrastructural analysis to assess the role of private actors in this context, mapping "the knowledge practices and relations of power that underlie global data governance and the process through which digital humanitarianism is assembled."[55] To address abuses, she argues for essentially a soft law principle of corporate responsibility that should govern the private sector role in humanitarian relief operations. Specifically, she identifies a principle of "negative responsibility" for corporations "to do no harm, by not assisting states that use

---

54. Sarfaty, *supra* note 13, at 276.

55. *Id.* at 277.

Introduction

data to commit human rights violations."[56] At the same time, she calls for a positive responsibility for corporations "to respect human rights by making available data that could prevent gross human rights abuses or humanitarian crises."[57]

For human rights advocates, one of the key promises of data, and Big Data in particular, is the ability to collect evidence of atrocities committed in (and beyond) conflict zones. The growing availability of such data, and its potential to serve both as a warning signal for atrocity prevention efforts and as an accountability tool, is the starting point for the chapter by Beth Van Schaack. Van Schaack surveys the myriad sources of such Big Data and the tools for Big Data analytics, including object recognition and event detection, facial recognition, statistical analysis of targeting patterns, artificial intelligence language assessment, social networking analysis, and 3-D modeling. She details how these analytic tools are already being deployed for both atrocity prevention and accountability, and she shows the potential for these tools to be used to an even greater extent in the future. For example, "these data sets can be exploited by prosecutors for multiple purposes, including geo-location of people and events, fugitive tracking, and social network analysis," which can provide "lead and crime base information but also critical linkage evidence, connecting particular actors to the commission of war crimes."[58] Yet, at the same time, she highlights some of the distinct challenges of using such "Big Data" for these purposes. She observes, for example, that if "amassing enough evidence to stage a viable war crimes trial was often a principal challenge" of an earlier era, "today, the problem may be the reverse: there is too much documentation, much of it unverified and duplicative, which can overwhelm legal actors seeking to impose individual criminal responsibility, defend against criminal charges, or make real-time policy interventions in the service of deterrence and prevention."[59] In addition to the problem of information overload, other challenges include information bias—which Big Data sets can amplify exponentially—and mis- and dis-information campaigns designed to corrupt or thwart the use of such data for accountability and prevention purposes. Furthermore, data is less likely to track some types of wartime atrocities, such as custodial abuses or sexual assaults, than others, such as massacres or air strikes with large civilian death tolls. Van Schaack notes that "the existence of . . . systemic false negatives may tilt overall conclusions about the nature of, and responsibility for, violence and disproportionately implicate particular actors or communities in criminal behavior."[60] Finally, she describes the challenges that can arise when corporate, governmental, or even NGO actors resist providing access to such data.

56. *Id.*

57. *Id.*

58. Van Schaack, *supra* note 16, at 299.

59. *Id.* at 293.

60. *Id.* at 302.

Yet, overall, she concludes that the rise of "Big Data" has the potential to reshape and improve atrocity prevention and accountability efforts on the battlefield.

PART FOUR: INTERNATIONAL HUMAN RIGHTS LAW

Finally, although questions about the extraterritoriality of IHRL obligations, and the extent to which IHRL intersects with IHL, have long been areas of contention and uncertainty, the rise of Big Data complicates those questions further. Whether IHRL rules and norms apply on the battlefield, and if so how, are particularly important questions as applied to data-based operations because IHRL rules and norms that pertain to data are much more developed that those found in IHL (or the *jus ad bellum*, for that matter). In addition, the growing use of Big Data might enable states and other actors to exploit gaps in both IHL and IHRL. Indeed, conflicting views about how these bodies of law intersect could create ever-expanding interpretive gray areas that potentially threaten the rule of law itself.

In his chapter on the *jus ad bellum* in Part One, Michael Schmitt introduces the complex questions surrounding the applicability of IHRL to operations below the armed conflict threshold that rely on or target data, as suggested by the introductory scenario. Schmitt details the IHRL rules and norms that protect data privacy and the use of biased data, as well as potentially applicable rules regarding derogation of human rights in times of emergency and limitations to such rights. He also spotlights the debates over whether states are obligated to protect such rights when they act extraterritorially, as well as questions surrounding the scope of state obligations to ensure respect of such rights by non-state actors. Although some of these questions and debates are not new, the use and targeting of Big Data present particularly challenging questions of legal interpretation and analysis. He also spotlights questions about how IHRL might intersect with IHL.

Fionnuala Ni Aolain also explores issues that emerge at the intersection of IHRL and IHL when states and private actors collect, target, and use data inside and adjacent to armed conflict. But rather than engaging in the sort of translation exercise that dominates many of the other chapters, she challenges us to address even deeper implications of the rise of Big Data. Specifically, she argues that the massive collection and use of data in service of global counterterrorism efforts has destabilized and ruptured both the IHL and IHRL frameworks themselves. She charts the rise of a supranational, multilateral, and national institutional counterterrorism architecture, which, like "the 'Pac-Man' action chase video game . . . eats up all around . . . without distinction."[61] In her view, data collection in the service of counterterrorism—from UN Security Council initiatives mandating and supporting states to collect terrorists' biometric data, to the vast quantities of data collected to support drone strikes, to the data harvested by authoritarian regimes

---

61. Fionnualla Ní Aoláin, "Chapter 12: The Datafication of Counterterrorism," this book, at 324.

Introduction

in the name of fighting terrorism—has in fact devoured human rights and humanitarian law frameworks.

To begin, Ni Aiolain argues that the global focus on counterterrorism post 9/11 has elevated the role of the Security Council over other more participatory supranational entities, engendered malleable interpretations of existing legal categories, enabled state freedom of action outside multilateral legal frameworks, reduced transparency, and supported bloated security sectors that involve not just states but the private sector. In addition, she maintains that the murky data-collection and retention practices that have anchored these developments threaten the IHRL and IHL paradigms. With respect to IHRL, the collection and use of Big Data not only undermines a large number of fundamental human rights, from privacy to the right to life, but even more, functions "as a lever for governments to undermine rights wholesale through expanding national policing, security and border capacity."[62] With respect to IHL, the data-fueled counterterrorism framework has justified the "tendency to consider any act of violence carried out by a nonstate armed group in a non-international armed conflict (NIAC) as being 'terrorist' by definition, sidestepping assessment of lawfulness under IHL as well as the addressing of the legal and political significance of internal armed conflicts on the territories of States."[63] Furthermore, she contends that the counterterrorism framing is "downgrading IHL" and its categories entirely, replacing them with an "exceptionalist" approach that results in "the practical downgrading of IHL as the relevant legal framework. In sites where armed conflict is present but states view the rules on such matters as impartial humanitarian access, status of combatants and detainee treatment as overly constraining counterterrorism is a more palatable and manipulable frame of legal and political action."[64] Counterterrorism, she maintains, gives states cover to use exceptionalist arguments that existing IHL categories do not apply or can be manipulated for self-serving ends.

Thus, Ni Aiolain's chapter broadens the framework of analysis significantly, by suggesting that the rise of Big Data not only requires translating existing IHL and IHRL frameworks to new contexts, but may actually create a new paradigm that threatens to undermine the rules-based international order altogether. Accordingly, it provides a fitting, though sobering, conclusion to the collection.

* * *

As all the chapters in the collection make clear, Big Data is radically reshaping the modern battlefield. Like many new military technologies and capabilities, the myriad uses of Big Data present broad questions about how best to translate existing rules and principles embedded in multiple bodies of law to these new

---

62. *Id.* at 344.

63. *Id.* at 320.

64. *Id.* at 327

contexts, both within armed conflict, as part of adversarial activities below the armed conflict threshold, and in a range of related operations that increasingly use, deploy, and target such data. Because Big Data is profoundly transforming modern life off the battlefield as well, these questions extend beyond the role of Big Data within weapons systems and other military capabilities to questions about the nature of civilian harm and scope of individual rights. The chapters in this book comprise the first comprehensive initiative to grapple with a wide swath of these questions. At the same time, because Big Data is so transformative, the uses of Big Data provoke deeper questions about the international legal order itself. The impact of Big Data on the battlefield exposes gaps and interpretive ambiguities in existing legal frameworks that generate critiques of those frameworks as inadequate. Accordingly, while Big Data holds enormous promise, it also has the potential to disrupt modern warfare and the legal regimes that seek to regulate it. This book confronts these issues directly, offers a range of approaches and ideas to this timely issue, and hopefully offers an initial road map for scholars, policy makers, and advocates to follow as they address the enormous challenges still to come.

Scenario

MARK A. VISGER* ∎

This scenario seeks to highlight international legal issues posed by the acquisition, storage, use, and targeting of large quantities of data ("Big Data") in military operations below and above the armed conflict threshold. Produced in consultation with the U.S. Army Cyber Institute at the U.S. Military Academy, West Point,[1] it is based on realistic real-world possibilities. The scenario inspired analyisis by the writers of this volume, and we hope it will be a useful tool for future scholarship and teaching in this area. Although many research initiatives and conferences have tackled legal issues arising from the use of artificial intelligence (AI) in military operations, few efforts have homed in on the issues that arise from the use of Big Data specifically.

The scenario is therefore intended to highlight some of the key challenges in applying existing international legal frameworks, including the jus ad bellum, *international human rights law (IHRL), the law of armed conflict (LOAC), and the law of state responsibility, to the use of Big Data in the operations described in the scenario. The scenario is divided roughly between operations prior to armed conflict and operations during armed conflict, although of course some legal questions arise when the operations cross the armed conflict threshold.*

A. Pre-Conflict Preparations

Outlandia and Newtropia are rival nations on the world stage. Both consider themselves to be rising global powers, but they have been historic adversaries, fighting several wars over the last several decades. Recently, the two countries have engaged in a territorial dispute that appears to be headed toward armed conflict. In the past few years, the Newtropian Armed Forces (NAF) leadership

---

* Academy Professor, Army Cyber Institute at U.S. Military Academy at West Point.

1. Lieutenant Colonel Mark Visger drafted the scenario in consultation with Lieutenant Colonel Doug Fletcher, Major Nate Bastian, Major Bryan Jonas, Lieutenant Colonel Nick Clark, Lieutenant Colonel Ed Berg, and Professor Laura Dickinson.

Mark A. Visger, *Scenario* In: *Big Data and Armed Conflict*. Edited by: Laura A. Dickinson and Edward W. Berg, Oxford University Press. © Mark A. Visger 2024. DOI: 10.1093/oso/9780197668610.003.0002

sought to modernize their forces through the incorporation of machine learning/artificial intelligence (ML/AI) into its military operations and decision-making. The Newtropian government possesses a ready supply of data to train these systems because Newtropian law does not protect privacy, and the government has been gathering data from its own citizens for years.

In order to support operational planning for a possible conflict, Newtropia focuses on additional data collection aimed at Outlandia. Newtropia first gathers all publicly available information about Outlandia's citizens, which includes purchases of data profiles on the open market. Then, Newtropia hacks and exfiltrates large amounts of Outlandian data. The purloined data includes government and private databases (including civilian and military medical records) and security camera streams, as well as the centralized personnel database for the Outlandia Defense Department, which contains sensitive security clearance information. Based on this enormous pool of accumulated data, the Newtropia Military Intelligence Directorate develops detailed profiles of 96% of Outlandian citizens to facilitate individualized micro-targeting information campaigns against Newtropia prior to the war. This data collection campaign also identifies Outlandian military members, civilian defense employees and defense contractors, as well as their families, focusing additional data collection on these persons in order to build highly detailed profiles for further personalized targeting and/or influence.

Shortly before hostilities break out, the Outlandian Military Forces (OMF) realize their shortcomings in machine learning/artificial intelligence. They begin building the data infrastructure necessary to support a robust machine learning capacity, engaging in an all-out blitz to catch up. Dubbed Operation Full Warp, begun 18 months before war breaks out, the OMF spends 8% of its defense budget on AI development, with a major focus being on building sufficient data resources to support the machine learning algorithms. Domestic privacy protections and international human rights commitments have restricted the Outlandian government's capacity to acquire data from its citizens. Many private contractors assist in the data effort, roaming far and wide to obtain both domestic and foreign data to feed the algorithms. Much of the data is stored in UWS, the ubiquitous cloud storage service offered by Ucayali Incorporated, the dominant online retailer in Outlandia. In addition, Outlandia stores some of the Full Warp data in commercial servers located in foreign countries. In response, the NAF maps Outlandian government networks and the data on UWS and foreign servers, probing for potential weaknesses.

This data serves as a major turning point in pushing the nations to war, when Newtropian cyber forces delete over three-fourths of all cloud storage on UWS. In addition to the military impacts, this operation causes significant ripple effects across the Outlandian economy. At the time of the operation, 15% of the UWS cloud storage is being utilized to support the Outlandian military data collection effort. Ninety-two percent of Outlandian military data housed on UWS is successfully deleted by Newtropian cyber forces. Newtropia also targets and deletes some of Outlandia's Full Warp data being housed in third countries, prompting

Scenario

diplomatic demarches, expulsion of its diplomats and complaints to the UN Security Council.

B. Armed Conflict

Despite attempts at diplomacy during the immediate aftermath of the UWS operation, hostilities erupt. The OMF responds to the UWS hack with a missile attack on Newtropia's military cyber headquarters, which ultimately precipitates full-scale combat between the two nations. Newtropia unleashes an incredibly effective digital opening salvo. With the massive database of Outlandian government and military records and civilian data, Newtropia begins a campaign of blackmail, disruption, and intimidation against specific military and civilian members, as well as their family members. Newtropian AI identifies these individuals as critical nodes of support necessary for the rapid mobilization and deployment of the OMF to the theater of combat.[2] Newtropia targets approximately 5,000 military members, civilian employees, defense contractors, and government officials in this manner. Optimized based on vulnerabilities identified in the data, these operations significantly prevent targeted individuals from attending to their mobilization duties. These individuals face severed communications, threatening messages delivered to their family members via smart speakers, deleted bank and retirement accounts, and even sabotage to their "Internet of things" devices such as smart devices, with self-driving cars being a favorite target. This opening salvo cripples a rapid OMF mobilization.

Despite the difficulty in mobilizing forces, Outlandia continues the fight, deploying forces piecemeal into the theater of combat due to the delays. Once in theater, the OMF face a new type of foe—the Newtropian AI Targeting System (NAITS). The NAITS utilizes facial recognition technology from the military and medical records of OMF personnel that had been purloined prior to the war. The system built a kill list of high-value OMF targets, which is fed to loitering aerial kill vehicles that automatically launch a missile upon a facial and/or voice recognition match. These operations are mostly successful, although news reports begin filtering out of the combat zone regarding mistaken strikes, with civilians and ICRC personnel suffering casualties as a result. The algorithm is not 100% accurate and even though it has been shown to have an error rate similar to a human operator, there is a real possibility for mistakes. Due to the black-box nature of the AI system, it is practically impossible to track the machine logic that led to the errors. The majority of the mistaken strikes take place against non-Caucasian personnel, as the facial recognition training data primarily utilized that of Caucasian individuals.

---

2. The description of this micro-targeting attack is modeled after a fictional attack outlined in the Modern War Institute Blog Post, Jared Wilhelm, *Autopsy of a Future War*, MODERN WAR INSTITUTE (Nov. 5, 2019), available at https://mwi.usma.edu/autopsy-future-war/. (This article highlights a number of different possible harmful effects that could be created through the use of data. The ones highlighted in this Scenario are representative of those found in the article.)

The NAITS increasingly makes targeting mistakes as the war progresses, likely due to the degraded data flow that Newtropia suffers once hostilities commence because of OMF targeting of Newtropian data streams. OMF data countermeasures had begun prior to the conflict and continued into the conflict. These actions successfully degraded the NAITS' effectiveness. Data countermeasures take a number of different forms. As the OMF began to apprehend the extent of AFN data theft prior to the war, the OMF began inserting false data into the purloined data streams. In addition, they also began "fuzzing" the data—adding random noise where possible to confuse the Newtropian systems.

OMF cyberattacks also begin targeting the data within the Newtropian networks. In one instance after hostilities commence, Outlandian cyber forces access and delete all military personnel and pay records (as well as their backups), causing administrative nightmares for NAF personnel. In addition to taking action against the data in cyberspace, OMF start looking for ways to confuse the NAITS sensors. Outlandian soldiers begin placing random digital patterns on their uniform in an attempt to fool the NAITS. Through a system of trial and error, and some "best guess" reverse-engineering of the Newtropian systems, researchers identify several effective random digital patterns to thwart the NAITS. These patterns are issued to OMF personnel on a mass scale. Unbeknownst to the OMF, the top three digital evasion patterns they adopt cause the NAITS to identify OMF soldiers as medical personnel, school-aged children and penguins, respectively.

In a particularly tragic episode, a NAITS missile targets and kills Dr. Jean-Marc Van Lanner, head of the Doctors Beyond Frontiers (a medical NGO) mission to the combat region. Investigators are unable to identify why the system targeted Dr. Van Lanner. Experts state that the error was likely due to the NAITS updates to its targeting algorithm following OMF usage of data evasion patterns simulating medical personnel. As a result, the NAITS incorrectly identifies him as a high value OMF commander, an error likely exacerbated by the fact that Dr. Van Lanner is non-Caucasian.

Some (though not all) of the legal questions implicated in the scenario include the following:

PRE-CONFLICT

- Jus ad bellum:
  - *To what extent do the extraterritorial acquisition, storage, and use operations conducted by Newtropia or Outlandia violate sovereignty (either understood as a rule or principle)?*
  - *To what extent do these operations by Outlandia or Newtropia constitute an unlawful intervention?*
  - *Do any of these operations constitute an* ad bellum *armed attack?*

Scenario

- What are the ad bellum *obligations of third-party states in the scenario—for example, those states where data is stored?*
- What are the ad bellum *obligations, if any, of Ucayali Incorporated or any other nonstate actors who participate in these operations, and/or to what extent do Newtropia or Outlandia bear responsibility for any of the operations undertaken by the nonstate actors?*

- *IHRL:*
  - *To what extent do the data acquisition, storage, and use operations by Newtropia or Outlandia violate IHRL rules such as those protecting privacy and nondiscrimination?*
  - *To what extent do any of these obligations extend to the extraterritorial operations described?*
  - *To what extent are Outlandia or Newtropia responsible for the actions of nonstate actors who carry out any of the operations and/or to what extent, if at all, do the nonstate actors bear any direct obligations?*

CONFLICT THRESHOLD

- *At what point is the armed conflict threshold triggered in the scenario?*
- *Do any of the operations targeting data cross the threshold?*

ARMED CONFLICT

- *LOAC: Do any of the operations either targeting data or using data in targeting implicate LOAC?*
  - *With respect to targeting data, do the operations with non-kinetic effects constitute an attack within the meaning of LOAC? Assuming the data-targeting operations do trigger LOAC rules such as necessity, distinction, proportionality, and precautions, how should the data-related harms be incorporated into the analysis? Do any of the operations constitute perfidy? For those data-targeting operations that don't constitute an attack, how does the LOAC, if at all, constrain those operations?*
  - *With respect to the use of data in targeting, do the operations implicate LOAC? Do LOAC rules govern the acquisition or storage of data for use in the AI systems? For example, is there any obligation deriving from LOAC that requires transparency or nondiscrimination in the collection, storage, or use of data that would apply, for example to the NAITS system? What obligations related to data, if any, derive from the LOAC weapons review process? Does the use of big data to conduct strikes with kinetic effects, such as through the NAITS system, affect the analysis of LOAC rules such as necessity, distinction, proportionality, and precautions? What are Newtropia's LOAC obligations related to*

targeting operations that rely on data degraded by Outlandia? Does Outlandia have any obligations related to Newtropia's targeting based on data that Outlandia degraded?

- IHRL:
  - *To what extent do Outlandia or Newtropia have any IHRL obligations related to the use of data in targeting or the targeting of data in the scenario?*

PART ONE

The *Jus ad Bellum* and Operations Below the Armed Conflict Threshold

Big Data

International Law Issues Below the Armed Conflict Threshold

MICHAEL N. SCHMITT* ■

In preparation for the annual Lieber Institute workshop upon which this volume was to have been based, the co-editors and members of the Institute worked closely with the U.S. Army Cyber Institute to build a scenario that highlights key international legal issues raised by the acquisition, storage, use, and targeting of large quantities of data ("Big Data") in military operations.[1] Big Data has been usefully defined as "the exponentially increasing amount of digital information being created by new information technologies such as mobile internet, cloud storage, social networking, and the 'internet of things'—and the advanced analytics used to process that data."[2] Although many research initiatives and conferences have tackled legal issues surrounding artificial intelligence (AI) in military operations, few have homed in on those that arise from the use of Big Data. Accordingly, the

---

* G. Norman Lieber Scholar, United States Military Academy at West Point; Professor of International Law, University of Reading; Professor Emeritus, United States Naval War College. The author is grateful to Professor Marko Milanovic of Reading University and Ms. Liis Vihul of Cyber Law International for the many extended discussions of issues discussed in this chapter and presentations on them, which the author had the good fortune to attend. Any errors or unattributed views, however, are the author's alone.

1. Lieutenant Colonel Mark Visger drafted the scenario in consultation with Lieutenant Colonel Doug Fletcher, Major Nate Bastian, Major Bryan Jonas, Lieutenant Colonel Nick Clark, Lieutenant Colonel Ed Berg, and Professor Laura A. Dickinson.

2. Paul B. Symon & Arzan Tarapore, *Defense Intelligence Analysis in the Age of Big Data*, 79 JOINT FORCE Q. 5 (2015).

Michael N. Schmitt, *Big Data* In: *Big Data and Armed Conflict.* Edited by: Laura A. Dickinson and Edward W. Berg, Oxford University Press. © Michael N. Schmitt 2024. DOI: 10.1093/oso/9780197668610.003.0003

scenario was designed to highlight challenges in applying existing international legal frameworks to that use.

This chapter analyzes the scenario activities involving Big Data that preceded the outbreak of hostilities. It pays particular attention to international human rights law (IHRL) and the international law rules governing sovereignty, intervention, and the use of force. Chapter 5 complements this contribution by examining aspects of the scenario occurring during international armed conflict.

I. SCENARIO: PRE-CONFLICT PREPARATIONS

Outlandia and Newtropia are rival nations on the world stage that consider themselves rising global powers. They have been historic adversaries, fighting several wars over the last several decades. Recently, the two countries have engaged in a territorial dispute that appears to be headed toward armed conflict. In the past few years, the Newtropian Armed Forces (NAF) leadership sought to modernize its forces by incorporating machine learning/artificial intelligence (ML/AI) into its military operations and decision-making. The Newtropian government possesses a ready supply of data to train these systems because Newtropian law does not protect privacy. The government has been gathering data from its citizens for years.

To support operational planning for a possible conflict, Newtropia engages in additional data collection aimed at Outlandia. Newtropia first gathers all publicly available information about Outlandia's citizens, including purchases of data profiles on the open market. Then, Newtropia hacks and exfiltrates large amounts of Outlandian data. The purloined data includes government and private databases (including civilian and military medical records), security camera streams, and the centralized personnel database for the Outlandia Defense Department, which contains sensitive security clearance information. Based on this enormous pool of accumulated data, the Newtropia Military Intelligence Directorate develops detailed profiles of 96% of Outlandian citizens to facilitate individualized microtargeting information campaigns against Newtropia before the war. The data collection campaign also identifies Outlandian military members, civilian defense employees, defense contractors, and their families. It focuses additional data collection on them to build highly detailed profiles for further personalized targeting and/or influence.

Shortly before hostilities break out, the Outlandian Military Forces (OMF) realize their machine learning/artificial intelligence shortcomings. They begin building the data infrastructure necessary to support a robust machine learning capacity, engaging in an all-out blitz to catch up. Dubbed Operation Full Warp and begun 18 months before the war, the OMF spends 8% of its defense budget on AI development, with a significant focus on building sufficient data resources to support the machine learning algorithms. Domestic privacy protections and international human rights commitments have restricted the Outlandian government's capacity to acquire data from its citizens. As a result, many private contractors assist in the data effort, roaming far and wide to obtain domestic and foreign data to feed the algorithms. Much of the data is stored in UWS, the ubiquitous cloud storage service offered by Ucayali Incorporated, the dominant online retailer in Outlandia. In addition, Outlandia stores some of the Full Warp data in commercial servers located in foreign countries. In response, the NAF maps Outlandian government networks and the data on UWS and foreign servers, probing for potential weaknesses.

This data serves as a major turning point in pushing the nations to war when Newtropian cyber forces delete over three-fourths of all cloud storage on UWS. In addition to the military impact, the operation causes significant ripple effects across the Outlandian economy. At the time of the operation, 15% of the UWS cloud storage was utilized to support the Outlandian military data collection effort. Newtropian cyber forces successfully deleted 92% of Outlandian military data housed on UWS. Newtropia also targets and deletes some of the Outlandia's Full Warp data housed in third countries, prompting diplomatic demarches, the expulsion of its diplomats, and complaints to the U.N. Security Council.

II. LEGAL ANALYSIS: PRE-CONFLICT PREPARATIONS

A. Newtropian Internal Collection Operations: International Human Rights Law

A key legal issue the scenario raises is the lawfulness under international human rights law (IHRL) of the Big Data collection program in Newtropia. In that regard, it is now universally accepted that IHRL applies to cyber activities.[3]

1. The Four-Step Analysis: To Whom Are Rights Owed?
Compliance with IHRL is assessed in a four-step analysis. The first is to determine whether the State taking action owes human rights obligations to the individual concerned at all. It has long been accepted that a State shoulders human rights obligations on its territory. Indeed, human rights treaties often set forth their scope in terms of territory and/or jurisdiction.[4] Therefore, as a general matter,

---

3. Group of Governmental Experts [GGE] on Developments in the Field of Information and Telecommunications in the Context of International Security, ¶ 70, U.N. Doc. A/76/135 (July 14, 2021) [hereinafter 2021 GGE]. Previous Groups of Governmental Experts also confirmed the applicability of international human rights law to cyber activities in reports that were endorsed by the UN General Assembly. *See, e.g.,* Group of Governmental Experts on Developments in the Field of Information and Telecommunications in the Context of International Security, ¶ 13(e), U.N. Doc. A/70/174 (July 22, 2015); G.A. Res. 70/237, Developments in the Field of Information and Telecommunications in the Context of International Security (Dec. 30, 2015) (endorsing the 2015 GGE report).

4. *See, e.g.,* International Covenant on Civil and Political Rights, Art. 2(1), Dec. 16, 1966, 999 U.N.T.S. 171 [hereinafter ICCPR] ("Each State Party to the present Covenant undertakes to respect and to ensure to all individuals within its territory and subject to its jurisdiction the rights recognized in the present Covenant.").

Newtropia owes human rights obligations to the individuals affected by its domestic collection program.

2. The Four-Step Analysis: Is a Right Implicated?

The second step is to identify the human right implicated by the State's action. That right may reside either in a treaty to which the State is Party or in customary international law. The question is whether the matter concerned is within the scope of a particular human right such that the State shoulders an obligation based on it. The State's obligation may be a negative obligation to "respect" the individual's right by not interfering with its enjoyment or exercise or a positive obligation to "protect" enjoyment or exercise of the right from interference by other States, entities, or individuals (often expressed as an obligation to "ensure" human rights[5]). As the State (Newtropia) is acting in this case, the obligation to respect is at issue.[6]

The primary right implicated by the scenario is privacy, which appears in numerous treaties, most prominently Article 17(1) of the International Covenant on Civil and Political Rights (ICCPR). That article provides, "No one shall be subjected to arbitrary or unlawful interference with his privacy, family, home or correspondence, nor to unlawful attacks on his honour and reputation."[7] Although there is no indication that Newtropia is Party to any relevant human rights treaty,

---

5. For instance, the ICCPR provides that States Parties have an obligation to "respect and to ensure to all individuals within its territory and subject to its jurisdiction the rights recognized in the present Covenant." *Id.*

6. If Newtropia had outsourced its collection efforts to private actors, or otherwise relied upon non-State entities to accumulate the data, it would also have the obligation to "protect" the privacy rights of those who were affected by the collection on its territory. In some cases, it would also bear responsibility for the actions of the non-State actor under the law of State Responsibility. *See, e.g.,* International Law Commission, Draft Articles on Responsibility of States for Internationally Wrongful Acts, with Commentaries, Art. 8, *reprinted in* [2001] 2 Y.B. INT'L L. COMM'N, pt. 2, U.N. Doc. A/56/10.

7. *Id.*, Art. 17(1). *See also* Universal Declaration of Human Rights Art. 12, G.A. Res. 217 (III), U.N. GAOR, U.N. Doc. A/810, at 73 (1948); American Convention on Human Rights, Nov. 22, 1969, Art. 11, Series no. 36, at 1, Organization of American States, Official Record, OEA/Ser.L/ V/II.23; European Convention for the Protection of Human Rights and Fundamental Freedoms, Nov. 4, 1950, Art. 8, 213 U.N.T.S. 221 [hereinafter ECHR]; Convention for the Protection of Individuals with regard to Automatic Processing of Personal Data, Art. 1, Oct. 1 1985, ETS No. 108; Report of the Special Rapporteur on the Promotion and Protection of the Right to Freedom of Opinion and Expression, ¶ 23, U.N. Doc. A/HRC/23/40 (Apr. 17, 2013); Report of the United Nations High Commissioner for Human Rights, The Right to Privacy in the Digital Age, ¶ 14, U.N. Doc. A/HRC/27/37 (June 30, 2014); The Right to Privacy in the Digital Age, GA Res. 69/ 166, U.N. Doc. A/RES/69/166 (Feb. 10, 2016). For an excellent analysis of privacy in the cyber context, *see* Marko Milanovic, *Human Rights Treaties and Foreign Surveillance: Privacy in the Digital Age*, 56 HARV. INT'L L.J. 81 (2015).

Article 17(1) reflects customary international law.[8] Clearly, Newtropia must respect the privacy of those individuals on its territory.

Newtropia's program is a mass (or "bulk"), as distinct from targeted, collection effort; it relies on "Big Data." The country presumably gathers content data and metadata (also known as "communications data"). The former refers to the content of communications like email and social media posts, while the latter is data concerning the communication itself, such as the means of creation, time of creation, and location of the system where the communication originated.[9] A helpful analogy is a letter that is mailed. The letter itself is analogous to content data, whereas the information on the outside of the envelope, like the sender and recipient's address, is comparable to metadata. At the very least, metadata can be pieced together to discern information about who is communicating with whom.

Although privacy is "a broad term not susceptible to exhaustive definition,"[10] the European Court of Human Rights has suggested it "encompass[es], *inter alia*, aspects of an individual's physical and social identity including the right to personal autonomy, personal development and to establish and develop relationships with human beings and the outside world."[11] More concretely, the right to privacy protects communications and personal data like health records or information contained in a security clearance application.[12] The scenario lacks information about the nature of the data collected, but it certainly includes communications and personal data, in light of Newtropia's uses of the data as described in the scenario.

There is no question that the right to privacy includes content data, even if the communication(s) in question contains no sensitive information.[13] However, the protection of metadata in IHRL is less settled. For example, in the 1984 case *Malone v. United Kingdom*, the European Court of Human Rights held that the European Convention on Human Rights' privacy protection extends beyond

---

8. TALLINN MANUAL 2.0 ON THE INTERNATIONAL LAW APPLICABLE TO CYBER OPERATIONS 189 (Michael N. Schmitt gen. ed., 2017), citing for support G20 Leaders' Communiqué, Antalya Summit, November 15–16, 2015; Council of Europe, Parliamentary Assembly, Resolution 2045, ¶¶ 4, 10 (Apr. 21, 2015); ASEAN Declaration, prin. 21, Nov. 19, 2012; The Right to Privacy in the Digital Age, GA Res. 69/166, *supra* note 7, pmbl.

9. PRESIDENT'S COUNCIL OF ADVISORS ON SCIENCE AND TECHNOLOGY, BIG DATA AND PRIVACY: A TECHNOLOGICAL PERSPECTIVE 19 (May 2014).

10. Peck v. U.K., Eur. Ct. H.R., App. No. 00044647/98, ¶ 57 (Jan. 28, 2003). European Court of Human Rights cases are available on the HUDOC database: https://www.echr.coe.int/pages/home.aspx?p=caselaw/hudoc&c/.

11. Evans v. U.K., Eur. Ct. H.R., App. No. 6339, ¶ 71 (Apr. 10, 2007).

12. *See, e.g.*, Human Rights Comm., General Comment No. 16, Art. 17 (Right to Privacy) The Right to Respect of Privacy, Family, Home and Correspondence, and Protection of Honour and Reputation, ¶¶ 8, 10, U.N. Doc. HRI/GEN/1/Rev.9 (Vol. I) (Apr. 8, 1988).

13. *See, e.g.*, Eur. Ct. Just., Cases C-293/12 and C-594/12, Digital Rights Ireland and Seitlinger and Others, ¶ 33, 2014 ECR 238 (Apr. 8).

content data to an analog of metadata—phone numbers dialed and duration of calls. But the court also indicated metadata enjoyed somewhat less protection than content data.[14]

That distinction has been questioned, for, as the European Union's Court of Justice pointed out in 2014, communications metadata "taken as a whole may allow very precise conclusions to be drawn concerning the private lives of the persons whose data has been retained."[15] For example, the U.N. High Commissioner for Human Rights has noted that communications metadata has been used to enable drone strikes.[16] Indeed, the High Commissioner argued, "[f]rom the perspective of the right to privacy, this distinction [between content data and metadata] is not persuasive. The aggregation of information commonly referred to as 'metadata' may give an insight into an individual's behaviour, social relationships, private preferences and identity that go beyond even that conveyed by accessing the content of a private communication."[17]

In 2021, the European Court of Human Rights again took on the distinction in *Big Brother Watch v. United Kingdom*. There, the Grand Chamber noted that it "is not persuaded that the acquisition of related communications data through bulk interception is necessarily less intrusive than the acquisition of content. It therefore considers that the interception, retention and searching of related communications data should be analysed by reference to the same safeguards as those applicable to content."[18] Accordingly, there appears to be no question that the

---

14. Malone v. U.K., Eur. Ct. H.R., App. No. 8691/79, ¶¶ 84, 87 (Aug. 2, 1984). The Inter-American Court of Human Rights had earlier likewise held that the right to privacy extended U.S. courts have expressed varying views as to whether there is an analogous constitutional privacy interest in metadata. A particular question is the extent to which the Supreme Court's decision in *Smith v. Maryland*, 442 U.S. 735 (1979), (no Fourth Amendment warrant required to collect pen register phone call record information) survives its more recent decision in *Carpenter v. United States*, 128 S. Ct. 2206 (June 22, 2018) (a Fourth Amendment warrant is required for the government to collect cell site location information). Lower courts have taken different views, with some suggesting that Fourth Amendment privacy rights include metadata, particularly if it is collected and retained in large quantities [compare *ACLU v. Clapper*, 785 F.3d 787 (2nd Cir. 2015) (invalidating government's extensive metadata collection on statutory grounds, but flagging constitutional concerns under the Fourth Amendment and noting the extent of privacy interests implicated] with the Foreign Intelligence Surveillance Court's decision in *In re: Application of the FBI*, 2019 WL 5637562 (relying on *Smith v. Maryland* to conclude there is no Fourth Amendment privacy interest in metadata). Note that *Clapper* was ultimately mooted out when the government ceased its broad metadata collection program and Congress rewrote the statutory authority for the program.

15. Digital Rights Ireland and Seitlinger and Others, *supra* note 13, ¶¶ 26–27.

16. The Right to Privacy in the Digital Age, *supra* note 7, ¶ 14.

17. *Id.*, ¶ 19.

18. Big Brother Watch and Others v. U.K., Eur. Ct. H.R., App. No. 58170/13, ¶ 363 (May 25, 2021). It is especially important in the Big Data context to note that the court found that the right to privacy can encompass collection, retention, and use of the data.

collection by Newtropia content data and (probably) metadata of individuals on its territory falls within the scope of the human right of privacy. The size and scale of the data—even metadata—may be relevant to determining whether IHRL privacy rights are implicated.

3. The Four-Step Analysis: Has the Right Been Adversely Affected?

This takes the analysis to the third step, in which it must be determined whether the State's action has adversely affected the right of privacy. In this regard, it is unclear precisely how Newtropia processes the data and who has access to it. Mass collection programs can rely on a machine to gather and process information and data. Such programs may also be mounted by ordering companies to hand over metadata that the companies have collected. In a mass collection surveillance operation, an algorithm could then be used to identify information that may be of value, some of which might then be processed for assessment by humans. The nature and execution of a collection program drive the legal evaluation.

Here, the data is collected to train Newtropian machine learning systems. It is possible that humans are not involved at any point. That said, the government has been collecting the data for years, and there is no suggestion in the scenario that it is regularly deleting the data. On the contrary, given its purpose, Newtropia might retain the data (both content and meta) for long periods.

As a matter of law, it remains unsettled whether the mere collection and retention of data by machine, with humans never accessing it, interferes with the right to privacy. On the one hand, the personal data remains entirely private. In a sense, nothing intrusive has occurred. But on the other, the government is using it for training purposes, and it might remain accessible to the government should it wish to access the data for other purposes.

Human rights cases addressing applicants' standing may shed some light on the matter. They signal judicial views regarding the nature of the nexus between the State's action and an individual's privacy right that merits inquiry into compliance with human rights obligations. For example, the European Court of Human Rights found in *Zakharov v. Russia* that the mere existence of a law allowing surveillance provides the basis for the standing of applicants who might be subject to that surveillance.[19] And in its earlier *Leander v. Sweden* judgment, the Court held that the storage of information could interfere with the right to privacy under the European Convention on Human Rights.[20]

Despite these European Court of Human Rights judgments, whether the collection and retention, without more, of data for potential future examination amounts to an interference with the right to privacy remains somewhat unsettled,

---

19. Roman Zakharov v. Russia, Eur. Ct. H.R., app. 47143/06, ¶ 171 (Apr. 12, 2015). *See also* Centrum För Rättvisa v. Sweden, Eur. Ct. H.R., app. 35252/08, ¶¶ 166–177 (May 25, 2021); Big Brother Watch, *supra* note 18, ¶¶ 464–65.

20. Leander v. Sweden, Eur. Ct. H.R., app. no. 9248/81, ¶ 48 (Mar. 26, 1987). *See also* The Right to Privacy in the Digital Age, *supra* note 7, ¶ 20.

as does algorithm-based collection and machine inspection of communications or personal data without human access. And in this case, the facts are even further afield, for the communications and data are not being collected for examination at all, and, presumably, humans would not be involved in the process of training the Newtropian systems.

4. The Four-Step Analysis: Is the Adverse Effect Justified?

Assuming solely for the sake of continued analysis that the mass collection program interfered with the right to privacy of individuals present on Newtropian territory, the final step in a human rights assessment is determining whether the State's interference with the right (or failure to comply with the obligation to protect it) is justified. It may be so because either the right is derogable under an applicable treaty regime, or because a treaty or customary IHRL allows for limitations on that right by the State.

As an illustration of derogation, the ICCPR provides the following:

> In time of public emergency which threatens the life of the nation and the existence of which is officially proclaimed, the States Parties to the present Covenant may take measures derogating from their obligations under the present Covenant to the extent strictly required by the exigencies of the situation, provided that such measures are not inconsistent with their other obligations under international law and do not involve discrimination solely on the ground of race, colour, sex, language, religion or social origin.[21]

Thus, derogation of the right to privacy is permitted (provided it is strictly required), although the derogating State must provide notice to other States Parties that includes its rationale.[22] In this case, there is no indication that Newtropia is Party to any human rights instrument providing for the right to privacy and permitting derogation. However, even if it is, the situation is unlikely to qualify as a state of emergency, at least not at the time the data was collected.

Therefore, the question is whether a limitation of the right is justified. Limitations must (1) be prescribed by law, (2) be for a legitimate aim, and (3) be necessary and proportionate.[23] As privacy is not an absolute right like the right to be free from torture or the right to hold an opinion, limitation consistent with these criteria is permissible. Indeed, applying the European Convention on Human Rights, the European Court of Human Rights has indicated that bulk collection programs involving communications and data of those to whom a State

---

21. ICCPR, *supra* note 4, Art. 4(1).

22. *Id.*, Arts. 17(1), 4(3). It must be cautioned that some rights, although not privacy, are non-derogable.

23. TALLINN MANUAL 2.0, *supra* note 8, r. 37 and accompanying commentary. *See also* Big Brother Watch, *supra* note 18, ¶ 322; Zakharov, *supra* note 19, ¶ 227; Kennedy v. U.K., Eur. Ct. H.R., app. no. 26839/05, ¶ 130 (May 18, 2010).

owes human rights obligations are not per se unlawful, so long as they comply with various requirements designed to preclude abuse and overreach.[24]

Concerning the first requirement, the Human Rights Committee observed in its 1988 General Comment 16 that "[t]he gathering and holding of personal information on computers, data banks, and other devices, whether by public authorities or private individuals or bodies, must be regulated by law."[25] The European Court has imposed six requirements for collection-related legislation in criminal cases: identification of the offenses that permit an interception order; a definition of the categories of persons who may have their communications intercepted; a time limit on interception; the procedure for examining, using, and storing the data obtained; the precautions required when transmitting the data to others; and the circumstances that require the communications collected to be erased.[26] In both *Zakharov* and *Big Brother Watch*, the Court adopted these criteria for national security-based interception.[27]

As an example, in *Zakharov*, the Court held that a Russian surveillance law provided insufficient oversight, even though it could only be initiated with a judicial warrant. In the situation under consideration, (1) the judge who authorized the surveillance failed to inquire into whether the program was necessary, (2) the State was able to obtain the records of calls and text messages without going through the service provider, (3) no logs were kept that would allow an assessment of whether the powers were being abused, and (4) there was no ongoing supervision of the program following the initial authorization. Essentially, the judge was rubber-stamping warrants.[28] And in *Big Brother Watch*, the court found that although reasonable suspicion, prior judicial approval, and subsequent notification are not required of the legal regime governing surveillance, there is a requirement of "end-to-end" safeguards.[29] There is no indication that Newtropia has adopted legislation or other appropriate authorization for the program. Moreover, even if it has, that legislation would have to satisfy the requirements identified earlier.

Again, assuming solely for the sake of continued analysis that such legislation exists, the aim of the legislation must be legitimate. National security is unquestionably a legitimate aim. Indeed, Article 8 of the European Convention makes this point explicitly vis-à-vis the right to privacy: "There shall be no interference

---

24. See discussion in Marko Milanovic, *The Grand Normalization of Mass Surveillance: ECtHR Grand Chamber Judgments in Big Brother Watch and Centrum för rättvisa*, EJIL:TALK! (May 26, 2021).

25. General Comment No. 16, *supra* note 12, ¶ 10.

26. These are known as the "Weber criteria" and were articulated by the court in Weber and Saravia v. Germany, Eur. Ct. H.R., app.54934/00, ¶ 95 (June 29, 2006).

27. Zakarov, *supra* note 19, ¶ 232; Big Brother Watch, *supra* note 18, ¶ 335.

28. Zakarov, *supra* note 19, ¶¶ 261–62.

29. Big Brother Watch, *supra* note 18, ¶ 350. See also Centrum, *supra* note 24, ¶ 264.

by a public authority with the exercise of this right except such as is in accordance with the law and is necessary in a democratic society in the interests of national security. . . ."[30] And in *Big Brother Watch*, the Court "consider[ed] that the decision to operate a bulk interception regime in order to identify unknown threats to national security or against essential national interests is one which continues to fall within [the States' margin of appreciation]."[31]

Of course, military capacity is directly related to national security, and the training of Newtropian NAITS enhances its military capability. However, a national security justification can only apply when the State's national security aims are lawful. The scenario does not expressly indicate that Newtropia intends to use the systems to attack Outlandia, an unlawful use of force under Article 2(4) of the UN Charter and customary law.[32] But if it does, the national security assertion would fail, for it cannot be the case that human rights may be infringed for unlawful purposes.

Finally, any infringement on human rights must be necessary and proportionate. As noted by the Human Rights Committee in General Comment 27, the action authorized by law to achieve a legitimate aim must be the "least intrusive instrument amongst those which might achieve their protective function; and they must be proportionate to the interest to be protected."[33] Generally considered together, necessity and proportionality require that the State's action be suitable to achieving the aim. Less intrusive means have to be used if available, and the degree and nature of the intrusion into privacy must be proportionate to that aim.

In a mass data collection program, significant volumes of data are collected, much of it having nothing to do with the purpose (here national security) motivating its collection. But since a great deal of data is required to train the Newtropian systems, bulk collection is likely the only way to achieve that objective. Moreover, it is unclear whether any means of bulk collection other than that engaged in by Newtropia is available. However, the scale and the duration of the program suggest Newtropia may have overreached; in other words, Big Data is the issue. And, of course, if the program does not support a legitimate aim, or if the aim is legitimate but the systems used do not contribute significantly to the military capacity of the Newtropian armed forces, the collection program would be disproportionate.

5. Conclusion

The Newtropian bulk collection program is highly questionable. It is subject to the human right of privacy and arguably interferes with the enjoyment of

---

30. ECHR, *supra* note 7, Art. 8(2).

31. Big Brother Watch, *supra* note 18, ¶ 340. *See also* Centrum, *supra* note 24, ¶ 252.

32. UN Charter Art. 2(4).

33. Human Rights Comm., General Comment No. 27, Article 12 (Freedom of Movement), ¶ 14, U.N. Doc. CCPR/C/Rev.1/Add.9, ¶ 14 (Nov. 2, 1999).

that right. Moreover, it is unclear whether the operation has been authorized by law or that it is in support of a legitimate aim. Finally, even if it is, the scale and scope of the program might render it disproportionate to, and potentially unnecessary for, the contribution the Newtropian collection program will make to that aim.

B. Newtropian External Collection Operations: International Human Rights Law

Newtropia's collection of Outlandian data also raises human rights concerns. The critical question is whether Newtropia owes human rights obligations to individuals in Outlandia (or elsewhere outside Newtropia) whose communications and personal data have been collected. It does if it collects on Newtropian nationals beyond its borders. But what about others located there?

1. Adversely Affected Right?

IHRL does not protect official communications of individuals performing government duties. As a general matter, nor would accessing publicly available information. Purchasing data profiles on the open market is less well-settled and, the issue of subsequent retention and search of the data raises further questions. However, with regard to the purchases, it would be problematic to attribute the original collection to Newtropia under the law of State responsibility (see discussion of State responsibility later in this chapter), and a reasonable argument can be fashioned that the purchase standing alone does not implicate privacy rights.

The most questionable activity is Newtropia's hacking and exfiltration of nongovernmental communications and data in Outlandia. The legal criteria set forth regarding the right of privacy apply *mutatis mutandis* to the collection of that data.

To begin with, the information collected is meant for use by Newtropia in an influence campaign and during a potential armed conflict rather than simply to train its systems. And the information consists of, at least, content data that clearly qualifies as protected communications and personal information. Thus, the operations certainly represent an interference with the right to privacy of affected individuals.

Accordingly, putting aside the question of territoriality that will be discussed, the collection efforts would need to be justified according to the conditions precedent to a State's limitation of human rights. The scenario does not indicate whether Newtropian law authorizes the collection program. Nor is it clear that Newtropia's aim is legitimate. As already discussed, if the program's purpose is to engage in unlawful use of force against Outlandia, the requirement for legitimate aim is not met. Moreover, if Newtropia intends to use the data in an armed conflict to target individuals protected from attack under international humanitarian law (IHL, see the laterdiscussion), as distinct from conducting influence (psychological) operations against them, the aim would be illegitimate.[34] The scenario is unclear on this issue.

But assuming solely for the sake of analysis that legislation authorizing the program exists and Newtropia had a legitimate national security interest in the information, the collection might be necessary and proportionate because the data would appear to be required to conduct the operation (a question of fact), and there is no indication in the scenario that alternative means of gathering it exists. Further, although the intrusion into privacy is substantial, it is unquestionably highly useful should an armed conflict break out. Although more facts would be required to render a definitive assessment of whether Newtropia's interference with the right to privacy is justified under IHRL, it would be unlikely to survive legal muster, especially with respect to the legitimate interest criterion.

2. Extraterritoriality

The critical issue in this scenario is whether that conclusion matters at all. In other words, does Newtropia even owe human rights obligations to individuals who are not Newtropian nationals and who are located outside Newtropia, including in Outlandia? Do human rights apply extraterritorially?

Some human rights treaties refer to "jurisdiction" to indicate their scope of application. For instance, under the ICCPR, "[e]ach state Party to the present Covenant undertakes to respect and to ensure to all individuals within its territory and subject to its jurisdiction the rights recognized in the present Covenant."[35] Similarly, the European Convention on Human Rights provides that "[t]he High Contracting Parties shall secure to everyone within their jurisdiction the rights and freedoms defined in Section I of this Convention."[36] The effect of these provisions is uncertain. And some treaties contain no jurisdiction clause.[37] The extraterritorial application of customary IHRL is also a point of contention.

Thus, the extraterritoriality of IHRL obligations is a fraught issue.[38] The United States has taken the position, for example, that, at least as to the ICCPR's jurisdictional clause, human rights obligations protect only individuals in the territory of the State concerned. Supranational human rights courts and treaty bodies generally interpret jurisdiction more broadly as denoting control over territory or

---

34. Protocol Additional to the Geneva Conventions of 12 August 1949, and Relating to the Protection of Victims of International Armed Conflicts Art. 51, June 8, 1977, 1125 U.N.T.S. 3 [hereinafter API]; 1 CUSTOMARY INTERNATIONAL HUMANITARIAN LAW, r. 1 (Jean-Marie Henckaerts & Louise Doswald-Beck eds., 2005).

35. ICCPR, *supra* note 4, Art. 2(1).

36. ECHR, *supra* note 7, Art. 1.

37. For instance, the International Covenant on Economic, Social and Cultural Rights, Dec. 16, 1966, 993 U.N.T.S. 3.

38. *See generally* MARKO MILANOVIC, EXTRATERRITORIAL APPLICATION OF HUMAN RIGHTS TREATIES (2011); YUVAL SHANY, THE EXTRATERRITORIAL APPLICATION OF INTERNATIONAL HUMAN RIGHTS LAW (2020).

the individual concerned (spatial and personal jurisdiction).[39] To illustrate, States owe human rights obligations on the former basis to those on its territory and territory it controls, like occupied territory, while on the latter, States owe human rights obligations to those whom they detain abroad.

By these approaches, Newtropia would not owe individuals in Outlandia any human rights obligations; the operations do not take place on Newtropian territory, Newtropia does not exercise control over the territory where its collection operations interfere with the right to privacy, and it does not control the affected individuals.

However, there are strong advocates for an even broader extension of human rights extraterritorially. From a scholarly perspective, Marko Milanovic has argued that the obligation to respect human rights should be territorially unrestricted.[40] According to Milanovic, "even in the cyber surveillance context involving no direct harm to life or health, . . . the right to privacy would apply extraterritorially, and the state engaging in such operations would need to justify any interferences with privacy."[41]

The U.N. Human Rights Committee is moving in the same direction. Dealing with the right to life under the ICCPR's Article 2(1), it has noted that States owe the obligation to "all persons over whose enjoyment of the right to life [the state] exercises power or effective control. This includes persons located outside any territory effectively controlled by the State, whose right to life is nonetheless impacted by its military or other activities in a direct and reasonably foreseeable manner."[42] After all, "it would be unconscionable to so interpret the responsibility under Article 2 of the Covenant as to permit a State party to perpetrate violations of the Covenant on the territory of another State, which violations it could not perpetrate on its own territory."[43] There is no principled reason to distinguish the right to privacy from the right to life vis-à-vis territoriality. But whether Newtropia has violated the right to privacy of individuals subject to its collection program in Outlandia turns on the resolution of this issue.

---

39. TALLINN MANUAL 2.0, *supra* note 8, at 183–84. For instance, see, Banković and Others v. Belgium and Others (decision as to admissibility), Eur. Ct. H.R., app. no. 52207/99, ¶¶ 74–82 (Dec. 12, 2001); Al-Skeini and Others v. U.K., Eur. Ct. H.R., app. no. 55721/07, ¶¶ 135–50 (July 7, 2011).

40. MILANOVIC, EXTRATERRITORIAL APPLICATION, *supra* note 38, at 209–28.

41. Marko Milanovic & Michael Schmitt, *Cyber Attacks and Cyber (Mis)information Operations During a Pandemic*, 11 J. NAT'L SEC. L. & POL'Y 247, 263–64 (2020); *see also* Marko Milanovic, *Human Rights Treaties and Foreign Surveillance: Privacy in the Digital Age*, 56 HARV. INT'L L.J. 81 (2015).

42. Human Rights Comm., General Comment No. 36, ¶ 63, CCPR/C/GC/36 (Oct. 30, 2018). Note that this assertion runs contrary to the holding of the ECHR in *Banković*. The Court avoided the issue in *Big Brother Watch*.

43. Human Rights Committee, Lopez Burgos v. Uruguay, ¶12.3, Communication No. R.12/52, U.N. Doc. Supp. No. 40 (A/36/40) at 176 (1981).

3. Conclusion

Ultimately, the lawfulness of the Newtropian operations in Outlandia depends on the extraterritoriality issue. If human rights apply extraterritorially based on control over the enjoyment of the right in question (privacy in this case), the operations would not satisfy the legitimate interest criterion for limitation.

Of course, with respect to Newtropian operations in both its own country and Outlandia, the challenge of enforcement would loom large. Formal and informal international human rights accountability mechanisms are relatively weak, de jure and de facto. This is especially the case for powerful States that wield weighty influence in international and regional organizations and bilaterally. Such influence can even hobble mechanisms such as naming and shaming or the imposition of policy-based sanctions.

C. Newtropian Operations: Sovereignty

Newtropia's cyber operations against Outlandia raise several other important legal issues. The first is whether they violated Outlandia's sovereignty. The United Kingdom has taken the position that remotely conducted cyber operations into the territory of another State do not violate the latter's sovereignty because no rule protecting sovereignty exists in international law; sovereignty is a principle of law from which rules of law derive, but not a rule in itself.[44] However, every State that has taken an unambiguous stance on the matter has rejected this assertion.[45] Indeed, the international community has long considered sovereignty a rule of law,[46] and the distinct trend among States opining on the issue is that the rule applies to cyber operations.[47]

---

44. Jeremy Wright, Attorney General, United Kingdom, Cyber and International Law in the 21st Century, Remarks at the Chatham House Royal Institute for International Affairs (May 23, 2018), https://www.gov.uk/government/speeches/cyber-and-international-law-in-the-21st-century.

45. Two early reactions affirming sovereignty as a rule came from NATO allies the Netherlands and France. Letter of July 5, 2019, from the Netherlands Minister of Foreign Affairs to the President of the House of Representatives on the International Legal Order in Cyberspace, Appendix: International Law in Cyberspace 2, https://perma.cc/ENU3-DFGV; France, Ministry of the Armies, International Law Applied to Operations in Cyberspace 6–7 (2019) (English version). NATO, except for the United Kingdom, has taken the same position in its Cyber Doctrine. NATO, AJP-3.20 (ed. A, v.1), Allied Joint Doctrine for Cyberspace Operations, at FN 26, 20 (2020).

46. Michael Schmitt & Liis Vihul, *Respect for Sovereignty in Cyberspace*, 95 Tex.L. Rev. 1639 (2017).

47. *See, for example,* the annex appended to the 2021 GGE Report, in which only the United Kingdom opposed sovereignty being characterized as a rule. All other States accepted it as such or did not offer an opinion. Official Compendium of Voluntary National Contributions on the

No consensus among these States has emerged concerning the nature of cyber operations that violate the rule. It would seem clear that those causing physical damage or injury on the territory of another State do so.[48] But below this threshold, uncertainty persists. For instance, whether a cyber operation that temporarily interferes with cyberinfrastructure functionality qualifies as a sovereignty violation remains to be settled.

That said, there is widespread consensus that espionage does not violate sovereignty. This consensus would include those operations targeting Outlandian government and private data. Moreover, putting the espionage issue aside, the fact that the operations do not physically damage any systems in Outlandia or affect their functionality, even temporarily, makes it highly unlikely that States would consider Newtropia's collection program a sovereignty violation.

Similarly, the Newtropian influence campaigns do not violate sovereignty even when involving mis- or disinformation. There is a long-standing practice of conducting influence campaigns against other countries.[49] So long as those campaigns do not generate qualifying consequences, such as physical damage or illness, there is no sovereignty violation.[50]

However, the Newtropian response to the Outlandian catch-up effort is to target the data that Outlandia has collected. As noted, the legal threshold at which a remotely conducted cyber operation violates the sovereignty of the State into which it is conducted remains unsettled. Although physical damage is generally considered a violation of territorial sovereignty, it is unclear whether deletion or alteration of data would fall into that category.[51]

Note that the territorial sovereignty analysis does not distinguish between public and private cyber infrastructure or data, nor does the nationality of the affected cyber infrastructure or data matter. Thus, it does not matter that the operation against UWS cloud storage affected both military and nongovernmental data; if deletion of data qualifies a cyber operation as a sovereignty violation, all deletions violate sovereignty. Similarly, the operations against Outlandian military data located in third countries would likewise violate the sovereignty of those States. If not, the opposite conclusion would result.

Sovereignty can also be violated through interference with, or usurpation of, inherently governmental functions,[52] one of which is providing for the nation's

---

Subject of How International Law Applies to the Use of Information and Communications Technologies by States, U.N. Doc. A/76/136, July 13, 2021.

48. TALLINN MANUAL 2.0, *supra* note 8, rule 4 and accompanying commentary.

49. Michael N. Schmitt, *Foreign Cyber Interference in Elections*, 97 INT'L L. STUD. 739, 741–42, 754 (2021).

50. TALLINN MANUAL 2.0, *supra* note 8, at 26.

51. *Id.*, at 21.

52. *Id.*, r. 4.

defense. Since the military data that Newtropia deleted relates to Outlandia's defense capability, its deletion interferes with an inherently governmental function and is resultantly a sovereignty violation.

As a matter of law, the more challenging question is whether the deletion of military data housed in third countries also constitutes a violation of sovereignty on this basis. Whether the necessary interference must occur on the territory of a state claiming violation remains unsettled. The better argument is that it need not so long as there is a clear nexus between the interference and an inherently governmental function. This is because the principle of sovereignty affords States control over both territory and activities.[53]

D. Newtropian Operations: Nonintervention

Nor does the Newtropian collection program in Outlandia violate the prohibition on intervention into other States' internal or external affairs. To constitute such a violation, the cyber operation in question must (1) coercively affect the (2) domaine réservé of a State.[54] The domaine réservé consists of those areas of activity left by international law to regulation by States.[55] Examples include elections and fiscal policy.

The Newtropian collection program is not designed to affect any Outlandian domaine réservé directly or indirectly; instead, its purpose is to enhance Newtropia's own capabilities. Moreover, the operation would have to be coercive in the sense of causing Outlandia to make policy choices it would otherwise not make concerning a domaine réservé or engage in activities contrary to its wishes as to one. There is no indication in this scenario that the Newtropian collection is forcing Outlandia's hand in any way.

However, the operations against the Outlandian military data could be characterized as intervention. Decisions regarding national defense are matters left to States by international law so long as those decisions do not violate

---

53. Max Huber famously set forth the classic definition of sovereignty in the 1928 Island of Palmas arbitration: "Sovereignty in the relations between States signifies independence. Independence in regard to a portion of the globe is the right to exercise therein, to the exclusion of any other State, *the functions of a State.*" Island of Palmas (Neth. v. U.S.) 2 R.I.A.A. 829, 838 (Perm. Ct. Arb. 1928) [emphasis added].

54. Military and Paramilitary Activities in and against Nicaragua (Nicar. v. U.S), Judgment, 1986 I.C.J. Rep. 14, ¶¶ 202, 205 (June 27) [hereinafter Nicaragua]. For an explanation, see TALLINN MANUAL 2.0 *supra* note 8, rule 66 and accompanying commentary.

55. Nicaragua, *supra* note 54, ¶ 205. *See also* Declaration on Principles of International Law concerning Friendly Relations and Cooperation among States in accordance with the Charter of the United Nations, G.A. Res. 2625 (XXV), principle (c) U.N. Doc. A/8082 (Sept. 28, 1970) (referring to "domestic jurisdiction"); Declaration on the Inadmissibility of Intervention and Interference in the Internal Affairs of States, G.A. Res. 36/103 annex, U.N. Doc. A/RES/36/103 (Dec. 9, 1981).

international rules such as disarmament agreements or the prohibition on the threat of the use of force found in Article 2(4) of the UN Charter. By deleting the data that is being collected for military purposes, Newtropia interfered with Outlandia's national defense decisions. The fact that it deleted the data qualifies as coercive for Outlandia can no longer field capabilities it had decided to acquire.

E. Newtropian Operations and Outlandian Response: Use of Force and Self-Defense

Article 2(4) of the UN Charter provides, "All Members shall refrain in their international relations from the threat or use of force against the territorial integrity or political independence of any state, or in any other manner inconsistent with the Purposes of the United Nations."[56] As a reflection of customary law,[57] it binds all States. There is no doubt that the prohibition applies in the cyber context.[58]

There are three accepted exceptions to the prohibition in the use of force— consent, authorization or mandate under Chapter VII of the UN Charter, and self- or collective defense pursuant to Article 51 of the UN Charter and customary international law. That article provides, in relevant part, that "[n]othing in the present Charter shall impair the inherent right of individual or collective self-defence if an armed attack occurs against a Member of the United Nations, until the Security Council has taken measures necessary to maintain international peace and security."[59] Of the three, this scenario raises only the right of self-defense.

1. The Use of Force

The Newtropian collection operation is not a prohibited "use of force." Although it enhances the ability of Newtropia to engage in military operations that could amount to an unlawful use of force (such as a kinetic attack), the mere acquisition of military capacity per se is not a use of force violation. A breach occurs only once the capacity is employed to mount qualifying military operations.

Newtropia's cyber operations against the data in UWS are more legally complex. Applicability of the prohibition to kinetic uses of force is relatively straightforward. So too is its relevance to cyber operations that produce significant physical damage, injury, or death. However, most cyber operations do not have these effects. The question, therefore, is whether a cyber operation that is neither physically destructive nor injurious, as in this case, ever may qualify as a use of force subject to the prohibition.

---

56. U.N. Charter Art. 2(4).

57. Nicaragua, *supra* note 55, ¶ 34.

58. For instance, the 2021 U.N. Group of Governmental Experts confirmed this, as had its predecessor. 2021 GGE, *supra* note 3, ¶ 71(d); 2015 GGE Report, *supra* note 3, ¶ 26.

59. U.N. Charter Art. 51.

In its *Nicaragua* judgment, the International Court of Justice found that training and arming guerrillas amounted to a use of force,[60] thereby indicating that, at least in the court's eyes, there are uses of force that are not directly destructive or injurious. The logic of this holding is even more compelling in the cyber context, for cyber operations can cause severe non-destructive and non-injurious consequences, such as nationwide transportation disruption or economic harm.[61]

During the *Tallinn Manual* project, the International Groups of Experts for both editions (2013 and 2017) suggested an approach by which various factors suggested whether States would be likely to view a cyber operation as a use of force.[62] Those nonexclusive factors included severity, immediacy, directness, invasiveness, measurability of effects, military character, state involvement, presumptive legality, prevailing political environment, whether the cyber operation portends the future use of military force, the identity of the attacker, any record of cyber operations by the attacker, and the nature of the target. The premise of the approach is that States faced with having to make a use of force assessment in the face of normative ambiguity would consider these and numerous other factors in concert and in context when making their determination.

Several states have adopted the *Tallinn Manual* approach. For instance, Germany suggests that,

> With regard to [exclusively cyber operations], Germany shares the view expressed in the Tallinn Manual 2.0. . . .
>
> The determination of a cyber operation as having crossed the threshold of a prohibited use of force is a decision to be taken on a case-by-case basis. Based on the assessment of the scale and effects of the operation, the broader context of the situation and the significance of the malicious cyber operation will have to be taken into account. Qualitative criteria which may play a role in the assessment are, inter alia, the severity of the interference, the immediacy of its effects, the degree of intrusion into a foreign cyber infrastructure and the degree of organization and coordination of the malicious cyber operation.[63]

The French Ministry of the Armies has taken a similar tack.

> France does not rule out the possibility that a cyber operation without physical effects may also be characterised as a use of force. In the absence of

---

60. Nicaragua, *supra* note 55, ¶ 228.

61. Michael N. Schmitt, *Cyber Operations and the Jus ad Bellum*, 56 Vill. L. Rev. 569, 573–78 (2011).

62. Tallinn Manual 2.0, *supra* note 8, at 333–37; Tallinn Manual on the International Law Applicable to Cyber Warfare 48–51 (Michael N. Schmitt gen. ed., 2013).

63. Germany, in Official Compendium, *supra* note 47, 31, 35–36.

physical damage, a cyber operation may be deemed a use of force against the yardstick of several criteria, including the circumstances prevailing at the time of the operation, such as the origin of the operation and the nature of the instigator (military or not), the extent of intrusion, the actual or intended effects of the operation or the nature of the intended target. This is of course not an exhaustive list.[64]

Although most States that have spoken to the issue are less granular, there is an identifiable trend to, like Germany, adapt the "scale and effects" test for identifying armed attacks in the self-defense context that was set forth by the International Court of Justice in its *Nicaragua* judgment to use of force determinations,[65] as did the *Tallinn Manual* experts.[66] As an example, Australia notes,

> In determining whether a cyber activity constitutes a use of force, States should consider whether the activity's scale and effects are comparable to traditional kinetic operations that rise to the level of use of force under international law. This involves a consideration of the intended or reasonably expected direct and indirect consequences of the cyber activity, including for example whether the activity could reasonably be expected to cause serious or extensive ("scale") damage or destruction ("effects") in the form of injury or death to persons, or damage or destruction (including to their functioning) to objects or critical infrastructure.[67]

Applying these approaches, the deletion of the data has caused significant economic effects in Outlandia. There has been considerable discussion about whether economic harm can qualify a cyber operation as a use of force. France has opined that a cyber operation causing "considerable physical or economic damage" could be categorized as an "armed attack" under the law of self-defense.[68] Since all armed attacks also qualify as wrongful uses of force, this confirms that France is of the view that at a particular level of severity, economic harm standing alone violates the use of force rule. Other countries are slowly beginning to adopt the same approach, as in the case of Norway's 2021 assertion that "the use of crypto viruses or

---

64. France, Ministry of the Armies, International Law Applied to Operations in Cyberspace 7 (2019), https://www.defense.gouv.fr/content/download/567648/9770527/file/international+law+applied+t o + operations+in + cyberspace.pdf [https://perma.cc/WJQ3-XBWT.

65. Nicaragua, *supra* note 54, ¶ 195.

66. Tallinn Manual 2.0, *supra* note 8, r. 69.

67. Australia, in Official Compendium, *supra* note 47, at 5.

68. France, *supra* note 47, at 8; *See also* Netherlands in Official Compendium, *supra* note 47, at 58 (In the view of the government, at this time it cannot be ruled out that a cyber operation with a very serious financial or economic impact may qualify as the use of force.).

other forms of digital sabotage against a State's financial and banking system, or other operations that cause widespread economic effects and destabilisation, may amount to the use of force in violation of Article 2(4).''[69]

Unfortunately, in this scenario, the only indication of economic scale and effects is that there were "significant ripple effects across the Outlandian economy." Without more information as to the gravity of the economic consequences, and in light of the gingerly manner in which States are approaching the issue of economic harm, it is unlikely that States would see the operation against the cloud storage as a use of force.

Another possibility is that the nature of the target justifies characterization as a use of force. Ninety-two percent of Outlandian military data housed on UWS was successfully deleted, as was Operation Full Warp data housed abroad. This aspect of the Newtropian cyber operations led to Outlandia's missile strike. France has warned that "penetrating military systems in order to compromise French defence capabilities, or financing or even training individuals to carry out cyberattacks against France, could also be deemed uses of force."[70] Thus, at least by the French approach, the Newtropian operation might qualify as an unlawful use of force, especially in light of the scale of the loss. Whether other States would see it as such is highly uncertain.

2. Self-Defense

Assuming solely for the sake of analysis that the counter-data operation is a use of force, the question becomes whether it was an "armed attack" to which Outlandia may respond with its own use of force (the missile strike) in self-defense under Article 51 of the UN Charter and customary international law.[71] Like the use of force, the threshold at which a cyber operation qualifies as an armed attack is unsettled. However, most States (the United States is an exception[72]) and scholars

---

69. Norway, in Official Compendium, *supra* note 47, at 70.

70. France, *supra* note 47, at 7.

71. U.N. Charter Art. 51 ("Nothing in the present Charter shall impair the inherent right of individual or collective self-defence if an *armed attack* occurs against a Member of the United Nations, until the Security Council has taken measures necessary to maintain international peace and security" (emphasis added)).

72. Office of the General Counsel, U.S. Department of Defense, Law Of War Manual § 16.3.3.1 (rev. ed. Dec. 2016) (citing Harold Hongju Koh, Legal Adviser, U.S. Department of State, International Law in Cyberspace: Remarks as Prepared for Delivery to the USCYBERCOM Inter-Agency Legal Conference (Sept. 18, 2012), *reprinted in* 54 Harv. Int'l L. J. Online 7 (Dec. 2012)).

To cite just one example of this, the United States has for a long time taken the position that the inherent right of self-defense potentially applies against any illegal use of force. In our view, there is no threshold for a use of deadly force to qualify as an "armed attack" that may warrant a forcible response. But that is not to say that any illegal use of force triggers the right to use any and all force in response—such responses must still be necessary and of course proportionate.

consider the armed attack threshold to lie above that of use of force. As noted by the International Court of Justice in its *Nicaragua* judgment, armed attacks are the "most grave" forms of the use of force.[73] This being so, the operation is unlikely to be characterized by States as an armed attack allowing for a forcible response by Outlandia.

Nor does it appear from the scenario that an armed attack on Outlandia was "imminent," thus allowing Outlandia to strike Newtropia in anticipatory self-defense.[74] In particular, it is unclear whether Newtropia had definitively decided to attack or whether this was the "last window of opportunity" for Outlandia to defend itself.[75] Therefore, the Outlandian missile strike is best characterized as an unlawful use of force.

F. Outlandian Operations and International Law

Outlandia's cyber operations in response to Newtropia's actions, especially in the field of machine learning/artificial intelligence, raise many of the legal questions already discussed; the points made there should be applied to Outlandian operations *mutatis mutandis*. In particular, with respect to the obligation to respect sovereignty and the prohibition on coercive intervention, Outlandia's operations are unlikely to be deemed a violation. Two legal issues, however, are unique.

1. Attribution under the Law of State Responsibility

First, the Outlandian government has outsourced collection efforts to private contractors because domestic law and IHRL commitments limit its ability to conduct the operations itself. This arrangement implicates the law of State responsibility's rules on attributing non-State actor conduct to a State. The International Law Commission's Articles on State Responsibility are a generally reliable restatement of those customary rules. According to Article 8, "The conduct of a person or group of persons shall be considered an act of a State under international law if the person or group of persons is in fact acting on the instructions of, or under the direction or control of, that State in carrying out

---

73. Nicaragua, *supra* note 54, ¶ 191.

74. Tallinn Manual 2.0, *supra* note 8, r. 73 and accompanying text.

75. The "last window of opportunity" approach was proposed in Michael N. Schmitt, *Preemptive Strategies in International Law*, 24 Mich. J. Int'l L. 513, 534–36 (2003). It was later adopted by the United States. *See, e.g.*, Dep't of Justice, Lawfulness of a Lethal Operation Directed Against a U.S. Citizen Who Is a Senior Operational Leader of Al-Qa'ida or an Associated Force 7 (Nov. 8, 2011) (draft), http://www.justice.gov/sites/default/files/oip/legacy/2014/07/23/dept-white-paper.pdf; Eric Holder, Attorney General, Remarks at Northwestern University School of Law (Mar. 5, 2012), https://www.justice.gov/opa/speech/attorney-general-eric-holder-speaks-north western-university-school-law.

the conduct."[76] While "instructions" generally refers to express instructions to engage in particular conduct on the State's behalf, directions and control are often considered together as denoting "effective control" over the group in question.[77]

The contractual relationship between the government and the entities gathering the data in question, both domestically and abroad, satisfies the "instructions" criterion for legal attribution of the contractors' collection efforts to Outlandia. Accordingly, those efforts must be judged against Outlandia's international law obligations.

The information collected implicates the human right of privacy, although whether Outlandia owes respect for that right to individuals located beyond its territory is subject to the same uncertainty regarding extraterritoriality as was previously discussed. Assuming for the sake of analysis that the obligation attaches extraterritorially, it is necessary to assess Outlandia's operations against the criteria justifying infringement of the right to privacy.

One point of distinction is that Outlandia's aim appears to enjoy greater legitimacy than Newtropia's, for the scenario paints a picture of Outlandia as a potential target of a wrongful Newtropian use of force at the armed attack level. If that is the case, Outlandia is enhancing its capability to defend itself in the face of a threat that, although perhaps not imminent, is likely. Developing defensive capability qualifies unambiguously as a national security interest. Moreover, given the nature of that threat, and in the absence of any indication that alternatives exist to acquire the data necessary to build its own AI/ML capacity, Outlandia's program also probably would survive an IHRL necessity and proportionality appraisal.

2. The Duty to Protect

The second unique issue is whether Outlandia shoulders a positive obligation under IHRL to counter the Newtropian operations that affect the enjoyment of individuals' right to privacy in Outlandia. Recall that States have a negative duty to refrain from human rights violations and a positive obligation to ensure third parties respect them.[78] The latter duty can range from taking law enforcement or other investigative and administrative measures to applying technical solutions that resolve the situation.

---

76. Articles on State Responsibility, *supra* note 6, Art. 8 ("The conduct of a person or group of persons shall be considered an act of a State under international law if the person or group of persons is in fact acting on the instructions of, or under the direction or control of, that State in carrying out the conduct.").

77. *Id.*, ¶¶ 4, 7, 8 of commentary accompanying Art. 8. *See also* Alexander Kees, *Responsibility of States for Private Actors, in* Max Plank Encyclopedia of International Law (Anne Peters gen. ed., last updated Mar. 2011), https://opil.ouplaw.com/view/10.1093/law:epil/9780199231690/law-9780199231690-e1092?rskey=UNK58U&result=3&prd=MPIL.

78. Gabor Rona & Lauren Aarons, *State Responsibility to Respect, Protect and Fulfill Human Rights Obligations in Cyberspace*, 8 J. Nat'l Sec. L. Pol'y 503 (2016).

Unfortunately, the scenario does not provide sufficient facts to draw a definitive conclusion on the matter. For instance, it neither develops the extent to which Outlandia was aware of the exfiltration of data protected by the right to privacy nor the feasibility of Outlandia taking measures to prevent that intrusion into privacy. Presumably, Outlandia was unable to put an end to the operations, for, given the tension between the two States, it is reasonable to conclude that Outlandia would have acted had it been able to do so. Note that precisely the same issue arises concerning third States in which the private contractors were collecting data on behalf of Outlandia.

3. Due Diligence by Third States

Finally, it might be questioned whether the third States in which the Outlandian data is stored have a so-called due diligence obligation. As noted in Rule 6 of *Tallinn Manual 2.0*, "a State must exercise due diligence in not allowing its territory, or territory or cyberinfrastructure under its governmental control, to be used for cyber operations that affect the rights of, and produce serious adverse consequences for, other States."[79] Rule 7 explains that this "requires a State to take all measures that are feasible in the circumstances to put an end" to such operations.

A majority of states that have opined on the issue believe that a due diligence obligation applies to cyber activities, although there are dissenters.[80] But in any event, the obligation would not apply in this case.[81] First, it is not clear that any right of Outlandia is affected. As noted, the operation may constitute a sovereignty violation or even a use of force, but this is highly questionable. Second, the scenario does not indicate the extent to which the loss of the data stored outside its territory affects Outlandia's ability to ensure its national security; the due diligence obligation only attaches when the consequences are serious. Third, there is no indication that the third States are aware of the operations against the data stored on their territory. In the absence of knowledge as to Newtropia's operations, any obligation imposed on the third States would, in effect, be an obligation to take preventive measures. As the law stands today, due diligence imposes no requirement to take steps to prevent offending operations.

III. CONCLUSION

The Newtropian and Outlandian Big Data operations raise an array of international law questions that frequently surface in situations short of armed conflict.

---

79. TALLINN MANUAL 2.0, *supra* note 8, r. 6.

80. Michael Schmitt, *Three International Law Rules for Responding Effectively to Hostile Cyber Operations*, JUST SECURITY (July 31, 2021), https://www.justsecurity.org/77402/three-internatio nal-law-rules-for-responding-effectively-to-hostile-cyber-operations/.

81. See discussion of limiting factors on attachment of the obligation in TALLINN MANUAL 2.0, *supra* note 8, commentary accompanying rule 6.

However, the "bigness" of the data concerned has only slight bearing on the application of international law in the scenario.

Most prominent among these questions are those regarding the IHRL obligations of States. As explained, assessing whether a cyber operation attributable to a State violates IHRL is a four-step process. The first is to determine whether the State concerned owes human rights obligations to those affected by its cyber operations. Clearly, it does when conducting operations involving individuals on its territory, as in the case of Newtropia's domestic data collection operations.

But whether States owe IHRL obligations to those outside their territory is unsettled. The prevailing view is that no such obligations attach unless the individuals are in the "effective control" of the State, as in detention abroad. However, there is a marked trend in scholarship and European case law toward an extension of IHRL obligations to situations in which a State controls the enjoyment or exercise of a human right outside its territory. For instance, in this scenario, Newtropia's operations against individuals in Outlandia could be characterized as exercising effective control over the enjoyment of their right to privacy.

The second step is determining whether cyber operations implicate a particular IHRL right. In this scenario, the primary right concerned is privacy. Although collecting content data by cyber means implicates the right, it is less certain that mere metadata collection does so.

If a human right is implicated, it must be determined in the third step whether the right has been adversely affected. In the collection context, there is an adverse effect if humans review the material. However, it is an open question whether machine inspection or mere collection and retention, without human examination, qualifies as an adverse effect.

Finally, if a right has been adversely affected, it must be determined whether the adverse effect is justified either because derogation of a treaty obligation is permitted or the State concerned has complied with the IHRL requirements for limitation of a right. These requirements are that the limitation (in this case, collection) (1) is prescribed by law; (2) advances a legitimate aim of the State such as national security; (3) is necessary; and 4) the extent of interference with the right is proportionate to the State's aim in engaging in this cyber operation (which raises the issue of the amount of data collected).

The scenario involves several other international law rules. Key among these is the obligation to respect the sovereignty of other States when conducting cyber operations. Although the United Kingdom denies the existence of such a right, all other States that have spoken to the issue confirm its existence. The challenge is that the threshold for violation is unclear. Physical damage or injury certainly qualify, whereas espionage standing alone does not. Between these extremes, the law is unsettled. In this scenario, the deletion of data, as distinct from its collection, falls within this gray zone.

Other issues raised in this scenario include the prohibition on intervention, a violation of which requires coercive cyber operations against a State's domaine réservé; the prohibition on the use of force, which is today assessed by reference to a cyber operation's "scale and effects"; the right of self-defense against an "armed attack," and the threshold at which a cyber operation qualifies as such; attribution of a non-State actor's cyber operations to a State according to the rules of State responsibility; and the controversial obligation of due diligence, which requires States to take action to put an end to hostile cyber operations mounted from or through their territory that adversely affect the international law rights of other States.

As this scenario illustrates, the law governing cyber operations outside unarmed conflict remains highly unsettled. Until States offer a more granular accounting of their interpretation of these and other international rules as applied in this cyber context, this unfortunate reality is unlikely to improve.

2

Threatening Force in Cyberspace

DUNCAN B. HOLLIS* AND TSVETELINA VAN BENTHEM† ∎

In 1974, the first of four "tunnels of aggression" running from North Korea underneath the demilitarized zone and into South Korean territory was discovered.[1] In his 1971 construction order, North Korea's president, Kim Il-Sung, suggested that just "one tunnel would be more effective than 10 atomic bombs and would thus be the best means to overwhelm a heavily fortified front."[2] Military experts suggested the third tunnel could accommodate 30,000 fully armed soldiers plus light artillery every hour.[3] U.S. President Jimmy Carter would later highlight the tunnels in listing North Korea's "threats and provocations" against its Southern adversary.[4]

But what exactly did these tunnels threaten? They were never used. North Korea did not accompany their (surreptitious) construction with any demands.[5] Nor

---

* Laura H. Carnell Professor of Law, Temple University School of Law; Non-Resident Fellow, Carnegie Endowment for International Peace.

† Lecturer in international law for the Oxford Diplomatic Studies Programme and researcher at the Oxford Institute for Ethics, Law and Armed Conflict and Merton College.

1. Hannah Fischer, *North Korean Provocative Actions, 1950–2007* (2007); *Seoul Uncovers a Border Tunnel*, N.Y. TIMES (Mar. 4, 1990). The authors thank Herb Lin for calling attention to the history of these tunnels and their potential lessons for cyberspace.

2. (주)라이크웹, INFILTRATION TUNNELS FOR SOUTHERN INVASION: INFILTRATION TUNNELS PANMUNJOM (DMZ) TRAVEL CENTER (판문점트레블센터), at http://panmunjomtour.com/en/tunnel/tunnel_1_0.asp.

3. Fischer, *supra* note 1.

4. Jimmy Carter, *Camp Casey, Republic of Korea–Remarks at the Welcoming Ceremony–June 30, 1979*, PUB. PAPERS 1201 (1979).

5. In other instances, North Korea announced plans to use force. *See, e.g.*, Jonathan Cheng, *North Korea Threatens "Absolute Force" as U.S., South Hold Military Drills*, WALL ST. J. (Aug. 22, 2017); Agence France Presse, *North Korea Releases "Ultimatum" Video Showing Attack Destroying Seoul*, THE GUARDIAN (Apr. 5, 2016).

Duncan B. Hollis and Tsvetelina van Benthem, *Threatening Force in Cyberspace* In: *Big Data and Armed Conflict*. Edited by: Laura A. Dickinson and Edward W. Berg, Oxford University Press. © Duncan B. Hollis and Tsvetelina van Benthem 2024. DOI: 10.1093/oso/9780197668610.003.0004

did it hold associated military exercises from which to infer a threatened invasion.[6] And history shows secret tunnels are not just vehicles for launching armed attacks; they can serve other functions in peacetime and wartime (e.g., smuggling of goods—or people—for humanitarian or criminal purposes, intelligence collection, defensive retreats).[7] That said, the cross-border nature of these tunnels combined with the legacy of conflict makes it difficult to ascribe to them anything but hostile intentions on North Korea's part. As recently as 2012, South Korea's Defense Ministry told the *New York Times* that the possibility of such tunnels "could determine the outcome of a war and our country's survival."[8]

Today, questions about cross-border tunnels and the threats they pose have renewed relevance when considering the rise of cyberthreats. Some cyberthreats are overt and readily apparent to victims (e.g., ransomware).[9] Others, however, function like virtual tunnels (e.g., web shells that afford access to targeted systems via hidden "back doors"). They thus analogize to physical tunnels, especially in that both earthly and virtual means of access may not dictate how—or who—will use them. Unauthorized access to computers or networks can effectuate varied outcomes—from espionage to physical destruction. Such access may be used, moreover, not only by those who built it but others who later discover and deploy it for similar (or different) purposes.[10]

Within this intricate web of digital interactions, the advent of "Big Data" and Big Data Analytics adds further layers of complexity with new risks and potential rewards.[11] On the one hand, Big Data is designed to deal with the "complex" and "undecipherable," offering analytical tools to recognize trends and patterns within large datasets. As such, Big Data Analytics may be a helpful tool in identifying and cataloging different types of cyberthreats. On the other hand, Big Data's very employment calls for a careful discussion of the risks inherent in our data, the algorithms used, and the human and machine assessments of algorithmic outputs. Indeed, Big Data collection and analysis of data may in certain circumstances

---

6. Tunnels have been used to conduct (and defend against) armed attacks for centuries. *See* Daphné Richemond-Barak, Underground Warfare, ch. 1 (2018). Modern examples include the first and second World Wars as well as conflicts in Afghanistan, Iraq, Israel, Libya, Mali, and Syria. *Id.*

7. *See, e.g., id.* at 22–30 (describing Hamas's tunnels under the Gaza/Egypt border and into Israel); *Agents Find Drug Tunnel to US*, N.Y. Times (May 19, 1990) (tunnel used to smuggle cocaine from Mexico into the United States).

8. *See* Choe Sang-Hun, *Hunting for Tunnels to Prove a Threat*, N.Y. Times (July 2, 2012).

9. *See infra* notes 84, 97, and accompanying text.

10. There are various cases where new forces used old tunnels. *See, e.g.*, Richemond-Barak, *supra* note 6, at 22–30 (recounting Mujahedeen and Al Qaida use of irrigation tunnels used by locals to escape Genghis Kahn's invasion in AD 1221).

11. For a discussion on the definition of Big Data and Big Data Analytics, see the section on Technical Capacities, *infra* notes 117 and 118.

itself constitute a form of threatening behavior. In either case, Big Data becomes an important piece of the puzzle in assessing cyberthreats.[12]

In this chapter, we propose to assess what threats look like in cyberspace and how international law, and in particular the *jus ad bellum*, regulates them.[13] North Korea's tunnels of aggression counsel us to consider not just explicit cyberthreats but the implicit ones as well. Indeed, our central claim is that both States and scholars must integrate an analysis of the potential for threats in *all* cyber operations. Doing so will widen international law's application in cyberspace beyond assessments of a cyber operation's specific effects to consider what other threats it conveys to victims or any third parties observing it.

When it comes to regulating threats, international law has one central tenet. Article 2(4) of the UN Charter famously prohibits States from using force unless they do so in self-defense or pursuant to UN Security Council authorization. Yet, Article 2(4) also expressly prohibits States from the "threat . . . of force." The first prohibition has had a featured (if not always effective) role in the operation of modern international law.[14] The prohibition on the threat of force, in contrast, has occupied a more "empty space."[15] It is "an area neglected by international lawyers"[16] with a "paucity of literature."[17] Scholars suggest this is due to

---

12. This second way of thinking about the use of "Big Data" becomes clear in the scenario this volume's editors have offered for discussion. On its facts, Newtropia "gathers all publicly available information about Outlandia's citizens," "hacks and exfiltrates large amounts of Outlandian data," and, on that basis, its Military Intelligence Directorate "develops detailed micro-targeting profiles of 96% of Outlandian citizens." These profiles are then used in targeting during the conflict. *See* Mark A. Visger, "Scenario," this book, at 22.

13. For our initial call for such an effort, see Duncan B. Hollis & Tsvetelina van Benthem, *What Would Happen if States Started Looking at Cyber Operations as a "Threat" to Use Force?*, LAWFARE (Mar. 30, 2021), at https://www.lawfareblog.com/what-would-happen-if-states-started-looking-cyber-operations-threat-use-force.

14. *See, e.g.,* THE OXFORD HANDBOOK ON THE USE OF FORCE IN INTERNATIONAL LAW (Marc Weller ed., 2015); Oliver Dörr, *Use of Force, Prohibition Of, in* MAX PLANCK ENCYCLOPEDIA OF PUBLIC INTERNATIONAL LAW (A. Peters ed., Aug. 2019) (including bibliography).

15. NIKOLAS STÜRCHLER, THE THREAT OF FORCE IN INTERNATIONAL LAW 3 (2007).

16. Marco Roscini, *Threats of Armed Force and Contemporary International Law*, 54 NETH. INT'L L. REV. 229, 231 (2007); *see also* Nigel D. White & Robert Cryer, *Unilateral Enforcement of Resolution 687: A Threat Too Far?*, 29 CALIF. W. J. INT'L L 243, 244 (1999) (threat prohibition is "the neglected younger sibling of the more well-known (and discussed) prohibition on the use of force").

17. F. GRIMAL, THREATS OF FORCE: INTERNATIONAL LAW & STRATEGY 31 (2013). For notable exceptions, see STÜRCHLER, *supra* note 15; Roscini, *supra* note 16; Nicholas Tsagourias, *The Prohibition of Threats of Force, in* RESEARCH HANDBOOK ON INTERNATIONAL CONFLICT AND SECURITY LAW 67 (Nigel White & Christian Henderson eds., 2013); J.A. Green & F. Grimal, *The Threat of Force as an Action in Self-Defence under International Law*, 44 VANDERBILT J. TRANS'L L. 239 (2011); Dino Kritsiotis, *Close Encounters of a Sovereign Kind*, 20 EURO. J. INT'L L. 299 (2009); Romana Sadurska, *Threats of Force*, 82 AM J. INT'L L. 239 (1988).

the post-threat environment; either a use of force follows the threat, shifting legal analyses into the mainstream of *jus ad bellum* issues, or the very absence of that escalation incentivizes States to avoid raising the prohibition lest it trigger the undesired outcome.[18]

When it comes to applying international law to cyberspace, therefore, it is not surprising to see the lion's share of attention devoted to the question of delineating cyber operations falling above (or below) the use of force threshold.[19] The dominant mode of legal analysis examines the "effects" of cyber operations along a spectrum ranging from the most wrongful "armed attacks" that trigger a right of self-defense to "mere" acts of espionage, which international law either allows or ignores.[20]

We believe, however, that there are good reasons to expand the current discourse to incorporate a theory of prohibited cyberthreats. To begin, as a *factual* matter, threats of force are frequently deployed by States; scholars suggest they are a "ubiquitous"[21] and "pervasive"[22] element of international relations. Second, as a *doctrinal* matter, there is no real question that international law prohibits threats of force. As such, an examination of this prohibition is long past due if only to set a

---

18. Roscini, *supra* note 16, at 247; White & Cryer, *supra* note 16, at 246; Sadurska, *supra* note 17, at 239. The latter rationale may explain why legal analysis of the tunnels of aggression focused on their violation of the Armistice Agreement rather than whether they threatened a use of force. *See* Richemond-Barak, *supra* note 6, at 12.

19. *See, e.g.*, Report of Group of Governmental Experts on Advancing Responsible State Behavior in Cyberspace in the Context of International Security (May 28, 2021), U.N. Doc. A/76/136 (July 13, 2021) Annex (a collection of official State views on international law in cyberspace); Michael N. Schmitt, *Noteworthy Releases of International Cyber Law Positions—Part I: NATO*, Articles of War (Aug. 27, 2020). For scholarly views, *see* Tallinn Manual 2.0 on the International Law Applicable to Cyber-Operations (Michael N. Schmitt gen. ed., 2017); Marco Roscini, Cyber Operations and the Use of Force in International Law (2014); Oona A. Hathaway et al., *The Law of Cyber-Attack*, 100 Calif. L. Rev. 817 (2012); Matthew C. Waxman, *Cyber-Attacks and the Use of Force: Back to the Future of Article 2(4)*, 36 Yale J. Int'l L. 421 (2011); Duncan B. Hollis, *Why States Need an International Law for Information Operations*, 11 Lewis & Clark L. Rev. 1023 (2007).

20. In between these poles, debates persist over which effects delineate a use of force, violate the duty of nonintervention, and/or breach sovereignty (assuming a rule of sovereignty exists in cyberspace). *See, e.g.*, Duncan B. Hollis (Rapporteur), *International Law and State Cyber Operations: Improving Transparency: Fifth Report*, OEA/Ser.Q, CJI/doc. 615/20 (July 17, 2020); Harriet Moynihan, *The Application of International Law to Cyberspace: Sovereignty and Nonintervention*, Just Security (Dec. 13, 2019), at https://www.justsecurity.org/67723/the-application-of-international-law-to-cyberspace-sovereignty-and-non-intervention/; Russell Buchan, Cyber Espionage and International Law (2019); Russell Buchan, *Cyber-Attacks: Unlawful Uses of Force or Prohibited Interventions*, 17 J. Conflict & Sec. L. 211 (2012).

21. Sadurska, *supra* note 17, at 266.

22. Oscar Schachter, *The Right of States to Use Armed Force*, 82 Mich. L. Rev. 1620, 1620 (1984) (threats pervade international relations); Kritsiotis, *supra* note 17, at 300 (same).

baseline for its operation in cyberspace. Third, the scale and scope of cyberthreats are rising, suggesting a *functional* need to regulate any such threats that implicate international peace and security. Indeed, we believe that the migration of threats to the cyber domain may generate an even greater need for a theory of prohibited threats. This is so for a host of reasons, including the polysemous nature of many cyberthreats (they can have multiple meanings for victims and observers) and the scale and reach of persistent cyber operations. Finally, *technical* developments— chiefly the rise of Big Data—will increasingly provide States and other actors with a capacity to apply the threat prohibition in more meaningful ways (albeit not without attendant risks/costs).

Thus, our chapter aims to foreground the under-examined issue of cyberthreats in current discussions of international law's application to cyberspace. Of course, many cyber activities are threatening in nature. We recognize that conveying a threat *of some sort* is not sufficient to trigger the prohibition on threats of force. Only cyber operations that credibly threaten an unlawful use of force qualify. Assessing credibility requires looking at, among others, the author's identity and capacities, the relationships between States, imminence, and the nature of the threat and what is threatened.

We believe, moreover, that credible threats of force can be found in behaviors other than the ultimatums and demonstrations of force that the *jus ad bellum* has emphasized to date. In certain contexts, implicit threats of force may be presumed in the construction of persistent access, whether through physical tunnels or virtual ones. Virtual tunnels, in addition to exploiting vulnerabilities in ways that may open systems to direct uses of force, ensure access to data, and such data can subsequently be instrumentalized and weaponized in cyber or kinetic operations. States and other stakeholders thus need to expand the extant discourse beyond "effects-based" reasoning and ask whether and how a cyber operation that does one thing (e.g., cyberespionage) might simultaneously threaten another (e.g., a prohibited use of force). Beyond mere discussion, moreover, we believe that international law requires States (and their lawyers) to recognize and accommodate the prohibition on threats of force in all their cyber operations. As such, understanding what threatening force looks like in cyberspace may broaden and deepen our understanding of how Article 2(4) operates *in toto* and its capacity to more effectively establish and maintain international peace and security.

The chapter proceeds as follows. Part I surveys the current doctrine surrounding the prohibition on threats of force. Part II explores the nature and scope of current cyberthreats to identify whether and when such threats might trigger the prohibition. In doing so, we highlight several features of cyberthreats that differentiate them from kinetic threats of force. In Part III, we examine the role Big Data may play in identifying prohibited threats while noting the attendant risks in using data-driven models in the *jus ad bellum* context. We conclude with a call for further research and dialogue on threatening force in cyberspace and beyond.

I. THE DOCTRINE: THE PROHIBITION ON THREATS OF FORCE

Risks and threats have always accompanied international relations. Yet, international law's regulation of threats is of recent origin, dating to the UN Charter itself. Article 2(4) of the Charter provides that:

> All Members shall refrain in their international relations from the threat or use of force against the territorial integrity or political independence of any state, or in any other manner inconsistent with the Purposes of the United Nations.

The prohibition on using force had earlier analogues, most notably the denunciation of warfare in the (in)famous Kellogg-Briand Pact.[23] In contrast, the prohibition on threats of force only emerged with the Charter's conclusion. The *travaux préparatoires* are sparse (and that may be an overstatement).[24] As a result, interpretations of the prohibition must derive from the text itself, the larger purposes behind the UN's creation (namely, "to maintain international peace and security"[25]), as well as from subsequent State practice that seeks to give it content.[26]

Although State invocations of the prohibition are less frequent than actual threats of force in international relations, they still occur relatively regularly.[27] State practice, moreover, affirms the prohibition on threats of force as customary international law.[28] The doctrine has also received some scrutiny before international

---

23. *Kellogg-Briand Pact*, 98 L.N.T.S. no. 1-4 (1928). The Pact emerged in reaction to the regulatory failure of the League of Nations, which had tried to impose procedural limitations before States could resort to warfare. *See* League of Nations Covenant, Art. 12.

24. Tsagourias, *supra* note 17, at 3 ("the *travaux préparatoires* reveal little about the content of the prohibition; instead, they demonstrate an overwhelming consensus . . . that the twin prohibition was necessary in order to maintain international peace and security"). Stürchler recounts how earlier versions of what became Article 2(4) indicated that "no nation shall be permitted to *maintain or use* armed force." STÜRCHLER, *supra* note 15, at 20. None of the records explain, however, why "threats" replaced the "maintenance" concept and the phrasing passed through "the rush of negotiations with scant consideration" other than clarifying it excluded threats of an economic or political character. STÜRCHLER, *supra* note 15, at 22, 23.

25. U.N. Charter, Art. 1(1).

26. Richard Gardiner, *The Vienna Convention Rules on Treaty Interpretation, in* THE OXFORD GUIDE TO TREATIES 478, 479 (D. Hollis ed., 2d ed. 2020); STÜRCHLER, *supra* note 15, at 105.

27. *See* Roscini, *supra* note 16, at 245 (dispensing with claims that condemnations of threats are rare, citing various protests against threats of force or conduct labeled as such, including objections to U.S. and U.S.S.R. threats during the Cold War, protests against French threats of intervention in Western Sahara; and protests that the U.K. exclusion zone around the Falkland Islands was an unlawful threat of force).

28. On the view that the prohibition on threats of force is customary international law, see Military and Paramilitary Activities in and Against Nicaragua (Nicaragua v. USA), Merits [1986] ICJ Rep. 14, ¶¶ 187–90 (Nicaragua Case); Legal Consequences of the Construction of a Wall

Threatening Force in Cyberspace

organizations and various international courts and tribunals.[29] The International Court of Justice (ICJ) directly addressed the threat prohibition in two cases, with the most important contributions coming in its Advisory Opinion on the *Prohibition of Nuclear Weapons*.[30] Most recently, the Independent International Fact-Finding Mission on the Conflict in Georgia (IIFFMCG) found both Georgia and Russia had engaged in behaviors threatening force in violation of Article 2(4).[31]

Taken together, the existing doctrine suggests a three-part test for identifying prohibited threats of force: (a) an explicit or implicit *threat*; (b) of *force*; that is (c) *credible* in the given context, based on factors such as the author's identity and capacities, relationships between States, imminence, and the nature of the threat and what is threatened. We believe, moreover, that this test should be assessed by reference to *objective* criteria.

Before addressing what a prohibited threat of force *is*, however, we should high-light what a threat of force is *not*. It would be a mistake to conflate our threat inquiry into the one for imminent attacks under the (contested) doctrine of an-ticipatory self-defense.[32] Even if States can invoke this latter doctrine—a point on which we reserve our position—doing so still differs significantly from identifying threats of force. After all, Article 2(4)'s concern lies with threats of *force*, while anticipatory self-defense requires an *armed attack*. Moreover, as we will discuss, there is no imminence requirement for threats of force. Indeed, a successful threat is one where a use of force becomes unnecessary.[33] As such, it is important to treat threats of force and anticipatory self-defense as separate questions.

---

in the Occupied Palestinian Territory, Advisory Opinion [2004] I.C.J. Rep. 136, ¶87; *see also* [1966] YBILC, vol. II, at 246; Declaration on Principles of International Law, Friendly Relations and Co-operation among States in Accordance with the Charter of the United Nations, G.A. Res. 2625 (XXV), U.N. Doc. A/RES/25/2625 ¶2 (Oct. 24, 1970); Roscini, *supra* note 16, at 252 (citing national statements that the threat prohibition is customary international law and noting the absence of any state claims denying it that status); *but see* GRIMAL, *supra* note 17, at 48 (suggesting the prohibition on threats of force is not customary international law). Scholars also continue to debate whether the *jus cogens* status accorded to the prohibition on the use of force extends to threats of force.

29. Roscini, *supra* note 16, at 250 (reviewing international organizations' practice of condemning threats of force).

30. Legality of the Threat or Use of Nuclear Weapons, Advisory Opinion [1996] I.C.J. Rep. 226, ¶¶47–48; Nicaragua Case, *supra* note 28, at ¶227.

31. Independent International Fact-Finding Mission on the Conflict in Georgia, REPORT, Vol. II, at 238 ("IIFFMCG").

32. *Compare* Jeremy Wright QC MP, *The Modern Law of Self-Defence*, EJIL:TALK! (Jan. 11, 2017) (U.K. endorses possibility of responding in self-defense to "imminent attacks"); *with* OLIVIER CORTEN, THE LAW AGAINST WAR: THE PROHIBITION ON THE USE OF FORCE IN CONTEMPORARY INTERNATIONAL LAW 407–11 (2010) (describing diverging views on anticipatory self-defense).

33. STÜRCHLER, *supra* note 15, at 56. The UN Secretary-General expressed a similar view: "the threat of force differs from the employment of force in the same way as the threat to kill differs from murder. The person who utters the threat may not intend to carry it out, and the threat

A. An Explicit or Implicit Threat

As a general matter, threats involve an "element of coercion deduced from the explicit or implicit promise . . . to inflict certain injury on its recipient."[34] Brownlie's early definition had linked threats to a "demand," but scholars have subsequently suggested the presence of a demand is not determinative of a threat's existence.[35] As such, when a State like Iran suggests its intention to wipe Israel off the face of the earth, it still constitutes a threat even if the statement is read unconditionally.[36] The essence of a threat, therefore, lies in its communicative nature—the signal of potential harm to the targeted victim(s).

How does such signaling happen? Threats may, of course, involve an express ultimatum. A well-known example of an explicit threat was that expressed by the United States and the United Kingdom against Iraq for its recalcitrant behavior in 1997. Strikingly, this threat of force was welcomed by then Secretary-General Kofi Annan who hailed the two threatening States as the "perfect U.N. peacekeepers."[37] More recently, social media platforms, and in particular Twitter, have become the new playground for threatening force, including the memorable 2018 tweet by former President Trump:

> North Korean Leader Kim Jong Un just stated that the "Nuclear Button is on his desk at all times." Will someone from his depleted and food starved

is then only a form of intimidation and 'blackmail.'" Report of the Secretary-General on the Question of Defining Aggression, U.N. Doc. A/2211 (Oct. 3, 1952), GAOR, seventh session, Annexes, Agenda item 54, at 68.

34. Tsagourias, *supra* note 17, at 13; STÜRCHLER, *supra* note 15, at 37 (drawing on dictionary definitions to define threats as a "hostile intent . . . communicated in some form"); Sadurska, *supra* note 17, at 241 ("A threat is an act that is designed to create a psychological condition in the target of apprehension, anxiety, and eventually fear, which will erode the target's resistance to change or will pressure it toward preserving the status quo."); Roscini, *supra* note 16, at 235 ("a threat of force under Article 2(4) can be defined as an explicit or implicit promise of a future and unlawful use of armed force against one or more states, the realization of which depends on the threatener's will").

35. *Compare* IAN BROWNLIE, INTERNATIONAL LAW AND THE USE OF FORCE 364 (1963) ("A threat of force consists in an express or implied promise by a government of a resort to force conditional on non-acceptance of certain demands of that government."); Michael Wood, *Use of Force, Prohibition of Threat*, in MAX PLANCK ENCYCLOPEDIA OF PUBLIC INTERNATIONAL LAW (R. Wolfrum, ed., June 2013) (adopts Brownlie) *with* TALLINN MANUAL 2.0, *supra* note 19, Commentary to Rule 70, ¶4 ("Although threats are usually intended to be coercive in effect, there is no requirement that a specific "demand" accompany the threat."); Tsagourias, *supra* note 17, at 13; Rossini, *supra* note 16, at 235 ("demands are not a necessary requirement for the existence of a threat of force under Article 2(4)"); White & Cryer, *supra* note 16, at 254 ("demands are certainly very strong evidence of a threat, but they are not the only evidence from which such a threat can be determined"); YORAM DINSTEIN, WAR, AGGRESSION AND SELF-DEFENSE 86 (2005).

36. Tsagourias, *supra* note 17, at 13.

37. Kritsiotis, *supra* note 17, at 308–16.

regime please inform him that I too have a Nuclear Button, but it is a much
bigger & more powerful one than his, and my Button works!

As observed by Grimal, such statements must still navigate the classical typology
of written/verbal ultimatums, albeit expressed through a new medium.[38]

Beyond the traditional verbal ultimatum—"comply or else"—international law
also accepts the possibility of implicit forms of threatening behavior satisfying the
prohibition. The threats prohibition clearly covers both words and deeds. To understand what is being communicated, therefore, it is not enough to be mindful of
what States say, but also to observe what they do.

Implicit threats are conveyed rather than expressed. In the kinetic sphere,
we have a good sense of the types of actions that convey threats. For instance,
the IIFFMCG found the existence of a prohibited threat of force based on its
examination of Georgian and Russian actions, including the launching of air
surveillance over the Abkhaz conflict zone in spring 2008; Georgian participation in repeated exchanges of fire in South Ossetia; and its engagement in a
comprehensive military buildup with the assistance of third parties, including
acquiring modern weaponry. Recently, we observed yet another "signaling"
from Russia, this time around Ukraine's border. Social media videos surfacing in
April 2021 showed armored convoys moving toward the general border area.[39]
An open-source intelligence team noticed "a congregation of likely hundreds of
vehicles not far from the Russian city of Voronezh."[40] Later, in February 2022,
we observed what the United States called "the biggest mobilization of troops
since the second world war,"[41] as Russia continued to send forces to its border
with Ukraine. On February 24, the threat of force morphed into an actual use of
force, as Russia's stationed troops were instructed to cross the border and commence an invasion.

Considering Russia's well-known aggressive playbook—observed in South
Ossetia, Abkhazia,[42] Crimea, and now the whole of Ukraine—there is little doubt
that Russia was threatening force from at least as early as April 2021. In contrast,
the ICJ found that U.S. military maneuvers adjacent to Nicaragua's borders did

---

38. F. Grimal, *Twitter and the* Jus ad Bellum: *Threats of Force and Other Implications*, 6 J. USE OF
FORCE & INT'L L 183, 187 (2019).

39. IIFFMCG, *supra* note 31, at 233–38.

40. *Russian Forces Are Massing on Ukraine's Border. Bluff or Not, Putin Is Playing with Fire*, CNN
(Apr. 9, 2021), https://edition.cnn.com/2021/04/09/europe/russian-forces-ukraine-border-
analysis-intl/index.html.

41. *Russia Has Amassed Up to 190,000 Troops on Ukraine Borders, US Warns*, THE GUARDIAN
(Feb. 18, 2022), at https://www.theguardian.com/world/2022/feb/18/russia-has-amassed-up-
to-190000-troops-on-ukraine-borders-us-warns.

42. A. Cohen & R.E. Hamilton, *The Russia Military and the Georgia War: Lessons and
Implications*, STRATEGIC STUDIES INSTITUTE (2011).

not amount to a prohibited threat of force "in the circumstances in which they were held."[43]

B. Threats "of Force"

Neither Article 2(4) nor international law prohibit all threats; rather the prohibition extends only to threats "of force." Through threats, a State indicates its readiness to resort to forcible action, and this stated readiness is intended to provoke a certain change in a target audience, whether it is a reaction in the form of an action or omission, or just the cognition of an existing threat.

The language of Article 2(4) is clear that the prohibited conduct extends to the threat of *force*. This means that the State's threatened action must qualify as a use of force—threats to intervene economically or politically in another State fall outside the prohibition.[44] Of course, one difficulty here lies in the continuing debates on the threshold of "force." Any uncertainties about the contours of the term "force" in the Charter will thus have a direct impact on the analysis of threats.[45]

At the same time, the threat of force prohibition is most likely co-extensive with the use of force prohibition. As the ICJ explained in *Nuclear Weapons*, there is a close connection of contingency between threats and uses of force. Threats will only be unlawful if the threatened force is unlawful: "The notions of 'threat' and 'use' of force under Article 2(4) of the Charter stand together in the sense that if the use of force itself in a given case is illegal—for whatever reason—the threat to use such force will likewise be illegal."[46] Conversely, if a use of force is permissible (for example, as an exercise of self-defense or action taken on the basis of a Chapter VII Security Council authorization), so too are threats to pursue it. The analysis is both hypothetical and retroactive: "if actual force is unlawful, then, retroactively, so is the threat to use that same force."[47]

C. Assessing Credibility in Context

The third criterion for the threat prohibition lies in its credibility. Just as not all threats will implicate force, not all threats of force may trigger the prohibition of Article 2(4). As the IIFFMCG explained:

43. Nicaragua Case, *supra* note 28, at ¶227.

44. For more on the clause's negotiating history, see *supra* note 24.

45. This has been debated at length in the context of uses of force. *See, e.g.*, Tom Ruys, *The Meaning of "Force" and the Boundaries of the* Jus Ad Bellum—Are "Minimal" Uses of Force Excluded from U.N. Charter 2(4)?, 108 Am J. Int'l L. 159 (2014); Mary-Ellen O'Connell, *The True Meaning of Force*, 108 AJIL Unbound 141 (2014).

46. Nuclear Weapons, *supra* note 30, at 47.

47. Green & Grimal, *supra* note 17, at 295.

Overall, the emphasis of the practice of states is on credibility. A threat is credible when it appears rational that it may be implemented, when there is a sufficient commitment to run the risk of armed encounter. It is enough to create a calculated expectation that an unnamed challenge might incur the penalty of military force within a dispute.[48]

States and other stakeholders have not devised any fixed criteria for assessing the credibility of threats. As a result, differentiating the credible from the non credible will depend largely on context. As Roscini explains, the "same conduct could thus be a threat in certain circumstances but not in others."[49] All relevant contextual factors need to be considered, such as the identity and capacities of the threat's author, past and present behavior of the parties involved, the threat's imminence, and the nature of the threat and what target is threatened.

1. The Identity and Capacities of the Threat's Author

For several scholars, the identity of the threat's author is key[50]—a proposition that seems reasonable on the basis of existing State practice.[51] For starters, a threat is more credible when it comes from a State's agents than from non-State actors. Nonetheless, the latter may trigger international legal responsibility if the non-State actors make their threats under the instructions or control of a State actor (or if the State later ratifies their threats).[52] Where a State's agent makes the threat, it may still matter where it emanates from *within* the State's hierarchy. For instance, if a threat originates from a Head of State, it will be more credible than, say, one originating from a local tax official.

What about the author's chosen vehicle for making a threat? In the context of social media threats, Grimal has emphasized the nature of the account used: "[i]f a tweet were to originate from a 'personal' account as opposed to a 'state' account, it is difficult to see how it would constitute a potential violation of Article 2(4); individual threats of force from a private actor will not trigger a violation of Article 2(4)."[53] However, that approach fails to differentiate between primary and secondary rules; that is, the elements of the prohibition and of its attribution. The

---

48. IIFFMCG, *supra* note 31, at 232.

49. Roscini, *supra* note 16, at 240. For Roscini, the most important criterion is the "intention of the state" undertaking the conduct. *Id.* We address this subjective approach in Part II.D below.

50. Grimal, *supra* note 38, at 188.

51. Kritsiotis, *supra* note 17, sections 2–5.

52. International Law Commission, Articles on the Responsibility of States for Internationally Wrongful Acts with Commentaries [2001] YBILC, vol. II(2), U.N. Doc A/56/10 (as corrected), Arts. 8, 11 (ASR). Although we do not address them here, we note that debates about the capacity of non-State actors to engage directly in uses of force/armed attacks might extend to threatening force.

53. Grimal, *supra* note 38, at 188.

use of a personal account may have some relevance in assessing a threat's credibility under Article 2(4) as a primary (prohibitory) rule, just as it would matter if a threat was issued at an intergovernmental conference versus on a late-night comedy talk show. Still, if a Head of State were to post a private tweet to the effect that force will be used against another State, it is unclear why this would automatically disqualify the statement from being a threat when considered alongside other contextual factors. That said, the use of a private account may have relevance to the attribution question raised above, that is, whether we are dealing with conduct that has the requisite link to a State for purpose of triggering State responsibility. Here again, however, the use of a private account does not automatically imply that we have a "private actor" at play. Under the customary rules of attribution, the conduct of State organs is attributed to the State even for *ultra vires* acts with *very limited* exceptions for purely private conduct.[54]

Beyond the author's identity, the capacity of the author to carry out the threatened conduct will also have a significant role in assessing the threat's credibility. The ICJ and the IIFFMCG have both emphasized the acquisition of certain capabilities may be relevant to the threat analysis. This is not to suggest that simply possessing (or developing) a particular means or method for using force will itself constitute a threat to use force. Instead, the capacity for force weighs in among multiple factors in assessing threat credibility. For instance, a State threatening the deployment of a nuclear missile if it does not possess such missiles will be less credible than a similar threat issued by nuclear States.[55] That said, Suriname's denials that it had neither the gunboats nor the weapons to exact force on a Guyanese ship if it did not leave Suriname's waters within 12 hours, was, according to the Arbitral Tribunal, still "an explicit threat that force might be used if the order was not complied with."[56]

In addition to the capacity to carry out the threatened conduct, the capacity to engage in preparations for forcible operations, including the gathering of information on vulnerabilities in the opponent's systems, has an important place in

---

54. ASR, *supra* note 52, at 45–47 (re Article 7 in connection to Articles 4–6).

55. While a discussion on whether the mere possession of nuclear weapons constitutes a prohibited threat of force is beyond the scope of this chapter, it is worth noting that there are different ways of thinking about the relationship between such weapons and the prohibition. First, it could be argued that such possession does indeed constitute a breach of the prohibition of threats of force, and that the lack of invocation and operationalization is rooted in either procedural obstacles or lack of political will. Second, it could be advanced that mere possession of nuclear weapons would not constitute a prohibited threat, if one commits to the view that general threats are excluded from the scope of the rule. Finally, it could be argued that States, through their practice, have carved out an exception for nuclear weapons. However, the test here would indeed be high—for such an exception to the Charter to emerge, this subsequent practice must show *agreement* by all States parties.

56. Arbitral Tribunal Constituted Pursuant to Article 287, and in Accordance with Annex VII, of the United Nations Convention on the Law of the Sea (Guyana v. Suriname), 30 RIAA 1, ¶439 (Perm. Ct. Arb. 2007).

the analysis. Acquiring capacities for large-scale data mining and targeted profiling of individuals and objects (both closely related to the increasing sophistication of Big Data Analytics) are likely to grow in relevance in future threat assessments.

2. Threats and Relationships between States

Beyond issues of author identity and capacity, past and existing relationships can shore up (or undercut) a threat's credibility. Historical relationships matter—their relevant histories suggest that a threat of force by North Korea against South Korea will be more credible than one by Canada against the United States. Similarly, the operational practices of the author may also help discern whether its words or deeds qualify as threats of force.[57] A first-time military maneuver around a border differs significantly from a pattern of repeated conduct over decades, especially if such conduct led to prior actual uses of force. For example, the history of past Russian interactions with Ukraine lent credibility to the threat of force implicit in its buildup at the Ukrainian border.[58] Patterns of State behavior emerge from prior interactions, and the February 2022 invasion of Ukraine followed the lines of conduct familiar from Georgia and Crimea.

Threats via a demonstration of force may also become more credible if they are exigent rather than routine. As the IIFFMCG explained, if manifestations of force "are non-routine, suspiciously timed, scaled up, intensified, geographically proximate, staged in the exact mode of a potential military clash, and easily attributable to a foreign-policy message, the hostile intent is considered present and the demonstration of force manifest."[59]

3. Imminence

Imminence—that is, the immediacy of the force threatened—forms another relevant contextual element. But is imminence required? According to Asrat, imminence is a constitutive element of the threat prohibition (i.e., absent imminence, State conduct cannot qualify as a prohibited threat of force).[60] Perceived through this lens, he concludes that the 1962 Soviet preparations of nuclear missiles on Cuba did not violate Article 2(4) since "[t]he missiles had not yet reached the completed and credible stage that could have made them usable for, hence capable of, manifesting immediate hostility to one or more States of the Americas."[61]

---

57. This has been discussed at length in the context of nuclear deterrence. *See* Brian Drummond, *UK Nuclear Deterrence Policy: An Unlawful Threat of Force*, 6 J. Use of Force & Int'l L. 193 (2019).

58. *See supra* notes 39–41 and accompanying text.

59. IIFFMCG, *supra* note 31, at 232.

60. Belatchew Asrat, Prohibition of Force under the UN Charter: A Study of Art. 2(4) 140 (1991).

61. *Id.*

This view, however, finds no support in the interpretations given by international bodies[62] and is contested in the literature.[63] The IIFFMCG denied that the threat prohibition requires "an urgent and imminent danger" of the use of force, let alone any certainty that force will really be used. Indeed, an approach that views imminence as a *necessary* criterion would be far too restrictive. If the lack of temporal immediacy could deprive a communication of its illegality under Article 2(4), a State could lawfully threaten a patently unlawful use of force upon its acquisition of a particular military capability[64] so long as its acquisition was not temporally proximate to the time of the threat.

While we deny imminence is a necessary requirement for the prohibition of threats, we readily accept its relevance in any credibility assessment.[65] The lack of imminence, therefore, is not an automatic disqualifier—it is instead a potentially crucial piece in the qualification process. Threatening imminent action has a strong communicative force that can have significant impacts on the perceptions of the victim and other observers. It can thus be a powerful indicator in the pool of contextual criteria used to assess credibility.

4. The Nature of the Threat and the Threatened

Beyond the identity and capacity of the threat's author and the relationship within which the threat materializes, the credibility analysis requires attention to the specificity of the threat or its concretization. Two levels of concretization are of particular relevance—first, a concretization in time and space and, second, a concretization of form.

In some cases, we may have an idea of the type of force expected but remain in the dark regarding its specific timing. This raises the question of latent threats. For instance, it could be argued that certain capabilities, such as nuclear weapons, are per se threatening. We know how the threat can materialize (a nuclear attack), but the mere possession of the capability gives no indication as to if, when, where and how it would be used. The *Nuclear Weapons* Advisory Opinion suggests, however, that the Court was not, at that time, prepared to accept possession of nuclear weapons as itself a violation of Article 2(4). At the same time, it is worth recalling that the Charter's threat prohibition evolved out of a desire to control the militarization of States—it was initially conceived as a way of exercising arms control.[66] Thus, coupled with other contextual circumstances, the acquisition of

---

62. For instance, there was no suggestion in the *Nuclear Weapons* Advisory Opinion that imminence is a necessary requirement for prohibited threats of force. Nuclear Weapons, *supra* note 30.

63. *See* STÜRCHLER, *supra* note 15, at 56, 57; White & Cryer, *supra* note 16, at 253, 254.

64. White & Cryer, *supra* note 16, at 254.

65. STÜRCHLER, *supra* note 15, at 57.

66. *Id.* at 21.

certain capabilities (for instance, AI-operated drone swarms[67] or capacities for bulk collection of data and target profiling) could, even without a temporal or spatial specification, provide evidence on the existence of a threat of force.

In other cases, it may be clear that something will happen at a particular point in time, but there is little certainty over the form that the action could take. Consider, for example, a statement to the effect that "if you do not extradite that person by Sunday, you will see what will happen." We can predict *when*, but not *what*. If this statement coincides with movements of troops or other indicators of force, it may fall within the scope of the prohibition. In certain cases, like the tunnels of aggression, we may neither know what form any actions will take (they could be used for surveillance, sabotage, or an armed attack) nor when they will occur. Yet, the tunnel's existence reveals a capacity to violate the territorial integrity of another State, which may in certain cases be enough to qualify it as a prohibited threat of force.[68]

The identity of the target threatened may further delineate credible threats. Specific threats of force against critical infrastructure (say, a civilian nuclear power facility) may be more credible than generalized promises even if they are framed in violent terms. As with previous indicators, much will depend on the context.

D. Threats: Between a Subjective and an Objective Analysis

That a (a) credible (b) threat (c) of force violates Article 2(4) provides a ready framework for legal analysis and application to specific cases. Important questions remain, however. Of particular significance is whether and what role subjective elements play in defining prohibited threats. Subjectivity may manifest either with respect to the threatener or the threatened. First, it could be argued that threats are, by definition, intentional acts, such that unintentional conduct, even if perceived as threatening, cannot amount to a threat of force. Second, the victim's own subjective perception of a threat could be deemed a necessary requirement for the threat's existence. The first element is agent-focused, and the second victim-focused.

The agent-focused inquiry begs the question of whether the concept of unintentional threats is a contradiction in terms? From the ICJ's "signaled intention"[69] to the IIFFMCG's discarding of "routine missions devoid of hostile intent," intention appears implicit in the idea of communicated threats.[70] In his *Nuclear Weapons*

---

67. For an overview of current developments in swarm technology and architecture, *see* Francis Grimal & Jae Sundaram, *Combat Drones: Hives, Swarms, and Autonomous Action?*, 23 J. CONFLICT & SEC. L. 105 (2018).

68. *See* RICHEMOND-BARAK, *supra* note 6, at 143 ("a completed cross-border tunnel would amount to both a threat of the use of force and a use of force . . .").

69. Nuclear Weapons, *supra* note 30, at ¶47.

70. IIFFMCG, *supra* note 31, at 232.

Dissent, Judge Weeramantry coupled the very notion of threat with intent, opining that "[s]uch intention provides the mental element implicit in the concept of a threat."[71] Even so, could a State that created an environment from which a credible threat was readily inferable claim lack of intention to escape responsibility? Or, even if some intention is required, should the methodology for determining its existence be an objective one? The latter position finds support in the IIFFMCG's analysis. According to the *Report*, when objective indicia for the existence of a threat are present, "the hostile intent is considered present and the demonstration of force manifest."[72] What this means is that the subjective element can be proven through a methodology relying on objective indicia; the existence of such objective indicia creates a *presumption* that a State has issued an unlawful threat of force.[73] Such an approach may help explain other interpretations of the prohibition that seem to do away with agent-based intention entirely, opting for a purely victim-based model. During debates on the 1970 Friendly Relations Declaration, for instance, Chile's representative stated a threat is "any action . . . which tends to produce in the other State a justified fear."[74] This view does not, however, comport with the authoritative interpretations of the ICJ and other bodies. The better view is that, while a subjective element of intent underlies the notion of threat, it can be established in an objective way.

As for victim-focused perceptions, scholars like Roscini and Tsagourias have gravitated toward a subjective position—a threat must be perceived by its addressee to constitute a threat. This view has two important consequences. First, it denies the status of threats to State conduct that is unknown by the threat's target. Thus, Roscini notes that "secret military exercises or maneuvers might amount to the preparation of aggression but are not threats under the terms of Article 2(4) if they are unknown to the victim."[75] Second, and more broadly, it means that the target's own views determine compliance with Article 2(4) even where it knows of the threat's existence. Adopting this view, Green and Grimal conclude that "it may be that even deliberately threatening military behavior should only be labeled as an unlawful threat if it can be (or is) *perceived* as a threat."[76]

71. Nuclear Weapons, *supra* note 30, at ¶54.

72. *Id.*

73. The IIFFMCG's international legal approach is not novel. When considering the existence of a treaty, for example, the ICJ has adopted an objective approach to find manifestations of inter-subjective agreement among the parties. *See* Malgosia Fitzmaurice, *The Practical Working of the Law of Treaties, in* INTERNATIONAL LAW 139–43 (Malcolm Evans ed., 2018).

74. U.N. GAOR 21st Sess., Annexes, U.N. Doc. A/AC 125/L23 (1966).

75. Roscini, *supra* note 16, at 237, 238. This view thus suggests that so long as their existence and location are unknown, any more North Korean tunnels of aggression would appear not to qualify as threats of force.

76. Green & Grimal, *supra* note 17, at 297 (emphasis added).

On reflection, both aspects of this view ought to be rejected. First, the prohibition of the threat of force is geared toward violations measured by conduct, not consequences, for victims. Article 2(4) is simply not structured to make compliance depend on whether the victim State believed itself to be actually coerced into action or inaction by a threat; it prohibits the threat not the state of mind it produces. Second, the existing case law does not feature a subjective test or a criterion of perception. To be sure, most State practice and *opinio juris* around threats arises in instances where a threat was, in fact, perceived to exist. After all, States are most likely to protest threats of force that actually affect them. However, it does not follow that Article 2(4) requires an element of perception. Consider a case where a victim faces a threat that can be observed by third States even as the victim State is unaware of the threat or misunderstands its implications.

Third, and more broadly, the Charter's underlying aim in prohibiting threats and uses of force was not merely to protect potential victims from such actions. Rather, it sets out a legal framework to benefit the international community as a whole. It constitutes an affirmation that force, whether actual or threatened, should have no role to play in the relations among States. In this sense, objectively threatening behavior, irrespective of any perception by the victim, already constitutes a threat to the Charter's regime.

Finally, we should not lose sight of inherent inequalities in the international system and potential issues of proof if conclusive evidence of perception is required to establish an unlawful threat. If such evidence of victim perception is indeed required, many instances of factual threats of force will remain unaccounted. Victim States may choose silence, afraid of the consequences of a potential protest. Financial and technological divides may also mean that some victims lack the capacity to perceive certain online threats. In other words, threatening force behaviors may be happening *sub rosa*. But just as domestic violence happens behind closed doors and victims may choose not to speak out, the lack of evidence *from the victim* does not mean no wrong has occurred. Taken together, these factors favor an objective test, where perception is not a prerequisite for breaching Article 2(4).[77]

II. PROHIBITING THREATS OF FORCE VIA CYBER MEANS

Understanding how the prohibition on threats of force applies to cyber operations necessarily requires some understanding of the wide range of harms they pose. These harms, however, often share a common cause—unauthorized access.

---

77. Of course, if there is to be an invocation of responsibility or enforcement (through, for example, countermeasures), someone would need to perceive the threat. This, however, is a separate question from that of the existence of a breach of the prohibition itself.

Without access to the targeted system, network, or data contained therein, cyber operations' capacity to harm is limited.[78] The shared need for unauthorized access means that a victim's discovery of a compromised system is *polysemous* (i.e., the fact of unauthorized access can have multiple meanings). It might signal what Herb Lin calls a "cyberexploit"—unauthorized surveillance or data exfiltration.[79] Or, it could signal a potential "cyberattack," denying access to a system, or degrading or destroying the integrity of its operation (or even the physical infrastructure it supports). The polysemous character of unauthorized access in cyber operations suggests that any typology of cyberthreats must consider their potential to convey both explicit and implicit threats. This typology, in turn, provides a framework for applying the existing doctrine prohibiting threats of force to cyber operations.

A. What Harms Can Cyberthreats Threaten?

Computer scientists have long grouped cyber harms under the "CIA" triad: losses to computer systems and networks of (i) confidentiality, (ii) integrity, and (iii) availability.[80] To this list, international lawyers and policy makers emphasize the (iv) indirect harms that may follow one or more of these losses. *Confidentiality* losses follow from access to data on or transiting information and communication technologies (ICTs) otherwise intended to remain private, whether as a means of surveillance or to access financial or personal information that can be leveraged for future gains.[81] For example, the 2020 breach of SolarWinds software has apparently only resulted in confidentiality losses to date.[82] *Integrity* losses, in contrast, do more than access data; they impact the functioning of computer systems, interfering with their expected operations. A decade on, Stuxnet serves as a paradigmatic example of this type of harm.[83] Meanwhile, losses of ICT *availability*

---

78. This is not to say that cyber operations cannot cause harm without access. Directed denial of service attacks can flood a target system with requests that render it inaccessible to legitimate users. Our focus here, however, involves those cyberthreats that involve unauthorized access to a computer system.

79. Herbert S. Lin, *Offensive Cyber Operations and the Use of Force*, 4 J. NAT'L SECURITY L. & POL'Y 63 (2010).

80. Mohammad N. Alam et al., *Security Engineering Towards Building a Secure Software*, 81 INT'L J. COMPUTER APPLICATIONS 32, 33–34 (2013).

81. *See* Lin, *supra* note 79, at 63.

82. The compromise of SolarWinds' routine software update reportedly resulted in extensive surveillance of various U.S. government agencies and private companies. *See* Dina Temple-Raston, *A "Worst Nightmare" Cyberattack: The Untold Story of The SolarWinds Hack*, NPR (Apr. 16, 2021), at https://www.npr.org/2021/04/16/985439655/a-worst-nightmare-cyberattack-the-untold-story-of-the-solarwinds-hack.

83. *See generally* KIM ZETTER, COUNTDOWN TO ZERO DAY: STUXNET AND THE LAUNCH OF THE WORLD'S FIRST DIGITAL WEAPON (2014). For more recent examples, *see* James Crump,

deny users access to ICTs themselves. This can occur via directed denial of service attacks (DDoS) or via the deployment of "ransomware," encrypting an ICT system and rendering it inaccessible (or threatening to release its secrets) until a ransom is paid. Ransomware attacks have generated global attention recently given the range of victims (e.g., pipelines, meat processors, health systems, and managed service providers).[84]

But the most significant threats of cyber operations are their *indirect* ones. Losses of confidentiality, integrity, and availability can generate knock-on effects that range from physically destructive impacts to economic losses to cognitive consequences among targeted audiences. Stuxnet's goal was not simply to breach the integrity of Natanz's industrial control systems, but to use that compromise to run centrifuges at unsustainable speeds, causing 1,000 of them to self-destruct, and thereby setting back Iran's nuclear ambitions.[85] Ransomware targeting Colonial Pipeline only disabled access to its IT infrastructure, but the company shuttered its operational infrastructure as well.[86] Access to data creates possibilities for information weaponization, for instance through its use in the targeting of persons or objects, which can generate further harms such as identity theft, extortion, or even physical harms. Moreover, each of these effects—on confidentiality, integrity, availability, and more indirect consequences—can occur in isolation or in concert. They may be immediately obvious or remain hidden (e.g., a victim may not be aware of the loss of confidentiality or write off integrity effects as the result of interoperability errors). Additionally, given the complexity and sophistication of certain cyber intrusions, their potential *effects* may not become immediately apparent to victims and external observers. Understanding that access at one point in time may produce a chain of subsequent harmful effects activated at a later date is essential to ensuring the development of adequate cyber defenses, reaction, and mitigation capabilities.

Hackers Tried to Poison California Water Supply in Major Cyber Attack, NEWSWEEK (June 18, 2021); Chris Bing, *Trisis has the security world spooked, stumped and searching for answers*, CYBERSCOOP (Jan. 16, 2018), at https://www.cyberscoop.com/trisis-ics-malware-saudi-arabia/.

84. *See, e.g.*, Matt Tait, *The Kaseya Ransomware Attack Is a Really Big Deal*, LAWFARE (July 5, 2021), at https://www.lawfareblog.com/kaseya-ransomware-attack-really-big-deal; Jacob Bunge, *JBS Paid $11 Million to Resolve Ransomware Attack*, WALL ST. J. (June 9, 2021); Sylvia Hui et al, *Irish Health System Struggling to Recover from Cyberattack*, AP NEWS (May 18, 2021), at https://apnews.com/article/europe-asia-health-technology-business-2cfbc82beb75d fede32fc225113131b3; Gloria Gonzalez et al., *Jugular of the U.S. Fuel Pipeline System Shuts Down After Cyberattack*, POLITICO (May 10, 2021), at https://www.politico.com/news/2021/05/08/colonial-pipeline-cyber-attack-485984 (describing ransomware used against Colonial Pipeline).

85. ZETTER, *supra* note 83, at 363.

86. *See* Gonzalez et al., *supra* note 84.

B. Unauthorized Access—A Common Feature of Cyberthreats

For all their varied impacts, cyberthreats regularly emerge from the same recipe: (i) knowledge of a vulnerability, (ii) access to it, and (iii) a payload.[87] Cyber operations generally require some vulnerability—that is, a flaw that makes the ICT susceptible to compromise—of which the adversary has knowledge.[88] That said, adversaries must not simply know about a vulnerability in a target's ICT; they must also be able to access it. The layered and distributed nature of ICTs affords multiple access vectors, including: (a) *remote access* or "hacking" via an Internet connection; (b) *supply chain access* via "back doors" baked into hardware or software during their creation or servicing; (c) *proximity access*, where physical proximity to boxes, wires, cables, or Wi-Fi gives adversaries opportunities to connect to the same network or convince unsuspecting targets to make the connection for them; and (d) *insider access*, whether provided willingly by disgruntled insiders or unwittingly through social engineering techniques.[89] Whatever the means, as a factual matter, access to an identified vulnerability constitutes a threat because of the "payload" an adversary can deploy, whether immediately or at a later date. Payloads take many forms, including viruses, worms, and Trojan Horses.[90] They may be selective or indiscriminate, targeting specific high-value targets as the SolarWinds breach did or exploiting all ICTs to which access can be gained as witnessed in the rapid attempt to leverage a Microsoft Exchange hack

---

87. *See* Martha Finnemore & Duncan B. Hollis, *Constructing Norms for Global Cybersecurity*, 110 Am J. Int'l L. 425, 432 (2016); Martin C. Libicki, Cyberdeterrence and Cyberwar 41 (2009).

88. Vulnerabilities are an inherent feature of ICTs; modern software, for example, regularly combines millions of lines of code in which errors may reside. Other vulnerabilities exist across all five layers at which ICTs operate. The bottom "Link" layer includes the physical media for transmitting data packets. Separate "network" and "transport" layers break data into packets and route them between networks through the use of a "naming" system. An applications layer converts the routed data into useful things like files, videos, and websites. Finally, on top of these coded layers, a final, "content" layer comprises "material that gets served across the Internet." *See* Lawrence Lessig, *The Internet Under Siege*, Foreign Policy 56, 59 (Nov.–Dec. 2001). Each layer functions independently; at the application layer, for example, Google Chrome works regardless of whether the link layer employs DSL or WIFI, let alone 4G or 5G. For other (better) explanations, see Forcepoint, *What Is the OSI Model*, at https://www.forcepoint.com/cyber-edu/osi-model; David G. Post, In Search of Jefferson's Moose 80–90 (2009).

89. Finnemore & Hollis, *supra* note 87, at 432–33.

90. Viruses spread by attaching themselves to programs or files and cannot infect a computer unless users open the program or file. Worms self-replicate, spreading without human interaction. Trojan Horses are seemingly innocent programs containing malware. Rootkit programs allow hackers access to computer functions as administrators while remaining hidden from operating systems and antivirus software. Mohamed Chawki et al., Cybercrime, Digital Forensics and Jurisdiction 39–51 (2015).

Threatening Force in Cyberspace

in 2021.[91] Importantly, they need not be static, as upgrades to the payload may transform it from a data exfiltration device to a destructive one. As Chris Krebs, who led the U.S. Cybersecurity and Infrastructure Security Agency described the Exchange hack, "adversaries figured out how to tunnel into domestic communications infrastructure and set up shop."[92]

The fact that cyber operations regularly feature the same criterion—unauthorized access—has significant implications for global cybersecurity generally and international law's prohibition on threats of force in particular. As Gary Brown summarizes the situation:

> It is often not immediately apparent whether the unauthorized access is intended for spying, for disruptive and destructive activities, or both. The potential damage is not limited to a physical location, as in the case of a saboteur, which ups the ante for cyber operations. To complicate the situation even more, the initial access may be for reconnaissance in advance of attack, so that the compromise and theft of data are preludes to future offensive operations. Finally, even if the initial purpose were espionage, access itself may embolden the hacker to commit a future attack.[93]

In other words, the existence of unauthorized access—just like a hidden tunnel—can threaten a range of different harms. Consider, for example, the different payloads employed after gaining access to systems susceptible to the Eternal Blue exploit. Originally authored by the NSA for surveillance, it later facilitated the deployment of both the WannaCry and NotPetya malware.[94] As a result, various threats

91. *See, e.g.,* Brian Krebs, *At Least 30,000 U.S. Organizations Newly Hacked Via Holes in Microsoft's Email Software,* KREBS ON SECURITY (May 21, 2021), at https://krebsonsecurity.com/2021/03/at-least-30000-u-s-organizations-newly-hacked-via-holes-in-microsofts-email-software/.

92. Jonathan Tepperman, *A "Crazy Huge" Hack,* FOREIGN POL'Y (Mar. 10, 2021).

93. Gary Brown, *Spying and Fighting in Cyberspace, Which Is Which?,* 8 J. NAT'L SEC. L & POL'Y 621, 625 (2016). In a seminal 2009 National Resources Council Report, Herb Lin and his co-authors were among the first to observe this phenomenon. WILLIAM A. OWENS, KENNETH W. DAM, & HERBERT S. LIN (eds.), TECHNOLOGY, POLICY, LAW, AND ETHICS REGARDING U.S. ACQUISITION AND USE OF CYBERATTACK CAPABILITIES 20–21 (2009) ("a successful cyberexploitation requires a vulnerability, access to that vulnerability, and a payload to be executed—the only difference is in the payload to be executed. These similarities often mean that a targeted party may not be able to distinguish easily between a cyberexploitation and a cyberattack—a fact that may result in that party's making incorrect or misinformed decisions."); *accord* Bruce Schneier, *There's No Real Difference Between Online Espionage and Online Attack,* THE ATLANTIC (Mar. 6, 2014) ("The problem is that, from the point of view of the object of an attack" cyber espionage and cyberattacks "look the same as each other, except for the end result. Today's surveillance systems involve breaking into the computers and installing malware, just as cybercriminals do when they want your money. And just like Stuxnet . . .").

94. *See* Nicole Perlroth & Scott Shane, *In Baltimore and Beyond, a Stolen N.S.A. Tool Wreaks Havoc,* N.Y. TIMES (May 25, 2019).

may be implicit in the very fact of a compromise. The technologist Bruce Schneir, for example, has highlighted that "[w]hen the Chinese penetrate U.S. computer networks . . . we don't really know what they're doing. Are they modifying our hardware and software to just eavesdrop, or are they leaving 'logic bombs' that could be triggered to do real damage at some future time? It can be impossible to tell."[95] At a minimum, the polysemous character of unauthorized access suggests it may be a mistake to assume that a cyber operation involving one type of threat (e.g., espionage) somehow denies the potential or existence of other threats involving different, more serious harms that, depending on the context, may include a use of force.

C. Prohibiting Cyberthreats of Force

Understanding the range of losses cyber operations threaten and the common features by which they do so provides a baseline to construct a typology of cyber "threats," including *explicit* threats whether by (i) speech acts (ultimatums) or (ii) other activity (ransomware) as well as (iii) *implicit* threats. First, we should not overlook the possibility of *explicit* threats to cause harm by cyber means. Ultimatums or demands may be accompanied by a threat to conduct one or more cyber operations in the absence of the desired response or outcome. While denying any link to the Russian Federation, Vladimir Putin has, for example, noted that "patriotic hackers" might launch cyber operations against those who criticize Russia.[96] In these cases, the threat is not via, but rather about, the use of cyber operations. In contrast, other cyber operations are themselves inherently threatening. Ransomware is the chief example, where unauthorized access leads to encryption of the target's systems with the threat to deny their future use or availability until the ransom is paid. In a number of recent cases, there is a second threat (i.e., double-extortion) where the failure to pay will lead to the disclosure of the encrypted material: materials that may contain intellectual property, trade secrets, personal secrets, or other communications that may cause reputational harm to the victims.[97] Finally, their polysemous character means that cyber operations that succeed in gaining unauthorized access implicitly threaten the full panoply of harms payloads might deliver via that access pathway. Where the access is persistent, these threats are particularly significant and may be less dependent on the actual payloads deployed.

How should international lawyers evaluate this typology in light of the prohibition on threats of force? For starters, many (if not most) cyberthreats have nothing

---

95. Schneier, *supra* note 93.

96. Ian Phillips & Vladimir Isachenkov, *Putin: Russia Doesn't Hack but "Patriotic" Individuals Might*, AP (June 1, 2017), at https://apnews.com/article/moscow-donald-trump-ap-top-news-elections-international-news-281464d38ee54c6ca5bf573978e8ee91.

97. *See* Shannon Vavra, *Ransomware Operators Now Threatening to Publish Stolen Data in Extortion Demands*, CYBERSCOOP (Jun 24, 2020), at https://www.cyberscoop.com/ransomw are-hack-leak-extortion-crowdstrike-falcon/.

Threatening Force in Cyberspace

to do with a use of force. President Putin's reference to "patriotic" hackers, for example, likely involved a threat of information operations, the cognitive quality of which will rarely, if ever, implicate the prohibition on the use of force.[98] Similarly, ransomware may always have a threatening quality, but its threats—unavailability of data/systems or their unwanted public disclosure—are primarily economic or reputational, without the violence a use of force requires. The same may be said of unauthorized access generally—whatever possible payloads an attacker might deploy with such access, in many cases they simply cannot directly or indirectly generate effects akin to force. The capacity of North Korean hackers targeting Sony Pictures to not only exfiltrate movies but to destroy the company's proprietary code may have been financially costly, but it was not a use of force.[99] And if an operation cannot generate force, it follows that the threat that operation poses will similarly avoid any issues under Article 2(4)'s threat prohibition.[100]

Nonetheless, several States and scholars have begun to recognize the potential for at least some cyberthreats to involve an unlawful use of force.[101] The Government of Japan focused specifically on this possibility in laying out its official views of international law's application to cyberspace in May 2021.[102] The

98. If an influence operation cannot constitute an unlawful use of force, neither will threats of such operation trigger Article 2(4)'s threats prohibition. Nonetheless, other rules and principles of international law still regulate such operations. *See The Oxford Statement on International Law Protections in Cyberspace: The Regulation of Information Operations and Activities* (May 2021), at https://www.elac.ox.ac.uk/the-oxford-statement-on-the-regulation-of-information-operations-and-activities#/.

99. *See* Andrea Peterson, *The Sony Pictures Hack, Explained*, WASH. POST: THE SWITCH (Dec. 18, 2014).

100. In addition to questions around the specification of the threat of force prohibition, difficulties remain with respect to establishing attribution, especially in cyberspace. Since the prohibition of threats of force is addressed to States, a precondition for its application is the existence of a link between the person or entity acting and the State. While a discussion of attribution tests and their application to cyberspace is beyond the scope of this chapter, the next section examines the ways in which Big Data may assist in drawing connections between particular actors and States.

101. All members of the *Tallinn Manual's* Independent Group of Experts, for example, accepted that the Stuxnet worm constituted a use of force, even as some of them resisted ascribing it the status of an armed attack. TALLINN MANUAL 2.0, *supra* note 19, at 342.

102. Ministry of Foreign Affairs of Japan, Basic Position of the Government of Japan on International Law Applicable to Cyber Operations (May 28, 2021), at https://www.mofa.go.jp/files/100200935.pdf ("Under certain circumstances, a cyber operation may constitute the threat or use of force prohibited by Article 2(4) of the UN Charter. Pursuant to this article, all States shall refrain in their international relations from the threat or use of force. The Government of Japan presumes that as a general rule the threat of force refers to a State's act of threatening another State by indicating its intention or attitude of using force, without actually using force, unless its arguments or demands are accepted. The obligation to refrain from the threat or use of force in international relations is an important obligation relating to cyber operations.")

Commentary to Rule 70 of *Tallinn Manual 2.0* provides that a prohibited cyberthreat of force can be "conveyed by any means (for instance, through public pronouncements)" where its substance is "to carry out cyber operations qualifying as a use of force."[103] However, despite the reference to "any means," the *Tallinn Manual* offers no examples of prohibited implicit threats. Its Independent Group of Experts agreed that the acquisition of cyber capacities alone will not constitute a threat of force, while dividing on the question of whether a State without such capacities can even violate Article 2(4) with its express statements.[104]

We believe that States and scholars must extend their analysis beyond express threats to use force by cyber means to assess cyber operations' implicit potential to do so. This means refocusing our attention to the actual threatened outcome (an unlawful use of force) and recognizing that it can be conveyed through various modalities, both explicit and implicit. Thus, while ransomware generally may not implicate a use of force, its deployment on the operational infrastructure of certain targets in certain contexts might do so. For example, ransomware that degrades the ability of critical infrastructure like a water filtration plant or a civilian nuclear power facility to function might comprise a threat of force.[105] There is also the possibility that a cyber operation like NotPetya (which appeared at first to operate as ransomware but ultimately targeted the integrity of its victims' systems) might threaten force if the destruction of the compromised system or the infrastructure it supports would do so.[106] Likewise, back doors or persistent tunneling into a victim's networks could be used to deploy payloads that constitute a use of force if the targeted system's degradation or destruction could so qualify.[107]

The critical question for applying the prohibition of threats of force to cyber operations comes in assessing the credibility of the threat.[108] We do not suggest

---

103. TALLINN MANUAL 2.0, *supra* note 19, at 338.

104. *Id.* at 338–339. The Experts also divided over whether a State with the capacity to carry out a threat but no intention of doing so would violate Article 2(4) where it makes threats "for purely domestic political reasons." *Id.* at 339.

105. The Colonial Pipeline ransomware incident raises the question of whether impacts on the operational infrastructure must be a direct consequence of the ransomware or, as there, an indirect outcome resulting from a victim's remedial measures. Whether a linkage to such an outcome could be made (and how foreseeable it might need to be) are questions we leave for further research. *See* Gonzalez et al., *supra* note 84.

106. *See* Alex Hern, *Ransomware Attack "Not Designed to Make Money," Researchers Claim*, THE GUARDIAN (June 28, 2017).

107. A more precise assessment of whether and when a cyber operation's indirect effects constitute a use of force implicate questions of causation and evidence that bear further study and discussion, including the necessity of kinetic effects versus a greater focus on functionality losses.

108. Of course, even if a threat is credible, additional analysis may be required to assess if the threatened use of force would itself be unlawful or it could be justified under the banners of self-defense or Chapter VII of the U.N. Charter.

that every hypothetical use of unauthorized access to generate destruction (or even deaths)—however fanciful—turns a cyber operation into a prohibited threat of force. The possibility of a use of force is a necessary—but far from determinative—condition for triggering the prohibition. Finding a credible threat of force will necessarily involve other context clues discussed in Part I above (including the identity and capacities of the threat's author, past and present behavior of the parties involved, their relationship, the threat's imminence, and the nature of the threat and the threatened). In particular, the context will need to show more than just a latent capacity to use force; a threat of force must have some signaling function.

But what if the cyberthreat is intended to be hidden, like the tunnels of aggression? We do not believe the covert nature of a cyberthreat should exclude it from a threat analysis any more than Article 2(4) should exclude assessing threats implicit in the construction of cross-border tunnels. Instead, the credibility of a threat may turn on whether once the victim (or a third party) discovers the operation would they regard it as a threat of force against the victim State. As explained in Part I, such threat perceptions involve an objective assessment that examines the perspective of both the agent and the victim. When it comes to cyber operations, the views of observers (be they States or ICT companies with a capacity to identify instances of unauthorized access, sometimes independent of the victim State's own awareness) may have particular relevance. To the extent observers may be as (if not more) likely than some victims to discover or identify unauthorized access, they can play a key role in situating that access and the threat(s) it poses. In other words, where observers discovering a cyberthreat view it as including a risk of future force, the cyber operation is more likely a credible trigger for Article 2(4).

D. The Relevance of the Prohibition on Threats of Force to Cyber Operations

Our analysis so far suggests that States must accommodate the Article 2(4) prohibition on threats of unlawful force in their own operational planning. Just as States construct and conduct cyber operations subject to the duty of nonintervention or the prohibition on the use of force, so too must they calibrate whether and when their operations—explicitly *or* implicitly—will threaten an unlawful use of force.

Nonetheless, we remain cognizant of the limited visibility of the prohibition on threats of force in past State practice. Where threats have matured into a use of force, such as Russia's February 2022 full-scale invasion of Ukraine, it is not surprising to see legal assessments focus on questions of the use of force threshold, armed attacks, anticipatory self-defense, imminence, necessity, and proportionality.[109] And where a State refrains from following through on threatened

---

109. *See supra* notes 19 and 20, and accompanying text.

behavior, it may be rationale for the threatened State (and other members of the international community) to refrain from protesting the threat lest it (re)escalate the situation. Similar factors may chill efforts by States to identify, let alone protest, explicit *and* implicit threats by other States via their cyber operations.

At the same time, whatever (dis)incentives exist for invoking the threat prohibition in past, kinetic contexts, several aspects of cyber operations suggest a greater opportunity (and thus need) to do so in cyberspace. We have already highlighted one of these—the *polysemous* character of cyber operations. If cyber operations' unauthorized access always includes threats of additional or different harms beyond the access itself (or whatever exploits have been deployed previously), cyberspace has the potential to have more implicit threats of force than in the kinetic context. Second, the capacity of cyber operations to be discovered and malware employed for divergent purposes by actors other than the original perpetrators widens the landscape from which a threat might be implied. Here, for example, the tunnel analogy may not hold since the means of unauthorized access are not fixed to their originally constructed contours but rather can be lifted and deployed in myriad other settings. In other words, as virtual tunnels, cyberthreats are easily reproduced and redistributed.

Finally, cyber operations are tied to foreign territory in ways not usually evident in traditional threats of force. Ultimatums and demonstrations of force suggest that the threatening State *may* cross a border to use force against the threatened State. Yet, the context of most such threats does not involve the State actually doing so; the territorial boundaries of the threatened State are usually not breached by the threatening State. The tunnels of aggression in this respect are outliers.[110]

In contrast, in the cyber context, cross-border conduct is the norm for cyber operations. Unauthorized access almost always involves a cross-border incursion (of code) that compromises the targeted system or network. By operating within a foreign State's networks or systems (which are associated with hardware physically located within that State's territory or jurisdiction), these operations exhibit a marked difference from classic threat scenarios involving troop movements or ships patrolling *outside* a State's borders. That difference suggests a need for greater public attention to the threat potential in the cyber context than witnessed to date under the *jus ad bellum*.[111]

---

110. And for some scholars at least, the existence of a cross-border tunnel actually goes beyond a threat of force to constitute an actual use of force. *See* RICHEMOND-BARAK, *supra* note 6, at 127–28 (treating the constructed tunnel as akin to the presence of troops in a foreign State's territory for armed attack purposes); *id* at 141 (tunnels actually crossing the border constitute a use of force).

111. We recognize, moreover, that the cross-border incursion involved in gaining unauthorized access may breach other rules or principles of international law, such as the duty of nonintervention. Such breaches may be among the factors that make a threat of force more credible.

III. TECHNICAL CAPACITIES: THE PROMISE AND PERILS OF USING BIG DATA TO IDENTIFY THREATS OF FORCE IN CYBERSPACE

To identify clear and compliance-guiding criteria for assessing threats of force in cyberspace, international lawyers need either a detailed, prescriptive legal standard or a wealth of practice from which to induce commonalities. To date, Article 2(4)'s prohibition of threats of force has neither. The extant doctrine gives, at best, limited guidance on the prohibition's constitutive elements. And relative to the practice generated around the *use of force*, the practice on threats of force is underwhelming.

We have already identified two reasons for the threat prohibition's limited visibility to date—(i) threats are often a prelude to uses of force that receive all the (legal) attention, and (ii) States fear that protesting threats may prove escalatory where uses of force do not occur.[112] But these are clearly not the only explanations.[113] Information gaps may play an equally large role in limiting attention to—and operation of—the prohibition (especially in anything approaching the objective methodologies we identified earlier).[114] Tsagourias, for instance, disavows applying agreed criteria to threats of force as they would

> definitely be "lost in translation" due to the imprecise or faulty nature of intelligence or other evidence that proves the existence or not of a threat, the confidential nature of such evidence which states prefer to keep secret, the inadequacy of intelligence assessments, the difficulty of predicting future state action, the difficulty of third party appraisal of ideological, political, or other assumptions that the target state makes with regard to the threat, the difficulty in appraising how the consequences of a threat play out in the specific state, or the credibility of the threat (unless it materializes).[115]

Of course, as we have seen from the IIFFMCG's work, some cases generate enough evidence to overcome such concerns.[116] Nonetheless, the relative dearth of claims of violations (let alone findings of breach) suggest that States are often reluctant to assess the credibility of threats of force with the information available to them.

---

112. *See supra* notes 18, 109, and accompanying text.

113. For example, where threats are not followed through, attention may dissipate as the threats themselves ebb away. Alternatively, being threatened may be perceived as a weakness, and States cherish their reputation. In cyberspace, for example, acknowledging a particular type of threatening conduct, such as the introduction of a back door, can create additional risks to the victim State, as this constitutes an implied acknowledgment of security concerns and vulnerabilities in its networks.

114. *See supra* notes 69–77, and accompanying text.

115. Tsagourias, *supra* note 17, at 78.

116. *See* IIFFMCG, *supra* note 31, at 233–38.

How can international law overcome such challenges? We believe Big Data offers one tool to change the existing calculus in identifying (and declaiming) threats of force.[117] The cyber context provides a particularly apt environment for doing so. The success of Big Data Analytics[118] depends on the availability of information. Today, information about cyberthreats continues to cumulate and aggregate. States are increasingly making accusations against other States concerning cyber operations, which offer everything from technical indicators of compromise to an overview of the nature of the threat and what was threatened.[119] Moreover, the role of non-State actors affords additional avenues to information unavailable in more traditional cases of inter-State threats. Cyber operations occur via ICTs owned and operated by private actors. Their incentives to disclose the existence and scope of cyber threats differ from States, providing additional informational resources for assessing the credibility of explicit and implicit threats.[120]

As data about cyber operations accumulates and evolves, so do the ways to collect and analyze it. Big Data Analytics offers mechanisms for assessing cyberthreats that may be, for their scope and speed, undecipherable to the human mind. The growing field of threat intelligence has already signaled the value of using Big Data to identify cyberthreats generally.[121] We believe these methods can extend to the *jus ad bellum*.[122] Simply put, Big Data has the potential to make the

---

117. In the past decades, we have witnessed an explosion in the production and retention of data. "Big data" refers to how data today contains greater variety, arriving in increasing volumes and with more velocity (the three Vs). Oracle, *What Is Big Data?*, at https://www.oracle.com/big-data/what-is-big-data/.

118. Big Data Analytics include models that define protocols and algorithms for Big Data analysis, like procedures, models, algorithms definitions down to the source code, and analysis's results. *See* EU Agency for Network and Information Security, *Big Data Threat Landscape and Good Practice Guide* 14 (Jan. 2016).

119. *See* Martha Finnemore & Duncan B. Hollis, *Beyond Naming and Shaming: Accusations and International Law in Cybersecurity*, 31 Euro. J. Int'l L. 969, 985 (2020).

120. For instance, Microsoft has played a key role in identifying and analyzing the mechanics of the breach of SolarWinds software. Microsoft, *Analysing Solorigate, the Compromised DLL File That Started a Sophisticated Cyberattack, and How Microsoft Defender Helps Protect Customers* (Dec. 18, 2020), at https://www.microsoft.com/en-us/security/blog/2020/12/18/analyzing-sol origate-the-compromised-dll-file-that-started-a-sophisticated-cyberattack-and-how-micros oft-defender-helps-protect/.

121. Webroot, *Threat Intelligence: What Is It, and How Can It Protect You from Today's Advanced Cyber Attacks?* (2014), at https://pdfsecret.com/download/threat-intelligence-what-is-it-and-how-can-it-protect-you-gartner_5a30800dd64ab21cdb5fa98a_pdf (defining threat intelligence as "evidence-based knowledge, including context, mechanisms, indicators, implications and actionable advice, about an existing or emerging menace or hazard to assets that can be used to inform decisions regarding the subject's response to that menace or hazard").

122. Although we focus on threats of force, we recognize that Big Data may facilitate identifying and applying other areas of the *jus ad bellum* (e.g., anticipatory self-defense) to say nothing of international law more generally. *See* Ashley Deeks, *High-Tech International Law*, 88 G.W. L. Rev. 574 (2020).

prohibition on threats of force actually effective for States and other stakeholders. It can further flesh out criteria for prohibited threats or develop threat indicators specific to cyberspace.

At the same time, for all its advantages, Big Data comes with risks. The literature on autonomous weapons suggests that there could be biases or errors in employing Big Data Analytics to identify cyberthreats of force. This suggests, as in the autonomous weapons context, that there is a need for a meaningful framework of human-machine interaction in the context of cyber threat analysis.

A. Criteria and Application

In 2014, Professor Charles Dunlap, Jr., warned of a "hyper-personalization of war"—a consequence of the exponential increase in available information and the availability of tools for rapidly assessing it. He argued that, just as corporations hold digital dossiers on consumers to tailor and target marketing campaigns, parties to armed conflicts may devise digital dossiers for the conduct of hostilities, especially for targeting purposes.[123] Those same Big Data tools may facilitate building digital dossiers on States and their cyber operations, for example, information on particular patterns of activity, means and methods used in conducting operations, and connections with non-State actors.

In the physical world, our conduct often leaves clear and discernible marks. Moving your missile launcher from location A to location B, for example, may leave marks on the road. These marks may indicate the model of the launcher, and thereby link the launcher to a manufacturer, and ultimately to its owner. Marks may indicate the direction of the launcher's route and perhaps even the temporal frame of its movement.[124]

Cyberspace has its own web of marks. Actors leave digital footprints, and these footprints often carry unique characteristics of their authors. Patterns of behavior can be linked to certain State agents through specific techniques used in carrying out cyber operations, the timing of operations, or coinciding with moments of tension with the target State. In the past, the available data was not always sufficient to sort through such marks to reach definitive conclusions. Thus, the famous DDoS attack against Estonia in 2007 generated competing assertions of responsibility for the Russian Federation and "patriotic" Russian hacktivists acting autonomously, both of whom may have been motivated by contemporaneous tensions between Estonians and Russians over the relocation of the Bronze Soldier of

---

123. Charles J. Dunlap Jr., *The Hyper-Personalization of War: Cyber, Big Data, and the Changing Face of Conflict*, 15 Georgetown J Int'l Aff. 108, 111–13 (2014).

124. Pieter van Huis, *"A Birdie Is Flying Towards You": Identifying the Separatists Linked to the Downing of MH17* (Bellingcat Investigation Team, 2018/2019), at https://www.bellingcat.com/app/uploads/2019/06/a-birdie-is-flying-towards-you.pdf.

Tallinn.[125] In today's "Big Data" era, there is a greater ability to gather and process data on techniques and other patterns of behavior. Such data formed a part of the recent U.S. attribution of the SolarWinds breach to the Russian government.[126] In analyzing such data, however, it is important to not lose sight of context; certain acts in cyberspace may indeed indicate threatening activity per se, but threats of force have strong relational components that should be kept in mind. Threats acquire their meaning in light of a particular geopolitical climate and past interactions. Just as a generally friendly relationship may indicate that an act is not, in fact, threatening, so may a past of hostile interactions indicate the opposite.

Deeks, Lubell, and Murray have argued that States should employ machine learning to create "early warning systems" for pre-attack detection.[127] These early warning systems could use traditional indicators, such as the movement of troops or military equipment, but they could also use Big Data to track suspicious patterns of communication on certain platforms or the exploitation of defense vulnerabilities. In addition, Big Data can be (and is) employed to assist in attribution inquiries. Questions of attribution have long plagued assessments of cyber operations due to the cloaks of anonymity the technical architecture often allows as well as the dispersed nature of many groups engaging in cyber operations.[128] Today's growing wealth of information, together with tools to discern patterns in that information, may allow building dossiers on *networks of actors*, based on assessments of their intensity of interactions, similarity in source code used, and evidence of communications.

Big Data can assist, moreover, not just in attributing responsibility for cyberthreats; it can also assist in assessments of their credibility. Even as all determinations on the existence of a threat of force are context-based, reliance on Big Data may facilitate the requisite "objectification" of that analysis. In the kinetic world, for example, movements of troops may be seen as either routine exercises or acts threatening force depending on surrounding contextual factors. Big Data Analytics can be employed in cyberspace to embed benchmarks for potential threats in the algorithms. As a result, from their very outset, certain patterns of behavior (including certain types of unauthorized access) could be labeled as "suspicious" or "threatening" per se. Their presence may, then, create a *presumption* of a threat against a victim State.

---

125. *See* Joshua Davis, *Hackers Take Down the Most Wired Country in Europe*, WIRED (Aug. 21, 2007); *Estonian Links Moscow to Internet Attack*, N.Y. TIMES (May 18, 2007).

126. *See* Temple-Raston, *supra* note 82; White House, *Fact Sheet: Imposing Costs for Harmful Foreign Activities by the Russian Government* (Apr. 15, 2021).

127. Ashley Deeks, Noam Lubell, & Daragh Murray, *Machine Learning, Artificial Intelligence, and the Use of Force by States*, 10 J. NAT'L SEC. L. & POL'Y 6 (2018).

128. *See, e.g.*, Kristen E. Eichensehr, *The Law & Politics of Cyberattack Attribution*, 67 UCLA L. REV. 520 (2020); Cordula Droege, *Get Off My Cloud, Cyber Warfare, International Humanitarian Law, and the Protection of Civilians*, 94 INT'L REV. RED CROSS 886 (2012).

Big Data, of course, need not supplant more traditional contextual analyses. A move to *hybrid assessments* can incorporate factors from the physical world alongside the digital footprint of actors. Algorithms could even be trained to deal with both types of factors at the same time. In such cases, Big Data would form an important, if not critical, element in differentiating among cyberthreats to identify those that constitute a prohibited threat of force.

Whether existing algorithms are capable of conducting such assessments is an empirical question rather than a legal one. However, we do not mean to suggest Big Data is some magic, silver bullet solution. Indeed, until such time as analytical tools are proven advanced enough to consider both cyber and kinetic elements in tandem without errors or biases, care must be taken not to overcommit to its use in practice.[129]

B. Trusting the Process: The Risks of Overreliance on Big Data Analytics

Being able to detect the previously undetectable and to identify objective benchmarks for processes that used to be prone to subjectivity and arbitrariness is an end state worth striving toward. Analyzing Big Data through machine learning algorithms growing in sophistication may be a way—perhaps the only way—to achieve this in a digital environment. However, we should not ignore the attendant risks of using information analytics. From concerns over biased data through the potential for automation bias to override contextual assessments, automation has already raised red flags in various sectors (e.g., criminal justice, lethal autonomous weapons systems). International legal scholars have similarly identified the risks of Big Data to international humanitarian law, international criminal law, and international human rights law.[130] The alarm bell they sound is just as relevant to the *jus ad bellum* generally and the prohibition on threats of force in particular. Using algorithmic tools to sift through vast amounts of information effectively requires a trusted framework. After all, for technology to deliver on its promise, it needs a robust system of governance, with accountable control chains and skilled users.[131]

---

129. Some have already sought to close a gap in the literature by linking, through quantitative and statistical analysis, cyber operations and kinetic ones. *See, e.g.,* Nadia Kostyuk & Yuri M. Zhukov, *Invisible Digital Front: Can Cyber Attacks Shape Battlefield Events?*, 63 J. Conflict Res. 317 (2019).

130. *See, e.g.,* Nema Milaninia, *Biases in Machine Learning Models and Big Data Analytics: The International Criminal and Humanitarian Law Implications*, 102 Int'l Rev. Red Cross 199 (2021); Galit A. Sarfaty, *Can Big Data Revolutionize International Human Rights Law*, 39 U. Pa. J. Int'l L. 73 (2017).

131. Sonia Lucarelli, Alessandro Marrone, & Francesco Niccolò Moro (eds.), Nato Decision-Making in the Age of Big Data and Artificial Intelligence 10 (NATO Allied Command Transformation, Universita di Bologna, Instituto Affari Internazionali, 2021).

To ensure this, meaningful human-machine interaction should accompany any Big Data Analytics' assessment of a cyberthreat of force. Three aspects of this interaction warrant particular emphasis.

First, as discussed earlier, the process of identifying a threat of force under Article 2(4) is highly context specific. The variables are many and include historical relationships between States, sudden tensions, alliances, the evolution of political ties, statements by a range of actors, suspiciously timed movements, the acquisition of military capabilities, etc. It is only through a holistic examination of these variables that international lawyers can understand whether (and which) behavior threatens force. To complicate matters even further, the pieces of evidence on threatening behavior may be held by a variety of private actors, making access to data and analysis more challenging. Tempting as it may be to automatically link the presence of certain objective patterns of behavior to classifications of a threat/non-threat, such assessments still must accommodate the context. Indeed, extreme objectification and automaticity in threat assessments could lead States to see everything as a potential "threat of force." That approach, however, runs counter to the text of Article 2(4) and its underlying purpose to the extent it risks dangerous escalations in language and, potentially, uses of force themselves.[132]

Second, extant geopolitical rivalries between States suggest a possibility that such rivalries could contaminate the information from which algorithmic assessments are made. For example, given an ongoing U.S. crisis with Iraq over admitting weapons inspectors, U.S. Defense officials presumed the Solar Sunrise cyber exploitation in 1998 had to be linked to a foreign government. In reality, the authors were three teenagers.[133] It is thus critically important to provide safeguards against biases in the information pool. It is also important to build in an ability to recognize attempts at deception.[134] That a State relies on Big Data Analytics may incentivize others to contaminate its data, or "trick" analytical algorithms to recognize or ignore certain types of conduct. All these risks ought to be factored in, and continuously monitored, across the life cycle of algorithmic use.

---

132. Stürchler, for example, highlights the spiral model of international relations: "the spiral model asserts that military threats and brinkmanship tend to escalate into war. States engage in arms races; in crisis, they raise the ante through threats only to discover later that these threats, having failed, need to be implemented for the sake of credibility, personal pride, or political necessity." STÜRCHLER, *supra* note 15, at 46.

133. Kim Zetter, *Israeli Hacker "The Analyst" Indicted in New York—Update*, WIRED (Oct. 29, 2008).

134. For instance, malicious actors may resort to "data poisoning," a practice through which they manipulate the datasets used by the AI system, thereby compromising the system's integrity. *See* Sue Poremba, *Data Poisoning: When Attackers Turn AI and ML Against You*, SECURITY INTELLIGENCE (Apr. 21, 2021), at https://securityintelligence.com/articles/data-poisoning-ai-and-machine-learning/.

Recognizing false positives, biases, and deceptive practices becomes crucial in any threat analysis given the close linkage between threats of force and potential claims to anticipatory self-defense where threatening behavior is assessed as an imminent armed attack. We have already highlighted above legal concerns with this risk, concerns that support decoupling any threat analysis from claims of anticipatory self-defense.[135] There is, however, a separate, and additional empirical worry: systems should be designed in ways that do not over-identify behavior as threatening. Any potential over-identification needs to be mitigated through meaningful procedural checks.

Third and finally, the limitations of both Big Data Analytics and how international lawyers use them need to be adequately acknowledged. Concerns over maintaining meaningful interaction between humans and systems have already been at the forefront of discussions on lethal autonomous weapons systems.[136] There, one of the key issues is automation bias—that is, the propensity of humans to over rely, or even hide behind, seemingly objective outputs generated by algorithms.[137] That same risk could very well arise in the context of assessing cyberthreats. Acknowledging this risk suggests the need for some accommodation, such as training that allows human supervisors to understand the process of pattern identification as well as grants them a capacity to contest automated findings, particularly if there are concerns over their reliability.[138] Meaningful human interactions should entail a meaningful role for the human in the process—teaming rather than replacement. Such possibilities generate a host of additional questions—who is in control, what is under control, when should control be exercised, and how is control to be exercised?[139] For present purposes, however, it is enough to highlight the potential of Big Data and Big Data Analytics to operationalize an international legal prohibition that has long operated in the shadows, while acknowledging the risks of over-relying on these methods. Both the possibilities and perils of Big Data hold significant implications for the future of the *jus ad bellum*.

---

135. See *supra* Part I.

136. *See* Final Report of the Meeting of the High Contracting Parties to the Convention on Prohibitions or Restrictions on the Use of Certain Conventional Weapons Which May Be Deemed to Be Excessively Injurious or to Have Indiscriminate Effects, U.N. Doc. CCW/MSP/2019/9 (Dec. 13, 2019), ¶¶16, 22(b), Guiding Principle (c).

137. *Id.*, ¶20(a).

138. For a discussion on already adopted models of human-machine interaction, *see* Ben Wagner, *Liable, but Not in Control? Ensuring Meaningful Human Agency in Automated Decision-Making Systems*, 11 Pol'y & Internet 104 (2019).

139. This classification of questions was elaborated by the ICRC and SIPRI. *See* Vincent Boulanin, Neil Davison, Netta Goussac, & Moa Peldán Carlsson, Limits on Autonomy in Weapons Systems: Identifying Practical Elements of Human Control (Stockholm International Peace Research Institute, June 2020).

IV. CONCLUSION

Our chapter has highlighted an under-explored element of the *jus ad bellum*—the prohibition on threats of unlawful force—and assessed its regulatory capacity in a cyber context incorporating Big Data Analytics. We provided a granular assessment of existing doctrine and the preference it reveals for objective methodologies. In the cyber context, we explored the potential for cyberthreats of force to exist in new vehicles beyond the ultimatums and demonstrations of force that have occupied the kinetic context. In particular, we find that the *polysemous* character of persistent unauthorized access to computer networks and systems suggests a need for States and scholars to assess all cyber operations for their capacity to implicitly threaten a use of force.

States have not relied much on the threats prohibition in their international relations to date. The nature, scale, and cross-border elements of cyberthreats, however, raises the relevance of this aspect of Article 2(4) in cyberspace. The corresponding potential of Big Data may create conditions for identifying threats of force in cyberspace where previous cases would have been left under-examined or unresolved. Taken together, we now have the tools to launch a new, reinvigorated dialogue on the role of the prohibition of threats of force in the cyber context.

At the same time, a more robust assessment of threats of force in cyberspace may have broader implications for understanding threats of force generally. At the time, international lawyers largely ignored the threat of force implicit in North Korea's tunnels of aggression. Our framework for assessing credible cyberthreats of force, however, need not be limited to cyber contexts. The same methodology, including the potential (and perils) of Big Data Analytics, can extend to a broader swath of behavior. It can address cases where credible threats of force can be implied from State behaviors like building secret tunnels (and to differentiate such threats from cases where State behavior may have other rationales, such as defensive or domestic functions). A broader resurgence in recognizing—and applying—the prohibition on threats of force may, in turn, enhance the purpose for which it exists—maintaining international peace and security for all.

To threaten force is to assert dominance. It is an act of creating inequality, of subjecting another State to one's will. In the past, suggestions have been made that "an effective threat of force will not have the same destructive consequences as the use of force" and that "threats of force can sometimes be beneficial to international relations."[140] Destruction, however, is not the sole benchmark for assessing the gravity of wrongfulness. Credible threats of force conflict with every value at the heart of the Charter—the sovereign equality of States,[141] the obligation to

---

140. Sadurska, *supra* note 17, at 250.

141. U.N. Charter, Art. 2(1).

settle disputes through peaceful means,[142] and the robust renunciation of force.[143] Threats, particularly credible ones, create a climate of fear and inequality in international relations. As such, whatever the reasons for the prohibition of threats to have remained in the shadows for so long, it is time for States and scholars to shine a light on Article 2(4) in its entirety.

142. *Id.*, Art. 2(3), pmbl.

143. *Id.*, Art. 2(4), pmbl.

3

"Attacking" Big Data

Strategic Competition, the Race for AI, and the International Law of Cyber Sabotage

GARY P. CORN* AND ERIC TALBOT JENSEN† ∎

I. INTRODUCTION

Prevailing in strategic competition with China is now the centerpiece of U.S. national security strategy and policy.[1] This should come as no surprise. For years the United States has been pivoting, albeit fitfully, to confront China's emergence as a near-peer competitor and now squarely recognizes China as its top national security threat.[2] According to the U.S. Intelligence Community, China is "challenging the United States in multiple arenas—especially economically, militarily, and technologically," all as part of its steady and increasing push for

---

* Program Director and Adjunct Professor, Technology, Law & Security Program, American University Washington College of Law; Senior Fellow, National Security and Cybersecurity, R Street Institute, Washington, D.C.; Consultant to the U.S. Department of Defense Office of General Counsel; Colonel U.S. Army (Retired) and former Staff Judge Advocate, U. S. Cyber Command. The opinions expressed herein are those of the author and do not necessarily reflect the views of the Department of Defense or any other organization or entity with which the author is affiliated.

† Robert W. Barker Professor of Law, Brigham Young University Law School.

1. White House, Interim National Security Strategic Guidance 19–22 (2021), https://www.whitehouse.gov/wp-content/uploads/2021/03/NSC-1v2.pdf (discusses evolution from pivot to Great Power Competition, to strategic competition).

2. See Julian E. Barnes, *China Poses Biggest Threat to U.S., Intelligence Report Says*, N.Y. TIMES (Apr. 13, 2021), https://www.nytimes.com/2021/04/13/us/politics/china-national-security-intelligence-report.html (citing 2021 IC Annual Threat Assessment).

Gary P. Corn and Eric Talbot Jensen, *"Attacking" Big Data* In: *Big Data and Armed Conflict.* Edited by: Laura A. Dickinson and Edward W. Berg, Oxford University Press. © Gary P. Corn and Eric Talbot Jensen 2024.
DOI: 10.1093/oso/9780197668610.003.0005

global power.[3] China is engaged in a multi-front effort, including through ever more aggressive gray-zone tactics, to undermine the United States' global influence and competitive advantages, drive wedges between the United States and its allies and partners, and disrupt the rules-based international order in favor of establishing international norms that align with Chinese authoritarianism and interests.

A key component of Beijing's strategy is to outpace and overtake the United States as the global leader in science and technology. While it has yet to succeed, it is quickly closing the gap. As the bipartisan National Security Commission on Artificial Intelligence (NSCAI) recently noted, "For the first time since World War II, America's technological predominance—the backbone of its economic and military power—is under threat."[4] The potential impacts of failing to maintain a competitive edge in technology and innovation over China and other adversaries are acute. Emerging technologies have the potential to fundamentally reshape key aspects of the international order such as the economic and military balance among states.[5] Artificial intelligence (AI) is chief among these emerging, potentially game-changing technologies.

The race to develop AI is fast becoming a central front in the strategic competition among the current great powers. According to Russian President Vladimir Putin, "Artificial intelligence is the future, not only for Russia, but for all humankind. It comes with colossal opportunities, but also threats that are difficult to predict. Whoever becomes the leader in this sphere will become the ruler of the world."[6] Although a bit hyperbolic in phrasing, Putin's warning in 2017 is not that far off the mark. It is now well recognized that AI is a transformative strategic technology with profound implications for national security.

Apart from commercial applications, states—the United States and China lead among them—are investing heavily in researching and developing AI applications for myriad national security functions including lethal combat systems, and AI-enhanced capabilities will likely "be the tools of first resort in a new era of conflict as strategic competitors develop AI concepts and technologies for military and other malign uses."[7] Artificial Intelligence capabilities are playing a role in the Russia-Ukraine conflict, and China and other adversaries are leveraging AI to enhance their ongoing, malicious cyber and information operations directed at the

---

3. Off. Dir. Nat'l Intel., Annual Threat Assessment of the US Intelligence Community 4 (Apr. 9, 2021), https://www.dni.gov/files/ODNI/documents/assessments/ATA-2021-Unclassified-Report.pdf.

4. Nat'l. Sec. Comm'n. on A.I., Final Report 7 (Mar. 1, 2021), https://www.nscai.gov/wp-content/uploads/2021/03/Full-Report-Digital-1.pdf.

5. *See* Interim National Security Strategic Guidance, *supra* note 1, at 8–9.

6. James Vincent, *Putin Says the Nation That Leads in AI "Will Be the Ruler of the World,"* VERGE (Sept. 4, 2017), https://www.theverge.com/2017/9/4/16251226/russia-ai-putin-rule-the-world.

7. Nat'l. Sec. Comm'n. on A.I., *supra* note 4, at 9.

United States, its partners, and allies: efforts China is committed to building on. China and Russia are also incorporating AI into their military weapons systems.[8] China's publicly announced strategy is to become the leading AI power by 2030,[9] and by some assessments, it "possesses the might, talent, and ambition to surpass the United States as the world's leader in AI in the next decade if current trends do not change."[10]

The Department of Defense is keenly aware of this sobering reality and the extreme risk attendant to losing the AI race. It recognizes that maintaining competitive advantage in the development of AI and other new technologies, including advanced computing, "Big Data" analytics, autonomy, and robotics, is critical to ensuring the United States will succeed in strategic competition today and will be able to fight and win the wars of the future.[11] United States strategy for winning this competition rightly emphasizes measures to foster innovation and enhance U.S. capability, capacity, and leadership—measures such as broad and sustained investment in the research and development (R&D) of these technologies. But R&D alone may not be enough. The United States may need to take steps, consistent with its international legal obligations, to prevent or retard China's ability to develop AI for purposes that threaten U.S. national security.

Developing effective AI systems is extremely complex and depends on myriad variables. One critical component of the development process is the availability of sufficiently large, relevant, and accurate datasets for AI systems and their underlying algorithms to train on. China's mass data collection and aggregation practices—through unconstrained domestic surveillance programs, nearly unfettered access to Chinese companies' datasets, and relentless theft and exploitation of foreign data—offer China at least one distinct point of comparative advantage in the AI race. Simply put, China is awash in Big Data. Yet this apparent strength also creates a vulnerability and hence an opportunity.

Like any digitally based system, AI systems, and especially the datasets they rely on, are vulnerable to attack. Cyber operations targeting machine learning and AI systems, and the R&D behind them are not theoretical. Reports of what

---

8. *See, e.g.*, Patrick Tucker, *New Drones, Weapons Get Spotlight in China's Military Parade*, Def. One (Oct. 1 2019), https://www.defenseone.com/technology/2019/10/new-drones-weapons-get-spotlight-chinas-military-parade/160291/; Franz-Stefan Gady, *Russia's New Nuclear Torpedo-Carrying Sub to Begin Sea Trials in June 2020*, Diplomat (Sept. 10 2019), https://thediplomat.com/2019/09/russias-new-nuclear-torpedo-carrying-sub-to-begin-sea-trials-in-june-2020/.

9. Paul Mozur, *Beijing Wants A.I.to Be Made in China by 2030*, N.Y. Times (July 20, 2017), https://www.nytimes.com/2017/07/20/business/china-artificial-intelligence.html.

10. Nat'l. Sec. Comm'n on A.I., *supra* note 4, at 7.

11. Dep't. Defense, National Defense Strategy, 3 (2018), https://dod.defense.gov/Portals/1/Documents/pubs/2018-National-Defense-Strategy-Summary.pdf.

have been dubbed "adversarial AI" attacks are already emerging in the commercial sector.[12] As the NSCAI notes in its report, "Given the reliance of AI systems on large datasets and algorithms, even small manipulations of these datasets or algorithms can lead to consequential changes for how AI systems operate."[13] Data poisoning—deliberately polluting the training data to mislead the underlying machine learning algorithms and skew results—and other cyber operations aimed at manipulating, corrupting, or denying the datasets China is using to advance its AI R&D (all methods of cyber sabotage) could, under the right circumstances, offer a non-forcible means of impeding China's progress.

States have long employed sabotage as a tool of statecraft, both during and outside of armed conflict.[14] There are numerous historical examples of states engaging in sabotage to ensure military competitive advantage, especially in the context of arms races over critical, highly impactful or destructive technologies. These actions, frequently taken in a preventive framework, have ranged from overt, highly destructive, and legally suspect actions like Israel's brazen airstrike in1981on Iraq's Osirak nuclear reactor, to far more subtle, covert operations like the so-called Farewell dossier during the Cold War.[15] With the emergence of AI, its national security implications, and the power of Big Data, the United States may very well find itself in the midst of just such a moment where cyber-enabled sabotage, such as data poisoning, may be an appealing course of action. In writing this chapter the authors are not advocating for nor opining as to the technical feasibility or policy suitability of conducting such operations. We consider only whether, as a theoretical means for offsetting China's data advantage, they could be conducted consistent with international law.

12. *See, e.g.*, Ram Shankar Siva Kumar & Ann Johnson, *Cyberattacks Against Machine Learning Systems Are More Common Than You Think*, Microsoft Sec. (Oct. 22, 2020), https://www.microsoft.com/security/blog/2020/10/22/cyberattacks-against-machine-learning-systems-are-more-common-than- you-think/; Paddy Smith, *Data Poisoning: A New Front in the AI Cyber War*, AI Mag. (Oct. 8, 2020), https://aimagazine.com/data-and-analytics/data-poison ing-new-front-ai-cyber-war.

13. Nat'l Sec. Comm'n. on A.I., *supra* note 4, at 52, note 33.

14. There is no single definition of sabotage. *Sabotage*, Oxford Learner's Dictionaries, https://www.oxfordlearnersdictionaries.com/us/definition/english/sabotage_1?q=sabotage (last visited Oct. 29, 2021) ("the act of doing deliberate damage to equipment, transport, machines, etc. to prevent an enemy from using them, or to protest about something; the act of preventing something from being successful or being achieved, especially deliberately"). For purposes of this chapter, we refer to the meaning generally ascribed to the term in the context of state conducted or sponsored sabotage: actions intended to impede a state's ability to prepare for or participate in war or national defense or otherwise present a national-security threat, by impeding through interference, subversion, obstruction, damage, or destruction, the development of its military or other potentially threatening capabilities.

15. Gus W. Weiss, *The Farewell Dossier*, Def. Tech. Info. Ctr. (1996), https://apps.dtic.mil/sti/pdfs/ADA527328.pdf.

Like espionage, there is no specific rule of international law prohibiting sabotage per se. Sabotage is a stratagem, not a legal term of art. It might involve a wide spectrum of tactical actions aimed at degrading an adversary's capabilities or capacity. When conducted in advance of a perceived threat actually manifesting, sabotage can raise challenging issues of international law depending on the means of sabotage employed and the nature of the effects generated. Understanding that the legal analysis of any act of sabotage will turn on a case-by-case review of the specific facts and circumstances attendant to the operation, this chapter considers some of the potential international law implications of conducting offensive counter-AI operations in and through cyberspace.[16] We argue that China's development of AI is not likely to be considered either an armed attack or a use of force, meaning the United States has no basis to act against this development in self-defense. Indeed, it is also unlikely that China's AI development would reach the threshold of a prohibited intervention in U.S. domaine réservé. However, this does not mean that the United States is precluded from any actions against China's AI R&D data.

This chapter begins with a discussion of the national security threat that China's AI development efforts pose and the importance of Big Data to those efforts. It then moves to a review of potential cyber-enabled operations, particularly as applied to data, that could impede or thwart China's AI development. The chapter then proceeds to a review of the international law implications of cyber sabotage, beginning with a discussion of the *jus ad bellum* and followed by a review of other relevant aspects of the international law of state responsibility such as the rule of prohibited intervention, principles of state sovereignty, and the doctrines of countermeasures and necessity.

Various cyber means allow for the sabotage of China's AI development in ways that do not violate the prohibition on the use of force, and may not, depending on how the cyber means are employed, implicate the doctrine of prohibited intervention. Carefully crafted precision tools might be used to poison China's progress in AI without crossing any thresholds barred by international law.

II. BIG DATA AND ARTIFICIAL INTELLIGENCE

It is impossible to speak about effective machine learning (ML) and AI without discussing data and the fundamental role "Big Data"[17] analytics plays in the

---

16. For purposes of this paper, by counter-AI we are referring to actions aimed at "attacking each technological component of AI. . . ." Nat'l. Sec. Comm'n. on A.I., *supra* note 4, at 56, note 33. For a discussion of broader counter-AI actions, such as passive countermeasures, see Dep't Airforce, *Time for a Counter-AI Strategy,* STRATEGIC STUD. Q. (Spring 2020), https://www.airuniversity.af.edu/Portals/10/SSQ/documents/Volume-14_Issue-1/thomas.pdf.

17. For the purpose of defining "Big Data," please refer to Mark Visger, "Chapter 6: Garbage In, Garbage Out: Data Poisoning Attacks and Their Legal Implications," this book, where the authors

development and application of these advanced capabilities. For myriad reasons, China is awash in Big Data and steadily increasing its access to more sources of new and larger datasets. China's aggressive data acquisition practices align with "top-level strategic plans and guidance on the need to develop China's Big Data analytic capability" as a necessary precursor to achieving AI dominance.[18] With technology playing a central role in strategic competition between the United States and China, this "evolution of data in Chinese strategic planning provides a window into how China aims to win that contest."[19] Logically, efforts to prevent or erode any competitive advantage in AI China has or may achieve should account for its "national Big Data strategy" and the critical role access to Big Data play in its AI development efforts.[20]

A. AI Reliance on Big Data

The backbone of artificial intelligence is data. As the NSCAI has stated, data is critical for most AI systems. Labeled and curated data enables much of current ML used to create new applications and improve the performance of existing AI applications. Though the underlying hardware provides the computing power to analyze ever-growing data pools, it is the data that provides the artificial intelligence with the ability to provide answers and perform functions.[21]

During the "first wave" of machine learning, much of the advancement in this area came from "handcrafted knowledge" defined by humans and then used by the machine for reasoning and interacting.[22] However, the "second wave" of development has been propelled by the use of large-scale data. The use of this data has enabled engineers to create models that can be trained to specific problem domains if given exemplar data or simulated interactions. It is only by learning from large datasets that these systems have been capable of "solv[ing] specific

provide the following definition: "Big Data is a combination of structured, semistructured and unstructured data collected by organizations that can be mined for information and used in machine learning projects, predictive modeling and other advanced analytics applications." Bridget Botelho & Stephen J. Bigelow, *Big Data*, TechTarget.com, https://searchdatamanagement.techtar get.com/definition/big-data (last visited Oct. 29, 2021).

18. Derek Grossman et al., *Chinese Views of Big Data Analytics*, RAND CORP. (2020), 4–5, https://www.rand.org/pubs/research_reports/RRA176-1.html.

19. Lindsay Gorman, *China's Data Ambitions Strategy, Emerging Technologies, and Implications for Democracies*, NAT'L. BUREAU OF ASIAN RSCH. (Aug. 14, 2021), https://www.nbr.org/publ ication/chinas-data-ambitions-strategy-emerging-technologies-and-implications-for-demo cracies/.

20. *Id.*

21. Nat'l. Sec. Comm'n. on A.I., *supra* note 4, at 32.

22. *Id.*

tasks and achiev[ing] particular goals with competencies that, in some respects, parallel the cognitive processes of humans: perceiving, reasoning, learning, communicating, deciding, and acting," but in a fraction of the time it would take a human.[23]

In an article designed to educate policy makers on the basics of machine learning and AI, Andrew Lohn writes:

> Data fuels machine learning systems [and] has to be collected or mined from somewhere, such as a surveillance drone, a Twitter feed, or computer data. During training, the machine learning system extracts patterns from this data. The system learns by adjusting the parameters of its model to correspond to these patterns. Different kinds of machine learning systems learn from data in distinct ways, but the idea of matching the model to the training data generally holds. Crucially, the system does not know which patterns are desirable to learn and which, like those corresponding to human biases, are not. It simply learns everything it can from the data. Once training is complete, the model can be used as a component in a larger system . . . In some cases, the model can continue to be updated and trained while deployed for use, but in other cases it is frozen as is before it is deployed.[24]

An important aspect of the continuing growth and effectiveness of ML and AI is both the quantity and quality of the available datasets.[25] In terms of quantity, it is almost impossible to have too much data. "In fact, it's quite the opposite."[26] As Melendez writes, "the more data, the better. Because AI systems have the ability to process enormous amounts of data, and their accuracy increases along with data volume, the demand for data continues to grow." It is only by providing as much data as possible to address different variables, that machine learning programs can most effectively and efficiently determine the actual cause of the problem.[27] The accuracy of outputs is affected by both the quantity and the quality of the input data. That is, "machine learning algorithms work on the basis

---

23. *Id.*

24. Andrew J. Lohn, *Hacking AI: A Primer for Policymakers on Machine Learning Cybersecurity*, Ctr. for Sec. & Emerging Tech. 1–2 (Dec. 2020), https://cset.georgetown.edu/wp-content/uploads/CSET-Hacking-AI.pdf.

25. Eur. Union Agency for Fundamental Rts., *Data Quality and Artificial Intelligence—Mitigating Bias and Error to Protect Fundamental Rights*, FRA 13 (June 11, 2019), https://fra.europa.eu/sites/default/files/fra_uploads/fra-2019-data-quality-and-ai_en.pdf (hereinafter "FRA").

26. Carlos Melendez, *Data Is the Lifeblood of AI, But How Do You Collect It?*, InfoWorld (Aug. 8, 2018) https://www.infoworld.com/article/3296044/data-is-the-lifeblood-of-ai-but-how-do-you-collect-it.html.

27. *Id.*

of correlation and so sufficient training data (that is, input data linked to associated outcomes) is required in order to train the model so that it can be applied to new situations."[28]

The European Union's LIBE Committee has noted that "the use of low-quality, outdated, incomplete or incorrect data at different stages of data processing may lead to poor predictions and assessments and in turn to bias, which can eventually result in . . . incorrect conclusions or false outcomes."[29] To some extent, the quantity of the data can help strengthen the quality of the data because large amounts of data can be used to mitigate errors through having more comprehensive measurement based on many observations. The number of observations used can decrease statistical uncertainty, but only if the data has low errors of representation and measurement. Otherwise, the application will just miss the correct answer consistently. For example, if only partial data is used, such as only data on a certain demographic group that is systematically different to other groups in the population, the quantity of the data will never be likely to correct inherent errors.[30] This reliance on quality of data has caused some to argue that the old "garbage in, garbage out" adage is true, as is its inverse.[31]

An imbalance between quantity and quality of data can have cascading effects. For example:

> [A]s algorithms become increasingly central to state decision-making processes, the number of algorithmic recommendations that inform—and therefore influence—a final decision is likely to increase. This means that the impact of any inadequacy within the underlying algorithm may be magnified. The potential exists for a cascade effect, whereby a small bias in the first algorithmic recommendation is fed into a second algorithmic recommendation, which in turn skews the input for a third recommendation, and so on. Within any inter-connected and inter-dependent process, the impact of even a small error may be extensive. This means that although a human may make the final decision, the basis on which that decision is made, and the range of available options, may have been heavily influenced by the underlying algorithm(s).[32]

---

28. Ashley Deeks, Noam Lubell, & Daragh Murray, *Machine Learning, Artificial Intelligence, and the Use of Force by States*, 10 J. NAT'L SEC. L. & POL'Y 1, 5 (2019).

29. FRA, *supra* note 25.

30. *Id.*

31. *Poor-Quality Data Imposes Costs and Risks on Businesses, Says New Forbes Insights Report*, FORBES (May 31, 2017), https://www.forbes.com/sites/forbespr/2017/05/31/poor-quality-data-imposes-costs-and-risks-on-businesses-says-new-forbes-insights-report/?sh=256be738452b.

32. Deeks et al., *supra* note 28.

"Attacking" Big Data

This quotation highlights why the great powers of today are in a race to gather, verify, and apply large quantities of quality Big Data to gain competitive advantage over their adversaries.

B. The United States and China Are in an AI Race

President Putin is not alone in his recognition of the game-changing importance of AI and his ambitions to achieve first-mover advantage. Governments around the world, including the United States and China, are striving to develop their ML and AI capabilities as fast as possible. As the NSCAI concluded,

> Ad-tech will become natsec-tech as adversaries recognize what advertising and technology firms have recognized for years: that machine learning is a powerful tool for harvesting and analyzing data and targeting activities. Using espionage and publicly available data, adversaries will gather information and use AI to identify vulnerabilities in individuals, society, and critical infrastructure. They will model how best to manipulate behavior, and then act.[33]

As an example of China's efforts in this area, according to the Chinese Academy of Information and Communications Technology, China's digital economy grew much faster in 2019 than its national gross domestic product, underscoring its significance to future growth. With respect to data, "market research firm IDC projected that China would hold around a third of the world's data by 2025, or roughly 48.6 zettabytes—about 60% more than the U.S."[34]

Cyber expert and former CEO of Google, Eric Schmidt has "urged lawmakers to ramp up funding for research and development in the artificial intelligence space in order to prevent China from becoming the biggest player in the global AI market—a development Schmidt warned would spark national security and privacy concerns that could ultimately constitute a national emergency."[35] These same sentiments were echoed by Glenn Gerstell of the National Security Agency:

> [O]ur nation will have no choice but to harness the collective capabilities of the government and the private sector to address the combined technologic

33. Nat'l. Sec. Comm'n. on A.I., *supra* note 4, at 22.

34. *Xi's Next Target in Tech Crackdown Is China's Vast Reams of Data*, BLOOMBERG (Apr. 22, 2021) https://www.bloomberg.com/news/articles/2021-04-23/xi-s-next-target-in-tech-crackdown-is-china-s-vast-reams-of-data .

35. Jonathan Ponciano, *Google Billionaire Eric Schmidt Warns of "National Emergency" if China Overtakes U.S. In AI Tech*, FORBES (Mar. 7, 2021), https://www.forbes.com/sites/jonathanponciano/2021/03/07/google-billionaire-eric-schmidt-warns-of-national-emergency-if-china-overtakes-us-in-ai-tech/?sh=30e888a199fa.

and economic threats posed by China. For the first time since the United States became a global power, it must now confront an adversary that presents not merely a political or military threat but also an existential economic one. But in the latter area, the playing field is not level, as China advances its national strategic goals through a unified effort harnessing its government and its business sectors (the latter being a mix of private and state-sponsored endeavors)—while our strategic goals are seen as the responsibility of the federal government, with our private sector largely free to pursue its capitalist interests as it sees fit.[36]

However, while China represents a significant threat, and may already have surpassed the United States in many ways with respect to ML and AI, it is hard to draw specific conclusions about the future. As experts note "AI is not a monolithic single piece of technology. . . . Saying that one country's ahead or behind in aggregate is hard . . . You have to take it on an individual technology basis."[37] Some conclusions can be drawn from a comparative analysis to the approaches the United States and China take to developing this emerging technology.

1. China's Approach

China's system of government gives it both different capabilities and a different focus than that of the United States. For example, China collects data that facilities its more centralized and directive method of governance—things like "video image recognition for population control, or Great Firewall content filtering."[38] China has immense datasets that support machine learning capabilities in the areas of facial recognition for universal surveillance and text analysis for Internet and media censorship.[39] China is in the process of nationalizing its data collection from Internet companies, fining companies like Alibaba and warning others to ensure compliance with national data regulation.[40]

This data and platform domination allows China to harvest the data of its users and "permits China to extend aspects of its domestic system of control. Wherever China controls the digital infrastructure, social media platforms, and e-commerce, it would possess greater leverage and power to coerce, propagandize,

---

36. Glenn S. Gerstell, *I Work for the N.S.A. We Cannot Afford to Lose the Cyber Revolution*, N.Y. Times (Sept. 10, 2019), https://www.nytimes.com/2019/09/10/opinion/nsa-privacy.html.

37. Sydney J. Freedberg Jr., *China Is Not Ahead of US On AI: JAIC Chief & Gen. Hyten*, Breaking Def. (Sept. 10, 2020), https://breakingdefense.com/2020/09/china-is-not-ahead-of-us-on-ai-jaic-chief-vcjsc-hyten/.

38. *Id.*

39. *Id.*

40. *Xi's Next Target in Tech Crackdown Is China's Vast Reams of Data*, Bloomberg (Apr. 22, 2021), https://www.bloomberg.com/news/articles/2021-04-23/xi-s-next-target-in-tech-crackd own-is-china-s-vast-reams-of-data.

"Attacking" Big Data

and shape the world to conform to its goals."[41] Through its telecom giants, China has expanded its access to data and is "extract[ing] AI knowledge from abroad through espionage, talent recruitment, technology transfer, and investments."[42] Recent research by the *Washington Post* discovered that China is collecting data both within and outside its borders, from both Chinese nationals and foreign nationals: "bidding documents and contracts for over 300 Chinese government projects since the beginning of 2020 include orders for software designed to collect data on foreign targets from sources such as Twitter, Facebook and other Western social media."[43] The net result is a nearly unconstrained and unlimited source of Big Data that China can leverage for its AI development efforts.

In military terms, China sees ML and AI as the way to offset U.S. conventional military superiority by "leapfrogging" to a new generation of technology. It relies on what it terms "intelligentized war," an example of which is developing swarming drones as a response to U.S. naval supremacy. China sees the future in using AI systems for "reconnaissance, electromagnetic countermeasures and coordinated firepower strikes." The military is already testing and training AI algorithms to run military games designed around real-world scenarios.[44] For China, the collection of data and the development of machine learning and AI is the method to catch up with and overtake the United States in every aspect of national power.

2. U.S. Approach

As noted earlier, data collection for machine learning and artificial intelligence is not a homogenous endeavor. Greater capability in one aspect of machine learning does not necessarily translate to other, even related aspects. For example, the acting director of the Pentagon's Joint AI Center, Nand Mulchandani, believes that China may lead the world in some aspects of AI, such as surveillance and censorship. But in the ways that matter most for future warfare, "the US is still ahead compared to China [in terms of] sophistication and breadth."[45]

---

41. Nat'l. Sec. Comm'n. on A.I., *supra* note 4, at 26.

42. *Id.* at 25.

43. Cate Cadell, *China Harvests Masses of Data on Western Targets, Documents Show*, WASH. POST. (Dec. 31, 2021), https://www.washingtonpost.com/national-security/china-harvests-mas ses-of-data-on-western-targets-documents-show/2021/12/31/3981ce9c-538e-11ec-8927-c39 6fa861a71_story.html. According to the article, these systems include "a $320,000 Chinese state media software program that mines Twitter and Facebook to create a database of foreign journalists and academics; a $216,000 Beijing police intelligence program that analyzes Western chatter on Hong Kong and Taiwan; and a cybercenter in Xinjiang, home to most of China's Uyghur population, that catalogues the mainly Muslim minority group's language content abroad."

44. Nat'l. Sec. Comm'n. on A.I., *supra* note 4, at 23.

45. Freedberg Jr., *supra* note 36.

Much of this is due to the data collected over the past two decades of war, data that China cannot easily replicate because it is tied directly to a transnational armed conflict.[46]

Another difference in approach is the U.S.' reliance on private industry. For example, the Joint AI Center is working with more than 120 private companies on its AI projects.[47] Similarly, the Department of Defense partnered with Google on an AI development initiative that became known as Project Maven. Though no longer running, the project and many like it are indicative of how the partnership between government and private industry typifies the U.S. approach.[48] The U.S. government benefits significantly from being able to partner with innovative and market-driven companies such as Google, but also has to realize that, unlike the situation with the Chinese government in a command-directed economy, companies may decide to not cooperate.

While the United States and China have very different approaches, which nation will come out on top is not a foregone conclusion. According to the NSCAI:

> The countries, companies, and researchers that win the AI competition—in computing, data, talent, and commercialization—will be positioned to win a much larger game. In essence, more and better data, fed by a larger consumer/ participant base, produce better algorithms, which produce better results, which in turn produces more users, more data, and better performance— until, ultimately, fewer companies will become entrenched as the dominant platforms. If China's firms win these competitions, it will not only disadvantage U.S. commercial firms, it will also create the digital foundation for a geopolitical challenge to the United States and its allies.[49]

Because of the strategic importance of AI development, the United States needs to act with urgency and adopt a holistic approach to ensuring it maintains its competitive edge in development and fielding of these transformative technologies. Such an approach should rightly emphasize measures to bolster the U.S.'s ability and capacity to be the global leader in ML and AI, such as investments in innovation and talent. But if history is a guide, it may be necessary to take measures aimed at countering China's anticompetitive practices, starting with its "national Big Data strategy."

---

46. *Id.*

47. *Id.*

48. Sean Hollister, *Project Maven: Nearly a Dozen Google Employees Have Reportedly Quit in Protest*, CNET (May 14, 2018), https://www.cnet.com/news/google-project-maven-drone-protect-resign/.

49. Nat'l. Sec. Comm'n. on A.I., *supra* note 4, at 26.

C. Operations to Corrupt Data Might Be a Viable Option to Offset the Competitive Advantage

Even accepting the assertions above that the United States currently maintains data superiority over China with respect to key machine learning and artificial intelligence development in armed conflict, China's commitment to narrow that gap, and its abundant resources to do so, should cause the United States to consider its options in order to preserve its advantage. Andrew Lohn has outlined risks associated with data and potential impacts from actions based on those risks.

> In cybersecurity, possible harms are typically grouped into three broad categories represented by the acronym CIA: confidentiality, integrity, and availability. All three categories also apply to machine learning. Integrity attacks alter data to cause machines to make errors and have attracted the most attention. Confidentiality attacks extract information meant to remain hidden; they also garner notable research focus. Availability attacks cause the machine learning component to run slowly or not at all. While availability attacks are starting to attract more attention, they have been the least popular.[50]

Lohn's quote presents three possible avenues that the United States could use to influence China's ability to leverage "Big Data" in support of its ML and AI development efforts. While all three options should be considered thoroughly, the analysis in this chapter focuses on one particular example of cyber sabotage: data poisoning.

In a recent posting by Microsoft, multiple actions against data are described and analyzed within a threat taxonomy. One of these actions is described as a poisoning attack. In a "[p]oisoning attack," the goal of the actor is to "contaminate the machine model generated in the training phase, so that predictions on new data will be modified in the testing phase."[51] The United States could employee this type of action to "taint" the datasets China uses in order to corrupt the inputs, resulting in incorrect outputs for both ML and AI applications.

---

50. Lohn, *supra* note 24, at 5.

51. *Failure Models in Machine Learning*, MICROSOFT CORP. (Nov. 11, 2019), https://docs. microsoft.com/en-us/security/engineering/failure-modes-in-machine-learning; *see also* Elham Tabassi et al., *A Taxonomy and Terminology of Adversarial Machine Learning*, NAT'L. INST. OF STANDARDS AND TECH. 22 (2019) (noting that data poisoning, "also known as Causative Attacks . . . Aims to increase the number of misclassified samples at test time by injecting a small fraction of carefully designed adversarial samples into the training data. Indirect poisoning manipulates data before any preprocessing, while direct poisoning the data are altered by Data Injection or Data Manipulation, or the model is altered directly by Logic Corruption. Also known as a contamination of the training data. Alternately, also includes tampering with the ML algorithm itself, to compromise the whole learning process).

Many other options are available to create the same or similar effects on the data, and resulting conclusions. These types of actions, then, would allow the United States to undermine China's confidence in its ML and AI development and execution. This chapter now turns to questions of international law as a potential constraint on such actions.

III. THE INTERNATIONAL LAW IMPLICATIONS OF OFFENSIVE, COUNTER-AI CYBER OPERATIONS

The terrorist attacks on 9/11, and the subsequent trial by military commission of several of the perpetrators, brought out of relative obscurity the somewhat forgotten story of eight Nazi "saboteurs" put ashore in New York and Florida in 1942.[52] The so-called Quirin eight were part of a failed plan to conduct a series of destructive attacks against critical infrastructure throughout the United States with the goal of disrupting and degrading U.S. war production and supply chains.[53]

This botched attempt at wartime sabotage was far from unprecedented. History is replete with examples of states and partisan groups using sabotage as a method of warfare to degrade the enemy's warfighting capacity through attacks on, inter alia, war-sustaining supplies, materiel, manufacturing, logistics routes, and communications systems. As *Ex Parte Quirin* teaches, although the *lex specialis* of the Law of War does not prohibit sabotage as a method of warfare per se, it does strip the perpetrators of certain protections normally accorded combatants.[54] In peacetime, international law has even less to say about sabotage as a method of statecraft.

A. Preventive Action, Sabotage, and International Law

Sabotage is not, however, an activity states have relegated to use in warfare. There are numerous examples of states engaging in sabotage as a tool of peacetime statecraft to subvert adversaries and deter or prevent war or other national security

---

52. *Ex Parte Quirin*, 317 U.S. 1 (1942) (the Supreme Court's 1942 decision upholding the saboteurs' trial and conviction by a military commission, served as precedent for prosecuting—also by military commission—perpetrators of the 9/11 attacks as unlawful belligerents); *see Hamdan v. Rumsfeld*, 548 U.S. (2006); *Hamdi v. Rumsfeld*, 542 U.S. (2004).

53. *Ex Parte Quirin*, 317 U.S. 1.

54. Rather, while those who engage in sabotage may, under certain circumstances, lose entitlement to the privilege of combatant status, the acts of sabotage themselves are measured against the same rules governing all other means and methods of warfare. *See* Office of the General Counsel, U.S. Department of Defense, Law Of War Manual ¶ 4.17 (June 2015) (hereinafter DoD LoW Manual).

"Attacking" Big Data

threats.[55] For example, in the years leading up to the U.S.' entry into World War I, Germany engaged in an extended campaign of disruptive attacks against and within the United States to stem the flow of war supplies to the Allied powers.[56] Perhaps the most notable of these attacks, the "Black Tom" bombing that destroyed two million tons of war materials stored at a train depot in New York Harbor, and even led to the enactment of the first iteration of the Sabotage Act.[57]

After World War II, sabotage, both political and actual, formed a key component of the Soviet Union's covert "active measures" against the United States and Western adversaries.[58] Only after the Soviet Union's collapse in 1991 did the full extent of its plans and preparations to conduct sabotage become more fully apparent.[59] In addition to direct acts of subversion, the Soviets had established complex and extensive networks of operatives and weapons caches in the United States, along the border, and in other Western states to be used in the event of war or serious international crisis.[60]

The United States also engaged in preventive sabotage during the Cold War. For example, in the early 1980s, the United States "supplied" the Soviet Union with Trojanized software that eventually led to a major pipeline disaster in what is commonly referred to as the Farewell Dossier.[61] Through recruited agents in Moscow, the United States had discovered that the Soviets were stealing emerging computer technology from the West. Having obtained a detailed list of the Soviet's planned targets for theft, the CIA implemented a covert program to inject

55. *See generally* John Arquilla, *An Ounce of (Virtual) Prevention?*, in UNDERSTANDING CYBER CONFLICT: 14 ANALOGIES (Oct. 16, 2017), https://carnegieendowment.org/2017/10/16/unders tanding-cyber-conflict-14-analogies-pub-72689.

56. *See* 1 CIA, *Intelligence Studies*, 46 CTR. FOR THE STUDY OF INTEL. (Mar. 2017), https://www. cia.gov/resources/csi/studies-in-intelligence/volume-46-no-1/.

57. 40 Stat. 533 (1918); *see also* Sam Bass Warner, *The Model Sabotage Prevention Act*, 54 HARV. L. REV. 602, 624–25 (1941) (discussing the Black Tom attack and the passage of the original Sabotage Act) and *Black Tom 1916 Bombing*, FBI (last visited Jan. 9, 2022), https://www.fbi.gov/ history/famous-cases/black-tom-1916-bombing (same). The Sabotage Act is currently codified at 18 U.S.C. §§ 2151–2156 (2018). Note that the term "sabotage," as used in this chapter, is not limited to the definition under United States domestic law.

58. *See generally* THOMAS RID, ACTIVE MEASURES: THE SECRET HISTORY OF DISINFORMATION AND POLITICAL WARFARE (2020); Gary P. Corn, *Covert Deception, Strategic Fraud, and the Rule of Prohibited Intervention*, HOOVER INST. 4–5, https://www.hoover.org/sites/default/files/resea rch/docs/corn_webready.pdf.

59. *See generally* CHRISTOPHER ANDREW & VASILI MITROKHIN, THE SWORD AND THE SHIELD: THE MITROKHIN ARCHIVE AND THE SECRET HISTORY OF THE KGB (2000); *see also Russian Threat Perceptions and Plans for Sabotage Against hte United States Before the Mil. Rsch. and Dev. Subcomm. of the H. Armed Serv. Comm.* [hereinafter HASC], 106 Cong. 1 (Oct. 26, 1999), http://commdocs.house.gov/committees/security/has299010.000/has299010_0f.htm.

60. HASC, *supra* note 59.

61. Weiss, *supra* note 15.

corrupted computer components and software into the supply chain of stolen items.[62] The Farewell Dossier episode served as a prelude to what some have dubbed "cybotage"—operations conducted in the cyber domain intended to sabotage computers, computer networks, and the data resident thereon to generate denial effects against those devices or possibly outside of cyberspace.[63]

According to various reports, Israel, and perhaps the United States, have already leveraged cyberspace as an alternative approach to achieving counter-proliferation objectives without resorting to more traditional, kinetic means of preventive sabotage. The notorious 2010 Stuxnet worm that infected Iran's Natanz uranium enrichment facility, an alleged Israeli-U.S. cyber operation that caused nearly a thousand centrifuges to spin out of control and self-destruct, is a clear example of preventive sabotage effected by cyber means.[64] Yet despite the significant damage that resulted from Stuxnet, neither Iran nor any other state has asserted that the event amounted to a use of force, at least as a matter of international law.[65] More recently, reports surfaced alleging that Israel again used cyber capabilities against the Natanz facility.[66] If true, these cyber operations were deliberate efforts to retard Iran's ability to develop nuclear technology and weapons.

In 2017, North Korea experienced exceptionally high failure rates during testing of the Musudan, intermediate-range ballistic missile. Some attributed

---

62. FCW, *Tech Sabotage during the Cold War* (Apr. 26, 2004), https://fcw.com/Articles/2004/04/26/Tech-sabotage-during-the-Cold-War.aspx?m=1&Page=2.

63. *See, e.g.*, John Arquilla, Bitskrieg: The New Challenge of CyberWarfare 10–13 (2021).

64. John Arquilla, *An Ounce of (Virtual) Prevention?, in* Understanding Cyber Conflict: 14 Analogies 100 (Oct. 16, 2017), https://carnegieendowment.org/2017/10/16/understanding-cyber-conflict-14-analogies-pub-72689.

65. *See infra*, notes and accompanying text. John Arquilla offers Stuxnet as an example of preventive force, and a number of international law experts have cited it as an example of a prohibited use of force. John Arquilla, *An Ounce of (Virtual) Prevention?, in* Understanding Cyber Conflict 14, 100, 107–08 (Perkovich & Levite eds., 2017); Michael N. Schmitt, Tallinn Manual 2.0 on the International Law applicable to Cyber Operations 342 (2d ed. 2017) [hereinafter Tallinn Manual 2.0].

66. According to various reports, Iran's ability to enrich uranium and move closer to producing nuclear weapons recently suffered a significant setback when, on April 11, 2021, its Natanz uranium enrichment site experienced a power failure caused, apparently, by an explosion at the site. Ronen Bergman et al., *Blackout Hits Iran Nuclear Site in What Appears to Be Israeli Sabotage*, N.Y. Times (Apr. 13, 2021), https://www.nytimes.com/2021/04/11/world/middleeast/iran-nucl ear-natanz.html. Reports immediately surfaced alleging the explosion was the result of an Israeli cyber operation. Although facts substantiating this claim are sparse, in an unusual step, Israel imposed no censorship restrictions on coverage of the incident and in the face of reports by Israel's public radio that the Mossad had been involved, the Israeli defense chief, Aviv Kochavi, said the country's "operations in the Middle East are not hidden from the eyes of the enemy." Martin Chulov, *Israel Appears to Confirm It Carried Out Cyberattack on Iran Nuclear Facility*, Guardian (Apr. 11, 2021), https://www.theguardian.com/world/2021/apr/11/israel-appears-confirm-cyberattack-iran-nuclear-facility.

these failures to U.S. cyber operations.[67] Whether true or not, sabotaging North Korea's missile capabilities would have been consistent with the Department of Defense's "Left-of-Launch" air and missile defense program announced in 2013, that envisions using cyber and other kinetic and non-kinetic capabilities to prevent adversaries "from effectively employing any of [their] air and missile weapons" against the United States or its allies.[68]

The foregoing examples are just a small sampling of state-conducted sabotage. When conducted outside of clear situations of armed conflict, sabotage generally takes the form of preventive force; that is, "using violence now in the hope of avoiding a full-blown war or to keep the strategic situation in an ongoing confrontation from deteriorating."[69] The admixture of cyber and other non-kinetic capabilities into the sabotage toolkit, with the attendant possibility of achieving prevention goals through less-than-obviously forcible means, further muddies an already murky area of international law. What follows is a discussion of some of the more pertinent aspects of international law relevant to assessing whether the United States could use cyber operations to preventively sabotage the data necessary for China's AI development efforts consistent with international law.

B. Preventive Sabotage and the *Jus ad Bellum*

The starting point for assessing the international law implications of a state engaging in preventive acts of sabotage is the *jus ad bellum*. This body of customary international law, reflected in Articles 2(4) and 51 of the UN Charter, governs the conditions under which states may resort to the use of force in their international relations.[70] Article 2(4) sets out the baseline prohibition against states threatening or using force "against the territorial integrity or political independence of any State, or in any other manner inconsistent with the Purposes of the United

---

67. David E. Sanger & William J. Broad, *Trump Inherits a Secret Cyberwar Against North Korean Missiles*, N.Y. Times (Mar. 4, 2017), https://www.nytimes.com/2017/03/04/world/asia/north-korea-missile-program-sabotage.html?smid=tw-share. *Cf.* Jeffery Lewis, *Is the United States Really Blowing Up North Korea's Missiles?*, Foreign Pol'y. (Apr. 19, 2017), https://foreignpolicy.com/2017/04/19/the-united-states-isnt-hacking-north-koreas-missile-launches/.

68. Martin E. Dempsey, Joint Integrated Air and Missile Defense: Vision 2020 (Dec. 5, 2013); *see also* Riki Ellison, *Left of Launch*, Missile Def. Advoc. All. (Mar. 16, 2015), http://missiledefenseadvocacy.org/alert/3132 ("The strategy is based on a preemptive strike with new non kinetic technologies, such as electromagnetic propagation, cyber as well as offensive force to defeat nuclear ballistic missile threats before they are launched, known as 'left of launch.' The strategy is to attack by electronic embedment or through the electronic radar signatures of the threat's command and control systems and the targeting systems of the threatening ballistic missiles").

69. Arquilla, *supra* note 62, at 1.

70. *See generally* U.N. Charter Art. 2, Art. 51.

Nations."[71] In contrast, Article 51 recognizes that in the face of an "armed attack," states have an inherent right to resort to force in self-defense.[72]

This general prohibition in Article 2(4) admits of only three exceptions. First, actions conducted with the consent of the affected state do not violate Article 2(4).[73] Second, states can lawfully use force under a Chapter VII enforcement action authorized by the Security Council.[74] Finally, as noted, states are permitted to use force in the face of an "armed attack" as an exercise of their inherent right of individual or collective self-defense.[75] Once triggered, the right of self-defense permits the victim state to respond with defensive force, subject to the principles of necessity and proportionality.[76]

This seemingly straightforward framework "is in fact rife with interpretive ambiguities" that make it difficult to apply neatly to cyberspace.[77] These range from questions as to the nature and threshold of "force" subject to the Article 2(4) prohibition, to the meaning of "armed attack" in Article 51, to the issue of whether, and under what circumstances, using force in self-defense can be justified prior to an armed attack actually manifesting. For reasons set out next, while conducting cyber sabotage operations including data poisoning aimed at impeding China's AI development might breach other rules of international law, it is unlikely that they would amount to a use of force. Before turning to those questions, we first address the international law boundaries of preventive uses of force.

71. U.N. Charter Art. 2, ¶ 4 ("All Members shall refrain in their international relations from the threat or use of force against the territorial integrity or political independence of any State, or in any other manner inconsistent with the Purposes of the United Nations").

72. U.N. Charter Art. 51.

73. *See* Int'l L Comm'n. Rep., Draft Articles on Responsibility of States for Internationally Wrongful Acts, Fifty-Third Session U.N. Doc. 10 A/56/10 (Nov. 2001) at Art. 20 ("Valid consent by a State to the commission of a given act by another State precludes the wrongfulness of that act in relation to the former State to the extent that the act remains within the limits of that consent") (hereinafter "Draft Articles on State Responsibility").

74. TALLINN MANUAL 2.0, *supra* note 65, at 329 ("[T]he lack of agreed-upon definitions, criteria, and thresholds for application creates uncertainty when applying the *jus ad bellum* to the rapidly changing realities of cyberspace."); Obama White House, Report on the Legal and Policy Frameworks Guiding the United States' Use of Military Force ad Related National Security Operations, White House 8 (Dec. 2016), https://obamawhitehouse.archives.gov/sites/whiteho use.gov/files/documents/Legal_Policy_Report.pdf.

75. U.N. Charter Art. 51 ("Nothing in the present Charter shall impair the inherent right of individual or collective self-defense if an armed attack occurs against a member of the United Nations until the Security Council has taken measures necessary to maintain international peace and security"). Several states, to include the United States, consider Article 51 as reflective of customary international law.

76. DoD LoW MANUAL, *supra* note 52, at 999–1000 ("As a matter of national policy, the United States has expressed the view that when warranted, it will respond to hostile acts in cyberspace as it would to any other threat to the country").

77. GARY P. CORN, NATIONAL SECURITY IN THE DIGITAL AGE (2020).

1. The Law of Preventive Force

In the summer of 1981, Israel made clear through word and deed that when faced with the prospect of a regional adversary developing nuclear weapons, it would not hesitate to disrupt those efforts, even by means of armed force. On June 7, 1981, Israel conducted a devastating airstrike against the Osirak nuclear reactor deep inside Iraq in what then Israeli Prime Minister Menachem Begin justified morally and legally as an act of "anticipatory self-defense at its best."[78] Setting out what became known as the Begin Doctrine, he reiterated days after the strike that the Osirak attack would serve as precedent for how Israel would approach such threats going forward. According to Begin, "every future Israeli prime minister [would] act, in similar circumstances, in the same way."[79]

The international community was not persuaded. Condemnation of the Osirak attack was swift, nearly universal, and grounded in the assertion that it had violated the UN Charter and international law. In the absence of evidence that Iraq presented an immediate threat of armed attack, Israel's invocation of anticipatory self-defense to justify the airstrike was roundly rejected as a misapplication of the doctrine.[80]

Unfazed by this international condemnation, Israel again took forcible preventive action against a potential nuclear threat in 2007 when it conducted a similar raid on the al-Kibar nuclear reactor in Syria—Operation Outside the Box.[81] In contrast to the Osirak attack, this time international reaction was far more muted. Syria itself offered no condemnation, downplayed the strikes, and sought to cover up any traces of the nuclear facility. Neither the UN generally, nor the Security Council specifically, took up the matter or offered any rebuke.[82]

---

78. Leonard S. Spector & Avner Cohen, *Israel's Airstrike on Syria's Reactor: Implications for the Nonproliferation Regime*, 38 ARMS CONTROL TODAY 15, 16 (July/Aug. 2008). Begin set out his rationale thus: "We chose this moment: now, not later, because later may be too late, perhaps forever. And if we stood by idly, two, three years, at the most four years, and Saddam Hussein would have produced his three, four, five bombs. . . . Then, this country and this people would have been lost, after the Holocaust. Another Holocaust would have happened in the history of the Jewish people. Never again, never again! Tell so your friends, tell anyone you meet, we shall defend our people with all the means at our disposal. We shall not allow any enemy to develop weapons of mass destruction turned against us." *Id.*

79. *Id.* (citing *"CBS News: An Interview with Prime Minister Menachem Begin,"* Face the Nation, CBS June 15, 1981).

80. Bernard D. Nossiter, *Israelis Condemned By Security Council For Attack On Iraq*, N.Y. TIMES (June 20, 1981), https://www.nytimes.com/1981/06/20/world/israelis-condemned-by-security-council-for-attack-on-iraq.html.

81. Barbara Opall-Rome, *Declassified: How an Israeli Operation Derailed Syria's Nuclear Weapons Drive*, DEFENSE NEWS (Mar. 4, 2018), https://www.defensenews.com/global/mideast-africa/2018/03/20/just-declassified-how-an-israeli-operation-derailed-syrias-nuclear-weapons-drive/; Gary P. Corn, *Israel, Cyber Sabotage and International Law*, MIRYAM INST. (Jul. 16, 2021), https://www.miryaminstitute.org/commentary-blog/israel-cyber-sabotage-and-international-law.

82. Chachko, *infra* note 85.

While some point to myriad practical and political considerations to account for the markedly different reactions to the two events,[83] others argue that the different reactions reflect an evolution in the *opinio juris* of states with respect to the parameters of the right of self-defense.[84] Specifically, this view posits that, at least in the case of nuclear weapons and perhaps other weapons of mass destruction, states may be more tolerant of uses of force intended to preempt threats that cannot be said to meet the strict *Caroline* standard of imminence required for a state to use force in anticipation of an actual attack.[85]

Recall that as set out in Article 51 of the UN Charter, the *jus ad bellum* limits the inherent right of self-defense to situations where "an armed attack occurs against a Member of the United Nations. . . ."[86] The Charter language raises disputed questions as to what constitutes an armed attack, and when such attacks "occur."

Neither the term "use of force" nor "armed attack" are defined in the Charter, and international consensus is lacking on their precise meanings.[87] As it will be discussed more fully, action causing death or injury to persons or physical damage or destruction to objects, regardless of the modality employed, will likely qualify as a use of force.[88] However, for a majority of states, the term "armed attack" conveys a quantitatively and qualitatively higher threshold of harm than does a mere use of force, with the right of self-defense being triggered only by the former.[89] For these states, defensive force is appropriate only to thwart certain

---

83. Some have pointed to, *inter alia*, the al-Kibar reactor posing a greater threat, different regional and international political considerations, and the failure of either party involved to openly acknowledge the open secret of operation Outside the Box.

84. Chachko, *infra* note 85.

85. This debate reignited with Israel's acknowledgment of Operation Outside the Box in 2018. *See, e.g.*, Elena Chachko, *The Al-Kibar Strike: What a Difference 26 Years Make*, LAWFARE BLOG (Apr. 2, 2018), https://www.lawfareblog.com/al-kibar-strike-what-difference-26-years-make; Kevin Jon Heller, *Why Al-Kibar Does Not Contribute to Pre-Emptive Self-Defense*, OPINIO JURIS (Mar. 4, 2018), http://opiniojuris.org/2018/04/03/why-the-al-kibar-strike-does-not-contribute-to-the-customary-jus-ad-bellum/.

86. U.N. Charter Art. 51.

87. Corn, *supra* note 77.

88. Michael N. Schmitt, *Grey Zones in the International Law of Cyberspace*, 42:2 YALE J. OF INT'L. L. ONLINE 1, 14 (2017); Gary D. Brown et al., *Military Cyberspace Operations*, 135, in U.S. MILITARY OPERATIONS: LAW, POLICY, AND PRACTICE (Geoffrey S. Corn et al. eds., 2016); *see also* TALLINN MANUAL 2.0, *supra* note 74, at 328 (quoting Legality of the Threat or Use of Nuclear Weapons (Advisory Opinion), 1996 I.C.J. 226, ¶ 39 (July 1996) (The *jus ad bellum* applies to "any use of force, regardless of the weapons employed.")).

89. These states and scholars base this view primarily on the ICJ's distinction in its *Nicaragua* decision between "the most grave forms of the use of force (those constituting an armed attack) from other less grave forms." Case Concerning Military and Paramilitary Activities in and Against Nicaragua (Nicar. V. U.S.), 1986 I.C.J. 14, ¶ 191 (June 27) [hereinafter Nicaragua Judgment].

undefined, "grave" uses of unlawful force, whether actual or expected. However, the United States' rejects this so-called response gap between a use of force and an armed attack, taking instead the position that the inherent right of self-defense potentially applies against *any* illegal use of force.[90] So for the United States, "cyber operations causing the same or similar effects as those that would be considered a use of force if caused through traditional physical means would be treated equally under the *jus ad bellum*."[91]

Given the obvious destructive nature of at least some of the foregoing examples, discussions about sabotage have tended to center more on the issue of whether, and if so, when states can resort to force to prevent an expected, but inchoate, armed attack. While some states reject the notion that, in accordance with the plain language of Article 51 of the UN Charter, self-defense can ever be legitimately exercised prior to an attack actually manifesting, many states consider the right of self-defense to include anticipatory actions as a matter of customary international law.[92] For these states, the United States being chief among them, a state is "not required to absorb the first hit before it can resort to the use of force in self-defense to repel an imminent attack."[93] Indeed, history offers numerous examples of states invoking self-defense to justify their use of force in the first instance.[94] In each case, the availability of the self-help remedy turns on the degree of immediacy of the threatened attack that must be present: a matter on which international consensus is also lacking.[95] Debates on this question align

90. DoD LoW MANUAL, *supra* note 54, at 1000 (citing Harold Hongju Koh, *Keynote Address at the U.S. Cyber Command Inter-Agency Legal Conference: International Law in Cyberspace* (Sept. 18, 2012)); *see also* LoC, *Operational Law Handbook*, Lib. of Cong. 4 (2017), https://www.loc.gov/rr/frd/Military_Law/pdf/operational-law-handbook_2017.pdf.

91. Gary P. Corn, *Cyber National Security: Navigating Gray Zone Challenges In and Through Cyberspace*, *in* COMPLEX BATTLESPACES: THE LAW OF ARMED CONFLICT AND THE DYNAMICS OF MODERN WARFARE (Corn et al. eds., 2019); DoD LoW MANUAL, *supra* note 54, at 1000. The *Department of Defense Law of War Manual* lists examples of cyber operations that would presumptively cross the threshold of a use of force—those that trigger a nuclear plant meltdown; open a dam above a populated area, causing destruction; disable air traffic control services, resulting in airplane crashes; or cripple a military's logistics systems—but emphasizes the context specific nature of the inquiry. *Id.* at 998–99. In addition to the nature of the effects, other factors such as the perpetrator, the target location, and the intent of the cyber operation would be relevant.

92. Gary P. Corn, *Developing Rules of Engagement: Operationalizing Law, Policy, and Military Imperatives at the Strategic Level*, *in* U.S. MILITARY OPERATIONS: LAW, POLICY, AND PRACTICE 232 (G.S. Corn et al. eds., 2016) [hereinafter *Developing Rules of Engagement*].

93. U.S. Army JAG Corps Int'l Operational L. Dep't, LAW OF ARMED CONFLICT DESKBOOK 334–35 (5th ed. 2015), https://www.loc.gov/rr/frd/Military_Law/pdf/LOAC-Deskbook-2015.pdf; *see also* Michael N. Schmitt, *Preemptive Strategies in International Law*, 24 MICH. J. INT'L L. 513, 535, (2003) ("It would be absurd to suggest that international law requires a State to 'take the first hit' when it could effectively defend itself by acting preemptively").

94. *See* YORAM DINSTEIN, WAR, AGGRESSION, AND SELF-DEFENSE 195 (6th ed. 2017).

95. *Developing Rules of Engagement, supra* note 92, at 232.

pre-armed-attack self-defense into three general categories that run along a temporal spectrum: anticipatory, preemptive, and preventive.[96]

Anticipatory self-defense is the most widely accepted standard of pre-attack self-defense. Drawn from the principle established in the famous 1837 *Caroline* case, in which British soldiers in Canada crossed the Niagara River to attack and send over Niagara Falls the American steamship *Caroline* that was assisting Canadian rebels, anticipatory self-defense permits a state "to respond to an attack before it is completed, but only where the need to respond is 'instant, overwhelming, and leaving no choice of means, and no moment for deliberation.'"[97] The *Caroline* standard of self-defense is generally understood as requiring strict temporal proximity to the expected armed attack to justify the necessity of force. The underlying intent of this standard is to allow as much opportunity as possible for non-forceful measures to work in averting a crisis.

Preemptive self-defense involves using force "to halt a particular tangible course of action that the potential victim state perceives will shortly evolve into an armed attack against it."[98] This approach extends the time horizon for action, loosening the requirement of temporal proximity. Although more distant in time relative to the perceived threat, "the potential victim state has good reasons to believe that the attack is likely, is near at hand, and, if it takes place, will result in significant harm."[99]

96. Note that Yoram Dinstein has also proposed the ability of states to exercise "interceptive self-defense" when an attacking state has "committed itself to an armed attack in an ostensibly irrevocable way." YORAM DINSTEIN, WAR, AGGRESSION, AND SELF-DEFENSE 191 (2005).

97. Ashley S. Deeks, *Taming the Doctrine of Pre-Emption, in* THE OXFORD HANDBOOK OF THE USE OF FORCE IN INTERNATIONAL LAW 662 (Marc Weller ed., 2015) (quoting Letter of Daniel Webster, US Secretary of State, to Lord Ashburton, British Plenipotentiary (Aug. 6, 1842), *quoted in* JOHN BASSETT MOORE, A DIGEST OF INTERNATIONAL LAW, vol. 2 (1906), § 217, at 412). The *Caroline* incident involved an exchange of diplomatic letters between the United States and Great Britain regarding an attack by the latter against Canadian rebels inside the United States. In 1837, British troops set fire to a steamer, the *Caroline*, on the U.S. side of the Niagara River, alleging self-defense in that the *Caroline* had been used to transport Canadian rebels across the border to attack British forces. Then U.S. Secretary of State Daniel Webster filed a strong objection to the British action and justification, stating "[i]t will be for . . . [Her Majesty's] Government to show a necessity of self-defence, instant, overwhelming, leaving no choice of means, and no moment for deliberation" and the action must not be "unreasonable or excessive, since the act, justified by the necessity of self-defense, must be limited by that necessity, and kept clearly within it." Elizabeth Wilmhurst, Principles of International Law on the Use of Force by States in Self–Defence 7 (Chatham House: The Royal Institute of Int'l Affairs Working Paper no. 05/01, 2005) (quoting letter of Daniel Webster); *see also* Martin A. Rogoff & Edward Collins Jr., *The Caroline Incident and the Development of International Law*, 16 BROOK. J. INT'L L. 493 (1990) (discussing the *Caroline* incident).

98. Deeks, *supra* note 97, at 662 (citing Sean Murphy, *The Doctrine of Preemptive Self-Defense*, 50 VILL. L. REV. 699, 704 (2005)).

99. *Id.* at 662–63.

Preventive self-defense places greater emphasis on the quantum of the threat than its actual immediacy or concreteness. It "refers to the use of force to avoid an emerging state of affairs in which a threat would be more likely or increasingly dire."[100] States might justify preventive force, even in the absence of specific evidence of the adversary's intent to attack, where the risk of inaction is deemed too consequential and there is "difficulty in ascertaining precisely when and how that threat will manifest itself as an armed attack."[101]

Whereas the strict imminence standard of the *Caroline* case is generally accepted among states as reflecting customary international law, the opposite is true with respect to preventive self-defense.[102] Many states consider actions falling within this category as illegitimate. However, as evidenced by the Begin Doctrine, it would appear that some nations reject strict application of the *Caroline* imminence standard, at least with respect to counter-proliferation of nuclear weapons and perhaps other weapons of mass destruction (WMD).[103] Whether that flexibility extends to or beyond what is described above as preemptive self-defense is highly contextual and uncertain.

Israel does not stand alone in seeking to evolve the law of self-defense and the notion of imminence to reflect the realities of modern weapons technology and national security threats.[104] For example, the 2002 National Security Strategy of the United States (2002 NSS) signaled a clear willingness to use force preemptively, stating that "[w]hen the consequences of an attack with WMD are potentially so devastating, we cannot afford to stand idly by as grave dangers materialize" and thus may use of force in self-defense "even if uncertainty remains as to the time and place of the enemy's attack."[105] This is, according to the 2002 NSS, "the principle and logic of pre-emption."[106] And although this shift met with criticism, especially after it was viewed at least in part as a misapplied justification for the U.S. invasion of Iraq in 2003, it retains currency to this day in the U.S.

---

100. Matthew C. Waxman, *The Use of Force Against States That Might Have Weapons of Mass Destruction*, 31 Mich. J. Int'l. L. 1, 13 (2009).

101. Alex Potcovaru, *The International Law of Anticipatory Self-Defense and U.S. Options in North Korea*, Lawfare Blog (Aug. 8, 2017), https://www.lawfareblog.com/international-law-anticipatory-self-defense-and-us-options-north-korea; Deeks, *supra* note 97.

102. *See* Tallinn Manual 2.0, *supra* note 74, at 353.

103. Deeks, *supra* note 97, at 670–72.

104. *Id.* at 670 ("Certain scholars and states deem it imperative to update the self-defence concept of imminence in response to efforts by rogue states (and potentially non-state actors) to acquire WMD.").

105. Nat'l. Sec. Council, Prevent Our Enemies from Threatening Us, Our Allies, and Our Friends with Weapons of Mass Destruction, White House 15 (June 1, 2002), https://georgewbush-whitehouse.archives.gov/nsc/nss/2002/nss5.html.

106. *Id.* at 77.

Standing Rules of Engagement's pronouncement that "[i]mminent does not necessarily mean immediate or instantaneous."[107] Other states, Australia, Japan, and the United Kingdom among them, have expressed varying degrees of solidarity with expanded standards of self-defense, at least to prevent WMD and terrorist threats from materializing.[108]

The logic of adapting the *jus ad bellum* to modern weapons technology and national security threats is compelling. The ability of adversaries to achieve surprise and inflict devastating blows bears little if any relationship to the threats of the 1830s, when the range of weapons was measured in miles and attacks depended on the "visible mobilization and deployment of armies and navies."[109] The "last feasible window of opportunity" standard is another approach to accounting for this reality. By this standard, a state may act in self-defense "when the attacker is clearly committed to launching an armed attack and the victim State will lose its opportunity to effectively defend itself unless it act."[110] This "window of opportunity" is not defined by temporal proximity to the threat, but instead turns on whether failure to act at a given moment would reasonably be expected to deprive the victim state of the ability to effectively defend itself when an attack actually occurs.[111] This approach aligns closely with preemptive self-defense. However, proponents of this view would not consider preventive force to be a legitimate exercise of self-defense.[112]

Wherever one falls on this spectrum, justifying as an exercise of self-defense, offensive counter-AI cyber operations that would themselves rise to the level of a use of force presents substantial difficulties. The instances where states have invoked an expanded interpretation of imminence to justify preventive action are limited in number and context. For example, Israel's strikes to impede Iraqi, Syrian, and Iranian nuclear ambitions presented unique cases of existential threats in terms of both the weapons capability and the perceived intentions of Israel's enemies. The

---

107. LOC, *Standing Rules of Engagement*, Libr. Cong. 84 (2015) [hereinafter "SROE"], https://www.loc.gov/rr/frd/Military_Law/pdf/OLH_2015_Ch5.pdf .

108. Deeks, *supra* note 97, at 667 and footnotes.

109. Michael N. Schmitt, *Cyber Operations and the Jud Ad Bellum Revisited*, 56 Vill. L. Rev. 569 (2011) (Legal scholars and international jurists often conditioned the legitimacy of pre-emption on the existence of an imminent threat-most often a visible mobilization of armies, navies, and air forces preparing to attack. We must adapt the concept of imminent threat to the capabilities and objectives of today's adversaries. Rogue states and terrorists do not seek to attack us using conventional means. They know such attacks would fail. Instead, they rely on acts of terror and, potentially, the use of weapons of mass destruction, weapons that can be easily concealed, delivered covertly, and used without warning).

110. Tallinn Manual 2.0, *supra* note 74, at 351.

111. *Id.*

112. *Id.* (noting that "a preventive strike, that is, one against a prospective attacker who has not initiated any preparations or expressed either impliedly or explicitly an intention to carry out an armed attack, does not qualify as a lawful exercise of anticipatory self-defense").

mere development of artificial intelligence does not, in and of itself, involve such circumstances. Further, even in the context of WMD threats, Israel's actions have been generally viewed as standing on weak legal footing.

Generally, simply enhancing one's military capabilities and capacity alone is insufficient evidence of attack planning, let alone intent. The United States' pursuit of AI dominance is not in preparation for initiating armed conflict, but rather to "deter war and ensure [the] nation's security."[113] Absent evidence that China is planning and has the intent to launch an attack, using force preventively to impede China's AI development would seem to stretch self-defense beyond accepted understandings.

Further, unlike nuclear weapons or other WMD, AI is not a single, discreet weapon or weapons system. It is the next evolution of computer programming technology that produces systems or machines that mimic human intelligence to perform tasks and can iteratively improve themselves based on the information they collect. It is "the quintessential 'dual use' technology" that can be put to beneficial civilian purposes as well as paradigm-altering national security, and especially military uses.[114] Some predict that conflicts of the future "will be dominated by AI and pit algorithms against algorithms" where advantage will ultimately "be determined by the amount and quality of a military's data, the algorithms it develops, the AI-enabled networks it connects, the AI-enabled weapons it fields, and the AI-enabled operating concepts it embraces to create new ways of war."[115] While China's development and integration of AI presents a substantial risk of military advantage, and may further compress warning time and decision space, it may be difficult to equate that risk with the existential consequence nuclear weapons present. That is, whereas the use of a nuclear weapon or other WMD would certainly meet the armed attack threshold in Article 51, the same cannot be said categorically for the use of AI. Thus, absent contextually specific and compelling facts, China's effort to develop AI, standing alone, does not present a compelling case for preemptive, let alone preventive self-defense.

However, as it will be set out more fully, it is unlikely that data-poisoning operations will rise to the level of a use of force. Thus, when it comes to data poisoning or many other types of cyber sabotage, debates over the rigidity or malleability of imminence and the parameters of self-defense can quickly fall away. That is not to say cyber sabotage can never rise to the level of a use of force.[116] For example, many argue that Stuxnet constituted a use of force, although to date no state has asserted that claim. But, the vast majority of cyber operations, even those that achieve some disruptive or denial effect, fall below the use-of-force threshold, effectively mooting the issue of self-defense. And for the other protective self-help

113. DoD, *Mission Statement*, Dep't. Def., https://www.defense.gov/About/.

114. Nat'l. Sec. Comm'n. on A.I., *supra* note 4, at 75–88.

115. *Id.*

116. *See infra* Section II.B.2.

remedy recognized in international law—countermeasures—the prevailing view is that they can never be employed anticipatorily, let alone preemptively or preventively.[117] As such, whether preventive cyber sabotage can be conducted consonant with international law turns first on a determination of whether a particular operation, as designed, would itself constitute a breach of the executing state's international legal obligations other than the prohibition on using force. It is to this question we turn next.

2. Cyber Sabotage Operating Below the Use of Force Threshold

The most concrete rule of international law imposing obligations on states is the prohibition on the use of force. Applying this long-standing prohibition in the cyber context has proved challenging but data-poisoning operations are unlikely to cross established thresholds. Because the prohibition on the use of force has long been understood to apply to states' adversarial interactions regardless of the weapons or other means employed, it follows that "[c]yber operations may in certain circumstances constitute uses of force within the meaning of Article 2(4) of the Charter of the United Nations and customary international law."[118] Yet despite Article 2(4) being one of the most consequential proscriptions in international law, the Charter contains no definition of the term "threat or use of force." Nor is there a generally agreed-on standard among states by which to determine whether an action crosses the use of force threshold. This is particularly true of cyber "threats."[119] As a result, states have yet to achieve consensus as to the contours of Article 2(4)'s prohibition generally; uncertainty that has carried over to and plagued application of the prohibition in the cyber context.[120]

The most commonly repeated refrain from states that have publicly addressed this question is that, at a minimum, cyber operations causing the same or similar effects as those that would be considered a use of force if caused through traditional physical means would be treated equally under the *jus ad bellum*.[121] The

---

117. The authors do not agree with this interpretation. *See infra* Section II.D.2.b.

118. DoD LoW Manual, *supra* note 54, at ¶ 16.3.1 (citing Koh); Tallinn Manual 2.0, *supra* note 74; Legality of the Threat or Use of Nuclear Weapons, Advisory Opinion, International Court of Justice (ICJ), July 8, 1996, ¶ 39.

119. Duncan B. Hollis & Tsvetelina van Benthem, "Chapter 2: Threatening Force in Cyberspace."

120. Corn, *supra* note 89; *see* Laurent Gisel et al., *Twenty Years On: International Humanitarian Law and the Protection of Civilians Against the Effects of Cyber Operations During Armed Conflicts*, 102 Int'l Rev. Red Cross 287, 307 (2020).

121. DoD LoW Manual, *supra* note 54, at ¶ 16.3.1 (Citing Koh, International Law in Cyberspace, *supra* note 74, at 4); Jeremy Wright, *Cyber and International Law in the 21st Century*, Gov.uk (May 23, 2018) (speech), https://www.gov.uk/government/speeches/cyber-and-international-law-in-the-21st-century; DFAT, *Australia's Position on the Application of International Law to State Conduct in Cyberspace*, Dep't. Foreign Aff. and Trade (2019), *https://www.internation alcybertech.gov.au/sites/default/files/2020-11/2019%20Legal%20Supplment_0.PDF.*

circularity of this truism should be apparent, and the examples generally offered, operations such as causing a nuclear power plant to melt down or causing destructive floods by opening a dam, are too obvious to provide much interpretive value.[122]

Ultimately, whether any particular cyber operation amounts to a use of force is a highly contextual question that can turn on multiple variables; the focus of the inquiry ultimately being on the consequences of the operation and the attendant circumstances, not the modality used.[123] Taking notice of the ICJ's *Nicaragua* judgment, in which the court employed a "scale and effects" test to measure whether an action amounted to an armed attack, the Tallinn Manual 2.0 recommends a similar approach for use of force determinations.[124] The Manual goes on to suggest a number of factors that states would likely consider in assessing the scale and effects flowing from a cyber operation: factors such as the severity of harm generated, the military character of the operation, the immediacy and directness of the impacts, and the measurability of the effects.[125] A growing number of states have similarly endorsed what is in effect a totality of the circumstances approach.[126]

Within this framing, a number of states and experts have coalesced around the view that generally, an action proximately causing death or injury to persons or physical damage or destruction to objects would likely qualify as an unlawful use of force regardless of the means used.[127] Some view this as a near bright-line test, relegating the totality-of-the-circumstances approach only to situations not involving such physical harms. For instance, the Tallinn Manual 2.0 states that "[a]cts that injure or kill persons or physically damage or destroy objects

---

122. *See* DoD LoW Manual, *supra* note 54, at ¶ 16.3.1.

123. DoD LoW Manual, *supra* note 54, at ¶ 16.3.1 (citing Koh); Tallinn Manual 2.0, *supra* note 74; Gov't. NL *Appendix: International Law in Cyberspace*, Gov't. NL (Sept. 26, 2019) ("The government endorses the generally accepted position that each case must be examined individually to establish whether the 'scale and effects' are such that an operation may be deemed a violation of the prohibition of use of force.") (hereinafter "Netherlands Statement"), https://www.government.nl/documents/parliamentary-documents/2019/09/26/letter-to-the-parliament-on-the-international-legal-order-in-cyberspace.

124. Tallinn Manual 2.0, *supra* note 74, at 330–31; *See also* Netherlands Statement, *supra* note 123.

125. Tallinn Manual 2.0, *supra* note 74, at 334–36.

126. *See, e.g.*, Netherlands statement, *supra* note 123; Jack Kenny, *France, Cyber Operations and Sovereignty: The "Purist" Approach to Sovereignty and Contradictory State Practice*, Lawfare (Mar. 12, 2021), https://www.lawfareblog.com/france-cyber-operations-and-sovereignty-purist-approach-sovereignty-and-contradictory-state-practice; DoD LoW Manual, *supra* note 54, at ¶ 5.9.3.

127. Tallinn Manual 2.0, *supra* note 74, at 328 (quoting Legality of the Threat or Use of Nuclear Weapons (Advisory Opinion), 1996 I.C.J. 226, ¶ 39 (July 1996) (The *jus ad bellum* applies to "any use of force, regardless of the weapons employed.")).

are uses of force."[128] However, neither state practice nor *opinio juris* "demonstrate that the borders of 'force' precisely coincide with armed force, i.e., physical or kinetic force applied by conventional weaponry."[129] Thus, while the use of "armed force" resulting in physical harms likely creates a strong presumption that an action constitutes a use of force, "the (actual or anticipated) physical destruction of property, injury and death" are better viewed as "[f]actors in considering the scale and effects. . . ." attendant to a particular operation.[130] Either way, by this measuring stick most of the historical examples of sabotage previously described would likely be considered uses of force, and, absent a qualifying exception, internationally wrongful acts. For this reason, international lawyers often cite Stuxnet as an instance of a use of force by cyber means, despite any official condemnations as such.[131]

However, while many consider death, injury, or physical damage or destruction to objects as the *sine qua non* of a use of force, determining what consequences amount to damage or destruction in the cyber context is no easy task. What types of cyber-generated effects qualify either qualitatively or quantitatively as damage or destruction is an open question, as is the meaning of "objects" in the cyber context.[132] According to U.S. military doctrine, offensive cyberspace operations (OCO) can "create noticeable denial effects (i.e., degradation, disruption, or destruction) in cyberspace or manipulation that leads to denial effects in the physical domains."[133] In other words, OCO can range from low-level, temporary impacts "deny[ing] access to, or operation of, a [targeted device or system] to a level represented as a percentage of capacity" to "completely and irreparably deny[ing] access to, or operation of" those devices or systems, and ultimately to causing through manipulation of those targets physical effects, including destruction, outside of cyberspace.[134] Given the wide range of impacts that cyber

---

128. TALLINN MANUAL 2.0, *supra* note 74, at 333. However, with regard to the severity factor, the *Tallinn Manual* qualifies this statement slightly, asserting it is "[s]ubject to a *de minimis* rule." *Id.* at 334.

129. Michael N. Schmitt, *Computer Network Attack and the Use of Force in International Law: Thoughts on a Normative Framework*, 37 COLUM. J. TRANSNAT'L L. 885, 908 (1999).

130. UK Gov't, *Application of International Law to States' Conduct in Cyberspace: UK Statement*, FOREIGN, COMMONWEALTH AND DEV. OFF. (June 3, 2021), https://www.gov.uk/government/publications/application-of-international-law-to-states-conduct-in-cyberspace-uk-statement/application-of-international-law-to-states-conduct-in-cyberspace-uk-statement.

131. TALLIN MANUAL 2.0, *supra* note 74.

132. *Id.* at 334; Brian J. Egan, *Remarks on International Law and Stability in Cyberspace*, U.S. DEP'T. STATE (Nov. 10, 2016) (speech), https://2009-2017.state.gov/s/l/releases/remarks/264303.htm.

133. Dep't of the Army, Joint Chiefs of Staff, JP 3-12 CYBERSPACE OPERATIONS, II-7 (June 8, 2018) [hereinafter JP 3-12], https://www.jcs.mil/Portals/36/Documents/Doctrine/pubs/jp3_12.pdf.

134. *Id.*

"Attacking" Big Data

operations can cause, both in the physical world and within cyberspace, the lack of an agreed taxonomy of qualifying harms is significant.[135]

While this issue has garnered much attention in the specific context of the *jus in bello* rules regulating "attacks,"[136] the same cannot be said when it comes to defining non-*de minimis* damage or destruction for purposes of applying the *jus ad bellum*. Even in the more developed discussions regarding *jus in bello* rules, interpretive questions about qualifying harms linger when it comes to cyber operations.

There is little question that cyber-generated denial effects causing damage and destruction in the physical world constitute *in bello* attacks. The same is true for operations that "completely and irreparably deny access to, or operation of" a target within cyberspace.[137] Causing damage to cyber infrastructure and devices entirely within cyberspace, one of the specified doctrinal objectives of offensive military cyberspace operations, is well understood to qualify as the requisite type of destructive harm.[138] However, it is presently far from certain that some lesser impact on the functionality of a targeted device or system is sufficient to satisfy the attack definition, especially where the restoration of functionality would not require the replacement of physical components of the affected device.[139] At least

135. Corn, *supra* note 91, at 354 ("[C]yber operations can generate a wide range of effects in both scope and scale, from subtle manipulation to significant destruction, directly within and against components of cyberspace as well as indirectly against the external systems and users that depend on it").

136. The prohibitions on attacking civilians or civilian objects, the ban on indiscriminate attacks, and the rules of precaution and proportionality are among the most central to the *jus in bello* framework regulating the conduct of hostilities, where the term attack bears specific legal meaning—"acts of violence against the adversary, whether in the offense or in the defence." Protocol Additional to the Geneva Conventions of 12 August 1949, and Relating to the Protection of Victims of International Armed Conflicts, Art. 49(1), June 8, 1977, 1125 U.N.T.S. 3 [hereinafter AP I]. As in the *jus ad bellum* context, the assessment of whether is something constitutes an act of violence focuses on the consequence, not the modality used. *See* TALLIN MANUAL 2.0, *supra* note 74 at 415. Violence, in turn, is widely understood to refer somewhat narrowly to the consequences of death or injury to persons or physical damage to or destruction of tangible objects. *See* TALLIN MANUAL 2.0, *supra* note 74 at 415–16; Roy Schöndorf, *Israel's Perspective on Key Legal and Practical Issues Concerning the Application of International Law to Cyber Operations*, 97 INT'L L. STUD. 395, 400 ("The requirement for physical damage has been accepted law since the introduction of the legal term of art "attack" into the LOAC discourse."). Applying the "act of violence" standard to traditional military operations is fairly straight forward, but has proved challenging in the cyber context with little publicly available evidence of state practice to draw from.

137. For example, irreversibly encrypting a computer hard drive or permanently rendering the logic board inoperable.

138. JP 3-12, *supra* note 133, at II-7 ("Cyberspace attack actions create noticeable denial effects (i.e., degradation, disruption, or destruction) in cyberspace or manipulation that leads to denial effects in the physical domains.").

139. *See* TALLIN MANUAL 2.0, *supra* note 74, at 417–18 (a majority, but not all, of the drafters, took the view that where restoration of functionality requires replacement of physical

one state, Israel, rejects the notion that loss of functionality alone constitutes damage within the meaning of the *jus in bello*.[140]

Of perhaps greater relevance to the present discussion is the prevailing view that data, because they are not tangible, do not qualify as an "object" within the meaning accorded that term in the *jus in bello*.[141] Therefore, data as such cannot be made the object of an attack or act of violence and, as a consequence, data poisoning or other operations to delete or alter data would not be subject to the *jus in bello* rules of distinction, precautions, or proportionality.[142] Other *jus in bello* principles might come into play, but the stricter prescriptions on targeting that flow from engaging in acts of violence against an adversary in armed conflict are simply not triggered.

Whether the debates over how to apply the *jus in bello* attack standards in the cyber context have any relevance to the *jus ad bellum* concept of force is a fair question.[143] Nevertheless, there is some overlap in these bodies of law where notions of armed force and harm share common roots.[144] It is not unreasonable to expect understandings of the concept of *jus in bello* attack to indirectly influence the issue of whether a cyber operation executed outside of or unrelated to an existing

---

components, damage or destruction is achieved. The drafters could reach no conclusions about other situations of loss or degradation of functionality.); Schöndorf, *supra* note 136, at 401 (The term "object" encompasses only tangible things, not data).

140. Schöndorf, *supra* note 136 ("In the same vein, the mere loss or impairment of functionality to infrastructure would be insufficient in this regard, and no other specific rule to the contrary has evolved in the cyber domain.").

141. *See, e.g.*, Schmitt, *Grey Zones*, *supra* note 88, at 17–19; TALLIN MANUAL 2.0, *supra* note 74, at 437 (taking the position that data does not constitute a tangible object that can be attacked within the meaning of article 49(1) of AP I).

142. Schöndorf, *supra* note 136, at 401 (As Israel correctly notes, however, "when an operation involving the deletion or alteration of computer data is still reasonably expected to cause physical damage to objects or persons and fulfills the other elements required to constitute an attack, the operation would be subject to LOAC targeting rules.").

143. As a body of *lex specialis*, the *jus in bello* applies in a different context, serves very distinct purposes, and the interpretive debates described above draw on specific treaty terms, travaux préparatoires, and official commentaries. Thus, "[a]s a strict matter of law . . . the [law of armed conflict], to include its concept and definition of attack, is inapplicable to . . . cyber operations conducted outside of armed conflict." Corn, *supra* note 91, at 407.

144. For example, an *ad bellum* use of force, in so much as it involves a resort to armed force, may concurrently initiate armed conflict between the responsible and victim states, and thus trigger application of the *jus in bello*. *See generally* DoD LoW MANUAL, *supra* note 54, ¶ 3.5 (discussing relationship between jus ad bellum and jus in bello); TALLINN MANUAL 2.0, *supra* note 74, at 381–83 (discussing armed hostilities requirement for triggering the *jus in bello*); Michael N. Schmitt, *Providing Arms and Materiel to Ukraine: Neutrality, Co-Belligerency, and the Use of Force*, ARTICLES OF WAR (Mar. 7, 2022), https://lieber.westpoint.edu/ukraine-neutrality-co-belligerency-use-of-force (discussing relationship between *jus ad bellum* and *jus in bello*).

armed conflict amounts to a use of force.[145] Applying these understandings to the *jus ad bellum* analysis, cyber operations directed against AI datasets, such as data poisoning, would not amount to damage or destruction of objects and thus not support the presumption of being a use of force.

Conversely, while armed force and physical harm are indicative elements of a use of force, the International Court of Justice has stated that actions short of actual armed interventions can violate the use-of-force prohibition, and there is a growing view among states that nonphysical cyber harms may also cross the use of force threshold. For example, in 2019 the Netherlands noted that "at this time it cannot be ruled out that a cyber operation with a very serious financial or economic impact may qualify as a use of force."[146] France adopted a similar position that same year.[147] In a similar vein, the U.S. Department of Defense notes that "cyber operations that cripple a military's logistics systems, and thus its ability to conduct and sustain military operations, might also be considered a use of force under the *jus ad bellum*."[148]

Based on the foregoing, one cannot exclude the possibility that an offensive, counter-AI cyber operation, even one designed only to corrupt, manipulate, or deny data being used to research and develop AI, would constitute a use of force or at least run the risk of the victim state construing it as such. Much might depend on the perceived criticality of the targeted data or AI system to the state's security or other core sovereign interests.[149]

For example, assume that China has developed a set of training data central to its ability to develop an AI tool that would create unacceptable risk to U.S. national security. In response, the United States gains access to the training data

---

145. *See, e.g.*, Netherlands Statement, *supra* note 123 (The government believes that cyber operations can fall within the scope of the prohibition of the use of force, particularly when the effects of the operation are comparable to those of *a conventional act of violence* covered by the prohibition. (emphasis added)).

146. Minister of Foreign Affairs to the President [Netherlands], *Letter to the Parliament on the International Legal Order in Cyberspace*, Gov. NL. (July 5, 2019), https://www.government.nl/documents/parliamentary-documents/2019/09/26/letter-to-the-parliament-on-the-internatio nal-legal-order-in-cyberspace.

147. French Ministry of the Armies, *International Law Applicable to Operations in Cyber Space*, Ministre Des Armees (Sept. 2019), https://www.defense.gouv.fr/content/download/567648/9770527/file/international+law+applied+to+operations+in+cyberspace.pdf.

148. DoD LoW Manual, *supra* note 52, at ¶ 16.3.1.

149. *See, e.g.*, Dep't Defense, Office of the General Counsel, An Assessment of International Legal Issues in Information Operations (2d ed., Nov. 1999), *reprinted in* 76 U.S. Naval War College Int'l. L. Stud. 459, 483 (2002) ("Even if the systems attacked were unclassified military logistics systems, an attack on such systems might seriously threaten a nation's security. For example, corrupting the data in a nation's computerized systems for managing its military fuel, spare parts, transportation, troop mobilization, or medical supplies may seriously interfere with its ability to conduct military operations. In short, the consequences are likely to be more important than the means used.").

and corrupts it, making it unusable to train the AI tool. While many might consider this action as too attenuated and lacking in scale and effects to rise to the level of a use of force, depending on the AI's stage of development and the importance China places on it, it may reach a different conclusion. Ultimately, the further along the development process of an AI system and the closer it is to actual procurement and deployment, the greater the risk that under a totality of the circumstances analysis, it will be perceived as, if not correctly deemed to be, a use of force. However, based on current understandings of the use-of-force prohibition, especially in the cyber context, operations that merely interfere with or corrupt training and development data will not likely reach the use-of-force threshold. That does not mean, however, that such an operation might not breach other established rules of international law.

C. The Prohibition on Intervention

Based on the above analysis, it seems unlikely that international law would preclude an act of non-destructive "cybotage" as a use of force in violation of article 2(4) of the UN Charter. However, that determination is not conclusive as to the legality of such an action against China's data. Other accepted restraints on the actions of states may present legal barriers to actions of sabotage. Primary among these is the rule of prohibited intervention.

The principle of nonintervention "forbids all States or groups of States to intervene directly or indirectly in internal or external affairs of other States."[150] It is a proscription with a long history and is well recognized in customary international law,[151] even if the exact parameters of the principle remain vague and elusive.[152] Like the use-of-force prohibition, there is broad and growing consensus among states that the nonintervention rule "applies with full force to states' activities in cyberspace."[153]

Many look to the ICJ's *Nicaragua* judgment[154] as presenting an authoritative description of this principle, where the Court stated:

150. Military and Paramilitary Activities in and Against Nicaragua (Nicar. v. U.S.), Judgment, 1986 I.C.J. Rep. 14, ¶ 206 (June 27).

151. *Id.* at ¶ 174, 202.

152. Chatham House, The Application of International Law to State Cyberattacks, ¶ 80 (Dec. 2, 2019), https://www.chathamhouse.org/2019/12/application-international-law-state-cyberattacks/3-application-non-intervention-principle; Gary P. Corn, *Punching on the Edges of the Grey Zone: Iranian Cyber Threats and State Cyber Responses*, Just Sec. (Feb. 11, 2020), https://www.justsecurity.org/68622/punching-on-the-edges-of-the-grey-zone-iranian-cyber-threats-and-state-cyber-responses/.

153. Corn, *supra* note 91, at 413; Tallinn Manual 2.0 *supra* note 74, at 312 (rule 66: "A State may not intervene, including by cyber means, in the internal or external affairs of another State.").

154. Nicar v. U.S., 1986, I.C.J.

"Attacking" Big Data

A prohibited intervention must accordingly be one bearing on matters in which each State is permitted, by the principle of State sovereignty, to decide freely. One of these is the choice of a political, economic, social and cultural system, and the formulation of foreign policy. Intervention is wrongful when it uses methods of coercion in regard to such choices, which must remain free ones. The element of coercion, which defines, and indeed forms the very essence of, prohibited intervention, is particularly obvious in the case of an intervention which uses force, either in the direct form of military action, or in the indirect form of support for subversive or terrorist armed activities within another State.[155]

This statement characterizes the principle of nonintervention as containing two necessary elements: an act of coercion aimed at the state's domaine réservé. This definitional construct has become the standard that is generally accepted in international law,[156] and is accepted as applicable to cyber operations as well.[157] As one of the authors has previously argued, the ICJ's description must be understood within the context of the unique facts presented in that case and thus against the backdrop of forcible military action.[158] But as the ICJ also made clear, the rule can be violated by both forcible and non-forcible means.[159] Therefore, an offensive counter-AI cyber operation to corrupt data may be precluded as unlawful if under the circumstances the operation impacts the domain réservé in a coercive manner. Key to this assessment is understanding these two ill-defined elements, which will be discussed in turn below.

1. Domain Réservé

Of the two elements of prohibited intervention, domaine réservé is likely the easiest one to conceptualize. The purpose of the rule is to prevent certain forms of

---

155. *Id.* at ¶ 206.

156. Philip Kunig, *Intervention, Prohibition of*, OXFORD PUBLIC INT'L. L. (Apr. 2008), https://opil-ouplaw-com.proxlaw.byu.edu/view/10.1093/law:epil/9780199231690/law-9780199231690-e1434?rskey=vGJhgS&result=1&prd=OPIL.

157. Group of Governmental Experts on Developments in the Field of Information and Telecommunications in the Context of International Security, A/70/174, ¶ 26 (July 22, 2015), which states 26. In considering the application of international law to State use of ICTs, the Group identified as of central importance the commitments of States to the following principles of the Charter and other international law: sovereign equality; the settlement of international disputes by peaceful means in such a manner that international peace and security and justice are not endangered; refraining in their international relations from the threat or use of force against the territorial integrity or political independence of any State, or in any other manner inconsistent with the purposes of the United Nations; respect for human rights and fundamental freedoms; and non-intervention in the internal affairs of other States.

158. Corn, *supra* note 152.

159. Military and Paramilitary Activities in and Against Nicaragua (Nicar. v. U.S.), Judgment, 1986 I.C.J. Rep. 14, ¶ 206 (June 27); *see also,* Corn, *supra* note 58, at 6.

"interference by one state in the affairs, internal or external, of another," where the "affairs" encompasses only those "matters which, as a function of sovereignty, are reserved in international law to the sole prerogative of states."[160] Thus, as stated by the ICJ in the quote above, a State's domaine réservé is a protected space within the sphere of sovereignty in which the State can dictate and enforce its own affairs (political, economic, social, etc.). Any actions by another state to coercively constrain this agency (a State's domaine réservé) are generally prohibited.[161]

Explained further, "[t]he quintessential example of a violation of the principle of nonintervention is one State coercively interfering in the internal political process of another State, such as by altering the votes recorded and thereby altering the results of an election."[162] The United Kingdom has stated that intervention in the fundamental operation of Parliament or in the stability of the financial system would "surely be a breach of the prohibition on intervention."[163] Indeed, some observers have claimed that the Russian meddling in both the U.S. and European elections,[164] as well as its misinformation campaign concerning Covid,[165] were examples of violations of the principle of nonintervention. The formulation and execution of policy regarding foreign affairs and national defense would plainly fall within each state's domaine réservé.

The concept of sovereign prerogative is not without limits, however, and those "domains or activities" not strictly reserved to the state are potentially subject to foreign action.[166] For example, matters otherwise subject to international legal regulation, such as human rights, may benefit from less protection or fall outside the rule's ambit all together.[167] Ultimately, "the full contours of a State's domaine

---

160. Corn, *supra* note 152 (quoting Openheim).

161. With the exception of interventions based on human rights violations that are conducted through the proper channels.

162. Chatham House, *The Principle of Non-Intervention in Contemporary International Law: Non-Interference in a State's Internal Affairs Used to be a Rule of International Law: Is it Still?*, (Feb. 28, 2007).

163. Wright, *supra* note 121.

164. Steven J. Barela, *Cross-Border Cyber Ops to Erode Legitimacy: An Act of Coercion*, JUST SEC. (Jan. 12, 2017), https://www.justsecurity.org/36212/cross-border-cyber-ops-erode-legitimacy-act-coercion/; Ellen Nakashima, *Russia's Apparent Meddling in U.S. Election Is Not an Act of War, Cyber Expert Says*, WASH. POST (Feb. 7, 2017), https://www.washingtonpost.com/news/checkpoint/wp/2017/02/07/russias-apparent-meddling-in-u-s-election-is-not-an-act-of-war-cyber-expert-says/.

165. Gary P. Corn, *Coronavirus Disinformation and the Need for States to Shore Up International Law*, LAWFAREBLOG (Apr. 2, 2020), https://www.lawfareblog.com/coronavirus-disinformation-and-need-states-shore-international-law; Jennifer Rankin, *Russian Media "Spreading Covid-19 disinformation,"* GUARDIAN (Mar. 18, 2020), https://www.theguardian.com/world/2020/mar/18/russian-media-spreading-covid-19-disinformation.

166. Jens David Ohlin, *Did Russian Cyber Interference in the 2016 Election Violate International Law?*, 95 TEXAS L. REV. 1579, 1588 (2017).

167. Corn, *supra* note 58, at 8–9.

réservé can only be discerned through a careful examination of State practice and *opinio juris* and the scope of a state's domaine réservé evolves over time."[168]

Also, and of particular relevance to the present discussion, it is generally accepted that a state's domaine réservé does not extend to purely commercial activities, even if engaged in by state-owned enterprises.[169] Where AI R&D is done in the labs of commercial tech companies, it may fall outside the zone of protection, especially where the AI is being developed for some general, undefined future use. However, this question is clouded by the nature and structure of China's command economy, where the line between commercial and state activities is often unclear. The division between purely commercial and sovereign government activities also breaks down when the R&D is done pursuant to government tasking, contracts, or funding, especially when the specific purpose of the R&D is to develop military or other national security applications or capabilities. Ultimately, it would take a deep factual analysis to assess the nexus of the relevant data and R&D efforts to a protected sovereign prerogative, and perhaps the stage of the R&D effort, in order to determine whether the activity falls within China's domaine réservé and is thus protected against coercive intervention.

2. Coercion

The second element of a wrongful intervention is that the action must be coercive in nature. Although frequently described in terms of interference, "international law only proscribes [intervention] as wrongful; '[i]nterference pure and simple is not intervention.'"[170] Indeed, the element of coercion serves as the dividing "line between minor interference and unfriendly acts on the one hand, and intervention sufficient to breach the prohibition on non-intervention on the other."[171] To constitute a prohibited intervention, it is often said that the state actions at issue "must be forcible or dictatorial, or otherwise coercive, in effect depriving the state intervened against of control over the matter in question."[172] Schmitt notes that,

> an act of coercion is one that deprives another State of choice by either causing that State to behave in a way it otherwise would not or to refrain from acting in a manner in which it otherwise would act. Merely influencing the other State's choice does not suffice; the choice to act or not has to effectively be taken off the table in the sense that a reasonable State in the same or similar circumstances would no longer consider it to be a viable option . . . [T]here

---

168. TALLINN MANUAL 2.0, *supra* note 74, at 314.

169. Schmitt, *Grey Zones, supra* note 11, at 7; TALLINN MANUAL 2.0, *supra* note 74, at 315.

170. Corn, *supra* note 91 (quoting 1 LASSA OPPENHEIM, OPPENHEIM'S INTERNATIONAL LAW, 432 (Sir Robert Jennings & Sir Arthur Watts eds., 9th ed. 1992) [hereinafter "Oppenheim"]).

171. Chatham House report, *supra* note 152, at ¶¶ 84–85.

172. Oppenheim, *supra* note 170, at 432.

must be a relationship between coercion and the domaine réservé; the State conducting the operation has to seek to deprive the target State of choice with respect to its behavior or policies involving a domaine réservé.[173]

Non-forceful, yet coercive, intervention is now well recognized as internationally wrongful, though the exact line between pressure or influence and coercion remains blurred and "will vary in each case according to the facts."[174] Nevertheless, a prohibited intervention "encompass[es] actions involving some level of subversion or usurpation of a victim state's protected prerogatives."[175] As one of the authors has argued, the rule is best "understood as prohibiting measures calculated and likely to deprive, subordinate, or substantially impair the right of independence in governance, and such interventions are wrongful even if inchoate or unsuccessful."[176]

Nevertheless, there is little in the way of concrete examples, let alone state practice, of non-forcible measures that have been deemed to be coercive within the meaning of the nonintervention rule, indicating that the requisite threshold of consequence remains high.

In the cyber context, the issue of coercion remains somewhat unclear. Schmitt provides two excellent examples to help clarify coercive versus non-coercive uses of cyber capabilities.

To illustrate, using autonomous cyber capabilities to spread disinformation during an election is a noxious form of influence, but it is not necessarily coercive, for voters (the State) retain their ability to decide for whom to vote. But using autonomous cyber capabilities to disrupt the operation of voting machinery or alter vote counts would certainly be coercive because the very ability of members of the electorate to exercise political choice has been denied. . . .

An often-misunderstood dynamic of the prohibition involves the relationship between the coercion and the domaine réservé. The domaine réservé is not the physical target of the operation. Rather, it is that area of activity that the cyber operation is meant to coerce. Consider a State's covert cyber operation that employs autonomous capabilities in a ransomware attack against the sole international port facility of another State. To assess whether the operation constitutes unlawful intervention, it is necessary to determine why the former is conducting that hostile activity. If it is merely a criminal

---

173. Michael N. Schmitt, *Autonomous Cyber Capabilities and the International Law of Sovereignty and Intervention*, 96 INT'L L. STUD. 549, 561, 567 (2020).

174. Chatham House report, *supra* note 152, at ¶ 86.

175. Gary Corn & Eric Jensen, *The Technicolor Zone of Cyberspace—Part I*, JUST SEC. (May 30, 2018), https://www.justsecurity.org/57217/technicolor-zone-cyberspace-part/.

176. Corn, *supra* note 58, at 12.

attempt to acquire funds, it is not coercive vis-a-vis any domaine réservé. However, if designed to force the State to, for instance, alter its trade practice by creating a situation in which there is no choice but to transship through the attacker's logistics network, the relationship between the coercive operation and a domaine réservé exists.[177]

These two examples shed light on the question of whether corruption of data is a coercive act. First, the nature of the data is not the key legal factor. Whether the data is private or public, government or non-government, may have significance with respect to the domaine réservé, but has little bearing on whether the act is coercive. Additionally, the act of corruption itself is not the key legal issue. Rather, what matters is the intended outcome of the data corruption. If the United States intends to dictate China's actions or deprive China of some option by corrupting the data, it may be coercive. This analysis would be done on a case-by-case basis, and would be analyzed against current state practice, of which there are, admittedly, few, if any, clear examples of coercive cyber interventions.

In assessing the potential that an offensive counter-AI operation involving data poisoning would breach the nonintervention rule, it would be necessary to determine, among other facts, whether the data targeted is part of R&D efforts being conducted by a commercial enterprise, the degree of state direction or involvement in the R&D process, the intended end use of the AI (i.e., whether it is intended for civilian, economic, or national defense purposes), and the proximity of the AI capability to actual employment. Given the overall uncertainty surrounding the rule's application in the cyber context, it difficult to rule out the possibility that a particular operation would be deemed wrongful. But neither is it possible to exclude the possibility that operations could be designed in ways that would fall outside of the rule's purview as either non-coercive actions or actions not aimed at elements of domaine réservé, or both. Where an operation implicates the nonintervention rule, a further assessment would be needed to determine whether it could proceed as a countermeasure as discussed next. For operations that would not amount to an intervention, at present international law would not stand as a clear bar to action.

D. A Note on Sovereignty in Cyberspace

The principle of sovereignty and how it applies in the realm of cyberspace is a complex and multifaceted issue. The United States has acknowledged for some time that when states conduct activities in cyberspace, they "must take into account the sovereignty of other States, including outside the context of armed conflict."[178] However, what exactly sovereignty connotes, how a state takes account of

177. Schmitt, *supra* note 173, at 561–622.

178. Egan, *supra* note 132 (quoting Koh speech).

another's sovereignty, and whether doing so stems from a binding legal obligation, are highly contested and unsettled questions.

Certainly sovereignty, "as a general principle, is a fundamental concept in international law."[179] It serves as a "basic constitutional doctrine of the law of nations," and is at the core of prohibitions like those in Article 2(4) and the rule of nonintervention.[180] In broad terms, it refers to "the collection of rights held by a state, first in its capacity as the entity entitled to exercise control over its territory and second in its capacity to act on the international plane, representing that territory and its people."[181] It is understood as encompassing "the whole body of rights and attributes which a state possesses in its territory, to the exclusion of all other states, and also in its relation with other states."[182]

But as much as sovereignty implicates freedom from certain outside interference, it also conveys freedom of action on the international plane.[183] Prohibitions on the activities of states in the conduct of their international relations cannot be presumed.[184] Rather, any prohibition, "whether in relation to cyberspace or other matters, must be clearly established either in customary international law or in a treaty binding upon the States concerned."[185]

According to the Tallinn Manual 2.0, sovereignty is more than just a general concept or the definer of a state's legal personality. It operates as just such a stand-alone rule of international law that proscribes certain state cyber operations; a view that some states have now publicly endorsed.[186] However, even among those states and experts that endorse this view, there is little consensus regarding the content of this purported rule, and some have indicted the Tallinn Manual 2.0

---

179. Application of international law to states' conduct in cyberspace: UK statement, *supra* note 130.

180. Corn, *supra* note 91, at 414 (quoting Crawford, *supra* note 362, at 447).

181. James Crawford, Brownlie's Principles of Public International Law 448 (8th ed. 2012).

182. Corfu Channel (U.K. v. Alb.), Merits, 1949 ICJ REP. 4, 43 (Apr. 9) (individual opinion by Alvarez J.).

183. James Crawford, *Sovereignty as a Legal Value, in* The Cambridge Companion to International Law, 118 (James Crawford & Martti Koskenniemi eds., 2012) ("[International law] regards each state as sovereign, in the sense that it is presumed to have full authority to act not only internally but at the international level, to make (or not to make) treaties and other commitments, to relate (or not to relate) to other states in a wide variety of ways, to consent (or not to consent) to resolve international disputes.") [hereinafter Crawford, *Sovereignty as a Legal Value*].

184. The S.S. Lotus (Fr. v. Turk.), 1927 P.C.I.J. (ser. A) No. 10, at 18 (Sept. 7) ("Restrictions upon the independence of States cannot therefore be presumed.").

185. Application of International Law to States' Conduct in Cyberspace: UK Statement, *supra* note 130.

186. Corn, *supra* note 77, at 969.

approach as lacking "any practical connection to the complex interplay of extensive state practice and *opinio juris* that constitutes customary international law."[187]

Other states, however, have tacked in a decidedly different direction. Lead among them is the United Kingdom, which in 2018 announced its view that as a matter of current international law, it could not "extrapolate from that general principle [of sovereignty] a specific rule or additional prohibition for cyber activity beyond that of a prohibited intervention."[188] It reiterated this stance in its 2021 submission to the United Nations Group of Governmental Experts (UNGGE) process.[189] Similarly, Israel has also gone on record as questioning whether cyber operations can ever constitute breaches of territorial sovereignty under existing international law, or whether "our understanding of territorial sovereignty in cyberspace is substantively different from its meaning in the physical world."[190]

While the United States has yet to take a definitive stance on the sovereignty question, neither has it been a fence sitter or completely opaque, and all indications are that it is not aligned with or prepared to endorse the Tallinn Manual 2.0 approach. In several official speeches on the subject, the United States has noted its clear position that "remote cyber operations involving computers or other networked devices located on another State's territory do not constitute a per se violation of international law."[191] And from the perspective of the Department of Defense, the public silence of states in the "face of countless publicly known cyber intrusions into foreign networks precludes a conclusion that States have coalesced around a common view that there is an international prohibition against all such operations" under a general rule of sovereignty.[192] In other words, the United Kingdom's view is the most accurate account of this issue, and one with which the DoD "shares similarities. . . ."[193] Therefore, there is little to indicate that the United States would consider sovereignty a bar to conducting counter-AI cyber

---

187. Jack Goldsmith & Alex Loomis, *"Defend Forward" and Sovereignty*, HOOVER INST. 2 (Apr. 29, 2021) https://www.hoover.org/research/defend-forward-and-sovereignty.

188. Wright, *supra* note 121.

189. Application of international law to states' conduct in cyberspace: UK Statement, *supra* note 127 ("The United Kingdom does not consider that the general concept of sovereignty by itself provides a sufficient or clear basis for extrapolating a specific rule or additional prohibition for cyber conduct going beyond that of non-intervention.").

190. Schöndorf, *supra* note 136, at 403.

191. Egan, *supra* note 132. According to the former Brian Egan, the former Legal Adviser to the U.S. Department of State, "This is perhaps most clear where such activities in another State's territory have no effects or de minimis effects." *Id.*

192. Hon. Paul C. Ney, Jr., *DOD General Counsel Remarks at U.S. Cyber Command Legal Conference*, DEP'T. DEFENSE (Mar. 2, 2020) (speech), https://www.defense.gov/News/Speeches/Speech/Article/2099378/dod-general-counsel-remarks-at-us-cyber-command-legal-conference//.

193. *Id.*

operations that fall below the threshold of a use of force or that do not violate the rule of nonintervention.

As we have seen, one cannot say that all sub-use of force, offensive counter-AI cyber operations would be per se violations of international law. But, as also demonstrated, depending on the circumstances some might risk violating the rule of prohibited intervention. Assuming arguendo that the *ex ante* review of a proposed operation determines it would amount to an internationally wrongful act, could the United States nevertheless proceed consistent with international law by invoking the justification of countermeasures? For the reasons that follow, that would be a steep climb.

Like national self-defense, the principle of countermeasures justifies state actions that would otherwise constitute breaches of international law. Countermeasures include unlawful actions below the use-of-force threshold that are rendered lawful when taken for the sole purpose of causing another state to desist in its unlawful conduct.[194] Countermeasures do not extend to acts of retaliation or retribution.[195] The purpose of countermeasures is to induce the breaching state to desist in its unlawful conduct and bring about a return to the *status quo ante* between the states involved. As such, the unlawful act triggering the countermeasure must be ongoing or reasonably assessed to be one in a series of wrongful acts, and the countermeasure or measures must be terminated as soon as the responsible state complies with its obligations.[196]

Thus, invoking countermeasures as a basis to preclude the wrongfulness of a counter-AI operation would first require an assessment of whether China's mere efforts to develop AI capabilities, even for military purposes, amount to an internationally wrongful act. If not, would those efforts present a sufficient enough threat of future violation to justify invoking countermeasures preventively? We next turn to these questions.

1. The Development of AI as an Internationally Wrongful Act

Because of the strict definition of a prohibited intervention explained above, the United States would have to determine that the compilation and development of data was, even at this embryonic stage, coercive against the United States' domaine réservé. This argument has little, if any, basis in international practice. By analogy, to make this argument, one would have to argue that gathering steel and other materials and drawing up plans for a new piece of weaponry such as a battle tank or artillery piece was sufficient to elicit a response from some other state that might feel threatened by this action. There is not historical basis for such a determination.

---

194. Michael N. Schmitt, *Peacetime Cyber Responses and Wartime Cyber Operations Under International Law: An Analytical Vade Mecum*, 8 Harv. Nat'l Sec. J. 253 (2017); Tallin Manual 2.0, *supra* note 74, at 111; Brown, *supra* note 88, at 139 & n. 81.

195. Schmitt, *supra* note 194, at 253.

196. *Id.*; Draft Articles on State Responsibility, *supra* note 73, at Art. 53.

With respect to China's AI at the R&D stage, the threat is too inchoate to be considered a prohibited intervention, even under an attempt theory. Though the eventual target may fall within the domaine résérve, there is unlikely to have been a sufficient substantial step toward coercion on behalf of China to meet the definition. As discussed, anticipating future violations of international law finds some support in the law of self-defense such as in the above-mentioned examples of preventive action, but there is nothing to indicate that this expanded temporal view has migrated from the self-defense realm to the law of countermeasures.

Supporting this argument that China's acts would not amount to an unlawful intervention, the United States and other countries are also anxiously engaged in their own AI R&D programs, as discussed earlier. For the United States to allege that China's program was an unlawful intervention, it would be similarly describing its own efforts in the same area of technology.

One more note worth clarifying concerns an attempted prohibited intervention. Most experts, including those who took part in the Tallinn Manual, agree that a State can be responsible for an attempt to unlawfully intervene in the domaine réservé of another State, even if that attempt fails.[197] Likewise, an act that is in progress but has not yet fully developed may amount to a prohibited intervention. However, in both cases, for the attempt to justify the resort to countermeasures, it would have to be more than speculative, perhaps requiring a substantial step having already been taken in order to justify an act. Given the lack of solid foundation for anticipatory countermeasures that will be discussed, China's development of AI is unlikely to cross this threshold.

2. Anticipatory Countermeasures?

Unlike the ability to act in anticipation of an armed attack as discussed earlier, convention holds that the doctrine of countermeasures contains no authority to act anticipatorily. As the authors have argued previously, "though customary law contemplates the use of anticipatory actions, including cyber actions, in self-defense to repel an imminent armed attack, there is no such option for countermeasures under international law."[198] In other words, international law requires the victim state to suffer the initial non-forcible wrong, or at least substantial step in an attempt, before authorizing otherwise illegal non-forcible responses.

Even when there is an attempt underway, anticipatory actions have not migrated to countermeasures.

For some, including the authors, this restraint on the use of countermeasures is counterproductive, particularly in the era of cyber operations.

The speed at which cyber actions occur argues for the acceptance of anticipatory countermeasures. Cyber actions occur at a speed not equaled by

---

197. Tallinn Manual 2.0, *supra* note 74, at 315.

198. Gary Corn & Eric Jensen, *The Use of Force and Cyber Countermeasures*, 32 Temple Int'l & Compar. L.J. 127, 130 (2018).

many other offensive systems. But these same cyber actions often take time to develop and require a persistent presence on the victim state's systems, including pre-attack probing and intrusions into intermediary systems. A victim state may be aware of such actions, and have the capabilities to take countermeasures in advance of the impending illegal act that would defeat or decrease its effectiveness. However, the victim state is unable to lawfully do so because the doctrine of countermeasures requires a previous illegal act prior to allowing any action. Allowing an anticipatory countermeasure that was proportional and tailored to thwart the impending illegal action would be a much better approach.[199]

However, the international community has not yet embraced the validity of anticipatory countermeasures, as it has anticipatory acts in self-defense. Thus, to the extent that poisoning China's data during the compilation and development stage is considered a non-forcible, but otherwise illegal act under international law, the United States would be legally precluded from conducting that form of non-forceful cybotage.

The above analysis elucidates that U.S. actions to corrupt data in order to prevent China from developing and employing artificial intelligence capabilities would only be a prohibited intervention under very limited and precise circumstances. For example, if the data was government data, particularly if currently held and maintained by the government with the purpose of building a capability that would support foreign policy or military action in armed conflict, and the United States corrupted that data in order to dictate a specific course of action or remove a potential course of action from potential foreign policy or armed conflict possibilities, it may be deemed a prohibited intervention.

Alternatively, if the United States believes that China is gathering data from private sources in order to create an ML or AI capability, the direct application of which is not clear or not determined, corrupting that data prior to the Chinese government's receipt of it is likely not a violation of the principle of nonintervention. However, as already discussed, it may be a violation of sovereignty, which some also view as a violation of international law.

E. The Doctrine of Necessity

Another possible option for lawfully corrupting data might be through a claim of necessity. The doctrine of necessity allows a State to act an in a manner that would otherwise be unlawful, but only under limited circumstances. In other words, an otherwise prohibited action is permissible if it:

---

199. *Id.*, 130–31 (2018).

"Attacking" Big Data

(a) is the only way for the State to safeguard an essential interest against a grave and imminent peril; and
(b) does not seriously impair an essential interest of the State or States towards which the obligation exists, or of the international community as a whole.[200]

Furthermore, the doctrine of necessity may not be invoked if:

(a) the international obligation in question excludes the possibility of invoking necessity; or
(b) the State has contributed to the situation of necessity.[201]

The Commentary to Article 25 of the Articles of State Responsibility makes clear that necessity applies only to "exceptional cases where the only way a State can safeguard an essential interest threatened by a grave and imminent peril is, for the time being, not to perform some other international obligation of lesser weight or urgency."[202] The commentary continues:

> The plea of necessity is exceptional in a number of respects. Unlike consent (art. 20), self-defence (art. 21) or countermeasures (art. 22), it is not dependent on the prior conduct of the injured State. Unlike force majeure (art. 23), it does not involve conduct which is involuntary or coerced. Unlike distress (art. 24), necessity consists not in danger to the lives of individuals in the charge of a
> State official but in a grave danger either to the essential interests of the State or of the international community as a whole. It arises where there is an irreconcilable conflict between an essential interest on the one hand and an obligation of the State invoking necessity on the other. These special features mean that necessity will only rarely be available to excuse non-performance of an obligation and that it is subject to strict limitations to safeguard against possible abuse.[203]

Prior claims of necessity include attempts to preserve natural resources or the environment[204] and attempts to delay payment of debts in order to prevent severe domestic hardship.[205] It is difficult to envision a circumstance where necessity

200. Draft Articles on State Responsibility, *supra* note 73, at Art. 25.

201. *Id.*

202. *Id.* at Art. 25, ¶ 1 (commentary).

203. *Id.* at ¶ 2.

204. *Id.* at ¶¶ 6, 9, 11, 12

205. *Id.* at ¶ 7, 8.

might be successfully claimed as a basis for violating international law in order to corrupt data. However, if a future AI capability influenced public opinion in a way that effectively removed free choice by the citizens so influenced, for example, the corrupting of the data that supported that AI would not be unlawful based on a plea of necessity.

IV. CONCLUSION

The race for global supremacy in the areas of ML and AI is well under way. China and the United States are leading contenders in that race, and see each other as competitors in what has become just another layer of strategic competition. One way which the United States might contemplate slowing down China's advancements in this area is "poisoning" its pre-AI data in an effort to prevent the actual development of usable AI.

We conclude that China's development of AI is extremely unlikely to meet the threshold of an armed attack or a use of force, denying the United States the option of responding in self-defense. We further conclude that in most cases, such R&D also does not amount to a prohibited intervention, allowing the use of countermeasures. However, this does not mean that the United States is precluded from any actions against China's AI R&D data.

We further conclude that whether military operations could be conducted consistent with international law against China's data would turn on a number of variables, because like espionage, it is not possible to identify a rule of international law that deems cyber sabotage an internationally wrongful act per se. Given current understandings and empirical evidence, cyber means could be employed to conduct sabotage in ways unlikely to rise to the level of a prohibited use of force. In some circumstances, however, such operations might constitute a form of coercive intervention into China's internal affairs, depending on the source of the data and the current position of the data on the spectrum of development, among other factors. On the other hand, carefully crafted sub-use of force counter-AI cyber operations might not implicate this rule and would not otherwise be barred by international law.

While not advocating for such actions, there appear to be legal methods to accomplish this task.

4

Attacking Big Data as a Use of Force

IDO KILOVATY* ■

I. INTRODUCTION

Since the advent of cyber operations, international law has operated on the assumption that state actors are not prohibited from breaching each other's systems to manipulate, and potentially destroy, digital data. This assumption is based on the common understanding that international law does not make acts of harm to data illegal. However, with decreasing storage costs and the emergence of large quantities of data, this assumption is increasingly questioned by both states and scholars.

This chapter seeks to challenge the assumption that all data is created equal. The current legal state of affairs affords states carte blanche to hack each other's computer systems and networks regardless of the type of data being targeted (personal vs. non-personal) and its volume (a single file vs. an entire database). Indeed, such action may lead to criminal charges initiated by the targeted state, but internationally, states rarely face any consequences or condemnation.

This chapter will argue that international law, generally, should treat Big Data differently from "small" data. More specifically, this chapter is focused on *jus ad bellum* questions pertaining to cyber operations against Big Data. Given the increasing volume of sensitive and personal data compromised by states, both pre-conflict and during conflict, the equilibrium between sovereignty (a state's

---

* Associate Professor of Law, University of Arkansas School of Law; Affiliate, Center for Law, Innovation and Creativity, Northeastern University Law School; Visiting Faculty Fellow, Center for Global Legal Challenges at Yale Law School; Affiliated Fellow, Information Society Project, Yale Law School. Many thanks to Ed Berg, Laura Dickinson, Debrae Kennedy-Mayo, and the participants of the 2021 Cybersecurity Law and Policy Scholars Conference for their helpful feedback.

Ido Kilovaty, *Attacking Big Data as a Use of Force* In: *Big Data and Armed Conflict*. Edited by: Laura A. Dickinson and Edward W. Berg, Oxford University Press. © Ido Kilovaty 2024. DOI: 10.1093/oso/9780197668610.003.0006

freedom of action in cyberspace) and the confidentiality, integrity, and availability of data ought to change.[1] To support this argument, this chapter will take two routes to conduct its analysis. First, this chapter will conceptualize Big Data, as compared to Small Data.

Second, this chapter will explore how cyber operations against data may be addressed by the *jus ad bellum*. This exercise will highlight that international law has an existing legal framework through which a subset of cyber operations against Big Data may be addressed.

Third, this chapter will offer a way to conceptualize the *jus ad bellum* in the context of cyber operations against Big Data. Today's big data is far more sensitive, revealing, and prone to misuse. For example, the compromise of a biometric data database may enable the adversary to misuse these credentials in future cyber operations as well as make powerful inferences based on the quality and quantity of the data. Therefore, Big Data should be treated differently by the use of force framework as compared to Small Data. The focus of this chapter, therefore, is on the use of force and armed attack thresholds and their application to Big Data.

Fourth, this chapter will explore some of the developments in the context of international law and cyberspace, in particular, official state statements on how the *jus ad bellum* applies to non-kinetic cyber operations. At the heart of this exploration is the observation that some states are ever more willing to extend existing *jus ad bellum* to cyber operations targeting data, though they do not dive any deeper into what they mean by "data." This deviation from the kinetic approach is heralding a shift in the way cyber operations against Big Data may be handled under the *jus ad bellum* in the future.

Finally, this chapter will make a normative argument and a methodological recommendation. Normatively, cyber operations targeting Big Data are much more devastating than cyber operations against Small Data; therefore the *jus ad bellum* framework should distinguish between the severities of the two scenarios. Methodologically, any State statements on how the use of force framework applies to non-kinetic cyber operations should explicitly distinguish between Small Data and Big Data, given the normative position that this chapter takes on the difference between the two.

This chapter therefore contributes to the current body of scholarship by arguing that not all data is created equal. Up to this point, scholarship has addressed data as a monolith, without acknowledging the changing nature, volume, and sensitivity of data which we are witnessing with the emerging Big Data environment. Scholarship to date has largely failed to distinguish between data and Big Data, which is a critical distinction to make as this chapter will argue. While the law has by and large tolerated the cyber operations against data, it has only addressed

---

1. This argument is relevant not only in the *jus ad bellum* context but also bodies of law. For example, are civilians protected during armed conflict from foreign data breaches? Does human rights law provide any protections against cyber operations implicating personal data? These questions have often, but not always, been answered in the negative for "data," but what about *big* data?

such operations against Big Data by analogy to Small Data. As will be shown in this chapter, the two operations cannot be analogized.

II. ON DATA: "SMALL" DATA AND BIG DATA

When international law scholars write about cyber operations against data, they usually refer to " "Small" Data, that is, a discrete, individualized source of data. Small Data can well consist of data from multiple sources: for example, a number of computers or servers, but the idea is that the victims can easily be identified, and the harm is somewhat isolated.[2]

In recent years, Big Data has become a concept of increasing interest in academia, industry, and government.[3] Definitions of Big Data vary depending on context, and international law does not currently have an agreed-upon definition of the term. This chapter will focus on two ways to understand Big Data — through its volume and nature.

First, Big Data can be understood by its volume. As the modifier "Big" suggests, Big Data's main characteristic is its vast volume. As one definition provides, Big Data is "the exponentially increasing amount of digital information being created by new information technologies such as mobile internet, cloud storage, social networking, and the 'internet of things'–and the advanced analytics used to process that data."[4] In other words, the technological ecosystem that we have created in the last decade is now also the biggest data mining operation in human history.

But there is a second approach to defining Big Data. Big Data can also be conceptualized through its networked nature.[5] Big Data's utility is not primarily in its volume, but rather in its nature, which reveals patterns, shows connections about an individual and between individuals, and more.[6] In other words, the vast volume of Big Data is undisputed; it is the analytical use of Big Data that makes it a phenomenon of opportunity and concern.

Big Data's networked nature, paired with tools like machine learning and algorithms, enhances our ability to make sense of the data. As one group of

---

2. *See* Duncan Hollis & Tsvetelina van Benthem, *What Would Happen If States Started Looking at Cyber Operations as a "Threat" to Use Force?*, Lawfare (Mar. 30, 2021) https://www.lawfareblog.com/what-would-happen-if-states-started-looking-cyber-operations-threat-use-force (showing that the SolarWinds breach "was limited to data exfiltration from a circumscribed group of victims").

3. Danah Boyd & Kate Crawford, *Critical Questions for Big Data: Provocations for a Cultural, Technological, and Scholarly Phenomenon*, 15 Information, Communication & Society 662, 663 (2012).

4. Paul B. Symon & Arzan Tarapore, *Defense Intelligence Analysis in the Age of Big Data*, 79 Joint Force Q. 5 (2015).

5. Boyd & Crawford, *supra* note 3, citing Lev Manovich (2012).

6. *Id.*

scholars has observed, "Algorithms are used to analyze these large and unconventional data streams in order to find ever-finer grained correlations between data points."[7] This ability has also been scrutinized for producing inaccurate, biased, and discriminatory results.[8]

What does the emergence of Big Data mean for the *jus ad bellum*? First, this body of law cannot treat "data" as a monolith anymore. Some data is discrete and individualized, other data is more voluminous, and some other data is Big Data both due to its analytical nature and volume. Over time, states are likely to set the boundaries between attacks targeting Big Data, the scale and effects of which are more likely to reach the use of force thresholds, and those that would not.[9] Second, the legal scholarship on cyber operations against data must acknowledge the differences in volume, effects, nature, and sensitivity between Small Data and Big Data. These differences suggest that not all cyber operations against data are alike.

III. ON INTERNATIONAL LAW AND CYBER OPERATIONS AGAINST BIG DATA

Cyber operations against data present a plethora of perplexing questions that international law fails to answer. And while each area of international law has its unique gaps, there are some common themes and characteristics surrounding cyber operations against data that lead to common shortfalls. This chapter seeks to unveil some of these themes and characteristics in light of the *jus ad bellum*.

International law is obsessed with physicality. Drop a bomb on a civilian hospital, and you're in trouble. Manipulate the same hospital's patient database, and you get a pass. With the increasing number of cyber operations exclusively targeting Big Data and databases, the devastating effects of such operations on cybersecurity, privacy, national security, and stability can no longer be overlooked. In the *jus ad bellum* context, the kinetic/non-kinetic distinction is largely at fault for this reality.[10] According to this distinction, operations that result in physical effects, such as property destruction, injuries, and deaths are likely to be in violation of Article 2(4) of the UN Charter,[11] prohibiting the threat or use

---

7. Caryn Devins, Teppo Felin, Stuart Kauffman, & Roger Koppl, *The Law and Big Data*, 27 Cornell J.L. Pub. Pol'y 357, 363–64 (2017).

8. *Id.*

9. *See* Michael Schmitt, *The Law of Cyber Warfare: Quo Vadis?*, 25 Stan. L. Pol'y Rev. 269, 296 (2014) (arguing that states will eventually create customary international law that would label certain data as "essential").

10. Reese Nguyen, *Navigating Jus Ad Bellum in the Age of Cyber Warfare*, 101 Cal. L. Rev. 1079, 1122 (2013). ("A cyber attack that produces physical destruction akin to that produced by a kinetic attack is more likely to qualify as the equivalent of force or armed attack.")

11. Art. 2(4) of the UN Charter reads "All Members shall refrain in their international relations from the threat or use of force against the territorial integrity or political independence of

of force by one state against another.[12] In more severe cases, the same operations might also constitute an armed attack, which entitles the victim state to respond in self-defense.[13] Conversely, any operation that falls short of the aforementioned kinetic effects is unlikely to trigger Article 2(4). While cyber operations that seek to acquire, manipulate, or delete sensitive data are undoubtedly damaging and destabilizing, the current law on the use of force is having a hard time catching up. Recently, many have begun to argue that the kinetic/non-kinetic distinction that the law on the use of force holds dear is antiquated and increasingly unattainable.[14] This is further reflected in some state statements on the international law applicable to cyber operations.[15] According to this argument, the many negative impacts of cyber operations against data can no longer be ignored. While states recently seem to have become more comfortable with the proposition that some cyber operations against data are wrongful, they have yet to acknowledge the matrix of Small Data, Big Data, and their different characteristics.

In recent years, cyber operations against data have been on the rise. Both states and non-state actors have realized the potential of accessing without authorization confidential data to advance their political, strategic, national security, financial, and sometimes personal goals.

Many such state-sponsored cyber operations have already taken place. Most notable was the data wiping operation against Ukraine, attributed to Russia, which preceded the Russian invasion of Ukraine in February of 2022 and was aimed to destabilize the computer systems in the country.[16] Another prominent example is the SolarWinds Orion software hack, which affected as many as 18,000 entities using the Orion monitoring software,[17] including the U.S. Commerce and Treasury Departments, the Department of Homeland Security (DHS), the National Institutes of Health, the State Department, the Energy Department, and the National Nuclear Security Administration, and many other private sector

---

any state, or in any other manner inconsistent with the Purposes of the United Nations." U.N. Charter Art. 2, § 4.

12. Harold Honhgu Koh, Legal Advisor of the Dep't of State, International Law in Cyberspace, Address to the USCYBERCOM Inter-Agency Legal Conference (Sept. 18, 2012), https://2009-2017.state.gov/s/l/releases/remarks/197924.htm. ("Cyber activities that proximately result in death, injury, or significant destruction would likely be viewed as a use of force.")

13. U.N. Charter, Art. 51.

14. *See* Marc Schack, *Did the US Stay "Well Below the Threshold of War" With Its June Cyberattack on Iran*, EJIL: TALK! (Sept. 2, 2019), https://www.ejiltalk.org/did-the-us-stay-well-below-the-threshold-of-war-with-its-june-cyberattack-on-iran; Ido Kilovaty, *Cyber Conflict and the Thresholds of War*, forthcoming in Is THE INTERNATIONAL LEGAL ORDER UNRAVELING? (David Sloss ed., 2022).

15. *See* Section IV of this chapter.

16. *Ukraine Computers Hit by Data-wiping Software as Russia Launched Invasion*, REUTERS, Feb. 24, 2022.

17. Hollis & van Benthem, *supra* note 2.

entities.[18] It is believed that the SolarWinds hack's purpose was solely to exfiltrate confidential and valuable data.[19]

Other prominent operations include the North Korean operation against Sony[20] and the Iranian malware targeting Saudi Aramco.[21] In both cases, the deletion of sensitive data was the goal and the actual result.

Cyber operations against Big Data have also been surfacing in recent years. The largest biometric ID database, India's Aadhaar, has become the target of a data breach.[22] The Aadhaar breach exposed the personal information of more than one billion people, with individual personal information offered for sale for less than $10 per record.[23]

This chapter is concerned with the question of whether a cyber operation against Big Data or a database containing it violates the prohibition on the use of force. Should such cyber operation be considered a prohibited use of force? These are some examples of the questions that need to be addressed in the era we live in.

Labeling such cyber operations as prohibited uses of force would stretch the scope of what qualifies as "force." In more extreme cases, some states might deem a non-kinetic cyber operation an armed attack, which would further escalate already existing tensions between the nations involved. Similarly, would a cyber operation against Big Data constitute a threat to use *actual*, kinetic force?[24] The purpose of this chapter is not to argue for more forceful retaliation against cyber operations targeting data, but rather ask whether these operations should be considered unlawful therefore wrongful under international law. By wrongfulness I mean an act that is unlawful, attributable to a state, and is likely to result in that state's responsibility for the violation of international law.[25]

---

18. Pam Baker, *The SolarWinds Hack Timeline: Who Knew What, and When?*, CSO ONLINE (June 4, 2021), https://www.csoonline.com/article/3613571/the-solarwinds-hack-timeline-who-knew-what-and-when.html.

19. *Id.*

20. Kim Zetter, *Sony Got Hacked Hard: What We Know and Don't Know So Far*, WIRED (Dec. 3, 2014).

21. Humeyra Pamuk, *Exclusive: U.S. Probe Of Saudi Oil Attack Shows It Came From North— Report*, REUTERS (Dec. 19, 2019).

22. Ashish Malhotra, *The World's Largest Biometric ID System Keeps Getting Hacked*, VICE (Jan. 8, 2018), https://www.vice.com/en/article/43q4jp/aadhaar-hack-insecure-biometric-id-system.

23. *Id.*

24. *See generally* Duncan Hollis & Tsvetelina van Benthem, *Threatening Force in Cyberspace, in* BIG DATA AND ARMED CONFLICT: LEGAL ISSUES ABOVE AND BELOW THE ARMED CONFLICT THRESHOLD (Laura Dickinson & Edward Berg eds., 2023).

25. See Art. 2 of the International Law Commission Draft Articles on the Responsibility of States for Internationally Wrongful Acts ("There is an internationally wrongful act of a State when conduct consisting of an action or omission: (a) is attributable to the State under international law; and (b) constitutes a breach of an international obligation of the State.").

Article 2(4) of the UN Charter offers a convenient framework through which that question could be assessed. First, the meaning of "force" is a contextual legal term of art that is constantly changing and should be dependent on existing technology, geopolitical trends, and values that the international community seeks to protect. Second, the wrongfulness of using force might prove effective in deterring cyber operations targeting data. And finally, the prohibition on the use of force already exists, which cannot be said about more cyber-specific norms and principles that the international community periodically fails to agree on, even on a non-binding basis.

Below the use of force threshold, cyber operations may nonetheless violate other bodies of international law: for example, the sovereignty of the state affected, as well as the human rights of the individuals whose date is compromised and abused. These are additional, existing frameworks through which such cyber operations can be addressed.

IV. CYBER OPERATIONS AGAINST BIG DATA: A USE OF FORCE OR ARMED ATTACK?

Cyber operations that target data, broadly speaking, present a difficult case for the *jus ad bellum*. Targeting digital data in a non-kinetic manner places cases of data deletion, manipulation, or corruption outside the scope of Article 2(4), as currently understood.[26] On the other hand, the case of cyber operations against Big Data may offer an easier opportunity to trigger the use of force framework, as the immediate and long-term consequences of the compromise of Big Data are far more devastating than any other category of data. In recent years, this debate has gained traction as the non-kinetic effects of some cyber operations targeting Big Data are becoming a matter of concern.

The kinetic effects argument holds that cyber operations against data cannot be considered uses of force or armed attacks because they do not usually manifest in the kinds of physical effects that are normally attributed to kinetic attacks, though there are exceptions. For example, Michael Schmitt argues that a cyber operations targeting data may be considered a use of force if the data targeted is "immediately convertible into tangible objects, like banking data."[27] This argument relies on convertibility to determine whether a cyber operation reaches the level of a use of force or armed attack.[28] According to this rationale, if data can be converted to

---

26. Marco Roscini, Cyber Operations and the Use of Force in International Law 55 (2014).

27. Michael N. Schmitt, *Cyber Operations in International Law: The Use of Force, Collective Security, Self-Defense, and Armed Conflicts, in* Proceedings of a Workshop on Deterring Cyberattacks: Informing Strategies and Developing Options for U.S. Policy 164 (2010).

28. Duncan Hollis, *Why States Need an International Law for Information Operations*, 11 Lewis & Clark L. Rev. 1023, 1039 (2007) (discussing translation of international law to information operations).

a physical item and also deprive the owner of control and access to that physical item, then the effects are equivalent to the physical destruction typically required to constitute a kinetic attack.

Similarly, as Catherine Lotrionte has argued regarding prohibited armed attacks, "Without any physical consequences such cyber operation [against data] will not meet the armed attack threshold."[29] However, if a cyber operation against data "were to result in the disruption of an air traffic control system causing it to fail and planes to crash, the computer operations would rise to the level of an armed attack."[30] In other words, are the scale and effects of the operation similar or identical to those resulting from a traditional kinetic attack? If not, the *jus ad bellum* analysis is over.

Some other scholars have made proposals to address this gap. For example, by treating cyber operations against data as threats to use force, thus in violation of Article 2(4) of the UN Charter[31] or by creating an entirely new international law of espionage to address the novel and challenging nature of cyber operations, by imposing restrictions both before and during espionage.[32]

For some time, there has been uncertainty as to whether the *jus ad bellum* captured the non-kinetic nature of most cyber operations. As the 2017 *Tallinn Manual 2.0* concluded, the "case of cyber operations that do not result in injury, death, damage, or destruction, but that otherwise have extensive negative effects, remains unsettled."[33] Ever since 2017, there have been some significant developments on that question. In particular, many states have released official statements on their interpretation of international law in light of cyber operations.[34] By expressing their official views on the prohibition on the use of force,

---

29. Catherine Lotrionte, Cyber *Operations: Conflict Under International Law*, GEO. J. INT'L AFF. 10, 20 (2012).

30. *Id.*

31. Hollis & van Benthem, *supra* note 2.

32. Asaf Lubin, *SolarWinds as a Constitutive Moment: A New Agenda for the International Law of Intelligence*, JUST SECURITY (Dec. 23, 2020), https://www.justsecurity.org/73989/solarwinds-as-a-constitutive-moment-a-new-agenda-for-the-international-law-of-intelligence/.

33. TALLINN MANUAL 2.0 ON THE INTERNATIONAL LAW APPLICABLE TO CYBER OPERATIONS, rule 71 and accompanying commentary (Michael N. Schmitt gen. ed., 2017), 342.

34. *See, e.g.*, Paul C. Ney, Jr., DOD General Counsel Remarks at U.S. Cyber Command Legal Conference (Mar. 2, 2020), https://www.defense.gov/Newsroom/Speeches/Speech/Article/2099378/dod-general-counsel-remarks-at-us-cyber-command-legal-conference/; Attorney General's Office, Cyber and International Law in the 21st Century (May 23, 2018), https://www.gov.uk/government/speeches/cyber-and-international-law-in-the-21st-century; The Federal Government, Position Paper on the Application of International Law in Cyberspace (Mar. 2021), https://www.auswaertiges-amt.de/blob/2446304/32e7b2498e10b74fb17204c54665bdf0/on-the-application-of-international-law-in-cyberspace-data.pdf; Australian Government, Annex B: Australia's position on how international law applies to State conduct in cyberspace, https://www.internationalcybertech.gov.au/our-work/annexes/annex-b; Ministère des Armées Droit, International Appliqué aux Opérations dans le Cyberspace (2019), https://www.justsecurity.org/wp-content/uploads/2019/09/droit-internat-appliqu%C3%A9-aux-op%C3%A9rations-cybe

sovereignty, and non-kinetic cyber operations, it is easier to hypothesize the possible trajectory, as well as potential disagreements, on this question. It is also not entirely clear at what point this particular question will be supported by a critical mass of state practice and *opinio juris*.[35]

V. STATE STATEMENTS ON THE USE OF FORCE PROHIBITION AND CYBER OPERATIONS AGAINST BIG DATA

States have recently become more vocal about their individual views of how international law applies in cyberspace, and more specifically, on whether cyber operations against data should be considered as violations of Article 2(4) of the UN Charter. Some of the states who have made their views known include the United States,[36] the United Kingdom,[37] Germany,[38] France,[39] Australia,[40] the Netherlands,[41]

respace-france.pdf; Ministry of Foreign Affairs, Letter to the parliament on the international legal order in cyberspace (July 5, 2019), https://www.government.nl/ministries/ministry-of-fore ign-affairs/documents/parliamentary-documents/2019/09/26/letter-to-the-parliament-on-the-international-legal-order-in-cyberspace; International Law and Cyberspace, Finland's National Positions, https://um.fi/documents/35732/0/KyberkannatPDF_EN.pdf/12bbbbde-623b-9f86-b254-07d5af3c6d85?t=1603097522727; New Zealand Foreign Affairs & Trade, The Application of International Law to State Activity in Cyberspace (Dec. 1, 2020), https://www.mfat.govt.nz/assets/Peace-Rights-and-Security/International-security/International-Cyber-statement.pdf; Roy Schöndorf, *Israel's Perspective on Key Legal and Practical Issues Concerning the Application of International Law to Cyber Operations*, 97 Int'l. L. Stud. 395 (2021).

35. Ryan Goodman, *Cyber Operations and the U.S. Definition of "Armed Attack,"* Just Security (Mar. 8, 2018), https://www.justsecurity.org/53495/cyber-operations-u-s-definition-armed-att ack/ ("This is an area where views are developing in one direction, but what happens in the limbo period between now and then, when some States and legal authorities hold one view and others hold different ones? That seems like a dangerous period for calibrating the use of force in cyber.").

36. Ney, *supra* note 34.

37. Attorney General's Office, *supra* note 34.

38. The Federal Government, *supra* note 34.

39. Ministère des Armées, International Appliqué aux Opérations dans le Cyberspace (2019), https://www.justsecurity.org/wp-content/uploads/2019/09/droit-internat-appliqu%C3%A9-aux-op%C3%A9rations-cyberespace-france.pdf; Ministère des Armées, International Law Applied to Operations in Cyberspace, https://www.defense.gouv.fr/content/download/567648/9770527/file/international+law+applied+to+operations+in+cyberspace.pdf.

40. Australian Government, *supra* note 34.

41. Ministry of Foreign Affairs, Letter to the parliament on the international legal order in cyberspace (July 5, 2019), https://www.government.nl/ministries/ministry-of-foreign-affairs/documents/parliamentary-documents/2019/09/26/letter-to-the-parliament-on-the-internatio nal-legal-order-in-cyberspace.

Finland,[42] Italy,[43] Japan,[44] New Zealand,[45] and Israel.[46] States expressing their views in these statements are not always aligned with each other. These views can be divided into two categories: the kinetic approach and the non-kinetic approach.

A. States Adopting the Kinetic Approach

For many states, international law in cyberspace is no different from international law in physical space. These states apply international law to cyberspace by analogy to the physical world. For example, the U.S. Department of Defense view holds that in assessing whether a cyber operation constitutes a use of force, "DoD lawyers consider whether the operation causes physical injury or damage that would be considered a use of force if caused solely by traditional means like a missile or a mine."[47]

Many other states hold the same view, though some have used a less categorical framing of their approach. For example, the German view adopts the "scale and effects" standard for use of force assessments developed by the ICJ in the *Nicaragua* case.[48] According to Germany's view, if a cyber operation has effects "comparable to those of traditional kinetic use of force," then it should be considered a use of force. In addition, Germany leaves some leeway on the cyber use of force question, which it characterizes as "a decision to be taken on a case-by-case basis,"[49] taking into account its severity, immediacy, degree of intrusion, and degree of organization and coordination.[50]

42. International Law and Cyberspace, Finland's National Positions, https://um.fi/docume nts/35732/0/KyberkannatPDF_EN.pdf/12bbbbde-623b-9f86-b254-07d5af3c6d85?t=160309 7522727.

43. Italian Position Paper on 'International Law and Cyberspace' (Nov. 2021), https://www.est eri.it/mae/resource/doc/2021/11/italian_position_paper_on_international_law_and_cybersp ace.pdf.

44. Ministry of Foreign Affairs of Japan, Basic Position of the Government of Japan on International Law Applicable to Cyber Operations (May 28, 2021), https://www.mofa.go.jp/files/100200935.pdf.

45. New Zealand Foreign Affairs & Trade, The Application of International Law to State Activity in Cyberspace (Dec. 1, 2020), https://www.mfat.govt.nz/assets/Peace-Rights-and-Security/International-security/International-Cyber-statement.pdf

46. Schöndorf, *supra* note 34.

47. *See* U.S. view, *supra* note 20.

48. *See* Germany's view, *supra* note 22, at 6; ICJ, Military and Paramilitary Activities in and against Nicaragua, para. 195.

49. *See* Germany's view, *supra* note 22, at 6..

50. *Id.*

Among these states, there is no consideration of the legality of cyber operations against Big Data, specifically, as compared to Small Data.

B. States Adopting the Non-kinetic Approach

A significant deviation from the kinetic approach is reflected in the French approach. While the French statement supports the kinetic argument by comparing the effects of cyber uses of force to "those that result from the use of conventional weapons,"[51] the statement notably opens the door to non-kinetic uses of force when it states that "France does not rule out the possibility that a cyberoperation without physical effects may also be characterised as a use of force."[52] In making this determination, the French approach proposes a set of non-exhaustive criteria, which include "the circumstances prevailing at the time of the operation, such as the origin of the operation and the nature of the instigator (military or not), the extent of intrusion, the actual or intended effects of the operation or the nature of the intended target."[53]

In other words, when a cyber operation would target an important French government database by manipulating its data, it is entirely possible that the French government would deem that cyber operation a use of force, though it is unclear whether the French position would ever characterize a cyber operation against Big Data as an armed attack. In such a circumstance, the cyber operation need not cause any physical effects to be considered wrongful.

France is not alone in its expansive view of the use of force prohibition and cyber operations targeting data. The Dutch Minister of Defense recently made clear that, if a "cyber-attack targets the entire Dutch financial system . . . or if it prevents the government from carrying out essential tasks such as policing or taxation . . . it would qualify as an armed attack."[54] While "armed attack" is a higher threshold that is more difficult to meet than use of force, the Dutch view reflects that cyber operations against Big Data, especially of sensitive financial nature, may qualify not only as a use of force, but an armed attack, which would entitle the Dutch government to respond in self-defense.[55] Therefore, these non-kinetic effects, in certain cases, may meet the relevant *jus ad bellum* thresholds.

---

51. *See* France's view, *supra* note 23, at 7.

52. *Id.*

53. *Id.*

54. Ministry of Defence, Keynote address by the Minister of Defence, Ms. Ank Bijleveld, marking the first anniversary of the Tallinn Manual 2.0 on the 20th of June 2018 (June 21, 2018), https://english.defensie.nl/downloads/speeches/2018/06/21/keynote-address-by-the-minister-of-defence-ms.-ank-bijleveld-marking-the-first-anniversary-of-the-tallinn-manual-2.0-on-the-20th-of-june-2018.

55. Art. 51 of the UN Charter allows the use of defensive force in response to an armed attack. While all armed attacks are also uses of force, not all uses of force are armed attacks.

Both the French and Dutch positions reflect similar concerns. First, some cyber operations that cause no physical effects are nonetheless damaging. Other states have advanced this view as well. Panama, for example, has observed that "an attack in which new information and telecommunications technologies are employed may cause more damage than, for instance, a conventional bombardment."[56] Many other states have made statements of similar nature.[57]

If the aforementioned cyber operations reach the threshold of use of force, it may allow the victim to use countermeasures in response to an internationally wrongful act. In more severe cases, if a cyber operation against Big Data reaches the level of an armed attack, the victim could lawfully use a forceful self-help remedy: self-defense. The use of force prohibition, while helpful to conceptualize damaging cyber operations against Big Data, is not a panacea. It is to be used sparingly only in cases where cyber operations cause devastating non-kinetic consequences, such as the manipulation of financial Big Data to the point of a complete shutdown of the entire economy. In that sense, certain cyber operations against Big Data, while damaging, may not be addressed by any existing legal framework.

France and the Netherlands will probably not be alone in reading Article 2(4) expansively. In response to the SolarWinds hack, which affected 300,000 customers including Fortune 500 companies and U.S. government agencies, Yevgeny Vindman argued that the United States should adopt a similar approach.[58] Vindman's op-ed gets at exactly the same concern as that of France and the Netherlands: "a country need not be subjected to a cyberattack tantamount to physical attack to suffer *casus belli*. Such an understanding of international law would be illogical and unsupportable in the digital age of warfare."[59] On this point, Yoram Dinstein's characterization of cyber operations as "a new means of warfare—in other words, a weapon: no less and no more than other weapons" seems reasonable.[60]

Notably, these expansive readings of Article 2(4) leave out some important details. How severe should the non-kinetic effects be to reach the use of force threshold? Are there any other criteria that should be used as part of the use of force assessment? And more. The next section offers some further ideas and criteria to be considered in this context.

---

56. UN Doc A/57/166/Add.1, 29 Aug. 2002, p. 5.

57. Roscini, *supra* note 26, at 51.

58. Yevgeny Vindman, *Is the SolarWinds Cyberattack an Act of War? It Is, If the United States Says It Is*, LAWFARE (Jan. 26, 2021), https://www.lawfareblog.com/solarwinds-cyberattack-act-war-it-if-united-states-says-it.

59. *Id.*

60. Yoram Dinstein, *Cyber War and International Law: Concluding Remarks at the 2012 Naval War College International Law Conference*, 89 INT'L. L. STUD. 280 (2013).

VI. NOT ALL DATA ARE CREATED EQUAL: SMALL DATA AND BIG DATA

In reading Article 2(4)'s prohibition as inclusive of cyber operations against data, some crucial questions to ask include the following: What kinds of data are targeted? What is the volume of the data involved? Does the data belong to a single individual (politician, businesswoman), a corporation, a government agency, a military?

The strict reading of Article 2(4) as exclusive of non-kinetic effects fails exactly for that reason—not all data are created equal. Indeed, there are isolated state-sponsored cyber operations that target a single entity's data for primarily commercial purposes: for example, theft of intellectual property, which would qualify as neither use of force nor armed attack.

Conversely, there have been a growing number of cyber operations targeting numerous entities at once, including their Big Data, with political or strategic goals. The scale and effects of these operations could be significant enough to reach the threshold of the use of force prohibition, though they would rarely reach the requisite level of armed attack. The major difference lies in the quality of Big Data. Specifically, the compromise of Big Data affects not a single individual or entity, but a large subsection (if not the entirety) of a given society. A cyber operation against a biometric ID database is arguably more devastating than a cyber operation targeting a single individual's computer device. The former is not only more revealing than a cyber operation targeting an individual's computer device containing data about a more limited group of people, but its vastness and sensitivity may allow the attacker to further magnify the impact by using tools like algorithms and machine learning techniques to reveal a magnitude of inferences based on the compromised Big Data.

Indeed, the exfiltration of Big Data through a cyber operation not only reveals the data contained in the Big Data targeted, but also a mass quantity of information pertaining to inferences that can be drawn from the Big Data processed by advanced analytical tools.

An example of a cyber operation against Big Data recently causing significant non-kinetic damage is the Colonial Pipeline ransomware attack, which led to a shutdown of vast portions of a gas pipeline stretching from Texas to New Jersey.[61] While this ransomware attack targeted Colonial's Big Data, it resulted in significant chaos and disruption. In the Colonial Pipeline, the harms are not limited to the immediate cyber operation, but they are also likely to materialize as the attackers process the Big Data compromised for additional inferences, such as, which regions use more electricity than others? Which households are more likely to suffer physical consequences in the case of a power outage? And more.

---

61. Michael Shear, Nicole Perloth, & Clifford Krauss, *Colonial Pipeline Paid Roughly $5 Million in Ransom to Hackers*, N.Y. TIMES (May. 13, 2021), https://www.nytimes.com/2021/05/13/us/politics/biden-colonial-pipeline-ransomware.html

The quality, volume, and type of Big Data may be determined by the main target of the operation. In this case, the effects-based approach may prove useful to distinguish between operations against Big Data falling below the use of force threshold and those that are above the threshold.[62] Among the criteria for the effects-based approach, set forth in the *Tallinn Manual*,[63] are (1) severity, (2) immediacy, (3) directness, (4) invasiveness, (5) measurability of effects, (6) military character, (7) state involvement, and (8) presumptive legality. These criteria may be adapted to address cyber operations against Big Data.

Furthermore, the argument as to the distinction between Small Data and Big Data is both normative and methodological. Normatively, cyber operations against Big Data are more damaging than cyber operations against Small Data. Therefore, the *jus ad bellum* should not address both categories of data indistinguishably. Methodologically, states making statements about international law and cyberspace should clarify what they mean by "data" and the distinction they would draw between Small Data and Big Data, as the two lead to vastly different consequences.

VII. CONCLUSION

Cyber operations against Big Data are on the rise. Despite not always causing any direct physical effects, recent years have demonstrated the dangers of state-sponsored data breaches taking place across borders. International law's outdated concern with physical effects does not match the reality in which foreign governments steal, manipulate, delete, or otherwise target Big Data belonging to another state or its citizens. Furthermore, Big Data should be treated differently from Small Data for not only qualitative and quantitative differences, but also the ability of Big Data to be processed by algorithms and other tools to produce powerful, and oftentimes damaging, inferences.

Methodologically, States should begin to differentiate between Big Data and Small Data. As I have argued in this chapter, the two are not alike and therefore cannot be considered under the more general and unnuanced umbrella of "data."

This chapter has offered several ways to conceptualize cyber operations against Big Data within the *jus ad bellum*. States have already begun to question the *jus ad bellum*'s kinetic status quo, and further state practice and *opinio juris* will likely clarify the boundaries and principles that will eventually guide state cyber operations against Big Data.

---

62. Michael N. Schmitt, *Computer Network Attack and the Use of Force in International Law: Thoughts on a Normative Framework*, 37 COLUM. J. TRANSNAT'L L. 885, 909 (1999).

63. TALLINN MANUAL 2.0, *supra* note 33, at 334–36.

PART TWO

International Humanitarian Law and Military Operations

5

Big Data

International Law Issues During Armed Conflict

MICHAEL N. SCHMITT* ∎

This chapter builds on the scenario and analysis set forth in Chapter 1, which dealt with cyber operations involving Big Data before the outbreak of armed conflict. Big Data has been usefully defined as "the exponentially increasing amount of digital information being created by new information technologies such as mobile internet, cloud storage, social networking, and the 'internet of things'—and the advanced analytics used to process that data."[1] As illustrated in the opening scenario chapter of the book, Big Data allows for the acquisition of unique military capabilities.

In this part of the scenario, an armed conflict between Newtropia and Outlandia breaks out. Accordingly, I will discuss the complex legal questions the scenario presents under international humanitarian law (IHL). I will begin by examining whether an armed conflict exists and, if so, whether that conflict is international or non-international in character. The discussion then moves on to a subject unique to cyber operations, the meaning of the IHL term "attack" as applied to cyber operations. Should a cyber operation qualify as an attack, it may only be directed at military objectives, the third subject considered. Finally, my analysis concludes with a *capita selecta* examination of other issues the scenario raises. I would note that while the scenario involves international armed conflict, much of the analysis applies *mutatis mutandis* to non-international armed conflict.

---

* G. Norman Lieber Scholar, United States Military Academy at West Point; Professor of International Law, University of Reading; Professor Emeritus, United States Naval War College.

1. Paul B. Symon & Arzan Tarapore, *Defense Intelligence Analysis in the Age of Big Data*, 79 JOINT FORCE Q. 5 (2015).

Michael N. Schmitt, *Big Data* In: *Big Data and Armed Conflict*. Edited by: Laura A. Dickinson and Edward W. Berg, Oxford University Press. © Michael N. Schmitt 2024. DOI: 10.1093/oso/9780197668610.003.0007

As will become apparent, the role of data in modern conflict has significant IHL implications. However, the fact of Big Data does not, at least not directly. It enables operations that might not otherwise be possible, but their nature and consequences drive legal analysis, not the fact that Big Data enabled them.

I. SCENARIO: ARMED CONFLICT

Despite attempts at diplomacy during the immediate aftermath of the UWS operation, hostilities erupt.[2] The OMF responds to the UWS hack with a missile attack on Newtropia's military cyber headquarters, which ultimately precipitates full-scale combat between the two nations. Newtropia unleashes an incredibly effective digital opening salvo. With the massive database of Outlandian government and military records and civilian data, Newtropia begins a campaign of blackmail, disruption, and intimidation against specific military and civilian members, as well as their family members. Newtropian AI identifies these individuals as critical nodes of support necessary for the rapid mobilization and deployment of the OMF to the theater of combat.[2] Newtropia targets approximately 5,000 military members, civilian employees, defense contractors, and government officials in this manner.[3] Optimized based on vulnerabilities identified in the data, these operations significantly prevent targeted individuals from attending to their mobilization duties. These individuals face severed communications, threatening messages delivered to their family members via smart speakers, deleted bank and retirement accounts, and even sabotage to their "Internet of things" devices, such as smart devices, with self-driving cars being a favorite target. This opening salvo cripples a rapid OMF mobilization.

Despite the difficulty in mobilizing forces, Outlandia continues the fight, deploying forces piecemeal into the theater of combat due to the delays. Once in theater, the OMF face a new type of foe—the Newtropian AI Targeting System (NAITS). The NAITS utilizes facial recognition technology from the military and medical records of OMF personnel that had been purloined prior to the war. The system built a kill list of high-value OMF targets, which is fed to loitering aerial kill vehicles that automatically launch a missile upon a facial and/or voice recognition match. These operations are mostly successful, although news reports begin filtering out of the combat zone regarding mistaken strikes, with civilians and ICRC personnel suffering casualties as a result. The algorithm is not 100% accurate and even though it has been shown to have an error rate similar to a human operator, there is a real

---

2. Lieutenant Colonel Mark Visger drafted the scenario in consultation with Lieutenant Colonel Doug Fletcher, Major Nate Bastian, Major Bryan Jonas, Lieutenant Colonel Nick Clark, Lieutenant Colonel Ed Berg, and Professor Laura Dickinson. For Part I of the scenario, see Mark A. Visger, "Scenario," this book, at 21-26.

3. The description of this micro-targeting attack is modeled after a fictional attack outlined in the Modern War Institute Blog Post, "Autopsy of a Future War" (Jared Wilhelm, Nov. 5, 2019), https://mwi.usma.edu/autopsy-future-war/.

possibility for mistakes. Due to the black-box nature of the AI system, it is practically impossible to track the machine logic that led to the errors. The majority of the, mistaken strikes take place against non-Caucasian personnel, as the facial recognition training data primarily utilized that of Caucasians individual.

The NAITS increasingly makes targeting mistakes as the war progresses, likely due to the degraded data flow that Newtropia suffers once hostilities commence because of OMF targeting of Newtropian data streams. OMF data countermeasures had begun prior to the conflict and continued into the conflict. These actions successfully degraded the NAITS' effectiveness. Data countermeasures take a number of different forms. As the OMF began to apprehend the extent of AFN data theft prior to the war, the OMF began inserting false data into the purloined data streams. In addition, they also began "fuzzing" the data—adding random noise where possible to confuse the Newtropian systems.

OMF cyberattacks also begin targeting the data within the Newtropian networks. In one instance after hostilities commence, Outlandian cyber forces access and delete all military personnel and pay records (as well as their backups), causing administrative nightmares for NAF personnel. In addition to taking action against the data in cyberspace, OMF start looking for ways to confuse the NAITS sensors. Outlandian soldiers begin placing random digital patterns on their uniform in an attempt to fool the NAITS. Through a system of trial and error, and some "best guess" reverse-engineering of the Newtropian systems, researchers identify several effective random digital patterns to thwart the NAITS. These patterns are issued to OMF personnel on a mass scale. Unbeknownst to the OMF, the top three digital evasion patterns they adopt cause the NAITS to identify OMF soldiers as medical personnel, school-aged children, and penguins, respectively.

In a particularly tragic episode, a NAITS missile targets and kills Dr. Jean-Marc Van Lanner, head of the Doctors Beyond Frontiers (a medical NGO) mission to the combat region. Investigators are unable to identify why the system targeted Dr. Van Lanner. Experts state that the error was likely due to the NAITS updates to its targeting algorithm following OMF usage of data evasion patterns simulating medical personnel. As a result, the NAITS incorrectly identifies him as a high value OMF commander, an error likely exacerbated by the fact that Dr. Van Lanner is non-Caucasian.

II. QUALIFICATION AS AN ARMED CONFLICT

The first step in any conflict legal analysis is classification—the determination of whether the situation qualifies as an "armed conflict" and, if so, whether that conflict is international or non-international. Should a situation not amount to armed conflict, it will be governed by general international law rules such as sovereignty, international human rights law, and the domestic law of States enjoying prescriptive jurisdiction. However, if an armed conflict is underway, IHL acts as the default law governing activities having a nexus to the conflict, including cyber and cyber-related operations.[4] The classification of the armed conflict as international or non-international will determine which aspects of that body of law apply.

This scenario is undoubtedly an international armed conflict. The condition precedent to such a conflict is the existence of "hostilities" (*armed*) between two or more states (*international*).[5] The missile attack by OMF against Newtropia's military cyber headquarters obviously qualifies as hostilities. Thus, at least by that point, an international armed conflict governed by IHL was underway between Outlandia and Newtropia.

The more challenging question is whether the earlier cyber operations,[6] such as those by Newtropia's cyber forces that deleted 92% of the Outlandian military data on UWS, triggered an international armed conflict. Although cyber operations standing alone can initiate such conflict,[7] IHL provides no definitive

---

4. The applicability of IHL to cyber operations occurring during an armed conflict has been the source of some discord among States. Michael Schmitt & Liis Vihul, *International Cyber Law Politicized: The UN GGE's Failure to Advance Cyber Norms*, JUST SECURITY (June 30, 2017), https://www.justsecurity.org/42768/international-cyber-law-politicized-gges-failure-advance-cyber-norms/. However, that discord was overcome in the Sixth GGE. Report of the Group of Governmental Experts on Advancing Responsible State Behaviour in Cyberspace in the Context of International Security, ¶ 71(f), U.N. Doc. A/76/135 (July 14, 2021). *See also* Office of the General Counsel, U.S. DEPARTMENT OF DEFENSE, LAW OF WAR MANUAL, §16.2 (updated as of Dec. 2016); ICRC, International Humanitarian Law and Cyber Operations during Armed Conflicts, Position Paper Submitted to the Open-Ended Working Group on Developments in the Field of Information and Telecommunications in the Context of International Security and the Group of Governmental Experts on Advancing Responsible State Behaviour in Cyberspace in the Context of International Security 4 (Nov. 28, 2019), https://www.icrc.org/en/document/international-humanitarian-law-and-cyber-operations-during-armed-conflicts. For an excellent in-depth discussion setting forth ICRC views on how IHL applies in the cyber context, *see* Laurent Gisel, Tilman Rodenhäuser, & Knut Dörmann, *Twenty Years On: International Humanitarian Law and the Protection of Civilians Against the Effects of Cyber Operations During Armed Conflict*, 102 (913) INT'L REV. RED CROSS 287 (2020).

5. Convention (I) for the Amelioration of the Condition of the Wounded and Sick in the Armed Forces in the Field Art. 2, Aug. 12, 1949, 6 U.S.T. 3114, 75 U.N.T.S. 31; Convention (II) for the Amelioration of the Condition of the Wounded, Sick, and Shipwrecked Members of Armed Forces at Sea Art. 2, Aug. 12, 1949, 6 U.S.T. 3217, 75 U.N.T.S. 85; Convention (III) Relative to the Treatment of Prisoners of War Art. 2, Aug. 12, 1949, 6 U.S.T. 3316, 75 U.N.T.S. 135; Convention (IV) Relative to the Protection of Civilian Persons in Time of War Art. 2, Aug. 12, 1949, 6 U.S.T. 3516, 75 U.N.T.S. 287 [hereinafter 1949 Geneva Convention I, II, III, and IV respectively]. For an analysis of the meaning of "hostilities," *see* YORAM DINSTEIN, THE CONDUCT OF HOSTILITIES UNDER THE LAW OF INTERNATIONAL ARMED CONFLICT 1–3 (3d ed. 2016).

6. See Visger, *supra* note 2. Immediately before and during the 2022 movement of additional forces into Ukraine, cyber operations likely attributable to Russia began targeting Ukrainian systems. *Ukraine Computers Hit by Data-Wiping Software as Russia Launched Invasion*, Reuters (Feb. 24, 2022), https://www.reuters.com/world/europe/ukrainian-government-foreign-ministry-parliament-websites-down-2022-02-23/.

7. TALLINN MANUAL 2.0 ON THE INTERNATIONAL LAW APPLICABLE TO CYBER OPERATIONS, rule 82 and accompanying commentary (Michael N. Schmitt gen. ed., 2017).

Big Data: Armed Conflict   155

threshold at which they do so. This complicates the problem of how to understand the notion of "hostilities" in the cyber context.

In the 1949 Geneva Conventions commentaries, the ICRC suggested that "any difference arising between two States and leading to the intervention of armed forces is an armed conflict . . . It makes no difference how long the conflict lasts or how much slaughter takes place."[8] Some commentators have argued that this threshold is too low and that the hostilities' extent, duration, and intensity must be considered.[9]

However one resolves that non-cyber debate, when cyber operations result in significant physical damage or injury, as in using cyber means to down an aircraft, the threshold has been crossed. Moreover, the armed forces need not conduct the operations to initiate an armed conflict. Rather, the determinative issue in that regard is whether either a State's organs (like the military or intelligence services) or proxies operating under the "overall control" of a State conducted the operations.[10]

Although State organs of Newtropia mounted the operations under consideration here, the operations caused no physical harm to persons or objects. This raises the question of whether non-destructive and non-injurious cyber operations by one State against another can ever initiate an armed conflict.

No consensus has coalesced among States or within the academic community. However, the fact that cyber operations can generate highly disruptive nonphysical consequences far more harmful to a State than minor physical damage or injury augurs toward an understanding of armed conflict that looks to the severity of operations, rather than their character (cyber or kinetic) or the nature of the resulting consequences (damage or injury). Moreover, IHL should always be interpreted to achieve a contextual balance between the needs of the armed forces

8. *See, e.g.*, Commentary to Geneva Convention I for the Amelioration of the Condition of the Wounded and Sick in the Armed Forces in the Field 32 (Jean Pictet ed., 1952). All subsequent Geneva Conventions commentaries have echoed this conclusion, most recently the International Committee of the Red Cross, Commentary on the Third Geneva Convention: Convention (III) Relative to the Treatment of Prisoners of War ¶ 269 (2020). *See also* Prosecutor v. Tadić, Case No. IT-94-1-I, Decision on the Defence Motion for Interlocutory Appeal on Jurisdiction ¶ 70 (Int'l Crim. Trib. for the Former Yugoslavia 2 October 1995; DoD Law of War Manual, *supra* note 4, § 3.4.2 (rev. ed., Dec. 2016) ("any situation in which there is hostile action between the armed forces of two parties, regardless of the duration, intensity or scope of the fighting").

9. Christopher Greenwood, *Scope of Application of Humanitarian Law, in* THE HANDBOOK OF INTERNATIONAL HUMANITARIAN LAW 45, 57 (Dieter Fleck ed., 2d ed., 2008); Howard S. Levie, *The Status of Belligerent Personnel Splashed and Rescued by a Neutral in the Persian Gulf Area*, 31 VA. J. INT'L L. 611, 613–14 (1991).

10. Prosecutor v. Tadić, Case No. IT-94-1-A, Appeals Chamber Judgment, ¶¶ 131–140, 145, 162 (Intl'l Crim. Trib. for the Former Yugoslavia July 15, 1999). On internationalization of conflict, *see* Dapo Akande, *Classification of Armed Conflicts: Relevant Legal Concepts, in* INTERNATIONAL LAW AND THE CLASSIFICATION OF CONFLICTS 32, 56–63 (Elizabeth Wilmshurst ed., 2012).

on the battlefield and humanitarian considerations.[11] Struggling with this issue, the *Tallinn Manual 2.0* International Group of Experts concluded that cyber operations could amount to hostilities satisfying the armed component of international armed conflict but failed to offer a bright-line test for when that would be so.[12]

Beyond noting that IHL applies to cyber operations in situations of armed conflict, no State has tackled the issue head-on. And States have never characterized cyber operations standing alone as initiating armed conflict, even when they were destructive, as in the case of Stuxnet.[13] Given this relative State silence, no definitive conclusion can be drawn regarding whether the cyber operations preceding Outlandia's missile attack triggered an international armed conflict.

In my estimation, the better view is that they did not, that the operations simply shifted the relative balance of cyber power *prior* to the outbreak of hostilities. The key lies in the distinction between so-called preparation of the battlefield and cyber operations that are integral to hostilities. To take a simple example, consider the placement of malware into a potential adversary's integrated air defense system (IADS). That step would not alone trigger an armed conflict. However, if the malware is activated to facilitate the penetration of that adversary's airspace by attacking aircraft, then doing so triggers the armed conflict even before the first bomb falls. The most defensible conclusion is that the Newtropian actions are neither hostilities in themselves nor an integral part of an operation qualifying as hostilities; they at most prepared the battlefield for future hostilities.

III. ATTACKS

As the situation is one of international armed conflict, it is necessary to assess whether the cyber operations by Newtropia and Outlandia following the start of the conflict complied with the IHL rules governing attacks, in particular those that prohibit attacks against civilians and civilian objects,[14] the rule of

---

11. *See* Michael N. Schmitt, *Military Necessity and Humanity in International Humanitarian Law: Preserving the Delicate Balance*, 50 Va. J. Int'l L. 795 (2010).

12. Tallinn Manual 2.0 *supra* note 7, at 384. Note that the Tallinn Manual 2.0 International Group of Experts adopted most of the IHL text previously developed by the International Group of Experts that authored Tallinn Manual on the International Law Applicable to Cyber Warfare (Michael N. Schmitt gen. ed. 2013).

13. Kim Zetter, Countdown to Zero Day: Stuxnet and the Launch of the World's First Digital Weapon (2015).

14. Protocol Additional to the Geneva Conventions of 12 August 1949, and Relating to the Protection of Victims of International Armed Conflicts Art. 51(2), 52(1), June 8, 1977, 1125 U.N.T.S. 3; 1 Customary International Humanitarian Law, rules 1, 7 (Jean-Marie Henckaerts & Louise Doswald-Beck eds., 2005) [hereinafter CIHL Study]; Office of the General Counsel, U.S. Department of Defense, Law of War Manual § 5.6.2 (rev. ed., Dec. 2016). In the cyber context, see Tallinn Manual 2.0, *supra* note 7, rules 94, 99.

proportionality,[15] and the requirement to take precautions in attack.[16] "Attack" is a term of art in IHL. The 1977 Additional Protocol I to the 1949 Geneva Conventions defines attacks as "acts of violence against the adversary, whether in offence or defence."[17]

Tallinn Manual 2.0's experts struggled with the question of how to apply this standard in the cyber context. The only consensus they could reach was that a cyber operation "that is reasonably expected to cause injury or death to persons or damage or destruction to objects" is an attack for IHL purposes (whether deletion or alteration of data amounts to damage to an object, is a separate issue dealt with below).[18] The experts were also willing to include cyber operations that cause relatively permanent loss of functionality on the basis that it is "damage" to the affected cyber infrastructure.[19] Beyond that point, agreement proved elusive. As an example, the experts could not agree on whether an operation that only temporarily interferes with functionality or causes targeted cyberinfrastructure to misfunction amounts to an attack. For its part, the ICRC has stated that a cyber operation "designed to disable a computer or a computer network constitutes an attack," a sensible approach.[20]

States have been struggling with the same issue. Some look to the effects of cyber operations and seek analogies to those of kinetic attacks. For instance, Australia has noted, "a cyber activity may constitute an 'attack' against an adversary under IHL if it rises to the same threshold as a kinetic 'attack' (or act of violence)."[21] Although the analogy approach has not been fleshed out by States adopting it, it would presumably include operations that cause the targeted infrastructure to lose functionality permanently or require repair even though there is no physical damage; it doesn't matter whether the system was bombed or was the target of a cyber operation—it no longer works.

Other States have taken a more limited approach. Israel, as an example, is of the view that "[o]nly when a cyber operation is expected to cause physical damage, will it satisfy this element of an attack under LOAC. In the same vein, the mere

---

15. Additional Protocol I, *supra* note 14, Arts. 51(5)(b), 57(2)(a)(iii), 57(2)(b); CIHL Study, *supra* note 14, rule 14; DoD Law of War Manual, *supra* note 4, § 5.12. In the cyber context, see Tallinn Manual 2.0, *supra* note 7, rule 113.

16. Additional Protocol I, *supra* note 14, art. 57(2); CIHL Study, *supra* note 14, rules 15–17, 20–21; DoD Law of War Manual, supra note 4, § 5.11. In the cyber context, see Tallinn Manual 2.0, *supra* note 7, rules 114–20.

17. Additional Protocol I, *supra* note 14, Art. 49.

18. Tallinn Manual 2.0, *supra* note 7, rule 92.

19. *Id.* at 417–18.

20. ICRC Position Paper, *supra* note 4, at 7–8.

21. Official Compendium of Voluntary National Contributions on the Subject of How International Law Applies to the Use of Information and Communications Technologies by States, Australia, 6, U.N. Doc. A/76/136, July 13, 2021.

loss or impairment functionality to infrastructure would be insufficient in this regard, and no other specific rule to the contrary has evolved in the cyber domain."[22]

Given the severe effects some cyber operations could generate if directed at civilian cyber infrastructure, the narrow approach does not reflect a fair balancing of military concerns and humanitarian considerations. Thus, some States have worked to adapt the notion of attack to the realities of cyber operations. France, for instance, "does not characterise a cyberattack solely on the basis of material criteria. It considers that a cyberoperation is an attack where the targeted equipment or systems no longer provide the service for which they were implemented, whether temporarily or permanently, reversibly or not. If the effects are temporary and/or reversible, the attack is characterised where action by the adversary is necessary to restore the infrastructure or system (repair of equipment, replacement of a part, reinstallation of a network, etc.)."[23] France also considers data to be an object, a contentious issue examined later. Thus, it would treat a cyber operation that deletes or alters data as an "attack" in IHL terms.

The matter is unlikely to be resolved any time soon, but its consequences are weighty. If the definition of cyberattacks is limited to operations that cause physical damage or injury, very few will be subject to the prohibition on targeting civilian cyber infrastructure. As this is an untenable result, I have suggested policy remedies elsewhere that take into account the disruption of civilian activities that would not be considered if a cyber operation fails to qualify as an attack or if data is not considered to be an object.[24]

In the scenario, most of Newtropia's blackmail, disruption, and intimidation campaign would not qualify as an IHL attack under any of these approaches. However, it is difficult to reach this conclusion definitively because the scenario fails to indicate the precise operations and full range of the campaign's effects, and

---

22. Roy Schöndorf, *Israel's Perspective on Key Legal and Practical Issues Concerning the Application of International Law to Cyber Operations*, 97 INT'L L. STUD. 395, 404 (2021). *See also* DANISH MINISTRY OF DEFENCE, MILITARY MANUAL ON INTERNATIONAL LAW RELEVANT TO DANISH ARMED FORCES IN INTERNATIONAL OPERATIONS 290 (2020), https://usnwc.libguides.com/c.php?g=86619&p=557511.

23. France, MINISTRY OF THE ARMIES, INTERNATIONAL LAW APPLIED TO OPERATIONS IN CYBERSPACE 13 (2019), https://perma.cc/WJQ3-XBWT.

24. Michael N. Schmitt, *Wired Warfare 3.0: Protecting the Civilian Population during Cyber Operations*, 101(1) INT'L REV. RED CROSS 333 (2019). The first proposal is for States to accord special protection as a matter of policy to certain essential civilian functions or services by committing to refrain from conducting cyber operations against civilian infrastructure or data that interfere with them. By the second, States would commit, as a matter of policy, to refraining from conducting cyber operations to which the IHL rules governing attacks do not apply when the expected concrete negative effects on individual civilians or the civilian population are excessive relative to the concrete benefit related to the conflict that is anticipated to be gained through the operation. These proposals are designed to accord de facto protection to essential systems and data in cases where the attacker believes either that its operation is not an attack or that the targeted civilian data is not an object that enjoys IHL's protection of civilian objects.

the attack threshold is, as discussed, ambiguous. Nevertheless, certain tentative conclusions are possible.

When Newtropia severed communications in the scenario, it was not an attack by any of the approaches already mentioned unless the way those communications were severed caused the requisite harm to communications cyber infrastructure, such as a loss of functionality requiring repair of the system. In such a case, for instance, France would style the operation an attack, while Israel would not. By contrast, Newtropia's deletion of the bank and retirement accounts was arguably (albeit not definitively) an attack, as data was damaged. Even if so, the applicability of key IHL targeting rules depends on the additional question of whether data is an "object," an issue explored later.[25] And Newtropia's cyber sabotage of the self-driving cars likely caused some of them to crash, clearly qualifying that aspect of the campaign as an attack.

The OMF countermeasures, such as inserting false data and fuzzing, might be considered attacks depending on where the threshold for attack lies. As a result of the insertion and fuzzing, the NAITS began to malfunction. A few of the *Tallinn Manual 2.0* experts were of the view that rendering a system unusable by cyber means amounts to an attack; this would appear to be the French position today. Here the NAITS was becoming increasingly unreliable. At a certain point, it will become useless because it is incapable of reliably distinguishing lawful from unlawful targets. More broadly, it is not unreasonable to suggest that a cyber operation that causes cyber infrastructure or systems that rely upon it to function in other than the intended manner is an attack since it is arguably "damaging." However, caution is merited because the only consensus among States today is that a physically damaging or injurious cyber operation is an attack.

Outlandia's use of random digital patterns on uniforms to fool the NAITS results in unintended attacks against medical personnel and children. This "ruse" (see below) is not an attack because it is not directed at the adversary or other protected persons or objects. This is so even though harm to those individuals is of a nature to generally qualify an operation as an attack. Instead, the use comprises a ruse gone wrong. Compare this situation with the use of weaponized honeypots[26]

---

25. Interestingly, the DoD Law of War Manual states, "a cyber attack that would destroy enemy computer systems could not be directed against ostensibly civilian infrastructure, such as computer systems belonging to stock exchanges, banking systems, and universities, unless those computer systems met the test for being a military objective under the circumstances." DoD Law of War Manual, *supra* note 4, § 16.5.1. It is unclear whether the passage refers to an operation affecting functionality of the system or one targeting data, or both, is envisaged.

26. "A deception technique in which a person seeking to defend computer systems against malicious cyber operations uses a physical or virtual environment designed to lure the attention of intruders with the aim of deceiving the intruders about the nature of the environment; having the intruders waste resources on the decoy environment; and gathering counter-intelligence about the intruder's intent, identity, and means and methods of cyber operation. Typically, the honeypot is co-resident with the actual systems the intruder wishes to target." TALLINN MANUAL 2.0, *supra* note 7, at 565. A weaponized honeypot contains a file that once exfiltrated will harm the attacker's system.

in which the exfiltrated data would generate effects at the level of an attack. Since the intent is to cause qualifying damage to the enemy, the tactic would be an attack that is subject to the attendant IHL rules. However, all that is occurring in this case is the frustration of effective NAITS-enabled attacks.

Finally, the kinetic targeting of individuals by employing the NAITS-enabled aerial kill vehicles is a classic attack.

IV. MILITARY OBJECTIVES

A. Persons

If an operation qualifies as an attack under IHL, the next question is whether the target is an individual subject to attack or a military objective.[27] Individuals may be attacked if they are combatants during an international armed conflict, such as members of the armed forces.[28] Civilians who have organized themselves into armed groups are also lawful targets,[29] although there is controversy surrounding those who do not have a "continuous combat function" in the group; the more defensible view is that they may be attacked.[30] Finally, civilians who "directly participate in hostilities" lose their protection from attack for such time as they so participate.[31] There is a degree of disagreement over which activities qualify as

27. The term "military objectives" is sometimes interpreted as including targetable individuals, although it technically only includes objects. DoD Law of War Manual, *supra* note 4, § 5.5.

28. Additional Protocol I, *supra* note 14, arts. 43, 48; DoD Law of War Manual, *supra* note 4, § 5.7.2. In the cyber context, see Tallinn Manual 2.0, *supra* note 7, rule 96 (a). The notion of combatancy does not apply in non-international armed conflict. Medical and religious personnel of the armed forces are protected from attack. 1949 Geneva Convention I, *supra* note 5, Art. 24; DoD Law of War Manual, *supra* note 4, § 4.10.1. They are not combatants. Additional Protocol I, *supra* note 14, Art. 43(2).

29. DoD Law of War Manual, *supra* note 4, § 5.7.3. In the cyber context, see Tallinn Manual 2.0, *supra* note 7, rule 96(b).

30. On the notion, see International Committee of the Red Cross, Interpretive Guidance on the Notion of Direct Participation in Hostilities under International Humanitarian Law (2009). For analysis, compare Michael N. Schmitt, *The Interpretive Guidance on the Notion of Direct Participation in Hostilities: A Critical Analysis*, 1 Harv. Nat'l Sec. J. 5, 21–24 (2010); and Kenneth Watkin, *Opportunity Lost: Organized Armed Groups and the ICRC "Direct Participation in Hostilities" Interpretive Guidance*, 42 N.Y.U. J. Int'l L. & Pol'y 641, 655–57 (2010), with Nils Melzer, *Keeping the Balance between Military Necessity and Humanity: A Response to Four Critiques of the ICRC's Interpretive Guidance on the Notion of Direct Participation in Hostilities*, 42 N.Y.U. J. Int'l L. & Pol'y 831, 846–50 (2010).

31. *See, e.g.*, Additional Protocol I, *supra* note 14, Art. 51(3); Protocol Additional to the Geneva Conventions of August 12, 1949, and Relating to the Protection of Victims of Non-international Armed Conflicts art. 13.3, June 8, 1977, 1125 U.N.T.S. 609; CIHL Study, *supra* note 14, rule 6; DoD Law of War Manual, *supra* note 4, § 5.8.1. In the cyber context, see Tallinn Manual 2.0, *supra* note 7, rule 96(c).

"direct" and the scope of the term "for such time."[32] Still, there is universal agreement that direct participants may be attacked.

In applying these categories to the scenario, we must identify the "object of attack," for the prohibitions are framed in that manner, as in the case of Additional Protocol I's Article 51(2): "The civilian population as such, as well as individual civilians, shall not be the object of attack." The object of attack is the entity upon which the attack's damaging or injurious force works. Consider Newtropia's "campaign of blackmail, disruption and intimidation against specific military and civilian members, as well as their family members." There, the object of attack to which the prohibitions on targeting civilian objects and civilians apply is the cyber infrastructure targeted by the operation, and, perhaps, data that is affected, but not the affected individuals. This is so as a matter of targeting law even though the effect sought is on individuals involved in mobilization and deployment. Thus, it is the cyber infrastructure, including that affected by operations involving data upon which it relies, that must be assessed against the criteria for military objectives that will be discussed when determining whether the operations targeted military objectives. Of course, that needs only to be done for aspects of the campaign that qualify as an attack.

In the scenario, the only individuals who plainly are made the "object of attack" are those targeted by the NAITS-enabled aerial kill vehicle missile strikes. All the intended targets appear to be OMF personnel. They are targetable as combatants regardless of the activity they might be engaged in at the time of attack. In other words, they are so-called status-based targets who may be attacked around the clock, subject to application of the rule of proportionality and the requirement to take precautions in attack. The issue of the mistaken strikes is addressed below.

The NAF operations against self-driving cars are more problematic. Assuming the operations cause the vehicles to crash while they are carrying individuals, the status of the individuals will determine Newtropia's compliance with IHL's prohibition on attacking civilians. As with the air strikes, there is no issue vis-à-vis targeting OMF personnel in this matter unless other persons or property are harmed (see later discussion of proportionality and precautions in attack).

Any attack on civilian employees, defense contractors, and government officials directly participating in hostilities is likewise lawful, subject to the proportionality and precautions rules. The ICRC has identified three elements of direct participation in its *Interpretive Guidance on the Notion of Direct Participation in Hostilities.*

1. the act must be likely to adversely affect the military operations or military capacity of a party to an armed conflict or, alternatively, to

---

32. Compare Michael N. Schmitt, *Deconstructing Direct Participation in Hostilities: The Constitutive Elements*, 42 N.Y.U. J. Int'l L. & Pol'y. 697, 725–34 (2010), and Bill Boothby, "*And for Such Time As*": *The Time Dimension to Direct Participation in Hostilities*, 42 N.Y.U. J. Int'l L. & Pol'y 741 (2010), with Melzer, *supra* note 30, at 865–69, 879–91.

inflict death, injury, or destruction on persons or objects protected against direct attack (threshold of harm), and

2. there must be a direct causal link between the act and the harm likely to result either from that act, or from a coordinated military operation of which that act constitutes an integral part (direct causation), and

3. the act must be specifically designed to directly cause the required threshold of harm in support of a party to the conflict and to the detriment of another (belligerent nexus).[33]

The elements appropriately set forth the criteria for direct participation, although, as noted, there is some disagreement with their application. According to the scenario, the individuals are involved in the mobilization and deployment of OMF personnel, thereby satisfying the first and third criteria. But without further information as to their roles in the execution of OMF military operations, it cannot be determined whether their activities are direct enough to result in a loss of their protection as civilians from attack. Speaking broadly, however, most are unlikely to qualify as direct participants.

Of course, family members are not direct participants and may not be directly attacked. If the operations cannot distinguish them from those who are combatants or direct participants, and injury or death is foreseeable as a result of any crashes, the attacks are indiscriminate and therefore unlawful. Indiscriminate attacks are discussed below in the context of mistaken attacks.

B. Objects

IHL defines civilian objects as those that are not military objectives.[34] Article 52(2) of Additional Protocol I, which restates customary international law, provides that "insofar as objects are concerned, military objectives are limited to those objects which by their nature, location, purpose or use make an effective contribution to military action and whose total or partial destruction, capture or neutralization, in the circumstances ruling at the time, offers a definite military advantage."[35] An object is a military objective by nature when its character is military. It is a military objective by use if it was originally civilian in character but is now used for military ends. And an object qualifies as a military objective by

---

33. Interpretive Guidance, *supra* note 30, at 46.

34. Additional Protocol I, *supra* note 14, art. 42(1). In the cyber context, see TALLINN MANUAL 2.0, *supra* note 7, rule 100.

35. As to the customary status of the definition, *see, e.g.,* CIHL Study, *supra* note 14, rule 8; DoD Law of War Manual, *supra* note 4, § 5.6.3.

purpose when it is not currently being used for military purposes but will be in the future.[36]

Much of the scenario raises the issue of conducting cyber operations against data. There is widespread agreement that if a cyber operation against data during an armed conflict directly causes the requisite consequences to persons or objects, the operation amounts to an attack. Examples include targeting the data upon which the cyber infrastructure relies in order to function, such as an operation against a reactor's cooling system, causing its meltdown or resulting in the requisite secondary effects, like a temporary denial of service attack against an electrical grid during a harsh winter storm that foreseeably causes the loss of heat, and individuals freeze to death.[37] In these cases, the object of attack is the nuclear reactor and the electrical grid, respectively. Such targets would be assessed against the military objective criteria.

The legal puzzle is how to assess an operation in which the data itself is the object of attack. Alteration, damage, or deletion of data, standing alone, arguably (although not definitively) satisfies the effects requirement for "attack," as the data is damaged. This being so, the determinative issue in targeting law is whether data is an "object" under IHL in the first place.

Before turning to that issue, it is necessary to dispense with one red herring. The "bigness" of Big Data, as such, is irrelevant. Data either is an object or not, and if so, it is either a military objective or a civilian object. In the same way that attacking a small civilian building and striking a large one are both treated as attacks on a civilian object, if data is an object, it makes no difference whether a lot or a little data is altered or deleted—an attack on a civilian object has occurred in both cases. Of course, the application of other IHL rules might be affected, especially the rule of proportionality.

The opposite is likewise the case. If data is not an object, the amount of data altered or destroyed is irrelevant; there is no attack on a civilian object. But as noted, if cyber infrastructure relies on that data, the IHL rules would apply to harm caused to the infrastructure and associated systems.

If data is treated as an object, an operation against data that does not qualify as a military objective would violate the IHL prohibition on attacking "civilian objects" and be a war crime.[38] For example, by this "data is an object" approach, a deep fake psychological cyber operation would be unlawful because it likely damages civilian data. Moreover, any harm collaterally caused to civilian data during a

---

36. On the four categories, see COMMENTARY ON THE ADDITIONAL PROTOCOLS OF 8 JUNE 1977 TO THE GENEVA CONVENTIONS OF 12 AUGUST 1949, ¶¶ 2020-2023 (Yves Sandoz, Christophe Swinarski, & Bruno Zimmermann eds., 1987).

37. TALLINN MANUAL 2.0, *supra* note 7, at 416. *See also, e.g.,* Schöndorf (Israel), *supra* note 22, at 400–01.

38. Additional Protocol I, *supra* note 14, arts. 52(1); CIHL Study, *supra* note 14, rule 7; DoD Law of War Manual, *supra* note 4, § 5.5.2; Rome Statute of the International Criminal Court art. 8.2(b)(ii), July 17, 1998, 2187 U.N.T.S. 90.

cyberattack directed against a military objective would need to be considered in the proportionality analysis and when assessing required precautions in attack.

In contrast, if data is not an object as a matter of IHL, conducting cyber operations intended to alter or delete civilian data is lawful so long as there are no damaging second-order effects to civilian cyberinfrastructure or other systems, or harm to civilians. By this approach, for instance, it would be lawful to mount operations that alter or delete civilian databases such as national archives, tax records, educational databases, and social service databases. Likewise, an attacker launching a cyberattack against a military objective expected to collaterally damage data residing in civilian systems would not have to consider that harm when doing the required proportionality and precautions assessments; only collateral damage to civilian objects and incidental injury of civilians is considered.

The matter is unsettled and contentious.[39] Israel, for example, has stated, "[o]bjects for the purposes of LOAC have always been understood to be tangible things and this understanding is not domain-specific. It is therefore our position that, under the law of armed conflict, as it currently stands, only tangible things can constitute objects."[40] It cautions, however, that "this does not mean that cyber operations adversely affecting computer data are unregulated. In particular, when an operation involving the deletion or alteration of computer data is still reasonably expected to cause physical damage to objects or persons and fulfills the other elements required to constitute an attack, the operation would be subject to LOAC targeting rules."[41] The approach is logical, for if civilian data is an object, many operations, such as psychological operations or those against social media, would be unlawful.

But as the ICRC has noted, "the assertion that deleting or tampering with such essential civilian data would not be prohibited by IHL in today's data-reliant world seems difficult to reconcile with the object and purpose of IHL."[42] This has led other countries to adopt the contrary approach. Romania, for example, asserts "that cyber operations against data do trigger the application of IHL. Therefore, cyber-attacks can only be directed against those data that represent military objectives according to IHL and cannot be directed against those data that represent a civilian object which must be protected under the principle of distinction."[43] And France has adopted a nuanced approach that distinguishes process data (that affecting the functioning of the associated cyber infrastructure and other systems) from content data (data containing information, such as the tax records): "Given the current state of digital dependence, content data (such as civilian, bank or medical data, etc.) are protected under the principle of

---

39. My views are set forth in Wired Warfare 3.0, *supra* note 24.

40. Schöndorf (Israel), *supra* note 22, at 401.

41. *Id.*

42. ICRC Position Paper, *supra* note 4, at 8.

43. Compendium, Romania, *supra* note 21, at 78.

distinction."[44] As to process data, France would look to the effect on the associated systems, but not on the data itself, to assess the lawfulness of the operation.

Assuming solely for the sake of illustration that the cyber operations targeting data in the scenario were attacks and that data is an object, the question then is whether the targets were military objectives and, therefore, lawfully subject to attack. Consider first the Newtropian disruption and intimidation campaign operations. The deleted bank and retirement accounts Newtropia targeted are not military objectives. To suggest that they might so qualify because they affect the morale of certain individuals who themselves might be targetable, or were designed to otherwise disrupt the mobilization, would unduly minimize the centrality of the "effective contribution to military action" and "definite military advantage" requirements for qualification as a military objective; the causal connection between the affected entities and the operations' military impact is too attenuated. Since they are not military objectives, they are civilian in character. The question, therefore, becomes whether data is subject to the prohibition on attacks against civilian objects.

By contrast, if the internet of things devices in Outlandia, particularly vehicles, are used for mobilization purposes and to transport military personnel and civilians involved in military operations to their place of duty, they amount to military objectives by virtue of their use for military purposes. And any Outlandian communications system used to pass mobilization-related information also undoubtedly qualifies as a military objective. This is so even if also used for civilian communications.[45] Accordingly, they may be the object of Newtropian cyber operations rising to the level of an attack, subject to the rule of proportionality and the requirement to take precautions in attack.

With respect to the OMF's operations, and again assuming for the sake of analysis that data is an object, the data targeted in Newtropian military networks, such as military personnel and pay records, is a military objective by "nature." Only military medical data would be shielded from interference by virtue of its so-called special protection under IHL and therefore cannot qualify as a military objective.[46]

The NAITS-related data that the OMF targets by inserting false data and fuzzing is a military objective by "use" if data is an object. This is true even though some of the data used by the NAITS was originally private civilian data collected by Newtropia. It became a military objective by "purpose" once Newtropia started collecting it to enable the NAITS and qualified as a military objective by "use" once Newtropia began to use it to train the system. The question regarding both this data and Newtropian military data is whether the operations against them were attacks in the first place. If so, it is lawful to delete, damage, or alter the data

---

44. France, Ministry of the Armies, *supra* note 22, at 14.

45. DoD Law of War Manual, *supra* note 4, § 5.6.12.

46. TALLINN MANUAL 2.0, *supra* note 7, rule 132.

because of qualification as a military objective. If not, it is lawful to do so because the operations are not subject to the conduct of hostility rules governing attacks.

C. Targeting Errors

The NAITS-enabled attacks that misidentified civilians and lawful targets illustrate the persistent real-world challenge of uncertainty during targeting. The mere fact that the wrong individuals were attacked, even though they enjoyed protected status as civilians, is not alone enough to amount to an IHL violation. Indeed, attacks based on honest and reasonable mistakes do not violate IHL.[47] This includes the use of weapons systems that unexpectedly malfunction, as in the case of a missile that loses its guidance capability while in flight.

Here, though, the issue is different. The NAITS algorithm is imperfect, and OMF's countermeasures, including uniforms containing random digital patterns, are causing a growing number of mistaken strikes. The mistaken strikes raise the issue of whether the NAF's use of NAITS-enabled aerial kill vehicles complies with the customary law requirement of distinction captured in Article 48 of Additional Protocol I: "In order to ensure respect for and protection of the civilian population and civilian objects, the Parties to the conflict shall at all times distinguish between the civilian population and combatants and between civilian objects and military objectives and accordingly shall direct their operations only against military objectives." Specifically, the issue is the level of acceptable uncertainty when identifying lawfully targetable individuals and military objectives for attack. In other words, was it lawful for NAF personnel to execute the strikes in the face of the growing unreliability of the system?

Those who plan, approve, and conduct attacks must understand the capabilities and shortfalls of a weapons system in the environment in which it is to be employed and use them appropriately considering that context.[48] Thus, once the propensity for errors should have been noticed, NAF personnel involved in the strikes were obligated to take the system's precision capability at the time, including the likelihood of misidentification, into account when assessing whether to launch the attacks.

When assessing their decision, it is incorrect to compare the NAITS-enabled kill vehicle's error rate to weapons systems having a human operator in the

---

47. Marko Milanovic, *Mistakes of Fact When Using Lethal Force in International Law: Part I*, Ejil: Talk! (Jan. 14, 2020), https://www.ejiltalk.org/mistakes-of-fact-when-using-lethal-force-in-international-law-part-i/.

48. *See generally* Michael N. Schmitt &Jeffrey Thurner, *"Out of the Loop": Autonomous Weapon Systems and the Law of Armed Conflict*, 4 Harv. Nat'l Sec. J. 231 (2013). *See also* the points made regarding the "human element" in Government of the United States, Statement to the Convention on Conventional Weapons Group of Governmental Experts on lethal autonomous weapons systems, Aug. 20, 2019, https://conf.unog.ch/digitalrecordings/index.html?guid=public/61.0500/53087D36-FA85-4050-88DB-27932ABEBFAA_15h12&position=7171.

Big Data: Armed Conflict 167

abstract. Instead, the issue when comparing systems is "precautions in attack," specifically that IHL rule's choice of "means" (weapons and weapons systems) element. International humanitarian law requires an attacker to select the available weapons system that causes the least incidental injury and collateral damage, so long as its use is feasible in the circumstances and military advantage is not sacrificed.[49] Feasibility is a complex issue that ranges from the availability of weapons systems and any need for them elsewhere to the employment environment and likelihood of success. As an illustration of the standard, consider a case in which an available human-enabled weapons system's use would have resulted in fewer civilian casualties than the NAITS-enabled aerial kill vehicles while achieving the same (or comparable) desired effect. If its use made sense militarily, the NAF would have been required to employ it instead of the kill vehicles.

Assuming that no viable alternative to the NAITS-enabled aerial kill vehicle existed, the question becomes whether the likelihood of mistaken attacks against civilians (mistaken attacks against lawfully targetable individuals are not unlawful) at the time the Newtropian forces planned, approved, and executed the operations was so high as to render the operation indiscriminate,[50] and therefore unlawful. This is the case when a system "cannot be directed at a specific military objective" reliably.[51] In other words, if civilians cannot be adequately distinguished in that particular battlefield environment from individuals who lawfully may be attacked, the weapon involved cannot be reliably "directed," and its use in those circumstances is indiscriminate. The operations against the self-driving cars raise the same issue.

The fact that the technology was misidentifying targets does not relieve those deciding to employ the NAITS-enabled kill vehicle of their obligation to refrain from utilizing a system so unreliable as to be indiscriminate. The question is, when does the degree of uncertainty about the reliability of the system's identification of targeted individuals reach a point where the use of the system is indiscriminate?

The ICRC has acknowledged, and correctly so, that targeting decisions are contextual.

---

49. Additional Protocol I, *supra* note 14, art. 57(2)(a)(ii); CIHL Study, *supra* note 14, rule 17; DoD Law of War Manual, *supra* note 4, § 5.11. In the cyber context, see TALLINN MANUAL 2.0, *supra* note 7, rule 116.

50. Additional Protocol I, *supra* note 14, Art. 51(4)(a)(b); CIHL Study, *supra* note 14, rules 11, 12; Dinstein, *supra* note 5, at 147–49; Michael N. Schmitt & Eric Widmar, *"On Target": Precision and Balance in the Contemporary Law of Targeting*, 7 J. NAT'L SEC. L. & POL'Y 379, 398–99 (2014). The International Court of Justice has labeled the prohibition on indiscriminate weapons as one of two "cardinal" principles, the other being the principle of unnecessary suffering. Legality of the Threat of Use of Nuclear Weapons, Advisory Opinion, 1996 I.C.J 226, ¶ 78 (July 8). *See also* Prosecutor v. Kupreskic´, Case Number IT-95-16-T, Judgment, ¶ 524 (Int'l Crim. Trib. for the former Yugoslavia Jan. 14, 2000).)

51. Additional Protocol I, *supra* note 14, Art. 51(4)(a). In the cyber context, see TALLINN MANUAL 2.0, *supra* note 7, rule 111.

Obviously, the standard of doubt applicable to targeting decision . . . must reflect the level of certainty that can reasonably be achieved in the circumstances. In practice, this determination will have to take into account, inter alia, the intelligence available to the decision maker, the urgency of the situation, and the harm likely to result to the operating forces or to persons and objects protected against direct attack from an erroneous decision.[52]

Adopting the same contextual approach, the experts who drafted the *Harvard Manual on International Law Applicable to Air and Missile Warfare* suggested that the point at which an attack must not be executed is when the degree of uncertainty "is that which would cause a reasonable attacker in the same or similar circumstances to abstain from ordering or executing an attack."[53] This conclusion applies equally to uncertainty as to the identification made by the NAITS technology.

The subject of how to deal with uncertainty in targeting has been the subject of significant scholarly consideration.[54] However, in practice, assessing uncertainty occurs through a flexible process involving the balancing of military considerations and humanitarian concerns. As I have explained elsewhere, the greater the value of a target, the more uncertainty may be countenanced in an attack, and vice versa.

[T]he risk posed by uncertainty when identifying a target is that the target will be misidentified as a valid military objective and the attack accordingly will harm persons or objects protected by IHL. This risk reflects the humanitarian concern that is present in the aforementioned balancing. But the military advantage anticipated to accrue if the target is attacked must also be considered. The objective is to determine when the risk of harm to protected persons or objects should the target be misidentified as a military objective is warranted relative to the anticipated value of the target; at that point, the prospective attack becomes lawful.[55]

In this case, the built-in kill list consisted of "high-value" OMF personnel. Therefore, greater uncertainty as to verification of the targets could be tolerated than, for instance, a system that would engage any OMF personnel in the database.

---

52. Interpretive Guidance, *supra* note 30, at 76.

53. Program on Humanitarian Policy and Conflict Research at Harvard University, Commentary on the HPCR Manual on International Law Applicable to Air and Missile Warfare 90 (2010) [hereinafter Harvard AMW Manual].

54. Adil Haque, *Killing in the Fog of War*, 86 S. Cal. L. Rev. 63 (2012); Geoffrey S. Corn, *Targeting, Command Judgment, and a Proposed Quantum of Information Component: A Fourth Amendment Lesson in Contextual Reasonableness*, 77 Brook. L. Rev. 437 (2012).

55. Michael N. Schmitt & Michael Schauss, *Uncertainty in the Law of Targeting: Towards a Cognitive Framework*, 10 Harv. Nat'l Sec. J. 148, 163 (2019).

Probabilities also enter the assessment. An attacker needs to consider both the probability of achieving the attack's desired effect and the likelihood of collateral damage or incidental injury. Accordingly, Newtropian forces must factor in the degraded precision of the NAITS-enabled kill vehicle because it lowers the probability of success and increases the likelihood of mistakenly causing incidental injury to civilians.

It is impossible to assess the use of the NAITS-enabled attacks either individually or together without more information. For example, beyond being high-value targets, what precise effects would their deaths likely have on the enemy's operations? What was the error rate at the time they were employed? What systems were in place to monitor the error rate? Could measures have been taken to minimize mistaken engagements, such as limiting the use of the kill vehicles to certain battlefield environments or narrowing the kill list to only the top OMF commanders such that the reliability was acceptable in the circumstances in which the system was being used?

Of course, the NAITS-enable aerial kill vehicle itself may become unlawful at some point along the continuum of unreliability.[56] This would be so once it became highly unreliable in *any* environment in which it was meant to be employed; the fact that the OMF countermeasures contribute to its unreliability does not relieve the NAF of its legal obligations. Yet, this is unlikely ever to be the case, for it is possible to envision circumstances in which it could adequately distinguish between civilians from targetable individuals, including the OMF forces. For instance, there may be areas where civilians are absent, such as ones from which the civilian population has fled or that are very remote. Absence of civilians in the target area would mean there is no opportunity for the attacks to be indiscriminate. As a general matter, then, the NAITS-enable kill vehicle is a lawful weapons system, although the decision to employ it in an environment in which civilians and lawfully targetable individuals were collocated is subject to the analysis set forth above.

V. CAPITA SELECTA

A. Proportionality and Precautions in Attack

The significance of civilian status extends beyond the issue of whether the target is a lawful "object of attack."[57] According to the rule of proportionality, "An attack which may be expected to cause incidental loss of civilian life, injury to civilians, damage to civilian objects, or a combination thereof, which would be excessive in relation to the concrete and direct military advantage anticipated," is prohibited

---

56. On the distinction between an indiscriminate weapon and the indiscriminate use of a discriminate weapon, *see* DoD Law of War Manual, *supra* note 4, § 6.1.1.

57. Additional Protocol I, *supra* note 14, Art. 51(2).

as indiscriminate.[58] The determination is made *ex ante*, not *post factum*; the actual harm caused or military advantage achieved is only evidence bearing on the issue of what the attacker should have concluded when doing the proportionality assessment before or at the time of the attack. It merits noting that neither this rule nor that requiring precautions in attack consider harm to data unless data is treated as an "object" under IHL (see earlier discussion). Moreover, irritation, inconvenience, and even intimidation do not qualify as incidental injury by mainstream approaches to proportionality and precautions in attack.[59]

Determination of whether the NAITS-enabled aerial kill vehicle strikes complied with the rule of proportionality depends on the anticipated advantage the NAF reasonably believed it would gain from killing the intended targets, considered in light of the likelihood of mistaken attacks on, or incidental injury to, civilians. The latter factor would include consideration of the system's reliability at the time. If the expected incidental injury was "excessive" to the anticipated military advantage, the strikes were unlawful.

This assessment is complicated because the strikes target different individuals on the kill list, but the NAF does not control individual strikes and does not necessarily know which person is being targeted at any one time. Thus, the anticipated military advantage factored into the analysis must be the lowest among those on the list. Additionally, the degree of military advantage in combat is often fluid. Because the reliability of NAITS is slipping, those involved with NAITS assessments should have frequently assessed whether use of the system remained compliant over time with the proportionality rule.

Even when "collateral damage" to civilian objects or "incidental injury" to civilians is proportionate, an attacker must take "feasible" measures to minimize it. This obligation includes choosing from among weapons, tactics, and targets that are likely to cause the least collateral damage and incidental injury, so long as likely military advantage is not sacrificed.[60]

The issue of precautions in attack was discussed earlier in the context of indiscriminate attacks. It was noted that if Newtropia has weapons systems that could target the individuals with greater reliability than the kill vehicles, it was feasible to use them in the circumstances, and they generated comparable military

---

58. *Id.*, Arts. 51(5)(b), 57(2)(a)(iii), 57(2)(b). *See also* CIHL Study, *supra* note 14, rule 14; DoD Law of War Manual, *supra* note 4, § 5.10. On proportionality generally, see Dinstein, *supra* note 5, at 149–62; A.P.V. ROGERS, LAW ON THE BATTLEFIELD 21–26 (3d ed. 2012). In the cyber context, see TALLINN MANUAL 2.0, *supra* note 7, rule 113.

59. Harvard AMW Manual, *supra* note 53, at 96; TALLINN MANUAL 2.0, *supra* note 7, at 472. The DOD Law of War Manual appropriately juxtaposes inconvenience and temporary disruption of civilian life in general with civilian loss of life, injury, and damage to objects. DoD Law of War Manual, *supra* note 4, § 5.12.1.2. *See also id.*, § 16.5.1.1.

60. Additional Protocol I, *supra* note 14, art. 57(2); CIHL Study, *supra* note 14, rules 15–17, 20–21; DoD Law of War Manual, *supra* note 4, § 5.11. *See also* Dinstein, *supra* note 5, at 164–72; Rogers, *supra* note 58, ch. 5. In the cyber context, see TALLINN MANUAL 2.0, *supra* note 7, rule 116.

advantage, the NAF would be obligated to use them. However, the scenario does not include any indication that such systems exist. Additionally, if the NAF could adjust its tactics to minimize the likelihood of mistakes or manipulate the NAITS somehow to improve reliability, it would be obliged to do so as no military advantage would be sacrificed.

Article 57(1) of Additional Protocol I also imposes a duty to take "constant care" during military operations. Whether this article restates customary IHL is an open question. Moreover, if there is such a duty under either treaty or customary international law, there is an ongoing debate over whether the duty only applies to operations qualifying as an attack, an issue examined earlier. This is because the title of Article 57 is "Precautions in *attack*," but Article 57(1), unlike the other sections of the article, uses the broader term "operations." And even if the obligation applies to all military operations, there is uncertainty about its precise meaning in concrete situations.

I have examined the issue in greater depth elsewhere, concluding that the most defensible position as a matter of law is that the obligation is customary, applies to all military operations, and by it "[c]ommanders and others with control over military operations cannot lawfully ignore any possibility of an impact on the civilian population. They may be able to dismiss the possibility very quickly, but the consideration thereof must always be part of the operational analysis."[61]

Thus, Newtropian and Outlandian cyber operations that do not qualify as attacks nevertheless would be subject to this obligation. For example, consider the OMF's NAITS countermeasures that caused the system to misidentify targets. The countermeasures would be unlikely to be characterized as attacks since none of them caused any physical or functional damage to Newtropian systems. But once the OMF knew civilians are being misidentified, it had to consider that fact in determining whether to continue or adjust the countermeasures.

B. Precautions against Attack

Precautions taken by an attacking force to minimize collateral damage and incidental injury are known as "passive precautions." IHL also imposes an obligation on defenders to take "passive precautions" to minimize harm to civilians and civilian objects. Article 58 of Additional Protocol I reflects this customary law obligation.[62] Sub-paragraph (c), which summarizes the entire article, provides,

---

61. Schmitt and Schauss, *supra* note 55, at 180. The DoD *Law of War Manual* takes a very broad view, and surprisingly so, of the obligation: "For example, even if a cyber operation is not an "attack" or does not cause any injury or damage that would need to be considered under the principle of proportionality in conducting attacks, that cyber operation still should not be conducted in a way that unnecessarily causes inconvenience to civilians or neutral persons." DoD Law of War Manual, *supra* note 4, § 16.5.2.

62. Additional Protocol I, *supra* note 14, art. 58; CIHL Study, *supra* note 14, rule 22; DoD Law of War Manual, *supra* note 4, § 5.14.

"The Parties to the conflict shall, to the maximum extent feasible . . . [t]ake . . .1 necessary precautions to protect the civilian population, individual civilians and civilian objects under their control against the dangers resulting from military operations."

There is no question that the obligation applies in the cyber context,[63] but the devil is in the details, as evidenced during the Tallinn Manual deliberations. A majority of the experts were of the view that the provision only applies to passive precautions against cyber operations that qualify as an attack under IHL. For them, there is no legal obligation to take measures against other forms of hostile cyber operations. They based this view on the reference to "attacks" in the title of Article 58. They further suggested that even if Article 58 applies to all hostile military operations, customary IHL does not extend that far. Accordingly, the legal obligation for non-Party States would be limited to passive precautions against cyberattacks.[64]

The minority looked to the object and purpose of the rule, suggesting that the reference to "operations" in Article 58(c) should be understood as imposing a broader requirement, much as the reference to "operations" in Article 57(1) suggests application to all operations vis-à-vis the constant care requirement.[65] Both views are reasonable, although the general trend in understanding how IHL applies in the cyber context is toward broad interpretation. Whichever view is correct, the obligation, unlike most other IHL obligations, attaches prior to the outbreak of hostilities; it may be too late to take effective passive precautions once hostilities occur.

This scenario does not provide sufficient granularity to determine whether Newtropia and Outlandia have complied with their passive precautions obligations. This is because the requirement is to take feasible measures, not prevent civilian harm altogether; the obligation is one of conduct, not result. However, the *Tallinn Manual* experts cited numerous passive cyber precautions, some of which would apply in this scenario. They include "segregating military from civilian cyberinfrastructure; segregating computer systems on which critical civilian infrastructure depends from the Internet; backing up important civilian data; taking advance arrangements to ensure the timely repair of important computer systems; digitally recording important cultural or spiritual objects to facilitate reconstruction in the event of their destruction; and using anti-virus measures to protect civilians systems that might suffer damage or destruction during an attack on military cyberinfrastructure."[66]

The obligation to take passive precautions is subject to a condition of feasibility. For example, backing up Big Data could present distinct logistical challenges.

---

63. TALLINN MANUAL 2.0, *supra* note 7, rule 121 and accompanying commentary.

64. *Id.* at 488.

65. *Id.*

66. *Id.*

Similarly, segregating systems storing Big Data likewise could prove difficult. And backing up civilian data might also implicate some human rights privacy issues discussed in the previous chapter.

C. Blackmail, Disruption, Intimidation

The threatening messages delivered by Newtropia to OMF family members and Outlandian civilians who are not direct participants in the hostilities implicate the prohibition on terrorizing the civilian population. According to Article 51(2) of Additional Protocol I, "acts or threats of violence the primary purpose of which is to spread terror among the civilian population are prohibited." This prohibition reflects customary international law and therefore governs the Newtropian cyber operations irrespective of Newtropia's Party status to the Protocol.[67] It is important to emphasize that the rule only prohibits terrorizing civilians who are protected from attack. Terrorizing military personnel, members of armed groups, or individual civilians directly participating in hostilities is lawful.

To assess the operations against any protected persons, it would be necessary to know the content of the intimidating messages. If they threatened violence in a manner that would cause reasonable individuals to become fearful, the communications would be unlawful. This is so even though the messages themselves would not qualify as an attack, the mere threat of an attack having the requisite consequences breaches the prohibition.

D. Perfidy and Misuse of Protective Indicators

The OMF's use of random digital patterns to thwart the Newtropian AWS raises several IHL issues. First, the use of these patterns does not amount to perfidy, which Article 37(1) of Additional Protocol I and customary IHL prohibit.[68] According to the article, "Acts inviting the confidence of an adversary to lead him to believe that he is entitled to, or is obliged to accord, protection under the rules of international law applicable in armed conflict, with intent to betray that confidence, shall constitute perfidy."

In some cases, the digital patterns cause OMF soldiers to appear to the NAITS as medical personnel, children, and penguins. Although medical personnel and civilians, including children, enjoy protection from attack, the OMF was not seeking to trick Newtropian forces into believing they were obligated to accord protection to the troops wearing the patterns; indeed, the OMF was unaware

---

67. CIHL Study, *supra* note 14, rule 2; DoD Law of War Manual, *supra* note 4, § 5.3.2; Tallinn Manual 2.0, *supra* note 7, rule 98.

68. Additional Protocol I, *supra* note 14, Art, 37(1); CIHL Study, *supra* note 14, rule 65; DoD Law of War Manual, *supra* note 4, § 5.22; Tallinn Manual 2.0, *supra* note 7, rule 122.

that this was occurring. Moreover, the OMF did not use the patterns to place Newtropian forces in a situation where they could be attacked.

On the contrary, the OMF designed the patterns to confuse the NAITS sensors so the aerial kill vehicle could not engage the OMF soldiers reliably. As such, they amounted to a "ruse." Ruses are expressly permitted by Article 37(2) of Additional Protocol I and have long been accepted as lawful in the practice of States on the battlefield.[69] The Protocol defines ruses as "acts which are intended to mislead an adversary or to induce him to act recklessly but which infringe no rule of international law applicable in armed conflict and which are not perfidious because they do not invite the confidence of an adversary with respect to protection under that law." It offers camouflage, decoys, mock operations, and misinformation as examples. In a sense, the patterns were intended to serve as camouflage because they make it difficult for the NAITS sensors to identify OMF troops.

Also note that although the NAITS sensors were incorrectly identifying OMF soldiers as medical personnel due to the digital patterns on their uniforms, the OMF ruse was not a violation of the prohibition on the misuse of medical emblems. The Red Cross, Red Crescent, and Red Crystal are recognized as distinctive emblems for medical personnel; the display of these emblems by those not entitled to wear them is prohibited irrespective of whether there is any intent to betray the confidence of the enemy in order to attack them.[70]

The *Tallinn Manual* experts were unable to achieve consensus on how this prohibition applied in the cyber context, as in using cyber means to feign medical status or trick cyberinfrastructure into concluding that individuals are medical personnel, as happened, albeit unintentionally, in this case.[71] One approach is to interpret the rule strictly to apply only to physical emblems, such as wearing the actual Red Cross emblem on a uniform. A teleological approach, by contrast, looks to the underlying object and purpose of the rule and argues that in the cyber context, the issue is whether there was an attempt to feign medical status.

However, by the facts in this scenario, neither approach would lead to a conclusion of misuse, either because no designated emblem was used or because there was no intent to feign status. If the OMF learned of the NAITS misidentification of its personnel as medical and nevertheless continued to employ the pattern, doing so would violate the prohibition by the latter interpretation, but not by the former.

---

69. *See, e.g.,* Regulations Respecting the Laws and Customs of War on Land, annexed to Convention No. IV Respecting the Laws and Customs of War on Land, art. 24, Oct. 18, 1907, 36 Stat. 2227, T.S. No. 539.

70. *Id.,* Art. 23(f); Additional Protocol I, *supra* note 14, Art. 38(1); Additional Protocol II, *supra* note 31, Art. 12; DoD Law of War Manual *supra* note 4, §§ 5.24.2, 7.15.4 and 16.5.4. CIHL Study, *supra* note 14, rule 59; Tallinn Manual 2.0, *supra* note 7, rule 124.

71. Tallinn Manual 2.0, *supra* note 7, at 498.

Big Data: Armed Conflict

E. Race

The mistaken attacks are disproportionately against non-Caucasians because the data used to train the NAITS was predominantly that of Caucasians. Various IHL rules expressly prohibit racial discrimination with respect to civilians and those who are *hors de combat*, prohibitions recognized by States such as the United States as customary international law. For instance, Common Article 3 of the 1949 Geneva Conventions provides, "Persons taking no active part in the hostilities, including members of armed forces who have laid down their arms and those placed hors de combat by sickness, wounds, detention, or any other cause, shall in all circumstances be treated humanely, without any adverse distinction founded on race, colour, religion or faith, sex, birth or wealth, or any other similar criteria."[72]

Although not all IHL rules contain a nondiscrimination clause, the ICRC's *Customary International Humanitarian Law* study observes, "Adverse distinction in the application of international humanitarian law based on race, colour, sex, language, religion or belief, political or other opinion, national or social origin, wealth, birth or other status, or on any other similar criteria is prohibited."[73] As this is a sound assertion, the prohibition of discrimination would bar attributing lesser value to specific racial groups when making target identification, proportionality, and precautions in attack assessments.

However, in this case, the NAITS-enabled kill vehicles are not valuing racial groups differently; instead, they are making technical errors based on the nature of the collected data. Moreover, Newtropia did not intentionally gather data that would result in disproportionate racial impact. It is essential to understand that IHL does not forbid disparate racial impact during combat operations. Rather, it prohibits treating racial groups differently in the same or similar circumstances to the detriment of a group. Thus, even if the differing frequency of mistakes comes to the attention of the Newtropian forces, continuing to engage in attacks would be lawful, at least so long as there were no feasible means to remedy the high number of mistakes against non-Caucasians. Of course, if such a means existed, its use would already be required by the obligation to take feasible precautions in attack to avoid harming civilians.

Disparate impact does raise international human rights law issues. However, although human rights obligations apply during armed conflict, they do so

---

72. Geneva Convention for the Amelioration of the Condition of the Wounded and Sick in Armed Forces in the Field Art. 3, Aug. 12, 1949, 6 U.S.T. 3114, 75 U.N.T.S. 31; Convention for the Amelioration of the Condition of the Wounded, Sick and Shipwrecked Members of Armed Forces at Sea Art. 3, Aug. 12, 1949, 6 U.S.T. 3217, 75 U.N.T.S. 85; Geneva Convention Relative to the Treatment of Prisoners of War Art. 3, Aug. 12, 1949, 6 U.S.T. 3316, 75 U.N.T.S. 135; Geneva Convention Relative to the Protection of Civilian Persons in Time of War Art. 3, Aug. 12, 1949, 6 U.S.T. 3516, 75 U.N.T.S. 287.

73. CIHL Study, *supra* note 14, rule 88.

according to the *lex specialis* principle. As noted by the International Court of Justice in its *Nuclear Weapons* Advisory Opinion,

> The Court observes that the protection of the International Covenant of Civil and Political Rights does not cease in times of war, except by operation of Article 4 of the Covenant whereby certain provisions may be derogated from in a time of national emergency. Respect for the right to life is not, however, such a provision. In principle, the right not arbitrarily to be deprived of one's life applies also in hostilities. The test of what is an arbitrary deprivation of life, however, then falls to be determined by the applicable lex specialis, namely, the law applicable in armed conflict which is designed to regulate the conduct of hostilities. Thus whether a particular loss of life, through the use of a certain weapon in warfare, is to be considered an arbitrary deprivation of life . . . can only be decided by reference to the law applicable in armed conflict and not deduced from the terms of the Covenant itself.[74]

Accordingly, the NAITS-enable strikes must be assessed by the IHL rules governing targeting discussed above, by which all feasible measures must be taken to ensure that (1) *every* target is a lawful one, (2) expected incidental injury to *all* civilians is not excessive relative to the anticipated concrete and direct military advantage of the attack, and that (3) *all* feasible measures to minimize incidental harm to any civilian have been taken.

F. Weapons Review

International humanitarian law requires a weapon review before fielding weapons and weapons systems. It is universally accepted that the obligation applies in the cyber context.[75] Article 36 of Additional Protocol I sets forth the obligation for States Party to the instrument: "In the study, development, acquisition or adoption of a new weapon, means or method of warfare, a High

Contracting Party is under an obligation to determine whether its employment would, in some or all circumstances, be prohibited by this Protocol or by any other rule of international law applicable to the High Contracting Party." "Means" of warfare refers to weapons and weapons systems, whereas "methods" refers to tactics, the way attacks are conducted. The requirement to review weapons prior to fielding them is generally considered customary in character, but the United

---

74. Nuclear Weapons Advisory Opinion, *supra* note 50, ¶ 25.

75. For a discussion, *see* TALLINN MANUAL 2.0, *supra* note 7, rule 110 and accompanying commentary.

States, and numerous other countries and commentators, do not draw the same conclusion regarding methods of warfare.[76]

The scenario does not indicate whether Newtropia or Outlandia have conducted weapons reviews of their cyber-enabled systems, like the NAITS-enabled kill vehicle, or particular types of cyber operations. However, it is clear that cyber-enabled systems capable of mounting an attack, as that term is understood in IHL, require a weapons review. Thus, a review would be required of the NAITS-enabled aerial kill vehicle.

A more difficult question is how the obligation applies to cyber operations in which cyber capability is not used to enable an associated weapon or weapons systems, as in the use of malware to target cyberinfrastructure. The *Tallinn Manual* experts took the position that cyber means of warfare "include any cyber device, material, instrument, mechanism, equipment, or software used, designed, or intended to be used to conduct a cyber attack."[77] For them, "methods of warfare" refers to how cyber operations are mounted," citing the example of a "botnet to conduct a destructive distributed denial of service attack."[78] Thus, for instance, the malware used in the operations against the self-driving cars would require a weapons review because it is a means of warfare.

A contrary view has begun to emerge by which cyber capabilities qualify as methods of warfare but not means of warfare unless integrated into an associated weapons system such as the NAITS-enabled kill vehicle.[79] As I have explained elsewhere,

> The physical damage (including loss of functionality) or injury that occurs as the result of malicious computer code used in a cyber attack is the result of actions ultimately undertaken by the targeted system itself. The code is but a communication to that system instructing it to undertake a harmful action, function in an unintended manner, or cease to function. In no other type of weapon is an intervening step by the target itself required to achieve the sought-after harm. Thus, the notion that a communication of code alone can constitute a damage mechanism fails to stand up to logical and legal analysis based on current understandings of means of warfare. That said, there is no question that categories of cyber operations are methods of warfare subject to relevant legal prohibitions and limitations, as well as policy restrictions.[80]

---

76. Jeffrey T. Biller & Michael N. Schmitt, *Classification of Cyber Capabilities and Operations as Weapons, Means, or Methods of Warfare*, 95 INT'L L. STUD. 179, 183–88 (2019).

77. TALLINN MANUAL 2.0, *supra* note 7, at 453.

78. *Id.*

79. Biller & Schmitt, *supra* note 76.

80. *Id.* at 224–25.

By this interpretation, no legal review of the cyber capabilities used in the scenario would be required of non-Parties to Additional Protocol I, except for that which is integral to the kill vehicles. However, it must be emphasized that an operation qualifying as an attack must still comply with the IHL rules governing the conduct of attacks even if employing a cyber capability that is not by the second approach subject to a weapons review before fielding.

VI. CONCLUSION

The use of data for military operations during an armed conflict presents numerous IHL issues. Two loom largest. First, operations targeting data in a manner that affects the functionality of cyber infrastructure raise the thorny question of whether that consequence, in the absence of physical damage or injury, qualifies as an *attack*, the condition precedent to the application of most IHL targeting rules. If not, the extent of the opportunity to mount cyber operations that will dramatically affect the civilian population is concerning.

Second, the issue of whether data is an object is fundamental. If it is not, a party to the conflict may freely alter or destroy civilian data even if the alteration or deletion is considered an attack, so long as there is no knock-on effect for civilian cyber infrastructure. This is because the relevant prohibition is on attacking civilian *objects*. Again, the potential for disruption of civilian activities is huge.

Finally, the "bigness" of data is generally irrelevant to application of the IHL rules considered above. Of course, if an operation targeting Big Data causes consequences to which IHL applies, the nature, extent, and scope of those consequences, which may result from the bigness of the data, matters, especially with regard to the assessment of proportionality. But as a rule, there is no legal significance to the size of the data concerned as such.

6

Garbage In, Garbage Out

Data Poisoning Attacks and Their Legal Implications

MARK A. VISGER* ◼

I. INTRODUCTION

With each new development in the cyber era, a corresponding attempt to "hack" the new technology has taken place. For example, in the case of self-driving cars, experts have demonstrated how such a car can be hacked, with the hacker able to assume control of the vehicle.[1] With the advent of Artificial Intelligence (AI) powered by machine learning and the prospect of deploying such tools into combat systems, the obvious question is raised—Can AI be hacked?

The process of hacking usually requires deep technological understanding of the structure and mechanics of the underlying technological system. The hacker needs to dive deep "under the hood," so to speak, to find flaws and bugs to exploit. In the case of artificial intelligence/machine learning, hackers seek to do the same thing. In the case of AI, and more specifically machine learning, when one looks under the hood, one finds Big Data. Many have said that "data is the new oil,"[2] in part because data is the underlying substance that is able to power analytic tools

---

* Academy Professor, Army Cyber Institute at U.S. Military Academy at West Point.

1. Eric A. Taub, *Carmakers Strive to Stay Ahead of Hackers*, N.Y. TIMES (Mar. 18, 2021), https://www.nytimes.com/2021/03/18/business/hacking-cars-cybersecurity.html.

2. This quote is widely attributed to Clive Humby. Charles Arthur, *Tech Giants May Be Huge, but Nothing Matches Big Data*, THE GUARDIAN (Aug. 23, 2013, 3:21 PM), https://www.theguardian.com/technology/2013/aug/23/tech-giants-data. The purpose of the analogy was twofold, to state its great value in driving these new processes but also to state the need for refinement, in order for big data to be valuable. *Id.*

Mark A. Visger, *Garbage In, Garbage Out* In: *Big Data and Armed Conflict.* Edited by: Laura A. Dickinson and Edward W. Berg, Oxford University Press. © Mark A. Visger 2024. DOI: 10.1093/oso/9780197668610.003.0008

such as machine learning and predictive analysis.[3] For purposes of this chapter, Big Data will be defined as "a combination of structured, semistructured and unstructured data collected by organizations that can be mined for information and used in machine learning projects, predictive modeling and other advanced analytics applications."[4] These analytic tools distill this Big Data into actionable information—such as the recommendations that are now ubiquitous on cyber commerce websites.[5] These machine learning systems digest large amounts of data as part of the "learning" process—making connections, discerning inferences, and ultimately drawing conclusions in a manner that looks somewhat like what we humans call "learning."[6] As a result, if one can hack the Big Data that powers machine learning, one can potentially also hack the machine learning process itself.

To help visualize this process, let's consider a somewhat absurd hypothetical. Suppose an archetypical villain from a James Bond movie develops a machine learning model to identify cats from real-time video feeds. This information is fed to a loitering weapon, which we'll call the de-catenator, which targets the cats for destruction. In order to develop an application that identifies cats in real time, the villain would need to create a machine learning model that is trained to identify cats by "watching" thousands of hours of cat videos. In one type of machine learning, the cats in these videos would be labeled so that the machine learning can discern the relevant features on the labeled cats and "learn" how to identify cats independently. When the learning process is complete, the system would be deployed operationally, able to identify cats from video feeds in real time and funneling this information to the loitering weapon, threatening the feline species with imminent destruction. Now suppose that a hacker, who loves cats but hates dogs, accesses the training data and swaps all of the "cat" and "dog" labels. This hack "poisons" the data, and it is now the dogs who will meet their demise.

It is not hard to make the leap from cats and dogs to soldiers and combatants. In fact, the short video *Slaughterbots* claims that such technologies are imminently available and presents a dystopian scenario where such weapons are deployed against civilian human rights activists using AI-enabled facial recognition technology.[7] In fact, a UN report states that lethal autonomous drones have been used on the battlefield in Libya.[8] One can easily visualize AI making its way onto the battlefield, one possible example being the AI-enabled targeting

---

3. Bridget Botelho & Stephen J. Bigelow, *Big Data*, TechTarget.com, https://searchdatamanagement.techtarget.com/definition/big-data (last visited Oct. 29, 2021).

4. *Id.*

5. *Id.*

6. Anthony D. Joseph et al., Adversarial Machine Learning 20–21 (2019).

7. Stop Autonomous Weapons, *Slaughterbots*, YouTube (Nov. 12, 2017), https://www.youtube.com/watch?v=9CO6M2HsoIA.

8. Final Rep. of the Panel of Experts on Libya (2021), transmitted by Letter dated 8 March 2021 to the President of the Security Council, ¶ 63, U.N. Doc. S/2021/229 (Mar. 8, 2021).

system described in the Scenario chapter. Because one would expect military machine learning systems themselves to be hardened with protections against cyberattacks, direct hacks of the machine learning algorithms are likely to be impossible. Instead, much like switching the cat and dog labels, attacking the large amounts of data being fed to the machine learning algorithms so that the targeting system's performance is degraded or completely inaccurate will be a likely way to counter them.

While many are thinking about the legal frameworks for using AI in combat, such as to support targeting, the scholarly literature is relatively devoid of discussion about the legal framework to apply to attacks on the *data* upon which the AI system relies—either during the training phase or when operationally deployed. This is a significant oversight. If AI artificial agents employed on the battlefield have the decisive effect that experts are predicting, then enemy forces will accordingly train their fires—both kinetic and cyber—to attempt to neutralize the AI agent. Further, cyber "virtual fires" on an AI system's data is likely to have physical impacts, such as weapons-systems malfunctions, which result in civilian casualties. Unfortunately, it is at best unclear how current legal frameworks apply to attacks on "mere" data. The dominant approach to this question is quite limited—to an analysis of whether or not an attack on data has impact in the physical environment.[9] As data becomes much more central to operations powered by AI, the legal approaches and frameworks must similarly account for the significant changes in how data is used to power AI.

The prospect of data poisoning attacks creates potential implications for the application of the Law of Armed Conflict (LOAC) that should be addressed before such attacks become a reality.[10] The nature of AI and the potential for attacks on the Big Data underlying the AI result in novel issues that have not yet been addressed. Three primary issues are immediately apparent. First, there is the very real prospect that data poisoning activities will take place before armed conflict even begins, while the machine learning models are being trained. Is such pre-conflict activity governed by the LOAC? If so, how? Second, the effects of such data poisoning efforts are highly uncertain and attenuated. How can a commander apply targeting concepts like proportionality and military necessity in operations targeting Big Data via data poisoning in such an uncertain environment? Third, do such operations create the potential for perfidy, particularly in situations where the data poisoning results in conclusions that enemy forces are in fact protected persons?

---

9. Tallinn Manual 2.0 on the International Law Applicable to Cyber Operations, 416 (Michael N. Schmitt & Liis Vihul eds., 2017) [hereinafter Tallinn 2.0].

10. In order to understand how data poisoning might be used in armed conflict, it will be helpful for the reader to review the scenario chapter at the outset of this volume. This chapter will draw from the scenario that describes data poisoning and data evasion activities by the fictional country Outlandia against its enemy Newtropia, who had deployed AI targeting, called the Newtropian AI Targeting System (hereinafter NAITS).

A new academic sub-discipline has been created to catalog the methods by which machine learning can be attacked and secured against attack—Adversarial Machine Learning.[11] Academic experts in this field have crafted a draft taxonomy that catalogues the technical challenges in adversarial machine learning.[12] The most likely attack vectors will be against the data. Similarly, legal experts must begin systematically considering the issues raised and begin developing legal frameworks for the deployment of adversarial machine learning in the context of armed conflict. This chapter will address the LOAC implications of data poisoning. It will begin with an overview of data poisoning and data evasion, along with potential military applications. It will then proceed to examine the three legal issues that use of these techniques will likely raise: (1) the applicability of the LOAC to pre-conflict data poisoning, (2) navigating the highly uncertain and attenuated effects of data poisoning during armed conflict, and (3) whether certain applications raise perfidy concerns.

II. WHAT IS ADVERSARIAL MACHINE LEARNING? TECHNICAL OVERVIEW AND LEGAL ROAD MAP

A. Introduction to Adversarial Machine Learning

Before delving into the legal analysis, it is necessary to provide a more detailed description of how Big Data powers processes such as machine learning and how data poisoning can corrupt machine learning. Artificial intelligence is defined as "computer systems able to perform tasks that normally require human intelligence."[13] Machine learning frequently powers this AI using computer components to "learn from data to perform such tasks."[14] Of course, AI standing alone is not all that useful. Instead, the application of AI to specific "use cases" is where the technology shows its value. In fact, AI can be considered as building blocks for a large variety of applications. Another valid comparison for AI is electricity— useful not in itself, but instead through the various ways that the electric current can be harnessed when there is general and widespread availability.[15] In the military context, the most high-profile (and controversial) use case would be in AI

---

11. *See generally* JOSEPH ET AL., *supra* note 6.

12. NAT'L INST. OF STANDARDS AND TECHNOLOGY, DRAFT NAT'L INST. OF STANDARDS & TECHNOLOGY INTERAGENCY OR INTERNAL REPORT 8269: A TAXONOMY AND TERMINOLOGY OF ADVERSARIAL MACHINE LEARNING (2019) [hereinafter Draft NISTIR 8269].

13. *Id.* at 1.

14. *Id.*

15. Shana Lynch, *Andrew Ng: Why AI Is the New Electricity*, Insights by Stanford Business (Mar. 11, 2017), https://www.gsb.stanford.edu/insights/andrew-ng-why-ai-new-electricity

Garbage In, Garbage Out

algorithms that engaged and executed targeting decisions with little to no human involvement.[16]

As with any new computer process, adversaries or other hostile actors will seek to "hack" this artificial intelligence.[17] The field of "adversarial machine learning" has emerged, predicated on the fact that AI/machine learning systems can and will be attacked, studying the ways in which attacks may be carried out and how systems may be hardened against such attacks.[18] This section will utilize the draft taxonomy published by the National Institute of Standards and Technology, Draft NISTIR 8269,[19] in order to classify and define the various types of attacks that can be used to poison the data powering the machine learning systems.

Generally, machine learning begins with a system processing large amounts of data in order to build a prediction model (or algorithm) able to perform a desired task independently.[20] This training phase is defined as taking place as the machine learning analyzes the training data to develop a model that can be applied in the real world.[21] The example cited before describes an instance of developing AI to identify cats: in one method, the system processes many photographs or videos where cats are labeled.[22] From this training data, the system can develop connections and inferences as to what features define a "cat." Data scientists term this learning process the testing, or inference phase. Once the testing phase is complete, the AI is deployed to conduct the task for which it was trained (this is termed the "operational phase"). Going back to our cat example, in the operational phase the AI will use the algorithm created in the testing phase and will monitor real-time video feeds to identify cats and feed the information to the de-catenator. The NISTIR 8269 framework distinguishes between attacks on data in these two phases, utilizing the term "data poisoning" for attacks on data taking place during the training phase and the term "evasion attacks" for attacks occurring during the operational or testing/inference phase.[23]

---

16. *See* HUMAN RIGHTS WATCH, LOSING HUMANITY: THE CASE AGAINST KILLER ROBOTS (2012), available at https://www.hrw.org/sites/default/files/reports/arms1112_ForUpload.pdf [hereinafter LOSING HUMANITY].

17. This is already being done in the context of machine-learning based cyber security use cases. Ilja Moisejevs, *Poisoning Attacks on Machine Learning*, TOWARDS DATA SCIENCE (July 14, 2019), https://towardsdatascience.com/poisoning-attacks-on-machine-learning-1ff247c254db.

18. JOSEPH ET AL., *supra* note 6, at 3.

19. Draft NISTIR 8269, *supra* note 12.

20. TREVOR HASTIE, ROBERT TIBSHIRANI, & JEROME FRIEDMAN, THE ELEMENTS OF STATISTICAL LEARNING 2 (2d ed. 2017).

21. Draft NISTIR 8269, *supra* note 12, at 2–3.

22. Liat Clark, *Google's Artificial Brain Learns to Find Cat Videos*, WIRED (JUNE 26, 2012, 11:15 AM), https://www.wired.com/2012/06/google-x-neural-network/. Note that this article details a technique by which the artificial intelligence is able to learn to complete this task without labels.

23. Draft NISTIR 8269, *supra* note 12, at 2–3.

Data poisoning is further broken down into attacks on the data and attacks on the actual machine learning algorithm, called "logic corruption."[24] This latter attack is very effective (albeit difficult to accomplish) but essentially gives the attacker control over the AI system and its outputs. (Going back to our cat example, in a "logic corruption attack," the dog hater would access the actual algorithm that had been developed to identify cats during the learning process and rewrite the algorithm to instead identify dogs). As military AI systems are likely to be hardened against attack with significant cybersecurity measures, a direct attack on the algorithm along these lines is highly unlikely and will not be considered in this chapter.

Attacks on the data are much more feasible and can take a number of different forms (with overly simplified examples from our cat scenario included in parentheses): (1) "data injection," where the adversary inputs additional data into the machine learning system in order to manipulate decision boundaries and outcomes (here, the dog hater would add additional training videos featuring cats that look like dogs); (2) "data manipulation," where existing data in the system is altered to manipulate decision boundaries and outcomes (here, the dog hater manipulates the data residing in the training set, perhaps by adding random data to the training videos that causes dogs to be identified as cats); (3) "label manipulation," where the attacker is able to modify the output labels produced by the algorithm as it is processed through the machine learning system (as described in the introduction, this would involve switching the dog and cat labels); and (4) "indirect poisoning," where the attacker modifies the data as it transits between the database and the machine learning system (accomplished, for example, by a wiretap that can alter the data in the cat videos as they travel from the training database to the machine learning system).[25]

Evasion attacks are similar to the data attacks outlined in the training phase, but they take place once the system is operational. These attacks seek to utilize "inputs that are able to evade proper output classification by the model."[26] In such attacks, the attacker attempts to identify "a small input perturbation [e.g., a manipulation or change to the data] that causes a large change in the loss function [model accuracy] and results in output misclassification."[27] Evasion can occur through one of two methods—through accessing and altering the digital data before it arrives at the algorithm for processing (much like the indirect poisoning described earlier, except that this poisoning takes place after the machine learning system is operational) or through adding items or images that will cause the artificial intelligence to produce an incorrect output.[28] Examples of adding "digital camouflage" to confuse machine learning systems are seen in media reports of digitally

24. *Id.* at 6–7.

25. *Id.*

26. *Id.* at 7.

27. *Id.*

28. *Id.* at 7–8.

patterned shirts that cause a machine learning agent to fail to identify the wearer as a person (in effect rendering them invisible to the artificial intelligence).[29] In another example, researchers added small, innocuous pieces of tape to a traditional American stop sign, which caused the AI agent to classify the stop sign as a speed limit sign instead (with the potential for devastating consequences).[30]

One additional consideration from the Draft NISTIR 8269 that will also impact the LOAC analysis is the level of knowledge that an adversary has of the machine learning system. It makes intuitive sense that the more an adversary knows about the functioning of an AI/machine learning system, the easier it will be to identify attack vectors through techniques such as data poisoning or evasion attacks. Additionally, the attacker with greater knowledge will have higher confidence levels in the outcomes of those attacks. The Draft NISTIR 8269 takes this level of adversary knowledge into account and classifies attacks accordingly: white box, gray box, and black box. In a white box scenario, the adversary has full knowledge of the machine learning system and data used to train it.[31] A white box situation would be unlikely for a hardened, combat-ready AI system, and a black box or gray box situation would be much more likely. In black box situations, an adversary has no knowledge except for the possibility of being able to observe input-output matches in real time (e.g., observing the operations of the AI and drawing conclusions from these observations about its internal workings).[32] In a gray box situation, the adversary will have some limited knowledge of the training model.[33] Under these situations of limited information, there is the potential for significant unintended outcomes due to uncertainty of how the AI systems operate—this could have significant effects on the legal analysis of such attacks in a black- or gray-box environment, as discussed below.

B. What Is the Legal Framework for These Attacks on Data?

Many scholars are focused on attempting to predict the future of AI and its applications to warfare.[34] In the comparison of AI to electricity—that is, an

---

29. Alex Lee, *This Ugly T-Shirt Makes You Invisible to Facial Recognition Tech*, WIRED (May 11, 2020, 06:00 AM), https://www.wired.co.uk/article/facial-recognition-t-shirt-block

30. *Id.*

31. Draft NISTIR 8269, *supra* note 12, at 8.

32. *Id.*

33. *Id.*

34. *See generally* JAMES JOHNSON, ARTIFICIAL INTELLIGENCE AND THE FUTURE OF WARFARE (2021); AI AT WAR (Sam J. Tangredi & Geoorge Galdorisi eds., 2021); LOUIS A. DEL MONTE, GENIUS WEAPONS: ARTIFICIAL INTELLIGENCE, AUTONOMOUS WEAPONRY, AND THE FUTURE OF WARFARE (2018).

enabling technology that allows for significant improvements when applied to different contexts—a critical question is how military organizations will apply this enabling technology in their combat operations? Everyone seems to agree that AI will lead to "profound" changes in warfare.[35] However, much will be dependent upon the nature and pace of progress and how different militaries elect to implement this technology. Much of the current scholarly literature focuses on the potential for an automated system that selects and engages targets without human involvement (so-called killer AI or killer robots).[36] While true "Terminator-style" AI is not likely in the foreseeable future, increasing AI support to the targeting process poses the potential for hyper-fast and hyper-accurate targeting that would overwhelm the enemy and result in a decisive and rapid victory.[37] In this context, countermeasures such as data poisoning or data evasion that degrade or slow enemy AI targeting systems will become quite useful.

This chapter identifies and reviews three main legal concerns that should be considered and addressed prior to the deployment of data poisoning attacks on the battlefield. First, how should data poisoning activities that take place prior to armed conflict be regulated? As discussed in the overview of the Draft NISTIR 8269 framework, a critical vulnerability for attack is during the training phase of the machine learning agent. These training phase preparations and corresponding data attacks will likely take place prior to armed conflict—but with impacts that will carry forward into the armed conflict. How does the law regulate such pre-conflict activity? What legal provisions are in place to provide appropriate limits?

Second, attacks on data in armed conflict will likely take place in a highly uncertain, even speculative, environment. While military operators engaged in data poisoning and data evasion will have a specific military objective in mind (specifically, to target the data driving the enemy's algorithms in order to degrade the enemy's AI targeting systems or render them inoperable), the practical effects on the battlefield are difficult if not impossible to predict, particularly in a black box or gray box environment. Artificial intelligence systems hobbled by data poisoning attacks may malfunction in unpredictable ways, which may result in unintended consequences to civilians. How does a data poisoning attacker engage in discrimination, proportionality and precautions analyses in such instances where outcomes cannot be predicted?

Third, how do the perfidy rules apply to data evasion attacks and the associated digital camouflage that armed forces will likely adopt to foil AI systems? With current technology, it is not that difficult to confuse or trick an AI system with minimal

---

35. Michael N. Schmitt & Jeffrey S. Thurnher, *"Out of the Loop": Autonomous Weapons Systems and the Law of Armed Conflict*, 4 Harvard Nat. Sec. J. 231 (2013).

36. *See* Losing Humanity, *supra* note 16.

37. Alexander Kott, U.S. Army Research Laboratory, ARL-TN-0901, Ground Warfare in 2050: How it Might Look 9 (2018).

Garbage In, Garbage Out

"digital camouflage" such as adding small pieces of tape to foil identification of a stop sign.[38] While military AI that is relied upon for targeting is likely to be more robust prior to operational deployment, one would expect adversaries to continue to focus on similar simple techniques to foil enemy targeting. Without knowing the inner workings of the enemy system, there is potential for "inadvertent" use of protective markings—situations where the AI/ML system misclassifies the enemy as a protected person or object due to evasion techniques.[39]

The pace of technological change has made it increasingly difficult for legal regimes to effectively regulate behavior, and the LOAC is just one body of law that has faced such challenges. Increased incorporation of Big Data and artificial intelligence is likely to make this problem worse. As will be seen in the discussion of these three issues, there are gaps and lacunae in the law that create real risks for some parties to take advantage of these "gray zones." On the other hand, the *lex lata* does give us a jumping off point for beginning to think about how to regulate data poisoning and evasion attacks and suggest approaches for future development of the law. The following three sections will examine each of these major areas in turn.

III. DATA POISONING ATTACKS PRIOR TO ARMED CONFLICT: *JUS PRE BELLO?*

One of the first features that is observed of data poisoning, especially if it takes place during the training phase of machine learning, is that such activities may take place well before the occurrence of hostilities. The LOAC generally applies only after armed conflict has commenced. If this is the case, it is unclear whether the LOAC governs pre-conflict data poisoning activities.[40] Such a dynamic creates a unique situation in warfare—the prospect of operations against data, conducted wholly before the armed conflict and without physical impact before the armed conflict, yet causing physical effects during the armed conflict. This section will address three questions that are raised by this possibility: (1) Does the LOAC apply to data poisoning taking place before armed conflict?; (2) Does data poisoning itself constitute the start of armed conflict?; and (3) Could data poisoning be regulated by the LOAC if effects manifest during conflict?

Building on the Scenario chapter, let us suppose that Outlandia engages in a successful data poisoning attack on Newtropia's AI Targeting System (NAITS) prior to the conflict. Outlandian officials do so by injecting compromised data

---

38. Lee, *supra* note 29.

39. Recognizing, of course, there is an intent component to perfidy.

40. Note that other legal regimes may apply to such situations, such as International Human Rights Law, *jus ad bellum*, international law related to sovereignty, or domestic law. These legal regimes will not be addressed in this chapter.

into the training data, which in turn undermines the algorithm's effectiveness and degrades the system's overall reliability. The NAITS performs well enough to pass Newtropian reliability tests prior to the fielding of the weapon, but the system's designers notice that NAITS is not as effective as their projections had indicated. Suppose that post-conflict analysis determines that this decrease in the NAITS effectiveness is due to Outlandian data poisoning efforts. However, this difference is not a mere statistic, as it directly led to an increase in mistargeting and corresponding increase in civilian casualties.

Assuming an extreme scenario in which Outlandian officials are aware that their pre-conflict data poisoning attack would result in excessive civilian casualties (in relation to the anticipated military advantage of "attacking" the data) and yet continue with the attack. Would their actions violate the LOAC where the data poisoning activities entirely took place prior to the conflict?[41] A similar problem would arise where Outlandian officials knew of feasible precautions that would reduce civilian casualties but failed to adopt the precautions. Because Outlandia would have taken such actions *before* the armed conflict, the LOAC would not seem to apply, and Outlandian officials would not likely be deemed culpable under the LOAC.[42] The remainder of this section will outline the possible approaches to resolve this potential legal gap.

A. Has Armed Conflict Been Triggered?

The well-known trigger for the applicability of the Geneva Conventions and the LOAC generally is armed conflict. Common Article Two of the Geneva Conventions establishes the trigger: "the present convention shall apply to all cases of declared war or of any other armed conflict which may arise between two or more of the High Contracting Parties, even if the state of war is not recognized by one of them."[43] While the primary focus of this provision was extending the

---

41. Recalling that Common Article 2 of the Geneva Conventions designated the time frame to which the Conventions apply: "In addition to the provisions which shall be implemented in peacetime, [none of which are apparently applicable to the present scenario] the present Convention shall apply to all cases of declared war or of any other armed conflict which may arise between two or more of the High Contracting Parties . . ."

42. Again, highlighting the limit of this chapter to the Law of Armed Conflict. Another argument that Outlandia might make is that the superseding and intervening act of Newtropia to deploy the NAITS despite its degraded effectiveness negated Outlandia's legal culpability. Outlandia would likely claim that they relied on Newtropia to act in good faith and comply with IHL by taking the system offline if its effectiveness were degraded to the point where its deployment would lead to excessive civilian casualties. This argument is considered in the proportionality analysis *infra*.

43. Common Article 2 of the Geneva Conventions (1949). Note that this portion is preceded by a qualifier, "In addition to the provisions which shall be implemented in peacetime . . ." *Id.* However, these are limited in scope to such things as marking protected and cultural property

applicability of the LOAC beyond cases of declared war, the commonly understood definition of armed conflict arising immediately after Geneva (e.g., "[a]ny difference arising between two States and leading to the intervention of armed forces"[44]) does not shed much light on the level of armed conflict required to trigger this threshold.

Resolving the ambiguity surrounding this issue is the focus of the 2010 International Law Association Final Report on the Meaning of Armed Conflict in International Law.[45] A data poisoning scenario is not likely to meet the criterion of intensity ("hostilities must reach a certain level of intensity to qualify as an armed conflict"[46]). Among the factors that the ILA cites to assess intensity based on their review of custom, commentary, and judicial opinions, none seem to even reach the level of a colorable claim for intensity in a data poisoning situation like that outlined in the Scenario chapter. Specifically, the ILA suggests the following factors to assess intensity: (1) "number of fighters involved"–in the case of data poisoning, none would actually be exchanging kinetic attacks, although there may be several involved in the data poisoning operation; (2) "type and quantity of weapons used"—in this case there would be cyber operations but with no immediate physical effects; (3) "the duration and territorial extent of fighting"— no fighting would be occurring because data poisoning is surreptitious, all operations associated with the data poisoning would take place in cyberspace with no physical effects prior to the commencement of armed conflict; (4) "extent of destruction of property"—no physical property would be destroyed, albeit data might be altered and/or deleted; (5) "displacement of the population"—none in this case; (6) "involvement of the Security Council or other actors to broker ceasefire efforts"—again, not likely.[47] In a situation like that described in the Scenario chapter, it is hard to envision a possible basis to make a good faith claim that hostilities have commenced such that the Common Article 2 Armed Conflict threshold has been triggered.

and training forces on the law of war. There appear to be no provisions applicable to peacetime that are relevant to the data poisoning problem.

44. Int'l Committee of the Red Cross, Commentary I Geneva Convention for the Amelioration of the Condition of the Wounded and Sick in Armed Forces in the Field 32 (Jean S. Pictet ed., 1952).

45. Int'l L. Ass'n, Final Report on the Meaning of Armed Conflict in International Law (2010) [hereafter ILA Armed Conflict Final Report]. Note that while a major concern in the report was determining when Non-International Armed Conflicts met the armed conflict threshold, the committee focused on a general definition of armed conflict and considered both Common Article 2 International Armed Conflict as well as Common Article 3 Non-International Armed Conflict. *Id.* at 3 n.7.

46. *Id.* at 29.

47. These factors are listed in the ILA Armed Conflict Final Report. *Id.* at 30.

B. Does Data Poisoning Standing Alone Meet Criteria for Armed Conflict?

Another option might be to consider whether data poisoning activities, standing alone, serve as the marker of the commencement of armed conflict. Because the current position of the Tallinn 2.0 experts is that an attack against data, standing alone, does not qualify as a cyberattack,[48] such a conclusion is unlikely. With data classified as intangible, and not a physical object whose destruction/deletion would implicate the *jus ad bellum-jus in bello* legal frameworks, it is hard to imagine a situation where the surreptitious insertion of fake data or manipulation of existing data would be sufficient standing alone to trigger an armed conflict. Even under the more expansive definition of attack considered by the International Group of Experts—specifically, cyber operations "result[ing] in large-scale adverse consequences"—data poisoning would not qualify.[49] It is unlikely that data poisoning would have such large-scale adverse effects prior to the commencement of conflict. That said, this position has proved controversial in the *jus in bello* context, with calls to expand the definition of cyberattacks to include attacks on data.[50] At this point, it does not appear that that custom has developed to the point where a conclusion could be drawn that an attack on data would either qualify as a use of force (in the *jus ad bellum* context) or cyberattack (in the *jus in bello* context). The prospect of data poisoning, however, serves as another layer of challenges in conceptualizing and articulating what cyber activities constitute a use of force or armed attack.

C. Continuing Crimes Doctrine as Vehicle for Legal Regulation

Another possible vehicle for regulating pre-conflict data poisoning would be the doctrine of continuing crimes. This doctrine relates to "a breach of a prohibition over a period of time."[51] An example of such a crime in International Criminal Law is enforced disappearance, in which the crime continues so long as the whereabouts of the disappeared person are not released.[52] A similar rule

---

48. Tallinn 2.0, *supra* note 9, at 416.

49. *See id.* at 418 (considering and rejecting the position that cyber operations resulting in "large-scale adverse consequences" qualify as an attack under the law of armed conflict).

50. Kubo Mačák, *Military Objectives 2.0: The Case for Interpreting Computer Data as Objects under International Humanitarian Law*, 48 Israel L. Rev. 55 (2015).

51. Alan Nissel, *Continuing Crimes in the Rome Statute*, 25 Mich. J. Int'l L. 653, 661–62 (2004).

52. *Id.* at 654.

exists for continuing State acts under the Draft Articles of State Responsibility.[53] In the common law within the United States, the doctrine of continuing effects also generally operates to extend or toll statutes of limitation that have expired for tort or criminal liability.[54] If a sufficient doctrine of continuing crimes could be identified, it might serve to encompass data poisoning taking place prior to armed conflict and render such activities subject to the LOAC.

Significant challenges would exist, however, to extending this principle to allow for a LOAC violation prior to armed conflict. While the Draft Articles of State Responsibility allow for continuing violations, they also explicitly disallow the retroactive application of the law: "An act of a State does not constitute a breach of an international obligation unless the State is bound by the obligation at the time the act occurs."[55] Similarly, the principle of *nullum crimen sine lege, nullum poene sine lege* would operate to restrict application of retroactive criminal liability for war crimes. A practical example of these principles is the Rome Statute, which applies only to offenses "committed after the entry into force of [the] Statute."[56] Even continuing crimes commencing prior to the entry of force of the Rome Statute are not clearly addressed by the Statute and would be subject to the limitations of *nullem crimen sine lege.*[57]

To better parse whether a continuing crimes/effects theory is viable, it will be necessary to examine the practical aspects of the specific type of data poisoning attack being used. The specific details of the poisoning attack will help to answer the question whether the poisoning is an ongoing event that might qualify as "continuing" or whether it is instead a discrete event with a defined end point. A training phase data poisoning attack would likely qualify as the latter where the poisoning concludes at the end of the training phase prior to the AI system becoming operational. Another consideration that might serve to classify a data poisoning attack as a "continuing" act is the degree it is possible for a data poisoning attacker to reverse the effects of data poisoning through removing the poisoned data. Generally, one might expect that the data poisoning would set off an irreversible sequence of events that cannot be remedied by an *ex post* fixing of the data (if fixing the data were even possible). In assessing whether an attack would be continuing in nature, it will be necessary to examine the details of the specific

---

53. International Law Commission, Draft Articles on Responsibility of States for Internationally Wrongful Acts, arts. 14 & 30, November 2001, Supplement No. 10 (A/56/10), chp.IV.E.1 [hereinafter Draft Articles of State Responsibility].

54. *See generally* Kyle Graham, *The Continuing Violations Doctrine*, 43 GONZAGA L. REV. 271 (2007).

55. Draft Articles of State Responsibility, *supra* note 53, art. 13.

56. Rome Statute of the International Criminal Court, *opened for signature* July 17, 1998, art. 11(1), 37 I.L.M. 999, 1010 (entered into force July 1, 2002) [hereinafter Rome Statute].

57. Nissel, *supra* note 51, at 656, 687.

type of attack, but in many cases it appears doubtful that an argument can be made for the poisoning to qualify as a continuing act.

Another significant objection that must be resolved before traveling further down the continuing crimes path is the fact that there is no LOAC violation that would apply to invalidate the original, pre-conflict data poisoning because the LOAC is not yet in effect. The doctrines noted above presuppose that the misconduct in question violated then-existing law. In other words, the act of data poisoning, which might be legal before armed conflict, might be transformed *ex post facto* into a LOAC violation and perhaps a war crime, by virtue of the superseding and intervening cause of armed conflict commencing and the corresponding applicability of the LOAC.[58] This objection poses significant challenges to retroactive application of the LOAC, making the applicability of the continuing crimes doctrine unlikely.

D. Applicability of the Martens Clause

The previous discussion leaves the Martens Clause as the most viable option for providing some meaningful legal regulation to pre-conflict data poisoning. While the clause exists in different forms depending on the treaty in which it is found, the original iteration provides:

> Until a more complete code of the laws of war has been issued, the High Contracting parties deem it expedient to declare that, in cases not including in the Regulations adopted by them, the inhabitants and the belligerents remain under the protection and rule of the principles of the law of nations, as they result from the usages established among civilized peoples, from the laws of humanity, and the dictates of the public conscience.[59]

Interpreting this clause has presented a challenge as there is no settled agreement on interpreting the reach and applicability of the Martens Clause. This chapter will not attempt to examine the various interpretive approaches in detail or defend a detailed theory of legal regulation of pre-conflict data poisoning attacks via the Martens Clause. Instead, this section will explore whether the Martens Clause might provide a method of regulating pre-conflict data poisoning attacks.

While scholars have asserted different interpretive approaches to the Martens Clause,[60] only one interpretation provides any real inroads toward regulating

---

58. Note that this analysis is restricted to the Law of Armed Conflict. The applicability of other bodies of law, such as Human Rights Law, are not under consideration in this chapter.

59. 1899 Hague Convention (II) Respecting the Laws and Customs of War on Land with Annex of Regulations, preamble, July 29, 1899, 32 Stat. 1803, 1 Bevans 247.

60. Four interpretive approaches can be ruled out at the outset as not providing substantial guidance to the problem of pre-conflict data poisoning. (1) The *a contrario* argument

Garbage In, Garbage Out

pre-conflict data poisoning. This theory asserts that the Martens Clause recognizes (or creates) a body of law with an expansive applicability, which might serve as a possible means of regulating pre-conflict data poisoning. The strong version of this theory—concluding that the clause raises principles of humanity and public conscience to the level of general principles of international law[61]—is likely not to be accepted as a basis for regulating data poisoning, as there does not appear to be widespread acceptance of this position. However, a weaker formulation of this argument is more defensible. Schmitt and Thurnher offer the best expression of this formulation: "By its own terms, though, the clause applies only in the absence of treaty law. In other words, it is a failsafe mechanism meant to address lacunae in the law; it does not act as an overarching principle that must be considered in every case."[62] In fact, this statement seems to directly address the problem created by pre-conflict data poisoning—it is a situation not governed by existing treaty and appears to be a lacuna in the law.

Under this approach, inquiry must be made to determine what law would apply to pre-conflict activities and the source of this law. There would be no customary law, as there is no state practice and *opinio juris* addressing pre-conflict data poisoning. However, a case could be made that principles of humanity woven into the LOAC could provide the outlines for a legal framework. Three threads or principles from the LOAC, woven together, outline the potential case that, under the Martens Clause, the LOAC should apply to pre-conflict data poisoning. First, Common Article 3 contains very expansive language: "[Noncombatants] shall *in*

---

states that the Martens Clause merely highlights that existing customary law continues to regulate armed conflict in the absence of an authoritative treaty provision. Antonio Cassese, *The Martens Clause: Half a Loaf or Simply Pie in the Sky?*, 11 EUR. J. OF INT'L L. 187, 192 (2000). This approach is not helpful due to the absence of customary Law of Armed Conflict provisions that might serve to regulate data poisoning pre-conflict. (2) Another tack is to argue that the Clause serves to elevate the value of *opinio juris* and loosen the requirements for concordant state practice in the field of International Humanitarian Law in order to establish custom, *id.* at 214; Theodor Meron, *The Martens Clause, Principles of Humanity and Dictates of Public Conscience*, 94 AM. J. INT'L L. 78, 88 (2000). This view does not assist in the absence of *opinio juris* and state practice in the arena of data poisoning in armed conflict. (3) Another interpretation is that the Martens Clause is interpretive gloss, "merely" serving to elevate considerations of humanity in close situations. Cassesse at 212; Meron at 88. This interpretive gloss would be of little effect if the trigger of armed conflict has not been met, as discussed earlier. (4) Finally, one might be able to import the argument forwarded by Human Rights Watch regarding the use of autonomous weapons; specifically, that certain weapons systems should be prohibited under the Martens Clause *ab initio* if they are determined to be contrary to humanity or public conscience. HUMAN RIGHTS WATCH, MAKING THE CASE: THE DANGERS OF KILLER ROBOTS AND THE NEED FOR A PREEMPTIVE BAN, 14–17 (2016), available at https://www.hrw.org/sites/default/files/report_pdf/arms1216_web.pdf. However, it would need to be shown that the use of data poisoning is contrary to the principles of humanity or public conscience.

61. Meron, *supra* note 60, at 80–82.

62. Schmitt & Thurnher, *supra* note 35, at 275.

all circumstances be treated humanely . . ." and ". . . the following acts are and shall remain prohibited *at any time and in any place whatsoever. . . .*" While the opening sentence of Common Article 3 contains the "armed conflict not of an international character" qualifier, the expansive language cited in the previous sentence ("in all circumstances" and "at any time and in any place whatsoever") suggests that there might be some aspects of Common Article 3 that extend beyond armed conflict. This position is further buttressed by the ICJ *Corfu Channel* decision, in which the ICJ stated that the violations of Albania were "obligations based, not on the Hague Convention of 1907, No. VIII, which is applicable in time of war, but on certain general and well-recognized principles, namely: elementary considerations of humanity, even more exacting in peace than in war . . ."[63] The United Nations Security Council used a second, parallel approach to condemn the targeting of civil aircraft as a violation of the LOAC even though the targeting took place in flight outside of the armed conflict environment, where such actions were described as "being incompatible with elementary considerations of humanity."[64] The third thread buttressing such a position was the ICJ's statement in the *Advisory Opinion on the Legality of the Threat or Use of Nuclear Weapons.* The Court stated there that that the Martens Clause "proved to be an effective means of addressing the rapid evolution of military technology."[65]

These three threads—the expansive language of Common Article 3, the recognition of considerations of humanity as existing in both peacetime and war, and the ICJ's identification of the Martens Clause as a tool to help address technological advances—provide an outline of a theory to regulate pre-armed conflict data poisoning. This outline is by no means unassailable, but it provides a useful starting point. In order to make a stronger case, one would need to better address the counter-argument that the Martens Clause is merely a gap filler within armed conflict (with no applicability outside of an armed conflict situation). One way to address this argument is to examine the degree to which the LOAC serves as *lex specialis*, with the Martens Clause referring to (and perhaps recognizing to a certain degree) the *lex generalis*, consisting of the principles of humanity universally applicable as noted in the *Corfu Channel* opinion. Given the increased blurring of the lines between conflict and non-conflict situations, further scholarly work in addressing how the Martens Clause might address these gray zones between peace and war would be helpful.

The next question to consider is the substantive content of the legal framework that the Martens Clause would import into a pre-conflict scenario. This topic itself could be the subject of an extensive article and goes beyond the scope of this chapter. In addition, as will be discussed in the next section, even the legal framework governing use of data poisoning in armed conflict contains gaps, primarily

---

63. Corfu Channel (UK v. Alb.) (Merits), 1949 I.C.J. Rep. 4, 22 (Apr. 9).

64. S.C. Res. 1067, ¶ 6 (July 28, 1996).

65. Legality of the Threat or Use of Nuclear Weapons, Advisory Opinion, 1996 I.C.J. 226, ¶ 78 (July 8).

Garbage In, Garbage Out

due to the indirect nature of the attack and the fact that the adversary has the ability to prevent bad outcomes by taking the compromised AI system offline. One possible guide, however, might be the UN Special Rapporteur's report on human rights in occupied Kuwait, which stated that the "elementary considerations of humanity" referenced in the Martens Clause incorporated these three principles: "(i) that the right of parties to choose the means and methods of warfare, i.e. the right of the parties to a conflict to adopt means of injuring the enemy, is not unlimited; (ii) that a distinction must be made between persons participating in military operations and those belong to the civilian population to the effect that the latter be spared as much as possible; and (iii) it is prohibited to launch attacks against the civilian population as such."[66] This list of elementary considerations of humanity is a good start, but further research is needed on whether and how the Martens Clause might apply to pre-conflict data poisoning.

IV. DATA POISONING DURING ARMED CONFLICT: TARGETING PRINCIPLES IN AN UNCERTAIN ENVIRONMENT

Once conflict has commenced, the traditional targeting legal analysis becomes more central. It is important at the outset to highlight that the attack on Big Data outlined in the Scenario chapter operates as a "hack"—a back door means to disrupt or degrade the artificial intelligence. This fact creates vexing challenges for prospective attackers and their legal advisers due to the uncertain effects and attenuated nature of the data poisoning attack.[67] The data poisoning attacker definitely seeks an effect—to degrade or deny the enemy use of their AI system as it targets their forces. But *how* data poisoning achieves this effect is murky at best and unknowable at worst. In some ways, data poisoning is a shot in the dark. This shot in the dark may be acceptable (and not considered an indiscriminate attack) if the data poisoning attack consisted of a "mere" cyber operation targeting data with no immediate kinetic effects.[68] On the other hand, the analysis may be different if there is the potential for the data poisoning attack to result in inaccuracies with the AI system, resulting in the targeting of civilians and civilian objects. This

---

66. Report on the Situation of Human Rights in Kuwait under Iraqi Occupation, para. 36, U.N. Doc. E/CH.4/1992/26.

67. For purposes of this section, I will operate from a working assumption that a data poisoning attack constitutes a cyberattack and is therefore governed by the Law of Armed Conflict.

68. *See generally* Michael N. Schmitt, *Rewired Warfare: Rethinking the Law of Cyber Attack*, 96 INT'L REV. RED CROSS 189 (2014) (outlining the debate over the two approaches to defining what cyber operations constitutes an attack, whether an attack on data constitutes an attack and describing the Tallinn Manual deliberations concluding that an attack on data, standing alone and without physical effect or effect on functionality would not constitute a cyber attack); *see also* TALLINN MANUAL 2.0, *supra* note 9, at 416 (stating the same conclusion).

section examines targeting principles in the highly uncertain data poisoning environment, by examining in turn whether data poisoning is an indiscriminate method of warfare, how to conduct a proportionality analysis, and the applicability of precautions in the attack.

A. Is a Data Poisoning Attack an Indiscriminate Means or Method of Warfare?

To provide context in analyzing whether data poisoning might constitute an indiscriminate attack, an analogy might be made to a GPS-guided precision bomb. If the targeted military elected to engage in GPS-jamming of the precision bomb, thus rendering the munition a "dumb" bomb with the potential for landing in civilian areas, is the GPS-jamming operation an indiscriminate attack?[69] Similarly, does a data poisoning attacker who disrupts or degrades an AI targeting system cause an indiscriminate attack?

From a strictly textual analysis of the three types of indiscriminate attacks found in Article 51(4) of Additional Protocol I,[70] an argument can be made that data poisoning does not constitute an indiscriminate attack. Because the data poisoning attacker is directing the poisoned data to a specific military objective,[71] the enemy's AI systems, it would not qualify as the first type of indiscriminate attack ("those which are not directed at a specific military objective"). The ultimate objective of the data poisoner is likely to reduce the number and effectiveness of AI-supported attacks on its own troops, or, in an extreme case, force the enemy to shut down its AI-targeting systems altogether. Nor would data poisoning likely constitute the second type of indiscriminate attacks, "those which employ a method or means of combat which cannot be directed at a specific military objective." The attacker can feed poisoned data by directing it at a specific military objective with little danger of spillover.[72] Unlike a worm or virus, which carries the risk of propagation beyond the intended military network being attacked, data poisoning is likely to be tailored to the system being poisoned, does not

69. Brigadier General (Retired) David Wallace, Professor Emeritus, U.S. Military Academy, provided this analogy.

70. Protocol Additional to the Geneva Conventions of 12 August 1949, art. 51 (June 8, 1977) [*hereinafter, Additional Protocol I*]. The three types or attacks are: 1. "those which are not directed at a specific military objective"; 2. "those which employ a method or means of combat which cannot be directed at a specific military objective"; or 3. "those which employ a method or means of combat the effects of which cannot be limited as required by this Protocol." *Id.* at art. 51(4).

71. *See id.* at art. 51(4)(a) (defining indiscriminate attacks as "those which are not directed at a specific military objective.").

72. *See id.* at art. 51(4)(b) (defining indiscriminate attacks as "a method or means of combat which cannot be directed a specific military objective.")

propagate, and does not have likely carryover effects to other AI systems utilizing different use cases.

The third type of indiscriminate attacks, "those which employ a method or means of combat the effects of which cannot be limited as required by this Protocol,"[73] does create potential issues. The expected outcome of a data poisoning attack would be to degrade performance in the AI system—most likely in the form of increased processing times (causing delayed targeting decisions) and lower accuracy (causing an increased likelihood of errors, to include the mistaken targeting of noncombatants). The most extreme outcome would be a situation in which the AI system targets wholly at random, creating the potential for truly indiscriminate and potentially devastating effects. Any such outcome is a second-order effect and not a direct effect of the data poisoning—the subsequent malfunction of the enemy AI system is what causes the adverse effects. In addition, this effect can be limited if the adversary elected to take the AI system offline either due to the observation of the malfunction by the AI system operators or due to notification of the data poisoning attack's effects by the data poisoning attacker. Given the attenuation of effects and potential to limit effects, the better answer is to conclude that a data poisoning attack is not indiscriminate.

Instead, the concerns for civilian collateral damage are better suited for regulation by the principle of proportionality. In such a proportionality analysis, the data poisoning attacker must evaluate the expected civilian losses against the anticipated military advantage of the data poisoning, much like the GPS-jamming combatant in the hypothetical presented earlier should engage in a similar analysis. The proportionality route offers several advantages, as (1) it does not require the combatants to remain so-called sitting-duck targets, and (2) it also takes into account the individual facts and circumstances of the GPS-jamming or data poisoning operation (e.g., GPS-jamming taking place in the desert vs. an urban environment). Further, the fact that potential adverse effects of data poisoning can be controlled by the AI-system operator through turning the system off can effectively be weighed in a proportionality analysis, lending further weight in favor of proportionality approach as the better way to evaluate the legality of data poisoning. The next section will address the nuances of that particular issue.

B. How to Apply Proportionality to the Data Poisoning Context?

Moving now into the nuts and bolts of a proportionality analysis, some of the features of data poisoning serve as significant challenges to the commander attempting to engage in a proportionality assessment prior to attack. Under the traditional Additional Protocol I formulation, which prohibits an attack "which may be expected to cause incidental loss of civilian life, injury to civilians, damage

---

73. *Id.* at art. 51(4)(c).

to civilian objects, or a combination thereof, which would be excessive in relation to the concrete and direct military advantage anticipated,"[74] both sides of this analysis pose challenges in the data poisoning context. What is "the concrete and direct military advantage anticipated"?[75] A data poisoning attacker would hope that the attack renders the enemy AI inoperable, although more realistically expects a degradation in the system's effectiveness. The outcome cannot be known at the outset, however. What civilian collateral effects "may be expected"?[76] This second question is even more difficult, as it is more attenuated from the immediate purpose of the data poisoning attack. Finally, as in all combat, "the enemy gets a vote." Here, how do the enemy's actions in operating the system work to mitigate potential collateral civilian damage? This section will examine first the traditional proportionality calculus and then will turn to how enemy activity might affect proportionality.

1. Proportionality Analysis Challenges.

Data poisoning, as a result of its indirect, uncertain, and attenuated nature, will challenge the commander's ability to conduct a proportionality analysis. In the first place, the data poisoning attacker cannot be sure of the ultimate effects that will be accomplished through the attack. An AI targeting system being attacked via data poisoning would be a military target. The desired effect of a data poisoning attack is to degrade the effectiveness of the targeting system—generally in terms of accuracy or timeliness. A degraded system will likely operate at a slower speed, thus giving the data poisoning attacker an advantage, perhaps even a decisive advantage. For example, a reduction in accuracy will likely provide a great advantage if the data poisoning reduces the enemy AI system to 72% accuracy instead of 98% accuracy. The data poisoning attacker's objective is to achieve a significant effect such as degrading the system to the point of ineffectiveness, but less significant effects such as minor degradation, or an effect lasting a short period of time, or no effect at all, are distinct possibilities. Due to the uncertainty of effect referenced in the previous paragraph, the concrete and direct military advantage is difficult to assess with any level of certainty.

Of course, by degrading AI targeting, data poisoning is likely to come with a cost on the collateral effects side. As an AI targeting system loses accuracy, one must consider the real-world targeting effects: Whom or what is being targeted in lieu of military targets? If combat takes place in a remote area, then such concerns are minimal. However, combat in populated areas become more problematic. The black box nature of most AI systems will further complicate matters, further limiting the ability to predict potential adverse effects. Much like the anticipated military advantage, the expected civilian collateral effects will be difficult to assess in advance.

---

74. *Id.* at art. 51(5)(b).

75. *Id.*

76. *Id.*

The debate over the interpretation of "may be expected" and the role of reverberating effects further hinders satisfactory resolution of these matters.[77] The nature of data poisoning is such that the most likely outcome would be a chain of events that results in collateral damage (e.g., poisoned data during the training phase alters the machine learning algorithm, which in turn causes errors in targeting). This chain of causation potentially extends beyond what one may expect a commander to anticipate, depending on one's interpretation of how causation applies in the proportionality context. On the other hand, while there is debate over interpretations of causation and foreseeability, a reasonable person or reasonable commander would likely expect some degree of civilian collateral effects to result from a successful data poisoning attack. Because of this fact, a proportionality analysis should be conducted by the data poisoning attacker.[78]

A possible solution to the problem of not being unable to precisely predict the outcome is to engage in a sliding scale proportionality analysis, analyzing the range of possible outcomes. For example, relatively minor effects of data poisoning on the enemy AI are likely to have relatively small civilian collateral damage. Similarly, a significant military advantage such as rendering the enemy AI inoperable would have great military advantage but would also carry with it a much higher chance of significant collateral damage. One difficulty to this approach would be if some outcomes were deemed disproportionate and others were not—which outcome would control whether the ultimate proportionality determination? An intuitive possible answer might be to select the outcome that was considered most likely by the data poisoning experts, but there are other approaches which should be considered and addressed. Further research and analysis are needed in applying the proportionality standards to data poisoning.

2. Proportionality and Enemy Responses to Data Poisoning.

The other factor complicating the proportionality analysis is the fact that the targeted enemy system itself will be the source of the collateral damage. On the one hand, from a pure causation view, this fact presents the possibility of a superseding

---

77. *See* Ian Henderson & Kate Reece, *Proportionality under International Humanitarian Law: The Reasonable Military Commander and Reverberating Effects*, 51 VAND. J. TRANSNAT'L L. 835, 846–54 (2018) (outlining the arguments and considerations regarding foreseeability and direct vs. indirect effects when assessing proportionality); Isabel Robinson & Ellen Nohle, *Proportionality and Precautions in Attack: The Reverberating Effects of Using Explosive Weapons in Populated Areas*, 98(1) INT'L REV. RED CROSS, 107, 116 (2016) (concluding that "certain reverberating effects" must be considered when assessing proportionality); YORAM DINSTEIN, THE CONDUCT OF HOSTILITIES UNDER THE LAW OF INTERNATIONAL ARMED CONFLICT 159 (3d ed., 2016) (restricting analysis to direct effects); Eric Talbot Jensen, *Cyber Attacks: Proportionality and Precautions in the Attack*, 89 INT'L L. STUD. 198, 208 (2013) (indirect effects should not be factored unless "expected").

78. *See, e.g.*, TALLINN MANUAL 2.0, *supra* note 9, at 472 (indicating that indirect effects should be considered as collateral damage where the damage is "expected" by those engaging in a cyberattack).

and intervening cause that removes responsibility from the data poisoning attacker, because the enemy is the entity that will be conducting the targeting operations. On the other hand, it does not seem advisable to conclude that the attacker lacks all responsibility for this reason. A middle ground seems more appropriate; in such an approach, a proportionality analysis could consider three factors.

The first factor is the degree to which the AI targeting system has a human operator in the loop. This factor intersects the current debate over autonomous weapons systems and the degree of active and continuing human oversight of AI-assisted or AI-directed targeting.[79] If there is a high level of human oversight, the potential for civilian collateral damage will be limited if an AI system malfunctions due to data poisoning. The higher degree of human oversight is likely to mitigate negative outcomes.[80] As a result, a data poisoning attacker could confidently assess a lower likelihood of collateral damage when conducting a proportionality analysis in a human "in the loop" scenario. Alternatively, in a human "out of the loop" situation, with the AI able to make substantive targeting decisions on its own, there is the potential for significant adverse consequences should the AI begin targeting at random as a result of the data poisoning attack. This is due to the significant time lag that is likely to occur before such a situation is identified and remedied. In such instances, the data poisoning attacker should expect a higher level of collateral damage.

Given the controversy surrounding autonomous weapons,[81] this analysis does create a potential problem whereby the entity operating the AI targeting system might be disincentivized to keep a human in the loop. An attack on an unmanned system may be foreclosed because the data poisoning attacker deems to the proportionality risk to be too great. There is a very real possibility of creating a moral hazard, protecting those who deploy AI weapons systems without meaningful human oversight, if proportionality is not implemented thoughtfully here. As the law surrounding the use of autonomous AI weapons continues to develop, it may be advisable to limit the reach of this factor in order to further the normative goal of minimizing unmanned weapons systems.

The second factor for consideration is the degree to which human oversight would be able to see the effects as they are occurring in real time. The data poisoner should also consider the degree of control and oversight that the enemy is

---

79. *See generally* Alan L. Schuller, *At the Crossroads of Control: The Intersection of Artificial Intelligence in Autonomous Weapon Systems with International Humanitarian Law,* 8 Harv. Nat'l Sec. J. 379 (2017); Lieutenant Colonel Christopher M. Ford, *Autonomous Weapons and International Law,* 69 S.C. L. Rev. 413 (2017); Marco Sassoli, *Autonomous Weapons and International Humanitarian Law: Advantages, Open Technical Questions and Legal Issues to be Clarified,* 90 Int'l L. Stud. 308 (2014); Schmitt & Thurnher, *supra* note 35; Hin-Yan Liu, *Categorization and Legality of Autonomous and Remote Weapons Systems,* 94 Int'l Rev. Red Cross 627 (2012).

80. *See* Schmitt & Thurnher, *supra* note 35, at 234–43 (outlining the different degrees of human oversight of autonomous systems).

81. *See generally id.*; Losing Humanity, *supra* note 16.

Garbage In, Garbage Out

able to exercise over the AI system. If the AI system operator has good visibility over the system and is readily able to take the AI system offline if the system begins targeting civilians due to the data poisoning, then proportionality concerns will be minimized. On the other hand, if the enemy has limited ability to observe the effects of the AI targeting, for example, due to other cyber operations against the AI system, this factor should be considered in the proportionality analysis that the data poisoner conducts.

Finally, the potential collateral effects of a data poisoning attack differ from those of other attacks because the side being poisoned has control over the targeting system and can turn it off should it the AI targeting system become too error prone (assuming they are able to see the effects of the data poisoning attack). An obvious call would be if a data poisoning attack resulted in an AI targeting system, as a result of the attack, to begin to target indiscriminately or at random. A human operator overseeing the system would immediately have the responsibility to take such a damaged system offline. But what about the attack mentioned above where the overall accuracy is reduced from 95% to 72%? Or 62%? Or 47%? At what point is the operator of the AI targeting system obliged to take the system offline? And if the operator continues to rely on a degraded AI system (because presumably they assess that the collateral damage is not excessive in relation to the military advantages of continuing to operate the system), can one maintain that the data poisoner is responsible for the adverse effects against civilian objects? The question that must be considered is whether a data poisoning attacker should be able to rely on the reasonable good faith of their adversary to take the AI system offline if the data poisoning is so effective that it results in either excessive civilian casualties or indiscriminate attacks.

When considering proportionality, the attenuated nature of the downstream effects of a data poisoning attack and enemy control of the AI creates challenges in applying the proportionality legal framework. If we reach a point where data poisoning attacks are actually used in combat, we will have real-world experience from which subsequent data-poisoning attackers will be able to draw in order to conduct a proportionality analysis. Until we reach that point, the unique nature of data poisoning will present challenges to a commander conducting a proportionality assessment. The factors identified in this section should assist the commander in making this determination in a way that mitigates the most serious potential harms.

C. What Precautions in the Attack Are Feasible for Data Poisoning?

In the arena of precautions in the attack, which requires that "constant care shall be taken to spare the civilian population, civilians and civilian objects,"[82] data

---

82. Additional Protocol I, *supra* note 70, art. 57(1).

poisoning poses similar challenges. These challenges center around the same uncertainty and attenuation issues discussed earlier. However, there are some unique considerations that may be applicable. To that end, I propose a number of guidelines that data poisoning attackers should consider when planning and executing a data poisoning attack. I intend these suggestions as a starting point, as the proposals are likely to be of limited utility with the current state of technology. At a minimum, the legal adviser should discuss the principle of precautions in the attack with the cyber operators developing a poisoning attack so precautions could be identified and built into the process where it was feasible.

Suggested Precautions Guideline 1: To the extent feasible, design data poisoning attacks with a view toward minimizing civilian casualties. This guideline may be hard to implement in reality at present, but those who conduct future data poisoning attacks may be able to implement this precaution. As discussed earlier, the data poisoning attack is likely to have uncertain, unpredictable, and highly variable downstream responses. In addition, the indirect, second- and third- order outcomes are the ones that will potentially result in civilian casualties. That said, in the technical process of developing the data poisoning attack, there may be opportunities to build in features or options or design the software in a way to minimize the possibility of an automated system targeting civilians or civilian objects. While a legal adviser might not be able to meaningfully understand the coding process and other technical aspects of designing such an attack, he or she can outline the requirements for precautions in the attack and engage in a conversation about potential precautions where such efforts might be feasible.

Suggested Precautions Guideline 2: Consider the feasibility of designing a reversal capacity for a data poisoning attack in the event the attack causes the targeted system to become uncontrollable and begin causing civilian attacks. Much like the first guideline, the capacity to reverse the effects of a data poisoning attack may be difficult to achieve with present technology. This would be the case particularly if the poisoned data were introduced into the dataset on a one-time basis (e.g., fire and forget data poisoning). If the data poisoning attacker were able to achieve an ongoing introduction of poisoned data into the enemy's system, then the data poisoning attacker might be under an obligation to attempt to observe the ongoing effects, if such observation were feasible, and turn off the flow of poisoned information if it became apparent that the poisoned data was resulting in civilian attacks that were excessive in relation to the military advantage. This is similar to the suggestion that a commander should engage in continuous monitoring of enemy networks, if feasible, in order to comply with his or her precautions obligations.[83]

Suggested Precautions Guideline 3: Adopt procedures for notifying the enemy if there are indicators that the targeted system is engaging or is about to engage in significant attacks on civilians. Much like the first two guidelines, this potential precaution will likely be of limited utility. First, the operators of the targeted AI

---

83. Jensen, *supra* note 77, at 202–03.

system will likely be in a better position to receive indicators of malfunction of this nature. Second, data poisoning or data evasion attacks generally do not involve ongoing monitoring of the enemy systems, although perhaps the data poisoning attacker may be in a position to see physical effects and link them to ongoing data poisoning operations—thus providing an opportunity for the data poisoning attacker to see effects being caused by the data poisoning. This approach would not be without controversy, however. Notifying an enemy that compromised data was adversely affecting their AI systems would provide the enemy an opportunity to scrub the data and unleash the re-tooled AI system on the armed forces of the data poisoner. This scenario would require close consultations between the data engineers and legal advisers to decide that such a notification would be feasible.

Despite the limitations discussed above, these suggested guidelines are a good starting point for building precautions into prospective data poisoning attacks. At a minimum, they can facilitate a discussion between the data engineers designing prospective attacks and the operational lawyers advising the commander. These examples may inspire other possible ideas for minimizing civilian casualties that would be both feasible and also have a practical ability to limit civilian casualties.

V. DATA EVASION DURING ARMED CONFLICT: PERFIDY CONSIDERATIONS

Once active hostilities begin in an armed conflict scenario, the focus of the efforts to undermine enemy AI will likely occur through data evasion, which seeks to poison the data being evaluated by the operational AI system. In such a battle-field, one could expect to see video feeds, motion detection sensors, and radio intercepts being piped to the Big Data servers, like streams feeding a reservoir. These streams have the potential to modify the machine learning, as the system continuously "learns" and updates itself based on the newly received data. Just as an individual can wear a shirt with digital patterns that causes the AI to misclassify the individual,[84] we should expect soldiers to seek to fool enemy AI targeting systems with similar random symbols (or perturbations, to use the technical terminology). Like the other types of data poisoning, use of this technique creates new legal issues, particularly centered around perfidy. The armed forces seeking to fool the enemy AI will not necessarily know *how* the AI is misclassifying the otherwise-legitimate target. They would just know that, once they poison the data that powers the enemy AI, the AI is no longer targeting their forces (and that would likely be enough from their point of view). The enemy might then seek to take advantage of the patterns used by the poisoned AI system, raising questions about perfidy. For example, the patterns adopted by the parties might cause the AI to conclude that the soldiers are protected parties, such as medical personnel or members of the Red Cross. The rules of perfidy, which one prominent scholar

84. Lee, *supra* note 29.

has critiqued as moving from a "general principle understood into a technically-bound, law of war prohibition,"[85] are not clearly designed to apply to effectively regulate these situations.[86]

As an example, suppose that all International Committee of the Red Cross (ICRC) personnel carry a distinctive messenger bag while engaged in their field work during an armed conflict, and the machine learning of one party's targeting system relies on the presence of the messenger bag to conclude that a person is a member of the Red Cross and therefore not targetable.[87] If the adversary is able to learn of this linkage, do they commit perfidy if they start carrying the same messenger bag? From a strict elements analysis of Article 37 of Additional Protocol I, a case could be made that perfidy was committed—specifically, that the combatant carried the messenger bag with the intent to invite the adversary to believe that the combatant was protected under the LOAC.[88]

A possible counterargument, and one that will become increasingly relevant in the era of greater reliance on AI in targeting decisions and data science-driven warfare, is that no perfidy occurred because no human refrained from attack. One can envision a situation in the not-too-distant-future where data is gathered directly by technological sensors and fed directly to the AI for processing and action with little to no human involvement. AI systems will be able to increasingly take significant actions, and much more quickly, without meaningful human input. Where the data goes directly to the machine learning algorithm and a

---

85. Sean Watts, *Law-of-War Perfidy*, 219 MIL. L. REV. 106, 167 (2014).

86. Generally speaking, perfidy is defined as "any attempt to gain the enemy's confidence by assuring his protection under the law of war, while intending to kill, wound, or capture him." GARY D. SOLIS, THE LAW OF ARMED CONFLICT 458 (2d ed. 2016). A ruse is considered lawful and is defined as "a deceit employed in the interest of military operations for the purpose of misleading the enemy." *Id.* at 464 (citation omitted).

87. This situation could be plausible if the AI had "learned" of the potential for misuse of the emblem or had been confused by data evasion and instead relied on a proxy characteristic it determined to be more effective. It is not unusual for machine learning to make conclusions based on nontraditional considerations. For example, AI has been shown to be able to determine the race of an individual solely by examining medical images (e.g., x-rays, CT scans) without reference to pictures showing the color of their skin. Banerjee et al., Reading Race: AI Recognises Patient's Racial Identity in Medical Images, arXiv>Computer Science>Computer Vision and Pattern Recognition (July 21, 2021), https://arxiv.org/abs/2107.10356.

88. Additional Protocol I, *supra* note 70, art. 37. Article 37 provides: "[i]t is prohibited to kill, injure or capture an adversary by resort to perfidy. Acts inviting the confidence of an adversary to lead him to believe that he is entitled to, or is obliged to accord, protection under the rules of international law applicable to armed conflict, with intent to betray that confidence, shall constitute perfidy." *Id.* To make the case in this hypothetical, one must prove that (1) the act (carrying the same messenger bag as ICRC personnel) is undertaken to invite the adversary that the soldier is protected by the Laws of Armed Conflict, (2) the adversary refrains from attacking because its AI concludes that the soldier is protected as a member of the ICRC, and (3) the soldier intentionally betrays the adversary's confidence by engaging in operations resulting in specified harmful consequences.

decision is made without human interaction, can there be perfidy? An argument can be made that there was no perfidy under a strict elemental analysis because "inviting the confidence of the adversary" presupposes a human adversary. Such an argument, on the other hand, seemingly runs counter to the basic object and purpose of the corpus of the LOAC. The danger of this approach is demonstrated by the fact pattern in the Scenario chapter, where the AI system attacked a doctor due to the confusion generated by enemy usage of data evasion patterns that unwittingly simulated medical personnel. Reconsideration of how perfidy applies in these circumstances should be considered in the data- and sensor-driven environment.

Recent scholarship has identified gaps in the perfidy rules which create confusion and the potential for problematic outcomes.[89] These gaps will only continue to grow with the introduction of machines into the decision cycle. This technological development will hopefully spur the accompanying development of custom and legal frameworks that appropriately address these developments.

VI. CONCLUSION: BIG DATA IS DIFFERENT

As we enter the era of Big Data and machine learning, it is important for legal scholars to view this technological development as more than simply the next step in the cyber revolution. In one sense, scholars are beginning to appreciate this fact as they begin to examine the legal implications of artificial intelligence in the battlefield. On the other hand, the current focus on artificial intelligence overlooks the Big Data that powers the artificial intelligence. Another risk is conflating Big Data with cyber operations generally. Big Data is not merely a subset of cyber; while Big Data is cyber-enabled, it is fundamentally distinct both in its functioning and application. The connections that machine learning draws from various pieces of data are central the data mining/analytics process:

> There is little doubt that the quantities of data now available are indeed large, but that's not the most relevant characteristic of this new data ecosystem. Big Data is notable not because of its size, but because of its relationality to other data. Due to efforts to mine and aggregate data, Big Data is fundamentally networked. Its value comes from the patterns that can be derived by making connections between pieces of data, about an individual, about individuals

---

89. *See generally* Watts, *supra* note 85 (tracing the development of the law and identifying gaps in the definition of perfidy); Gary P. Corn & Peter P. Pascucci, *The Law of Armed Conflict Implications of Covered or Concealed Cyber Operations: Perfidy, Ruses, and the Principle of Passive Distinction, in* The Impact of Emerging Technologies on the Law of Armed Conflict 273 (Eric Talbot Jensen & Ronald T.P. Alcala eds., 2019); John C. Dehn, *Permissible Perfidy? Analyzing the Colombian Hostage Rescue, the Capture of Rebel Leaders and the World's Reaction,* 6 J. of Int'l Crim. Just. 627 (2008).

in relation to others, about groups of people, or simply about the structure of information itself.[90]

In other words, it's not about the size of the data or its use in cyber operations alone, but instead the connections that can be derived from linking many disparate parts of the data, with applications far beyond the cyber realm. Attacks on Big Data in the future will focus on this feature, as can be seen by the rise of the field of Adversarial Machine Learning. The advent of Big Data will require legal frameworks that address this underlying foundational dynamic.

Data poisoning is but one aspect of Adversarial Machine Learning and can be expected on the battlefield before long. The analysis provided in this chapter demonstrates the inadequacy of merely "copying and pasting" preexisting legal frameworks to this tactic. Legal scholars will need to become versed in the basic technical functioning of these systems, much like it was necessary to understand the basic functioning of computer networking in order to develop legal frameworks for cyber operations such as that found in the *Tallinn Manual*. Further, thoughtful consideration of the applicability of existing legal doctrines to Big Data will be required. As was demonstrated in this chapter, concepts such as proportionality or perfidy do not neatly map onto data poisoning attacks. Instead, novel and thoughtful analyses are needed. Similarly, the time frame of the applicability of a *lex specialis* such as the LOAC will be impacted by the practical realities of the time frames of data poisoning operations.

The purpose of this chapter was to identify and frame some of the legal issues that are raised, not to provide definitive answers to these questions. These preliminary thoughts will hopefully be a starting point to begin working out the finer details of the needed legal analysis.

---

90. Danah Boyd, Kate Crawford, *Six Provocations for Big Data*, OSF Preprints (Jan. 4, 2017), https://osf.io/nrjhn.

7

Data Centers and International Humanitarian Law

FRANÇOIS DELERUE* ■

On Wednesday, March 10, 2021, the French cloud computing company OVHcloud suffered a large fire incident at the site housing its data centers located in Strasbourg. Among the four data centers located on the Strasbourg site, one was totally destroyed (SBG2) and another was partially destroyed (SBG1), while the two others remained untouched (SBG 3 and SBG 4). The fire alarm went off at 1:00 a.m., and the firefighters contained the blaze by 7:00 a.m. Yet, the consequences for the four data centers of the Strasbourg site, and thus for their customers, lasted for much longer. When the fire broke, the four data centers located in Strasbourg were turned off. SBG 3 and SBG 4, the two undamaged data centers, restarted on Monday, March 15, but the progressive restart of the servers lasted for months.[1]

This local incident also had consequences for the worldwide activities of OVHcloud. The fire and the switching off of the data centers made the stored data

---

* Assistant Professor of Law at IE University. He is also an Associate Fellow of The Hague Program on International Cyber Security (Leiden University) and the GEODE Center (Paris 8 University). His book titled Cyber Operations and International Law was published by Cambridge University Press in February 2020 and was awarded the 2021 Book Prize of the European Society of International Law. This chapter has been written in the context of the EU Cyber Direct project funded by the European Union. The contents of this chapter are the sole responsibility of the author and can under no circumstances be regarded as reflecting the position of the EU or any other institution.

1. On this incident, see generally the dedicated thread and OVHcloud website: Strasbourg datacentre: latest information, OVHCLOUD (Mar. 18, 2021), https://www.ovh.com/world/news/press/cpl1787.fire-our-strasbourg-site. See also Dennis Cronin, *Give OVH a Break. And Use the Data Center Fire as a Teachable Moment*, DATACENTER KNOWLEDGE (Mar. 23, 2021), https://www.datacenterknowledge.com/industry-perspectives/give-ovh-break-and-use-data-center-fire-teachable-moment.

François Delerue, *Data Centers and International Humanitarian Law* In: *Big Data and Armed Conflict.*
Edited by: Laura A. Dickinson and Edward W. Berg, Oxford University Press. © François Delerue 2024.
DOI: 10.1093/oso/9780197668610.003.0009

inaccessible. Most of this data was only temporarily inaccessible the time the concerned servers were switched offline. Some data was destroyed when the servers hosting the data were incinerated in the fire. As it is common practice for cloud service providers, most of this data was backed up by OVHcloud on other servers located in another location, and it was thus possible to retrieve that data. Yet, it appears that some data was backed up at the same location and thus both the original data and the backup were destroyed by the fire, rendering them impossible to retrieve.[2] During the fire, 18 percent of the IP addresses attributed to OVHcloud were unresponsive and around 3.6 million websites were taken offline. In addition to numerous private and governmental French websites, it also affected websites belonging to foreign entities, such as the Polish Financial Ombudsman, the Ivorian Ministry of Economic Affairs, the UK Government's Vehicle Certification Agency, and the Welsh Government's Export hub.[3] This example, therefore, shows how the destruction or even the mere temporary outage of a data center may have important consequences on numerous actors.

In the event of an armed conflict, a data center may be considered as an appealing target because of the importance of the data it houses or because of the applications operating on its servers. In that sense, a data center may be compared to a warehouse. This useful yet imperfect analogy helps describe how a data center may contribute effectively to military action, one of the elements (described below) for determining whether an object of attack is a military objective under international humanitarian law (IHL). In simple terms, a data center is a building filled with servers and networking equipment, which by themselves are of limited interest in respect of their eventual contribution to military action. This chapter demonstrates, however, the importance of the data and applications stored and processed in these servers, and how they may be decisive in determining whether a data center constitutes a military objective. This leads to the observation that, in some cases, data centers may effectively contribute to military action and thus are likely to constitute lawful military objectives. Building on this observation, this chapter then discusses related questions regarding the targeting of data centers under IHL.

The chapter is comprised of three sections: the first section introduces and presents the history and different types of data centers; the second section questions whether data centers are likely to constitute civilian objects or military objectives under IHL; the third section discusses how other IHL rules might apply to the targeting of data centers.

---

2. Claude Uruganda, *Incendie et perte de données, les clients d'OVH confrontés aux limites contractuelles*, L'USINE NOUVELLE (Mar. 23, 2021), https://www.usinenouvelle.com/article/incen die-et-perte-de-donnees-les-clients-d-ovh-confrontes-aux-limites-contractuelles.N1073929.

3. Paul Mutton, *3.6 million websites taken offline after fire at OVH datacenters*, NETCRAFT (Mar. 10, 2021), https://news.netcraft.com/archives/2021/03/10/ovh-fire.html; Mathieu Rosemain & Raphael Satter, *Millions of websites offline after fire at French cloud services firm*, REUTERS (Mar. 10, 2021), https://www.reuters.com/article/us-france-ovh-fire-idUSKBN2B20NU.

I. THE SCOPE OF THE DISCUSSION: DEFINITION OF DATA CENTERS

The history of data centers is closely related to the development of computers. Indeed, the large size of the first computers required dedicated rooms entirely filled with their components. The Electronic Numerical Integrator and Computer (ENIAC), for instance, the first digital computer, built at the University of Pennsylvania in 1945, occupied a surface of 167 m[2] and weighted 30 tons.[4] In the following decades, technological advances reduced the size of computers, leading to an evolution from large-size computers housed in dedicated rooms to personal computers as we know them today.[5] Yet, today certain types of computers still fill entire room—that is, supercomputers—which may themselves be considered as a type of data center and thus are also discussed in this chapter.

In the 1990s, the development of the Internet, which relies on a client-server model,[6] led to the development of the data centers as we know them today. Indeed, the data was no longer stored on local computers but rather on servers located elsewhere and accessible through the interconnection of computers and computer networks. The massive growth of Internet use between 1995 and 2000 was accompanied by a massive development of data centers to make possible the exponential development of websites and webmail.[7] An important new wave of development of data centers accompanied the development of cloud computing, which heavily relies on the client-server model.

Building on this brief introduction, this chapter will rely on the following definition: a data center is a physical facility that houses computer systems; networking equipment; and associated components for the purposes of storing, processing, and disseminating data and applications.[8] This facility may be owned

---

4. Martin Pramatarov, *The History of Data Centers*, CLOUDWARE (Aug. 14, 2018), https://blog.cloudware.bg/en/the-history-of-data-centers/.

5. Cynthia Harvey, *What Is a Data Center? History, Design, Cooling & Types*, DATAMATION (July 10, 2017), https://www.datamation.com/data-center/what-is-data-center/.

6. The client-server model "describes how a server provides resources and services to one or more clients. Examples of servers include web servers, mail servers, and file servers. Each of these servers provide resources to client devices, such as desktop computers, laptops, tablets, and smartphones. Most servers have a one-to-many relationship with clients, meaning a single server can provide resources to multiple clients at one time," Client-Server Model, TECHTERMS, https://techterms.com/definition/client-server_model; Andrew Butterfield, Gerard Ekembe Ngondi & Anne Kerr, *client/server (c/s)*, OXFORD DICTIONARY OF COMPUTING (7th ed. 2016).

7. John Holusha, *Commercial Property/Engine Room for the Internet; Combining a Data Center with a "Telco Hotel*," N.Y. TIMES (May 14, 2000), https://www.nytimes.com/2000/05/14/realestate/commercial-property-engine-room-for-internet-combining-data-center-with-telco.html.

8. Rihards Balodis & Inara Opmane, *History of Data Centre Development, in* REFLECTIONS ON THE HISTORY OF COMPUTING: PRESERVING MEMORIES AND SHARING STORIES 179–202, 179–202 (2012). See also *What Is a Data Center?*, CISCO, https://www.cisco.com/c/en/us/solutions/

by a company or a governmental entity, either for its own use or to be used by others. Generally, the owner of the building is also the owner of the servers. But the owner of the data may be different from the owner of the building or the servers on which they are stored. Today, an important market for cloud services is fueling the exponential development of data centers all over the world. With the emergence of cloud computing, it is not uncommon that data of a customer, including governmental data, might be stored, either primarily or as a backup, in a different country. Another important feature of these different developments is the exponential increase of data created, stored, and exchanged. This world of data is marked by large and complex datasets, generally referred to as Big Data.[9]

In addition to the servers and the networking equipment, which are the core components, data centers also rely on important support infrastructure, including Uninterruptible Power Sources (UPS); environmental controls such as the heating, ventilation, and air-conditioning (HVAC) systems; and physical security systems.[10] Servers are indeed very fragile, and thus this infrastructure is essential to ensure their functioning. For this reason, data centers are generally built where a reliable source of energy is available and in an area that is not subject to environmental hazards. In addition, in most cases, the data stored on a data center is backed up in one or more other data centers, preferably at another location, to ensure that even in the event of the servers are wiped or physically destroyed, the data is still retrievable.

II. DATA CENTERS AS OBJECTS UNDER INTERNATIONAL HUMANITARIAN LAW

There is no specific regulation on data centers under IHL and more broadly under international law. Indeed, most rules and principles of international law are anterior to the dawn of the information and communication technologies and the creation of the first data center. It is thus necessary to question how the existing legal framework might apply and regulate military activities that impact data centers.

The principle of distinction is a cornerstone principle of IHL. Belligerents have the obligation to distinguish at all times between civilians and combatants as well

---

data-center-virtualization/what-is-a-data-center.html (last visited Apr. 5, 2022); IBM Cloud Education, *What Is a Data Center*, IBM (Jan. 24, 2020), https://www.ibm.com/cloud/learn/data-centers.

9. Big data can be described as "the exponentially increasing amount of digital information being created by new information technologies such as mobile Internet, cloud storage, social networking, and the "internet of things"–and the advanced analytics used to process that data." Paul B. Symon & Arzan Tarapore, *Defense Intelligence Analysis in the Age of Big Data*, 79 JOINT FORCE Q. 5 (2015).

10. *What Is a Data Center?*, PALO ALTO NETWORKS, https://www.paloaltonetworks.com/cyb erpedia/what-is-a-data-center (last visited Apr. 5, 2022).

Data Centers and IHL 211

as between civilian objects and military objectives.[11] Both civilians and civilian objects are defined *ex negativo* as, respectively, those who are noncombatants[12] and objects as those which are not military objectives.[13] In case of doubt, a person is presumed noncombatant and an object is presumed not to be a military objective.[14] I will not elaborate further on the general description of the principle of distinction, on which an important literature exists.[15]

The first question to be addressed in this chapter is whether data centers should be considered as civilian objects and thus shall not be the object of attack. According to the negative definition adopted in Article 52 of Additional Protocol I, "Civilians objects are all objects which are not military objectives." The third paragraph of this Article adds the presumption already mentioned: in case of doubt, the object is to be presumed not to be a military objective. Thus, the question must be reversed, and we must consider whether data centers should be considered as military objectives.

A. Data Centers as Military Objectives

The definition of military objectives is to be found in the second paragraph of Article 52 of Additional Protocol I:

> [. . .] In so far as objects are concerned, military objectives are limited to those objects which by their nature, location, purpose or use make an effective contribution to military action and whose total or partial destruction, capture or neutralization, in the circumstances ruling at the time, offers a definite military advantage.[16]

This article establishes a two-pronged test.[17] Under the first prong, the object must "make an effective contribution to military action" of the enemy. Under the second

---

11. Article 48, Additional Protocol to the Geneva Conventions of 12 August 1949, and relating to the Protection of Victims of International Armed Conflicts, adopted at Geneva (Switzerland) on 8 June 1977 by the Diplomatic Conference on the Reaffirmation and Development of International Humanitarian Law applicable in Armed Conflicts and entered into force on 7 December 1979 [hereinafter Additional Protocol I].

12. Article 50(1), Additional Protocol I.

13. Article 52, Additional Protocol I.

14. Articles 43, 50, and 52, Additional Protocol I.

15. On the principle of distinction, *see generally* Nils Melzer, *The Principle of Distinction between Civilians and Combatants*, in THE OXFORD HANDBOOK OF INTERNATIONAL LAW IN ARMED CONFLICT 296–332 (Andrew Clapham & Paola Gaeta eds., 2014); HELEN M. KINSELLA, THE IMAGE BEFORE THE WEAPON: A CRITICAL HISTORY OF THE DISTINCTION BETWEEN COMBATANT AND CIVILIAN (2015).

16. Article 52(2), Additional Protocol I.

17. COMMENTARY ON THE ADDITIONAL PROTOCOLS OF 8 JUNE 1977 TO THE GENEVA CONVENTIONS OF 12 AUGUST 1949 635 (Claude Pilloud et al., 1987), para. 2018.

prong, the object's "total or partial destruction, capture or neutralization, in the circumstances ruling at the time," must "offer [. . .] a definite military advantage" for the attacking side. In the following paragraphs, we will focus on the first prong.

B. The Potential Contribution of Data Centers to Military Action

Under the first prong, one must consider whether a data center is likely to make an effective contribution to military action. The assessment, in turn, relies on four additional elements set forth in the text of Article 52(2): the location, nature, purpose, or use of the concerned object.

1. The Location of Data Centers

The location of a data center is generally carefully chosen according to different factors. Three factors, in particular, are very important in selecting a construction site for a data center: first, whether the data center can be connected to a reliable and important source of energy, which is necessary for the center to operate well; second, whether the location provides reliable and good access to the Internet; third, whether the site has optimal environmental conditions, notably an environment in which natural hazards are rare and in which it is possible to keep the data center infrastructure cool.[18]

These factors explain why the region of Lake Baikal in Russia is a hotspot for cryptocurrency mining today.[19] These activities rely on numerous data centers built in the region. According to Hugo Estecahandy and Kévin Limonier, different factors explain why the conditions in this region are so attractive: good Internet connectivity, a favorable cool dry climate and; more importantly, a cheap and reliable source of energy provided by the hydroelectric dams built during the Soviet era.[20]

The location of a data center is thus not left to chance. Yet, it can be observed that the factors dictating the location of the construction site of a data center differ from the element of location in Article 52(2). The commentary to Additional Protocol I clarifies the latter:

> [. . .] Clearly, there are objects [. . .] which, by virtue of their location, make an effective contribution to military action. This may be, for example, a bridge

---

18. Henry Bakis, *Les facteurs de localisation d'un nouveau type d'établissements tertiaires: les datacentres*, 27–3/4 NETCOM 351–84, 351–84 (2013); Moises Levy & Daniel Raviv, *A Novel Framework for Data Center Metrics using a Multidimensional Approach*, in 15TH LACCEI INTERNATIONAL MULTI-CONFERENCE FOR ENGINEERING, EDUCATION, AND TECHNOLOGY: "GLOBAL PARTNERSHIPS FOR DEVELOPMENT AND ENGINEERING EDUCATION", 6 (2017).

19. Hugo Estecahandy & Kévin Limonier, *Cryptomonnaies et puissance de calcul: la Sibérie orientale, nouveau territoire stratégique pour la Russie?*, 177–78 HÉRODOTE 253–66, 253–66 (2020).

20. *Id.* at 257.

or other construction, or it could also be, [. . .] a site which is of special importance for military operations in view of its location, either because it is a site that must be seized or because it is important to prevent the enemy from seizing it, or otherwise because it is a matter of forcing the enemy to retreat from it.[21]

Bridges, for instance, are likely to be built on sites that are "of special importance for military operations in view of [their] location." Conversely, the factors dictating the selection of the construction site for a data center are not relevant to identify whether this location is of special importance for military operations.

Additionally, the data housed in a data center may be easily accessible from a remote location through the Internet or other networks. In that sense, the contribution of a data center to military action cannot be presumed from its physical proximity to the battlefield. A data center located on another continent may contribute to military action while a data center located in the middle of the battlefield may not.

In conclusion, the location of a data center does not presume its eventual contribution to military action. For this reason, I will not discuss the element of location further in this chapter.[22] Yet, it should be noted that, in some cases, data centers may be built at a location of special importance for military operations: for instance, if they are located within a military compound, and thus be considered as military objectives due to their location.

2. The Nature of Data Centers
The element of "nature" refers to the "intrinsic character of an object"[23] as highlighted by the International Law Association Study Group on the Conduct of Hostilities in the 21st Century. This group also clarified that:

> It is not only a question of use because the qualification of military objective by nature may remain even if the object is not actually used at the time of the attack (a military plane in a hangar remains a military objective).[24]

The Commentary to Additional Protocol I provides a list of examples of such "objects directly used by the armed forces: weapons, equipment, transports, fortifications, depots, buildings occupied by armed forces, staff headquarters, communications centres etc."[25] Yet, such a military object is not to be automatically

---

21. PILLOUD ET AL., *supra* note 18 at 636, para. 2021.

22. On the element of location of Article 52(2) of Additional Protocol I, see notably: International Law Association Study Group on the Conduct of Hostilities in the 21st Century, *The Conduct of Hostilities and International Humanitarian Law: Challenges of 21st Century Warfare*, 93 INT. LAW STUD. 322–88, 331 (2017).

23. *Id.* at 329.

24. *Id.* at 329.

25. PILLOUD ET AL., *supra* note 18 at 636, para. 2020.

considered as a military objective, and its specific use may affect such a qualification.[26] The question whether a data centers is likely to contribute to military action by its nature is therefore a difficult assessment, but it is likely to be answered negatively in most cases.

It can be observed that most data centers are owned by private companies, either for their own use or to the use of their clients, and are used predominantly to store data from civilians. The OVHcloud data center in Strasbourg mentioned in the introduction is a prime example.

Some armed forces around the world have developed their own storage and processing capacities and thus have established their own data centers. An illustration can be found in the recent inauguration by the French Minister of the Armed Forces, on April 29, 2021, of the renovated data center named "Sous-Lieutenant Marie-Louise Cloarec," located in Bordeaux and which is managed by the Joint Directorate of Infrastructure Networks and Information Systems (DIRISI— *Direction Interarmées des Réseaux d'Infrastructure et des Systèmes d'Information*) of the Armed Forces.[27] In such cases of military-owned and managed data centers, we may be tempted to consider that they are automatically contributing to military action due to their nature. Yet, these centers form only a small portion of existing data centers and also in such a case, it is important to assess the actual purpose and use of the infrastructure within these centers. The data center of the French Armed Forces, to continue with the same example, houses human resources applications for the staff of the Ministry of the Armed Forces and the aeronautical maintenance in operational conditions (MCO-A).[28] This example illustrates that even a military-owned data center, storing and processing military data, may be used for activities that are less likely to contribute to military action, such as human resources management.

By contrast, a data center owned and managed by a private company may serve military uses and thus be considered as a military data center. An example of a military data center run by a private company can be found as part of the United States Department of Defense (U.S. DoD) "Cloud Strategy."[29] The Joint Enterprise Defense Infrastructure (JEDI), a project for a "Commercial General Purpose enterprise-wide cloud solution," led to a call for tenders issued in 2017

---

26. Yoram Dinstein, The Conduct of Hostilities Under the Law of International Armed Conflict 94 (3d ed. 2016).

27. France, Ministry of the Armed Forces, *Speech by Florence Parly, Minister of the Armed Forces—Inauguration of the "Sous-lieutenant Marie-Louise Cloarec" data center in Bordeaux*, Ministère des Armées (Apr. 29, 2021), https://www.vie-publique.fr/discours/279722-flore nce-parly-29042021-numerique; DC Mag, *Inauguration du nouveau datacenter du ministère des Armées à Bordeaux*, Data Center Mag. (May 7, 2021), https://datacenter-magazine.fr/inaug uration-nouveau-datacenter-ministere-des-armees-a-bordeaux/.

28. France, Ministry of the Armed Forces, *supra* note 28.

29. United States Department of Defense, *DOD Cloud Strategy* 12 (A–1) (Dec. 2018), https:// media.defense.gov/2019/Feb/04/2002085866/-1/-1/1/DOD-CLOUD-STRATEGY.PDF.

and adjudicated to Microsoft in 2021, after a juridical fight with its main competitor, Amazon. In July 2021, the U.S. DoD canceled the contract with Microsoft.[30]

In sum, this subsection has illustrated the diversity of data centers and shown that they may constitute military objectives because of their nature in only a limited number of cases.

3. The Purpose and the Use of Data Centers

The element of "purpose" assesses the intended future use of an object, while the element of "use" focuses on its current function.[31] Regarding data centers, a difficulty arises because they may be "dual-use objects," which are objects that can be used for military or civilian purposes, either simultaneously or at different times.[32] There is neither a definition of dual-use objects nor a specific category of such objects under IHL. I have already discussed the potential dual nature of data centers, as well as the possible decoupling between their nature and their use, were in the section dedicated to the nature element.

This observation leads to refine our approach. To assess the contribution to military action of a data center, therefore, it might be necessary to analyze separately its three constitutive elements: the nature of the building, the servers and networking equipment, and finally the data and applications stored and processed within the data center.

a. The Contribution to Military Action of the Building Housing a Data Center

On the first constitutive element, a data center is a building, a facility, which might be either a civilian or military object. I have already addressed this first element above in the discussion of the nature element, which showed that data centers may constitute military objectives because of their nature in a limited number of cases.

b. The Contribution to Military Action of the Servers and Networking Equipment

A data center building houses different servers and networking equipment. These servers might be the property of, or used by, one or more actors within a data center, who may be distinct from the owner of the building. While it is unlikely that nongovernmental entities will use military-owned data centers, privately owned data centers may have armed forces as clients. As part of the implementation of their cloud strategy, different armed forces may decide to store or process some of their data in privately owned data centers, either temporarily while

---

30. Kate Conger & David E. Sanger, *Pentagon Cancels a Disputed $10 Billion Technology Contract*, N.Y. Times (July 6, 2021), https://www.nytimes.com/2021/07/06/technology/JEDI-contract-cancelled.html.

31. Pilloud et al., *supra* note 18 at 636, para. 2022; International Law Association Study Group on the Conduct of Hostilities in the 21st Century, *supra* note 23 at 332–40.

32. Pilloud et al., *supra* note 18 at 636, para. 2023; International Law Association Study Group on the Conduct of Hostilities in the 21st Century, *supra* note 23 at 335–40.

they are developing their own capabilities or more permanently. We have already mentioned the example of the U.S. DoD's JEDI project, which aimed at developing a military data center owned and managed by a private company.

c. The Contribution to Military Action of the Stored Data and Applications

Third, within these servers, different types of data and applications are stored and processed. These data and applications may be the property of, and used by, a variety of actors, military or civilian, with different purposes and objectives. There are two distinct questions, therefore, that arise regarding the data and applications housed in a data center. On the one hand, a debate exists as to whether data might be considered as an object under IHL. On the other hand, the specific nature and function of these data and applications may be taken into account in assessing the military contribution of a data center.

With respect to the first question, there is a developing body of literature on whether data may be considered as an object under IHL.[33] The discussion in the Commentary to Rule 100 of *the Tallinn Manual 2.0 on the International Law Applicable to Cyber Operations*[34] offers a good illustration of the current state of the debate on that question:

> The majority of the International Group of Experts agreed that the law of armed conflict notion of "object" is not to be interpreted as including data, at least in the current state of the law. [. . .] Therefore, an attack on data per se does not qualify as an attack. [. . .] A minority of the Experts was of the opinion that, for the purposes of targeting, certain data should be regarded as an object. [. . .] For these Experts, the key factor, based on the underlying object and purpose of Article 52 of Additional Protocol I, is one of the severity of the operation's consequences, not the nature of harm. Thus, they were of the view that, at a minimum, civilian data that is "essential" to the well-being of the civilian population is encompassed in the notion of civilian objects and protected as such.[35]

In short, the academic literature appears divided on the matter. It seems, however, unlikely that all data is to be considered as an object under IHL. Rather, the debate

---

33. Robin Geiß & Henning Lahmann, *Protection of Data in Armed Conflict*, 97 Int. Law Stud. 556–572, 562–67 (2021); Heather Harrison Dinniss, *The Nature of Objects: Targeting Networks and the Challenge of Defining Cyber Military Objectives*, 48 Isr. L. Rev. 39–54, 39–54 (2015); Kubo Mačák, *Military Objectives 2.0: The Case for Interpreting Computer Data as Objects under International Humanitarian Law*, 48 Isr. L. Rev. 55–80, 55–80 (2015); Michael N. Schmitt, *The Notion of 'Objects' during Cyber Operations: A Riposte in Defence of Interpretive and Applicative Precision*, 48 Isr. L. Rev. 81–109, 81–109 (2015); International Law Association Study Group on the Conduct of Hostilities in the 21st Century, *supra* note 23 at 338–40.

34. The Tallinn Manual 2.0 on the International Law Applicable to Cyber Operations, 435–45 (Michael N. Schmitt & Liis Vihul eds., 2d ed. 2017).

35. *Id.* at 437, para. 6–7.

focuses on whether certain data would benefit from a specific status and thus be likely to be considered as an object. This discussion departs from the scope of this chapter, and I will not develop it further. Yet, in discussing whether data may qualify as an object under IHL, some experts of the *Tallinn Manual Process* agreed that "a cyber operation targeting data may sometimes qualify as an attack when the operation affects the functionality of cyber infrastructure,"[36] which, to some extent, relates to the second question.

Turning to the second question of the data center's contribution to military action, it is important to note that, without the data and applications it houses, a data center may be seen as an empty shell. In that sense, it may be compared to a warehouse. This analogy is useful but not perfect since the structure, function, and uses of a data center are more diverse. Certain warehouses may be considered as a military objective because of their nature; in most cases, however, it is necessary to assess their purpose and use to determine whether they are making an effective contribution to the military action. The situation is similar regarding data centers, and to assess their purpose and use it might be necessary to assess the purpose and use of the data and applications they house. The following discussion will distinguish the storage of data from the applications in discussing their eventual contribution to military action.

One of the important functions of data centers is to store data, either as a primary storage facility or as a backup. Some of this data storage may be highly strategic, such as the storage of military satellite images. Yet, it seems difficult to consider data that is merely stored (and not accessed or processed by a specific application at the considered moment) to contribute to military action. Moreover, what has been described as "the resilient character of the Internet" in IHL literature may also have consequence here and limit the potential military advantage of targeting such data.[37] Indeed, data that is merely stored can be relatively easily moved to another storage location, with limited effort and in a short period of time. The transfer of data from one location to another is not visible unless there is monitoring of the traffic. Moreover, data may have been backed up at one or more other locations limiting the possible effect of targeting it.

The situation is different regarding applications running in a data center and accessed remotely through a client-server model. It is important to distinguish, from a technical point of view, two types of applications that may be housed in data centers. The first type consists of applications that do not require specific characteristic or processing capacity and that may thus be easily moved to another location. The development of a cloud-based model of computing in the recent years leads to a situation where an increasing number of applications are partially or fully stored and processed on servers and accessed remotely through a client-server model by their end users. Some of these applications, either housed

36. *Id.* at 437, para. 6.

37. International Law Association Study Group on the Conduct of Hostilities in the 21st Century, *supra* note 23, at 328, 338.

on a military or privately owned data centers, may be used by armies in relation to their military activities. As already mentioned, the data center of the French Armed Forces houses notably the aeronautical maintenance in operational conditions (MCO-A) of the French Air Force.[38] In some cases, and depending on the circumstances at the time, the use of such applications may contribute to military action and are thus likely to lead to the characterization of the concerned data center as a military objective. In most cases, however, these applications that are remotely accessible to their end users do not require a specific server or installation and thus, as for stored data, may be easily moved to another storage and processing facility. Moreover, as for the data, these applications and their data may have been backed up at one or more other locations.

The second type of applications requires specific capabilities from the data center, such as processing power and storage capacity, and they can be stored and processed only on specific servers. The best example of such installations are supercomputers, which offer extremely fast and important processing capacities allowing them to perform complex calculation and simulation. They are notably used in meteorology, engineering, and astronomy, but they can also be used for military purposes. In November 2014, for instance, the United States Department of Energy commissioned three companies—IBM, NVIDIA, and Mellanox—to build two supercomputers, named Summit and Sierra.[39] While Summit is tasked with civilian scientific research, Sierra is used for nuclear weapons simulations.[40] Such an installation is likely to be considered as contributing to military action both for their purpose and their use. Indeed, in addition to their purpose, such as nuclear weapon simulations, their important calculation and processing capacities could also be used during an armed conflict for specific simulations in relation to the conduct of hostilities.

In discussing the potential contribution of data centers to military action, we have showed that this contribution is unlikely, in most cases, to be related to the location or nature of the concerned data centers. Conversely, we have demonstrated that the purpose and use of the data centers constitutes the decisive element in assessing the contribution to military action in most circumstances.

C. Data Centers and Protected Objects

Another important question is whether data centers might qualify as specially protected objects under IHL. IHL does not provide a definition of civilian objects,

---

38. France, Ministry of the Armed Forces, *supra* note 28.

39. Meet two of the most powerful supercomputers on the planet, IBM, https://www.ibm.com/it-infrastructure/hpc (last visited Apr. 5, 2022).

40. William Poor, *America's nuclear arsenal relies on this brand-new supercomputer*, THE VERGE (Nov. 20, 2018), https://www.theverge.com/science/2018/11/20/18097534/nuclear-weapons-supercomputer-sierra-california-classified-stockpile-simulations.

which instead are defined negatively as those *not* contributing to military action. Yet, under IHL some specific categories of objects benefit from specific protection. For example, the First Additional Protocol to the Geneva Conventions provides specific protection for cultural objects and of places of worship (Article 53), objects indispensable to the survival of the civilian population (Article 54), the natural environment (Article 55), and works and installations containing dangerous forces (Article 56). Data centers, in general, are unlikely to be considered as part of one of these categories by themselves.

Data centers may, however, house data and applications belonging to such protected objects, most notably cultural or medical institutions.[41] While discussing the status of data as an object under IHL, the International Law Association Study Group on the Conduct of Hostilities in the 21st Century noted that:

> On the other hand, the [Study Group] as a whole agreed that the special protection afforded to certain classes of objects (medical units, cultural property, water systems, etc.) should be understood as extending to data pertaining to them and thus prohibiting operations directed at deleting, damaging, manipulating or otherwise tampering with such data. [. . .] Similarly, the prohibition to "render useless" objects indispensable to the survival of the population will prohibit operations directed against the data that enable their proper functioning. A similarly special protection may apply to culturally important data.[42]

Thus, the protection of certain objects may also affect the protection of their data. In the case of data centers, however, the data are typically not housed on the site of the concerned protected object but are stored in another facility at another location. In such cases, the question is whether the protection status of the protected object, which extends to its data, also extends to a remote site of storage. This is an open question.

On that note, it can be observed that an increasing number of companies are developing health-related products and applications, notably as part of their smartwatches and smartphone applications. The e-health market today is fast growing and incorporating an increasing quantity of health-related data, such as heart rate or blood pressure monitoring, to be stored in different data centers. An added issue for this type of health data is the feasibility of identifying where such data are stored and how the specific nature of such data may affect the status of the concerned data centers.

41. On cyber operations against healthcare institutions, see notably: CYBERPEACE INSTITUTE, *Playing with Lives: Cyberattacks on Healthcare are Attacks on People* (Mar. 9, 2021), https://cyberpeaceinstitute.org/publications/sar001-healthcare/.

42. International Law Association Study Group on the Conduct of Hostilities in the 21st Century, *supra* note 23 at 339–340.

In conclusion, it is unlikely that a data center is considered as a protected object per se; however, the nature of the data it houses may, in some specific circumstances, leads to such a qualification.

D. Partial Contribution to Military Action of a Data Center

A key challenge in analyzing the status of a data center under IHL is the fact that a data center may be used for different activities and by different end users at the same time. In such cases, some activities may be contributing to military action while others may not. Thus, it may be the case that only a certain portion of the use and purpose of the concerned data center may be considered as contributing to military action.

This observation leads to the question of how that dual use may affect the characterization of the data center as a military objective. A similar situation may be observed in the case of a building such as a warehouse, to continue with a same analogy described earlier, in which some rooms may be used by civilians and others may be the site of activities contributing to military action. The prevailing approach in such cases is to assess the object as a whole: even if only some portions are contributing to military action, the whole building, or data center, may be considered as a military objective.[43] At the same time, the fact that portions of the building or data center are not contributing to military action is relevant to an assessment of the proportionality and the discriminate character of an eventual attack against that infrastructure.[44]

E. Concluding Remarks on the Characterization of Data Centers as an Object under International Humanitarian Law

This section has assessed whether data centers are likely to be considered as military objectives or, on the contrary, civilian objects. In many cases, data centers may not constitute military objectives. Yet, it appears clear that in some cases data centers can indeed be considered as military objectives and thus be the object of attacks. Such an assessment relies on four elements: the location, the nature, the purpose, and the use of the data center. Navigating these different elements, I have shown that, in the case of a data center, the most relevant elements are its purpose and its use. Building on this observation, I have emphasized the necessity of analyzing the purpose and the use of the different constitutive elements of a data center, namely the building, the housed equipment, and finally the data and applications stored and processed there. This second step in the reasoning leads to

43. *Id.* at 334–35.

44. *Id.* at 335.

the conclusion that, in assessing the data center's effective contribution to military action, the decisive element is the purpose and use of the data and applications. Conversely, the other elements are of little, if any, importance in such an assessment in most cases.

III. TARGETING DATA CENTERS

As the preceding discussion makes clear, data centers can constitute military objectives in some circumstances, and thus may be the object of an attack. Interestingly, because data centers are cyber infrastructure, they might be targeted both in the "real world" as well as through cyberspace. In either case, because data centers can be the object of attack, it is important to analyze how the IHL rules regarding such attacks might apply to data centers. The principle of distinction, which sets forth protections for civilians and civilian objects, is a foundational rule that governs the targeting process. Under this rule, belligerents must direct their operations only against military objectives.[45] Moreover, IHL prohibits direct and deliberate attacks against civilians as well as indiscriminate attacks.[46] The principles of proportionality[47] and feasible precautions[48] are additional IHL principles that govern attacks. The objective of this section is to analyze the different forms and objectives that an attack against a data center may have, as well how the principles of proportionality feasible precautions might apply to data centers.

A. The Different Ways to Target a Data Center

To assess the possible types of attacks on data centers, I use examples of incidents and threats to have affected data centers in the past. There are two main ways to target a data center, either through kinetic attacks against its infrastructure or by conducting cyber operations against the applications and data it stores. Furthermore, in attacking a data center, either through kinetic or cyber means and methods, two objectives may be contemplated: on the one hand, damage or destroy parts or the entirety of the targeted data center; on the other hand, disrupt or temporarily block its functioning.

1. Targeting the Physical Infrastructure of a Data Center
The servers and networking equipment housed in a data center are very fragile, and thus they may be easily damaged or even destroyed through kinetic means and

45. Article 48, Additional Protocol I.

46. Article 51, Additional Protocol I.

47. Article 51(5), Additional Protocol I.

48. Article 57(1), Additional Protocol I.

methods. There are plenty of examples of incidents that have led to the physical destruction of the whole or parts of a data center, such as the OVHcloud example used in introduction. The massive amount of heat produced by servers in operation renders them particularly vulnerable to fire. There are plenty of examples of data centers being totally or partially destroyed by fire,[49] which appears to be one of the main risks. These examples show that a kinetic attack against a data center would easily cause damage to its servers and equipment.

Targeting the support infrastructure, notably the heating, ventilation, and air-conditioning systems, can be an effective way to produce non-reversible damage as well as temporary outage of the functioning of a data center. The accidental triggering of the fire suppression system or a water pipe burst in the facility, for instance, may damage some servers located in the concerned data center.[50] The malfunction of support infrastructure may be caused by a kinetic attack but also resulting from a cyber operation. A distributed denial-of-service (DDoS) attack disturbing the managing system of the support infrastructure might, in some specific circumstances, lead to the overheating and physical damaging of the data center.[51]

It should be noted that, in some cases, the temporary disruption of the service may be decided by the owner of the data center or its support infrastructure. Indeed, in some cases, the servers may be switched off to protect them against a specific event. In the example of the fire at OVHcloud, for instance, the two untouched data centers (SBG 3 and SBG 4) were switched off to limit the risk of spread of the fire. Thus, in such case the support infrastructure created the outage of the data center, but it is not the result of a malfunction as the objective was to protect the concerned servers. It is an interesting observation for this chapter, indeed, since the targeting of a small part of a data center may lead to the switching off of the whole infrastructure. It may thus offer a useful alternative to

49. See, for instance: Paul Kunert, *Multiple customers knocked offline as firefighters tackle flames at Telstra's London Hosting Centre bit barn*, THE REGISTER (Aug. 27, 2020), https://www.ther egister.com/2020/08/27/telstra_london_hosting_centre_fire/; Sebastian Moss, *Ghanaian MoH server room catches fire; security blocked by biometric locks*, DATA CENTER DYNAMICS (July 8, 2019), https://www.datacenterdynamics.com/en/news/ghanaian-moh-server-room-catches-fire-security-blocked-biometric-locks/; Max Smolaks, *Fire at Georgetown University data center brings campus to a standstill*, DATA CENTER DYNAMICS (Apr. 6, 2018), https://www.datacen terdynamics.com/en/news/fire-at-georgetown-university-data-center-brings-campus-to-a-sta ndstill/.

50. Dan Swinhoe, *NOAA issues continue after data center flood*, DATA CENTER DYNAMICS (Apr. 7, 2021), https://www.datacenterdynamics.com/en/news/noaa-issues-continue-after-data-center-flood/; Alex Alley, *Global Switch's fire safety "malfunction" damages Sydney data center servers*, DATA CENTER DYNAMICS (Nov. 9, 2020), https://www.datacenterdynamics.com/en/news/global-switchs-fire-safety-malfunction-damages-sydney-data-center-servers/.

51. Zahid Anwar & Asad Waqar Malik, *Can a DDoS Attack Meltdown My Data Center? A Simulation Study and Defense Strategies*, 18 IEEE COMMUN. LETT. 1175–1178, 1175–78 (2014).

the destruction of the entire facility and thus mitigate the risk of collateral damage in the vicinity.

Data centers are particularly sensitive to power outages, which are often responsible for temporary outage of data centers. If there is no alternative source of energy available, the servers and networking equipment will no longer function during a power outage. Such temporary outages of data centers have occurred, for instance, during the 2021 winter storm in Texas and the 2020 wildfires in Australia.[52] Thus, from a targeting perspective, it would be conceivable to target the power supply source of a data center rather the data center itself. In such a case, it would be necessary to assess the other objects relying on this source of energy as well as the possible collateral and reverberating effects beyond the data center itself.

2. Targeting the Data and Applications Stored in a Data Center

Cyber operations also constitute an effective way to target a data center. It is conceivable that a cyber operation aims at wiping or rendering unavailable a specific set of data, or an application, stored in a data center. Yet, that objective might be difficult to achieve because there is also a possibility that the targeted data and applications are backed up at other locations, mitigating such a risk. Such cyber operations might, however, be an effective way to disrupt online services relying on the targeted data centers. In July 2020, for instance, ransomware targeted data centers belonging to Garmin and led to a significant outage of its services.[53] Sometimes, data centers are switched off to mitigate the risks linked to a cyber operation of this type. In March 2021, for instance, Brown University shut down both its data center and its supercomputer to protect them against a cyber threat affecting its operating system.[54] Similarly, in the spring of 2020, different supercomputers notably involved in Covid-19-related research

---

52. Sebastian Moss, *1,390 telecoms sites impacted by Australian wildfires, outages mostly due to power cuts*, DATA CENTER DYNAMICS (May 4, 2020), https://www.datacenterdynamics. com/en/news/1390-telecoms-sites-impacted-australian-wildfires-outages-mostly-due-power-cuts/; Sebastian Moss, *Texas data center outages knock out Greyhound, Availity, Cali Medical Association, and more amid storm*, DATA CENTER DYNAMICS (Feb. 18, 2021), https://www.dat acenterdynamics.com/en/news/texas-data-center-outages-knock-out-greyhound-availity-cali-medical-association-and-more-amid-storm/.

53. Sebastian Moss, *Garmin admits major outage was due to ransomware attack*, DATA CENTER DYNAMICS (July 28, 2020), https://www.datacenterdynamics.com/en/news/garmin-adm its-major-outage-was-due-ransomware-attack/. See also the case of CyrusOne data center in 2019: Peter Judge, *Ransomware attack hits CyrusOne data center and customers*, DATA CENTER DYNAMICS (Dec. 6, 2019), https://www.datacenterdynamics.com/en/news/ransomware-attack-hits-cyrusone-data-center-and-customers/.

54. Dan Swinhoe, *Brown University disconnects & shuts down data center amid cybersecurity threat*, DATA CENTER DYNAMICS (Mar. 31, 2021), https://www.datacenterdynamics.com/en/ news/brown-university-disconnects-shuts-down-data-center-amid-cybersecurity-threat/.

were shut down temporarily because they were infected by a cryptocurrency mining malware.[55]

The digitalization of our lives during the Covid-19 pandemic provides numerous examples of online services temporarily outed due to too many connections, such as Zoom outages or disruption of the French online schooling system.[56] There also several examples of DDoS attacks having rendered data centers temporarily inaccessible.

In sum, this subsection has shown that it is possible to target a data center through a wide range of means and methods with different goals. The next subsection will discuss these different options in the light of the principle of proportionality and the obligation to take feasible precautions.

B. Assessing the Different Options for Targeting

There are two related elements that should not be underemphasized while contemplating targeting a data center: the dual-use nature of data centers and the risk of reverberating effects. Both aspects of data centers have significant consequences for the application of the principles of proportionality and feasible precautions to the targeting of such centers.

Most data centers that may be contributing to military action may be dual-use objects. That is, they are likely to be used simultaneously by civilians. As discussed earlier, dual use does not affect the classification of a data center as a military objective. Even if the use contributing to military action is very limited in comparison to the civilian use, the data center may be considered a military objective. Yet, in any targeting operation, the proportionality rule requires an assessment of harm to civilians and civilian objects. Thus, even if the data center is identified as a military objective, it might be unlawful to target it because of the risk of consequences for civilians.

The second element is the risk of reverberating effects from destroying or tampering with the operation of a data center. Two examples to illustrate that risk: in 2015, a fire at a data center in Azerbaijan caused an Internet outage in that country;[57] in 2019, a power outage at a data center led to the malfunction of

---

55. *Recent Attacks Against Supercomputers*, CADO SECURITY (May 15, 2020), https://www.cadosecurity.com/post/recent-attacks-against-supercomputers.

56. Corentin Bechade, *Crash des sites d'éducations à distance: que s'est-il passé?*, NUMERAMA (Apr. 6, 2021), https://www.numerama.com/politique/702220-crash-des-sites-deducations-a-distance-que-sest-il-passe.html; Peter Judge, *Zoom has a global outage*, DATA CENTER DYNAMICS (Aug. 24, 2020), https://www.datacenterdynamics.com/en/news/zoom-has-global-outage/.

57. Max Smolaks, *Data center fire kills Internet in Azerbaijan*, DATA CENTER DYNAMICS (Nov. 17, 2015), https://www.datacenterdynamics.com/en/news/data-center-fire-kills-internet-in-azerbaijan/.

a hospital system in Oregon and the postponing of surgical interventions.[58] Thus, in addition to the direct collateral effects, it is necessary to assess the potential indirect effects on the civilian population.

Whether or not a proportionality analysis must assess the indirect effects of an attack is a matter of debate in the literature. The majority view is that indirect effects that are "of reasonable foreseeability" should be taken into account.[59] This question is particularly important when evaluating the legality of targeting data centers. Indeed, most data centers are used by numerous actors at the same time for various activities. It might then be difficult to identify all of them and the possible effects resulting from an attack on a specific data center. This also includes an important risk of grave reverberating effects, for instance, if targeting a data center were to destroy or make inaccessible the data and applications on which hospitals or critical infrastructure rely.

Building on the analysis from the previous section, the main type of harm caused by targeting a data center can be grouped into three categories:

1. Non-reversible damage:
   a. A kinetic attack to produce non-reversible physical damage to parts of or the whole infrastructure.
   b. A cyber operation aiming at wiping a specific set of data stored in the data center.
   c. A kinetic attack or a cyber operation on the support infrastructure of a data center with the expected outcome that it will malfunction and cause non-reversible damage.
2. Temporary outage or disruption:
   a. A kinetic attack on a specific part of the data center with the expected effect that the support infrastructure will switch off the entire facility as a protective measure.
   b. A cyber operation on the support infrastructure with the expected effect that it will switch off the entire facility as a protective measure.
   c. A cyber operation on the servers of the data center with the expected effect that the support infrastructure will switch off the entire facility as a protective measure.
3. Attack on another object with effect on a data center:
   a. A kinetic attack or a cyber operation causing a power outage aiming at disrupting the functioning of a data center.

---

58. Peter Judge, *Power outage at Tier III facility postpones surgery at Oregon hospital*, DATA CENTER DYNAMICS (Feb. 8, 2019), https://www.datacenterdynamics.com/en/news/power-out age-tier-iii-facility-postpones-surgery-oregon-hospital/.

59. International Law Association Study Group on the Conduct of Hostilities in the 21st Century, *supra* note 23, at 352–55.

Assessing which option to be selected to target a data center leads to question what the expected outcome is in targeting a data center. In this assessment, it is necessary to distinguish the specific case of supercomputers, which will be discussed later. Regarding data centers housing data and cloud-based applications, two objectives may be contemplated: first, rendering a specific set of data or cloud-based applications permanently unavailable; second, rendering a specific set of data or cloud-based applications temporarily unavailable.

The first objective might me highly difficult to achieve due to the resilient character of the Internet and most notably the fact that in most cases the data and applications housed in a data center are likely to be backed up in other data centers located somewhere else. Moreover, regarding the most sensitive data, there is also a possibility that they have been duplicated and stored in an infrastructure that may not be easily identified and that is disconnected from the Internet. Thus, if the expected effect in targeting a data center is to wipe a set of data, such an objective may be tempered by the existence of backups. These observations highlight the difficulty of achieving the first objective in targeting a data center. In that sense, the targeting options aiming at physically destroying the whole infrastructure appear of little interest.

By contrast, if the objective is to disturb the availability of data and cloud-based applications, targeting a data center seems more feasible. It might be possible to switch off of the entire data center with a limited kinetic attack or cyber operation on the support infrastructure. In addition to making the data and applications housed in the concerned data center unavailable for a certain time, it may also affect the functioning of other data centers due to the rerouting of the traffic. The possibility to achieve such an objective with limited kinetic force or a low-intensity cyber operation may also contribute to limiting eventual side effects and collateral damage.

Concerning supercomputers, the situation might be a bit different since the infrastructure is designed to a specific use. In that sense, the risk of reverberating effects might be more limited. Moreover, the main interest of a supercomputer being its calculation and processing capacities, its destruction may also constitute an advantage that is less likely to be tampered by the resilient character of the Internet.

IV. CONCLUSION

Data centers are objects under IHL. Following up on this observation, this chapter assessed the circumstances in which they are likely to constitute civilian objects or military objectives and the consequences of this classification.

In assessing whether data centers are military objectives, the second section of this chapter highlighted the wide diversity of location, nature, purpose, and use of data centers. These are the four elements that comprise the assessment of whether an object contributes to military action according to Article 52(2) of the Additional Protocol I. Navigating these different elements, this chapter has demonstrated that, in determining the effective contribution to military action of a data center, the decisive element is the purpose and use of the data and applications. Conversely, the other elements are of little, if any, importance in such an assessment in most cases.

Finally, building on the observation that, in some circumstances, data centers are likely to be considered as military objectives and thus be the object of an attack, the third section of the chapter discussed the targeting of data centers. It notably analyzed the different possibility to target a data center, either physically or through cyberspace, and discussed them in the light of the principle of proportionality and the obligation to take feasible precautions. One of the important observations here is that it might be difficult to identify the indirect and reverberating effects resulting from the targeting of a data center, due to the number and diversity of its users and activities.

The observations made in this chapter may have consequences on decision-making regarding the storage of data and applications in third-party data centers, notably regarding governmental and strategic data. On the one hand, data may be endangered if other data or applications stored in the same data center render it a military objective. On the other hand, storing data and applications that may be considered as contributing to military action in civilian data centers may have important consequences for the civilian population. These observations might be particularly relevant in the context of the exponential development of cloud computing and Big Data.

8

The Duty of Constant Care and Data Protection in War

ASAF LUBIN* ■

I. INTRODUCTION

Militaries have always operated in data-intensive environments. In fact, one of the earlier usages of the English word "computer" was in reference to "the (mostly) women in charge of 'computing' target coordinates for military assaults."[1] But belligerents' fascination with data has morphed in recent years. As processes of data production, collection, and assessment have become more ubiquitous and pervasive in everyday life, militaries have begun responding to new challenges and new opportunities in the datasphere. Wartime actors are now employing "machine learning and artificial intelligence to enhance their military capabilities and decision-making."[2] They use "Big Data" and algorithmic tools to both predict enemy actions[3] and to enhance their own command-and-control capacities.

The White House defines "Big Data" as the "growing technological ability to capture, aggregate, and process an ever-greater volume, velocity, and variety of

---

* Associate Professor of Law at Indiana University Maurer School of Law, Fellow at IU's Center for Applied Cybersecurity Research, Faculty Associate at the Berkman Klein Center for Internet and Society at Harvard University, Affiliated Fellow at the Information Society Project at Yale Law School, and a Visiting Scholar at the Federmann Cyber Security Center at Hebrew University of Jerusalem. I wish to thank both Laura Dickinson and Edward W. Berg for inviting me to contribute to this book and for providing such excellent feedback on earlier versions of this chapter.

1. Stephanie Ricker Schulte, Cached: Decoding the Internet in Global Popular Culture 43 (2013).

2. Ashley S. Deeks, *Predicting Enemies*, 104 Virginia L. Rev. 1529, 1531 (2018).

3. *Id.*

Asaf Lubin, *The Duty of Constant Care and Data Protection in War* In: *Big Data and Armed Conflict.*
Edited by: Laura A. Dickinson and Edward W. Berg, Oxford University Press. © Asaf Lubin 2024.
DOI: 10.1093/oso/9780197668610.003.0010

data."[4] Together these three Vs introduce endless opportunities for algorithmic research that may highlight previously undiscovered correlations in large and complex datasets. As the Federal Trade Commission noted, "the present scope and scale of data collection enables cost-effective, substantial research of even obscure or mundane topics."[5] Militaries can use Big Data solutions and associated technologies to improve their procurement, transportation, and redeployment of material and personnel. They can also use it to engage the varied aspects of warfare: manage detention facilities, launch targeted killing operations, and automate the collection and analysis of military intelligence, if to name but a few applications. This fast-paced evolution in the development and deployment of Big Data in the military is not free of casualties.

Consider, for example, reports concerning action taken by the Canadian Military, the U.S. Department of State, and the U.S. Agency for International Development, in the wake of the Taliban takeover of Afghanistan. Following the takeover, the United States and Canada began a complex process of scrubbing the digital presence of Afghan supporters from their websites out of fear of retribution by the new regime.[6] Even more troubling is that the U.S.-led coalition forces have previously relied on "portable scanners that collect eye, fingerprint, photographic and biographical data," which are also being used by the Taliban, further threatening the safety of those Afghans who've been left behind.[7] The story is a surreal example of where privacy, data protection, biometric information, and armed conflict intersect.

The Russian war of aggression against Ukraine offers another disturbing reminder of the urgent need to address this problem. In the lead up to the invasion, "the U.S. exposed multiple attempts by Russia to create false pretexts for invading Ukraine, and Putin continues to spread disinformation to justify his war."[8] Such disinformation is only going to increase in sophistication and sinisterness in the age of deepfake technology, which "will become too useful and effective in armed conflict to resist."[9] These computer-generated manipulations

---

4. EXEC. OFFICE OF THE PRESIDENT, BIG DATA: SEIZING OPPORTUNITIES, PRESERVING VALUES, THE WHITE HOUSE 2 (May 2014), https://obamawhitehouse.archives.gov/sites/default/files/docs/big_data_privacy_report_may_1_2014.pdf.

5. FED. TRADE COMM'N, BIG DATA: A TOOL FOR INCLUSION OR EXCLUSION? 2 (Jan. 2016), https://www.ftc.gov/system/files/documents/reports/big-data-tool-inclusion-or-exclusion-understanding-issues/160106big-data-rpt.pdf.

6. Colin Freeze, *Fearing Reprisals, Afghans Rush to Scrub Digital Presence after Taliban Takeover*, GLOBE & MAIL CANADA (Aug. 21, 2021), https://www.theglobeandmail.com/canada/article-fearing-reprisals-afghans-rush-to-scrub-digital-presence-after-taliban/.

7. *Id.*

8. Jill Goldenziel, *How Ukraine Can Win The Information War Against Russia*, FORBES (Feb. 26, 2022), https://www.forbes.com/sites/jillgoldenziel/2022/02/26/how-ukraine-can-win-the-information-war-against-russia/?sh=124815635c90.

9. Eric Jensen & Summer Crockett, *"Deepfakes" and the Law of Armed Conflict: Are they Legal?*, ARTICLES OF WAR (Aug. 19, 2020), https://lieber.westpoint.edu/deepfakes/.

of video could have devastating effects on civilians and may result in terrorizing whole populations.[10] Moreover, the war in Ukraine has also shown the effectiveness of using viral videos of captured soldiers to control narratives and advance the military's propaganda. Human Rights Watch has reported that Ukrainian authorities have posted on various social media and messaging apps "videos of captured Russian soldiers that expose them to public curiosity, in particular those that show them being humiliated or intimidated."[11] In the videos, the soldiers, under clear conditions of duress, are forced to share personally indefinable information about themselves. Such dignitary harms, reverberated by social media, could have real-life flow-on effects as the soldiers are told to share not only their names but also "their parents' names and addresses," thereby exposing them to potential future threats.[12]

Yet another troubling example is illustrated by Israeli data collection policies in the occupied Palestinian territories. Consider in this regard the decision of the Israeli Coordinator of Government Activities in the Territories (COGAT)[13] to mandate the downloading of the al-Munasiq (المنسق, Arabic for "The Coordinator") phone app by Palestinian workers.[14] In the days following the decision, "more than 50,000 Palestinians" downloaded this app and used it to access a set of digital services, including for example, the ability to check on the status of their applications for entry permits into Israel.[15] As part of their registration, these Palestinians were forced to consent to COGAT accessing their geolocation, phone's camera, and other "messages and files stored on the phone."[16] Only after a civil society organization in Israel petitioned against the terms of use of the app

---

10. Protocol Additional to the Geneva Conventions of 1949, and Relating to the Protections of Victims of International Armed Conflicts, Art. 51(2), June 8, 1977, 1125 U.N.T.S 3 [hereinafter API].

11. *Ukraine: Respect the Rights of Prisoners of War*, HUMAN RIGHTS WATCH (Mar. 16, 2022), https://www.hrw.org/news/2022/03/16/ukraine-respect-rights-prisoners-war.

12. *Id.* Note, that in past clashes in Ukraine the shoe was on the other foot and it was Russian-backed forces who used this tactic. In 2015, for example, viral videos were posted across social media platforms appearing to show the "brutal treatment of Ukrainian soldiers at the hands of separatist groups." Carl Schreck, *Video Raises Concerns over Ukraine's Treatment of Russian Prisoners*, THE GUARDIAN (May 20, 2015), https://www.theguardian.com/world/2015/may/20/ukraine-russia-pow-video-war-crimes.

13. COGAT is a unit within the Israeli Ministry of Defense responsible for implementing the government's civilian policy within the west bank and Gaza strip. For further reading, see COGAT's website at https://www.gov.il/en/departments/coordination-of-government-activities-in-the-territories/govil-landing-page.

14. Hagar Shezaf, *Israel Tells Court Would Stop Forcing Palestinian Laborers to Give Access to Phone Data*, HAARETZ (May 15, 2020), https://www.haaretz.com/middle-east-news/palestinians/.premium-over-50-000-palestinians-forced-to-give-phone-data-to-israel-1.8844580.

15. *Id.*

16. *Id.*

in court, did Israel officially commit to making changes to both the terms and practice.[17]

Even more drastically, Israel has relied on data governance policies for years as a tool for enhancing its oppression of the territories. Israeli authorities "remain in total control of the electromagnetic waves as well as [the] importing and installation of any equipment by Palestinian telcos and ISPs."[18] Israel has relied on national security claims to delay Palestinian adoption of 3G networks and has yet to authorize the setup of either 4G or wireless broadband networks.[19] One driver of this policy is Israel's own intelligence capacity in penetrating the existing networks, and its desire to maintain this level of surveillance and control within the occupied territories.[20]

These examples show that the possibility for humanitarian mistreatment and human rights abuses by militaries has fully extended into the digital realm. With the advancements of new technologies of war, militaries are now capable of effectuating digital harms, thereby eroding individual rights to privacy, anonymity, access to information, online freedom of expression, digital autonomy and dignity, and intellectual property. It is for this reason that some scholars have proposed a "paradigm shift," calling to reconceptualize the place of data protection frameworks in war. For example, Geiß and Lahmann have advocated the following:

> Given the significance of data for modern digitalised societies, we propose a paradigm shift: To date, the prevalent debate has taken the rules and principles of existing IHL and applied them to "data." A novel approach would

17. *Following HaMoked's demand: the military amended the invasive terms of use of the mobile app enabling Palestinians to check the status of permit requests*, HAMOKED (June 2, 2020), http://www.hamoked.org/Document.aspx?dID=Updates2175 (the "petition explained that the application's terms of use constitute a severe infringement of the users' right to privacy and dignity, were contrary to Israeli and international law; and compelled Palestinians to disclose information that could be exploited by the occupying power." In light of the petition "COGAT announced that the terms of use had been substantively changed, so as to make clear that a person's consent upon downloading the application relates strictly to the provision of the specific data required for the service in use, and that the application has no access to files, contacts, photos and so on." The petition itself was ultimately dismissed outright with the Court finding that "actual harm remained unproven.").

18. *Exposed and Exploited: Data Protection in the Middle East and North Africa*, ACCESS NOW 24 (Jan. 2021), https://www.accessnow.org/cms/assets/uploads/2021/01/Access-Now-MENA-data-protection-report.pdf.

19. *Connection Interrupted: Israel's Control of the Palestinian ICT Infrastructure and Its Impact on Digital Rights*, 7AMLEH 16 (Dec. 2018), https://7amleh.org/wp-content/uploads/2019/01/Repo rt_7amleh_English_final.pdf

20. *Id.* at 30 (citing to a 2014 letter by 43 reserve Israeli intelligence officers, which confirms that Palestinians are currently "completely exposed to espionage and surveillance by Israeli intelligence.").

be to take, as a starting point, the principles of existing data protection, data security, and other pertinent legal frameworks and attempt to apply them to contemporary armed conflict.[21]

Unfortunately, as I have discussed in prior work, such a paradigm shift is difficult to implement wholesale. Existing data protection regimes (and broader digital rights frameworks) are limited in their wartime application as a *lex lata* matter.[22] As a result, they are unable to properly restrain the negative externalities of these evolving data-invasive military practices. Three primary limitations are worth repeating: (1) data protection regimes are generally understood as local or regional and non-customary; (2) data protection regimes are generally perceived as peacetime domestic frameworks, thereby raising questions about their extraterritorial application concurrent with armed conflict; and (3) data protection regimes have built-in provisions which allow for derogation and exclusion for national security reasons.[23]

While we should, of course, continue to call for the urgent evolution and expansion of data protection frameworks into military operations, as a matter of future and desired law,[24] we must also look for practical intermediate solutions. We therefore should ask what data protection restraints, if any, may be found in existing frameworks of IHL. In this chapter I explore one such restraint: the duty of constant care as established under the general customary principle of precautions in attack.

It was Eric Jensen who proposed, almost a decade ago, that "all cyber operations are governed by the constant-care standard"[25] and that the standard requires, as a baseline, that commanders take into account the "effects on civilian population" from their cyber activity.[26] This position was reaffirmed by the international group of experts (IGE) who drafted *Tallinn Manual 2.0*. The IGE noted that the constant

---

21. Robin Geiß & Henning Lahmann, *Data Protection in Armed Conflict*, VERFASSUNGSBLOG (Feb. 15, 2021), https://verfassungsblog.de/data-protection-in-armed-conflict/.

22. *See generally* Asaf Lubin, *The Rights to Privacy and Data Protection Under International Humanitarian Law and Human Rights Law*, in RESEARCH HANDBOOK ON HUMAN RIGHTS AND HUMANITARIAN LAW: FURTHER REFLECTIONS AND PERSPECTIVES 462-491, (Robert Kolb, Gloria Gaggioli & Pavle Kilibarda eds., Edward Elgar, 2022) [Lubin, Research Handbook Chapter]; Asaf Lubin, *Big Data and the Future of Belligerency: Applying the Rights to Privacy and Data Protection to Wartime Artificial Intelligence*, in HANDBOOK ON WARFARE AND ARTIFICIAL INTELLIGENCE (Geiss & Lahmann eds., forthcoming, Edward Elgar, 2023).

23. Lubin, *supra* note 22 at 475–82.

24. See, for example, our recent book published under the auspices of the NATO Cooperative Cyber Defense Centre of Excellence (CCDCOE), THE RIGHTS TO PRIVACY AND DATA PROTECTION IN TIMES OF ARMED CONFLICT (Buchan & Lubin eds., NATO CCDCOE, 2022).

25. Eric Talbot Jensen, *Cyber Attacks: Proportionality and Precautions in Attack*, 89 INT'L L. STUD. 198, 204 (2013).

26. *Id.* at 202.

care standard introduces a "general duty to 'respect' the civilian population, that is, to consider deleterious effects of military operations on civilians," and that such a duty also applies in cyberspace.[27]

In this short chapter, I hope to expand and build on Jensen's proposal as reaffirmed in the *Tallinn Manual*. While both Jensen and the IGE focused solely on cyberattacks, I argue that the duty applies to a larger universe of informational activity conducted by belligerents. Such activity may even extend temporally to periods before the armed conflict had broken out. This could include broader acts of data collection, processing, analysis, storage, and dissemination, that go beyond direct offensive operations. Such an extension is necessary to operationalize the duty of constant care in the digital age. In fact, I go as far as to suggest that the "precautions in attack" principle, as was originally envisaged by the drafters of the First Additional Protocol to the Geneva Conventions (AP), itself reflects, at least in part, a primeval and elementary data protection rule. I thus argue that the duty of constant care may serve as a temporary gap filler to the lacuna that exists around data protection in IHL, at least until more expansive and restrictive data protection regimes are implemented through treaty evolution and custom formation.

The chapter proceeds in the following order. Section I describes the binding nature of the duty of constant care and its temporal and subject matter scope.[28] Section II then examines the duty's possible data protection applications, focusing specifically on two primary obligations: legality and transparency and storage specification and data integrity.

II. THE DUTY OF CONSTANT CARE

A. The Binding Nature of the Duty

The duty of constant care is enshrined in Article 57(1) of API and reads as follows: "In the conduct of military operations, constant care shall be taken to spare the civilian population, civilians and civilian objects."[29] This provision imposes an "important duty on belligerents"[30] and is part of the broader principle of precautions in attack. The ICRC Customary International

---

27. Tallinn Manual 2.0 on the International Law Applicable to Cyber Operations 477 (Michael N. Schmitt gen. ed., 2017) [hereinafter TM2.0].

28. Section I.A. and certain limited parts in section I.B. were first produced and published in Asaf Lubin, *The Reasonable Intelligence Agency*, 47 Yale J. Int'l. L. 119 (2022).

29. *See* API, *supra* note 10, at Art. 57(1).

30. International Committee of the Red Cross, Commentary on the Additional Protocols of June 8 1977 to the Geneva Conventions of 12 August 1949, at 680, ¶ 2191 (1987) [hereinafter Commentary to API].

Humanitarian Law Study (CIHL) confirms in rule 15, that Article 57 reflects "a norm of customary international law applicable in both international armed conflicts [IACs] and non-international armed conflicts [NIACs]."[31] Notably, the United States, a non-party to API and one of its most vocal opponents, has never once challenged the binding nature of the principle of precautions.[32] Indeed, as the ICTY noted in *Prosecutor v. Kupreškić*, Article 57 reflects custom not only because it specifies "general pre-existing norms" but also because it does "not appear to be contested by any state, including those which have not ratified the Protocol."[33]

While the duty of constant care only applies to those parties engaging in offensive operations, it is matched by a parallel (albeit not identical)[34] duty for defenders. Article 58(c) of API confirms that parties to a conflict must "to the maximum extent feasible" adopt "necessary precautions to protect the civilian population, individual civilians, and civilian objects under their control against the dangers resulting from military operations."[35] The ICRC CIHL study confirms that this rule, too, is reflective of custom and applicable in both IACs and NIACs.[36] I stress the similarities between the two sister duties only because we may be able to learn more about the scope of the obligation under Article 57 by comparing it to the obligation under Article 58.[37]

---

31. ICRC, CUSTOMARY INTERNATIONAL HUMANITARIAN LAW, Rule 15 (vol. I, 2005) [hereinafter ICRC CIHL].

32. *See, e.g.*, Michael J. Matheson, *The United States Position on the Relation of Customary International Law to the 1977 Protocols Additional to the 1949 Geneva Conventions*, 2 AM. J. INT'L. L. & POL'Y 419, 427 (1987) (accepting the precautions principle as binding on the United States); COL. THEODORE T. RICHARD, UNOFFICIAL UNITED STATES GUIDE TO THE FIRST ADDITIONAL PROTOCOL TO THE GENEVA CONVENTIONS OF 12 AUGUST 1949, 117–29 (May 2019) (providing an array of citations all confirming the U.S. commitment to the precautions principle); OFF. GEN. COUNSEL DEP'T OF DEFENSE, LAW OF WAR MANUAL, § 5.11 (June 2015, Updated Dec. 2016) (confirming the obligation of combatants to "take feasible precautions in planning and conducting attacks").

33. *Prosecutor v. Kupreškić et al.*, Case No. IT-95-16-T T.Ch.II, Judgment, para. 524 (2000).

34. Since Article 58 begins with the caveat "to the maximum extent feasible," some commentators have viewed this article as introducing a general recommendation rather than a strict obligation (*see* YORAM DINSTEIN, THE CONDUCT OF HOSTILITIES UNDER THE LAW OF INTERNATIONAL ARMED CONFLICT 145 (2d ed., 2010).

35. *See* API, *supra* note 10, at Art. 58(c).

36. *See* ICRC CIHL, *supra* note 31, at Rule 22.

37. William Boothby has in fact suggested that an equivalent duty of constant care also extends to all defensive preparations. *See* WILLIAM BOOTHBY, THE LAW OF TARGETING 119 (2012). But *cf.* Eric Talbot Jensen, *Cyber Warfare and Precautions against the Effects of Attacks*, 88 TEX. L. REV. 1533, 1553 (2009) (acknowledging that "it is not feasible to protect everything all the time" and applying that notion in cyberspace).

B. The Duty's General Scope

The drafting history of Article 57 tells a complicated tale about the scope and nature of the duty of constant care. The drafting of the Article "required lengthy discussions and difficult negotiations" with the final wording being the "fruit of laborious compromise."[38] It is therefore not surprising that Article 57 ultimately only "prescribes generic precautions and is not prescriptive as to exactly how they should be accomplished."[39] This was to the dismay of some states, who considered the provision "deficient in clarity" and "vague" in wording.[40] The ICRC representative to the Diplomatic Conference, Mr. Mirimanoff-Chilkine, saw this flexible terminology as a feature, not a bug. He believed that, over time, belligerents would produce more "precise" guidance on how to apply these rules in practice.[41] Mr. Mirimanoff-Chilkine never got his wish. As one commentator notes, contemporary military manuals and rules of engagement do little to provide such guidance, let alone "list criteria for commanders" as to how to apply Article 57.[42]

One thing is certain though: the principle of precautions in attack is not limited to the specific list of precautions provided in Article 57 (e.g., the obligation to verify the objects of attack, the obligation to minimize incidental civilian harm in the choice of means and methods, the obligation to suspend or cancel apparently disproportionate attacks, and the obligation to provide advance warning).[43] Quite the opposite, it was always intended that Article 57(1) affirmed a general and flexible duty that applied as a catch-all provision. Such interpretation is reaffirmed by the general maxim of "*Verba accipienda ut sortiantur effectum*" (words are to be construed so that they obtain effect). Under this surplusage canon, Article 57(1) "should not be construed as useless or redundant," and therefore should not be interpreted in a way which empties it from meaning. If the entirety of the obligations that Article 57(1) imposed were subsumed by the following provisions of Article 57, then the clause would have no independent function.

Having concluded that Article 57(1) establishes a general, broad, and flexible duty, we should explore its specific scope of application for informational and data-intensive activities.

---

38. Commentary to API, *supra* note 30, at 678, ¶ 2191.

39. *See* Boothby, *supra* note 37, at 123.

40. Italy, Statement at the CDDH, *Summary Record of the 42nd Plenary Meeting: Adoption of the Articles of Draft Protocol I*, Vol. VI, CDDH/SR. 42, 231 (May 27, 1977).

41. ICRC, Statement at the CDDH, *Committee III Summary Record of the 21st Meeting: Consideration of Draft Protocols I and II*, Vol. XIV, CDDHI III/SR. 21, 182 (Feb. 17, 1975).

42. Tetyana Krupiy, A Toolbox for the Application of the Rules of Targeting 129 (2016).

43. For further reading on these obligations, *see, e.g.*, Stuart Casey-Maslen & Steven Haines, Hague Law Interpreted: The Conduct of Hostilities under the Law of Armed Conflict 197–207 (2018).

1. What Military Activities Trigger the Duty?

As a preliminary matter we must first understand the set of circumstances that triggers the application of the duty. The duty to spare the civilian population applies "in the conduct of military operations."[44] The reference to "military operations" indicates that the duty extends beyond "attacks," and applies to "any movements, manoeuvres, and other activities whatsoever carried out by the armed forces with a view of combat."[45] As Eric Jensen writes, the term military operations "imposes a general legal requirement on militaries even when not attacking."[46] This is an expansive definition that captures all military activities with a general nexus to combat.

What this means for military operations in the digital age is still subject for evolving interpretation. One possible reading, the one I advocate in this chapter, interprets the rule encompassed in Article 57(1) as covering all informational operations necessary to support military activity. In this regard, intelligence collection, in any of its forms and conducted by any actor (including private contractors or civilian intelligence agencies), as well as other broader data collection and management activities should trigger the application of the duty, so long as the information in question is collected, stored, processed, or disseminated with the general purpose of advancing combat.

Applying the rule, in this way, will entail an assessment of proximity. It is true that evaluating whether the informational activity in question is sufficiently connected in space, time, and relationship with the goals of advancing military combat will be subject to some discretion, and there will certainly be quite a few close calls. On the other hand, there will also be cases that squarely and clearly fall outside the margins of this rule. For example, a criminal investigation against a soldier for drug use or sexual assault within the military—even where it involves certain data collection as part of the investigation—is not the kind of informational activity that will trigger the application of the duty as it is too far removed and disassociated from the zone of active or future combat and does not concern sparing the "civilian population" or "individual civilians."

As noted, it may not always be easy to determine whether a particular informational operation meets this "proximity test." The fluidity surrounding data collection and processing—the fact that information may serve different masters for different purposes at different times—makes the assessment particularly complex. Data transfers between agencies and across borders, common in the age of Big Data, only further compound the problem. While this poses an evidentiary challenge, it does not negate from the reasonableness of the interpretation as a textual matter, nor from its normative appeal as a possible built-in check within IHL on military cyber powers.

---

44. *See supra* note 29 and accompanying text.

45. Commentary to API, *supra* note 30, at 678, ¶ 2191.

46. *See* Jensen, *supra* note 25, at 202.

I recognize that this is a controversial argument, but such an interpretation is in line with the purpose of the Conventions and Additional Protocols to provide minimum protections to victims of armed conflict by setting standards of humane treatment. In fact, any interpretation of the rule that would set artificial distinctions based on the entity doing the collection and processing (civilian vs. military, contractor vs. members of the armed forces), or the nature of the collection and processing (commercial v. governmental) will muddy the waters. That is because such distinctions dilute the function that the drafters intended for the duty of constant care as a tool for sparing civilians from the harms of war.

2. When Does the Duty Apply?

The duty is a duty of *constant* care. As is alluded to by the adjective, it means that the duty has no temporal limitations; it simply applies "at all times." As the IGE noted in *Tallinn Manual 2.0*, the duty has a "continuing nature," and as such "[t]he law admits no situation in which, or time when, individuals involved in the planning and execution process may ignore the effects of their operations on civilians or civilian objects. In the cyber context, this requires situational awareness at all times, not merely during the preparatory stage of an operation."[47]

One important derivative conclusion is that the obligation extends beyond situations of active armed conflict and applies in peacetime, both before the armed conflict begins and after it ceases.[48] Whenever the military engages in certain informational operations that support its war efforts, the duty of constant care will latch on. I have written about this phenomenon in the context of "targeting banks."[49] These are archives where the air force stores and routinely updates intelligence cards with information about future targets in preparation for war.[50] As one Israeli major describes, the target bank must be routinely checked to ensure continued accuracy:

47. *See* TM2.0, *supra* note 27, at 477.

48. A similar reading is suggested by Mark Visger in his contribution to this volume. Mark offers three theories to support the conclusion that LOAC norms could govern data poisoning pre-conflict: (1) a broad reading of Common Article 3; (2) a theory of continuous crimes (where data poisoning is a criminal act); and (3) an application of the Martens Clause.

49. *See* Lubin, *supra* note 28, at 127 fn. 29 and accompanying text.

50. Interview with Major S., the deputy commander of the Israeli Air Force 200 Squadron, *reprinted in* Ann Rogers, *Investigating the Relationship between Drone Warfare and Civilian Casualties in Gaza*, 7 J. Strategic Sec. 94, 101 (2014); The 2014 Gaza Conflict (7 July–26 August 2014): Factual and Legal Aspects, Israeli Ministry of Foreign Affairs, ¶ 246 (May 2015), https://mfa.gov.il/ProtectiveEdge/Pages/default.aspx (noting that the "target planning process begins with the collection of intelligence" and describing how that intelligence is preserved in a "Target Card." The card includes operational directives and is subject to legal review that takes into account, among other things, precautions that could be taken upon execution).

Duty of Constant Care

[e]very few months, it is essential to check that the target is still relevant. If you find a weapons storage facility today, tomorrow they could take all of the weapons out of the building and build a kindergarten. If I don't know about that change, I might accidentally target it. That's why we don't only find new targets; we also keep track of the existing ones.[51]

In other words, the duty of constant care, and the specific precaution of target verification (enshrined in Article 57(2)(a)(i)), introduce peacetime obligations on the party collecting and processing that data. Specifically, in this example, the collector and processor of the data is required to monitor the database to ensure the accuracy of the data stored. Accuracy of personal data is a common data protection standard. The *principle of accuracy* in data protection establishes "a qualitative requirement and entails a responsibility that the data be accurate, and necessarily complete and up to date for the purpose intended."[52] By requiring the military to take every reasonable step to rectify inaccurate or incomplete data in targeting, Article 57's verification standard is an early articulation of a data protection concept. This is a crucial finding. If Article 57 is truly a data protection regime in disguise, what other standards might be hiding at plain sight between its four corners? It may therefore be in line with the drafters' intuitive intention that we interpret the duty of constant care as one that shines a data-protective light on the military's informational activity.

But while this inquiry may ultimately lead to new data protection obligations on militaries, it may also raise new and complex questions. Here is one: the "targeting banks" example speaks directly to intelligence collected by the military for a clear wartime purpose. How far along the data supply chain should we extend Article 57's data protection reach? What about intelligence originally collected for a noncombat purpose that is later found of use for a military aim? At what point should the duty of constant care latch on and should it retroactively introduce certain data protection standards? I am unable to offer a definitive answer at this point. As guidance I can only suggest that we employ a fact-intensive analysis that takes into account the varied circumstances surrounding each case, so to apply the general "proximity test" I proposed before.

3. What Harms Is the Duty Meant to Prevent?

As some commentators argue, the duty of constant care "should be taken literally," which means that "total avoidance of damage to the civilian population is the standard that combatants should seek to achieve in all cases."[53] But the provision is

---

51. *See* Interview with Major S., *supra* note 50, at 103–04.

52. Report of the International Law Commission on the Work of its Fifty-Eighth Session, Annex IV: Protection of Personal Data in Transborder Flow of Information (2006) UN Doc. Supplement No. 10 (A/61/10) (2006), 503 https://legal.un.org/ilc/reports/2006/english/anne xes.pdf [hereinafter ILC Data Protection Report].

53. Frits Kalshoven & Liesbeth Zegveld, Constraints on the Waging of War: An Introduction to International Humanitarian Law 113 (4th ed., 2011).

silent as to the categories of damages that the duty is meant to prevent. Certainly, in the context of attacks, damage is easily understood to mean kinetic harm, including loss of civilian life, injury to civilians, and physical harms to civilian objects.

There could indeed be many cases in which the reckless mishandling of data will trigger abhorrent physical harms. Suffice to consider the fictional scenario at the center of this book. The Newtropian AI Targeting System (NAITS) had a bias against non-Caucasians baked into its facial recognition algorithms that resulted in civilian casualties based on mistaken identification by the automated system. Similarly, a failure to properly test an update to the NAITS targeting algorithm (an update that was ultimately found to have been developed based on poisoned sets of data) resulted in the now updated NAITS mistakenly killing the head of a medical NGO. What both these examples show is that gross errors in the operating procedures surrounding the management of data could lead to actual death and injury of individuals, and physical destruction of property, in a military environment where data is weaponized.

But the duty of constant care could theoretically be said to extend beyond physical harms. Indeed, the parallel duty of defenders, in Article 58, refers to an even broader category of "dangers" and not mere damages. This extension of the harms prong of the duty also echoes the language of the 1970 UN General Assembly Resolution 2675. That resolution introduced an obligation on those engaging in military operations to make "every effort . . . to spare the civilian population from the *ravages of war*."[54]

It may be suggested that the "damage" prong behind the duty should be read broadly to include a range of "dangers" and "ravages of war" that go beyond the physical. If our goal is to "diminish the evils of war as far as military requirements permit"[55] then it follows that commanders must comply with "the laws of humanity, and the dictates of the public conscience"[56] wherever possible—even where the harms are dignitary rather than kinetic. In my introduction I listed a set of individual rights that have digital manifestations—privacy, anonymity, access to information, freedom of expression, autonomy and dignity, and the protection of property. As the examples provided in the introduction show, these rights are constantly at risk of abuse in the age of informational warfare. In the midst of the turmoil of war, it might seem strange to discuss these rights. Yet, the prohibition of "outrages upon personal dignity," which extends to acts of humiliation

---

54. Basic Principles for the Protection of Civilian Population in Armed Conflicts, UNGA Res. 2675, U.N. Doc. A/RES/2675(XXV), para. 3 (1970) (adopted by 109 votes in favor, none against and 8 abstentions) (emphasis added).

55. Convention (IV) Respecting the Laws and Customs of War on Land, 36 Stat. 2277, 207 Consol. T.S. 277, 18 October 1907 (Hague Convention IV), Preamble. See also Convention (II) with Respect to the Laws and Customs of War on Land, 32 Stat. 1803, Martens Nouveau Recueil, Series 2, Vol. 26, 29 July 1899, Preamble.

56. Hague Convention IV, *id.*, Preamble; API, *supra* note 10, at, Art. 1(2) (the Martens Clause).

and degrading treatment, is fundamental to the laws of war. If we committed to an obligation to minimize suffering, we must be mindful of assaults on the human spirit, not just the human body. In that regard, it seems to me that the duty of constant care may be able to serve a protective role for some of these digital rights at this intermediate stage of technological advancement, until more developed prescriptive frameworks take hold.

4. When Is the Duty Breached?

It is true that the duty of constant care is "poorly defined"[57] and therefore that extracting actual requirements may be difficult. Nonetheless, it is well established that the duty introduces a general obligation on a commander "to bear in mind the effect on the civilian population of what he is planning to do and take steps to reduce that effect as much as possible."[58]

The duty thus imposes a balancing act between "both the humanitarian considerations in favor of taking a precaution and the military considerations against taking that precaution."[59] In balancing between the two considerations, "there may be occasions when a commander will have to accept a higher level of risk to his own forces in order to avoid or reduce collateral damage to the enemy's civilian population."[60] In other words, "[m]ilitary necessity cannot always override humanity."[61]

Given the ambiguities surrounding "care" and lack of specific jurisprudence on its application as a standard, we may draw some inspiration from yet another historically ambiguous obligation: the obligation of "due regard" in the EEZ and high seas under UNCLOS. After all, the words "care" and "regard" are synonymous, and a familiar balance of interests test is expected under both. In the Chagos Marine Protected Area Arbitration (*Mauritius v. United Kingdom*), the Annex VII Tribunal clarified the following:

> [T]he ordinary meaning of "due regard" calls for [State A] to have such regard for the rights of [State B] as is called for by the circumstances and by the nature of those rights. The Tribunal declines to find in this formulation any universal rule of conduct. The Convention does not impose a uniform obligation to avoid any impairment of [State B's] rights; nor does it uniformly permit the [State A] to proceed as it wishes, merely noting such rights.

---

57. Michael N. Schmitt, *Wired Warfare 3.0: Protecting the Civilian Population during Cyber Operations*, 101 INT'L REV. RED CROSS 333, 354 (2019).

58. UK Ministry of Defence, The Manual of the Law of Armed Conflict, 2004 (UK Law of War Manual), para. 5.32.1.

59. ADIL AHMAD HAQUE, LAW AND MORALITY AT WAR 155 (2017).

60. *Id.* at 158 (citing a British defense doctrine).

61. A.P.V. Rogers, *Conduct of Combat and Risks Run by the Civilian Population*, 21 MIL. L. & L. WAR REV. 293, 310 (1982).

Rather, the extent of the regard required by the Convention will depend upon the nature of the rights held by [State B], their importance, the extent of the anticipated impairment, the nature and importance of the activities contemplated by [State A], and the availability of alternative approaches.[62]

This multi-factor test aligns with the duty of constant care under IHL. Lacking specific criteria, States are left with a general "zone of reasonableness"[63] within which they are called to "employ reasonably available resources and to gather reasonably available information."[64] Those states are merely asked to exercise basic due diligence, to do what is "practicably possible, taking into account all circumstances ruling at the time."[65]

Applying this approach, the breach of the duty of constant care may be found where a commander fails to consider the nature of the rights of the civilian population; their importance; the extent of the anticipated impairment upon those rights, while considering alternative approaches; and the military objectives to be achieved by the impairment. The commander needs to consider these factors at any point throughout the life cycle of an informational operation. For example, consider a belligerent occupier who collects extensive personally identifiable information on the civilian population in the occupied territory to advance the goals of the occupation. Now what if that occupier fails to introduce even the most basic of cybersecurity practices, and as a result of its gross negligence, the data is ultimately breached or exposed and certain economic, societal, and reputational harms ensue. It would seem to me to be the case that that occupier was in breach of its basic duty of care. The failure to introduce basic security measures over the data, where those measures are feasible and not burdensome, reflects a failure by the occupier to take reasonable precautions to spare the civilian populations from harm and thus a possible breach of the duty of contact care has occurred.

III. THE DUTY OF CONSTANT CARE AND DATA PROTECTION

A. The Duty of Constant Care as a Data Protection Rule

Another obligation derived from the duty of constant care is the obligation on commanders "to set up *an effective intelligence gathering system to collect and*

---

62. *In re* The Chagos Marine Protected Area Arbitration ¶519 (Mar. 18, 2015), http://www.pcacases.com/pcadocs/MU-UK%2020150318%20Award.pdf.

63. Amichai Cohen & David Zlotogorski, Proportionality in International Humanitarian Law: Consequences, Precautions, and Procedures 199 (2021).

64. *See* Krupiy, *supra* note 42, at 126.

65. *See* ICRC CIHL, *supra* note 31, Practice Relating to Rule 15.

evaluate information concerning potential targets. The commander must also direct his forces *to use available technical means to properly identify* targets during operations."[66] In this sense, Article 57 is the primary (if not only) "information collection" provision of the treatises of IHL. It thus makes great sense to rely on this provision as a potential gateway through which to introduce data protection norms into doctrinal IHL discourses.

Put another way, Article 57 mandates militaries to establish *effective* data collection, processing, verification, assessment, and dissemination frameworks and agencies. Those data arms, formed in response to this requirement, operate year-long to produce data to all echelons of the military machine. The effectiveness of this apparatus will be determined by objectively examining the methodologies of data management it employs. In this data-intensive environment, which Article 57 singlehandedly erected, the duty of constant care stands as the only possible lighthouse that could guide militaries in discharging of their duties.

In the final section of this chapter, I try to propose specific ways by which the duty of constant care may serve to restrain particular types of informational activity. To be clear, I do not argue that the duty of constant care as currently understood already encompasses a sufficiently clear menu of *lex lata* rules and obligations on member States. I only think that it *may* be read to encompass such rules through progressive interpretation. I argue that this interpretation would be textually reasonable and in line with the historical function that the duty of constant care was intended to serve since its drafting. I also think that such an interpretation could serve as a temporary gap filler, either as a matter of recommended best practice or as a matter of binding law, until such time as more formidable treaty frameworks and customary rules are introduced by the international community through formal rulemaking.

B. Specific Applications of the Duty in the Age of Big Data

For this final section I suggest that we follow an actual case study that might help demonstrate important ways by which a progressive interpretation of the duty of constant care could assist in constraining certain military informational activities. Consider in this regard biometric data processing. The UN Security Council introduced a Chapter VII resolution that required Member States, as part of the fight against terrorism, to "develop and implement systems to collect biometric data, which could include fingerprints, photographs, facial recognition, and other relevant identifying biometric data."[67]

---

66. Final Report to the Prosecutor by the Committee Established to Review the NATO Bombing Campaign Against the Federal Republic of Yugoslavia, ¶ 29 (June 2, 2000) https://www.icty.org/sid/10052 [hereinafter ICTY Expert Committee Report] (emphasis added).

67. Threats to International Peace and Security Caused by Returning Foreign Terrorist Fighters, S.C. Res. 2396, U.N. Doc. S/RES/2396, para. 15 (2017) (voted unanimously).

Responding to this obligation, the German Federal Government "has admitted that German soldiers collected biometric data in Afghanistan as part of the International Security Assistance Force (ISAF). It was stated that biometric data consisting of fingerprints, iris images and 'face geometry' has been collected from Afghan citizens and handed over to U.S. authorities. Mobile devices were afterwards used to identify people by matching the collected biometric data against a U.S. database."[68]

In conducting this operation, the German government applied no data protection standards. Quite the opposite, the government concluded that its domestic data protection law "did not apply to foreigners abroad,"[69] and therefore that there was no need to consider data protection law in the context of collecting this biometric data. But the recent developments in Afghanistan with which this article began highlight the potential horrific consequences to the civilian population from poorly managing data. The way personally identifiable information is collected, stored, disseminated, and ultimately deleted matters. Especially before, during, and after war. Not only that, but the specific features of this operation— (1) the fact that data was transferred between multiples members of a coalition force; (2) the fact that data was processed against another external dataset; (3) the fact that the data processing involved automated features; and (4) the fact that the data in question included particularly sensitive and personally indefinable information—make the lack of data protection standards particularly troubling. Many of these features are well-documented in the age of Big Data. They demonstrate just how little attention militaries have given to data protection in their rush to incorporate Big Data solutions in every segment of their activities.

So far, I have tried to show that a progressive interpretation of the duty of constant care could require commanders to take reasonable steps to reduce, where feasible, the negative effects on the civilian population from their informational operations. To determine what is reasonable and feasible we have no choice but to rely on existing well-tested benchmarks. The only way to determine whether alternative precautions were available and reasonable to employ, is by examining those alternatives. Existing data protection regimes offer us a rich menu from which to build on. I therefore suggest that the adoption of my progressive interpretation of the duty of constant care would allow us to import data protection principles currently excluded from IHL discourse. These principles could set clearer guidelines to belligerents who engage in Big Data practices, of the kind that the German biometric data processing involved. Below I offer two possible examples: (1) how the duty of constant care may introduce the data protection requirements of legality and transparency; and (2) how the duty of constant care may introduce the data protection requirements of storage specification and limitation and data integrity.

---

68. Sebastian Cymutta, *Biometric Data Processing by the German Armed Forces during Deployment*, CCDCOE 4 (2021), https://ccdcoe.org/uploads/2021/05/Cymutta_Biometric-data-processing-by-the-German-armed-forces-during-deployment_05.2021.pdf.

69. *Id.*

Duty of Constant Care

This is not an exhaustive list. Rather, I hope my chapter begins a necessary conversation about the way existing IHL could further cement data protection rules for military operations.

1. Legality and Transparency

A foundational data protection principle is the obligation of data processors to respect the rule of law and ensure transparency around the collection, processing, and dissemination of data, wherever feasible. This entails the adoption of primary or secondary legislation, and often additional other public-facing regulation that grounds the scope and nature of these data collection efforts, further establishing procedural safeguards to prevent abuse.[70] One such safeguard is the promulgation of *ex post* reviews that ensure greater transparency and accountability surrounding these efforts and increases societal trust.

In certain circumstances military data collection programs may not be disclosed to the data subjects, nor is seeking their consent practicable, for national security reasons. Certainly, where the very purpose of the operation will be hindered by the disclosure, rules of effectiveness should control and may justify some degree of secrecy. But this does not mean that a State must keep silent on all aspects of the operation. "While there may be legitimate public interest reasons for maintaining the secrecy of technical and operational specifications, these do not justify withholding from the public generic information."[71] As the Special Rapporteur on Counterterrorism noted, "without such information it is impossible to assess the legality, necessity, and proportionality of these measures."[72]

Information about German practices on biometric data collection in Afghanistan only came to light through *ex post* parliamentary inquiries.[73] The failure to articulate the policy, even at the most general level, through *ex ante* public statements and external policies shows a lack of care not in compliance with my proposed interpretation of the general duty enshrined in Article 57.

2. Storage Specification and Limitation and Data Integrity

Another common data protection principle is the data minimization principle. Under this principle "the purpose for which the data are collected should be specified . . . Data should not be disclosed, made available or otherwise used for purposes other than those specified."[74] This principle establishes that "the data

---

70. *See generally* ICRC Rules on Personal Data Protection, ICRC (2019), https://www.icrc.org/en/publication/4261-icrc-rules-on-personal-data-protection.

71. Report of the Special Rapporteur on the Promotion and Protection of Human Rights and Fundamental Freedoms While Countering Terrorism, U.N. Doc. A/69/397, para. 40 (Sept. 23, 2014).

72. *Id.*

73. *See* Cymutta, *supra* note 68, at 4.

74. *See* ILC Data Protection Report, *supra* note 52, at 503.

collected is not intended to be more far-reaching than is necessary for the purposes for which the data will be used. The test should be that the least intrusive method is used to achieve a legitimate aim."[75] A second data protection principle is the principle of data integrity. Under this principle personal data, especially sensitive data, as well as the infrastructure used to collect and store that data, "should be protected by security safeguards against risks such as unlawful or unauthorised access, use and disclosure, as well as loss, destruction, or damage of data."[76]

These sister principles of data minimization and data integrity may introduce a set of corollary and derivative obligations on the data processor depending on the circumstances. Commanders will need to assess what cybersecurity measures as well as data retention and storage limitation rules they wish to employ to reduce the risk of possible abuses. Such decisions will be based, in part, on capacity and available resources. This is a fact-intensive analysis that can only be applied on a case-by-case basis. One obvious general minimum threshold which could be easily applied is the following: a military should not use less security measures to protect the data it collects on foreigners than that which it uses to protect its own information. Where a military has already demonstrated a capacity to protect data at a certain high level (H), there should be a presumption against applying a second lower level (L) for foreign data that it collected. Like all presumptions it may be rebutted. There certainly could be reasons to apply diverging degrees of protection in certain circumstances (say due to certain resource limitations) but then any choice of application of either level H or level L security should depend on objective and nondiscriminatory criteria.

In the context of the German operation, no information was ever provided about the kind of measures the German authorities employed in the context of collecting and storing these biometric records. Again, the total lack of transparency as exemplified by a failure to publicly state basic security measures that were employed to protect highly sensitive data demonstrates a potential abdication of my proposed interpretation of the duty of care.

IV. CONCLUSION

In this short chapter I tried to suggest that IHL already possess a set of legal hooks on which we may be able to rest contemporary data protection best practices, thereby futureproofing the Geneva Conventions and Additional Protocols. I clarified that my proposal is one of progressive interpretation and that its utilization should be temporary, until such time as more robust frameworks and rules are developed to guide militaries in developing and deploying Big Data solutions.

---

75. *The Keys to Data Protection: A Guide for Policy Engagement on Data Protection*, PRIVACY INTERNATIONAL, 41 (Aug., 2018), https://privacyinternational.org/sites/default/files/2018-09/Part%203%20-%20Data%20Protection%20Principles.pdf.

76. *Id.* at 45.

Duty of Constant Care

To conclude, let us revisit for one final time to the fictional countries of Newtropia and Outlandia from the book's underlying hypothetical. Consider operation "Full Wrap" as described in the scenario. The operation was launched 18 months before the war broke out. It involved private contractors collecting huge amounts of data both domestically and globally to feed the algorithms developed by the military. The operation further relied on foreign commercial servers and a corporate cloud service provider for storing the data. The operation thus perfectly demonstrates yet another feature of the Big Data revolution—an overreliance on public/private partnerships. Contracting with the tech sector expands and speeds up existing trends in the privatization of warfare. But where the corporate sector has been the primary target of data protection rules, and therefore an early adopter of data protection language (not least because of the Brussels Effects of European data protection rules, like the GDPR), the military complex and intelligence agencies have mostly persisted in their objections to it.[77] Here lies the danger. By contracting with the military, certain corporate activity which was up until recently prohibited under evolving data protection norms, may be shielded under a cloak of national security. The introduction of data protection rules for the military, through the duty of constant care, could thus have the positive consequence of nipping this growing reality in the bud.

This chapter has offered a very technical and surgical expansion of an IHL obligation through a progressive interpretation of the treatises of IHL. But I do not want to end this chapter with only "desiccated concepts, devoid of connection."[78] Instead, I wish to end this short chapter with a passionate plea. As Naz Modirzadeh has noted, "passionate reasoning gives the reader a sense of why the author cares about the topic . . . Contextual, connected, passionate writing allows, and even demands of, the author to reflect upon the responsibilities that law, legal structures, and wartime legal scholars themselves may bear in seemingly endless war."[79]

So here goes. I spent roughly five years as an intelligence analyst within the Israeli military. My daily routine consisted of a myriad of assignments: identifying new potential intelligence sources, guiding collection efforts, analyzing raw surveillance material, developing and publishing intelligence briefs and larger research memos, consulting on specific ground and aerial operations, and (mostly

---

77. *See, e.g.*, Theodore Christakis & Kenneth Propp, *How Europe's Intelligence Services Aim to Avoid the EU's Highest Court—and What It Means for the United States*, LAWFARE (Mar. 8, 2021), https://www.lawfareblog.com/how-europes-intelligence-services-aim-avoid-eus-highest-court-and-what-it-means-united-states (exploring the current EU debates around the scope of the national security exception in data protection regimes). *Cf.* Council of Europe, Convention for the Protection of Individuals with Regard to Automatic Processing of Personal Data, Jan. 28, 1981, EST 108, Art. 11 (extending certain limited data protection obligations to data processing conducted for national security purposes).

78. Naz K. Modirzadeh, *Cut These Words: Passion and International Law of War Scholarship*, 61 HARV. INT'L. L. J. 1, 64 (2020).

79. *Id.* at 62.

toward the end of my service) training new generations of intelligence cadets. It has been argued that "service in the intelligence profession [. . .] involves doing things that in other times and places most would agree would be horribly immoral."[80] In all my years of service, not once have I felt like I've done anything unethical or illegal. Quite the opposite. Entering the profession at the age of 18, I accepted as inherent the "cloak and dagger" nature of the trade and rarely challenged my superiors. I saw each of my assignments as a Rubik's Cube or a 1000-piece puzzle that I was entrusted with solving. Once fully immersed in the work, I did not trouble myself with questions of law or morality (nor did I possess the vocabulary and mental stamina to understand them fully). Instead, I focused all of my energy on finishing the task at hand. At times, it felt like occupational therapy.

I understand perfectly well how churning data as a clog in a massive data-churning machine can distance and disassociate. Data protection rules and procedures are therefore not a panacea for all the ills and misfortunates that could materialize in this complexly wired and layered process. But the alternative is looking at an abyss of nothingness, embracing a false assumption that treaties that were written in a different time have nothing to teach us about the technological challenges of tomorrow. I vehemently oppose the thought that we will let the lacuna control and suffer the consequences of an unregulated infowar. This chapter is part of a broader research agenda that seeks to understand where privacy and data protection intersect with international humanitarian law. It is a research project and mission that will quite likely outlive me.

$$* * *$$

---

80. Tony Pfaff, *Bungee Jumping off the Moral Highground: Ethics of Espionage in the Modern Age, in* 1 ETHICS OF SPYING: A READER FOR THE INTELLIGENCE PROFESSIONAL 66, 68 (Jan. Goldman ed., 2006). Elsewhere Pfaff writes: "not only have [intelligence agents] felt that the deceiving and harming they have done in service to their country have corrupted their integrity, they feel this corruption is exacerbated by the "cloudy moral purpose" their agency serves." *Id.*

9

Cyborg Soldiers

Military Use of Brain-Computer Interfaces and the Law of Armed Conflict

NOAM LUBELL* AND KATYA AL-KHATEEB† ■

I. INTRODUCTION

Recent years have seen a spotlight aimed at new technologies and how they might be used by the military. Scholars and policy makers have given much attention to autonomous weapons systems and artificial intelligence (AI), as well as to cyber operations, but far less notice is paid to a host of other technologies that may also transform the way conflicts are conducted. One of these other areas of technological advancement is human enhancement. Enhancements can occur in a myriad of ways, from pharmaceutical to mechanical and even through gene modification. In this chapter, we focus on one particular method of enhancing human capabilities: the use of brain-computer interfaces (BCI). These systems open a direct link for the transfer of data between the human brain and a machine[1] and create possibilities for an extraordinary range of new abilities and actions. While it is still early days for this technology, BCI systems, including in many military-oriented projects, are currently in development.[2] The uses of BCIs range from

---

* Professor of International Law of Armed Conflict, University of Essex; Senior Research Fellow, Johns Hopkins University Applied Physics Laboratory; Research Associate, Federmann Cyber Security Research Center, Hebrew University. The authors wish to thank Erin Hahn, Daragh Murray, Clara Scholl, Yahli Shereshevsky, and Brock Wester, for their valuable comments. The final product is the responsibility of the authors alone.

† Senior Research Officer, School of Law & Human Rights Centre, University of Essex.

1. *See infra*, "BCI Definition."

2. *See infra*, "Military Uses."

Noam Lubell and Katya Al-Khateeb, *Cyborg Soldiers* In: *Big Data and Armed Conflict*. Edited by: Laura A. Dickinson and Edward W. Berg, Oxford University Press. © Noam Lubell and Katya Al-Khateeb 2024.
DOI: 10.1093/oso/9780197668610.003.0011

one-way transfer of sensory data from the brain to a computer, to two-way data exchanges between the brain and artificial intelligence systems, providing the human with almost instantaneous access to the power of AI.

The advanced capabilities of BCI will create previously unimaginable opportunities, as well as risks, on the battlefield. They will also present new challenges to the application of the law of armed conflict (LOAC, also referred to as International Humanitarian Law or IHL). Consider the following hypothetical future scenario: soldiers from State A are equipped with BCI systems designed to collect sensory data (sight and sound) from the soldiers, and they share this data directly with AI-based weapon platforms, including unmanned aerial vehicles. These systems also allow the soldiers to control the drones with commands issued directly from the brain to the weapon system. State B is aware of these functions and seeks to disrupt the data exchange between the soldiers and the drones, but corrupting the data communication could cause permanent brain damage to any BCI user in the vicinity, including persons other than the soldiers operating the drones. In a separate incident, State B detains a BCI-enhanced soldier from State A. However, the captors are uncertain if the BCI is still active and if the soldier should be considered hors de combat and entitled to protection, or whether the soldier's brain is still transmitting data back to headquarters; indeed, it is possible that the soldier may still be able to launch a strike through the BCI. These types of situations present complex challenges to the application of the rules on conduct of hostilities and protection of individuals during armed conflict.

As we will discuss in this chapter, much of the technology in this area is still in its infancy. Our chapter aims to identify the legal issues arising from future military uses based on potential technological development, rather than the current state of the science. As such, the scenarios we present are by and large hypothetical, and we cannot predict if and when they might become a reality. Nonetheless, we believe it is precisely at this early stage that an analysis based on the possible direction of travel can be most useful. Too often, technologies are developed and deployed—including by militaries—only to face a host of legal and other challenges to their use. By understanding and foreseeing the legal obstacles that may arise in the future, we aim to identify ways in which such risks can be mitigated through appropriate design and development of the nascent technology.

The literature on the international legal questions surrounding human enhancement is relatively sparse. A very small number of publications have begun to explore the legal issues arising from military applications in this field. Their focus, in most cases, has been on human enhancement technologies more generally, and has provided an excellent start to the debates.[3] This chapter takes a different

---

3. *See*, e.g., Heather A. Harrison Dinniss & Jann K. Kleffner, *Soldier 2.0: Military Human Enhancement and International Law*, 92 INT'L L.STUD. 432–482 (2016); Patrick Lin et al., *Enhanced Warfighters: Risk, Ethics, and Policy*, SSRN ELECTRONIC JOURNAL 1–19 (2013); NEW TECHNOLOGIES AND THE LAW IN WAR AND PEACE (W. H. Boothby ed., Cambridge University Press) (2018); Rain Liivoja & Luke Chircop, *Are Enhanced Warfighters Weapons, Means, or Methods of Warfare? or Methods of Warfare?*, 94 INT'L L.STUD. 161–185 (2018); EMILY JONES, FEMINIST THEORY AND INTERNATIONAL LAW: POSTHUMAN PERSPECTIVES, (forthcoming 2022);

approach, by delving deeper into the issues surrounding one class of technologies. As we will show, BCI systems have the potential to fundamentally transform the battlefield. While military human enhancements generally raise questions about the dividing line between the weapon and the human operator,[4] it is hard to conceive of a greater blurring of the lines than that created by the human-machine symbiosis of brain-computer interfaces. Moreover, the use of brain-computer interfaces raises many of the challenging legal questions posed by AI and the growing use of data as well as complex new issues specific to the unique brain-computer connection. By providing one of the first in-depth examinations of this subject, this chapter aims to lay the foundation for applying international humanitarian law to the use of BCIs. Following an explanation of BCI technology and some of its potential uses by militaries in the future, the chapter provides an analysis of a wide range of legal issues from the regulation of weapon development to specific rules of targeting and protection. As we will show, solutions to certain challenges may require consideration in the actual development and configuration of BCI systems. We hope that, by tackling these issues here at this point in time, we may still be able to influence the development of the systems to ensure they can operate within the confines of international law.

II. WHAT IS A BCI?

A. BCI Definition

A BCI "is a system that measures [central nervous system] CNS activity and converts it into artificial output that replaces, restores, enhances, supplements, or improves natural CNS output and thereby changes the ongoing interactions between the CNS and its external or internal environment."[5] Accordingly, there are five types of applications that a BCI output might control: (1) it might *replace* a natural output that has been lost due to injury/disease; (2) it might *restore* lost natural output; (3) it might *enhance* natural CNS output; (4) it might *supplement* natural CNS output; and (5) it might conceivably *improve* natural CNS output.[6]

Yahli Shereshevsky, *Are All Soldiers Created Equal?—On the Equal Application of the Law to Enhanced Soldiers*, VA. J. INT'L L., 271–324 (2020).

4. Lin et al., *supra* note 5, at 29–30; Liivoja & Chircop, *supra* note 5, at 176–8.

5. JONATHAN R. WOLPAW & ELIZABETH WINTER WOLPAW, BRAIN-COMPUTER INTERFACES: PRINCIPLES AND PRACTICE 5 (J. R. Wolpaw & E. W. Wolpaw ed., 2012). *See also*, Stefan Reschke et al., *Neural and Biological Soldier Enhancement: From SciFi to Deployment*, NATO, RESEARCH AND TECHNOLOGY ORGANISATION RTO 33.1–33.11, 33.2 (2009); (BCIs are also synonymous with the concept of "technointegration" referring to the "symbiotic coupling of humans with technology to amplify human physical and cognitive capabilities.").

6. A BCI output might *replace* a lost natural output; for example, a person who has lost limb control might use a BCI to operate an electric wheelchair. A BCI output might *restore* lost

In *improving* the natural CNS output, which is the primary focus of this chapter, possible BCI applications might include enabling a wide range of superhuman abilities such as extrasensorial perception, superstrength, or super-precision.[7] Some applications aim to allow a device to send sensory data to the user or facilitate bilateral communication involving both sensory data and motor control.[8] A more advanced hypothetical application in the future might enable multilateral cognitive collaboration, where, for example, a soldier with a brain implant can stream live data from the battlefield to the Command Base and receive communication back from commanders directly to the brain. In certain circumstances, the implant might both be remotely controlled by commanders and control a prosthetic attachment with an offensive capacity.[9]

A subset of BCI systems, particularly with exogenously driven operational modes, could potentially translate the user's intentions into actions through a correlation between brain and computer. For this correlation to happen, a device modulates the user's brain signals, and in turn the BCI identifies and interprets the neural signals. BCIs can be classified into those that use non-invasive, minimally invasive, partially invasive, and invasive BCIs.[10] EEG

natural output; for example, a person with spinal cord injury (limbs paralysis) might use a BCI to stimulate the paralyzed muscles via implanted electrodes so that the muscles move the limbs. A BCI output might *enhance* natural CNS output; for example, a person performing a task that requires continuous attention over a prolonged period (e.g., flying a combat aircraft) might use a BCI that detects the brain activity preceding declines in attention and then provides an alerting output (e.g., a sound) to restore attention. A BCI output might *supplement* natural CNS output such as *supplementing* natural neuromuscular output with an additional artificial output; for example, a person might use a BCI to control third (i.e., robotic) arm and hand. Finally, a BCI output might conceivably *improve* natural CNS output; for example, a person whose arm movements have been impaired by a damage to the sensorimotor cortex might use a BCI that measures signals from the damaged cortical areas and then stimulates muscles so as to improve arm movements. A repeated use of such BCI may induce activity-dependent CNS plasticity that *improves* the natural CNS output and thereby helps the person to regain more normal arm control. This type of BCI changes the continuous interactions between the CNS and its external or internal environment. It reflects an ongoing hybrid mode of operation that may improve both sensory input from the environment and CNS output. WOLPAW & WOLPAW, *supra* note 7, at 4–5.

7. *See* possible operational and applied capabilities in ANIKA BINNENDIJK ET AL., BRAIN-COMPUTER INTERFACES: U.S. MILITARY APPLICATIONS AND IMPLICATIONS, AN INITIAL ASSESSMENT 7 (RAND Corporation) (2020), https://www.rand.org/pubs/research_reports/RR2 996.html (last visited Jan 24, 2022).

8. Jeneva A. Cronin et al., *Task-Specific Somatosensory Feedback via Cortical Stimulation in Humans*, 9 IEEE TRANSACTIONS ON HAPTICS 515–522, 519 (2016).

9. For more examples, *see* PETER EMANUEL ET AL., CYBORG SOLDIER 2050: HUMAN/MACHINE FUSION AND THE IMPLICATIONS FOR THE FUTURE OF THE DOD 7–10 (Oct. 2019), https://apps. dtic.mil/sti/pdfs/AD1083010.pdf.

10. Otto et al, "Acquiring Brain Signals from within the Brain," *in* BRAIN-COMPUTER INTERFACES: PRINCIPLES AND PRACTICE 81 (J. R. Wolpaw & E. W. Wolpaw ed., 2012); Forian

(electroencephalogram), for example, obtains electrical signals from the scalp and is considered the dominant and safest method for noninvasive BCIs.[11] Invasive BCIs, by contrast, retrieve electrical signals via microelectrodes surgically implanted in the cortical layers of the brain.[12] Partially invasive BCIs could use ECoG (electrocorticography), which is a type of signal platform that enables electrodes to be placed on the attainable edge of the brain to detect electrical impulses originating from the cerebral cortex, without the need for brain surgery.[13] While most invasive and partially invasive BCIs require high-risk neurosurgical implantation, minimally invasive BCIs[14] are low risk surgical procedures such as implants that could be inserted into the blood stream while they travel to a particular organ by themselves.[15]

Using an EEG-based system, humans have been able to control a computer cursor and to command robots to manipulate objects and operate limb prosthetics.[16] The EEG devices, however, are fundamentally limited by their signal

---

Heinrichs, *Introduction to Brain-Computer Interfaces: When Technology from Science Fiction Movies Becomes Reality*, TOWARDS DATA SCIENCE (Oct. 19, 2021), https://towardsdatascience.com/introduction-to-brain-computer-interfaces-d05d533e3543 .

11. Otto et al., *supra* note 12.

12. *Id.*

13. *Id., see also* M. F. Mridha et al., *Brain-Computer Interface: Advancement and Challenges*, 21 SENSORS (BASEL, SWITZERLAND) 5746 (2021), https://pubmed.ncbi.nlm.nih.gov/34502636; Eric C. Leuthardt et al., *Defining Surgical Terminology and Risk for Brain Computer Interfaces Technologies*, 15 FRONTIERS IN NEUROSCIENCE 1–9, (Mar. 26, 2021) https://doi.org/10.3389/fnins.2021.599549.

14. Such as the "stentrode"; Department of Defense - Congressionally Directed Medical Research Programs (CDMRP), *Stentrode: A SCIRP-Funded Device to Facilitate Independence After Paralysis* (Sept. 22, 2021), https://cdmrp.army.mil/scirp/research_highlights/21opie_hi ghlight (last visited Apr. 4, 2022).

15. Yuhao Zhou et al., *Implantable Thin Film Devices as Brain-Computer Interfaces: Recent Advances in Design and Fabrication Approaches*, 11 COATINGS 1–26 (2021); Jonathan R. Wolpaw & Dennis J. McFarland, *Control of a Two-Dimensional Movement Signal by a Noninvasive Brain-Computer Interface in Humans*, 101 PROCEEDINGS OF THE NATIONAL ACADEMY OF SCIENCES OF THE UNITED STATES OF AMERICA 17849–17854 (2004), https://pubmed.ncbi.nlm.nih.gov/15585584 .

16. Paulette Campbell, *Quadriplegic Patient Uses Brain Signals to Feed Himself with Two Advanced Prosthetic Arms*, JOHNS HOPKINS U. HUB (Dec. 28, 2020), https://hub.jhu.edu/2020/12/28/quadr iplegic-man-feeds-himself-with-brain-controlled-prosthetic-arms/; Sebastian Olsen et al., *An Artificial Intelligence that Increases Simulated Brain–Computer Interface Performance*, 18 J. OF NEURAL ENGINEERING 046053 1–16 (May 13, 2021), http://dx.doi.org/10.1088/1741-2552/abfaaa; Sung Phil Kim et al., *Neural control of computer cursor velocity by decoding motor cortical spiking activity in humans with tetraplegia*, 5 J. OF NEURAL ENGINEERING 455–476 (2008); Michael Kryger et al., *Flight simulation using a Brain-Computer Interface: A pilot, pilot study*, 287 EXPERIMENTAL NEUROLOGY 473–478 (Jan. 2017), https://www.sciencedirect.com/science/article/pii/S0014488616301248 .

content, and recordings are prone to interference from the electromyographic activity.[17] Invasive and partially invasive BCIs, on some dimensions, enable higher performance limits.[18] For instance, patients with locked-in syndrome are able to move cursors and execute basic control over robotic devices, such as opening and closing a prosthetic hand.[19] Invasive and partially invasive BCIs hold greater potential for functionality than their noninvasive counterparts, but there are also risks and limitations associated with their implantation, some of which could affect the legal analysis conducted in this chapter. A skullcap that is worn and removed like a hat will create far less challenges than an implant surgically inserted into the brain. From the legal perspective, the latter type of BCI can most obviously affect matters such as the lawfulness of risk to the individual but also, as will be seen later, raises specific LOAC questions of targeting and protection. Accordingly, the attributes of any given BCI system must be considered when analyzing the legal issues it may raise. There are a number of different ways to categorize and differentiate between the various BCI systems in this regard. As we will discuss in the legal analysis, factors to consider include whether the BCI is attached in an invasive or noninvasive manner; where the BCI sits on the scale from wearable and easily removable to permanently implanted; whether the BCI's effects are temporary or ongoing; the direction of data flow to/from the device and whether it is bidirectional. These are not, as it may at first seem, overlapping categories; a removable device may, for example, nonetheless have caused changes in the brain that are not easily reversible even after the use of the BCI is ended.

B. AI, Data, and BCI

The introduction of AI and machine learning in the data collection and communication of BCIs provides for further enhancement of the system and the potential for new capabilities for the human using it.[20] For example, in a future hypothetical capability, the integration of AI in the BCI would enable the analysis of large volumes of data to improve the soldier's efficiency when assessing a situation on the battlefield. The AI enhances the techniques for data acquisition, monitoring,

---

17. Didar Dadebayev et al., *EEG-Based Emotion Recognition: Review of Commercial EEG Devices and Machine Learning Techniques*, J. OF KING SAUD U. - COMPUTER AND INFO. SCI. 1–17, 13 (2021).

18. *Id.*

19. Alberto J. Molina-Cantero et al., *Controlling a Mouse Pointer with a Single-Channel EEG Sensor*, 21 SENSORS, 4 (2021).

20. Xiayin Zhang et al., *The Combination of Brain-Computer Interfaces and Artificial Intelligence: Applications and Challenges*, 8 ANNALS TRANSLATIONAL MED. 712 (June 2020), https://pubmed.ncbi.nlm.nih.gov/32617332; Zehong Cao, *A Review of Artificial Intelligence for EEG-based Brain–Computer Interfaces and Applications*, 6 BRAIN SCIENCE ADVANCES (2020) https://journals.sagepub.com/doi/full/10.26599/BSA.2020.9050017.

and analysis. This can include a system capable of receiving sensory input data from the soldier's vision. The AI would then analyze this input to identify threats and relay findings and recommendations back to the soldier's brain as well as to the commanders. The sensory data could itself be augmented by systems capable, for example, of higher resolution perception or UV/IR spectrum readings. By combining the processing power of AI and the brain with direct flow of data between the two, such BCI systems are blurring the human-machine divide and raising questions across the spheres of law, ethics, and social policy. Our focus here is on the legal aspects, in particular LOAC. As we will demonstrate, there are significant complexities in categorizing all such systems as weapons, with legal and practical concerns in relation to both the conduct of hostilities and protection of those hors de combat, as well as accountability for violations. In addition to the issues raised by potential physical integration of human and machine, there are unique challenges related to data in this context, and to data reliability in targeting and to the possibility of attacks aimed at the data streams used by the BCI. The following sections will address these concerns. First, however, we must develop an initial understanding of how these systems might be deployed in a military context.

III. MILITARY USES

BCIs have the potential to affect every aspect of military operations, from providing a wealth of previously inaccessible information to battlefield actors, to enhancing the performance of individual soldiers, to conferring superior abilities on commanders to influence the actions of their troops. While a significant amount of the research focuses upon medical advantages,[21] this section will detail other, operational uses of BCI systems.

A. Monitoring

At the (relatively) simpler end of the scale, a BCI combined with other biotech could monitor brain and body functions of the soldier and transmit this information to the commander or a special monitoring unit.[22] Real-time soldier physiological monitoring is not a new concept. In 2004, U.S. officials noted that

---

21. *For example,* in 2013, DARPA launched the Restore Active Memory (RAM) program with the goal to develop a "fully implantable, closed-loop neural interface capable of re-storing normal memory function to military personnel suffering from the effects of brain injury or illness." DARPA, *Progress in Quest to Develop a Human Memory Prosthesis*, DARPA, 2018, https://www.darpa.mil/news-events/2018-03-28 (last visited Jan 19, 2022).

22. For the purpose of this chapter, "BCIs" also include assistive devices that are subject to remote control, in a broader biotech landscape.

monitoring is necessary to ensure that operational personnel are as physically fit as possible because success on the battlefield is to a great extent dependent on the ability of combat service members [...] to endure a host of physical stresses and strains that could easily overwhelm unfit individuals. [...] An alert or warning signal to the individual and to his or her squad leader could permit prompt intervention to alleviate the physiological danger and potentially save a mission.[23]

Detailed data could include hormonal readings of cortisol and adrenaline to indicate levels of stress and mental state in situations of danger, or other readings to provide information on fatigue and physical well-being.[24] This information would allow commanders to make better informed decisions on directing their troops, taking into account the exact state of the soldiers and possibly also determining which soldiers are in a better condition to carry out particular missions and tasks at any given moment. Moreover, the monitoring unit may also have the ability to trigger a function in the implant designed to affect the hormonal levels of the soldier and counteract undesirable readings or enhance particular functions. This could be achieved through brain stimulation mechanisms or in combination with other implants physically releasing chemicals. Commanders could, in theory, give their soldiers an "energy" jolt or heighten their situational awareness in particular circumstances.

B. Control

Recently, in the field of precision medicine, there have been significant advances in the use of biosensors and biotelemetry. Biosensors are "analytical devices containing a biological sensing element that transforms a biological response into electrical signals."[25] They can sensitively and rapidly detect a wide range of biomarkers, including molecular signatures, phenotype, environment, and lifestyle. Biotelemetry is the remote measurement of an activity, function or condition, and it utilizes the implantable technology of biosensors as a means of obtaining data such as electromyogram (EMG), electroencephalogram (EEG), electrocardiogram (ECG), heart rate, blood pressure, body temperature, activity, and circadian rhythm.[26] Moreover, biosensors have been developed to have the ability to deliver

23. INSTITUTE OF MEDICINE OF THE NATIONAL ACADEMIES, MONITORING METABOLIC STATUS: PREDICTING DECREMENTS IN PHYSIOLOGICAL AND COGNITIVE PERFORMANCE 15 (2004).

24. M Gray et al., *Implantable Biosensors and Their Contribution to the Future of Precision Medicine*, 239 THE VETERINARY J. 21–29, 21 (Sept. 2018), https://www.sciencedirect.com/science/article/pii/S1090023318304180 .

25. *Id.* at 22.

26. *Id.* at 23.

Cyborg Soldiers

drugs in response to biosensor readings.[27] Scientists at Johns Hopkins Electrical and Computer Engineering lab are currently developing "wireless biotelemetry using ultra-wideband communications."[28] These BCIs could be utilized in the future for significant control and monitoring of soldiers on the battlefield; not only to gauge the level of stress or fatigue but to potentially allow commanders to issue orders to the brain and control implants that could release chemicals or stimulate brain activities-influencing behavior and decisions of individual soldiers. As we will discuss later, such interventions raise several legal concerns.

C. Communications

There are several ongoing and planned projects aimed at using BCI systems as an advanced means for communication. These include a system/algorithm that would translate the thoughts or intentions of a soldier into a signal suitable for operating devices. This would enable silent communication or "silent speech" through a process in which a user imagines speaking a word without actually vocalizing any sound.[29] Using such technologies to enable silent speech among soldiers can provide a number of advantages on the battlefield. During hostilities when giving verbal commands is difficult due to the level of noise and chaotic surroundings, or during reconnaissance when silence is critical due to the stealth nature of a mission, silent communication will offer a significant benefit.

BCI designed for communication purposes could be a faster, more efficient, and safer method of communication not only among soldiers on the battlefield, but also between soldiers and their commanders.[30] The ability of commanders

---

27. *Id.* at 23–4. *Also see*, Gemma Church, *How Hacking the Human Heart Could Replace Pill Popping*, BBC (Dec. 16, 2019), https://www.bbc.com/future/article/20191216-how-hacking-the-human-heart-could-replace-pill-popping.

28. Ivana Čuljak et al., *Wireless Body Sensor Communication Systems Based on UWB and IBC Technologies: State-of-the-Art and Open Challenges*, 20 Sensors 3587, 1 (June 25, 2020), https://pubmed.ncbi.nlm.nih.gov/32630376.

29. N. Birbaumer et al., *The thoThought Translation Device (TTD) for Completely Paralyzed Patients*, 8 IEEE Transactions on Rehabilitation Engineering 190–193, 190 (2000); Benjamin Blankertz et al., *The Berlin Brain-Computer Interface: Progress Beyond Communication and Control*, 10 Frontiers in Neuroscience 1–24, 1 (Nov. 21, 2016), https://www.frontiersin.org/article/10.3389/fnins.2016.00530; Francis R. Willett et al., *High-performance brain-to-text communication via handwriting*, 593 Nature 249–254, 249 (May 12, 2021), https://doi.org/10.1038/s41586-021-03506-2; Ian Sample, *Paralysed Man Uses 'Mindwriting' Brain Computer to Compose Sentences*, The Guardian (May 12, 2021), https://www.theguardian.com/science/2021/may/12/paralysed-man-mindwriting-brain-computer-compose-sentences; Lauran Neergaard, *Device Taps Brain Waves to Help Paralyzed Man Communicate*, Tech Explore (July 15, 2021), https://techxplore.com/news/2021-07-device-brain-paralyzed.html .

30. There will, however, be other safety and security concerns, for example over hacking and other interference.

to receive information from soldiers and transmit orders directly to their brains could transform commanders' ability to direct operations from a distance. The communication from the soldiers could include data that goes far beyond what they might have been able to send verbally over the networks. Their "words" could be accompanied by simultaneous real-time sensory data, as well as other information described before.[31] With this technology, a soldier engaging in hostilities on the battlefield might, for example, be able to summon a drone and issue a firing command on a specific target with extreme precision through thought alone. With the aid of BCIs, soldiers may also be able to directly communicate with a drone in the air while it is surveying the surroundings, thereby avoiding—or preparing for—any perceived danger.

D. Enhanced Functions

In addition to improved communications, BCI systems provide a myriad of possibilities to enhance soldiers' battle-related capabilities. For example, The Neurotechnology for Intelligence Analysts and Cognitive Technology Threat Warning System visual interface programs both "utilized non-invasively recorded 'target detection' brain signals to improve the efficiency of imagery analysis and real-time threat detection, respectively";[32] where cognitive algorithms could highlight many events that would otherwise be considered irrelevant, but are actually indications of threats or targets. Moreover, DARPA's The Neural Engineering System Design also sought to develop "high-resolution neurotechnology capable of mitigating the effects of injury and disease on the visual and auditory systems of military personnel."[33] The aim of this program was to develop neural implants that make it possible for the human brain to precisely communicate directly to computer interfaces.[34]

The military has also taken an interest in transcranial direct current stimulation (tDCS)[35] for enhancing/amplifying the soldier's core cognitive capabilities or baseline performance, independent of auxiliary conditions, such as fatigue

---

31. Cf sub-section on *Monitoring* under "Military uses".

32. Robbin A. Miranda et al., *DARPA-Funded Efforts in the Development of Novel Brain–Computer Interface Technologies*, 244 J. Neuroscience Methods 52–67, 60 (Apr. 15, 2015), https://www.sciencedirect.com/science/article/pii/S0165027014002702

33. AI Emondi, *Neural Engineering System Design (NESD)*, Darpa, 2018, https://www.darpa.mil/program/neural-engineering-system-design (last visited Jan 19, 2022).

34. *High-resolution, Implantable Neural Interface,* Today's Medical Developments (August 3, 2017) https://www.todaysmedicaldevelopments.com/article/darpa-neural-system-design-manufacturing-device-8317/ (last visited Mar. 26, 2022).

35. Transcranial direct current stimulation (tDSCs), or transcranial electric stimulation (tES), is a form of non-invasive brain stimulation, usually through the application of a low-intensity electrical current via electrodes placed on the scalp.

Cyborg Soldiers

or environmental factors (e.g., noise exposure). In 2018, the Air Force Research Laboratory noted that tDCS "significantly improves the participants' information processing capability, which results in improved performance compared to sham tDCS."[36] Although several parameters were identified and studies suggested that this type of stimulation can also increase creativity and cognitive flexibility, perception, attention, accuracy, and boosts memory, further work is required before this type of technology can be recommended for operational use.[37]

Researchers are also studying systems affecting memory, including not only systems that encode and recall memories, but also those that rewrite memories with new data.[38] While these efforts to manipulate, decode, and rewrite memory are publicly directed at treating combatants' post-traumatic stress disorder, their military utility goes far beyond treating and preserving the fighting force. For example, manipulation of memories can directly influence soldiers' behavior and affect their decision-making.[39] Moreover, while each BCI has its own application, it is important to note that it could be possible to combine the working of several BCIs and unlock potentials hitherto unconsidered. For example, the combination of biosensors and memory data manipulation has the potential to alter perception and affect a soldier's decision-making far more effectively than either of these systems could do alone.

IV. LOAC IMPLICATIONS

The use of BCIs in military operations raises numerous questions under LOAC. Perhaps the most obvious one surrounds their categorization as a means or

36. MARK W. VAHLE, OPPORTUNITIES AND IMPLICATIONS OF BRAIN-COMPUTER INTERFACE TECHNOLOGY 13 (July 2020) https://www.airuniversity.af.edu/Portals/10/AUPress/Papers/ WF_0075_VAHLE_OPPORTUNITIES_AND_IMPLICATIONS_OF_BRAIN_COMPUTER_I NTERFACE_TECHNOLOGY.PDF .

37. Kathryn A. Feltman et al., *Viability of tDCS in Military Environments for Performance Enhancement: A Systematic Review*, 185 MIL. MED. e53–e60, e57–8 (Jan.—Feb. 2020), https:// doi.org/10.1093/milmed/usz189; Steven E. Davis & Glen A. Smith, *Transcranial Direct Current Stimulation Use in Warfighting: Benefits, Risks, and Future Prospects*, 13 FRONTIERS IN HUMAN NEUROSCIENCE 1–18 (2019).

38. Steve Ramirez, *Crystallizing a Memory*, 360 SCIENCE 1182–1183 (2018); Pablo Uchoa, *Could Hackers "Brainjack" Your Memories in Future?*, BBC (Feb. 19, 2019), https://www.bbc. co.uk/news/business-47277340; Wake Forest Baptist Medical Center, *Prosthetic Memory System Successful in Humans*, SCI. DAILY (Mar. 27, 2018), https://www.sciencedaily.com/releases/2018/ 03/180327194350.htm; Theo Austin Bruton, *Mind-Movies: Original Authorship as Applied to Works From "Mind-Reading" Neurotechnology*, 14 J. INTELL. PROP. CHICAGO-KENT J. OF INTELL. PROP. 263–286 (2014).

39. Joshua J. Tremel et al., *Manipulating Memory Efficacy Affects the Behavioral and Neural Profiles of Deterministic Learning and Decision-Making*, 114 NEUROPSYCHOLOGIA 214–230 (2018), https://www.ncbi.nlm.nih.gov/pmc/articles/PMC5989004/.

method of warfare and how they are to be regulated under the weapon review process. But the issues to be addressed are far wider. The aforementioned blurring of the human-machine divide also creates challenges in relation to the rules on targeting and complex new problems in the protection of individuals hors de combat, as well as concerns over accountability for violations. Although intriguing philosophical questions can be asked about the metamorphosis of the human body and the human-machine divide in the age of BCI systems, the blurring of lines is not just a conceptual problem of theory, but fast becomes a practical matter with significant legal repercussions. When the machine in this case is a military human enhancement technology—possibly categorized as a means or method of warfare—differentiating between it and the human to which it is attached will be of critical importance for a number LOAC rules.[40] Moreover, the problem runs deeper when we turn to BCI systems with an AI component. In such cases, the brain-computer interaction may include AI-generated data affecting the thought process and decision-making of the soldier. The breaking down of divisions between human and machine will, therefore, involve more than concerns over the lack of physical separation between the two. The extent to which the individual's decisions are based on AI data, and the possibility that the BCI system may even affect the decision-making process itself, create new challenges to how we measure the control the individual has over their actions on the battlefield, including determining their intent and legal responsibility.[41]

A. BCI Reliance on Data from AI Systems

As noted at the outset, by allowing for the bidirectional flow of data between the brain and a computer system, BCIs can effectively integrate AI and human capacities. For example, an AI system could be utilized to supplement and enhance individual perception and decision-making in a targeting situation. This could involve BCI systems designed to speed up the ability of soldiers to detect and respond to threats. Such a system may include a link to an AI mechanism that alerts the soldier to something their eyes have captured but they had not consciously noticed, by transmitting the images registered by the individual to the AI system for immediate analysis and determination of threat.[42] The system would essentially be the same as a comrade shouting a warning "enemy to your left," but in the form of an internal communication direct to the brain. The soldier could instinctively respond by quickly turning toward the enemy and firing.

40. *Cf* section on "LOAC Implications".

41. *Cf* section on "Accountability and Responsibility".

42. *See* section on "Enhanced Functions".

While these combinations of the brain and AI may be designed to provide the best of both worlds, there is also the risk of them achieving the exact opposite. Ensuring that such systems do not cause violations of the principle of distinction will necessitate examination of the reliability of the AI threat detection mechanisms.[43] The extensive debates surrounding AI in recent years have examined in great detail the potential risks of delegating certain functions to machines, for example, in relation to algorithmic biases.[44] There are many forms and causes of bias in this context, including conscious or unconscious bias of the human programmers, which finds itself built into the AI systems they design. Algorithmic bias can also occur when a machine learning AI system is trained on limited datasets.[45] For example, if the machine learning process for the AI system relied on data from previous conflicts that all took place in the same part of the world, it may associate certain ethnicities with enemy status.[46] These concerns are among the key reasons that many commentators (and States) advocate for maintaining human judgment in the targeting process, to ensure oversight and mitigate risk of flaws.[47]

If the BCI system utilizes AI analysis, this opens up the all the familiar problems regarding use of AI data in targeting, since the human in this case could become a conduit for carrying out a targeting action on the basis of a determination made by—and data received from—the AI. Because the objective of using such systems would be to enhance and speed up the reaction time of the soldiers, it is unrealistic to expect them to question the calculations of the system before acting. Moreover, the integration of AI data with the BCI further compounds the existing AI concerns, given that it may become more difficult to differentiate the

43. *Cf* section on "Weapon Review".

44. MICHAEL ROVATSOS ET AL., LANDSCAPE SUMMARY: BIAS IN ALGORITHMIC DECISION-MAKING 11–13 (2019); INTERNATIONAL LEGAL AND POLICY DIMENSIONS OF WAR ALGORITHMS: ENDURING AND EMERGING CONCERNS, https://pilac.law.harvard.edu/internatio nal-legal-and-policy-dimensions-of-war-algorithms (last visited Jan. 19, 2022); Ashley Deeks, *Will Autonomy in U.S. Military Operations Centralize Legal Decision-Making?*, ARTICLES OF WAR (Aug. 5, 2020), https://lieber.westpoint.edu/autonomy_military_operations_decision-making/; Wenlong Sun et al., *Evolution and Impact of Bias in Human and Machine Learning Algorithm Interaction*, 15 PLOS ONE 1–39 (Aug. 13, 2020), https://doi.org/10.1371/journal.pone.0235502

45. ARTHUR HOLLAND MICHEL, THE BLACK BOX, UNLOCKED: PREDICTABILITY AND UNDERSTANDABILITY IN MILITARY AI 19 (2020);*Will Knight, Forget Killer Robots—Bias Is the Real AI Danger*, MIT TECHNOLOGY REVIEW (Oct. 3, 2017); Jonathan Vanian, *Unmasking A.I.'S Bias problem*, 178 FORTUNE (June 25, 2018).

46. Yasmin Afina, *International Humanitarian Law Considerations for the Development of AI-enabled Technologies for Military Targeting Operations*, PhD thesis in progress, on file with the authors.

47. Dustin A. Lewis et al., *War-Algorithm Accountability*, SSRN ELECTRONIC JOURNAL 1–244 (2017); United Nation Institute for Disarmament Research UNIDIR, *Algorithmic Bias and the Weaponization of Increasingly Autonomous Technologies About the Project "The Weaponization of Increasingly Autonomous Technologies,"* 9 1–18 (Aug. 22, 2018), www.unidir.org.

information sources and could lead to confusing human thought processes with AI calculations.[48] Accordingly, the debates over the risks of biased AI in the targeting cycle, and any measures adopted to reduce such risks,[49] will need to equally inform the development and use of AI-based BCI systems.

B. Weapons Review

How we categorize BCI systems will affect their legal regulation. Notably, if these are weapons systems, then they must undergo the review process mandated by Article 36 of Additional Protocol I.[50] Not all the envisaged systems and uses would require such a review, as their function could, for example, constitute monitoring purely for medical care. There are also, undoubtedly, numerous bio-ethical concerns that must be considered in the development of these systems.[51] However, taking the monitoring function as an example, if the same system is also capable of affecting the soldier's performance (e.g., through brain stimulation, as discussed earlier), then it may also require a framework of analysis designed for weapon systems. This may also be the case for a BCI that provides a link between the soldier and an AI system for increased perception and faster decision-making in the targeting process.[52]

48. See discussion in section on accountability, *infra*.

49. Neil Davison, *A Legal Perspective: Autonomous Weapon Systems under International Humanitarian Law*, *in* PERSPECTIVES ON LETHAL AUTONOMOUS WEAPON SYSTEMS, UNODA Occasional Papers No. 30 5–17, 16–17, https://www.un.org/disarmament/publications/occasionalpapers/unoda-occasional-papers-no-30-november-2017/; Algorithmic Bias and the Weaponization of Increasingly Autonomous Technologies About the Project "The Weaponization of Increasingly Autonomous Technologies" 472–6 (2018), www.unidir.org; Dustin A. Lewis et al., *War-Algorithm Accountability*, SSRN ELECTRONIC JOURNAL 1–244, 103–4 (2017); Klaudia Klonowska, *Shifting the Narrative: Not Weapons, but Technologies of Warfare*, ICRC HUMANITARIAN LAW AND POLICY BLOG (Jan. 20, 2022), https://bit.ly/3qLLBLC; ICRC Position Paper: Artificial Intelligence and Machine Learning in Armed Conflict: A Human-Centred Approach, International Review of the Red Cross 463–479, 471–2 (Mar. 2021), https://international-review.icrc.org/articles/ai-and-machine-learning-in-armed-conflict-a-human-centred-approach-913 .

50. Article 36 establishes an obligation to review new weapons, stating that "In the study, development, acquisition or adoption of a new weapon, means or method of warfare, a High Contracting Party is under an obligation to determine whether its employment would, in some or all circumstances, be prohibited by this Protocol or by any other rule of international law applicable to the High Contracting Party": Protocol Additional to the Geneva Conventions of 12 August 1949, and relating to the Protection of Victims of International Armed Conflicts (Protocol I), art.36, 8 June 1977, [hereinafter API].

51. These are outside the scope of this paper. For discussion in the context of human enhancement and BCI see, for example Thibault Moulin, *Doctors Playing Gods? The Legal Challenges in Regulating the Experimental Stage of Cybernetic Human Enhancement*, 54 ISRAEL LAW REVIEW (2021).

52. *Also see* Klonowska, *Supra* note 51.

None of the terms "weapon, means or method of warfare" in Article 36 are explicitly defined in established LOAC instruments. "Weapon" is generally understood as a device constituting a "means of warfare" or "means of combat" that inflicts injury, death of persons, or damage to or destruction of objects. "Means of warfare" can also appear in conjunction with the expression "methods of warfare,"[53] and it is used in a broader sense than just referring to a weapon or combat "for it extends also to platforms and equipment which make possible an attack."[54] Whereas "means" are the tools used during military operations, "methods" refers to the operations themselves and how these means and weapons are used.[55]

Recent writings on human enhancement technologies in the context of weapons review obligations tend to focus on the physical integration of the human and the machine, and whether the fact that they cannot be easily separated might result in the soldier being considered part of the weapon system.[56] The challenge, in fact, goes much further and requires consideration of the fundamental distinction between weapons as tools and humans as individuals with independent agency. "Weapon" has a relatively straightforward meaning as "an instrument through which an offensive capability that can be applied to a military object or enemy combatant."[57] But for BCI systems, this understanding of "weapon" presents new difficulties, since the use of "instrument" is rendered ambiguous by the cybernetic relationship between the BCI and the soldier.[58] There is a general understanding that weapons are tools subject to human intention, but in the case of certain BCIs the roles may be reversed: the weapon itself can affect the intention. For example, in the case of a BCI system designed to scan for threats, there is a dynamic two-way flow of data influencing the soldier's thought process even prior to action. Accordingly, the reliability and accuracy of the BCI system for processing and alerting to threats may need to undergo a weapons review, especially when data input may influence offensive decisions on the battlefield. Moreover, the manner in which the BCI affects the soldier's actions will also require in-depth consideration.

53. Justin McClelland, *The Review of Weapons in Accordance with Article 36 of Additional Protocol I*, 85 REVUE INTERNATIONALE DE LA CROIX-ROUGE/INTERNATIONAL REVIEW OF THE RED CROSS 397–420, 405 (2003).

54. PROGRAM ON HPCR AT HARVARD UNIVERSITY, HPCR MANUAL ON INTERNATIONAL LAW APPLICABLE TO AIR AND MISSILE WARFARE 50 (2013).

55. *Id.* at xxiv.

56. Liivoja & Chircop, *supra* note 5, at 180.

57. Justin McClelland, *The review of weapons in accordance with Article 36 of Additional Protocol I*, 85 CIAC 397, 404 (2003). Some argue that it is unnecessary to include the wordings of "military object" and "combatant", Liivoja & Chircop, *supra* note 5, 175.

58. *See also* Dinniss & Kleffner, *supra* note 5, at 438; Lin et al., *supra* note 5, at 31–2.

C. Targeting the BCI

While only certain types of BCIs could be categorized as weapon systems, even the ones that are not weapons might nevertheless be considered as military equipment, with implications for the rules of targeting and protection. Military communications systems, for example, would in most cases be considered a legitimate military objective,[59] and BCI communication devices would therefore likely fall into the same category. Firing a missile at a shipment of BCI crates on an army truck would not entail too many legal problems, but might this assessment change when the BCI is already connected to the individual soldier? At first glance, it would not appear to present a problem, given that the soldier could also be a lawful target: a classic case of two birds with one stone. But there are certain circumstances that may complicate this assessment. For example, let us assume a situation in which it is known that the enemy relies heavily on BCI systems for a combination of communications and enhanced capabilities. In this scenario, it may be possible to damage the BCIs and prevent their functioning by transmitting a strong electromagnetic pulse or by intercepting the data flow and inserting a malicious code into the software. Let us assume that doing so will take down hundreds of BCIs at once and provide a significant military advantage. However, given that these systems are directly connected to the brains of the enemy soldiers, there may be a risk that causing a BCI malfunction would lead to brain damage of the users. This raises two legal questions: first, one of the oldest rules of LOAC prohibits causing superfluous injury and unnecessary suffering.[60] Certain technologies, such as blinding lasers, have been prohibited in large part on this basis.[61] If targeting the BCI systems would lead to excruciating inter-cranial pain or to severe brain damage, this would need to be considered in light of this rule.[62] Second, BCI systems might be in use by soldiers who are not themselves legitimate targets of attack. This could include medical forces, or even combatants who are injured and incapacitated but still have implanted BCIs.[63]

---

59. As a digital device purposely built to military specifications and used to organise and coordinate military operations, making effective contribution to military action. *See also* Heather A. Harrison Dinniss, *The Nature of Objects: Targeting Networks and the Challenge of Defining Cyber Military Objectives*, 48 ISRAEL L. R., 53 (2015).

60. API, art. 52(2), *supra* note 52.

61. Louise Doswald-Beck, *New Protocol on Blinding Laser Weapons*, 36 INTERNATIONAL REVIEW OF THE RED CROSS 272–299, 273 (1996).

62. It should be noted in this context that while the rule applies to all weapons, when there is relatively wide agreement on the need to prohibit or regulate a particular weapon, this often leads to attempts at drafting a new dedicated legal instrument on the matter.

63. A divergence of views exists on whether the proportionality rule applies only to civilians or also to combatants hors de combat. *E.g., Military Collaterals and Jus in Bello Proportionality*, 48 ISRAEL YEARBOOK ON HUMAN RIGHTS, 43–61 (2018) Geoffrey Corn & Andrew Culliver,

Cyborg Soldiers

Operations to disrupt and damage BCI systems should, therefore, only take place after a review of all the possible foreseeable effects, and it may be that certain expected outcomes would limit the ability to conduct attacks of this kind.

D. Protection of Individuals Hors de Combat

As noted previously, an injured soldier may still be connected to an active BCI. In fact, BCI-enhanced soldiers present significant challenges to the protections of individuals hors de combat for a number of reasons. Most apparent is the potential for abuse and ill treatment of detainees.[64] For example, research into systems affecting memory—not only encoding and recalling memories, but also rewriting memories with new data—has been developing rapidly.[65] In the future, there might be a possibility for a military to try and use such systems on captured enemy soldiers to extract data or implant new information. Actions of this type may fall afoul of a number of prohibitions, including those that ban experimenting on detainees, as well as ill treatment and torture.[66] Conversely, detaining powers aiming to abide by their obligations and provide appropriate medical care to detainees will face challenges of a different nature. BCI systems could be integrated in the individual's body in such a way that requires knowledge of their operation in order to provide medical treatment. If this arises in the case of seriously wounded or sick prisoners of war, then there is an obligation to repatriate them for treatment.[67] However, there may be prisoners who are not in a medically "serious" condition and nevertheless require treatment that depends on understanding the

---

Articles Wounded Combatants, Military Medical Personnel, and the Dilemma of Collateral Risk, 45 Ga, J. INT'L COMP. L. 445–473, 445 (2017).

64. Dinniss & Kleffner, *supra* note 5, at 446–7.

65. *E.g.*, Ramirez; Yasmin Anwar et al., *Scientists Use Brain Imaging To Reveal the Movies in Our Mind,* BERKELEY NEWS (2011); Robert E. Hampson et al., *Developing a Hippocampal Neural Prosthetic to Facilitate Human Memory Encoding and Recall,* 15 J. NEURAL ENGINEERING 1–15 (2018); *and* Wake Forest Baptist Medical Center; Vassilis Cutsuridis, Memory Prosthesis: *Is It Time for a Deep Neuromimetic Computing Approach?*, 13 FRONTIERS IN NEUROSCIENCE 1–9 (2019); Rockefeller University, *Scientists Discover a New Class of Memory Cells for Remembering Faces,* SCIENCES DAILY (July 1, 2021), https://www.sciencedaily.com/releases/2021/07/21070 1140929.htm (last visited Apr. 1, 2022); Massachusetts General Hospital, *Source of Remarkable Memory of 'Superagers' Revealed,* SCIENCE DAILY (July 6, 2021), https://www.sciencedaily.com/ releases/2021/07/210706133136.htm.

66. *E.g.*, Rome Statute of the International Criminal Court, art. 8(2)(a)(ii), July 17, 1998, 2187 U.N.T.S. 90 [hereinafter Rome Statute]; Geneva Convention (IV) relative to the Protection of Civilian Persons in Time of War, art. 32, Aug. 12, 1949, 6 U.S.T. 3516; 75 U.N.T.S. 287 [hereinafter GCIV]; API Article 11(5), *supra* note 52; Shereshevsky at 304–307, *Supra* note 5.

67. Geneva Convention Relative to the Treatment of Prisoners of War, art. 109(1), Aug. 12, 1949, 6 U.S.T. 3316, 75 U.N.T.S. 135 [hereinafter GCIII].

workings of the BCI. Given that the BCI will not have a publicly available operating manual for obvious security and proprietary reasons, the detaining power may find it difficult to fulfill its obligation of medical care.[68] While this obligation is generally understood as one that takes into account reasonable expectations and available resources,[69] the question arises whether due diligence requires the detaining power to communicate with the enemy (possibly through the ICRC) in a request for information that may be necessary for treatment, or allow remote treatment. If such a communication is received, the duty of care of the soldier's own State will also need to be considered. These situations need to be taken into account in the development stages of BCI systems to ensure, to the maximum extent possible, that the design of the BCI allows for detained soldiers to receive medical care by providers who do not have operating knowledge of the system.[70]

Beyond the specific challenges surrounding medical care, the future use of BCI systems, along with other enhancement technologies, could have a more profound effect by potentially jeopardizing the common understanding of who is entitled to protection—whether they are surrendering forces, wounded and sick, or detained. The protection status of individuals hors de combat rests on the fundamental principles of military necessity and humanity.[71] Persons clearly indicating that they no longer intend to engage in hostilities, or who are incapacitated and unable to engage, no longer represent a threat and there is no military necessity in targeting them.[72] However, a particular problem arising from the use of BCIs, especially if they involve embedded technology, is that soldiers may not be able to lay down their arms/devices, potentially leaving them unable to gain protected status and permanently open to targeting by the enemy. To avoid this result, it might be necessary to ensure that any such technology can be "switched off" by the individual soldier. This solution notwithstanding, there will remain a difficulty when the soldier is wounded: consider a scenario in which the soldier has a surgically implanted BCI that is transmitting information back to headquarters. That information includes not just location data, but potentially also elements of whatever the soldier is seeing and hearing. The BCI continues to operate even after the soldier is incapacitated, continuously transmitting information of military value.

---

68. Geneva Convention (I) for the Amelioration of the Condition of the Wounded and Sick in Armed Forces in the Field art. (12), Aug. 12, 1949, 6 U.S.T. 3114, 75 U.N.T.S. 31[hereinafter GCI].

69. INTERNATIONAL LAW COMMITTEE OF THE RED CROSS, COMMENTARY ON THE CONVENTION (I) FOR THE AMELIORATION OF THE CONDITION OF THE WOUNDED AND SICK IN ARMED FORCES IN THE FIELD OF 12 AUGUST 1949, art. 12, paras 1381-1385 (Jean Pictet ed., 1960).

70. *See also* discussion of the possibility for an 'off switch', *infra*.

71. David Luban, *Military Necessity and the Cultures of Military Law*, 26 LEIDEN J. INT'L L. 315–349, 343 (2013).

72. Stefan Oeter, *Methods and Means of Combat, in* THE HANDBOOK OF INT'L HUMANITARIAN L. 170–245, 186–7 (Dieter Fleck ed., 2021).

How should the detaining power act in this context? Addressing this type of situation may require the development of a process (formally agreed or voluntary) between parties to a conflict, providing some sort of assurance that BCI systems can be deactivated when soldiers are otherwise hors de combat. Doing so without compromising security will be a particular challenge.

E. Risk of Perfidy and Its Consequences

The inability to be certain whether the BCI is in operation causes not only protection concerns but might also facilitate certain war crimes. In particular, BCI-enhanced soldiers could be in a unique position of committing perfidious acts. Additional Protocol I Article 37(1) defines perfidy as "acts inviting the confidence of an adversary to lead him to believe that he is entitled to, or obliged to accord, protection under the rules of international law applicable in armed conflict, with intent to betray that confidence" and prohibits doing so in order to "kill, injure or capture an adversary."[73] Perfidious acts include feigning surrender or an incapacitating injury, to invite protection. BCI-enhanced soldiers are in a unique position to invite the confidence of the enemy to believe they are hors de combat because the enhancement is not physically apparent. A soldier could lay down their visible weapons while silently using a BCI to send information and coordinate a strike. The risk is twofold: in addition to the concern over an enhanced soldier committing perfidy, if and when the use of BCIs becomes commonplace, the opposing side might assume that soldiers have active, hidden BCIs, and therefore be less ready to afford protection.

A perfidious act contains an element of intent to deceive;[74] likewise, the affordance of protection relies upon the trust that the opposing individual does not possess this malicious intent. For a BCI-enhanced soldier to surrender, it may be incumbent upon them to perform a "positive act," to demonstrate the absence of any foul intent.[75] Accordingly, the design and use of BCIs must take into account the need for the individual soldier to convey that their actions are not deceitful, while also providing their enemy the assurance that the trust is not misplaced. There are a number of ways in which this could be achieved, and a combination of measures might be necessary. First, BCI-enhanced soldiers could, in such situations, explicitly declare the existence of their BCI. Second, they would need to demonstrate that the BCI is no longer usable as a weapon and does not present a threat. This would be analogous to a soldier demonstrably laying down their arms. Third, the opposing forces may need to have a way of verifying the

---

73. API art.37(1), *supra* note 52.

74. Yoram Dinstein, The Conduct of Hostilities Under the Law of International Armed Conflict 264 (2004).

75. Hilaire McCoubrey & Nigel D. White, International Law and Armed Conflict 227 (1992).

nonactive status of the BCI, for example, by being able to check that the BCI is not transmitting data (which might be possible without having access to the content of the data stream). This last stage, for obvious security reasons, will be the most challenging one to implement.[76] Utilizing an approach of this type would allow for BCI-enhanced soldiers to gain protection status where appropriate and reduce the risk of them being accused of perfidy. The consequences of failing to do so may be that opponents cease to accept that enemy forces suspected of having BCIs can ever be hors de combat. This could subsequently result in extensive denial of protection for those who need it.

F. Accountability and Responsibility

The use of BCIs also provides a unique twist to the debates taking place over autonomous weapons systems and military AI. A recurring theme in these debates has been the extent to which humans retain control when AI is deployed.[77] Indeed, while the concept of human control remains the subject of disagreement, most States and commentators appear to accept its centrality in the resolution of concerns over the use of AI.[78] Placing a human at the junction of critical decisions (such as engagement of targets) is, for many in these debates, a desirable—and even required—step to ensuring the legality of action.[79] In theory, BCI systems that make use of AI and Big Data might be answering these demands by connecting the AI to the human and leaving the decision in the hands of the latter. The operation of BCI might therefore serve as a form of keeping a human "in the loop," and be preferable to a system in which humans are "on" or "out of the loop." The concern in these circumstances, however, is whether the direct flow of data from the AI to the human's brain ultimately renders the human decision as nothing more than the execution of AI commands. The phenomenon of humans trusting machine decisions has been well-documented and is particularly acute with systems designed to provide rapid reaction to incoming threats, such as missile defense systems.[80] BCIs exacerbate these concerns: although the BCI-enhanced human is

---

76. As discussed in the previous section.

77. Lewis et al, *supra* note 47, at v–vi.

78. United Nation Institute for Disarmament Research UNIDIR, *supra* note 49, at 8–9.

79. Convention on Prohibitions or Restrictions on the Use of Certain Conventional Weapons Which May Be Deemed to Be Excessively Injurious or to Have Indiscriminate Effects, Group of Governmental Experts on Emerging Technologies in the Area of Lethal Autonomous Weapons System 96 (Apr. 19, 2021), https://documents.unoda.org/wp-content/uploads/2020/07/CCW_GGE1_2020_WP_7-ADVANCE.pdf.

80. United Nations Institute for Disarmament Research UNIDIR, *The Weaponization of Increasingly Autonomous Technologies: Considering how Meaningful Human Control Might Move the Discussion Forward*, 2 (Nov. 13, 2014), https://unidir.org/publication/weaponization-increasingly-autonomous-technologies-considering-how-meaningful-human.

Cyborg Soldiers

now technically *in* the loop, the speed and format by which the individual receives the data is such that there may be less room and time to process and question it. Indeed, insofar as the data from the AI is transmitted directly to the brain, the individual may experience the AI input in a manner that is hard to differentiate from the data and brain processes generated from their own senses and thoughts. Further research is required in this area to determine the extent to which the individual is able—experientially and practically—to recognize data received from the AI and maintain control and agency over their own actions. The training in use of BCI systems must therefore include specific elements designed to guide individuals in this regard.

The use of BCIs may also affect the responsibility of commanders. Systems with a monitoring element could provide commanders with a continuous data stream direct from the brains of soldiers on the battlefield. Some of this data could be of use in early detection of soldiers' behavior or impending action in violation of the law. Such systems could therefore provide a new mechanism for prevention of war crimes. While this application serves as an important and positive tool, increased capabilities will also lead to increased responsibilities. Access to such data could implicate commanders in accordance with the "should have known" standard applicable to some war crimes.[81] The responsibility of commanders will be even greater if they also have the ability to intervene remotely and affect the soldiers' actions through the BCI (for example, through brain stimulation, "uploading data," or triggering hormone release).[82] In such cases, the responsibility of commanders may be equivalent to issuing direct orders, which would implicate them in violations committed by the soldiers. However, from the soldiers' perspective, BCI-enabled orders may be more consequential than those received in the "old-fashioned" way.

The use of BCIs problematizes individual criminal responsibility of the soldiers themselves in relation to notions of free will and, more specifically, to the mental element of criminal responsibility. The traditional paradigm in criminal law defines actions in binary terms, that is, persons are expected to either be in control of their actions (liable) or not in control (not liable). There must be a culpable state of mind for liability to hold.[83] Depending on how the BCI functions, interventions by commanders could affect the soldier's free will and control over their own actions, thus reducing the latter's criminal culpability. Multilayered decisions are not new to LOAC; even without technology many

81. Command responsibility is contingent upon the ability to determine that the commander "either knew or, owing to the circumstances at the time, should have known that the forces were committing or about to commit such crimes." Shereshevsky, *supra* note 5, at 282; Rome Statute, *supra* note 68.

82. *See* section on "Monitoring," *supra*.

83. In other words, a person should intend to cause the harm; a principle notoriously coined by Edward Coke 'actus non facit reum nisi mens sit rea', (the act is not guilty unless the mind is also guilty). EDWARD COKE, INSTITUTES OF THE LAWS OF ENGLAND 45 (1797).

decisions have different levels of military hierarchy.[84] In this scenario, however, there is an added complexity to the layering of such decisions. While the traditional understanding of the relationship between "intention," "mind," and "responsibility" is already evolving through new findings in neuroscience,[85] BCIs expand the notion of legal personhood[86] and have the potential of altering the notion of criminal responsibility itself. These challenges to personhood and responsibility arise not only from the involvement of commanders and others in triggering or controlling an individual's brain functions, but also as a result of the above-mentioned combination of BCI and AI, which can equally destabilize our conception of what is a conscious and voluntary act and have implications for individual liability.[87]

V. CONCLUSION

BCI systems will provide militaries—and individual soldiers—with a world of new possibilities. Everything from communications to targeting could be affected, and with these changes will come a host of new situations previously unenvisaged. The dividing lines between human and machine will not be merely mechanical questions relating to the individual's body and a weapon to which they are attached, but go to the core of our being, to a melding of human thoughts and sensations with machine-generated data.

LOAC has a long history of adjusting to new technologies and novel means and methods of combat. The fact that BCIs will raise new questions does not necessarily mean that the law cannot answer them. Finding these answers will, however, take some effort. The above sections have begun the work of identifying the legal conundrums that are likely to arise when BCIs are deployed on the battlefield. As we have demonstrated, these questions implicate a wide range of rules relating to everything from the regulation of weapon development, to specific rules of targeting and protection. In addition to the need to consider these specific rules, there is a real risk that the use of BCIs would invite mistrust on the battlefield,

---

84. Ian Henderson, The Contemporary Law of Targeting 233–41 (2009).

85. Nick J. Davis, *Efficient Causation and Neuroscientific Explanations of Criminal Action*, in Neurolaw and Responsibility for Action: Concepts, Crimes, and Courts 124–140, 125–6 (Bebhinn Donnelly Lazarov ed., 2018); Bebhinn Donnelly Lazarov, *Intention as Non-Observational Knowledge: Rescuing Responsibility from the Brain*, in Neurolaw and Responsibility for Action: Concepts, Crimes, and Courts 104–123, 104 (Bebhinn Donnelly Lazarov ed., 2018).

86. Susan W. Brenner, *Humans and Humans+: Technological Enhancement and Criminal Responsibility*, 19 B. U. J. Sci. Tech. L. 1–73, 25–6 (2013).

87. Stephen Rainey et al., *When Thinking is Doing: Responsibility for BCI-Mediated Action*, 11 AJOB Neuroscience 46–58, 47–8 (2020).

leading to potential lower adherence to the rules on protection from attack for those hors de combat.

A number of the solutions proposed in this chapter, such as the built-in ability for soldiers to self-disable their BCIs in order to safeguard their protected status when captured, would require implementation at the development and manufacture stage of the technology. While it is not within the authors' remit nor expertise to propose the precise technological implementation of such solutions, we hope that our analysis and suggestions will aid in the development of systems that can be used lawfully, and reduce the risk of those which are more likely to lead to violations.

There are, undoubtedly, further issues to be examined beyond the scope of this chapter. International human rights law, as a separate legal framework, will present additional concerns to be addressed. The most obvious of these is the question of privacy in relation to data recorded from the brain of individual soldiers,[88] as well as matters of equality and nondiscrimination that could arise among enhanced and unenhanced soldiers, as well as after their return to civilian life.[89] Attention is slowly turning to these issues, many of which arise in relation to human enhancement more generally, on and off the battlefield. Our focus was intentionally narrower, using the case of BCIs—one of the most transformative of these technologies—to delve deeper into an examination of the legal concerns under the law of armed conflict, and help progress the debate into the next stage of finding solutions so that the technology may contribute to adherence to the law rather than become a mechanism for violation.

88. Dinniss & Kleffner, *supra* note 5, at 463–4.

89. *Id.*, at 471–2.

PART THREE

International Humanitarian Law and the Conduct of Humanitarian Operations and Atrocity Investigation

10

Corporate Data Responsibility

GALIT A. SARFATY* ■

Big data is playing an important role in the global economy, with corporations commonly using data analytics to forecast customer preferences, identify trends, innovate new business models, boost their productivity, minimize risks, and improve decision-making. Big data is "the exponentially increasing amount of digital information being created by new information technologies such as mobile Internet, cloud storage, social networking, and the 'internet of things'–and the advanced analytics used to process that data."[1] The term commonly refers to new technologies and software tools used to create, aggregate, and analyze large data sets.[2] While big data is increasingly being used in various areas of law, its application to armed conflict and international human rights law is relatively new. Data analytics tools are being mobilized to filter large amounts of data in order to identify signals of potential atrocities and provide humanitarian aid. Such data includes data exhaust (e.g., cell phone records), online activity (e.g., social media), sensing technologies (e.g., satellite data), and crowdsourced information.[3]

The predictive power of big data can potentially facilitate early warning systems and provide real-time awareness of human rights violations and emerging

---

* Canada Research Chair in Global Economic Governance & Associate Professor, Allard School of Law, University of British Columbia.

1. Paul B. Symon & Arzan Tarapore, *Defense Intelligence Analysis in the Age of Big Data*, 79 JOINT FORCE Q. 5 (2015).

2. James Manyika et al., *Big Data: The Next Frontier for Innovation, Competition, and Productivity* 1, MCKINSEY GLOBAL INST. (2011), http://www.mckinsey.com/business-functions/business-technology/our-insights/big-data-the-next-frontier-for-innovation [https://perma.cc/8NAK-T2XQ].

3. Bapu Vaitla, *The Landscape of Big Data for Development: Key Actors and Major Research Themes*, at ii (May 2014), https://data2x.org/wp-content/uploads/2019/09/LandscapeOfBigDataForDevelopment_10_28-1.pdf.

Galit A. Sarfaty, *Corporate Data Responsibility* In: *Big Data and Armed Conflict*. Edited by: Laura A. Dickinson and Edward W. Berg, Oxford University Press. © Galit A. Sarfaty 2024. DOI: 10.1093/oso/9780197668610.003.0012

humanitarian crises that arise out of armed conflicts.[4] One noteworthy project is Syria Tracker, which is a crisis-mapping system that has used crowdsourced text, photo and video reports, and data-mining techniques to form a live map of the Syrian conflict since March 2011.[5] Syria Tracker is able to collate data and illustrate trends in violence, which helps relief teams and citizens address human rights abuses and emerging humanitarian crises. It shows where human rights abuses are happening in Syria, including exactly when and where violence such as murders, rapes, and chemical attacks have taken place, as well as instances where food and water supplies have been tampered with. The crisis map also provides the rest of the world with otherwise nonexistent, accurate, and up-to-date information.

Big data is particularly useful for addressing refugee crises related to armed conflict. International organizations are using analytical tools in different phases of these crises: identifying potential refugee/migration exoduses, tracking refugee/migrant movements, and resettling or integrating refugees/migrants. For instance, the International Organization for Migration has developed the Displacement Tracking Matrix, which uses big data to track and monitor population mobility and displacement to target assistance.[6] Many of the locations of interest, such as Libya and the Democratic Republic of Congo, have experienced armed conflict. Most recently, the Displacement Tracking Matrix has been used in Ukraine to gain insights into internal displacement and mobility flows during the armed conflict in the region. A number of nongovernmental organizations are also focused on the harnessing of analytic technologies to address data gaps in the migration aid context. For example, the Humanitarian OpenStreetMap Team has used crowdsourced data mined from mobile phones to both map the expanding refugee influx in East Africa as well as improve aid delivery in South Sudan and Syria.[7]

Yet a major risk in "digital humanitarianism" (the mobilization of data in pursuit of humanitarian goals) is the extent to which the global community is reliant on the cooperation of companies.[8] While the use of big data is facilitating the mapping of conflict and the delivery of humanitarian aid, it is also transforming the corporation into a primary gatekeeper of rights protection. The private sector

---

4. *See* U.N. Global Pulse, *Big Data for Development: Challenges & Opportunities* (May 2012), http://www.unglobalpulse.org/sites/default/files/BigDataforDevelopment-UNGlobalPulseJune2012.pdf.

5. *See Syria Tracker*, Humanitarian Tracker, http://www.humanitariantracker.org/#!syria-tracker/cj00 (last visited Mar. 13, 2022).

6. *See* Int'l Org. Migration, Displacement Tracking Matrix, https://dtm.iom.int/about (last visited Mar. 13, 2022).

7. *See* Refugee Response, Humanitarian OpenStreetMap Team, https://www.hotosm.org/impact-areas/refugee-response/ (last visited Mar. 13, 2022).

8. Patrick Meier, Digital Humanitarians: How Big Data Is Changing the Face of Humanitarian Response Threshold (2015).

is playing a critical role as the mediator of information by exerting control over access to and analysis of big data. Large companies are providing data donations and leading the way in the Data for Good movement. Big data projects that rely on such data as cell phone logs, online content, and satellite images would not be possible without the participation of companies who voluntarily share the data for the public good—thus engaging in "data philanthropy."[9] However, some companies may be reluctant to share data even in situations of mass atrocities and humanitarian crises, whether inside or outside armed conflict.[10] Furthermore, they may be complicit in human rights abuses committed by authoritarian regimes when they engage in digital surveillance and other forms of data manipulation.

This chapter analyzes the role of corporations in the mobilization of big data for humanitarian aid. First, I describe the phenomenon of digital humanitarianism and analyze it through an infrastructural analysis. This interdisciplinary approach, borrowed from science and technology studies, conceptualizes infrastructures as a set of relations, networks, and techniques that are infused in politics and power relations. An infrastructural lens can highlight the role of private actors that operate in the shadows of digital humanitarianism yet nevertheless wield significant control over access to and analysis of big data. Next, I describe the knowledge practices and relations of power that underlie global data governance and the process through which digital humanitarianism is assembled. I argue that quantitative data practices should be supplemented with qualitative contextual knowledge in the humanitarian context. Finally, in order to ensure accountability to vulnerable populations, I argue for the promotion of corporate data responsibility in the name of the corporate responsibility to respect human rights. Corporate data responsibility includes two components. The first is a negative responsibility to do no harm by not assisting states that use data to commit human rights violations. The second is a positive responsibility to respect human rights by making available data that could prevent gross human rights abuses or humanitarian crises.

I. THE INFRASTRUCTURE OF DIGITAL HUMANITARIANISM

By analyzing digital humanitarianism through the lens of infrastructures, we can better understand its regulatory effects and political implications. An infrastructural analysis is an approach from science and technology studies that conceptualizes infrastructures as technical-social assemblages infused in politics

---

9. *See* Matt Stempeck, *Sharing Data Is a Form of Corporate Philanthropy*, Harv. Bus. Rev. (July 24, 2014), https://hbr.org/2014/07/sharing-data-is-a-form-of-corporate-philanthropy (last visited Mar. 28, 2022).

10. *See* Beth Van Schaack, *Leveraging Big Data for LOAC Enforcement: Finding the Needle in a Stack of Needles*, *in* Big Data and Armed Conflict: Legal Issues Above and Below the Armed Conflict Threshold (Laura A. Dickinson ed., 2022).

and power relations.[11] An infrastructure is defined as a dynamic network that connects disparate places, objects, people, and ideas across space and controls the flow of goods, people, and information. Infrastructures may be physical (e.g., roads or bridges), informational (e.g., databases or indicators), or digital (e.g., e-commerce platforms or Internet protocols). As Brian Larkin observes, "Their peculiar ontology lies in the facts that they are things and also the relation between things."[12] "Thinking infrastructurally" about digital humanitarianism entails "understanding infrastructure not simply as a thing, but as a set of relations, processes and imaginations."[13] These relations and processes include technical, social, and organizational dimensions.[14] An infrastructural analysis thus sheds light on the regulatory effects of infrastructures that shape behavior as well as the distributional dimensions that are implicated in power relations.

Digital humanitarianism involves engagement with data in particular assemblages involving public and private actors, which exercise authority through a variety of mechanisms and technologies.[15] An infrastructural analysis highlights how power relations shape how "networks are imagined, put in place, and mobilized for different ends."[16] It encourages us to look not only at the technical levels of global data governance but also the ideological and political dimensions, particularly with respect to the use of big data in humanitarianism. For instance, it helps us understand how the use of big data to prevent human rights violations or to address humanitarian crises emerging from armed conflicts can potentially reproduce power asymmetries between the Global North and Global South, entrench inequalities, and lead to a marketization of humanitarianism.[17]

As with other types of infrastructures, digital humanitarianism exhibits a tension between aspiration and failure as part of a process of doubling, where "systems and practices operate in variance with their purported objective."[18] There is a

---

11. See Benedict Kingsbury & Nahuel Maisley, *Infrastructures and Laws: Publics and Publicness*, 17 Annu. Rev. L. & Soc. Sci. 353 (2021).

12. Brian Larkin, *The Politics and Poetics of Infrastructure*, 42 Annu. Rev. Anthro. 327, 329 (2013).

13. Benedict Kingsbury, *Infrastructure and InfraReg: On Rousing the International Law "Wizards of Is,"* 8 Cambridge Int'l L.J. 171, 179 (2019).

14. *Id.*

15. See Fleur Johns & Caroline Compton, *Data Jurisdictions and Rival Regimes of Algorithmic Regulation*, 16 Regul. Gov. 63 (2022).

16. Jean-Christophe Plantin & Aswin Punathambekar, *Digital Media Infrastructures: Pipes, Platforms, and Politics*, 41 Media, Culture, & Soc'y 163, 166 (2019).

17. Mira Madianou, *Technocolonialism: Digital Innovation and Data Practices in the Humanitarian Response to Refugee Crises*, Social Media + Soc'y 1, 2 (2019).

18. See, e.g., Nikhil Anand et al., The Promise of Infrastructure (2018); Larkin, *supra* note 12, at 334.

sense of possibility through the use of big data to address human rights violations and emerging humanitarian crises in countries ravaged by armed conflict. Yet despite hopes of promoting development or humanitarian protection, digital humanitarianism has an underbelly that is lined with relations of power, inequality, and even human rights abuses. Scholars have argued that the use of data practices in humanitarian crises can foster "technocolonialism" by reinvigorating and reshaping colonial relationships of dependency:[19]

> The reworking of colonial relations of inequality occurs in a number of ways: through the extraction of value from the data of refugee and other vulnerable people; the extraction of value from experimentation with new technologies in fragile situations for the benefit of stakeholders, including private companies; by materializing the intangible forms and "ruins" of colonial legacies such as discrimination; by contributing to the production of social orders that entrench the "coloniality of power"; and by justifying some of these practices under the shibboleth of "emergencies."[20]

Yet technocolonialism operates along a continuum, and there are ways to reduce the risk of reproducing colonial relations of inequality. Later in this chapter, I will discuss the need to ensure accountability to vulnerable populations by promoting corporate data responsibility.

An infrastructural analysis can also shed light on the "technopolitics" behind global data governance and the process through which digital humanitarianism is assembled.[21] Technopolitics refers to the set of knowledge practices, administrative techniques, and relations of power that underlie governance.[22] This approach uncovers the practices, networks, and techniques embedded within human rights governance and humanitarian operations linked to armed conflict. Moreover, it highlights the corporate actors who operate in the shadows but nevertheless wield significant control as the gatekeepers of big data and rights protection.

II. CORPORATE GATEKEEPERS OF QUANTITATIVE DATA

Central to infrastructures are the role of experts and the use of technologies. In the case of digital humanitarianism, companies are imbricated in a variety

---

19. Madianou, *supra* note 17.

20. *Id.* at 2.

21. Larkin, *supra* note 12, at 328.

22. *See* Fleur Johns, *Data Detection and the Redistribution of the Sensible in International Law,* 111 AM. J. INT'L L. 57 (2017); Gavin Sullivan, *"Taking on the Technicalities" of International Law: Practice, Description, Critique: A Response to Fleur Johns,* 111 AJIL UNBOUND 181 (2017).

of dimensions of global data governance, including the mediation of information, control over access to data and analysis of data, and knowledge transformation processes. The rise of datafication, quantification, and digitization has "combined with increasing marketization, professionalization, pressure for humanitarian accountability, and, crucially, the dynamic entry of the private sector in the humanitarian field."[23] As corporations seek to deliver technocratic solutions to development problems and humanitarian crises emerging from armed conflict, they are exercising new forms of bureaucratic control and economic restructuring.[24]

The power imbalance between corporations and data subjects highlights the risks of relying on quantitative data for human rights governance and humanitarian operations linked to armed conflict. The use of big data in the international human rights field is part of an increasing focus on quantification in global governance.[25] In the humanitarian sphere, technocratic solutions based on quantitative data are often valued more highly than other types of knowledge.[26] Yet this emphasis on statistical data can reify power inequalities, lead to a concentration of decision-making power in the hands of technical experts, and risk distorting or obscuring the phenomena they are meant to take account of.[27] Numbers are political resources that serve as a "technology of distance,"[28] whose authority comes from "their capacity to create and overcome distance, both physical and social."[29] They abstract away the individual and the local while also creating a universal language that transcends distance.[30] In this way, objectivity through numbers and statistics becomes a proxy for truth and fairness, and it is privileged over local contextual knowledge.

---

23. Madianou, *supra* note 17, at 2.

24. Laura Mann, *Left to Other People's Devices? A Political Economy Perspective on the Big Data Revolution in Development*, 49 DEVELOPMENT & CHANGE 3, 28 (2017).

25. *See, e.g.*, Kevin E. Davis et al., *Introduction: Global Governance by Indicators, in* GOVERNANCE BY INDICATORS 3, 12 (Kevin E. Davis et al. eds., 2012); Kevin E. Davis et al., *Introduction: The Local-Global Life of Indicators: Law, Power, and Resistance, in* THE QUIET POWER OF INDICATORS 1, 1 (Sally Engle Merry et al. eds., 2015).

26. Roísín Read, Bertrand Taithe & Roger Mac Ginty, *Data Hubris? Humanitarian Information Systems and the Mirage of Technology*, 37 THIRD WORLD Q. 1314, 1320 (2016).

27. *See* Margaret L. Satterthwaite, *Rights-Based Humanitarian Indicators in Post-Earthquake Haiti, in* GOVERNANCE BY INDICATORS, *supra* note 25, at 365, 391; David Nelken, *Conclusion: Contesting Global Indicators, in* THE QUIET POWER OF INDICATORS, *supra* note 25, at 317, 318–19.

28. THEODORE M. PORTER, TRUST IN NUMBERS: THE PURSUIT OF OBJECTIVITY IN SCIENCE AND PUBLIC LIFE ix (1995).

29. Wendy Nelson Espeland, *Authority by the Numbers: Porter on Quantification, Discretion, and the Legitimation of Expertise*, 22 LAW & SOC. INQUIRY 1107, 1107 (1997).

30. PORTER, *supra* note 28, at 77.

Quantitative measurement creates "a promise of control" through the administration of everyday life—for instance, it reassures citizens "against the uncertainties of poverty, crime, unemployment, and more recently environmental and technological risk."[31] Yet, in reality, statistical data is not neutral but serves as a technology of power that constitutes populations and makes individuals calculable and therefore governable—both by others and themselves. The knowledge produced through big data projects "is always partial and reflects the geographical and social contexts of the people producing those knowledges."[32] In other words, it matters who is deciding what is counted as data (and what is not), how it is interpreted, what measurements and indicators are used, and the purposes to which such data is put.[33]

Because big data involves the aggregation and analysis of large data sets, there are additional risks when data analytics tools are used to prevent human rights violations or to address humanitarian crises emerging from armed conflicts. This method may privilege certain rights subject to quantitative measurement and fail to incorporate the necessary contextual information for data interpretation. For instance, data-driven human rights projects have focused on the prevention of macro violations (i.e., large-scale human rights abuses affecting many individuals, such as humanitarian crises), perhaps at the expense of micro violations (i.e., individualized human rights abuses occurring on a smaller scale). Big data aggregation will tend to capture those human rights violations that take place on a major scale, affecting a great number of people and occurring over a period of time. This is because these features lend themselves to trend analysis and pattern identification. By contrast, a data-driven approach to addressing human rights abuses, mass atrocities, and emerging humanitarian crises will not be useful for those areas where there is little (or no) data generated for collection or where there is insufficient opportunity to identify trends over time.[34] For example, sporadic accounts of unconnected instances of discrimination are not amenable to preventing similar abuses in the future through a data-driven approach. Big data may not live up to its promise in these latter contexts. Furthermore, basing policy decisions on partial data sets with unknown biases can be misleading.[35]

It is therefore important to incorporate local contextual information into decision-making to help interpret quantitative data, which may be fraught with

---

31. Sheila Jasanoff, *Ordering Knowledge, Ordering Society, in* STATES OF KNOWLEDGE: THE CO-PRODUCTION OF SCIENCE AND THE SOCIAL ORDER 13, 33 (Sheila Jasanoff ed., 2004).

32. Ryan Burns, *Rethinking Big Data in Digital Humanitarianism: Practices, Epistemologies, and Social Relations*, 80 GEOJOURNAL 477, 484–85 (2015).

33. SALLY ENGLE MERRY, THE SEDUCTIONS OF QUANTIFICATION: MEASURING HUMAN RIGHTS, GENDER VIOLENCE, AND SEX TRAFFICKING 4–6 (2016).

34. *See* Van Schaak, *supra* note 10.

35. Megan Price & Patrick Ball, *Big Data, Selection Bias, and the Statistical Patterns of Mortality in Conflict*, 34 SAIS REV. OF INT'L AFFAIRS 9, 10 (2014).

concerns over representativeness due to sampling selection bias.[36] Big data analysis offers insights about correlation, but not causation or objectivity.[37] By using qualitative, participatory methods (e.g., interviews, focus groups, or direct interpretation of the data itself by stakeholders including the community), states, agencies, and corporations can facilitate a better understanding of the data that takes into account local variation and cultural context.[38] Cultural practices with regard to data vary widely, as "[d]ifferent populations use services in different ways, and have different norms about how they communicate publicly about their lives."[39] Big data sources should thus be triangulated with other data sources including ethnographic information.[40] When we lose sight of this, we risk relying on a data-driven approach that exacerbates power imbalances, creates the potential for misinterpretation or manipulation, and fails to protect vulnerable populations.

III. THE PATH TO CORPORATE DATA RESPONSIBILITY

Due to the central role played by the private sector in global data governance and digital humanitarianism that arises out of situations of armed conflict, it is critical to ensure corporate data responsibility and provide accountability to vulnerable populations. Corporate data responsibility arises out of the corporate responsibility to respect human rights, enshrined in the U.N. Guiding Principles on Business and Human Rights, which is the internationally accepted framework for preventing and addressing the risk of adverse impacts on human rights linked to business activity.[41] The U.N. Human Rights Council unanimously endorsed

---

36. *See* Megan Price & Patrick Ball, *Big Data, Selection Bias, and the Statistical Patterns of Mortality in Conflict*, 34 SAIS REV. OF INT'L AFFAIRS 9, 10 (2014); Patrick Ball, *The Bigness of Big Data, in* THE TRANSFORMATION OF HUMAN RIGHTS FACT-FINDING 425, 436–37 (Philip Alston & Sarah Knuckey eds., 2015).

37. *See* Mark Latonero & Zachary Gold, *Data, Human Rights and Human Security*, DATA & SOCIETY RESEARCH INSTITUTE 3 (June 22, 2015), http://www.datasociety.net/pubs/dhr/Data-HumanRights-primer2015.pdf.

38. *See* Emilie Hafner-Burton & James Ron, *Seeing Double: Human Rights Impact Through Qualitative and Quantitative Eyes*, 61 WORLD POL. 360 (2009); Ball, *The Bigness of Big Data*, *supra* note 36; Sally Jackson, *Monitoring and Evaluation (M&E) for Big Data*, U.N. BLOG (June 20, 2014), http://www.unglobalpulse.org/using-big-data-MandE.

39. U.N. Global Pulse, *supra* note 4.

40. *Id.*

41. *See* John Ruggie (Special Representative of the Secretary-General on the Issue of Human Rights and Transnational Corporations and Other Business Enterprises), *Guiding Principles on Business and Human Rights: Implementing the United Nations "Protect, Respect and Remedy" Framework*, UN Doc. A/HRC/17/31 (Mar. 21, 2011), https://documents-dds-ny.un.org/doc/UNDOC/GEN/G11/121/90/PDF/G1112190.pdf?OpenElement [hereinafter *U.N. Guiding Principles*].

the Guiding Principles on Business and Human Rights in 2011.[42] The Guiding Principles include the "Protect, Respect, and Remedy Framework," which is grounded on three pillars: "(1) states' existing obligations to respect, protect, and fulfil human rights and fundamental freedoms; (2) the role of business enterprises as specialized organs of society performing specialized functions, required to comply with all applicable laws and to respect human rights; and (3) the need for human rights and obligations to be matched to appropriate and effective remedies when breached."[43] The Guiding Principles are not limited to peacetime operations and govern corporate conduct within, or linked to, armed conflict. The second pillar of the Guiding Principles is the global standard for expected conduct for all business enterprises wherever they operate and includes principles relevant to the private sector's responsible use of data. It is thus applicable to companies in the communications and information technology sector that provide metadata or supply the technology and equipment that make digital communications possible. It also applies to companies that supply data to authoritarian regimes and armed groups, which they use to commit gross human rights abuses, war crimes, and other atrocities.

Corporate data responsibility includes two components. The first is a negative responsibility to do no harm by not assisting states that use data to commit human rights violations or atrocities within armed conflict. The second is a positive responsibility to respect human rights by making available data that could prevent gross human rights abuses or humanitarian crises.

A. Mitigating Corporate Complicity in Human Rights Violations and Atrocities Linked to Armed Conflict

As part of the principle of corporate data responsibility and in line with the U.N. Guiding Principles, companies should avoid infringing on the human rights of others and ensure that they address potential adverse human rights impacts associated with their business operations.[44] In many ongoing humanitarian and conflict situations, the state has a notable role to play in managing who, how, and when the public can access data (e.g., states can hinder access to the Internet). Companies may be complicit when states manipulate data in ways that violate civilians' human rights—companies "build and market technologies that both enable and prevent surveillance, cooperate (or refuse to cooperate) with government requests to monitor activists or political dissidents, and create algorithms and

---

42. *See* The UN Working Group on Business and Human Rights, The UN Guiding Principles on Business and Human Rights: An Introduction, 2, http://www.ohchr.org/Documents/Issues/Business/Intro_Guiding_PrinciplesBusinessHR.pdf (last visited Mar. 13, 2022).

43. *U.N. Guiding Principles, supra* note 41.

44. *Id.*

weapons systems that may determine whether people live or die."[45] Technology managed by data companies can be used by states as tools of harassment and tools of surveillance that can infringe on the freedoms and privacy rights of citizens.[46] Yet complicity in surveillance-based repression by states is but one risk facing the information and communications technology sector.

There is also a risk that big data can be used to target specific individuals in armed conflict, thus leading to a "hyper-personalization of war."[47] Authoritarian regimes and armed groups can weaponize big data by building databases of potential opponents' militaries that includes profiles of individual members identified through facial recognition software.[48] For instance, in 2008, heavily armed members of a Kashmiri separatist group employed algorithms (e.g., Twitter search and the link analysis in Google's PageRank system) to attack several public sites in Mumbai, India, which killed and wounded hundreds of people.[49] Data mining the Internet and social media gave the attackers an intelligence advantage by allowing them to target particular individuals during conflicts.[50] This raises the question of complicity by companies that supply the data used by armed groups in this context.

Companies can also be complicit in states' human rights abuses when big data is used in the migration context, including migration spawned by armed conflict. Authoritarian regimes may use personal data gathered from technology companies to track civilians' locations when they are fleeing conflict. When doing so, they may misuse migrants' data by usurping their right to privacy and data protection. In addition, states may use big data to "identify and locate migrants heading towards their territory."[51] They may deny protection to vulnerable migrants and engage in refoulement, which is the forcible return of refugees or asylum seekers to a state where they are liable to be subjected to persecution.[52] Under international human rights law, the prohibition against refoulement is included in article 33 of the Convention relating to the Status of Refugees, the Convention against Torture and Other Cruel, Inhuman or Degrading Treatment or Punishment (Article 3), and the International Convention for the Protection

---

45. Molly K. Land & Jay D. Aronson, *Human Rights and Technology: New Challenges for Justice and Accountability*, 16 ANNU. REV. LAW & SOC. SCI. 223, 226 (2020).

46. *Id.*

47. Charles J. Dunlap Jr., *Cyber, Big Data, and the Changing Face of Conflict*, 15 GEORGETOWN J. INT'L AFFAIRS 108 (2014).

48. *Id.* at 110.

49. Andrej Zwitter, *Big Data and International Relations*, 29 ETHICS & INT'L AFFAIRS 377, 277 (2015).

50. *Id.*

51. Ana Beduschi, *The Big Data of International Migration: Opportunities and Challenges for States under International Human Rights Law*, 49 GEORGETOWN J. INT'L LAW. 981, 1010–11 (2018).

52. *Id.*

Corporate Data Responsibility

of All Persons from Enforced Disappearance (Article 16).[53] States may also use communicate big data about location to extremist groups who could then incite violence against specific migrant groups.[54]

Given the risk of corporate complicity in states' human rights abuses involving big data, including in situations linked to armed conflict, companies must ensure that they identify and address potential adverse human rights impacts associated with their business operations. According to the former U.N. Special Rapporteur on the Promotion and Protection of the Right to Freedom of Opinion and Expression:

> It is . . . essential that companies immediately cease the sale and transfer of and support for such technologies, until they have provided convincing evidence that they have adopted sufficient measures . . . concerning due diligence, transparency and accountability to prevent or mitigate the use of these technologies to commit human rights abuses.[55]

The responsibility to do no harm means that companies should conduct human rights due diligence to "assess whether and how their terms of service, or their policies for gathering and sharing customer data, may result in an adverse impact on the human rights of their users."[56] Impact assessments must occur before new technology is deployed in order to limit the risks of harm to vulnerable populations. Meaningful consultation with affected stakeholders would ensure transparency to potentially affected individuals and communities about how their data is being gathered, stored, used, and potentially shared with others.[57] Consultation should be conducted with a view to enabling potential data subjects to make informed decisions about the collection and use of data pertaining to them. Furthermore, business enterprises faced with government demands for access to data should comply with international human rights standards, which may mean "seeking clarification from a government with regard to the scope and legal foundation for the demand" and "communicating transparently with users about risks and compliance with government demands."[58] The same is true with

53. *See* U.N. Conventions Relating to the Status of Refugees, Art. 33, Apr. 22, 1954, 189 U.N.T.S. 150; Convention Against Torture and Other Cruel, Inhuman or Degrading Treatment or Punishment, Art. 3, Dec. 10, 1984, 1465 U.N.T.S. 85; International Convention for the Protection of All Persons from Enforced Disappearance, art. 16, Jan. 12, 2007, U.N. Doc. A/RES/61/177.

54. Beducsci, *supra* note 51, at 1011.

55. Human Rights Council, Report of the Special Rapporteur on the Promotion and Protection of the Right to Freedom of Opinion and Expression, UN Doc. A/HRC/41/35 (2019).

56. U.N. High Commissioner for Human Rights, *The Right to Privacy in the Digital Age*, ¶ 15, U.N. Doc. A/HRC/27/37 (June 30, 2014), available at http://www.ohchr.org/EN/HRBodies/HRC/RegularSessions/Session27/Documents/A.HRC.27.37_en.pdf.

57. *Id.*

58. *Id.*

regard to demands for data from aid agencies, NGOs, and academics. Companies should construe all demands for access to data narrowly—oversharing should be discouraged—and should have a clear understanding of the uses to which the information they supply is being put, lest they be complicit in committing human rights abuses arising from the use of the information.

B. Beyond Data Philanthropy

Corporate data responsibility means that corporations have a proactive responsibility to provide access to data when there is an impending humanitarian crisis. While the responsibility to respect human rights under the U.N. Guiding Principles is primarily focused on the negative responsibility to avoid contributing to adverse human rights impacts, there is also a positive ethical duty on corporations to facilitate the fulfillment of human rights through their own activities. Positive corporate duties are especially triggered when the primary duty-bearers (i.e., states) fail to protect the rights of citizens and yield political power to the companies that operate within those states.[59] As quasi-governmental institutions, corporations have an ethical duty to protect, promote, and fulfill human rights. In the context of big data and development, this means that companies should make available data that could prevent humanitarian crises, gross human rights abuses, war crimes, and other atrocities.[60] They should take active steps to increase the amount and detail of the data they collect, and to seek ways of making the data they collect more amenable to preventing human rights abuses.

Currently, select corporations are engaging data philanthropy by voluntarily sharing data for the public good (e.g., to prevent human rights abuses and war crimes) rather than keeping data "locked up" as proprietary information.[61] While data philanthropy is becoming more of a priority for the private sector,[62] it is still limited in scope for a number of reasons. Existing obstacles include "legal or reputational considerations, a need to protect their competitiveness, a culture of secrecy, . . . the absence of the right incentive and information structures [, and] . . . institutional and technical challenges—when data is stored in places and ways that make it difficult to be accessed, transferred, etc."[63] Companies may not

---

59. *See* Florian Wettstein, *For Better or For Worse*, 20 Bus. Ethics. Q. 275 (2010); Florian Wettstein, *CSR and the Debate on Business and Human Rights: Bridging the Great Divide*, 22 Bus. Ethics. Q. 739 (2012).

60. *See* Van Schaack, *supra* note 10.

61. For a comprehensive account of data philanthropy and different models of data-sharing, see Yafit Lev-Aretz, *Data Philanthropy*, 70 Hastings L.J. 1491 (2019).

62. Robert Kirkpatrick, *A New Type of Philanthropy: Donating Data*, Harv. Bus. Rev. (Mar. 21, 2013), https://hbr.org/2013/03/a-new-type-of-philanthropy-don.

63. U.N. Global Pulse, *Big Data for Development: Challenges & Opportunities*, *supra* note 4, at 25.

fully appreciate the extent to which the data in their possession can be a valuable resource for preventing human rights abuses. That is, companies may not be fully aware of big data's potential to transform lives by uncovering trends and patterns that assist in protecting human rights and generating positive social outcomes.

I argue that a model of corporate data responsibility requires companies to go beyond data philanthropy. The corporate responsibility to provide access to data can be facilitated through several possible frameworks—for example, "[a] data commons where some kinds of data are shared publicly after adequate anonymization and aggregation; and an alerting network where more sensitive data that can never be shared publicly is nevertheless analyzed by companies behind their firewalls for specific smoke signals."[64] The responsibility is particularly acute when there is a threat of mass atrocities, whether inside or outside armed conflict, and a need for assistance in providing humanitarian aid. Furthermore, some scholars argue that companies should take on a greater responsibility given their substantial economic and political power. According to political theories of corporate social responsibility, corporations have an inherent responsibility to society as "corporate citizens" given their power and position.[65]

The argument to go beyond data philanthropy is also based on the concept of a "global data commons," whereby "access to user-generated data possessed by platform companies would not only be available to these companies, but to a broader range of stakeholders."[66] A global data commons regime would grant data access and usage to public authorities and civil society organizations for the public good, while protecting users' privacy rights and without jeopardizing the market interests of data companies.[67] Such an approach should be reserved for limited circumstances when there is a compelling public interest in data being shared. Providing humanitarian aid to prevent grave human rights violations and address emerging humanitarian crises that arise out of armed conflicts would certainly warrant a global data commons approach.

Notably, European data protection legislation makes space for the use of personal data for the public good that goes beyond the original purpose for which the data was collected. Under the EU General Data Protection Regulation, there is a derogation to the principle of purpose limitation, under which personal data

---

64. Robert Kirkpatrick, *Data Philanthropy: Public & Private Sector Data Sharing for Global Resistance*, U.N. GLOBAL PULSE BLOG (Sept. 16, 2011), http://www.unglobalpulse.org/blog/data-philanthropy-public-private-sector-data-sharing-global-resilience.

65. *See* Elisabet Garriga & Domènec Melé, *Corporate Social Responsibility Theories: Mapping the Territory*, 53 J. Bus. ETHICS 51, 57 (2004); Dirk Matten & Andrew Crane, *Corporate Citizenship: Toward an Extended Theoretical Conceptualization*, 30 ACAD. MGMT. REV. 166, 166–67 (2005); Donna J. Wood & Jeanne M. Logsdon, *Business Citizenship: From Individuals to Organizations*, 3 RUFFIN SER. BUS. ETHICS 59, 66 (2002).

66. Jennifer Shkabatur, *The Global Commons of Data*, 22 STAN. TECH. L. REV. 354, 357 (2019).

67. *Id.* at 384; *see also* Alberto Alemanno, *Big Data for Good: Unlocking Privately-Held Data to the Benefit of the Many*, 9 EUR. J. RISK REG. 183, 186 (2018).

is to be collected for specified, explicit, and legitimate purposes, and not to be processed further in a manner incompatible with those purposes.[68] Under Article 5.1(b), the regulation allows for a derogation in case of "further processing for archiving purposes in the *public interest*, scientific or historical research purposes or statistical purposes."[69]

While there is a positive responsibility to share data for humanitarian aid, there are also internal benefits to companies in doing so. These efforts can be deployed to generate sustainable competitive advantages for the company, not just the public good.[70] Certain types of corporate philanthropy can lead to better bottom-line results by significantly improving the competitive business environment within which the company operates.[71] A company that minimizes the risk of human rights abuses occurring in its business environment is arguably better positioned to generate profit and avoid liability than one that does not. To the extent that the prevention of human rights abuses mitigates the risk of external shocks to the company's business operating environment, it is in the company's, and the public's, best interests. Additionally, being seen as a leader in corporate data responsibility may help a company attract and retain high-performing employees who place a premium on their employer's social, environmental, and human rights policies. This same "corporate halo effect" applies equally to consumer purchasing decisions, which may be shaped by a company's ethical behavior.

In promoting corporate data responsibility, it is of course important to protect the privacy of the individual emitters of the data and balance those concerns against the benefits of using the data for the public good. States and international agencies should develop specific criteria for evaluating the benefits and risks to determine how and in which specific circumstances data should be shared, in order to decrease the risks of inappropriate use of the data. For companies, this may mean obtaining prior informed consent from individuals or providing an opt-in or opt-out decision regarding the use of data.[72] At the same time, there might also be a risk that such data might be misappropriated by those who seek to commit war crimes or atrocities. It is essential that companies conduct due

---

68. *See* Regulation (EU) 2016/679, of the European Parliament and the Council of 27 April 2016 on the Protection of Natural Persons with Regard to the Processing of Personal Data and on the Free Movement of Such Data, and Repealing Directive 95/46/EC (General Data Protection Regulation), Art. 83(5), 2016 O.J. (L 119) 1, Art. 5(1)(b).

69. *Id.* (emphasis added); *see* Alemanno, *supra* note 67, at 189.

70. Michael E. Porter & Mark R. Kramer, *The Competitive Advantage of Corporate Philanthropy*, 80 Harv. Bus. Rev. 56, 57 (2002).

71. *Id.*

72. *See* Emmanuel Letouzé & Patrick Vinck, *The Politics and Ethics of CDR Analytics*, Data-Pop Alliance White Paper Series 11–12 (Dec. 10, 2014), http://static1.squarespace.com/static/531a2b4be4b009ca7e474c05/t/54b97f82e4b0ff9569874fe9/1421442946517/WhitePaperCDRs EthicFrameworkDec10-2014Draft-2.pdf.

diligence to ensure that their data is not misused and weaponized for digital surveillance and targeting operations during armed conflicts.

IV. CONCLUSION

As big data is mobilized to pursue development goals, corporations are playing a key role in the mapping of conflict, the identification of potential atrocities, and the delivery of humanitarian aid. Private actors operate in the shadows of digital infrastructures yet nevertheless wield significant control over access to and analysis of big data and have become a primary gatekeeper of rights protection. It is therefore critical to promote corporate data responsibility, including a negative responsibility to do no harm by not assisting states that use data to commit human rights violations, and a positive responsibility to respect human rights by making available data that could prevent gross human rights abuses or humanitarian crises. Moreover, big data should supplement, but not replace, existing tools and approaches to human rights and needs to be analyzed in the context of other data sources such as field-based research and qualitative knowledge. By doing so, we can maximize the benefits and minimize the risks of adopting a data-driven approach to humanitarianism.

11

Leveraging Big Data for LOAC Enforcement

Finding the Needle in a Stack of Needles

BETH VAN SCHAACK[1] ■

"We live in a world of near-ubiquitous data collection."[2] The battlefield is no different. Given the combined impact of pervasive smart phone use, social media participation, the Internet of things, mass digitization, and remote sensing, modern conflict zones are generating vast quantities of data. The sheer volume of digital information has quickly outpaced the ability of humans to review and process the material produced. In parallel, dramatic enhancements in storage capacities, advanced analytical software (including optical character recognition (OCR) of non-Latin scripts, machine learning, other forms of artificial intelligence, and predictive algorithms), and the exponential growth of computational power are helping to not only make sense of these mass data collections, but also to discern non-obvious patterns, trends, anomalies, and correlations that would otherwise be invisible to the human eye. This Big Data landscape offers new routes to ascend the epistemological pyramid from data to information to knowledge and, ultimately, to wisdom about today's armed conflicts.[3]

1. Leah Kaplan Visiting Professor in Human Rights, Stanford Law School.

2. White House, *Fact Sheet: Big Data and Privacy Working Group Review* (May 1, 2014), https://obamawhitehouse.archives.gov/the-press-office/2014/05/01/fact-sheet-big-data-and-privacy-working-group-review (last visited Mar. 14, 2022).

3. Russell Ackoff, *From Data to Wisdom*, 16 J. APPLIED SYSTEMS ANALYSIS 3, 3 (1989); Jay H. Bernstein, *The Data-Information-Knowledge-Wisdom Hierarchy and Its Antithesis*,

Beth Van Schaack, *Leveraging Big Data for LOAC Enforcement* In: *Big Data and Armed Conflict.* Edited by: Laura A. Dickinson and Edward W. Berg, Oxford University Press. © Beth Van Schaack 2024. DOI: 10.1093/oso/9780197668610.003.0013

Although "Big Data" has been defined multiple ways, it can be helpful to think about it in terms of four "v's": an expanding volume of highly varied and variable information, produced at increasing velocity, which makes human review virtually impossible and thus invites machine assistance.[4] As this volume and its scenario chapter reveal, Big Data and its accompanying analytics have the potential to dramatically alter how war is waged,[5] how the international community responds to conflicts,[6] and how artificial intelligence-enabled capabilities can help parties enhance (or evade) compliance with the law of armed conflict (LOAC).[7] Big Data and Big Data analytics are already revolutionizing the practice of law—including processes of litigation discovery,[8] sources of proof,[9] and sentencing[10]—in times of peace. This chapter surveys the opportunities and challenges presented by Big Data when it comes to the enforcement of LOAC, the prosecution of war crimes, and—to a lesser extent—the prevention of abuses.[11] The war in Syria—the first conflict in the modern social media era and once the most documented crime base in human history—is illustrative.[12] These issues will be equally acute in the

https://journals.lib.washington.edu/index.php/nasko/article/viewFile/12806/11288 (last visited Mar. 14, 2022).

4. National Institute of Standards & Technology Big Data Public Working Group, NIST Big Data Interoperability Framework: Volume 1, Definitions, NIST Special Publication 1500-1, at 4 (Sept. 2015).

5. *See* Laurie R. Blank et al., *Technology, Humanity, and the End of War*, ARTICLES OF WAR (Nov. 12, 2020), https://lieber.westpoint.edu/technology-humanity-end-war/ (last visited Mar. 14, 2022).

6. *See generally* Junaid Qadir et al., *Crisis Analytics: Big Data-Driven Crisis Response*, 1 J. INT'L HUMANITARIAN ACTION 12 (2016).

7. *See* Peter Margulies, *The Other Side of Autonomous Weapons: Using Artificial Intelligence to Enhance IHL Compliance, in* THE IMPACT OF EMERGING TECHNOLOGIES ON THE LAW OF ARMED CONFLICT 147 (Eric Talbot Jensen & Ronald T. P. Alcala eds., 2019); Anna Ahronheim, *Israel's Operation Against Hamas Was the World's First AI War*, JERUSALEM POST (May 27, 2021).

8. Christine Taylor, *Trends in Information Governance: eDiscovery and Big Data*, DATAMATION (Apr. 30, 2015), https://www.datamation.com/applications/trends-in-information-governance-ediscovery-and-big-data/ (last visited Mar. 14, 2022).

9. *See generally* Sarah Brayne, *The Criminal Law and Law Enforcement Implications of Big Data*, 14 ANNUAL REV. L. & SOC. SCIENCE 293, 294–95 (2018) (exploring the use of big data in law enforcement in both directed (i.e., against persons of suspicion) and dragnet (i.e., unparticularized) surveillance).

10. *See generally* Michael E. Donohue, *A Replacement for Justicia's Scales? Machine Learning's Role in Sentencing*, 32 HARV. J.L. & TECH. 657, 673 (2019) (discussing the use of big data risk scores during bail and sentencing determinations to help judges both predict which offenders are most like to recidivate and better understand the sentencing practices of their brethren).

11. For further discussion of the preventative potential of big data, see Galit A. Sarfaty's chapter in this volume on Corporate Data Responsibility.

12. *See* BETH VAN SCHAACK, IMAGINING JUSTICE FOR SYRIA 339–96 (2020) (discussing new documentation techniques and mechanisms being deployed in Syria).

war in Ukraine.[13] In prior conflicts, amassing enough evidence to stage a viable war crimes trial was often a principal challenge; today, the problem may be the reverse: there is too much documentation, much of it unverified and duplicative, which can overwhelm legal actors seeking to impose individual criminal responsibility, defend against criminal charges, or make real-time policy interventions in the service of deterrence and prevention.[14]

This chapter explores this conundrum in several parts. It first discusses the sources and potential utility of the mixed masses of evidence emerging from today's armed conflicts. It then sketches out several new technological methods for identifying, processing, and analyzing Big Data in war crimes prosecutions, including object recognition and event detection, facial recognition and reconstruction, statistical analysis of targeting patterns, social networking analysis, and 3-D modeling. Notwithstanding these promising opportunities to enhance the criminal enforcement of LOAC, a number of challenges remain to fully exploiting Big Data in the service of accountability and prevention. Further, this chapter does not engage the privacy issues implicated by Big Data, which deserve their own focused consideration.[15] Even with emerging Big Data analytics capable of transforming voluminous datasets into actionable information, modern armed conflicts—being complex, cross-domain, dynamic, and unpredictable—simply do not lend themselves to easy analysis.

I. THE SOURCES AND UTILITY OF CONFLICT-RELATED BIG DATA

As a feature of the Fourth Industrial Revolution, terabytes of data are being generated in modern conflicts, in a spontaneous and decentralized fashion, by

---

13. AP, *Frontline Launch 'War Crimes Watch Ukraine*, AP (Mar. 25, 2022), https://www.ap.org/press-releases/2022/ap-frontline-launch-war-crimes-watch-ukraine (last visited Mar. 14, 2022).

14. Lindsay Freeman, *Weapons of War, Tools of Justice: Using Artificial Intelligence to Investigate International Crimes*, 19 J. INT'L CRIM. JUSTICE 35, 40 (2021) ("In today's age of information . . . the key challenge has moved from data scarcity to data overload.").

15. *See* Mark Latonero, *Big Data Analytics and Human Rights: Privacy Considerations in Context, in* NEW TECHNOLOGIES FOR HUMAN RIGHTS LAW & PRACTICE 149 (Molly Land & Jay Aronson eds., 2018). Although the U.N. General Assembly has advanced a global "right to privacy," particularly regarding the sanctity of digital communications and the abuse of surveillance technology, there are no detailed international privacy standards. The Right to Privacy in the Digital Age, U.N. Doc. A/RES/68/167 (Dec. 18, 2013) ("*Deeply concerned* at the negative impact that surveillance and/or interception of communications, including extraterritorial surveillance and/or interception of communications, as well as the collection of personal data, in particular when carried out on a mass scale, may have on the exercise and enjoyment of human rights"). That said, in a fully networked world, the European Union's General Data Protection Regulation (GDPR) in many respects serves this purpose. *See generally* ANU BRADFORD, THE BRUSSELS EFFECT: HOW THE EUROPEAN UNION RULES THE WORLD (2020).

machines acting autonomously, by the parties to the conflict, and by other impacted people recording events around them in real time on their devices and self-publishing these digital artifacts—both untouched and enhanced—on their social networks.[16] Tools that were previously only available to national militaries and the law enforcement personnel of well-resourced states are now in the hands of ordinary people, leveling the documentation playing field for members of civil society but also malevolent actors.[17] Free or subsidized storage platforms, such as YouTube and cloud computing, have allowed for large-scale storage, but the quality and evidentiary value of those data vary enormously. Alongside ordinary media reporting, social media and messaging platforms are becoming dense repositories of potential war crimes evidence uploaded by witnesses, survivors, and perpetrators alike.[18] As such, they are ripe for data mining by criminal investigators.

For example, national prosecutors have convicted fighters who have fled the war in Syria for war crimes, including murder[19] and mistreating a corpse,[20] based almost exclusively on trophy photos shared on Facebook, found on their phones,

---

16. Madelaine Bair, *Is It Authentic? When Citizens and Soldiers Document War*, WITNESS, https://blog.witness.org/2012/11/is-it-authentic-when-citizens-and-soldiers-document-war/ (last visited Mar. 14, 2022). Civil society groups are curating and disseminating citizen videos for advocacy purposes, such as through Witness's Human Rights Channel. *Id.* According to one source, almost all of the data in the world has been produced in the last two years. *See* Christo Petrov, *25 + Impressive Big Data Statistics for 2021*, TECHJURY (Sept. 9, 2021), https://techjury.net/blog/big-data-statistics/#gref (last visited Mar. 14, 2022).

17. On the flip side, national authorities can turn to commercial services marketing connected devices for "deep well[s] of data," undermining settled expectations of privacy. *See* Ángel Díaz, *When Police Surveillance Meets the "Internet of Things,"* Brennan Center for Justice (Dec. 16, 2020). For example, in the United States, there are lessened expectations of privacy around information people voluntarily provide to third parties. *See Smith v. Maryland*, 442 U.S. 735 (1979); *but see Carpenter v. United States*, 585 U.S. 138 S.Ct. 2206 (2018) (limiting the third-party doctrine when information shared is not truly voluntary).

18. Such content often runs counter to the platforms' community standards and terms of service, leading to takedowns that have drawn controversy for hindering justice processes. Human Rights Watch, *"Video Unavailable": Social Media Platforms Remove Evidence of War Crimes* (Sept. 10, 2020); Rebecca Hamilton, *Social Media Platforms in International Criminal Investigations*, 52(1) CASE WESTERN RES. J. INT'L L. 213 (2020) (noting tendency of private companies to over-remove content). Civil society organizations are working to build an evidence vault where social media platforms can deposit this problematic content so it can be analyzed for actionable evidence. *See* U.C. Berkeley Human Rights Center, *Digital Lockers: Archiving Social Media Evidence of Atrocity Crimes* (June 2021).

19. The U.S. indictment against the so-called Beatles was built upon propaganda videos showing the beheading of U.S. journalists. United States v. Kotey, Indictment, Case 1:20-cr-00239-TSE (Oct. 6, 2020). The two are serving life sentences.

20. *See* Eurojust Network, *Prosecuting War Crimes of Outrage upon Personal Dignity based on Evidence from Open Sources—Legal Framework and Recent Developments in the Member States of the European Union* (Feb. 2018).

or discovered online.[21] Likewise, the International Criminal Court's arrest warrant in the *Al-Werfalli* case hinged on video footage showing the defendant engaged in what appeared to be extrajudicial executions in Libya.[22] Although much can be gleaned from it, aggregated user-generated data offers a non-probabilistic sample susceptible to selection biases, manipulation, and efforts to suppress reporting.[23] So far, courts have been willing to admit such evidence, even where provenance is sketchy,[24] although it is still early days.[25]

Data generated from sensing and "smart" technologies—including high-frequency remote sensing and the more proximate "Internet of things"—may soon outpace these forms of social media data.[26] Indeed, high resolution and synthetic aperture radar (SAR) satellite imagery has never been more accessible (in terms of availability, range, and cost) and can provide real-time, historical, and longitudinal insights into conflict dynamics, including the location and impact of attacks, the movement of people (combatants, civilians, and refugees), and transnational supply chains.[27] Hala Systems, for example, combines data from a network of trained civilian observers, remote sensors, and open media sources for threat detection and to provide early warning to schools, hospitals, and other vulnerable

21. Such evidence also undergirds the January 6th prosecutions given the propensity of participants to post incriminating videos of their actions breaching the U.S. capital and the prevalence of security cameras in the area. *See* Roger Parloff, *What Do—and Will—the Criminal Prosecutions of the Jan. 6 Capitol Rioters Tell Us?* LAWFARE (Nov. 4, 2021).

22. Prosecutor v. Al-Werfalli, Case No. ICC-01/11/01/17, Warrant of Arrest, ¶¶ 3, 11–22 (Aug. 15, 2017). Werfalli was subsequently assassinated and so the case against him was terminated. https://www.icc-cpi.int/libya/al-werfalli (last visited Mar. 14, 2022).

23. U.N. GLOBAL PULSE, BIG DATA FOR DEVELOPMENT: CHALLENGES AND OPPORTUNITIES 27–29 (May 2012), https://www.unglobalpulse.org/document/big-data-for-development-opport unities-and-challenges-white-paper/ (last visited Mar. 14, 2022). U.N. Globe Pulse seeks to harness the power of big data for development and humanitarian purposes.

24. *See* Riccardo Vecellio Segate, *Cognitive Bias, Privacy Rights, and Digital Evidence in International Criminal Proceedings: Demystifying the Double-Edged AI Revolution*, 21 INT'L CRIM. L. REV. 1, 3 (2021). The international tribunals are governed by omnibus admissibility rules that do not distinguish between types of evidence. *Id.*

25. *See* Patrick Nutter, *Machine Learning Evidence: Admissibility and Weight*, 21 UNIV. PENN. J. CONST. L. 919 (2019) (discussing potential evidentiary issues around machine learning outputs).

26. Qadir et al., *supra* note 6, at 4.

27. Optical satellite imagery is more difficult to gather at night or with cloud cover, whereas space-borne SAR sensors use microwaves that can operate regardless of the atmospheric conditions. The two provide complementary information, and SAR-optical image matching can yield useful insights into the observed scene. *See* Lloyd Haydn Hughes et al., *A Deep Learning Framework for Matching of SAR and Optical Imagery*, 169 ISPRS J. PHOTOGRAMMERTY AND REMOTE SENSING 166, 176 (2020).

populations in Syria when airstrikes are threatened.[28] Advocates are using before-and-after imagery to investigate the destruction of villages, the location of mass graves, and the targeting of cultural property or medical facilities. As just one example, a report co-produced by UNESCO relied upon information collected by the United Nations' Operational Satellite Applications Programme (UNOSAT) to detail the devastation of the ancient city of Aleppo, a World Heritage Site, during the war in Syria.[29] Likewise, satellite imagery is documenting the real-time destruction of Ukraine.[30]

Additional informational compilations are being purposefully generated by digitizing found or exfiltrated documents and scraping social media platforms.[31] Investigators with the Commission on International Justice & Accountability (CIJA), for example, have acquired over one million pages of documents generated by the Syrian regime and the Islamic State of Iraq and the Levant (ISIL). CIJA has secured these files in an evidence management system that has been shared with law enforcement authorities bringing war crimes cases in Europe and elsewhere.[32] Similar efforts are ramping up for Ukraine with lessons learned from Syria.[33]

---

28. *See Hala Systems: Blockchain Case Study for Saving Lives and Mitigating War Crimes*, CONSENSYS, https://consensys.net/blockchain-use-cases/social-impact/hala-systems-case-study/ (last visited Mar. 14, 2022). Hala is exploring the potential for uploading the raw information generated to a distributed ledger database like blockchain (rather than placing these data on its own servers) to prove that these artifacts have not been altered since the point of collection, effectively removing itself from the evidentiary chain of custody. *Id.*

29. UNESCO, UNITAR-UNOSAT, *Five Years of Conflict: The State of Cultural Heritage in the Ancient City of Aleppo* (2018), https://whc.unesco.org/en/activities/946/ (last visited Mar. 14, 2022).

30. Chris Young, *Ukraine's Crisis: 8 New Satellite Images Reveal the Devastation on the Ground*, INTERESTING ENGINEERING (Mar. 23, 2022), https://interestingengineering.com/satellite-images-reveal-the-devastation (last visited Mar. 14, 2022).

31. The courts continue to grapple with the permissibility of web scraping, particularly in the commercial sector given the platforms' terms of service, copyright and computer fraud laws, and data protection policies. *See hiQ Labs, Inc. v. LinkedIn Corp.*, 938 F.3d 985 (9th Cir. 2019) (upholding preliminary injunction allowing hiQ to access publicly available LinkedIn member profiles and suggesting that such activity likely does not violate the Computer Fraud and Abuse Act (CFAA)). The Electronic Frontier Foundation appeared as an *amicus curiae* and argued that the CFAA, which was enacted as an anti-hacking cybercrime tool, should not be invoked to police access to publicly available information or to enforce private terms of service. *See* Brief of Amicus Curiae Electronic Frontier Foundation, DuckDuckGo, and Internet Archive in Support of Plaintiff-Appellee, hiQ Labs, Inc. v. LinkedIn Corp., Case: 17-16783 (Nov. 27, 2017).

32. *See* CIJA, *What We Do*, https://cijaonline.org/model-of-work (last visited Mar. 14, 2022).

33. Rebecca Hamilton & Lindsay Freeman, *The Int'l Criminal Court's Ukraine Investigation: A Test Case for User-Generated Evidence*, JUST SECURITY (Mar. 2, 2022), https://www.justsecurity.org/80404/the-intl-criminal-courts-ukraine-investigation-a-test-case-for-user-generated-evidence/ (last visited Mar. 14, 2022).

Human rights documentation organizations, such as Mnemonic and eyeWitness, are establishing secure evidence vaults to preserve all this information and enable the aggregated analysis of fused data streams while also training local actors to maximize the utility of digital documentation.[34] Many organizations are starting to amass their information in storage solutions that rely on encryption and distributed ledgers, such as blockchain, to ensure data integrity and transparency and to establish an unimpeachable chain of custody.[35] These collections are being further curated for accountability processes in national and international courts.[36]

Battlefield evidence[37] and other material created by the parties to the conflict—such as after actions, strike logs, body camera feeds, detention rolls, captured enemy material, enlistment pledges, and disciplinary records—are often generated to support military tasks and objectives but may also contribute to prevention and accountability.[38] Added to these conflict-specific sources are native datasets

---

34. *See* Mnemonic, *Methods*, mnemonic.org/en/about/methods (last visited Mar. 14, 2022). Similar evidence vaults have been created for the conflict in Yemen using tools such as Uwazi's open-source software, which was designed to enable the sharing of document collections and compliance with chain of custody obligations. *See* Yemeni Archive, *Methods and Tools*, https://yemeniarchive.org/en/about/methods-tools (last visited Mar. 14, 2022); Uwazi, https://www.uwazi.io/about/ (last visited Mar. 14, 2022); HURIDOCS, *Developing Uwazi, a Human Rights Database Application*, https://huridocs.org/initiatives/developing-uwazi-a-human-rights-datab ase-tool/ (last visited Mar. 14, 2022).

35. Distributed ledgers store copies of data on multiple nodes on a peer-to-peer network subject to cryptographic keys and signatures and often operating without a central authority. Because the various sites store an identical copy of the information, distributed ledgers are more impervious to malicious tampering than legacy storage solutions. *See* Raoul Wallenberg Institute, *Human Rights and Blockchain*, https://rwi.lu.se/2018/02/12/blockchain-human-rights/ (last visited Mar. 14, 2022). Advocates are exploring other potential uses of blockchain in the promotion and protection of human rights. *See* Christina Comben, *How Blockchain Is Being Applied to Human Rights*, COINCENTRAL, May 31, 2020, https://coincentral.com/blockchain-and-human-rights/ (last visited Mar. 14, 2022); STANFORD BUSINESS SCHOOL CENTER FOR SOCIAL INNOVATION, BLOCKCHAIN FOR SOCIAL IMPACT: MOVING BEYOND THE HYPE, https://www.gsb.stanford.edu/sites/gsb/files/publication-pdf/study-blockchain-impact-moving-beyond-hype.pdf (last visited Mar. 14, 2022).

36. *See, e.g.*, Chiara Gabriele et al., *The Role of Mobile Technology in Documenting International Crimes: The* Affaire Castro et Kizito *in the Democratic Republic of Congo*, 19 J. INT'L CRIM. JUST. 107 (Mar. 2021).

37. *See* NATO, *NATO Allies agree [on] Policy on Battlefield Evidence from Operational Theatres to Boost Efforts Against Terrorism* (Oct. 22, 2020), https://www.nato.int/cps/en/natohq/news_179194.htm?selectedLocale=en (last visited Mar. 14, 2022); Eurojust, *Eurojust Memorandum on Battlefield Evidence* (Sept. 2020), https://www.eurojust.europa.eu/publication/eurojust-mem orandum-battlefield-evidence (last visited Mar. 14, 2022).

38. Researchers at Human Rights Watch, for example, uncovered thousands of documents from the abandoned headquarters of the *Directorate de Documentation et Securité* in Chad. These archives enabled experts to construct a command structure, track the movement and mistreatment of victims, and demonstrate that former President Hissène Habré had received

and "data exhaust" produced in the ordinary course of modern life—such as cell phone and financial records, Internet search histories, bureaucratic reports, and administrative archives.[39] Some of these repositories are proprietary or classified and would need to be obtained from corporate[40] or governmental entities[41] (although a surprising amount of such information is already available online). Nongovernmental organization (NGOs) may also hold datasets that they consider their intellectual property. Depending upon the nature and location of the jurisdiction that is seized of a particular matter, these sources of data may or may not be subject to the court's discovery or subpoena powers.

If they can be obtained, these datasets can be exploited by prosecutors for multiple purposes, including geolocation of people and events, fugitive tracking,[42] and social network analysis.[43] For example, the Prosecutor of the Special Tribunal for Lebanon (STL) proffered telecommunications evidence (call data

over 1,000 direct communications about harm to detainees. *See* Reed Brody, *Victims Bring a Dictator to Justice: The Case of Hissène Habré*, Analysis 70, BREAD FOR THE WORLD 1, 14 (June 2017), https://www.brot-fuer-die-welt.de/fileadmin/mediapool/2_Downloads/Fachinformatio nen/Analyse/Analysis70-The_Habre_Case.pdf (last visited Mar. 14, 2022).

39. *See* Megan Price et al., *A Statistical Analysis of the Guatemalan National Police Archive: Searching for Documentation of Human Rights Abuses*, https://hrdag.org/wp-content/ uploads/2013/02/JSM-GT-estimates.pdf (last visited Mar. 14, 2022) (discussing sampling and coding methodology of millions of archival records from the Guatemalan National Police to discern the prevalence of international crimes and official knowledge thereof). A truth commission relied upon these data to conclude that genocide was committed in Guatemala against indigenous communities during the dirty war era. GUATEMALAN HISTORICAL CLARIFICATION COMMISSION, GUATEMALA: MEMORIA DEL SILENCIO (1999), https://hrdag.org/wp-content/ uploads/2013/01/CEHreport-english.pdf (last visited Mar. 14, 2022).

40. The movement for data philanthropy aims to encourage corporations to make privacy-protected data available to advance the public good. Igor Tulchinsky & Robert Kilpatrick, *The Power of Data Philanthropy*, MILKEN INSTITUTE, May 10, 2019. *See also* Sarfaty's chapter in this volume for arguments fleshing out the negative and positive obligations of corporations when it comes to data regarding human rights abuses and humanitarian aid.

41. *See* Tarak Shah, *Processing Scanned Documents for Investigations of Police Violence*, HRDAG (July 13, 2021) (discussing utility of sampling techniques for analyzing large administrative collections to identify patterns of state violence). *See, e.g.*, Green v. Chicago Police Dep't, 2021 IL App. (1st) 200574 (Mar. 31, 2021) (ordering the release of thousands of pages of documents concerning police misconduct).

42. Abigail W. Xavier et al., *Where in the World Is Q? Clues from Image Metadata*, BELLiNGCAT (May 10, 2021), https://www.bellingcat.com/news/rest-of-world/2021/05/10/where-in-the-world-is-q-clues-from-image-metadata/ (last visited Mar. 14, 2022).

43. A U.S. court, for example, admitted a Google Earth image showing the defendant's location, reasoning that this was not a hearsay "statement" because Google Earth automatically generated the pinpoint graphic without human involvement. U.S. v. Lizarraga-Tirado, 789 F.3d 1107, 1110 (2015). *See also Carpenter*, 585 U.S. (holding that a warrant supported by probable cause is required to obtain third party cell phone location data because it implicates Fourth Amendment privacy interests).

and call sequence records coupled with user contact profiling) drawn from five interconnected and overlapping mobile phone networks in an effort (ultimately only partially successful) to prove that the *in absentia* defendants had former Lebanese Prime Minister Rafik Hariri under surveillance, coordinated his 2005 assassination, and staged an attempted coverup.[44] All of these types of data are susceptible to "function creep" wherein data originally collected for one purpose can be used for other unanticipated, unintended, or abusive purposes.[45] Accordingly, governments can misuse such approaches at the expense of human rights and civil liberties[46] and can subvert any equality of arms between the prosecution and the defense.[47] This is particularly so as we all become desensitized to being subjected to constant data collection, which can morph into pervasive surveillance.[48]

These various unstructured data streams can be aggregated and fused with insider and eyewitness testimony to undergird a whole range of transitional justice purposes. From the perspective of individual criminal accountability, these collections will include lead and crime base information but also critical linkage evidence, connecting particular actors to the commission of war crimes.[49] In addition to supporting individual claims and charges, Big Data can also identify macro trends to provide context for particularized charges. University verification labs, NGOs, and autonomous investigative organizations around the globe are training young people to authenticate key conflict artifacts using digital open-source investigative techniques, such as reverse image searches, sun-shadow

---

44. *See* Prosecutor v. Ayyash et al., Case No. STL-11-01/T/TC, Decision on the Admission of Call Sequence Tables related to the Movements of Mr. Rafiq Hariri and Related Events, and Four Witness Statements (Oct. 31, 2016); STL, *Primer on Telecommunications Evidence*, https://www.stl-tsl.org/images/Documents/PrimerZonZTelecommunicationsZEvidence.pdf (last visited Mar. 14, 2022). In the end, the Tribunal was unable to conclude beyond a reasonable doubt that some of the accused operated the phones that were used by the members of the conspiracy to assassinate Hariri. Prosecutor v. Ayyash et al., Case No. STL-11-01/T/TC, Judgment (Aug. 18, 2020). The acquittals were partially reversed on appeal. Prosecutor v. Ayyash, Case No. STL-11-01/A-2/AC, Appeal Judgement (Mar. 10, 2022).

45. Brayne, *supra* note 9, at 294–95.

46. *See generally* Emmanuel Letouzé et al., *The Law, Politics and Ethics of Cell Phone Data Analytics*, The World Bank Group (Apr. 2015) (discussing ethical issues with using call data records).

47. Serena Quottrocolo et al., *Technical Solutions for Legal Challenges: Equality of Arms in Criminal Proceeding* [sic], 20(1) GLOBAL JURIST (2020).

48. Peter Chertoff, *Facial Recognition Has Its Eye on the U.K.*, LAWFARE (Feb. 7, 2020), https://www.lawfareblog.com/facial-recognition-has-its-eye-uk (last visited Mar. 14, 2022) (discussing stealth rollout of facial recognition in the United Kingdom).

49. *Video as Evidence: To Be Evidence, What Does Video Need?*, NEW TACTICS FOR HUMAN RIGHTS (July 18, 2014), https://www.newtactics.org/comment/7430#comment-7430 (last visited Mar. 14, 2022).

calculators, heat and infrared signatures, metadata extraction, and geospatial data processing.[50]

II. THE HAZARDS OF CONFLICT-RELATED BIG DATA

Although there is great potential here, exploiting Big Data to assist with war crimes prosecutions is no easy feat. Big Data and accompanying analytics give the impression of greater objectivity and accuracy, but there is an ever-present risk of false precision. Any number of common informational and human biases can taint all data analytics, which may be amplified with Big Data sets.[51] This includes biases in all senses of the word: statistical biases inherent to reporting and collection patterns that do not accurately reflect the real-world prevalence of the phenomenon in question;[52] cognitive and perceptual biases associated with digital images and assumptions about the inherent credibility and infallibility of technology;[53] and prejudicial biases around race, gender, or political inclination.[54] It has already been amply demonstrated that facial recognition, speech recognition, and emotion detection tools contain racial biases.[55] In addition, machine learning assumes a "single, ground-truth label" that may be elusive in the "noisy" real world where Big Data collections of human speech may be misinterpreted, contradictory, and inconsistent.[56]

50. *See, e.g., The Digital Verification Corps: Amnesty International's Volunteers for the Age of Social Media,* https://citizenevidence.org/2019/12/06/the-digital-verification-corps-amnesty-internationals-volunteers-for-the-age-of-social-media/ (last visited Mar. 14, 2022).

51. *See* Nema Milaninia, *Biases in Machine Learning Models and Big Data Analytics: The International Criminal and Humanitarian Law Implications,* 102 INT'L REV. RED CROSS 199, 202 (2020).

52. For example, victims and survivors will strategically tailor their reporting to the expectations and priorities of humanitarian actors. *See* Mats Utas, *Victimcy, Girlfriending, Soldiering: Tactical Agency in a Young Women's Social Navigation of the Liberian War Zone,* 78 ANTHROPOLOGICAL Q. 403, 409 (2005). Likewise, the collection patterns of NGOs may be influenced by donor expectations, media reporting, the reach of an authoritarian state, and Internet shutdowns.

53. Eric Van Buskirk & Vincent T. Liu, *Digital Evidence: Challenging the Presumption of Reliability,* 1(1) J. DIGITAL FORENSIC PRACTICE 19, 20 (2006).

54. Jay D. Aronson, *Mobile Phones, Social Media, and Big Data in Human Rights Fact-Finding: Possibilities, Challenges, and Limitations, in* THE TRANSFORMATION OF HUMAN RIGHTS FACT-FINDING 441, 447 (Philip Alston & Sarah Knuckey eds., 2016) (noting that harm to marginalized groups may be excluded from social media convenience samples).

55. Díaz, *supra* note 17. This reality features in this book's Scenario chapter.

56. Chuying Huo, *"People with Always Disagree": HAI Researchers Tackle Hate Speech Moderators,* THE STANFORD DAILY (Sept. 20, 2021), https://stanforddaily.com/2021/09/20/people-will-alw ays-disagree-hai-researchers-tackle-hate-speech-moderators/ (last visited Mar. 14, 2022).

In addition, given how easy it is to manipulate digital information and disseminate deep fakes, investigators must continually contend with mis- and dis-information aimed at diverting scrutiny, influencing public opinion, and manipulating the international response to a crisis situation.[57] In conflict settings, strategic mis-information, influence campaigns, and "flooding the zone" with bogus information can complicate efforts to map violations, generate confusion and conspiracy theories, deflect attention from actual perpetrators, and unfairly taint principled actors.[58] Indeed, in Syria, the "arms race between information and disinformation" became integral to the conflict.[59] The White Helmets, for example, were subjected to a comprehensive "smear campaign."[60] Likewise, in connection with the 2017 chemical weapons attacks in Khan Sheikhoun, bots and state-sponsored Twitter accounts flooded social media platforms with denials under the hashtag #SyriaHoax that spread faster than more accurate or corroborated narratives.[61] Deep fakes are also emerging in connection with the conflict in Ukraine.[62] Such systemic tactics and the weaponization of Big Data create major distractions and require the expenditure of significant analytical energy to debunk.[63] At the same time, unmasking such premeditated coverups can help prove culpability.

Even taking malign intent out of the picture, while artificial intelligence is extraordinarily good at completing repetitive tasks within defined parameters, many algorithms must be trained before they can be deployed.[64] As such, machines are

---

57. Alexa Koenig, *"Half the Truth Is Often a Great Lie": Deep Fakes, Open Source Information, and International Criminal Law*, 113 AJIL UNBOUND 250, 251 (Aug. 19, 2019).

58. *See* Sean Illing, *"Flood the Zone with Shit": How Misinformation Overwhelmed Our Democracy*, Vox (Feb. 6, 2020), https://www.vox.com/policy-and-politics/2020/1/16/20991 816/impeachment-trial-trump-bannon-misinformation (last visited Mar. 14, 2022).

59. Karl Nicolas Lindenlaub, *The Syrian Online War of Narratives*, ATLANTIC COUNCIL (July 8, 2020).

60. Emma Grey Ellis, *Inside the Conspiracy Theory that Turned Syria's First Responders into Terrorists*, WIRED (Apr. 30, 2017).

61. Sarah P. White, *Information Warfare in the Digital Age: A Study of #SyriaHoax*, JOTS (Nov. 12, 2019).

62. Makena Kelly, *Facebook Removes 'Deepfake' of Ukrainian President Zelenskyy*, THE VERGE (Mar. 16, 2022), https://www.theverge.com/2022/3/16/22981806/facebook-removes-deepf ake-ukraine-zelenskyy-meta-instagram (last visited Mar. 14, 2022) (noting removal of a video showing President Zelenskyy surrendering to Russian forces).

63. *The Khan Sheikhoun Chemical Attack, The Evidence So Far*, BELLiNGCAT (Apr. 5, 2017); Eliot Higgins, *The First Images of the Type of Chemical Bomb Used in Syria's Sarin Attacks*, BELLiNGCAT (Sept. 24, 2019).

64. Unsupervised machine learning is not premised on training data and can be useful in independently finding hidden patterns in unstructured data sets by automatically clustering related items, such as documents based upon particular templates. *See* Elena Radeva, *The Potential for Computer Vision to Advance Accountability in the Syrian Crisis*, 19 INTL CRIM. L. 131 (2021)

only as smart as the training sets that are available. Common sampling and participation biases may result in skewed training datasets, which will undermine the results produced in subsequent applications.[65] For example, a computer trained to track combatants wearing identifiable insignia would "miss" images of combatants who do not display such recognizable traits.[66] Likewise, large-scale events (such as a massacre or airstrike) tend to receive greater coverage in all media sources, thus obscuring smaller scale events (such as a single death).[67] In the same way, certain forms of civilian harm—custodial abuses and sexual violence—are routinely concealed and chronically underreported.[68] The existence of these systemic false negatives may tilt overall conclusions about the nature of, and responsibility for, violence and disproportionately implicate particular actors or communities in criminal behavior. Some such biases may be obvious, whereas others may be less observable. There are techniques to address these concerns, but it may be impossible to eliminate data bias entirely, even with technological developments.[69] All told, Big Data has the potential to both increase and decrease information uncertainty when it comes to the enforcement of the law of war.[70] Where the fulcrum settles depends upon future developments.

III. BIG DATA AND THE ENFORCEMENT OF LOAC

With these caveats in mind, there are a number of potential use cases for Big Data and its enabled analytics in the enforcement of LOAC, including in preventative action ex ante and war crimes prosecutions ex post. This includes automating

(discussing the use of structured and unstructured computer vision techniques on the holdings of the Syrian investigative mechanism).

65. *See* Julianna Photopoulos, *Fighting Algorithmic Bias in Artificial Intelligence*, PHYSICSWORLD (May 4, 2021) (discussing race and gender bias in commercial facial recognition software).

66. Megan Price & Patrick Ball, *Data Collection and Documentation for Truth-Seeking and Accountability*, SYRIA JUSTICE & ACCOUNTABILITY CENTRE (Jan. 23, 2014).

67. Nils B. Weidman, *A Closer Look at Reporting Bias in Conflict Event Data*, 60 AM. J. POL. SCI. 211 (2015) (discussing the risk of systemic measurement error in micro-level analyses of conflict violence, particularly given variations in cell phone prevalence, which impacts media coverage).

68. Megan Price & Patrick Ball, *Big Data, Selection Bias, and the Statistical Patterns of Mortality in Conflict*, XXXVI SAIS REV. 9 (2014) (discussing event-size bias); Alexa Koenig & Ulic Egan, *Power and Privilege: Investigating Sexual Violence with Digital Open Source Information*, 19 J. INT'L CRIM. JUST. 55 (2021) (discussing challenges of investigating sexual violence with open source investigations).

69. Price & Ball, *supra* note 68, at 20 n.23.

70. *See* Christoph Koettl, *Sensors Everywhere: Using Satellites and Mobile Phones to Reduce Information Uncertainty in Human Rights Crisis Research*, 11 GENOCIDE STUDIES & PREVENTION: AN INT'L J. 36 (2017).

the review and analysis of digital material for potential incriminating, and exculpatory, evidence and using statistical techniques to verify, or estimate, the prevalence of particular conduct. The potential of more advanced artificial intelligence capabilities—including neural networks and deep learning processes that mimic human reasoning—remains undeveloped in this realm and more work needs to be done to consider how such often opaque algorithmic processes can be subjected to discovery and interrogatory practices in the context of an adversarial legal process.

A. Object Recognition, Event Detection, and Scene Synchronization

Using techniques associated with machine learning and computer vision—including object detection and classification (the ability of a computer to detect an object of interest in a digital image)—computers can be trained to review and code complex image datasets and identify patterns, trends, and correlations. This ability of machines is particularly useful with noisy data, that is, when a majority of the items are irrelevant. These processes can be deployed to identify the commission of potential war crimes, such as the use of prohibited weapons (e.g., chemical, biological, or indiscriminate weapons and weapon systems),[71] the intentional or reckless targeting of civilians or civilian objects,[72] the laying of improvised explosive devices (IEDs), or the commission of harm to protected persons who are hors de combat. Such techniques can also provide attribution evidence to support individual and state accountability, for example, by mapping the movement of armed vehicles or combatants or collecting documents bearing certain official stamps. As just one example, artificial intelligence is being used to identify seagoing vessels based upon their geometric attributes. Machines have proven to be effective at this task even if the crew has disabled, or tried to spoof, the ship's Auto Identification System (AIS) transponder or otherwise engaged in measures to mask its appearance.[73]

Supervised machine learning can require thousands of diverse and manually labeled images per class and an iterative training process to create a custom object detection model. The necessary training can be accomplished using existing

71. Kelly Geoghegan, *On the Utility of Weapon Bans and Restrictions—Anti-Personnel Mines, Cluster Munitions and Blinding Lasers*, INTERCROSS (Nov. 5, 2015).

72. By way of example, an analysis of satellite imagery coupled with open-source research on media reports and ISIL publications revealed the destruction and pillage of farms as a form of collective punishment meted out by vestigial ISIL fighters. Wim Zwijnenburg, *Torching and Extortion: OSINT Analysis of Burning Agriculture in Iraq*, BELL³NGCAT (June 3, 2019).

73. Michael S. Treacy, *Ship Identification and AI*, Disruptive Technologies and International Law, U.S. Naval War College (Dec. 7, 2020), https://www.youtube.com/watch?v=zWdSXCZH q4o&feature=youtu.be (last visited Mar. 14, 2022).

datasets (many of which have been developed for commercial purposes) or customized synthetic training sets. The latter are particularly relevant to the LOAC context because there are few publicly available training pipelines relevant to conflict events or, for that matter, the quantities of ground truth imagery necessary to construct one. To account for this deficit of exemplars, human rights groups are resorting to 3D printing and rendering to create bespoke training data for computers engaged in object detection in combat zones. For example, Visual Forensics & Metadata Extraction (VFRAME) and Mnemonic have begun employing this methodology in Syrian, Yemeni, and Sudanese conflict zones, primarily to track munitions deployed in these theaters.[74] One use case involves tracking the detonation of cluster munitions in Syria, such as Soviet-era AO-2.5RT submunitions.[75] Three-dimensional printed replicas are photographed in a natural environment to match the target domain. Software to (de)compress data (so-called codec tools) subsequently degrade and recompress the imagery to mimic real digital relics. An annotation tool, such as Intel's open-source Computer Vision Annotation Tool (CVAT),[76] then appropriately labels the images in order to train the algorithms in object detection.[77] Once a computer has "learned" to recognize a particular submunition (and eliminate distractors), it can be put to work on real-world conflict imagery. This automation offers huge efficiency gains, because computers are able to analyze images at a rate that dwarfs even the most capable investigator. Human researchers can then verify the relevance of the filtered images. Furthermore, by obviating the need for humans to review every image, machine learning coupled with synthetic training sets also protects against secondary trauma in researchers who would otherwise have to review hours of often distressing footage.[78]

Even more complex than image recognition is event detection, which involves more dynamic attributes (including visual and acoustic semantics) and is more computationally expensive. Carnegie-Mellon University's Event Labeling through

---

74. Adam Harvey, *Research: 3D Printed Training Data*, VFRAME (Jan. 23, 2021), https://vframe.io/research/3d-printed-training-data/ (last visited Mar. 14, 2022).

75. Kenton Fulmer, *Renewed Use of AO-2.RT Submunitions in Syria*, THE HOPLITE, Armament Research Service (Oct. 15, 2015), https://armamentresearch.com/renewed-use-of-ao-2-5rt-submunitions-in-syria/ (last visited Mar. 14, 2022). A similar effort is afoot with respect to the Saudi-led coalition's use of U. S.-manufactured BLU-63 in Yemen. *See* Karen Hao, *Human Rights Activists Want to Use AI to Help Prove War Crimes in Court*, MIT TECH. REV. (June 25, 2020).

76. *See* INTEL, *Computer Vision Annotation Tool: A Universal Approach to Data Annotation* (Mar. 2, 2019), https://software.intel.com/content/www/us/en/develop/articles/computer-vision-annotation-tool-a-universal-approach-to-data-annotation.html (last visited Mar. 14, 2022).

77. *See The Best Image Labeling Tools for Computer Vision of 2020*, HUMANS IN THE LOOP, https://humansintheloop.org/the-best-image-labeling-tools-for-computer-vision-of-2020/ (last visited Mar. 14, 2022).

78. *See* Elise Baker et al., *"Safer Viewing" A Study of Secondary Trauma Mitigation Techniques in Open Source Investigations*, 22 HEALTH & HUM. RTS. J. 293 (2020).

Analytic Media Processing (E-LAMP) system can detect predefined events—such as the firing of munitions, a structure collapsing, or demonstrative human behaviors (such as people fleeing)—and undertake content analysis of multimedia collections.[79] These include unconstrained full motion videos (like those uploaded by citizen journalists) using enabling devices, such as documentation apps[80] or miniaturized cameras.[81] E-LAMP's creators have discovered that the system works even when the video's resolution is reduced to a certain degree (but not more), which increases processing efficiency without degrading performance.[82]

When thousands of hours of video are on hand, computers can dramatically reduce video processing times and help investigators find the "best evidence" of a particular event through de-duplication and scene summarization. Because similar digital images of key events are often posted, enhanced, edited, and reposted by different individuals, advocacy organizations, and media outlets, de-duplication has emerged as a key challenge to organizing fused data collections. Technologists developed scene summarization techniques for reviewing long-form videos in structured scenarios, such as security camera footage. Content compression algorithms identify the most representative and high-quality frames and obviate the need for viewing potentially millions of hours of collected content.[83] The tool will identify relevant changes of scene, which helps to weed out irrelevant or repetitive content and focus object detection on the frames most likely to yield results.[84] Benetech, for instance, is working with the International, Impartial and Independent Mechanism devoted to Syria (IIIM) to analyze the thousands of hours of video in the latter's repository to identify copies and segments of the same video file.[85] Bellingcat has also turned its attention to Ukraine.[86]

79. *See* Wei Tong et al., *E-LAMP: Integration of Innovative Ideas for Multimedia Event Detection*, MACHINE LEARNING AND APPLICATIONS (2013).

80. For example, eyeWitness has developed an app for observers to capture and freeze footage of human rights violations and the accompanying metadata to maximize admissibility. *See* https://www.theeyewitnessapp.com/.

81. *See Secretive Human Rights Group Fights Abuses with Video*, AL JAZEERA, Apr. 15, 2016 (discussing *Videre est Credere* ("seeing is believing"), which is disseminating clandestine cameras to empower people to record violations of international law and acts of corruption).

82. Tong et al., *supra* note 79, at 2–3.

83. *See* Adam Harvey, *Research: Scene Summarization*, VFRAME (Oct. 1, 2019), https://vframe.io/research/scene-summarization/ (last visited Mar. 14, 2022).

84. *See* PySceneDetect, Overview of Features, https://pyscenedetect.readthedocs.io/en/latest/features/#features-in-current-release (last visited Mar. 14, 2022).

85. IIIM, *Message from the Head of IIIM*, Bulletin No. 5 (Feb. 2021), https://iiim.un.org/wp-content/uploads/2021/03/IIIM-Syria-Bulletin-5-ENG-Feb-2021.pdf.

86. The Conversation, *Digital Sleuths Are Changing the Course of the Ukraine War*, THE NEXT WEB (Mar. 23, 2022), https://thenextweb.com/news/digital-sleuths-are-changing-course-ukraine-war (last visited Mar. 14, 2022).

Similarly, scene synchronization techniques can align evidence from multiple sources, perspectives, and vantage points in the service of event reconstruction.[87] Investigators can compare information from different formats and angles to construct a more stereoscopic, multi-perspectival impression. Such synchronization can focus on images, but also audio signatures (e.g., gunshots, voices, explosions, aircraft). The latter are proving to be more amenable to synchronization, particularly when videos are shot from different points of view.[88]

B. Facial Recognition

Facial recognition is another sub-domain of computer vision. There are several use cases for facial recognition technology in conflict situations, including for improving the accuracy of targeting.[89] In the prevention and accountability realms, it can be equally useful for identifying perpetrators, potential witnesses, and victims from visual images produced during conflict events. The system is not foolproof, however. Whereas humans can recognize an individual from a single in-person exposure or interaction, standard facial recognition software is premised on having access to multiple images of a particular face under a range of different conditions, a predicate that may not exist in many conflict settings.[90] The next generation software is able to use a single image for identification, even in profile, etc., and scan the web for matches to make an identification.[91] Facial reconstruction can help identify perpetrators from historical or partial images as well.[92]

Crowdsourcing provides a low-tech alternative to facial recognition software, particularly in communities in which large portraiture and biometric datasets

---

87. *See* Jay D. Aronson et al., *Reconstructing Human Rights Violations Using Large Eyewitness Video Collections: The Case of Euromaidan Protester Deaths*, 10 J. HUM. RTS. PRACTICE 159, 162 (2018).

88. *See* Junwei Liang et al., *Video Synchronization and Sound Search for Human Rights Documentation and Conflict Monitoring*, CARNEGIE MELLON CENTER FOR HUMAN RIGHTS SCIENCE (June 2016).

89. Charles J. Dunlap Jr., *The Hyper-Personalization of War: Cyber, Big Data, and the Changing Face of Conflict*, 15 GEORGETOWN J. INT'L AFF. 108, 110 (2014) (noting potential for facial recognition-enabled drones to target particular individuals).

90. *See* Kimberly J. Del Greco, *Law Enforcement's Use of Facial Recognition Technology*, Statement before the House Committee on Oversight and Government Reform (Mar. 22, 2017).

91. *See* Kashmir Hill, *The Secretive Company That Might End Privacy as We Know It*, N.Y. TIMES (Jan. 18, 2020) (discussing law enforcement use of Clearview AI).

92. Jesus Diaz, *How VR Is Helping Convict Nazis in Court*, FAST COMPANY (Jan. 10, 2018), https://www.fastcompany.com/90156138/how-vr-is-helping-convict-nazis-in-court (last visited Mar. 14, 2022).

are unavailable. For example, a Syrian regime defector, code-named "Caesar," exfiltrated 50,000 images from military hospitals where he worked as a forensic photographer. The Federal Bureau of Investigations confirmed the authenticity of the images, and a multidisciplinary team of lawyers and forensic anthropologists retained by Qatar (which was aligned with the opposition) reviewed the injuries depicted to conclude that the majority of the victims had been subjected to physical trauma or starvation and thus were not likely battlefield deaths.[93] Some of the photos were distinct enough to subject those photos to facial recognition software, but not all the victims could be identified. Consequently, the Syria Association for Missing and Conscience Detainees posted the entire collection online in order to allow family and friends of the disappeared to search for their loved ones,[94] although this approach was subject to criticism given the potential infringement of privacy rights and the risk of retraumatization.[95] Similarly, Adalmaz is using the wisdom of the crowd to identify potential perpetrators in Syria (and elsewhere) from digital images.[96] Such efforts can be effective for known persons but dangerously inaccurate if those doing the identifying lacked prior interactions with those depicted in the imagery.

C. Text and Social Network Analysis

Advances in computational linguistics, statistical learning models, and natural language processing now enable computers to understand (and translate) text and spoken words. Such analyses can be useful for found documents (e.g., employment records), signals intercepts, social media posts, or text messages extracted from devices associated with a particular regime or warring party.[97] The next

---

93. *A Report into the Credibility of Certain Evidence with Regard to Torture and Execution of Persons Incarcerated by the Current Syrian Regime*, Prepared for Carter-Rusk and Co., https://www.theguardian.com/world/interactive/2014/jan/20/torture-of-persons-under-current-syrian-regime-report (last visited Mar. 14, 2022). Because Qatar has supported the armed Syrian opposition, and the report was issued prior to an important negotiation, the process generated concerns about bias.

94. Syrian Association for Missing Persons and Detainees of Conscience, *Martyrs of Torture*, https://safmcd.com/martyr/confirm (last visited Mar. 14, 2022). *See also* Red Cross/Red Crescent, *Trace the Fact—Migrants in Europe*, https://familylinks.icrc.org/europe/en/Pages/home.aspx (last visited Mar. 14, 2022) (compiling a photo gallery for people searching for lost relatives).

95. Syria Justice & Accountability Centre, *The Publication of Victims Photographs Online Jeopardizes Security and Accountability in Syria* (Mar. 26, 2015).

96. *See* Adalmaz: Justice for the Oppressed, https://adalmaz.org/ (last visited Mar. 14, 2022).

97. Natural language processing his highly developed for Latin-based language, less so for other languages and scripts. *See* Chenchen Ding et al., *Statistical Romanization for Abugida Scripts: Data and Experiment on Khmer and Burmese* (2017).

frontier involves sentiment analysis, which can reveal attitudes and emotions.[98] A computer can be taught to scan text or voice data and flag particular "selectors," such as items that mention violence; seem to be conveying, or acknowledging receipt of, orders; suggest a threat or incitement;[99] or reveal a person's connection to known perpetrators.[100] The process of training machines to tag relevant text is labor-intensive and context-specific since human communication is filled with ambiguities, metaphors, disambiguation, and coded language. As such, acute challenges of application and interpretation arise in areas where people communicate in a vernacular that might be resistant to natural language processing and text mining. Constructing, for example, a "dictionary" for textual and sentiment analysis in incitement circumstances is intensely circumstantial.[101]

In addition to reviewing the text of online posts, Big Data processes can be used to mine and map social media links and interactions to reconstruct social networks; establish the (in)credibility of witnesses and corroborate other evidence; and shed light on group membership, the chain of command, communication patterns, and turf boundaries of belligerents.[102] Such social network analyses can gauge the nature and strength of the bonds between individuals as well as the evolution of such relationships over time.[103] This is particularly helpful in understanding the organization and operation of opposition groups and other nonstate actors that may be structured in unorthodox ways as compared with formal armed forces, although the operative structures of the latter are also in flux.[104] Such information could assist with prevention, by identifying key actors in a conflict zone, and can also explicate potential forms of responsibility. Prosecutions based on ordering offenses, superior responsibility, or acting pursuant to a common purpose, for example, depend on proof of a particular relationship between the

---

98. *See* Gregorios Kalliatakis et al., *GET-AID: Visual Recognition of Human Rights Abuses via Global Emotional Traits*, IEEEAccess (2019). For a discussion of the dangers of this technology, *see* Jane Wakefield, *AI Emotion-Detection Software Tested on Uyghurs*, BBC News (May 26, 2021).

99. *See* Jenny Domino, *Crime as Cognitive Constraint: Facebook's Role in Myanmar's Incitement Landscape and the Promise of International Tort Liability*, 52 Case W. Res. J. Int'l L. 143, 146 (2020).

100. *See* Patrick Ball & Tarak Shaw, *Indexing Selectors from a Collection of Chat Messages*, HRDAG (Apr. 23, 2019), https://hrdag.org/tech-notes/indexing-selectors-from-collection-chat-messages.html (last visited Mar. 14, 2022).

101. *See* Edmund L. Andrews, *Why AI Struggles to Recognize Toxic Speech on Social Media*, Stanford Center for Human-Centered AI (July 13, 2021), https://hai.stanford.edu/news/why-ai-struggles-recognize-toxic-speech-social-media (last visited Mar. 14, 2022).

102. *See* Raúl Valencia, *Artificial Intelligence in Command and Control Systems*, GMV Blog (June 16, 2020).

103. Jennifer Johnson et al., *Social Network Analysis: A Systemic Approach for Investigating*, Law Enforcement Bulletin (Mar. 5, 2013).

104. Michael Piellusch, *Is the "Chain of Command" Still Meaningful*, War Room (Sept. 6, 2018).

defendant and the direct perpetrators and that the defendant had knowledge of the commission of abuses—all of which can be illuminated with the help of Big Data analytics.

D. Conflict Mapping and 3-D Rendering

Big Data can also be utilized to engage in conflict mapping in the sense of reconstructing the chain of events as a conflict unfolds, both chronologically and geographically. Compiling this so-called POLE data (of critical people, objects, locations, and events) can be useful for determining the commencement of the conflict (and thus the applicability of LOAC); conflict classification; the involvement of outside actors; evolving alliances; party strongholds and checkpoints; and the details of particular incidents, including the involvement of potential defendants. Such analyses can pull from a range of open and closed sources (from social media feeds to the output of major media outlets to call records) as well as percipient and expert witness testimony and the insight gleaned from field investigations.[105] Humanitarian Tracker, for example, has been using crowdsourcing and micro-tasking coupled with other open-source information to map the Syrian crisis since March 2011 and assist with the provision of aid.[106] Researchers also conducted a hyper-local assessment of the conflict dynamics in Aleppo, including restraints on humanitarian assistance and the targeting of bakeries as a proxy for attacks on civilian objects.[107] The Center for Information Resilience has launched a Ukraine conflict map.[108]

Using data visualization techniques and connective databases, the information gathered can be displayed graphically any number of ways—including in 3-D renderings—that are much more compelling than traditional testimony or even old-fashioned spreadsheets.[109] Forensic Architecture (FA), a multidisciplinary collective of investigators based at the University of London, has employed

---

105. New evidence protocols have been developed to address the proliferation of digital evidence. *See* Human Rights Center, University of California, Berkeley/UN Office of the High Commissioner for Human Rights, Berkeley Protocol on Digital Open Source Investigations, Dec. 1, 2020 ("Berkeley Protocol").

106. *Syria Tracker*, Humanitarian Tracker, https://www.humanitariantracker.org/syria-tracker (last visited Mar. 14, 2022). For a discussion of their methodology, *see* Taha Kass-Hou et al., *Syria Tracker: Crowdsourcing Crisis Information* (Jan. 5, 2012). The system leverages the Ushahidi platform. *See* Simon Jeffrey, *Ushahidi: Crowdmapping Collective That Exposed Kenyan Election Killings*, The Guardian (Apr. 7, 2011).

107. Caerus, *Mapping the Conflict in Aleppo, Syria* (Feb. 2014).

108. Russia-Ukraine Monitor Map, Cen4infoRes., https://maphub.net/Cen4infoRes/russian-ukraine-monitor (last visited Mar. 14, 2022).

109. *See* Syria Live Map, https://syria.liveuamap.com/en/2021/26-may-russian-warplanes-launched-several-air-strikes-targeting (last visited Mar. 14, 2022).

architectural rendering software to create groundbreaking computer models of putative crime scenes. These can shed light on the circumstances of particular armed attacks on civilians and civilian objects and, where necessary or possible, identify the perpetrators. With respect to the Syrian conflict, FA has recreated the sites of chemical attacks and built a three-dimensional rendition of Saydnaya Prison where detainees have credibly alleged they were tortured.[110] In addition, FA examined the destruction of the Sayidina Omar Ibn Al-Khattab Mosque in Al-Jinah, Syria, which was hit by U.S. air strikes on March 16, 2017. The United States originally insisted that the venue was a community hall where regional members of Al Qaida were meeting on the night in question.[111] Based on a reconstruction of the building prior to the attack and other data, FA concluded that the building was a mosque being used for religious purposes and that 38 congregants were killed. Following these civil society investigations, the United States admitted that the strike had hit part of a "mosque complex" and that "a more deliberative pre-strike analysis should have identified that the target was part of a religious compound," but continued to argue that appropriate precautions were undertaken.[112] The Syrian Commission of Inquiry (COI) disagreed and concluded that although munitions designed to inflict minimal casualties were employed, the United States still "failed to take all feasible precautions to avoid or minimize incidental loss of civilian life, injury to civilians and damage to civilian objects, in violation of international humanitarian law."[113] Incidentally, this conclusion has its detractors, with one set of commentators arguing that the COI applied the wrong legal standard—and had inadequate information—to accurately evaluate the lawfulness of the attack.[114] They cite the *Rendulic* rule developed in World War II in this regard, which dictates that

---

110. Michael Kimmelman, *Forensics Helps Widen Architecture's Mission*, N.Y. TIMES (Apr. 6, 2018); Forensic Architecture, Investigations, https://forensic-architecture.org/location/syria (last visited Mar. 14, 2022). FA has also worked in Eastern Ukraine to demonstrate that Russia was involved in separatist violence prior to the 2023 re-invasion. *See* FA, *The Battle of Ilovaisk: Verifying Russian Military Presence in Eastern Ukraine*, https://forensic-architecture.org/investigation/the-battle-of-ilovaisk# (last visited Mar. 14, 2022).

111. *Al-Jinah Mosque*, Forensic Architecture, https://forensic-architecture.org/investigation/airstrikes-on-the-al-jinah-mosque (last visited Mar. 14, 2022). FA worked in conjunction with Bellₗngcat and Human Rights Watch in this investigation. *See* Bellₗngcat, *The Al-Jinah Mosque Complex Bombing—New Information and Timeline* (Apr. 18, 2017); HUMAN RIGHTS WATCH, ATTACK ON THE OMAR IBN AL-KHATTAB MOSQUE: US AUTHORITIES' FAILURE TO TAKE ADEQUATE PRECAUTIONS (Apr. 18, 2017).

112. *Transcript of Pentagon's Al Jinah Investigation Media Briefing*, AIRWARS (June 27, 2017); Barbara Starr, *Pentagon Investigation: US Hit Mosque Complex in Syria*, CNN (May 5, 2017).

113. Report of the Independent International Commission of Inquiry on the Syrian Arab Republic, U.N. Doc. No. A/HRC/36/55, ¶¶ 52–61 (Aug. 8, 2017).

114. Shane Reeves & Ward Narramore, *The UNHRC Commission of Inquiry on Syria Misapplies the Law of Armed Conflict*, LAWFARE (Sept. 15, 2017), https://www.lawfareblog.com/unhrc-commission-inquiry-syria-misapplies-law-armed-conflict (last visited Mar. 14, 2022). *But see* Adil Ahmad Haque, *A Careless Attack on the UN's Commission of Inquiry on Syria*, JUST SECURITY

the legality of wartime attacks should not be judged by their results but by what the commander reasonably knew at the time the attack was launched.[115]

E. Statistical Analyses

Machine learning allows for in-depth analysis of patterns of behavior and violence (including demographic trends among victims) in Big Data sets, which can be relevant in evaluating the legality of targeting practices or proving the elements of crimes, such as the existence of a widespread or systematic attack against a civilian population, the predicate for a crimes against humanity charge. A quantitative analysis of large target datasets can provide statistical evidence that civilian objects were deliberately attacked rather than merely subject to random collateral harm. Big Data might also operate as a sort of "time machine" to reveal information a commander would have had at their disposal at the time an attack was planned in keeping with the *Rendulic* rule.[116]

The Syrian Archive, for example, has compiled a database of attacks—including air strikes and the use of indiscriminate weapons, such as barrel bombs and chemical weapons—on over 400 medical facilities,[117] many of which are in de-escalation zones or on humanitarian deconfliction/no-strike lists managed by the U.N. Office for the Coordination of Humanitarian Affairs (OCHA).[118] Such targeting datasets can be aggregated with information from other observation tools—such as on-the-ground civilian aircraft observers and remote sensors collecting audio recordings of exchanges between pilots and air traffic controllers—to identify the responsible parties.[119] Following a multidisciplinary investigation, a U.N. board of inquiry concluded that it was highly probable that "the government of Syria or its allies" committed the majority of the hospital attacks examined.[120] Needless-to-say,

---

(Sept. 21, 2017), https://www.justsecurity.org/45213/syria-commission-inquiry/ (last visited Mar. 14, 2022) (defending the COI's conclusions).

115. *See generally* Brian J. Bill, *The Rendulic "Rule": Military Necessity, Commander's Knowledge, and Methods of Warfare*, 12 Y.B. INT'L HUMANITARIAN L. 119 (2009).

116. I am grateful to Carmen Cheung for this observation.

117. *Targeting Health: Attacks Against Medical Facilities in Syria*, SYRIAN ARCHIVE, https://syrianarchive.org/en/datasets/medical-attacks (last visited Mar. 14, 2022).

118. Evan Hill & Whitney Hurst, *The U.N. Tried to Save Hospitals in Syria. It Didn't Work*, N.Y. TIMES (Dec. 29, 2019).

119. Evan Hill et al., *Russia Bombed Four Syrian Hospitals. We Have Proof*, N.Y. TIMES (Oct. 13, 2019).

120. The full report is confidential, but a summary was presented to the U.N. Security Council. *See Summary by the Secretary-General of the report of the United Nations Headquarters Board of Inquiry into certain incidents in northwest Syria since 17 September 2018 involving facilities on the United Nations deconfliction list and United Nations supported facilities* (Apr. 6, 2020),

a standard of "high probability," while potentially appropriate for setting policy or imposing sanctions, would be insufficient to convict in a criminal proceeding. But it could shape a prosecutor's investigative trajectory and contribute to a conviction when combined with utterances from the defendant, forensic investigations, witness testimony, and other corroborating evidence.

Big Data invites the utilization of statistical analytical techniques to draw conclusions from information gathered, which can also—perhaps paradoxically—shed light on the prevalence of undocumented events. For example, the Human Rights Data Analysis Group (HRDAG) analyzed data—using human review coupled with computer probability modeling—from the collections of multiple documentation organizations and other information streams to determine the number of conflict-related deaths in Syria.[121] In their investigation of deaths in detention, HRDAG deduplicated existing databases and linked multiple records that referred to the same victim. They were able to estimate the number of missing records using multiple systems estimations (MSE), a technique developed to generate estimates about difficult-to-observe populations by forming statistical inferences from the overlap between incomplete or convenience samples.[122] Mortality data premised on ethnicity, gender, and race can reveal relevant trends for proving the commission of crimes against humanity or genocide,[123] including the *chapeau* elements of such crimes.[124] An exclusive focus on lethal violence,

https://www.un.org/sg/sites/www.un.org.sg/files/atoms/files/NWS_BOI_Summary_06_April_2020.pdf. The board only focused on seven incidents, generating criticism for being too limited in scope.

121. The Office of the High Commission for Human Rights contracted with HRDAG to estimate the number of conflict-related deaths (including of combatants) in Syria by collating information gleaned from multiple governmental and non-governmental documentation organizations. *See* Megan Price et al., *Updated Statistical Analysis of Documentation of Killings in the Syrian Arab Republic* (Aug. 2014).

122. Convenience samples are non-random or non-representative samples that are selected for their ease of compilation and analysis. *See* Anita Gohdes, *Different Convenience Samples, Different Stories: The Case of Sierra Leone*, BENETECH (Apr. 6, 2010) (revealing discrepancies in the violations recorded between three data sources covering the same period of time). *See* Megan Price et al., *Technical Memo for Amnesty International Report on Deaths in Detention* (Aug. 18, 2016).

123. *See* Patrick Ball & Megan Price, *Using Statistics to Assess Lethal Violence in Civil and Inter-State War*, 6 ANNUAL REV. STATISTICS & ITS APPLICATION 63 (2019). HRDAG utilized similar techniques in Latin America (and elsewhere) to analyze multiple datasets and link senior government figures to particular war crimes committed during the region's "dirty wars." *See* Mark Leon Goldberg, *How Big Data Can Put War Criminals Behind Bars*, UN DISPATCH (Mar. 17, 2014).

124. The *chapeau* elements of genocide, for example, require evidence of violence against a racial, ethnic, religious, or national group; by contrast, proving crimes against humanity only requires a showing of an attack against any civilian population. Göran Sluiter, "Chapeau Elements" *of Crimes Against Humanity in the Jurisprudence of the UN Ad Hoc Tribunals, in* FORGING A CONVENTION FOR CRIMES AGAINST HUMANITY 102 (Leila Sadat ed., 2011).

however, will divert attention from other potential war crimes, such as torture, sexual violence, or even disappearances where the victim's death cannot be definitively proven (often by design).[125] And, it may be difficult to fully understand the dynamics of conflict-related violence if no record of baseline levels and patterns of violence are available as a comparison in a particular society.[126]

So far, although machines can be trained to analyze large quantities of targeting data, tribunals have struggled to develop the kind of objective metrics that would enable a machine to definitively determine liability for indiscriminate, no less disproportionate, attacks under LOAC. A Trial Chamber of the International Criminal Tribunal for the former Yugoslavia (ICTY) generated controversy in connection with its analysis of artillery targeting decisions during Operation Storm, a sustained assault by Croatian forces aimed at retaking the Serb-held Krajina region in the summer of 1995.[127] A guilty verdict against Lieutenant General Ante Gotovina was premised on a finding that although all of the objects placed under attack were proper military objectives, just under 5% of artillery shells fell outside a 200-meter radius of error. From this, the Trial Chamber concluded that his forces made civilians the direct object of attack or that the attacks were criminally indiscriminate.[128] This singular finding undergirded the Trial Chamber's conviction for war crimes and crimes against humanity. In one of only a few opinions addressed to the means and methods of warfare, the Appeals Chamber ultimately reversed, ruling that the Trial Chamber did not adequately justify the basis on which it arrived at this margin of error.[129]

IV. BIG DATA IN COURT

The results of Big Data-enabled analyses, such as conflict mapping and 3D rendering, are already being admitted into evidence in legal proceedings.[130] For

125. Yvonne McDermott et al., *Open Source Information's Blind Spot*, 19 J. Int'l Crim. Justice 85, 93 (2021).

126. Aronson, *supra* note 54, at 447.

127. *See generally* Beth Van Schaack, *ICTY Appeal & U.S. Suit Review Operation Storm*, IntLawGrrls (Aug. 13, 2011); Laurie R. Blank, *Operational Law Experts Roundtable on the Gotovina Judgment: Military Operations, Battlefield Reality and the Judgment's Impact on Effective Implementation and Enforcement of International Humanitarian Law* (Jan. 28, 2012), Emory Public Law Research Paper No. 12-186, https://ssrn.com/abstract=1994414 or http://dx.doi.org/10.2139/ssrn.1994414 (last visited Mar. 14, 2022).

128. Prosecutor v. Gotovina et al., Case No, IT-06-90-T, Judgement (Apr. 15, 2011).

129. Prosecutor v. Gotovina, Case No. IT-06-90-A, Judgement, ¶ 58–61 (Nov. 16, 2012).

130. An early example occurred in the Special Court for Sierra Leone. *See* Prosecutor v. Norman et al., Case No. SCSL-040140t, Decision on Prosecution's Request to Admit into Evidence Certain Documents Pursuant to Rules 92bis and 89(C) (July 14, 2005) (admitting conflict map prepared by No Peace Without Justice).

example, in a legal challenge to the United Kingdom's weapons sales to Saudi Arabia, NESTA is using machine learning to pinpoint incriminating footage of Yemeni airstrikes and cluster munitions use from all potentially relevant videos uploaded onto YouTube.[131] Likewise, the International Criminal Court employed an interactive spaciotemporal dashboard created by SITU Research to explicate the destruction of ancient mausoleums deemed "idolatrous" by Ansar Dine groups in the war crimes case against Ahmad Al Faqi Al Mahdi.[132] Prior to the current crisis in Ukraine, similar efforts were underway to reconstruct the 2014 Euromaidan protests in Ukraine and the ensuing government crackdown, the subject of an ICC investigation as well as domestic legal proceedings.[133] Because these efforts reside on the cutting edge, it remains to be seen whether they will contribute meaningfully to accountability before these various judicial forums. When it comes to the commission of international crimes in Syria, there are no prospects for an international tribunal to systematically adjudicate those responsible; as such, much of this work remains limited to advocacy purposes and domestic proceedings.

V. CONCLUSION

The data ecosystem of modern conflicts is complex, but it yields intriguing possibilities for Big Data applications and tech-enabled analysis in accountability processes. Big Data can be harnessed for lead and background purposes, to corroborate other evidence, to prove particular evidentiary points, to corroborate or impeach witnesses, to track fugitives, and even to establish the elements of war crimes charges levied against a particular defendant. However, it will likely never replace traditional criminal investigations or sources of evidence, including the testimony of witnesses—the soft underbelly of any war crimes prosecution. As such, there is an enduring need to keep humans "in the loop" in this wartime context as well.[134]

At the same time, investigators must understand, and account for, the enduring limitations of Big Data in their work. Besides the inherent challenges posed by

---

131. *See Documenting Mass Human Rights Violations Through Collective Intelligence*, https://www.nesta.org.uk/feature/collective-intelligence-grants/documenting-mass-human-rights-violations-through-collective-intelligence/; Dearbhla Minogue & Ruwandzano Makumbe, *Digital Accountability Symposium: Harnessing User Generated Content in Accountability Efforts for International Law Violations in Yemen*, OPINIO JURIS (Dec. 18, 2019).

132. *See* http://icc-mali.situplatform.com/.

133. *See* SITU/Research, Euromaidan Event Reconstruction, https://situ.nyc/research/projects/euromaidan-event-reconstruction. The current conflict is the subject of an investigation as well following the referral of the situation by over 40 states.

134. Robert Mazzolin, *Artificial Intelligence and Keeping Humans "in the Loop*," CENTER FOR INTERNATIONAL GOVERNANCE INNOVATION (Nov. 23, 2020).

the four v's, investigators and prosecutors must contend with incomplete data, informational and observational biases, and dis-information campaigns.[135] In addition, many legal actors do not have access to the technological tools, expertise, or computational power to fully exploit the Big Data that is available, and judges are often hesitant to adopt new evidentiary approaches.[136]

This chapter has focused on some potentially beneficial use cases for preventing harm and advancing LOAC accountability; it remains to be seen if these positive effects are eclipsed by negative externalities. In addition, most of the discussion in this chapter refers to descriptive or diagnostic analytics. We are not yet at the point of having the necessary historical data to fully exploit predictive algorithms to anticipate where war crimes are likely to occur[137] or anticipate how a court will rule on any particular evidentiary matrix.[138] But there is no question that Big Data has the potential to enhance accountability processes and contribute to the enforcement of LOAC.

* * *

135. *See* Megan Price & Patrick Ball, *The Limits of Observation for Understanding Mass Violence*, 30 CANADIAN J. LAW & SOC'Y 237, 239 (2015).

136. Amelia Hoover Green, *Learning the Hard Way at the ICTY: Statistical Evidence of Human Rights Violations in an Adversarial Information Environment*, *in* COLLECTIVE VIOLENCE AND INTERNATIONAL CRIMINAL JUSTICE—AN INTERDISCIPLINARY APPROACH 325 (Alette Smeulers ed., 2010) (discussing the ICTY's rejection of statistical evidence and expert testimony).

137. Indeed, predictive policing in the domestic realm remains controversial, in part because it is based upon algorithms premised on near-repeat modeling (the idea that once a crime occurs in one location, the immediate surroundings are at risk), which can perpetuate discriminatory patterns and miss other risk factors. Brayne, *supra* note 9, at 296. *See generally* Leda Tortura et al., *Neuroprediction and A.I. in Forensic Psychiatry and Criminal Justice: A Neurolaw Perspective*, 11 FRONTIERS IN PSYCHOLOGY (2020).

138. *But see* Masha Medvedeva et al., *Using Machine Learning to Predict Decisions of the European Court of Human Rights*, ARTIFICIAL INTELLIGENCE & THE LAW 237, 248 (2020).

PART FOUR

International Human Rights Law

12

The Datafication
of Counterterrorism

FIONNUALA NÍ AOLÁIN* ∎

Counterterrorism practices, institutions, and discourses have deepened and expanded over the past 20 years. This enlargement has come with extraordinary costs for international law's integrity and traction especially revealed in the pushback against the classification and regulation of non-international armed conflicts under a laws of war framework. There are particularly adverse consequences for the integrity of human rights and humanitarian law norms because the institutional and political interests represented by counterterrorism seek to displace these norms and reclaim complex conflict and fragile space as primarily subject to exceptional and nationally defined counterterrorism legal regimes.

To state the obvious, states frequently undertake counterterrorism measures and operations in the context of armed conflict where international humanitarian law applies. This reality is further illustrated by the number of non-international armed conflicts involving nonstate armed groups subject to United Nations terrorist designation and targeted sanctions regimes including on regional and national terrorist sanctions lists.[1] But beyond evident sites of contested low-intensity armed conflict, counterterrorism practice is increasingly intermeshed with authoritarian and repressive governance in multiple countries, and its tools,

---

* Regents Professor and Robina Chair in Law, Public Policy and Society University of Minnesota Law School and Professor of Law, The Queens University of Belfast, Northern Ireland. Thanks to Marine Loison for research assistance. All opinions and errors in this article are the responsibility of the author.

1. Position of the UN Special Rapporteur on the Promotion and Protection of Human Rights and Fundamental Freedoms while Countering Terrorism on the Human Rights and Rule of Law Implications of the United Nations Security Council Counter-terrorism Sanctions Regimes, OHCHR (2021), https://www.ohchr.org/sites/default/files/2021-11/position-paper-unsrct-on-unsc-use-of-ct-targeted-sanctions.pdf

Fionnuala Ní Aoláin, *The Datafication of Counterterrorism* In: *Big Data and Armed Conflict*. Edited by: Laura A. Dickinson and Edward W. Berg, Oxford University Press. © Fionnuala Ní Aoláin 2024. DOI: 10.1093/oso/9780197668610.003.0014

including new technologies and data collection, are in expanded use by counter-terrorism actors and institutions to fight State classified "terrorists" and "terrorist groups."[2]

In line with this expansionist and securitizing trend there is an evidenced tendency to consider any act of violence carried out by a nonstate armed group in a non-international armed conflict (NIAC) as being "terrorist" by definition, sidestepping assessment of lawfulness under IHL as well as the addressing of the legal and political significance of internal armed conflicts on the territories of States. Such practices have gone hand in hand with expansive militarism and security sector bloating justified by counterterrorism discourses and Security Council regulation.[3] Counterterrorism efforts are accompanied by a rhetoric including, but not limited to, the now maligned terminology of a "war on terror" that deliberately conflates armed conflict and terrorism as a means to weaken the application of both IHL and IHRL norms. The qualifier of "terrorism," which should be applied to the most serious and violent acts defined by treaty law, has regrettably been embraced with enthusiasm to legitimize a range of State action placed in the counterterrorism frame, in some contexts precisely, it would appear, to justify the exclusion of the protective norms of both international humanitarian law and international human rights law. These political moves have downstream and specific effects on the protection of individuals, and ultimately on the protection of group and individual rights.[4]

Over the past two decades of post 9/11 global counterterrorism regulation, several patterns in State responses to terrorism have emerged. These patterns represent sizable legal and institutional modifications at the United Nations and beyond, many of which impact the application of human rights and humanitarian law norms. They include the establishment of a supranational global counterterrorism architecture to regulate and support state responses to perceived terrorism threats.[5] Parts of this architecture are increasingly laying claim to interpretive

---

2. Human Rights Council, U.N. Doc A/HRC/43/45/Add.1 (Jan. 2, 2020); Human Rights Council, U.N. Doc A/HRC/40/52/Add.2 (Dec. 13, 2018); Human Rights Council, U.N. Doc A/HRC/40/52/Add.3 (Dec. 14, 2018).

3. Conference Report, *International Committee of the Red Cross, International Humanitarian Law and the Challenges of Contemporary Armed Conflict*, ICRC 17 (Oct. 31, 2015). Noting that the expansion of counter-terrorism norms, in parallel with under-enforcement of IHL norms has *inter alia* contributed to this impasse. *Id.*; Ornella Moderan, Habibou Souley Bako & Paul-Simon Handy, *Sahel Counter-Terrorism Takes a Heavy Toll on Civilians*, Inst. for Security Studies (Apr. 14, 2021).

4. *See, e.g., UN Experts Urge Indian Authorities to Stop Targeting Kashmiri Human Rights Defender Khurram Parvez and Release him Immediately*, OHCHR (Dec. 22, 2021).

5. The International Federation for Human Rights, *The United Nations Counter-Terrorism Complex, Bureaucracy, Political Influence and Civil Liberties*, Int'l Fed'n for Human Rights (Sept. 26, 2017), https://www.fidh.org/IMG/pdf/9.25_fidh_final_compressed.pdf; Ali Altiok & Jordan Street, *A Fourth Pillar for the United Nations?*, Saferworld (June 2020); Fionnuala Ní Aoláin, *How Can States Counter Terrorism While Protecting Human Rights?*, 45 Ohio N.U. L. Rev. 389 (2019); Fionnuala Ní Aoláin (Special Rapporteur on the Promotion and Protection

authority over international humanitarian law, agitating to cede classification of conflict status to political bodies charged with giving counterterrorism advice to states.[6] Concurrently, another trend is an elevated role for the Security Council legislating to prompt and support national and regional regulation of terrorism including express regulation on new technologies (where metadata collection is integral to counterterrorism action).[7] A third trend is the emergence of "soft law" as a dominant modality for states to regulate terrorism.[8] "Soft law" is formally non-binding on States but in the counterterrorism realm, "soft" standards including principles, toolkits, and guidance function as "hard" in practice and are frequently adopted by States at the expense of binding IHL norms. The interface of counterterrorism and new data-based technologies is significantly operationalized by standard setting that does not conform to traditional international law modalities.[9] Such new norm making is human rights and humanitarian law "lite" by design. Fourth is the overarching way in which new regional

of Human Rights and Fundamental Freedoms while Countering Terrorism), *Promotion and Protection of Human Rights and Fundamental Freedoms while Countering Terrorism*, U.N. Doc. A/74/335 (Aug. 29, 2019) [hereinafter A/74/335 (2019)]; Fionnuala Ní Aoláin (Special Rapporteur on the Promotion and Protection of Human Rights and Fundamental Freedoms while Countering Terrorism), U.N. Doc. A/75/337 (Sept. 3, 2020) [hereinafter A/75/337 (2020)].

6. Annabelle Bonnefront, Agathe Sarfati & Jason Ipe, *Continuity Amid Change: The 2021 Mandate Renewal of the UN Counter-Terrorism Committee Executive Directorate*, GLOB. CTR. ON COOP. SEC. (Nov. 2021), https://www.globalcenter.org/publications/continuity-amid-cha nge-the-2021-mandate-renewal-of-the-un-counter-terrorism-committee-executive-director ate; S.C. Res. 2617 (Dec. 30, 2021).

7. *See generally* S.C. Res. 1267 (1999); S.C. Res. 1333 (Dec. 19, 2000); S.C. Res. 1363 (July 30, 2001); S.C. Res. 1373 (Sept. 28, 2001); S.C. Res. 1455 (Jan. 17, 2003); S.C. Res. 1526 (Jan. 30, 2004); S.C. Res. 1535 (Mar. 26, 2004); S.C. Res. 1540 (Apr. 28, 2004), S.C. Res 1566 (Oct. 8, 2004) and S.C. Res. 1617 (July 29, 2005); S.C. Res. 1618 (Aug. 4, 2005); S.C. Res. 1624 (Sept, 14, 2005); S.C. Res. 1699 (Aug. 8, 2006); S.C. Res. 1735 (Dec. 22, 2006); S.C. Res 1822 (June 30, 2008); S.C. Res. 1904 (Dec. 17, 2009); S.C. Res. 1988 (June 17, 2011); S.C. Res. 1989 (June 17, 2011); S.C Res. 2082 (Dec. 17, 2012); S.C. Res. 2083 (Dec. 17, 2012); S.C. Res. 2160 (June 17, 2004); S.C. Res. 2161 (June 17, 2014); S.C. Res. 2253 (Dec. 17, 2015); S.C. Res. 2255 (Dec. 22, 2015); S.C. Res. 2322 (Dec. 12, 2006); S.C. Res. 2368 (July 20, 2017); S.C. Res. 2462 (Mar. 28, 2019); S.C. Res. 2482 (July 19, 2019); S.C. Res. 2501 (Dec. 16, 2019); S.C. Res. 2557 (Dec. 18, 2020); S.C. Res. 2560 (Dec. 29, 2020).

8. Fionnuala Ní Aoláin, *"Soft Law," and "New" Institutions in the Global Counter-Terrorism Architecture*, EUROPEAN J. INT'L L. 1–23 (2021).

9. Fionnuala Ní Aoláin, *The New UN Security Council, Global Watchlists, Biometrics and the Threat to the Rule of Law*, JUST SECURITY (Jan. 17, 2018), https://www.justsecurity.org/51075/ security-council-global-watch-lists-biometrics/; Krisztina Huszti-Orbán & Fionnuala Ní Aoláin, *Use of Biometric Data to Identify Terrorists: Best Practice or Risky Business?* U. MINN. L. SCH. HUM. RIGHTS. CTR. (2020), https://law.umn.edu/sites/law.umn.edu/files/2020/07/21/ hrc-biometrics-report-july2020.pdf; *International Expert Group Meeting on Vulnerable Targets and Unmanned Aircraft Systems*, UNITED NATIONS OFFICE OF COUNTER-TERRORISM (2021), https://www.un.org/counterterrorism/events/international-expert-group-meeting-vulnerable-targets-and-unmanned-aircraft-systems.

and global counterterrorism institutions function outside the traditional multilateral system supporting and enabling state freedom of action in counterterrorism and extremism action including by enabling a permissive environment for metadata collection and the new technologies that rely on them.[10] The ascendency of counterterrorism constricts and limits the scope of application for both human rights and humanitarian law and is being peddled in some extremes as a competitive alternative to regulate situations of non-international armed conflict. Fifth is the expanded scope of counterterrorism as the preferred framework of action for States to address complex conflict situations evidenced by the ouster of impartial humanitarian action, the wide-ranging application of countering terrorist finance rules to conflict sites, the unwillingness to apply either human rights or IHL standards to detention practices, and the labeling of all acts of violence even those directed at military targets in conflict contexts as acts of terrorism.[11] Sixth, in numerous conflict sites that may meet NIAC classification, there has been a displacement of "boots on the ground" for "drones in the air" as a preferred means to disrupt and kill persons alleged to be terrorists bypassing conflict status assessment.[12] Finally, across all these trends has been the linear if slow development of coordination and cooperation between States, particularly States that did not traditionally cooperate on security challenges, as a means to enhance global counterterrorism action.[13] These shifts have been glacier-like, lurking behind the

10. *See* discussion on the Global Terrorism Forum. A/74/335 (2019); *Generation of Law through Silence: The Global Counterterrorism Forum and Its Good Practices,* SAFERWORLD (July 2021), https://www.saferworld.org.uk/resources/publications/1357-generation-of-law-through-sile nce-the-global-counterterrorism-forum-and-its-good-practices; Alejandro Rodiles, *Coalitions of the Willing in Context: The Interplay between Formality and Informality,* in COALITIONS OF THE WILLING AND INTERNATIONAL LAW: THE INTERPLAY BETWEEN FORMALITY AND INFORMALITY 148–209 (2018).

11. *See* A/75/337 (2020), *supra* note 5.

12. *US Military Admits Killed Civilian in Yemen After NGO Investigations, But Refuses to Provide Remedy,* MWATANA FOR HUMAN RIGHTS (June 3, 2021), https://mwatana.org/en/us-military-admits-killed-civilian-in-yemen.

13. A/74/335 (2019), *supra* note 5, ¶11. S.C. Res. 1373 (2001) ("Calling on States to work together urgently to prevent and suppress terrorist acts, including through increased cooperation and full implementation of the relevant international conventions relating to terrorism, recognizing the need for States to complement international cooperation by taking additional measures to prevent and suppress, in their territories through all lawful means, the financing and preparation of any acts of terrorism."); S.C. Res. 1456, ¶ 4 (Jan. 20, 2003) ("The Counter-Terrorism Committee must intensify its efforts to promote the implementation by Member States of all aspects of resolution 1373 (2001), in particular through reviewing States' reports and facilitating international assistance and cooperation, and through continuing to operate in a transparent and effective manner."); S.C. Res. 1566, ¶¶ 5-6 (Oct. 8, 2004) ("Calls upon Member States to cooperate fully on an expedited basis in resolving all outstanding issues with a view to adopting by consensus the draft comprehensive convention on international terrorism and the draft international convention for the suppression of acts of nuclear terrorism; 6. Calls upon relevant international, regional and subregional organizations to strengthen international cooperation

now abandoned rhetoric of a "war on terror"[14] but have redefined legal and political landscapes from counterterrorism as exceptional regulation into counterterrorism practice as embedded into the regular laws and practices of States at multiple levels. These institutional and normative shifts frame the analysis in this chapter, which is focused on the central role new technologies play in counterterrorism. Specifically, I address the ways in which data collection has enabled new modalities of counterterrorism action with significant consequences for the regulation of non-international armed conflicts as well as the protection of individual and group rights.

This chapter asserts that the costs of counterterrorism expansion in the past two decades have been manifold. They include fueling new cycles of conflict by failing to address the underlying conditions conducive to the production of violence in multiple sites;[15] the systematic and pervasive misuse of counterterrorism measures against civil society actors, minorities, political oppositions, and human rights defenders in multiple countries leading to sustained human rights violations;[16] the consolidation of corruption in bloated security sectors supported by counterterrorism based technical assistance and capacity building;[17] and pervasive impunity for serious violations of international law including war crimes and crimes against humanity by States that have used counterterrorism measures in situations of armed conflict without regard to their international

in the fight against terrorism and to intensify their interaction with the United Nations and, in particular, the CTC with a view to facilitating full and timely implementation of resolution 1373 (2001)."); S.C. Res. 1631 (Oct. 17, 2005); S.C. Res. 2178 (Sept. 24, 2014) (requiring States to address the threat of foreign terrorist fighters); S.C. Res. 2185 (calling for increased sharing of information between Member States); S.C. Res. 2220 (May 22, 2015) (urging heightened cooperation to address illicit transfer of small arms); S.C. Res. 2309 (Sept. 22, 2016) (calling for closer collaboration to prevent terrorist attacks).

14. George W. Bush, President, Address to the Nation (Sept. 12, 2001).

15. United Nations Development Programme, *Journey to Extremism in Africa: Drivers, Incentive and the Tipping Point for Recruitment*, UNDP (2017), https://journey-to-extremism.undp.org/content/downloads/UNDP-JourneyToExtremism-report-2017-english.pdf; Olivier Guiryanan, Lucia Montanaro & Tuuli Räty, *European Security Assistance: The Search for Stability in the Sahel*, SAFERWORLD (Sept. 2021), https://www.saferworld.org.uk/resources/publications/1368-european-security-assistance-the-search-for-stability-in-the-sahel.

16. Fionnuala Ní Aoláin (Special Rapporteur on the Promotion and Protection of Human Rights and Fundamental Freedoms while Countering Terrorism), *Report of the Special Rapporteur on the Promotion and Protection of Human Rights and Fundamental Freedoms while Countering Terrorism on the Role of Measures to Address Terrorism and Violent Extremism on Closing Civic Space and Violating the Rights of Civil Society Actors and Human Rights Defenders*, U.N. Doc. A/HRC/40/52 (Feb. 18, 2019).

17. Fionnuala Ní Aoláin, (Special Rapporteur on the Promotion and Protection of Human Rights and Fundamental Freedoms while Countering Terrorism), *Promotion and Protection of Human Rights and Fundamental Freedoms while Countering Terrorism*, U.N. Doc A/76/261 (Aug. 3, 2021).

law obligations. Counterterrorism's trajectory is like the "Pac-Man" action chase video game, in which an eponymous character eats up all around her without distinction. Ascendant counterterrorism is similarly devouring human rights and humanitarian law frameworks, leaving conflict sites vulnerable to a legal framework that operates in the vacuum of non-consensus on what constitutes terrorism, and producing both an accountability and regulatory deficit with abysmal consequences.

With these cautions to the fore, the chapter turns to address the ways in which counterterrorism practice is moving to deploy new technologies from artificial intelligence, to biometrics, to dynamic databases, which extend and entrench the patterns of harm and impunity defining the post 9/11 counterterrorism landscape. New technology deployment opens new vistas of harm, consolidates existing patterns of concern, and pervasively operates in legal gray zones. Furthermore, metadata collection is spawning the datafication of counterterrorism and the central role technology plays in consolidating its practices and institutions.

This chapter proceeds in three parts. Section 1 addresses the broader expanding landscape of counterterrorism regulation and notes the ways in which this inflating terrain is having downstream and negative effects on IHL and IHRL application. Section 2 addresses new technologies and their increased centrality to counterterrorism efforts, with a particular emphasis on data collection. Section 3 warns about the normalization of new technologies justified on the basis of exceptionalism in the counterterrorism context and expanded data collection practices in counterterrorism contexts from both a rights and security perspective. The chapter identifies the problems that arise for human rights and humanitarian law as datafication in counterterrorism contexts drives practices of counterterrorism response on the ground.

I. THE EVOLVING LANDSCAPE OF COUNTERTERRORISM AND ITS IMPACT ON IHL AND IHRL

As the ash continued to billow around the ruins of the Twin Towers, President George W. Bush declared, "Either you are with us or you are with the terrorists."[18] Governments quickly adopted and mainstreamed the nomenclature of a "global war on terror,"[19] the "war" paradigm was embraced and endures to manage terrorism threats, torture memos were produced,[20] torture was then widely and egregiously

---

18. *Text: President Bush Addresses the Nation,* WASH. POST. (Sept. 20, 2001), https://www.was hingtonpost.com/wp-srv/nation/specials/attacked/transcripts/bushaddress_092001.html.

19. *Id.*

20. ANTHONY LEWIS, THE TORTURE PAPERS: THE ROAD TO ABU GHRAIB (Karen J. Greenberg & Joshua L. Dratel eds., 2005).

practiced,[21] individuals were rendered across borders,[22] a detention camp was established in Guantanamo Bay, Cuba,[23] military commissions were established,[24] surveillance expanded,[25] ethnic and religious profiling was magnified,[26] and the assault on civil liberties and human rights righteously led by the United States appeared to be comprehensive and unstoppable.[27] Embedded in egregious human rights harms were more subtle practices, including the creeping reliance on new technologies and data collection to ground and enable the infliction of military-based responses and the paradigm of countering terrorism in warlike mode. Information collection, use, sharing, and storage would be a central if largely unseen plank of the counterterrorism agenda. The long-term costs of a military-led human rights "lite" response to the terrorist attacks of 9/11 have yet to be fully counted in terms of the degradation of the rule of law within the United States. Moreover, the broader codependencies it established, with the production of the conditions conducive for further violence in fragile and conflict setting, are under-mapped.[28]

As the U.S. domestic response to counterterrorism was entrenching, an international counterterrorism architecture was emerging and consolidating. Its focal point was initially at the United Nations, spearheaded by the newly established Counter-Terrorism Committee, and supported by a special political mission the Counter-Terrorism Executive Directorate.[29] In parallel, an expansion of counterterrorism

21. S. REP. NO. 113-288 (2014).

22. Human Rights Council, *Promotion and Protection of all Human Rights, Civil, Political, Economic, Social and Cultural Rights, Including the Right to Development*, A/HRC/13/42 (Feb. 19, 2010).

23. Archive of Columns by Carol Rosenberg, N.Y. TIMES, https://www.nytimes.com/by/carol-rosenberg (last visited Nov. 12, 2021).

24. Office of Military Commissions, https://www.mc.mil, (last visited Nov. 12, 2021). The Military Commissions Act of 2006, HR-6166, Oct. 17, 2006. https://www.mc.mil/ABOUTUS/USCMCRHistory.aspx).

25. *Surveillance Under the Patriot Act*, ACLU, https://www.aclu.org/issues/national-security/privacy-and-surveillance/surveillance-under-patriot-act (last visited Nov. 12, 2021).

26. *Sanctioned Bias: Racial Profiling Since 9/11*, ACLU (Feb. 2004), https://www.aclu.org/sites/default/files/FilesPDFs/racial%20profiling%20report.pdf.

27. RICK ABEL, LAW'S WARS: THE FATE OF THE RULE OF LAW IN THE US "WAR ON TERROR" (2018).

28. *See generally* Mike Nelson, *It Was the Best of Coin, It Was the Worst of Coin: A Tale of Two Surges*, MOD. WAR INST. (June 24, 2021), https://mwi.usma.edu/it-was-the-best-of-coin-it-was-the-worst-of-coin-a-tale-of-two-surges; Beth Daley, *Is the U.S. Military Strategy Doing More Harm or Good in the Middle East?*, THE CONVERSATION (May 12, 2016); Christopher P. Freeman, *Dissonant Discourse: Forging Islamist States through Secular Models: The Case of Afghanistan*, 15 CAMBRIDGE REV. INT'L AFFAIRS 533 (2002); Richard L. Armitage, Samuel R. Berger & Daniel D. Markey, *U.S. Strategy for Pakistan and Afghanistan*, COUNCIL ON FOREIGN RELATIONS (2010), https://ciaotest.cc.columbia.edu/wps/cfr/0020267/f_0020267_17141.pdf.

29. Naz K. Modirzadeh, *The Dark Sides of Convergence: A Pro-Civilian Critique of the Extraterritorial Application of Human Rights Law in Armed Conflict*, HARV. HUMANITARIAN INITIATIVE (2010).

coordination and support from the General Assembly involved the creation of a body called The Counter-Terrorism Implementation Task Force (CTITF), now reconstructed as the United Nations Office of Counter-Terrorism.[30] The consolidation of the existing institutional setting in 2017 led to an increasingly complex United Nations counterterrorism architecture, now bound together through the Global Counter-Terrorism Coordination Compact, which comprises 44 member entities. The compact engages in significant counterterrorism capacity building and assistance. This assistance has many facets but importantly provides, supports, or enhances the use of new technologies for Member States in the counterterrorism arena.[31] The UN architecture is also in the data business, because its office of Counter-Terrorism is providing ever-growing capacity building and technical assistance to States to help them datify their responses to perceived terrorism threats. In parallel, the oversight role played by the United Nations Counter-Terrorism Committee Executive Directorate (UNCTED), in relying on the UN Security Council's support for data collection, sharing and use (insofar as observes can assess publicly as only one country assessment since 2006 has been made public), falls far short of a robust human rights response to widespread adoption and misuse of data tools in national settings. This is particularly the case for widespread metadata collection, as intelligence and security sectors are increasingly adopting and using spyware surveillance against civil society, journalists[32] and dissenters.

In parallel, outside the United Nations, the global counterterrorism architecture was deepening and embedding itself within Member States or groups of Member States. A variety of offshoots and decentralized initiatives of diverging forms have emerged, some utilitarian and functional, undertaking work that States prefer to remove from the United Nations umbrella; others are more aptly described as profile-raising projects, with the aim of raising the status of a particular State or

---

30. United Nations Office of Counter-Terrorism, *About Us,* https://www.un.org/counterterrorism/about (last visited Nov. 12, 2021).

31. General Assembly, *Review of the Functioning of the Reinvigorated Resident Coordinator System, Including its Funding Arrangement.* U.N. Doc. A/76/XXX (Oct. 7, 2021); *see, e.g.,* The October 6 and 7th, 2021 International Expert Group Meeting on the Protection of Vulnerable Targets and Unmanned Aircraft Systems is poised to examine the role of unmanned aircraft systems to protect critical infrastructure in the context of multiple Security Council resolutions. While it is undisputed that the United Nations Global Counter-Terrorism Strategy highlights the need for Member States to improve security and protection of vulnerable targets, including "soft targets" and critical infrastructure (including its seventh review resolution A/RES/75/291, PP and OPs 69, 71, 73, 74) and United Nations Security Council Resolution 2396 (2017) stresses the need for Member States to develop, review or amend national risk and threat assessments to consider "soft targets," and to develop appropriate contingency and emergency response plans for terrorist attacks it is not clear that the deployment of new technologies is the necessary solution to the problem identified. *International Expert Group Meeting on Vulnerable Targets and Unmanned Aircraft Systems, supra* note 9.

32. *Cf.* Pegasus used to Target El Salvador Activists, Journalists: Report, ALJAZEERA (Jan. 13, 2022), https://www.aljazeera.com/news/2022/1/13/pegasus-spyware-used-to-target-el-salvador-activists-journalists-report.

The Datafication of Counterterrorism

group of States by association with a leading role in countering and preventing terrorism; and some are best viewed as the solidification of existing pathways to norm creation, monitoring, capacity building, and oversight. In addition to State-centered initiatives, the landscape is augmented by public-private partnerships, such as Tech Against Terrorism[33] or institutions modeled after the Global Counterterrorism Forum. These initiatives reflect the increasingly crucial role of the private sector in the area of counterterrorism. They underscore the priority given to intersectoral cooperation in effectively tackling related threats absent a legal set of binding international law standards to give the cooperative enterprise. While there are many interfaces between the private and public sectors in counterterrorism, processes that enable, support, and provide the means to undertake data collection may be the most significant from a human rights standpoint. The privatization of counterterrorism data collection remains largely out of public view but underscores the underregulated nature of counterterrorism data work and its invisibility in practice to both human rights and humanitarian law oversight.

It is important to understand this institutional landscape in order to comprehend the shifting regulatory terrain of counterterrorism. The spaces and alliances described above operate as expanders of legal capacity. They view their roles as "service"-oriented, to enable states to tackle counterterrorism in new and innovative ways and provide important nodal points for cooperation and intersection for States. It is precisely these assemblages,[34] these pathways and configurations of public and private actors, that give counter-terrorism norms and practices, even when they appear to be legally 'soft' in form, their fluidity and quick adoption capacity. It is precisely the malleability of these norms that makes them so attractive to States and which has made counterterrorism regulation preferable over the perceived rigidity of human rights and humanitarian law. The shifts to a counterterrorism framing are not merely rhetorical but result in practical downgrading of IHL as the relevant legal framework. In sites where armed conflict is present but states view the rules on such matters as impartial humanitarian access, status of combatants and detainee treatment as overly constraining counterterrorism is a more palatable and manipulable frame of legal and political action.[35]

---

33. Tech Against Terrorism is a public-private partnership initiated by the Counter-Terrorism Committee Executive Directorate and the ICT4Peace Foundation and referenced in Security Council resolutions 2395 (2017) and 2396 (2017). *See* Tech Against Terrorism, *Project Background,* TECH. AGAINST TERRORISM, https://www.techagainstterrorism.org/project-bac kground (last visited Nov. 12, 2021); S.C. Res. 2395, (Dec. 21, 2017); S.C. Res. 2396 (Dec. 21, 2017).

34. Gavin Sullivan & Alejandro Rodiles, *Global Security Assemblages and International Law: A Socio-legal Study of Emergency in Motion,* BRITISH ACADEMY (2021); Alejandro Rodiles & Gavin Sullivan, *Global Security Assemblages: Studying International Counterterrorism Law in Motion* (unpublished paper) (on file with author); INFORMAL INTERNATIONAL LAWMAKING (Joost Pauwelyn, Ramses Wessel & Jan Wouters eds., 2012).

35. Dustin A. Lewis, Radhika Kapoor & Naz K. Modirzadeh, *Advancing Humanitarian Commitments in Connection with Countering Terrorism: Exploring a Foundational Reframing*

These institutional pathways also provide entry points for technology sharing and adoption, through which counterterrorism emerges as an arena of exceptionality validating the use of technology forms that have distinct human rights and rule of law impact. Justified as exceptions to norms, permissive regulatory terms move quickly to become the new norm, a point illustrated below by analyzing technology adoptions, including unmanned aerial vehicles (UAVs), Advance Passenger Information (API), Passenger Name Record (PNR), and biometric data practices. I note the obvious, that data collection, storage, use, and transfer are essential to these technologies. Furthermore, in the counterterrorism realm, the lack of normative constraint on privacy and data protection[36] functions as a positive incentive for States to invoke this legal framework when addressing security or conflict challenges instead of armed conflict or human rights derogations / limitations frames.[37] This in turn strengthens and consolidates the counterterrorism architecture through ongoing iteration and validation.

As I outline further below, technology use grounded on systematic and large-scale data collection also plays a critical role for States in repurposing and reframing the regulation of counterterrorism and conflict. This trend is evidenced in the appetite for "tech" solutions to complex social and political challenges. It also appears in the mutual admiration between private sector tech companies and States who are "solution" oriented and have clear fatigue with traditional multilateral or multi-stakeholder approaches to "solving" of terrorism or conflict challenges. In parallel, new and repurposed multilateral institutional responses to terrorism have seized on technology as a shiny new object to bring value in their technical assistance and capacity building support to States, thus "proving themselves worthy" of State attention as they offer "new" solutions to intractable problems.

The institutional and normative pathways created and consolidated since 9/11 have therefore served an important function in mainstreaming tech and data-based solutions in the counterterrorism arena. For example, the broader regulation of foreign (terrorist) fighters by the Security Council[38] instantly

---

Concerning the Security Council, PROGRAM ON INT'L L. & ARMED CONFLICT (Dec. 2021), https://pilac.law.harvard.edu/advancing-humanitarian-commitments-web-version.

36. Noting that none of the Security Council Resolutions requiring the adoption of API and PRN mention any obligations for States in respect of either privacy or data collection.

37. Noting that many data protection regimes, for example, GDPR have carve-outs for security or counterterrorism exceptions. European Parliament Regulation 2016/679 of Apr. 27, 2016, General Data Protection Regulation, 2016 O.J. (L 119) 2. The EU lacks competence to directly legislate in this area as the Treaty on European Union provides that "national security remains the sole responsibility of each Member State." *See* Consolidated Version of the Treaty on European Union (TEU), art. 4(2), Oct. 26, 2012, 2012 O.J. (C 326) 15).

38. Fionnuala Ní Aoláin, *The New UN Security Council, Global Watchlists, Biometrics and the Threat to the Rule of Law*, JUST SECURITY (Jan. 17, 2018), https://www.justsecurity.org/51075/security-council-global-watch-lists-biometrics/.

mainstreamed the use of biometric technology into global and national regulatory practice. United Nations Security Council 2396, adopted under chapter 7 of the Charter, primarily focused on addressed the threat of such fighters moving across borders, including paragraph 15, which decided that "all Member States shall develop and implement systems to collect biometric data."[39] Simply translated, this phrase introduced a global Security Council mandate requiring all governments to collect high-risk, highly personal biometrics data for millions of people traveling within their territorial borders. Adopted with virtually no consultation in the accelerated and closed space of Security Council negotiations, this global dictate on biometrics paid little attention to the broader rule of law, human rights, data protection and security implications.[40] Counter-terrorism was the edge of the knife: the persuasiveness of taking exceptional measures in fraught circumstances framing the conversation, plus the enthusiasm of security actors, meant that the broader costs and downstream effects of this move had minimal consideration. As it will be discussed, once the Security Council mandate was in place, counterterrorism actors and the private security sector enthusiastically took to the task, accelerating the use of this high-risk technology in multiple national settings where the rule of law deficits are extreme, and the frame of counterterrorism gives sizable cover to authoritarians and abusers of human rights to operate with effective impunity in their adoption and use of such technologies. For example, the United Nations Office of Counter-Terrorism reports that it currently supports 38 States to adopt mass data collection technologies including Advance Passenger Information and Passenger Name Recognition capacities,[41] many of whom have the distinction of egregious human rights records in their countering terrorism practices.[42]

39. S.C. Res. 2396 ¶ 15 (2017) ("*Decides that* Member States shall develop and implement systems to collect biometric data, which could include fingerprints, photographs, facial recognition, and other relevant identifying biometric data, in order to responsibly and properly identify terrorists, including foreign terrorist fighters, in compliance with domestic law and international human rights law, *calls upon* other Member States, international, regional, and subregional entities to provide technical assistance, resources, and capacity building to Member States in order to implement such systems and *encourages* Member States to share this data responsibly among relevant Member States, as appropriate, and with INTERPOL and other relevant international bodies. . . .").

40. I note the positive and transformative capacity of biometric data use in certain contexts. *See* Katja Lindskov Jacobsen, *New Forms of Intervention: The Case of Humanitarian Refugee Biometrics, in* HANDBOOK ON INTERVENTION AND STATEBUILDING 283–93 (Nicolas Lemay-Hébert ed., 2019).

41. United Nations Office of Counter-Terrorism, *Fifth Year of the UNCCT 5-Year Programme,* UNCCT (Jan.–Dec. 2021), https://www.un.org/counterterrorism/sites/www.un.org.counterterrorism/files/uncct_annual_report_2020.pdf.

42. Human Rights Council, U.N. Doc A/HRC/40/52/Add.2 (Dec. 13, 2018).

International human rights and humanitarian law scholars, with some notable exceptions, have largely failed to notice the insidious evolution of counterterrorism institutional consolidation and normative developments.[43] Counterterrorism is the preferred framework of discourse and practice for many States in non-international armed conflict and increasingly in contexts of domestic unrest and mobilization.[44] The activation of counterterrorism, along with its methods and means, relies heavily and opaquely on massive and sustained practices of data collection, carried out by a range of security actors but most often led by intelligence actors, increasingly in cooperation with private actors. In turn, the domestic agencies that deliver counterterrorism are the least accessible and transparent to the reach of the rule of law. So much of the day-to-day business of counterterrorism is, in fact, unseen and unattended to by independent oversight, such as by parliaments and courts. The implication of this layered institutional complexity means that the murkiness and impenetrability of the counterterrorism architecture is maintained, even as the legal regimes of human rights and humanitarian law maintain a facade of legality. But, in reality, the motif of the emperor's new clothes is apt, because in fact, counterterrorism is nakedly ascendant.

II. NEW TECHNOLOGIES AND COUNTERTERRORISM: THE ALLURE OF BRIGHT AND SHINY OBJECTS

In the embrace of a global war on terror a new era of surveillance technologies, States adopted widespread data collection and tech solutions to violent challenges.[45] Vast quantities of data collection across multiple technologies underpin and pervade the operationalization of counterterrorism practice across the globe. My analysis does not suggest that there was a singular moment of counterterrorism tech embrace. Rather, I identify a confluence of broader trends in technology development, use, co-option, sharing, and transfer resulting in the overlap of counterterrorism practice with technology deployment and acceleration, the vast majority of which are data collection dependent. In parallel, arguments about the exceptional use of such technologies in specific circumstances to specific threats have created the illusion of restraint in the endorsement of these technologies at the global

43. Ben Saul, *From Conflict to Complementarity: Reconciling International Counter-terrorism Law and International Humanitarian Law*, INTERNATIONAL REVIEW OF THE RED CROSS (Feb. 2022), https://international-review.icrc.org/articles/from-conflict-to-complementarity-916; FIONA DE LONDRAS, THE PRACTICE AND PROBLEMS OF TRANSNATIONAL COUNTER-TERRORISM (2022); Lewis et al., *supra* note 35.

44. *UN Experts decry US Rhetoric on Designation of Terrorist Groups*, OHCHR (June 19, 2020), https://www.ohchr.org/EN/NewsEvents/Pages/DisplayNews.aspx?NewsID=25980&LangID=E.

45. Privacy International, *Biometrics Collection under the Pretext of Counter-Terrorism*, PRIV. INT'L. (2020), https://privacyinternational.org/long-read/4528/biometrics-collection-under-pretext-counter-terrorism.

The Datafication of Counterterrorism

normative level.[46] In practice, those justifications of exceptionality had little value when the technologies themselves were wholesale responses to retail challenges. Nonetheless, their framing as retail measures provided the illusion of restraint. It is also relevant to note that many of these new technologies were being tested and deployed in sites that were synonymous with armed conflict, raising fundamental legal questions about technology use justified for counter-terrorism purposes in sites where an armed conflict is the appropriate *primus inter partes* legal regime.[47]

To understand this confluence is not only to address the specific trajectories of new technology capacities in surveillance, social media, biometrics, artificial intelligence, unmanned aerial systems and 3D printing, but rather to see the ways in which counterterrorism as a practice offered pathways for these technologies to gain early adoption and legitimacy. Channeling Ulrich Beck,[48] I would contend that the concentration on "terrorism" as a ubiquitous threat in the decades after 9/11, with the emphasis on its global insecurity, paved the way for a variety of institutional, normative, and practice responses. In this universe of action-oriented, forward-focused responses to terrorism, technology discourses and use premised on massive data collection, synthesis, and storage came to occupy an elevated importance. United Nations Security Council Resolutions adopted under chapter 7 of the UN Charter accelerated this new technology employment by embracing tech solutions to terrorism threats allied with reinforcing "soft law" standards.[49]

In broad-brush terms, counterterrorism post 9/11 initially manifested in "old-fashioned" practices of preventing, confronting, and destroying terrorism. The articulation of terrorism as a threat to peace and security under Chapter VII of the United Nations charter emerged pre 9/11,[50] but then consolidated as a collective

46. *See* Fionnuala Ní Aoláin (Special Rapporteur on the Promotion and Protection of Human Rights and Fundamental Freedoms while Countering Terrorism), *Report of the Special Rapporteur on the Promotion and Protection of Human Rights and Fundamental Freedoms while Countering Terrorism on the Human Rights Challenge of States of Emergency in the Context of Countering Terrorism,* U.N. Doc. A/HRC/37/52 (Mar. 1, 2018).

47. *See* Fionnuala Ní Aoláin (Special Rapporteur on the Promotion and Protection of Human Rights and Fundamental Freedoms while Countering Terrorism), *Report of the Special Rapporteur on the Promotion and Protection of Human Rights and Fundamental Freedoms while Countering Terrorism.,* U.N. Doc. A/75/337 (Sept. 3, 2020).

48. ULRICH BECK, RISK SOCIETY: TOWARDS A NEW MODERNITY (1986). Building on the concept adduced by Anthony Giddens, a risk society is "a society increasingly preoccupied with the future (and also with safety), which generates the notion of risk." Beck defines a risk-based approach as "a systematic way of dealing with hazards and insecurities induced and introduced by modernisation itself." *See* Anthony Giddens, *Risk and Responsibility,* 62 MODERN L. REV. 1, 3 (1999).

49. *See, e.g.,* S/Res/2178 (2014).

50. A notable change was the Council's practical enlargement of the notion of "threat to international peace and security." This move, prompted by new challenges to global peace and security, included situations that would have traditionally fallen outside of the understanding of the scope of collective action under the Charter. This included situations of non-international armed conflict, gross violations of human rights amounting to crimes against humanity, humanitarian

332   INTERNATIONAL HUMAN RIGHTS LAW

security response to the destruction of the Twin Towers and the Pentagon with the deployment of troops to Afghanistan and the waging of (mostly) conventional warfare on the ground.[51] In parallel, the well-honed if subverted use of tools of detention and interrogation were heavily relied upon to anticipate and respond to the manifest terrorist threat. Those tools were so abjectly tainted by practices of systematic torture,[52] arbitrary detention, and rendition that both their usefulness and legitimacy brought profound embarrassment and discredit to the United States and those countries who had aided and abetted in their sustained breaches of international law.[53]

---

crises, coups d'état, or other serious threats to the democratic order of a state. In obvious ways, the broadening of "threats to peace and security" laid the groundwork for the expansion of such threats to include global, regional and national experiences of terrorism.

51. H.R.J. Res. 114, 107th Cong. (2002). *See also* Nigel D. White, *On the Brink of Lawlessness: The State of Collective Security Action*, 13 IND. INT'L & COMP. L. REV. 237 (2002); Christopher Greenwood, *International Law and the Pre-emptive Use of Force: Afghanistan, Al-Qaida, and Iraq*, 4 SAN DIEGO INT'L L.J. 7 (2003); Michael Byers, *Terrorism, the Use of Force and International Law After II September*, 51 INT'L & COMP. L.Q. 401 (2002).

52. Memorandum from John C. Yoo on the President's Constitutional Authority to Conduct Military Operations against Terrorists and Nations Supporting Them to Timothy Flanigan, the Deputy Counsel to the President (Sept. 25, 2001); Memorandum to William J. Haynes II, General Counsel, Department of Defense (Dec. 28, 2001); Memorandum from John Yoo & Robert J. Delabunty on the Application of Treaties and Laws to Detainees to William J. Haynes II, General Counsel, Department of Defense (Jan. 9, 2002); Memorandum from Jay S. Bybee on Application of Treaties and Laws to al Qaeda and Taliban Detainees to Alberto R. Gonzales, Counsel to the President & William J. Haynes II, General Counsel, Department of Defense (Jan. 22, 2002); Memorandum from Alberto R. Gonzales on the Decision Re Application of the Geneva Convention on Prisoners of War to the Conflict with Al Qaeda and the Taliban to the President (Jan. 25, 2002); Memorandum from Colin L. Powell on the Applicability of the Geneva Convention to the Conflict in Afghanistan to the Counsel to the President (Jan. 26, 2002); Memorandum from Jay S. Bybee on Status of Taliban Forces Under Article 4 of the Third Geneva Convention of 1949 to Alberto R. Gonzales, Counsel to the President (Feb. 7, 2002); Memorandum from Jay S. Bybee on Potential Legal Constraints Applicable to Interrogations of Persons Captured by U.S. Armed Forces in Afghanistan to William J. Haynes II, General Counsel, Department of Defense (Feb. 26, 2002); Memorandum on Standards of Conduct for Interrogation under 18 U.S.C. §§ 2340-2340A to Alberto R. Gonzales, Counsel to the President (Aug. 1, 2002); Memorandum from William J. Haynes II, General Counsel on Counter-Resistance Techniques to Secretary of Defense (Nov. 27, 2002); Memorandum on Detainee Interrogations to the General Counsel of the Department of Defense (Jan. 15, 2003); Memorandum from William J. Haynes II on Working Group to Assess Legal, Policy, and Operational Issues Relating to Interrogation of Detainees Held by the U.S. Armed Forces in the War on Terrorism to the General Counsel of the Department of the Air Force (Jan. 17, 2003); Memorandum from John C. Yoo on Military Interrogation of Alien Unlawful Combatants Held Outside the United States to William J. Haynes II, General Counsel, Department of Defense (Mar. 14, 2003) (arguing that the United States would not be acting in breach of its international law obligations by engaging in "enhanced interrogation" techniques).

53. For some of the challenges to the maintenance of the torture prohibition, see Manfred Nowak, *Challenges to the Absolute Nature of the Prohibition of Torture and Ill-Treatment*, 23 NETH. Q. HUM. RTS. 674 (2005).

A. Drones, Data, and Counterterrorism

As detention became costly, politically compromised, and legally challenging, new approaches were needed to further contain the ongoing pursuit of accountability for 9/11 and address the constant terrorism threat. Among those approaches was the use of armed drones worldwide, both within the confines of formal armed conflicts in particular geographical locations and as part of an asserted global counterterrorism response. Big data, data analytics, and filtering were harnessed to the surveillance and selection that assessed, defined, and targeted individuals deemed to be terrorists, those "associated" with terrorists, or supporters of terrorism. The legal basis for the deployment of this technology remains opaque and under-defined.[54] One key continuum analysis is that drones provided an apparent technological solution to a practical counterterrorism problem, namely the legal, political, and military costs of engaging suspected terrorists directly on the territory of other states. This technologically driven solution remains a matter of substantial legal controversy and poses an ongoing and increasingly documented risk to civilians.[55] In parallel, lack of independent oversight of drone data collection,

54. The legal framework applying to the use of armed drones remains a matter of debate rather than global consensus. That said, formal statements have been made by the United States (United States Government, "Report on the Legal and Policy Frameworks Guiding the United States' Use of Military Force and Related National Security Operations" (December 2016); Brian Egan (the Legal Adviser, US Department of State), "International Law, Legal Diplomacy, and the Counter-ISIL Campaign," speech at the 110th Annual Meeting of the American Society of International Law (1 April 2016)) and United Kingdom (Rt Hon Jeremy Wright QC, UK Attorney General, "The Modern Law of Self Defence," speech at the International Institute for Strategic Studies (11 January 2017) shed some light on the use of drones in self-defense. The same position has been endorsed by Australia. See Hon George Brandis QC, Australian Attorney General, "The Right to Self-Defence Against Imminent Attack in International Law," speech at the University of Queensland School of Law (11 April 2017)) which shed light on one particular issue, namely the approach of those States to the criteria for self-defense at international law, particularly the role of the traditional condition of imminent threat of attack.

55. *See* Special Rapporteur on the Promotion and Protection of Human Rights and Fundamental Freedoms while Countering Terrorism, *Promotion and Protection of Human Rights: Human Rights questions, including alternative approaches for improving the effective enjoyment of Human Rights and Fundamental Freedoms,* U.N. Doc. A/68/389 (Sept. 18, 2013); Ben Emmerson (Former Special Rapporteur on the Promotion and Protection of Human Rights and Fundamental Freedoms while Countering Terrorism), *Report of the Special Rapporteur on the Promotion and Protection of Human Rights and Fundamental Freedoms while Countering Terrorism, Ben Emmerson,* U.N. Doc. A/HRC/25/59 (Mar. 11, 2014); Ben Emmerson (Former Special Rapporteur on the Promotion and Protection of Human Rights and Fundamental Freedoms while Countering Terrorism), *Report of the Special Rapporteur on the Promotion and Protection of Human Rights and Fundamental Freedoms while Countering Terrorism,* U.N. Doc. A/HRC/34/61 (Feb. 21, 2017); Agnes Callamard (Special Rapporteur on Extrajudicial, Summary or Arbitrary Executions), *Use of Armed Drones for Targeted Killings,* U.N. Doc A/HRC/44/38 (June 29, 2020); The New York Times, *How the U.S. Hid an Airstrike that Killed Dozens of Civilians in Syria* Nov. 15, 2021.

assessment, and use has been starkly illuminated by the hapless and brutal drone strike in Kabul, Afghanistan, on August 29, 2021, killing ten civilians including seven children.

I also observe an expansion of drone capacity to "garden-variety" counter-terrorism, namely the use of unmanned aerial vehicles in domestic counterter-rorism prevention efforts related to critical infrastructure. This expansion, which is heavily endorsed by the United Nations Office of Counter-Terrorism,[56] runs multiple risks of misuse, particularly when domestic definitions of terrorism en-compass acts squarely protected by international law.[57] In many countries, the use of such technologies by unaccountable and bloated security sectors risks the "stabilization of a militarized status quo."[58] A clear human rights problem in this arena is the transfer of drone technology to States that do not maintain rule of law standards in their counterterrorism regulation, lack adequate legal protections for the vast amount of data they collect and then use for targeting, store indef-initely, and sometimes transfer to other states. In numerous drone deployment contexts, there is no legal protection of privacy found in the relevant national system. Because multiple States have systematically misused counterterrorism measures against civil society and human rights defenders,[59] it is alarming that another means to collect data on those groups is being bolted to augmented legal force capacity in highly repressive or authoritarian settings and is enabled under the guise of counterterrorism in domestic law enforcement. In tandem, the risks of technology transfer from state to nonstate actors in precarious and fragile settings are high, with corruption and inadequate oversight fueling the transfer of state military stocks to armed groups.[60]

56. *International Expert Group Meeting, supra* note 31.

57. Fionnuala Ní Aoláin, Special Rapporteur on the Protection and Promotion of Human Rights and Fundamental Freedoms while Countering Terrorism at the International Expert Group Meeting on the Protection of Vulnerable Targets and Unmanned Aircraft Systems (Oct. 6–7 2021).

58. Guiryanan et al., *supra* note 15, at ii.

59. Between 2019 and January 2022, the Special Rapporteur on Counter-Terrorism and Human Rights has intervened in over 119 cases in 20 countries on behalf of women human rights defenders targeted under the guise of counterterrorism. More broadly, 66% of all com-munications sent by Special Procedure mandate-holders since 2005 have dealt with the use of counterterrorism measures against civil society actors. *See* Fionnuala Ní Aoláin (Special Rapporteur on the Promotion and Protection of Human Rights and Fundamental Freedoms while Countering Terrorism), *Report of the Special Rapporteur on the Promotion and Protection of Human Rights and Fundamental Freedoms while Countering Terrorism on the Human Rights Challenge of States of Emergency in the Context of Countering Terrorism,* U.N. Doc. A/HRC/40/52 (Feb. 18, 2019).

60. Rachel Stohl, *The Tangled Web of Illicit Arms Trafficking,* AM. PROGRESS 21 (2005), https://cdn.americanprogress.org/wp-content/uploads/kf/TerrorinShadows-Stohl.pdf.

B. Global Counterterrorism Cooperation and Data Collection

Data collection increasingly became an essential, indispensable, and necessary part of the counterterrorism landscape in the years following 9/11, and its importance is only growing. Ubiquitous data collection was a defining feature of Internet-driven, consumer-satiated, economic and social life in the same decades. The many ready sources of information, which were the byproduct of broader societal trends, offered extraordinary advantages to the security state. Large data sets, enhanced computing capacity, and innovative data analysis methods not only prompted significant social changes in many societies but dramatically affected security practices and assumptions.

The focus on building multiple and interrelated terrorism databases in many countries,[61] which allowed more security (and generic) information to be collected, on wider groups of persons (enabled by broad definitions of extremism and terrorism), and with access to much wider groups of security (and non-security) actors, massively enabled the investment in and use of data collection for counterterrorism purposes.[62] In practice, this meant new pathways for the allocation of resources, resulting in deeper reliance on databases in particular as the indispensable counterterrorism tool. Inclusion on such databases is often secret but has wide-ranging consequences for an individual's (and their families) human rights. Affected rights include the rights to life, work (because data base inclusion may be a barrier to employment), travel, family life, and access to government subsidies and support. In addition, because the government often conducts extensive surveillance of such individuals (and their families), they face potentially severe restrictions on their right to privacy. Inclusion on a data base is not a criminal law measure, and therefore does not directly implicate the liberty rights affected by criminal proceedings, but it may have commensurate effects particularly as regards de facto deprivation of liberty through limitations on freedom of movement in certain circumstances. Removal from a terrorism data base is generally difficult, and some individuals, for example, children who have returned from conflict zones in Syria and Iraq, may find that they are permanently condemned to remaining on such databases due to their birth circumstances and their "family associations."

The adoption of United Nations Security Council Resolution 2178 (2014) illustrates the normative affirmation of global counterterrorism-led data

---

61. *See, for example* the role of multiple counterterrorism databases in the Belgian context, including the hate preachers, dynamic and joint terrorist fighters databases—significant augmentation of data collection following the terrorist attacks of 2015. Human Rights Council Res., U.N. Doc. A/HRC/40/55, ¶53–62 (Jan. 8, 2019).

62. United Nations Office on Drugs and Crime, *The Use of the Internet for Terrorist Purposes*, UNODC (2012), https://www.unodc.org/documents/frontpage/Use_of_Internet_for_Terrorist_Purposes.pdf.

collection.[63] The resolution is, in part, defined by its emphasis on information gathering and information sharing among states. Specifically, this resolution creates several new obligations for states, including the requirement that states shall develop watch lists and databases of known and suspected terrorists ("including but not limited to foreign terrorist fighters").[64]

In principle, the principle of human rights and rule of law-based information sharing between states is not per se objectionable. However, global counterterrorism cooperation rhetoric is defined by a rhetorical illusion that all states value privacy equally; do not misuse information to target individuals outside of the rule of law; and that information practices including integrity, anonymity, and destruction as appropriate are rule of law based. In reality, this is simply not the case.[65] For example, the category of "suspected" terrorists is particularly opaque due to the wide-latitude national within legal systems to define terrorism or terrorist actors, and often in ways that press egregiously on the principle of legal certainty. The broader point is well illustrated by the finding made by the European Data Protection Supervisor (EDPS) in January 2022 that the EU's police agency (Europol) has unlawfully gathered and stored vast quantities of data, including sensitive personal data.[66] The agency holds much of the data on persons currently or formerly suspected of terrorism and people with whom they had contact. Europol has defended the scale and nature of the data collection and appears to argue that the EDPS in unrealistic in the expectations of policing and intelligence services.[67]

In parallel, the well-documented practices of multiple states in targeting civil society activists, writers, dissenters, and human rights defenders as terrorists have hardened the practices of lists and proscription (of groups) being used as tools of repression under the guise of countering terrorism. The fallout in multiple countries has been that states are relying on Security Council dictate to nefariously target those who disagree with them in new and highly coercive ways, not only within their borders but across borders with cooperation and impunity of other states. It is worth stressing that the language of the resolution is expansive:

---

63. S.C. Rec. 2178 (Sept. 24, 2014).

64. *See generally*, Helen Duffy, *Foreign Terrorist Fighters; A Human Rights Approach?*, 29 SECURITY & HUM. RTS. 120–72 (2018).

65. *See, e.g., Pegasus Used to Target El Salvador, supra* note 32.

66. Some privacy experts have named the collection efforts a "big data ark" containing billions of points of information drawn from crime reports hacked from encrypted phones and sampled from asylum seekers who have never been engaged in any crime. Apostolis Fotiadis, Ludek Stavinoha, Giacomo Zandonini & Daniel Howden, "*A Data Black Hole*": *Europol Ordered to Delete Vast Store of Personal Data*, THE GUARDIAN (Jan. 10, 2022), https://www.theguardian.com/world/2022/jan/10/a-data-black-hole-europol-ordered-to-delete-vast-store-of-personal-data?CMP=twt_gu&utm_source=Twitter&utm_medium#Echobox=1641819085.

67. *Id.*

The Datafication of Counterterrorism

> Decides that Member States shall develop watch lists or databases of known and suspected terrorists, including foreign terrorist fighters, for use by law enforcement, border security, customs, military, and intelligence agencies to screen travellers and conduct risk assessments and investigations, in compliance with domestic and international law, including human rights law, and encourages Member States to share this information through bilateral and multilateral mechanisms, in compliance with domestic and international human rights law, and further encourages the facilitation of capacity building and technical assistance by Member States and other relevant Organizations to Member States as they seek to implement this obligation;

The information-collection capacities that states are required to develop and implement (including but not expressly limited to "foreign fighters") are wide, and many involve inherently high-risk technologies that could restrict fundamental rights, including nondiscrimination:

> biometric data, which could include fingerprints, photographs, facial recognition, and other relevant identifying biometric data, in order to responsibly and properly identify terrorists, including foreign terrorist fighters.

It bears mentioning that human rights and humanitarian lawyers have long raised concerns about the terminology of "foreign fighters" (nationals of one country who travel abroad to fight alongside a nonstate armed group in the territory of another State) because the term appears to skirt recognition of status for combatants in situations of armed conflict and thus avoid obligations in the conduct of hostilities or detention at the end of hostilities.[68] The term foreign fighter is not a "term of art of IHL."[69] IHL applicability to a situation of violence in which such fighters are engaged depends on the facts on the ground, and a full assessment of Common Article 2 or 3 is necessary. Moreover, IHL would also require an assessment of whether the individual is taking a direct part in hostilities, a process that can be avoided when mere association with a group under national counterterrorism legislation is unlawful in many countries. Aside from IHL concerns, the use of this nomenclature has been the basis to authorize massive and sustained metadata collection across the globe, primarily authorized by Security Council chapter 7 resolutions with few meaningful human rights protections.

In a parallel universe, multiple security stakeholders including States enthusiastically adopted metadata collection with few overarching legal constraints in place as a tech-led solution to preventing terrorism.[70] Notably, collection was bolted

---

68. International Committee of the Red Cross, *supra* note 3.

69. *Id.* at 62.

70. Erik Dahl, *It's Not Big Data, but Little Data, That Prevents Terrorist Attacks*, STUDY OF TERRORISM & RESPONSES TO TERRORISM (July 25, 2013), https://www.start.umd.edu/publicat ion/its-not-big-data-little-data-prevents-terrorist-attacks.

to a preemptive model of criminal regulation with a move away from holding persons legally accountable for acts of terrorism and instead extending the use of inchoate offenses, and focused on preemption, as the leading edge of criminal and administrative regulation. The result was the collection and analysis of vast amounts of personal data, with the result of extending or entrenching forms of indiscriminate or arbitrary "mass surveillance," chilling the exercise of fundamental rights.[71] Case studies from Somalia[72] to the Occupied Palestinian Territories[73] illuminate the ways in which surveillance and constant data collection function in sites of conflict, rhetorically framed a counterterrorism arenas to undermine life choices, shape personal and familial movement, and distort intimate life as well as profoundly reshaping public space and interactions within targeted communities. From fingerprint collection to facial images to iris scans, we see functional creep and gradual widening of the data collection technology beyond its original defended use. Many human rights observers continue to fear an ongoing "digital arms race"[74] among States.[75]

C. Airline Passenger Information and Passenger Name Recognition in the Counterterrorism Universe

In the scheme of counterterrorism data collection technologies, Airline Passenger Information (API) and Passenger Name Recognition (PNR) play a starring role. Triggered by the fear that foreign fighters would travel from conflict site to other locales, Security Council Resolution 2178, augmented and extended by UNSCR 2396, required States to establish information systems to detect departure, travel

---

71. "Mass surveillance" involves the placing of taps on fiber-optic cables through which the majority of digital communications travel, enabling States to access the content of communications content and metadata, as well as mandatory data retention laws that require telecommunications and Internet service providers to preserve communications data for inspection and analysis. *See* Ben Emmerson (Former Special Rapporteur on the Promotion and Protection of Human Rights and Fundamental Freedoms while Countering Terrorism), *Promotion and Protection of Human Rights and Fundamental Freedoms while Countering Terrorism*, U.N. Doc. A/69/397 (Sept. 23, 2014); Daragh Murray & Pete Fussey, *Bulk Surveillance in the Digital Age: Rethinking the Human Rights Law Approach to Bulk Monitoring of Communications Data*, 52 Isr. L. Rev. 31 (2019).

72. Privacy International, Biometrics and Counter-Terrorism: Case Study of Somalia, Priv. Int'l. (May 28, 2021), https://privacyinternational.org/long-read/4528/biometrics-collection-under-pretext-counter-terrorism.

73. Nadera Shalhoub-Kevorkian, Security Theology, Surveillance and the Politics of Fear (2015).

74. CEPS, *Europe and the Digital Arms Race*, CEPS (June 6, 2019), https://www.ceps.eu/europe-and-the-digital-arms-race/.

75. TrendMicro, United Nations Interregional Crime and Justice Research Institute & Europol, *Malicious Uses and Abuses of Artificial Intelligence* (Nov. 2020), http://www.unicri.it/sites/defa ult/files/2020-11/Abuse_ai.pdf.

The Datafication of Counterterrorism   339

from, or transit through their territories by air.[76] In parallel, Resolution mandated States to collect, process, and analyze PNR data "for the purpose of preventing, detecting and investigating terrorist offences and related travel."[77] A notable feature of these data collection edicts was the encouragement to States to share PNR data:

> with relevant or concerned Member States to detect foreign terrorist fighters returning to their countries of origin or nationality, or traveling or relocating to a third country, with particular regard for all individuals designated by the Committee established pursuant to resolutions 1267 (1999), 1989 (2011), and 2253 (2015).

The expansive emphasis on "sharing" was without regard for the rule of law or human rights records of the States concerned and emerged with no specific requirements on data protection or even data security. While exhortations to create PNR and API systems often came with the stock phase, "with full respect for human rights and fundamental freedoms," the specific meaning of that phrase and how precisely it should be practiced in respect of new technologies for which there remains limited specific normative rules was in practice highly abstract. The abstraction is not without function: it precisely avoids entanglement with the specific requirements of rights-based obligations, enabling vague affirmations of compliance without ever requiring states to engage the specific requirements of human rights due diligence, obligations, and assessment in application.

From a human rights perspective, it would seem logical that a minimal human rights protection threshold would require effective privacy protection in the national legal system, operating independently of API national legislation. More concretely, any domestic legislation should specify the purpose of API collection in concrete terms, with a narrow definition of terrorism and terrorist acts. Transfer would be strictly regulated; retention of

---

76. S. Rec. 2396, *supra* note 33, ¶ 11 ("[A]nd *further calls upon* Member States to report any such departure from their territories, or such attempted entry into or transit through their territories, by sharing this information with the State of residence or nationality, or the countries of return, transit or relocation, and relevant international organizations as appropriate and in accordance with domestic law and international obligations, and to ensure API is analysed by all relevant authorities, with full respect for human rights and fundamental freedoms for the purpose of preventing, detecting, and investigating terrorist offenses and travel.").

77. *Id.* ¶ 12. *See also* S. Rec. 2482, ¶ 15 ("*Calls upon* Member States, including through relevant central and competent authorities, to: (c) implement obligations to collect and analyze Advance Passenger Information (API) and develop the ability to collect, process and analyse, in furtherance of International Civil Aviation Organization (ICAO) standards recommended practices, Passenger Name Record (PNR) data and to ensure PNR data is used by and shared with competent national authorities, with full respect for human rights and fundamental freedoms, which will help security officials make connections between individuals associated to organized crime, whether domestic or transnational, and terrorists, to stop terrorist travel and prosecute terrorism and organized crime, whether domestic or transnational, including by making use of capacity building programmes.").

API/PNR data should be necessary and proportionate and justified by a clear evidence base; prevention of abuse should be specifically regulated, and notification mechanisms for individuals whose data have been retained, independent oversight should be integrated into any such system, and adequate remedies should exist so that individuals can access their own API/PNR data. The United Nations[78] and the European Union[79] have led broad PNR and API standard-setting initiatives, but in practice the work has been decidedly human rights "lite." In parallel, PNR/API use has also come with capacity building and implementation practices that have raised numerous human rights concerns.[80] The United Nations Human Rights Committee has articulated its concerns about the export of technological capacities without human rights protections.[81] PNR cases pending before Austrian and German domestic courts raise fundamental questions about the compatibility of the EU PNR Directive and its transposition with the EU Charter on Fundamental Rights.[82] Judicial reckoning may lie ahead for these counterterrorism-grounded data collection practices, as disquiet grows about the lack of protection evidenced in their daily use.

D. Artificial Intelligence and Counterterrorism

Finally, we see new technology developments bolted onto counterterrorism imperatives and specifically the emergence of artificial intelligence as one of the

78. The UN has launched a flagship initiative "United Nations Countering Terrorist Travel Programme," being implemented in partnership with the Counter-Terrorism Committee Executive Directorate (CTED), the International Civil Aviation Organisation (ICAO), the United Nations Office on Drugs and Crime (UNODC), and the United Nations Office of Information Communication Technology (OICT). *See* United Nations Countering Terrorist Travel, *Programme Partners*, https://www.un.org/cttravel/content/programme-partners.

79. Council Directive 2016/681 of April 27, 2016, The Use of Passenger Name Record (PNR) Data for the Prevention, Detection, Investigation and Prosecution of Terrorist Offences and Serious Crime (L119).

80. A/76/261, ¶ 24 (Aug. 3, 2021).

81. Human Rights Committee, U.N. Doc. CCPR/C/ITA/CO/6, ¶ 36 (May 1, 2017). The Human Rights Committee calls on the State party to take measures to ensure that all corporations under its jurisdiction, such as technology corporations, respect human rights standards when engaging in operations abroad. Reminding the State Party of its regulatory functions vis-à-vis private actors affirming the Covenant's transnational application even where companies act abroad); Human Rights Committee, U.N. Doc. CCPR/C/131/D/3163/2018, ¶ 7.3–8 (Sept. 16, 2021).

82. De Capitani & others v. Federal Republic of Germany, Criminal Police Office of Austria and others, https://digitalfreedomfund.org/wp-content/uploads/2019/09/De-Capitani-and-others-case-study.pdf.

The Datafication of Counterterrorism 341

primary disruptive technologies of the 21st century.[83] The seventh biannual review of the global counterterrorism strategy recognized the capacities that AI offers to counterterrorism.[84]

In parallel, the OHCHR has observed:

> Law enforcement and counter-terrorism agencies are also exploring the benefits that AI can bring. From algorithmic systems that assist investigators in the curation and analysis of their databases and support operational decision-making to "smart" surveillance tools that promise to predict terrorist activities or identify suspects, many authorities believe that AI has the potential to enhance their capabilities and better allocate resources.[85]

From a human rights perspective, the use of such technologies, whether in counterterrorism or armed conflict contexts, should go hand in hand with the establishment of robust human rights protections that are institutionally embedded in recipient States.[86] At the very least, as I have set out elsewhere,[87] the mutually reinforcing relationship between IHL and human rights in the context of counterterrorism mandate the optimization of both normative regimes.

The need for human rights protection exists in precise relationship to the danger of human rights violations that follow from the misuse of such technologies. The danger is particularly acute when governments and other actors apply the data generated from these counterterrorism initiatives to perpetuate, enable, or support human rights violations or prevent accountability. Individuals suffer human rights consequences across a range of fundamental rights, including, but not limited to, the rights to life; to liberty and security of person; the right to be free from torture, cruel, inhuman or degrading treatment; the rights to a fair trial; privacy and family life; freedom of expression or movement; and more. It is the scale of impingement, together with the interconnected nature of these rights, that leads to manifold, interrelated effects

---

83. David Kaye, the former Special Rapporteur on the promotion and protection of the right to freedom of opinion and expression, has defined AI as a "constellation of processes and technologies enabling computers to complement or replace specific tasks otherwise performed by humans" through "computer code [. . .] carrying instructions to translate data into conclusions, information or outputs." David Kaye (Special Rapporteur on the Promotion and Protection of the Right to Freedom of Opinion and Expression), *Promotion and Protection of the Right to Freedom of Opinion and Expression of Human Rights,* U.N. Doc. A/73/348 (Aug. 29, 2019).

84. G.A. Res. 60/288 (Sept. 20, 2006).

85. United Nations Human Rights Office of the High Commissioner, *Artificial Intelligence Human Rights & Counterterrorism Report Draft* (2021).

86. A/73/438, ¶41-42 (Oct. 17, 2018).

87. A/75/337, (Sept. 3, 2020).

across a series of individual and collective freedoms and makes the necessity for human rights compliant regulation of the use both imperative and urgent. Human rights protections are not static in this space. Rather, they are relevant at every stage of the data process, from collection to retention to processing and sharing. Governments and other actors should protect human rights at all these points in a manner consistent with international human rights law standards given the evidenced dangers of abuse.

For example, the right to privacy is enshrined in international and regional human rights instruments that demonstrate a "universal recognition of [its] fundamental importance, and enduring relevance, [. . .] and of the need to ensure that it is safeguarded, in law and in practice".[88] Notwithstanding the arguably universal nature of the right to privacy, about one-third of the world's jurisdictions have not incorporated adequate (or any) privacy protections in law and practice.[89] Even in the case of countries with relevant protections embedded in domestic law, a comparative analysis shows consistent shortcomings in safeguarding the right to privacy in practice, together with a trend toward stepping up data collection and retention—a trend that risks "creating surveillance states."[90]

Finally, from a rule of law and human rights perspective, it seems obvious that certain high-risk technologies ripe for abuse in the counterterrorism arena should be subject to licensing requirements when included in counterterrorism capacity-building or technical assistance by States. Here, relevant oversight frameworks such as the Wassenaar Arrangement on Export Controls for Conventional Arms and the dual-use goods and technologies regulation of the Council of the European Union provide a pathway to think about the transfer and use of these technologies among States, particularly in the context of transfers to fragile, conflicted, and post-conflict settings.

In the absence of such protections, the use of new technologies runs not only the risk of violating rights but also contributing to the weakening of governance and oversight systems. It is worth noting that governments and other actors repurposed many of these technologies during the COVID-19 pandemic without adequate safeguards or oversight, leading to the securitization of

---

88. *See* Office of the United Nations High Commissioner for Human Rights, *The Right to Privacy in the Digital Age*, ¶ 13, U.N. Doc. A/HRC/27/37 (June 30, 2014). *See also* Frank la Rue, *Report of the Special Rapporteur on the Promotion and Protection of the Right to the Freedom of Opinion and Expression*, ¶ 20, U.N. Doc. A/HRC/23/40 (Apr. 17, 2013).

89. *See, e.g.*, United Nations Conference on Trade and Development, *Data Protection and Privacy Legislation Worldwide*, UNCTAD, https://unctad.org/page/data-protection-and-priv acy-legislation-worldwide (last visited Feb. 19, 2022).

90. *See* Paul Bischoff, *Data Privacy Laws & Government Surveillance by Country: Which Countries Best Protect Their Citizens?*, Comparitech (Oct. 15, 2019), https://www.comparitech. com/blog/vpn-privacy/surveillance-states.

The Datafication of Counterterrorism 343

health care, with particularly disparate effects on vulnerable and marginalized communities.[91]

It is also worth highlighting the expanding role played by private companies in the design, delivery, and implementation of these tools.[92] Their presence and investment have added to the unrestrained growth trajectory of these technologies in counterterrorism use. Obviously, many governments enter into diverse partnerships with private companies, and many such partnerships hold substantial social and economic benefits for society. While many of these companies have not per se developed their tools with the primary aim of security deployment, security actors increasingly find these tools attractive and transferable.

III. BUYER BEWARE: THE FALLACY OF TECHNOLOGICAL SOLUTIONS TO COMPLEX CONFLICTS AND TERRORISM

For multiple human rights, rule of law, and governance reasons, there should be uneasiness about the supply of new technologies justified and supported by counterterrorism imperatives bilaterally, multilaterally, and through UN capacity building and technical assistance.[93] These high-risk technologies include but are not limited to biometric data collection, application programming interface (API), and passenger name record (PNR) infrastructure capacity. The use of these technologies has triggered concerns from several human rights actors, including United Nations Special Procedure Mechanisms and the United Nations Human Rights Committee.[94] As outlined earlier, many of these technologies are inherently high-risk, with broad implications for a range of fundamental human rights

91. Fionnuala Ní Aoláin, *Exceptionality: A Typology of Covid-19 Emergency Powers*, UCLA J. INT'L. L. & FOREIGN AFFAIRS (2022) (forthcoming).

92. *See* Galit A. Sarfaty, *Can Big Data Revolutionize International Human Rights Law*, 39 U. PA. J. INT'L L. 73 (2017) (describing the private sector as a mediator of information by exerting control over access to and analysis of big data).

93. Highlighting expanding technologies used to collect, process and analyze expanding categories of biometric data fingerprints, DNA, facial analysis, plus additional biological and behavioral biometrics, including gait and voice recognition; acknowledges the relevance of other new technologies, such as artificial intelligence, integrated data platforms, blockchain, 3D printing, inter alia; and notes the requirement in S.C. Res. 2396, for States to responsibly adopt biometric data tools. S.C. Res. 2396, *supra* note 33, ¶ 15.

94. Human Rights Committee, U.N. Doc. CCPR/C/ITA/CO/6, ¶ 37 (May 1, 2017) (calling on the State party to take measures to ensure that all corporations under its jurisdiction, such as technology corporations, respect human rights standards when engaging in operations abroad and reminding the State Party of its regulatory functions vis-à-vis private actors affirming the Covenant's transnational application even where companies act abroad); Human Rights Committee, U.N. Doc. CCPR/C/131/D/3163/2018, ¶ 7.3–8 (Sept. 16, 2021).

from the right to life to the right to privacy. Counterterrorism initiatives increasingly function as a lever for governments to undermine rights wholesale, through expanding national policing, security and border capacity.[95]

The deployment of these technologies in domestic contexts has increasingly and consistently led to repression and systematic human rights violations that governments and others justify by reference to extremism, terrorism, separatism, and unacceptable dissent.[96] A prominent example is found in the Xinjiang Autonomous region of China, in which the government has utilized what has been described as an Orwellian monitoring system (CCP) to systematically document the daily private and public moves of the Uyghur people.[97] The surveillance cameras that litter the region utilize facial recognition and collect vast amounts of biometric data. Allied with an expansive and pervasive police presence,[98] these practices have transformed Xinjiang into a "security state."[99] The government has justified technology use with the need to regulate extremism, terrorism and "separatism," utilizing the broader global frameworks on counterterrorism as cover for quashing domestic dissent and minority expression of culture and religious practice.

It is worth further reflection on the deployment of these technologies in complex conflict, post-conflict, and other fragile contexts where counterterrorism provides legal and political justification for their use.[100] In multiple conflict

95. Krisztina Huszti-Orbán & Fionnuala Ní Aoláin, *Use of Biometric Data to Identify Terrorists: Best Practice or Risky Business?* U. MINN. L. SCH. HUM. RIGHTS. CTR. (2020), https://law.umn.edu/sites/law.umn.edu/files/2020/07/21/hrc-biometrics-report-july2020.pdf.

96. Human Rights Watch, *China's Algorithms of Repression: Reverse Engineering a Xinjiang Police Mass Surveillance App*, HUM. RTS. WATCH (May 2019), https://www.hrw.org/sites/default/files/report_pdf/china0519_web.pdf.

97. Fionnuala Ní Aoláin (Special Rapporteur on the Promotion and Protection of Human Rights and Fundamental Freedoms while Countering Terrorism), *Promotion and Protection of Human Rights and Fundamental Freedoms while Countering Terrorism*, U.N. Doc. A/HRC/49/45 (Follow-up report on the Joint Study (2010) on Global Practices in Relation to Secret Detention in the Context of Countering Terrorism); Kenneth Roth, *China's Global Threat to Human Rights*, *in* HUMAN RIGHTS WATCH: WORLD REPORT, 130–31 (2020).

98. Amnesty International, *China: "Where are They?" Time for Answers about Mass Detentions in the Xinuang Uighur Autonomous Region*, AMNESTY INT'L 1, 11 (2018).

99. Vicky Xiuzhong Xu, Danielle Cave, James Leibold, Kelsey Munro & Nathan Ruser, *Uyghurs For Sale: "Re-education," Forced Labour and Surveillance Beyond Xinjiang*, 26 AUSTL. STRATEGIC POL'Y INST., INT'L CYBER POL'Y CTR. (2020).

100. In the context of the withdrawal of American forces from Afghanistan, there is already evidence of repurposing the assets of surveillance and drone technology to address the "new" threats emanating from a jurisdiction with no military assets on the ground. Thomas Spahr, *Adapting Intelligence to the New Afghanistan*, WAR ON THE ROCKS (Sept. 30, 2021), https://warontherocks.com/2021/09/adapting-intelligence-to-the-new-afghanistan ("Amid the broader debate over the U.S. withdrawal from Afghanistan, policymakers should remain focused on one crucial fact: terrorist groups in Afghanistan now have greater freedom to operate. To monitor this threat, Washington should re-posture its intelligence assets in the region.").

The Datafication of Counterterrorism

contexts, counterterrorism regulation allied with massive investments in and international support to extensive data collection has reframed the management of conflict to surveillance, force, and containment over and above conflict resolution and identifying conditions conducive to violence.

There is a distinct stratification of humanitarian law norms applicable in international armed conflicts (IACs) as compared to NIACs, with a far more extensive and broadly accepted set of norms applicable in IACs. A sparse and contested set of rules applicable in NIACs partly explains the allure of counterterrorism regulation in situations that objectively meet the legal threshold for NIAC norms. For example, the Geneva Conventions of 1949 devote only one common article, common Article 3, to such conflicts and States have been consistently unwilling to accept its formal applicability to internal armed conflicts. Additional Protocol II, which fleshes out specific rules for NIACs in more detail, is not widely ratified, and rarely accepted as applicable during ongoing internal armed conflicts by States. That noted, international courts and tribunals have in recent years augmented the legal obligations in NIACs. For example, the ad hoc international criminal tribunals have developed a rich jurisprudence on the subject, and rules for NIACS have further flourished with the adoption of the ICC Statute and the consolidation of the ICC's docket.[101] Stating the obvious, international humanitarian law is acutely relevant to the protection of individuals and the enforcement of duties in NIACs. There is a distinct value and importance to sustaining both State and non-State armed groups observance of international humanitarian law norms in these contexts, particularly to protect the civilian population. Conversely, human rights and humanitarian law "lite" counterterrorism frameworks offer few protections to civilians and little by way of meaningful oversight and accountability of norm breaches. This may explain precisely why counterterrorism frameworks are far more attractive to States in their contemporary conflict management practices.

The resistance to the application of IHL in non-international armed conflicts is a persistent thread of State practice. It is not new per se. What is new since 9/11 is that State resistance to IHL NIAC application has an alternative body of legal norms to rely upon which is forcefully supported by two decades of Security Council chapter 7 counterterrorism resolutions, a biannual global counterterrorism strategy review,[102] and a growth industry in "soft law" norms to enable

---

101. Ezequiel Heffes & Marcos D. Kotlik, *Special Agreements as a Means of Enhancing Compliance with IHL in Non-international Armed Conflicts: An Inquiry into the Governing Legal Regime*, 96 Int'l Rev. Red Cross 1195 (2014); Allison M. Danner, *When Courts Make Law: How the International Criminal Tribunals Recast the Laws of War*, 59 Vand. L. Rev. 1 (2006); Vijay M. Padmanabhan, *Norm Internalization through Trials for Violations of International Law: Four Conditions for Success and their Application to Trials of Detainees at Guantanamo Bay*, 31 U. Pa. J. Int'l. L. 427 (2009); Prosecutor v. Tadić, Case No. IT-94-1-T, Judgment, ¶ 80 (July 17, 1995).

102. The UN Global Counter-Terrorism Strategy (UN General Assembly Resolution A/RES/60/228) was first adopted in 2006, and completed its 7th Review in 2022, adopted by General Assembly Resolution A/RES/75/291.

States to justify applying counterterrorism norms to situations of complex violence and conflict. Moreover, the ascendent global counter-terrorism architecture, which includes the United Nations Counter-Terrorism Committee, the UN Office of Counter-Terrorism conjoined with new (and old) counterterrorism entities like the Global Counter-Terrorism Forum and the Financial Action Task Force, provide extraordinary institutional legitimacy for the displacement of IHL. The broad criminalization of terrorism and related acts through Security Council Resolutions[103] has significantly incentivized domestic terrorism prosecutions over war crimes accountability and adds to this bleak displacement narrative. Overall, the exclusion of IHL norms, or their displacement by counterterrorism frameworks (that are distinctly "soft" in nature)[104] is profoundly troublesome to the integrity of international law but also operated to undermine the protection of individuals in conflict settings.

The proliferation of low-intensity conflicts and the historic unwillingness of States to acknowledge the applicability of IHL to them, including Common Article 3, increasingly goes hand in hand with the view that "terrorism" is a means to displace protective legal norms. The danger of such displacement is not merely formalistic, but has concrete effects on humanitarian action, the provision of humanitarian assistance, the protection of non-derogable rights, and essential judicial guarantees, as well as the principle of nondiscrimination in armed conflict. As we watch the deepening deployment of counterterrorism-based technological tools, justified by the threat of "terrorism" but not grounded by reference to broader armed conflict status, we need to be aware of the wide-ranging legal and political displacements that are playing out. In my view, it is imperative that the humanitarian law norms applicable to NIACs are robustly defended from counterterrorism encroachment. States must be encouraged to apply these norms in practice and challenged not to the misuse of counterterrorism discourse and norms to avoid the application of humanitarian law's customary and treaty rules. States and other actors in the international community should explicitly define the appropriate legal limits of counterterrorism regulation both normatively and institutionally, and prohibit overreach by States, counterterrorism institutions, and nonstate actors engaged in implementing counterterrorism measures, including corporate entities.[105]

---

103. *Cf.* S.C. Res. 1373 (Sept. 28, 2001) and its progeny. *See also* Agate Sarfati, *International Humanitarian Law and the Criminal Response to Terrorism: From the UN Security Council to the National Courts*, INT. REV. RED CROSS (2022).

104. Fionnuala Ní Aoláin, *"Soft Law," Informal Lawmaking and "New Institutions" in the Global Counter-Terrorism Architecture*, 32 (3) EUROPEAN J. INT'L L. (2021).

105. Ronald C. Slye, *Corporations, Veils and International Criminal Liability*, 33 BROOKLYN J. INT'L. L (2008); United Nations Office of the High Commissioner, *The Corporate Responsibility to Respect Human Rights*, OCHCR (2012), https://www.ohchr.org/documents/publications/hr.pub.12.2_en.pdf; Anita Ramastry, *Corporate Complicity: From Nuremberg to Rangoon, An Examination of Forced Labor Cases and Their Impact on the Liability of Multinational*

One important dimension of IHL displacement and the use of counterterrorism defended technologies is the argument that such technology "solves" the problem at hand, namely the resort to terrorism in the first place. Such magical thinking has little empirical or practical traction. Rather, the deployment of dignity-invading technologies, in situations already characterized by rights deficits, political grievance, lack of accountability and transparency, tends to bolster existing negative security practices rather than "fix" them. As a separate matter, the transfer of such high-risk technologies to broadly unaccountable and bloated security sectors[106] institutionalizes bad practices with new (and ever more dangerous) tools, and ultimately contributes to the broader conditions conducive producing the violence at hand.[107] In short, the use of new technology in counterterrorism, and the role it plays in conflict production, consolidation, and entrenchment, needs greater attention and analysis. The abuse of such technologies in these contexts is also ripe for transparency, accountability, and remedy for those harmed by misuse.

IV. CONCLUSION

Ubiquitous data collection is an undeniable feature of our contemporary global reality. As numerous contributions to this book have identified, there are extraordinary benefits to be gleaned from data collection in conflict and post-conflict settings, enabling, for example, knowledge exchange, accountability, delivering impartial humanitarian aid, and facilitating the effective implementation of the core rules of protection. In parallel, there is no escape from the vast quantities of

---

Corporations, BERKELEY J. INT'L L. 20, 91 (2002); Jonathan Kolieb, *Through the Looking-Glass: Nuremberg's Confusing Legacy on Corporate Accountability under International Law,* 32 AM. U. INT'L L. REV. 569 (2015).

106. A/75/337 (2020), *supra* note 5, ¶33; *Amid Unprecedented Violence, Escalation of Terrorist Attacks in West Africa, United Nations Regional Office Needs Greater Role, Speakers Tell Security Council,* UNITED NATIONS (Jan. 8, 2020); Bowie Sonnie Bowei, *Evaluating the Effects of Counterterrorism Strategies on Insurgency in Nigeria,* WALDEN U. (2019); Dona J. Stewart, *What Is Next for Mali? The Roots of Conflict and Challenges to Stability,* U.S. ARMY WAR COLLEGE STRATEGIC STUDIES INST. (Nov. 2013), https://publications.armywarcollege.edu/pubs/2257.pdf; Stephanie Savell, *The Costs of United States' Post-9/11 "Security Assistance": How Counterterrorism Intensified Conflict in Burkina Faso and Around the World,* WATSON INST. (Mar. 4, 2021), https://watson.brown.edu/costsofwar/files/cow/imce/papers/2021/Costs%20of%20Counterterror ism%20in%20Burkina%20Faso_Costs%20of%20War_Savell.pdf; Rida Lyammouri, *For Mali and the Sahel, New Tensions and an Old—and Worsening—Security Problem,* MIDDLE EAST INST. (Nov. 8, 2021), https://www.mei.edu/publications/mali-and-sahel-new-tensions-and-old-and-worsening-security-problem. Mwangi Kimenyi, Jideofor Adibe, Moussa Djiré, Abigail J. Jirgi, Alpha Kergna, Temesgen T. Deressa, Jessica E. Pugliese & Andrew Westbury, *The Impact of Conflict and Political Instability on Agricultural Investments in Mali and Nigeria,* AFR. GROWTH INITIATIVE 1, 16 (July 2014) ("Human Rights Watch (2013) has recorded a series of human rights abuses by the counterterrorism campaign.").

107. United Nations Development Programme, *supra* note 15.

data that are available to security actors who see its relevance to addressing the scourge of terrorism in multiple societies across the globe.

Nonetheless, this contribution urges caution on two grounds. The first is the increasing slippage between NIACs and counterterrorism arenas, and the strong preference of many states to replace the legal rules that have emerged in the past two decades from the latter, to regulate the former. The lack of an agreed definition of terrorism makes this move legally and politically dangerous, not least that the certainties of the law of armed conflict are replaced with the slippery slopes and non-definition of terrorism. In parallel, the second caution is the entrenched reliance by counterterrorism actors on new technologies and data collection as the foundational block to the counterterrorism edifice. Two decades of unrestrained metadata collection premised on countering terrorism and security justifications have illustrated the pitfalls of enabling security actors to define the ways in which the security state and security should be legitimized to gobble up fundamental and interrelated rights, from privacy to free movement. Counterterrorism has moved from the center to the periphery in national, regional, and global legal practice. As a result, not only have more permissive counterterrorism norms formally displaced other legal regimes, specifically human rights and humanitarian law, but societies that are, in this author's view, overall less free and less secure.

This leads to two interlocking conclusions. First, there is a robust need to defend IHL and IHRL from the encroachment of normative counterterrorism regulation. Counterterrorism must remain a complementary legal tool, exercised in compliance and compatibility with States' international human rights and humanitarian law obligations. Second, every society engaged in substantive counterterrorism work must repair the damage caused by sustained, invasive, human rights "lite" or absent data collection that has grounded counterterrorism initiatives across the globe.

INDEX

For the benefit of digital users, indexed terms that span two pages (e.g., 52–53) may, on occasion, appear on only one of those pages.

Aadhaar (biometric database), 140
Adalmaz (crowdsourcing), 306–7
adversarial machine learning, 182–85, 206
Afghanistan
  autonomous drones in, 333–34
  counterterrorism and, 344n.100
  data collection in, 244
  International Security Assistance Force (ISAF), 244
  scrubbing of data and, 230
  Taliban in, 230
  war in, 331–32
AI. *See* artificial intelligence (AI)
Airline Passenger Information (API), 328–29, 338–40, 343–44
Albania, Martens Clause and, 193–94
Alibaba, 100
Al-Khateeb, Katya, 3, 15–16
Al Mahdi, Ahmad Al Faqi, 313–14
Al Qaida, 309–11
Amazon, 214–15
Annan, Kofi, 62
Ansar Dine, 313–14
anticipatory countermeasures, 131–32
anticipatory self-defense, 61, 112
armed attack
  cyber sabotage as, 119–21
  self-defense, armed attack requirement, 110–11
  use of force versus, 141–43

armed conflict. *See also* international humanitarian law (IHL)
  generally, 12, 119–21
  attack requirement, 156–60
  blackmail, 173
  data poisoning attacks during
    generally, 186, 195–96
    indiscriminate means or method of warfare, as, 196–97
    perfidy and, 181, 186–87, 203–5
    precautionary principle and, 201–3
    proportionality principle and, 197–201
  disruption, 173
  hypothetical scenario, in, 23–24, 152–53
  intimidation, 173
  military objectives (*see* military objectives)
  perfidy, 173–74, 203–5
  policy recommendations, 158, 158n.24
  precautionary principle in
    generally, 156–57
    precautions against attack, 171–73
    precautions in attack, 169–71
  proportionality principle in, 156–57, 169–71
  protective indicators, misuse of, 173–74
  qualification as, 153–56
  race and, 175–76
  terrorism versus, 320
  weapons review, 176–78

"arms race" in AI

generally, 4–5, 91–94, 95–96, 99–100, 134
Chinese approach, 100–1
US approach, 101–2

artificial intelligence (AI)

generally, 1–3, 4–5, 9–10
"arms race" in
generally, 4–5, 91–94, 95–96, 99–100, 134
Chinese approach, 100–1
US approach, 101–2
availability, cyber threats against, 103
BCI technology and
generally, 254–55
reliance on data from AI systems, 260–62
Big Data, importance of, 95–99
confidentiality, cyber threats against, 103
counterterrorism and, 340–43
cyber sabotage against (*see* cyber sabotage)
defined, 182–83, 341n.83
integrity, cyber threats against, 103
internationally wrongful act, development as, 130–31, 134
military applications of, 92–93
quality and quantity of data, 97–99
use of force, development of AI as, 115
vulnerabilities of, 93–94

Asrat, Belatchew, 67

atrocity investigation

generally, 4, 17–18, 291–93, 314–15
bias in, 300
chapeau elements of atrocity crimes, 312–13, 312n.124
deep fakes and, 301
hazards of using Big Data in, 300–2
legal proceedings, in, 313–14
machine learning and, 291, 300, 301–2n.64, 303–4, 311, 313–14
methods of
generally, 303
conflict mapping, 309–11
event detection, 293, 303–6

facial recognition, 293, 306–7
object recognition, 293, 303–6
satellite imagery, 295–96, 295n.27
scene synchronization, 303–6
social network analysis, 293, 307–9
statistical analysis, 293, 311–13
text analysis, 307–9
3-D rendering, 293, 309–11
sources of Big Data on, 293–300

Australia

attack, on cyber operations as, 157
autonomous drones, on, 333n.54
self-defense, on, 113–14
use of force and, 47, 143–44

Austria, counterterrorism and, 339–40

autonomous drones

generally, 180–81
counterterrorism and, 320–23, 328, 331, 333–34, 333n.54
availability, cyber threats against, 72–73, 103

Azerbaijan, data centers in, 224–25

banks, targeting, 238–39
BCI technology. *See* brain-computer interface (BCI) technology
Beck, Ulrich, 331
Begin, Menachem, 108n.77, 109
Begin Doctrine, 113
Bellingcat (investigative site), 305
Benetech (investigative site), 305

Big Data. *See also specific topic*

generally, 1–4, 19–20
AI, importance to, 95–99
defined, 1–2, 1n.1, 95n.16, 137–38, 229–30, 292–93
duty of constant care and
generally, 243–45
data integrity, 245–46
data minimization, 245–46
legality, 245
transparency, 245
legal challenges, 5–8, 19–20
machine learning, importance to, 95–99
networked nature of, 137–38
"small data" versus, 135–38, 147–48
volume of, 137

INDEX

biometric data
  generally, 2–3
  counterterrorism and, 328–29, 331,
    343–44, 343n.93
blackmail, 173
blockchain, 296–97
Boothby, William, 235n.37
brain-computer interface (BCI) technology
  generally, 3, 15–16, 249–52, 270–71
  AI and
    generally, 254–55
    reliance on data from AI
      systems, 260–62
  challenges of, 250–51
  data and, 254–55
  defined, 252–54
  enhancing central nervous system
    output, 251–52, 251n.5
  IHL, implications for
    generally, 259–60
    accountability, 268–70
    individuals *hors de combat,* protection
      of, 265–67
    perfidy and, 267–68
    reliance on data from AI systems, 260–62
    responsibility, 268–70
    targeting of BCI, 263–65
    weapons review, 262–63, 262n.49
  improving central nervous system
    output, 251–52, 251n.5
  invasive BCI, 252–53
  military uses
    generally, 255
    communications, 257–58
    control, 256–57
    enhanced functions, 258–59
    monitoring, 255–56
  minimally invasive BCI, 252–53
  non-invasive BCI, 252–53
  partially invasive BCI, 252–53
  perfidy and, 267–68
  replacing central nervous system output,
    251–52, 251n.5
  restoring central nervous system output,
    251–52, 251n.5
  supplementing central nervous system
    output, 251–52, 251n.5

  torture and, 15–16
  transcranial direct current stimulation
    (tDCS), 258–59
bridges as military objectives, 213
Brown, Gary, 75
Brownlie, Ian, 62, 62n.35
Brown University, 223–24
Bush, George W., 324–25

Canada
  anticipatory self-defense and, 112
  scrubbing of data in, 230
  threat of force and, 67
Carnegie Mellon University, 304–5
Caroline incident, 112, 112n.96
Carter, Jimmy, 55
Chile, threat of force and, 69–70
China
  Academy of Information and
    Communications Technology, 99
  AI in
    generally, 2–3
    centralization of data, 100–1
    development of, 131
    "intelligentized war," 101
    leveraging, 100–1, 103
    military applications of, 92–93
    threat from, 93, 95
  anticipatory countermeasures and, 132
  "arms race" in AI
    generally, 4–5, 91–94, 95–96, 99–
      100, 134
    Chinese approach, 100–1
    US approach contrasted, 101–2
  counterterrorism and, 344
  cyber sabotage and, 9–10
  cyber threats and, 75–76
  growth of digital economy in, 99
  human rights in, 344
  IHRL and, 4–5
  Uyghurs in, 344
civilian objects, 211
civilians, attacks on, 119n.135
client–server model, 209, 209n.5
coercion
  cyber sabotage and, 125–27, 134
  election misinformation as, 126

INDEX

coercion (*cont.*)
  nonintervention and, 125–27
  ransomware attacks as, 126–27
Colonial Pipeline (ransomware attack), 73, 78n.105, 147
combatant status, 104, 104n.53
Commission on International Justice & Accountability (CIJA), 296–97
Computer Vision Annotation Tool (CVAT), 303–4
confidentiality, cyber threats against, 72–73, 103
conflict mapping, 309–11
conflict threshold
  hypothetical scenario, in, 25
  IHL and, 11–12
continuing crimes doctrine, 190–92
Convention against Torture and Other Cruel, Inhuman or Degrading Treatment or Punishment, 284–85
Convention on the Law of the Sea (UNCLOS), 241–42
Convention relating to the Status of Refugees, 284–85
Corn, Gary P., 5, 9–10, 118n.134
corporate data responsibility
  generally, 17–18, 275–77, 289
  cultural context and, 281–82
  "digital humanitarianism" and, 276–79
  due diligence and, 285–86
  evolution of
    generally, 282–83
    "data philanthropy," beyond, 276–77, 286–89
    mitigating corporate complicity, 283–86
  gatekeepers of quantitative data, 279–82
  local context and, 281–82
  macro violations versus micro violations, 281
  right to privacy and, 288–89
  UN Guiding Principles on Business and Human Rights, 282–84, 286
countermeasures
  anticipatory countermeasures, 131–32
  cyber sabotage and, 95, 129–30, 131–32
  sovereignty and, 129–30, 131–32

  use of force, as, 115–16
counterterrorism
  generally, 18–19, 319–24, 347–48
  costs of, 323–24
  evolution of, 324–30
  fallacy of technological solutions, 343–47
  foreign fighters and, 337
  global architecture of, 320–23
  IHL, impact on, 324–30
  IHRL, impact on, 324–30
  international armed conflicts (IACs) versus noninternational armed conflicts (NAICs), 345–46, 348
  interstate cooperation in, 320–23
  mass surveillance, 338n.71
  national and regional regulation, 320–23
  new technology and
    generally, 330–32
    AI, 331, 340–43
    Airline Passenger Information (API), 328–29, 338–40, 343–44
    autonomous drones, 320–23, 328, 331, 333–34, 333n.54
    biometric data, 328–29, 331, 337, 343–44, 343n.93
    data collection, 335–38
    DNA analysis, 343n.93
    facial recognition technology, 337, 343n.93
    Passenger Name Recognition (PNR), 328–29, 338–40, 343–44
    social media, 331
    3-D printing, 331
  right to privacy and, 342
  "soft law" and, 320–23
  torture and, 324–25
COVID-19, 124, 223–24, 342–43
Crawford, James, 128n.182
crimes against humanity. *See* atrocity investigation
Croatia, atrocity investigation in, 313
crowdsourcing, 3–4, 276, 306–7
Cryer, Robert, 62n.35
cryptocurrency mining, 212, 223–24
Cuba, nuclear weapons in, 67

INDEX

*Customary International Humanitarian
Law* (ICRC), 175, 234–35
cyber sabotage
  generally, 5, 9–10, 94–95, 104
  ambiguous nature of in international
    law, 107
  armed attack, as, 119–21
  coercion and, 125–27, 134
  countermeasures and, 95, 129–
    30, 131–32
  defined, 94n.13
  domain réservé and, 123–25
  jus ad bellum versus *jus in bello*, 119–21
  "left of launch," 106–7, 107n.67
  "near-peer" tensions, 9–10
  necessity doctrine and, 95, 132–34
  nonintervention and
    generally, 95, 122–23
    coercion, 125–27, 134
    domain réservé, 123–25
  objects of, 120
  self-defense, as, 111–12
  sovereignty and
    generally, 95, 127–30
    countermeasures, 129–30, 131–32
    development of AI as internationally
      wrongful act, 130–31, 134
  state responsibility doctrine and, 95
  traditional use of force
    compared, 116–17
  use of force, as, 115–16, 119–22, 134
cyborg soldiers. *See* brain-computer
  interface (BCI) technology

Dam, Kenneth W., 75n.93
data centers
  generally, 2–3, 13–14, 207–8, 226–27
  defined, 209–10
  dual-use nature of, 224
  military action, potential
    contributions to
      generally, 212
      buildings, 215
      location, relevance of, 212–13
      nature, relevance of, 213–15
      networking equipment, 215–16
      partial contribution, 220

purpose and use, relevance of, 215–18
  servers, 215–16
  stored data and applications, 216–18
networking equipment, 209–10, 215–16
objects, as
  generally, 210–11, 220–21
  buildings, 215
  location, relevance of, 212–13
  military objectives, 211–12
  nature, relevance of, 213–15
  networking equipment, 215–16
  protected objects, 218–20
  purpose and use, relevance of, 215–18
  servers, 215–16
  stored data and applications, 216–18
private centers, 214–15
servers, 209–10, 215–16
stored data and applications, 216–
  18, 226
supercomputers, 226
support infrastructure, 210, 221–23
targeting of
  generally, 221
  assessment of options, 224–26
  attacks on other objects, 225
  data and applications stored
    in, 223–24
  dual-use nature and, 224
  non-reversible damage, 225
  proportionality principle and, 225
  reverberating effects of, 224–25
  stored data and applications, 226
  supercomputers, 226
  support infrastructure, 221–23
  temporary outage or disruption, 225
data collection
  generally, 51–53
  counterterrorism and, 335–38
  due diligence and, 51
  duty to protect and, 50–51
  external data collection, IHRL and
    generally, 39, 42
    adverse affect justified, 52
    effective control and, 52
    extraterritoriality, 40–41
    four-step analysis, 52
    right adversely affected, 39–40, 52

data collection (*cont.*)
  right implicated, 52
  internal data collection, IHRL and
    generally, 31, 38–39
    adverse affect justified, 36–38
    four-step analysis, 31–38, 52
    right adversely affected, 35–36
    right implicated, 32–35
    whom rights owed to, 31–32
  legitimacy, 37–38
  machine learning and, 35
  necessary and proportionate, 38
  nonintervention and, 44–45, 52–53
  prescribed by law, 37
  right to privacy and
    adverse effect justified, 36–38
    right adversely affected, 35–36
    right implicated, 32–35
  self-defense, as, 48–49
  sovereignty and, 42–44, 52
  state responsibility doctrine and, 49–50
  targeting and, 57n.12
  use of force, as, 45–48
data exhaust, 297–98
data injection, 184
data manipulation, 184
"data philanthropy," 276–77, 286–89
data poisoning attacks
  generally, 6–7, 12–13, 86n.134, 103,
    103n.50, 179–82
  adversarial machine learning and, 182–
    85, 206
  armed conflict, during
    generally, 186, 195–96
    indiscriminate means or method of
      warfare, as, 196–97
    perfidy and, 181, 186–87, 203–5
    precautionary principle and, 201–3
    proportionality principle and,
      197–201
  Big Data, distinct nature of, 205–6
  continuing crimes doctrine, 190–92
  data injection, 184
  data manipulation, 184
  evasion attacks, 183, 184–85
  "gray zones," 187
  indirect data poisoning, 184

jus ad bellum
  generally, 181, 186, 187–88
  data poisoning alone, 190
  label manipulation, 184
  legal framework, 185–87
  logic corruption attacks, 184
  Martens Clause and, 192–95, 192n.59
  necessity doctrine and, 181
  nonintervention and, 127
  perfidy and, 181, 186–87, 203–5
  proportionality principle and
    generally, 181, 197–98
    enemy responses, 199–201
    proportionality analysis
      challenges, 198–99
  use of force, as, 115–16
Deeks, Ashley, 84
deep fakes, 301
Delerue, François, 2–3, 13–14
"digital humanitarianism," 276–79
Dinstein, Yoram, 146
disinformation, 230–31, 231n.12, 301
Displacement Tracking Matrix, 276
disruption, 173
distinction principle, 210–11
distributed ledgers, 296–97, 297n.35
DNA analysis, 343n.93
domain réservé, 123–25
  cyber sabotage and, 123–25
  nonintervention and, 123–25
  research and development (R&D)
    and, 125
  sovereignty and, 123–25
drones. *See* autonomous drones
due diligence
  corporate data responsibility
    and, 285–86
  data collection and, 52
Dunlap, Charles, Jr., 83
duty of constant care
  generally, 14–15, 229–34, 246–48
  banks, targeting, 238–39
  Big Data and
    generally, 243–45
    data integrity, 245–46
    data minimization, 245–46
    legality, 245

INDEX

transparency, 245
binding nature of, 234–35
breach of duty, 241–42
data protection rule, as, 242–43
harms meant to prevent, 239–41
military activities triggering, 237–38
peacetime, during, 238–39
precautionary principle and, 14–15, 234
principle of accuracy, 239
proximity test, 237
scope of, 236
when duty applies, 238–39
"zone of reasonableness," 242
duty to protect, data collection and, 50–51

Egan, Brian, 129n.190
election misinformation, 126
Electronic Frontier Foundation, 296n.31
Electronic Numerical Integrator and
Computer (ENIAC), 209
Ellison, Riki, 107n.67
encryption, 296–97
enforced disappearance, 190–91
enforcement. *See* atrocity investigation
espionage, sovereignty and, 43
Estecahandy, Hugo, 212
Estonia, cyber threats and, 83–84
Eternal Blue, 75–76
European Convention on Human Rights
extraterritoriality under, 40
right to privacy under, 33–34, 35, 36–38
European Court of Human Rights, right to
privacy and, 33–37, 38
European Court of Justice, 34
European Union
counterterrorism and, 339–40
Data Protection Supervisor (EDPS), 336
General Data Protection Regulation
(GDPR), 247, 287–88, 293n.15,
328n.37
LIBE Committee, 98
Passenger Name Recognition
Directive, 339–40
Europol, 336
evasion attacks, 183, 184–85
event detection, 293, 303–6

Event Labeling through Analytic Media
Processing (E-LAMP), 304–5
extraterritoriality, 40–41
eyeWitness (human rights
organization), 296–97

Facebook, 100–1, 101n.42, 294–95
facial recognition technology
generally, 3
atrocity investigation and, 293, 306–7
counterterrorism and, 337, 343n.93
Farewell Dossier, 94, 105–6
Financial Action Task Force, 345–46
Finland, use of force and, 143–44
Forensic Architecture (FA), 309–11,
310nn.110–11
France
attack, on cyber operations as, 158, 159
data centers in, 214, 217–18
Directorate of Infrastructure
Networks and Information Systems
(DIRISI), 214
Ministry of the Armed Forces, 46–47, 214
objects as military objectives,
on, 164–65
Sous-Lieutenant Marie-Louise Cloarec
(data center), 214
sovereignty, on, 42n.45
threat of force and, 60n.27
use of force and, 10–11, 46–47, 48, 121,
143–44, 145–46
Friendly Relations Declaration, 69–70

Garmin, 223–24
Geiß, Robin, 232–33
Geneva Conventions
Additional Protocol I
attack under, 156–57
blackmail, disruption, and
intimidation under, 173
civilian objects under, 211
duty of constant care under, 234–36, 235n.34, 237, 238, 239, 243,
245, 246
indiscriminate means or methods of
warfare under, 196–97, 196n.69

Geneva Conventions (*cont.*)
location of object, 212–13
military objectives under, 211–12
nature of object, 213–14
objects as military objectives under, 162–63, 226–27
perfidy under, 173, 174, 204, 204n.87, 267
persons as military objectives under, 161
precautionary principle under, 14–15, 171–72, 234
proportionality principle under, 197–98
protected objects under, 218–19
targeting errors under, 166
weapons review under, 176–77, 178, 262, 262n.49
Additional Protocol II, 12–13, 345
armed conflict under, 155, 188–89
Common Article 2, 187n.40, 188–89, 188n.42, 337
Common Article 3, 175, 193–94, 337, 345, 346
gaps in IHL and, 12–13
Martens Clause and, 193–94
race, IHL and, 175
genocide. *See* atrocity investigation
Georgia, threat of force and, 60–61, 63
Germany
counterterrorism and, 339–40
data collection by, 244–45, 246
sabotage and, 104–5
use of force and, 46, 143–44
Gerstell, Glenn, 99–100
Giddens, Anthony, 331n.48
Global Counter-Terrorism Coordination Compact, 325–26
Global Counter-Terrorism Forum, 326–27, 345–46
Google, 284
Google Earth, 298n.43
Gotovina, Ante, 313
Grimal, F., 63, 65–66
Guatemala, atrocity investigation in, 298n.39
Guyana, threat of force and, 66

hacking, 179–81
Hague Convention of 1907, 193–94
Hala Systems, 295–96, 296n.28
Hariri, Rafik, 298–99
Harvard Manual on International Law Applicable to Air and Missile Warfare, 168
Hollis, Duncan, 5, 9
honeypots, 159–60, 159n.26
Huber, Max, 44n.53
Humanitarian OpenStreetMap Team, 276
humanitarian operations
generally, 3–4, 16–18
atrocity investigation (*see* atrocity investigation)
corporate data responsibility (*see* corporate data responsibility)
"digital humanitarianism," 276–79
IHL and, 6–7
Humanitarian Tracker, 309
human rights. *See* international human rights law (IHRL)
Human Rights Data Analysis Group (HRDAG), 312–13
Human Rights Watch, 230–31
Hussein, Saddam, 108n.77
"hyper-personalization of war," 284

ICCPR. *See* International Covenant on Civil and Political Rights (ICCPR)
ICJ. *See* International Court of Justice (ICJ)
IHL. *See* international humanitarian law (IHL)
IHRL. *See* international human rights law (IHRL)
Independent International Fact- Finding Mission on the Conflict in Georgia (IIFFMCG), 60–61, 63, 64–65, 66, 67, 68, 69–70, 70n.73, 81
India
cyber operations and, 140
separatist violence in, 284
indirect data poisoning, 184
indiscriminate attacks, 119n.135
indiscriminate means or methods of warfare, 196–97, 196n.69

INDEX

individuals *hors de combat,* protection of, 265–67
integrity, cyber threats against, 72–73, 103
Intel, 303–4
Inter-American Court of Human Rights, 34n.14
International, Impartial and Independent Mechanism devoted to Syria (IIIM), 305
International Civil Aviation Organisation (ICAO), 340n.78
International Committee of the Red Cross (ICRC), 155, 157, 161–62, 167–68, 175, 234–35
International Convention for the Protection of All Persons from Enforced Disappearance, 284–85
International Court of Justice (ICJ)
  Martens Clause and, 193–94
  nonintervention, on, 122–24, 123n.156
  race, IHL and, 175–76
  self-defense, on, 110n.88
  threat of force, on, 60–61, 63–64, 66, 68–70, 70n.73
  use of force on, 46, 48–49, 117, 121, 144
International Covenant on Civil and Political Rights (ICCPR)
  extraterritoriality under, 40–41
  race, IHL and, 175–76
  right to privacy under, 31n.4, 32–33, 36
International Criminal Court (ICC), 294–95, 313–14, 345
International Criminal Tribunal for the former Yugoslavia (ICTY), 234–35, 313
International Group of Experts (IGE), 46, 77–78, 190, 216, 233–34, 238
international humanitarian law (IHL)
  generally, 11–16, 151–52
  armed attack in, 12, 119–21
  BCI technology (*see* brain-computer interface (BCI) technology)
  blackmail, 173
  civilians, attacking, 119n.135
  combatant status in, 104, 104n.53
  conflict threshold and, 11–12
  counterterrorism, impact of, 324–30
  data centers (*see* data centers)

data poisoning attacks (*see* data poisoning attacks)
definition of armed conflict, 153-56
disruption, 173
distinction principle, 210–11
duty of constant care (*see* duty of constant care)
humanitarian operations and, 6–7
IHRL and, 18
indiscriminate attacks, 119n.135
intimidation, 173
legal challenges of Big Data, 6–7, 11–12
military objectives (*see* military objectives)
necessity doctrine
  cyber sabotage and, 95, 132–34
  data poisoning attacks and, 181
  exceptions, 133
  permissible actions, 132–33
  state responsibility doctrine and, 133
perfidy, 173–74, 203–5
policy recommendations, 158, 158n.24
precautionary principle
  generally, 119n.135, 156–57
  duty of constant care and, 14–15, 234
  precautions against attack, 171–73
  precautions in attack, 169–71
proportionality principle (*see* proportionality principle)
protective indicators, misuse of, 173–74
qualification as armed conflict, 153–56
race and, 175–76
terrorism and, 320–23
weapons review, 176–78
international human rights law (IHRL)
  generally, 18–20
  China and, 4–5
  counterterrorism (*see* counterterrorism)
  external data collection
    generally, 39, 42
    adverse affect justified, 52
    effective control and, 52
    extraterritoriality, 40–41
    right adversely affected, 39–40, 52
    right implicated, 52
  IHL and, 18

international human rights law (IHRL)
(*cont.*)
  infringements on
    legitimacy, 37–38
    necessary and proportionate, 38
    prescribed by law, 37
  internal data collection
    generally, 31, 38–39
    adverse affect justified, 36–38
    four-step analysis, 31–38, 52
    right adversely affected, 35–36
    right implicated, 32–35
    whom rights owed to, 31–32
  legal challenges of Big Data, 7, 16, 18
  mitigating corporate complicity, 283–86
  refoulement, 284–85
  terrorism and, 320–23
  UN Guiding Principles on Business and
    Human Rights, 282–84, 286
International Law Association
  Final Report on the Meaning of Armed
    Conflict in International Law, 189
  Study Group on the Conduct of Hostilities
    in the 21st Century, 213, 219
International Law Commission, Draft
    Articles on State Responsibility, 49–
    50, 50n.76, 133, 190–91
International Organization for
    Migration, 276
*Interpretive Guidance on the Notion of
    Direct Participation in Hostilities*
    (ICRC), 161–62
intimidation, 173
Iran
  cyber operations and, 106, 140
  Natanz nuclear reactor attack, 73, 106,
    106n.65, 114–15
  threat of force and, 62
Iraq
  cyber operations and, 94
  cyber threats and, 86
  Osirak nuclear reactor attack, 94, 109–
    10, 114–15
  threat of force and, 62
  US invasion of, 113–14
Islamic State of Iraq and the Levant
    (ISIL), 296–97

Israel
  attack, on cyber operations as, 157–58
  Coordinator of Government Activities
    in the Territories (COGAT), 231–32,
    231n.13, 232n.17
  cyber operations and, 106, 106n.65
  data collection by, 231–32
  duty of constant care and, 238–39
  Mossad, 106n.65
  objects as military objectives, on, 164
  self-defense, on, 113, 114–15
  sovereignty, on, 129
  threat of force and, 62
  use of force and, 10–11, 143–44
Italy, use of force and, 143–44

Japan
  cyber threats and, 77–78, 77n.101
  self-defense, on, 113–14
  use of force and, 143–44
Jensen, Eric, 5, 9–10, 233–34, 237
Johns Hopkins University, 256–57
jus ad bellum
  generally, 8–11, 29–30
  cyber sabotage (*see* cyber sabotage)
  data collection as pre-conflict
    preparation (*see* data collection as
    pre-conflict preparation)
  data poisoning attacks
    generally, 181, 186, 187–88
    armed conflict triggered, 188–89
    continuing crimes doctrine, 190–92
    data poisoning alone, 190
    Martens Clause and, 192–95, 192n.59
  legal challenges of Big Data, 7, 8–9
  nonintervention and, 44–45
  sovereignty and, 8–9, 42–44
  threat of force (*see* threat of force)
  use of force (*see* use of force)
jus in bello. See international humanitarian
    law (IHL)

Kaye, David, 341n.83
Kellogg–Briand Pact, 60
Kilovaty, Ido, 5, 10–11
Kim Il-Sung, 55
Kim Jong Un, 62–63

INDEX

Kochavi, Aviv, 106n.65
Krebs, Chris, 74–75
Kuwait, human rights in, 194–95

label manipulation, 184
Lahmann, Henning, 232–33
Larkin, Brian, 277–78
Law of Armed Conflict (LOAC). *See*
    international humanitarian law (IHL)
"left of launch," 106–7, 107n.67
lex lata, 233
lex specialis, 120n.142
Libya
    atrocity investigation in, 294–95
    autonomous drones in, 180–81
Limonier, Kévin, 212
Lin, Herbert S., 75n.93
logic corruption attacks, 184
Lohn, Andrew, 97, 103
Lotrionte, Catherine, 142
Lubell, Noam, 3, 15–16, 84
Lubin, Asaf, 2–3, 14–15

machine learning
    generally, 1–3, 5
    adversarial machine learning, 182–
        85, 206
    atrocity investigation and, 291, 300,
        301–2n.64, 303–4, 311, 313–14
    Big Data, importance of, 95–99
    data collection and, 35
    first wave, 96–97
    identification of threats, use in, 84
    quality and quantity of data, 97–99
    second wave, 96–97
Martens Clause, 12–13, 192–95, 192n.59,
    238n.48
mass surveillance, 338n.71
Melendez, Carlos, 97–98
Microsoft, 82n.120, 103, 214–15
Microsoft Exchange, 74–75
migrants, 276
Milanovic, Marko, 41
military objectives
    bridges as, 213
    data as object, 162–66
    data centers as

generally, 211–12
    buildings, 215
    location, relevance of, 212–13
    nature, relevance of, 213–15
    networking equipment, 215–16
    partial contribution, 220
    purpose and use, relevance of, 215–18
    servers, 215–16
    stored data and applications, 216–18
    defined, 211–12
    direct participation requirement, 161–62
    objects, 12, 120, 162–66, 226–27 (*see
        also* objects)
    persons, 160–62
    self-driving cars, 161
    targeting errors, 166–69
Mirimanoff-Chilkine, J., 236
Mnemonic (human rights organization),
    296–97, 303–4
Mulchandani, Nand, 101–2
Murray, Daragh, 84

necessity doctrine
    cyber sabotage and, 95, 132–34
    data poisoning attacks and, 181
    exceptions, 133
    permissible actions, 132–33
    state responsibility doctrine and, 133
NESTA, 313–14
Netherlands
    sovereignty, on, 42n.45
    use of force and, 10–11, 47n.68, 117n.122,
        120n.144, 121, 143–44, 145–46
Netherlands Statement, 117n.122,
    120n.144
Neural Engineering System Design, 258
Neurotechnology for Intelligence Analysts
    and Cognitive Technology Threat
    Warning System, 258
New Zealand, use of force and, 143–44
Nguyen, Reese, 138n.10
Ni Aolain, Fionuala, 2–3, 18–19
Nicaragua, threat of force and, 63–64
nonintervention
    coercion and, 125–27
    cyber sabotage and
        generally, 95, 122–23

nonintervention (*cont.*)
    coercion, 125–27, 134
    domain réservé, 123–25
    data collection and, 44–45, 52–53
    data poisoning attacks and, 127
    domain réservé and, 123–25
    military data, cyber operations
        against, 44–45
    sovereignty and, 128
non-state actors
    counterterrorism and, 19
    state responsibility doctrine and, 7
    terrorism and, 320
North Korea
    cyber operations and, 106–7, 140
    cyber threats and, 76–77
    threat of force and, 55–56, 57, 67
    tunnels, 55–56, 70n.75, 88
Norway, use of force and, 47–48
NotPetya (malware), 75–76, 78
nuclear weapons, 66n.55

object recognition, 293, 303–6
objects
    armed conflict, in, 162–66
    civilian objects, 211
    cyber sabotage, of, 120
    data as, 162–66
    data centers as
        generally, 210–11, 220–21
        buildings, 215
        location, relevance of, 212–13
        military objectives, 211–12
        nature, relevance of, 213–15
        networking equipment, 215–16
        protected objects, 218–20
        purpose and use, relevance of, 215–18
        servers, 215–16
        stored data and applications, 216–18
    military objectives, as, 12, 120, 162–
        66, 226–27
OVHcloud (cloud computing company),
    207–8, 214, 221–23
Owens, William A., 75n.93

Palestinians
    counterterrorism and, 337–38

data collection and, 231–32
Passenger Name Recognition (PNR), 328–
    29, 338–40, 343–44
perfidy
    armed conflict, during, 173–74, 203–5
    BCI technology and, 267–68
    data poisoning attacks and, 181, 186–
        87, 203–5
    defined, 204n.85, 267
persons as military objectives, 160–62
Pfaff, Tony, 248n.80
precautionary principle
    generally, 119n.135, 156–57
    duty of constant care and, 14–15, 234
    precautions against attack, 171–73
    precautions in attack, 169–71
pre-conflict preparation. See *jus ad bellum*
preemptive self-defense, 112, 113–14,
    114n.108
preventive self-defense, 113, 114,
    114n.111
privacy, right to
    corporate data responsibility
        and, 288–89
    counterterrorism and, 342
    data collection and
        adverse affect justified, 36–38
        right adversely affected, 35–36
        right implicated, 32–35
    derogation of, 36
proportionality principle
    generally, 119n.135, 156–57
    armed conflict, in, 169–71
    data centers, targeting of, 225
    data poisoning attacks and
        generally, 181, 197–98
        enemy responses, 199–201
        proportionality analysis
            challenges, 198–99
protective indicators, misuse of, 173–74
Putin, Vladimir, 76–77, 92, 230–31

Qatar, atrocity investigation and, 306–7,
    307n.93

race, IHL and, 175–76
ransomware attacks, 126–27

INDEX

Red Crescent, 174
Red Cross, 174
Red Crystal, 174
refoulement, 284–85
refugees, 276
research and development (R&D), *domain réservé* and, 125
Rome Statute, 191
Rootkit programs, 74n.90
Roscini, Marco, 60–61nn.27–28, 70
Russia. *See also* Soviet Union
  AI in
    generally, 2–3
    military applications of, 92–93
  "arms race" in AI, 4–5
  cryptocurrency mining in, 212
  cyber operations and, 9–10, 139–40
  cyber threats and, 83–84
  disinformation and, 230–31, 231n.12
  nonintervention and, 124
  threat of force and, 60–61, 63–64, 67
  Ukraine, invasion of, 63–64, 79–80, 92–93, 139–40, 230–31

sabotage
  cyber sabotage (*see* cyber sabotage)
  defined, 94n.13
  historical background, 104–6
  preventive sabotage, 104–6
Sadurksa, Romana, 62n.34
Sarfaty, Galit, 3–4, 16–17
satellite imagery, 295–96, 295n.27
Saudi Arabia, UK arms sales to, 313–14
Saudi Aramco, 140
scene synchronization, 303–6
Schmidt, Eric, 99
Schmitt, Michael N., 8–9, 11–12, 18, 114n.108, 125–27, 138n.9, 141–42, 192–93, 195n.67
Schneier, Bruce, 75–76, 75n.93
Schöndorf, Roy, 119n.135, 119–20n.139, 120n.141
self-defense
  generally, 45
  anticipatory self-defense, 61, 112
  armed attack requirement, 110–11
  Caroline incident, 112, 112n.96

cyber sabotage as, 111–12
data collection as, 48–49
"last window of opportunity," 49, 49n.75
preemptive self-defense, 112, 113–14, 114n.108
preventive self-defense, 113, 114, 114n.111
use of force, as exception to prohibition, 45, 107–8, 108n.74
self-driving cars, 161, 179
SITU Research, 313–14
Slaughterbots (video), 180–81
"small data," 135–38, 147–48
social media
  atrocity investigation, network analysis in, 293, 307–9
  counterterrorism and, 331
Solar Sunrise (software hack), 86
SolarWinds Orion (software hack), 5, 72–73, 72n.82, 74–75, 83–84, 139–40, 146
Somalia, counterterrorism and, 337–38
Sony Pictures (software hack), 76–77, 140
South Korea
  Defense Ministry, 55–56
  threat of force and, 55–56, 67
South Sudan, crowdsourcing in, 276
sovereignty
  generally, 8–9
  countermeasures and, 129–30, 131–32
  cyber sabotage and
    generally, 95, 127–30
    countermeasures, 129–30, 131–32
    development of AI as internationally wrongful act, 130–31, 134
  data collection and, 42–44, 52
  defined, 44n.53
  domain réservé and, 123–25
  espionage and, 43
  governmental functions, interference with, 43–44
  nonintervention and, 128
  territoriality and, 43
Soviet Union. *See also* Russia
  sabotage and, 105–6
  threat of force and, 60n.27, 67
Special Tribunal for Lebanon (STL), 298–99

state responsibility doctrine
  generally, 7
  attribution, 49–50
  cyber sabotage and, 95
  data collection and, 49–50
  necessity doctrine and, 133
statistical analysis, 293, 311–13
Stürchler, Nikolas, 60n.24, 62n.34, 86n.132
Stuxnet (cyber attack), 72–73, 106,
    106n.64, 115–16
Sudan, atrocity investigation in, 303–4
supercomputers, 226
Suriname, threat of force and, 66
Syria
  al-Kibar nuclear reactor attack, 109–10,
    109n.82, 114–15
  atrocity investigation in, 292–93, 294–
    97, 303–4, 305, 306–7, 309–13
  casualties in, 312n.121
  crowdsourcing in, 3–4, 276
  disinformation and, 301
  US airstrikes in, 309–11
  war crimes in, 4
  White Helmets, 301
Syria Association for Missing and
    Conscience Detainees, 306–7
Syrian Archive, 311–12
Syrian Commission of Inquiry
    (COI), 309–11
Syria Tracker, 3–4, 275–76

Tabassi, Elham, 103n.50
Tallinn Manual
  armed conflict under, 155–56
  attack under, 157, 159
  data as objects under, 216–17
  data poisoning attacks and, 190
  due diligence under, 51
  duty of constant care under, 233–34, 238
  perfidy under, 174
  precautionary principle under, 172
  sovereignty under, 128–29, 131
  use of force under, 46, 47, 77–78, 117–
    18, 142–43, 148
  weapons review under, 177
targeting errors, 166–69
Tech Against Terrorism, 326–27

"technocolonialism," 278–79
"technopolitics," 279
terrorism. *See also* counterterrorism
  armed conflict versus, 320
  IHL and, 320–23
  IHRL and, 320–23
  non-state actors and, 320
text analysis, 307–9
threat of force
  generally, 9, 55–59, 88–89
  anticipatory self-defense
    distinguished, 61
  credibility, assessing
    generally, 61, 64
    identity and capacity of author of
      threat, 64–67
    imminence, 67–68
    nature of threat , 68–69
    relationships between states and, 67
  cyber threats
    generally, 71–72
    attribution, 77n.100
    availability, against, 72–73, 103
    confidentiality, against, 72–73, 103
    cross-border conduct, 80
    explicit versus implicit threats, 76
    harms threatened by, 72–73
    indirect harms, 73
    insider access, 74–75
    integrity, against, 72–73, 103
    prohibiting, 76–79
    proximity access, 74–75
    relevance of prohibition to cyber
      operations, 79–80
    remote access, 74–75
    supply chain access, 74–75
    unauthorized access, 74–76
  doctrine and, 58–59, 60–61
  explicit or implicit threat, 61, 62–64
  factual existence of, 58–59
  force requirement, 61, 64
  functional need to regulate, 58–59
  identification of threats, use of Big
    Data in
    generally, 56–57, 81–83
    context specific nature of, 86
    criteria and application, 83–85

INDEX

information contamination
    and, 86–87
machine learning and, 84
risks of overreliance, 85–87
implicit threats, 63
lack of clear definition, 116
maintenance of force
    distinguished, 60n.24
nuclear weapons as, 66n.55
prohibition generally, 60–61
signaling, 62–63
subjective versus objective
    analysis, 69–71
technical developments and, 58–59
virtual tunnels as, 56, 59
3-D printing, 331
3-D rendering, 293, 309–11
Thurnher, Jeffrey S., 192–93
torture
    brain-computer interface (BCI)
        technology and, 15–16
    Convention against Torture and Other
        Cruel, Inhuman or Degrading
        Treatment or Punishment, 284–85
    counterterrorism and, 324–25
transcranial direct current stimulation
    (tDCS), 258–59
Trojan Horses, 74–75, 74n.90
Trump, Donald, 62–63
Tsagourias, Nicholas, 60n.24, 70, 81
tunnels, 55–56, 56n.6, 70n.75, 88
Twitter, 100–1, 101n.42, 284

Ukraine
    atrocity investigation in, 292–93, 295–
        97, 305, 313–14
    cyber operations and, 139–40
    disinformation and, 230–31,
        231n.12, 301
    displacement in, 276
    Russian invasion of, 63–64, 79–80, 92–
        93, 139–40, 230–31
    threat of force and, 63–64, 67
United Kingdom
    nonintervention and, 124
    Saudi Arabia, arms sales to, 313–14
    self-defense, on, 113–14

sovereignty, on, 42, 42–43n.47, 129–30,
    129n.188
threat of force and, 60n.27, 62
use of force and, 143–44
United Nations
    Charter
        counterterrorism and, 328–29
        self-defense under, 45, 48–49
        threat of force under, 9 (see also threat
            of force)
        use of force under, 44–45 (see also use
            of force)
    Convention on the Law of the Sea
        (UNCLOS), 241–42
    Countering Terrorist Travel Programme,
        340n.78
    counterterrorism and, 325–26,
        326n.31, 339–40
    Counter-Terrorism Committee, 325–
        26, 345–46
    Counter-Terrorism Committee
        Executive Directorate (UNCTED),
        325–26, 340n.78
    Counter-Terrorism Implementation
        Task Force (CTITF), 325–26
    General Assembly Resolution 2675, 240
    Group of Governmental Experts
        (UNGGE), 129
    Guiding Principles on Business and
        Human Rights, 282–84, 286
    Human Rights Committee, 41, 339–40,
        340n.81, 343–44
    Human Rights Council, 282–83
    Office for the Coordination
        of Humanitarian Affairs
        (OCHA), 311–12
    Office of Counter-Terrorism, 328–29,
        334, 345–46
    Office of Information Communication
        Technology (OICT), 340n.78
    Office of the High Commission
        for Human Rights (OHCHR),
        312n.121, 341
    Office on Drugs and Crime (UNODC),
        340n.78
    Operational Satellite Applications
        Programme (UNOSAT), 295–96

United Nations (*cont.*)
  Security Council
    generally, 18–19, 109
    counterterrorism and, 320–23, 328–
      29, 329n.39, 331–32n.50, 335–37,
      338–39, 339nn.76–77, 345–46
    duty of constant care and, 243
    Martens Clause and, 193–94
    use of force authorized by, 108n.74
  Special Rapporteur on Counter-
    Terrorism and Human Rights, 194–
    95, 334n.59
  Special Rapporteur on the Promotion
    and Protection of the Right
    to Freedom of Opinion and
    Expression, 285
  terrorism and, 319–20
  UNESCO, 295–96
United States
  Agency for International
    Development, 230
  AI in
    generally, 2–3
    development of, 131
    heterogeneity of data, 101–2
    military applications of, 92–93
    private industry and, 102
    sophistication and breadth of, 101–2
  anticipatory countermeasures and, 132
  anticipatory self-defense and, 112
  "arms race" in AI
    generally, 4–5, 91–94, 95–96, 99–
      100, 134
    Chinese approach contrasted, 100–1
    US approach, 101–2
  Army Cyber Institute, 7–8
  autonomous drones, on, 333n.54
  Central Intelligence Agency
    (CIA), 105–6
  Commerce Department, 139–40
  Computer Fraud and Abuse Act
    (CFAA), 296n.31
  continuing crimes doctrine, on, 190–91
  counterterrorism and, 324–25, 331–32
  cyber operations and, 9–10, 106 7, 139–40
  Cybersecurity and Infrastructure
    Security Agency, 74–75

  cyber threats and, 86
  DARPA, 254n.20, 258
  data centers in, 214–15, 224–25
  Defense Department, 86n.134, 93, 121,
    129–30, 144, 214–15
  Department of Defense Law of War
    Manual, 111n.90, 159n.25
  Energy Department, 139–40
  extraterritoriality, on, 40–41
  Federal Bureau of Investigation, 306–7
  Federal Trade Commission, 229–30
  Foreign Intelligence Surveillance
    Court, 34n.14
  Fourth Amendment, 34n.14
  Guantanamo Bay detention
    camp, 324–25
  Homeland Security Department
    (DHS), 139–40
  Iraq, invasion of, 113–14
  January 6 insurrection, 4n.16, 295n.21
  Joint AI Center, 101–2
  Joint Enterprise Defense Infrastructure
    (JEDI), 214–15
  military commissions in, 103n.51
  National Institute of Standards and
    Technology, 183, 185, 186
  National Institutes of Health, 139–40
  National Nuclear Security
    Administration, 139–40
  National Security Agency (NSA), 75–76
  National Security Commission on
    Artificial Intelligence (NSCAI), 92,
    93–94, 96, 99, 102
  National Security Strategy of the United
    States (2002), 113–14
  9/11 attacks, 324–25, 331–32
  nonintervention and, 124
  Project Maven, 102
  right to privacy in, 34n.14
  Sabotage Act, 104–5, 105n.56
  sabotage and, 103n.51, 104–6
  scrubbing of data in, 230
  self-defense, on, 48–49, 48n.72, 111–
    12, 113–14
  sovereignty, on, 127–28, 129–30
  Standing Rules of Engagement, 113–14
  State Department, 139–40

INDEX

Syria, airstrikes in, 309–11
threat of force and, 60n.27, 62, 63–64, 67
Treasury Department, 139–40
use of force and, 10–11, 121, 121n.148, 143–44
University of London, 309–11
University of Pennsylvania, 209
use of force
generally, 8–9, 10–11, 45, 107–8
ambiguities regarding, 108
conflict threshold and, 48–49, 58
consent exception, 108
countermeasures, as, 115–16
cyber operations as
generally, 135–37, 148
armed attack versus, 141–43
Big Data versus "small data," 135–38, 147–48
international law, in, 136, 138–41
kinetic approach, 144–45
non-kinetic approach, 145–46
state statements, 143–46
cyber sabotage as, 115–16, 119–22, 134
data collection as, 45–48
data poisoning attacks as, 115–16
death or injury as *sine qua non*, 117–19
development of AI as, 115
economic harm, 47–48
exceptions to prohibition, 45, 108
guerrillas, arming and training as, 46

kinetic versus non-kinetic effects, 138–39, 140, 141–43
lack of clear definition, 116
nature of target and, 48
self-defense exception, 45, 107–8, 108n.74
Uwazi (open source software), 297n.34

van Benthem, Tsvetelina, 5, 9
Van Schaack, Beth, 4, 17–18
Vindman, Yevgeny, 146
virtual tunnels, 9, 56, 59
viruses, 74–75, 74n.90
Visger, Mark, 6–8, 12–13, 95n.16, 238n.48
Visual Forensics & Metadata Extraction (VFRAME), 303–4
vulnerabilities, 74n.88

WannaCry (malware), 75–76
war crimes. *See* atrocity investigation
Wassenaar Agreement on Export Controls for Conventional Arms, 342
weapons review
armed conflict, in, 176–78
BCI technology and, 262–63, 262n.49
Weeramantry, C.G., 69–70
White, Nigel D., 62n.35
"worms" in cyber-operations, 74–75, 74n.90

Yemen, atrocity investigation in, 297n.34, 303–4, 313–14